BRUCE SPRINGSTEEN
ALL THE SONGS

BRUCE SPRINGSTEEN ALL THE SONGS

THE STORY BEHIND EVERY TRACK

PHILIPPE MARGOTIN & JEAN-MICHEL GUESDON

CASSELL ILLUSTRATED

CONTENTS

ALBUM
GREETINGS FROM ASBURY PARK, N.J.

ALBUM
THE WILD, THE INNOCENT, & THE E STREET SHUFFLE

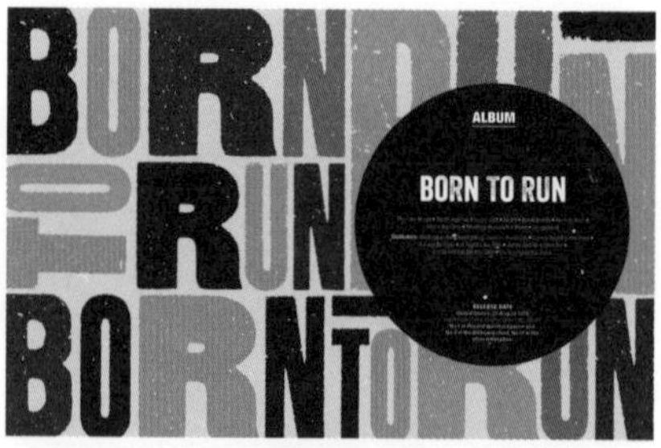
ALBUM
BORN TO RUN

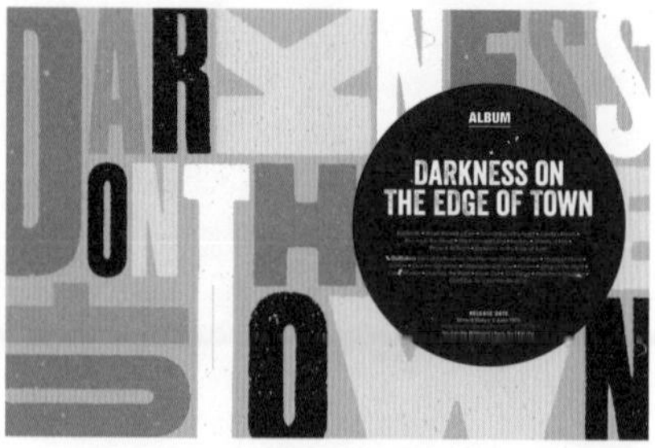
ALBUM
DARKNESS ON THE EDGE OF TOWN

ALBUM
THE RIVER

ALBUM
NEBRASKA

ALBUM
BORN IN THE U.S.A.

ALBUM
TUNNEL OF LOVE

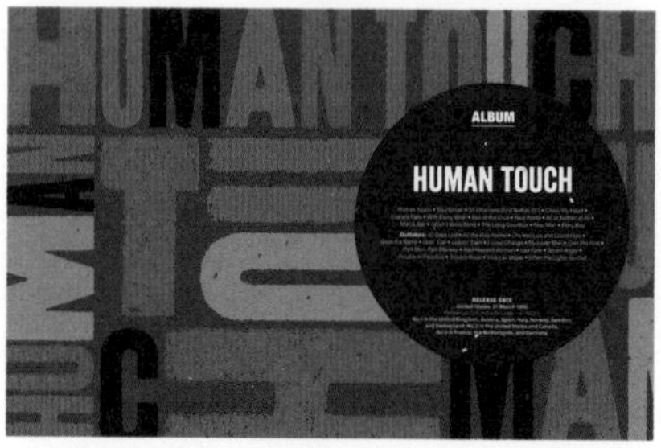
ALBUM
HUMAN TOUCH

ALBUM
LUCKY TOWN

ALBUM
GREATEST HITS

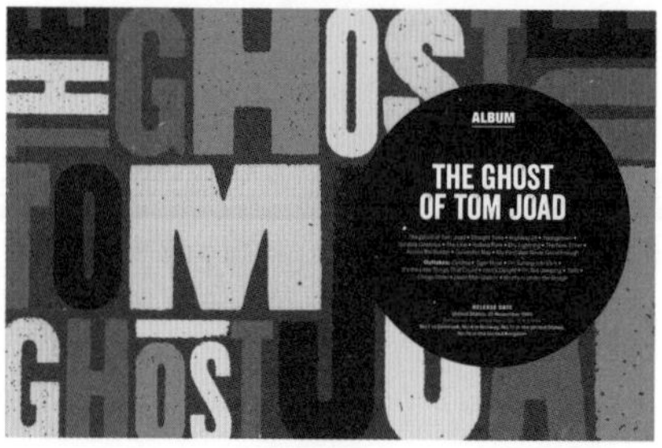
ALBUM
THE GHOST OF TOM JOAD

390

414

418

426

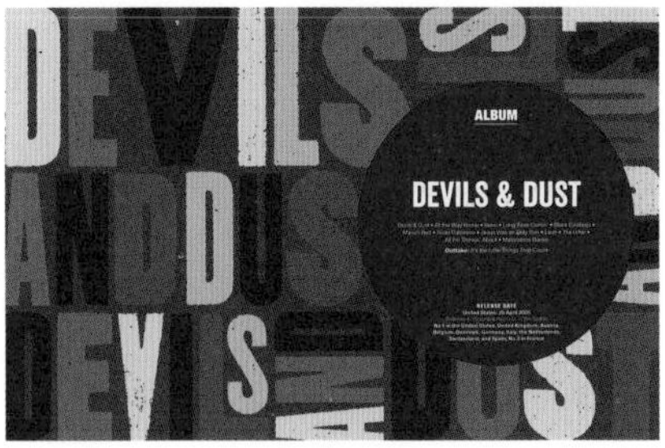

456

478

502

526

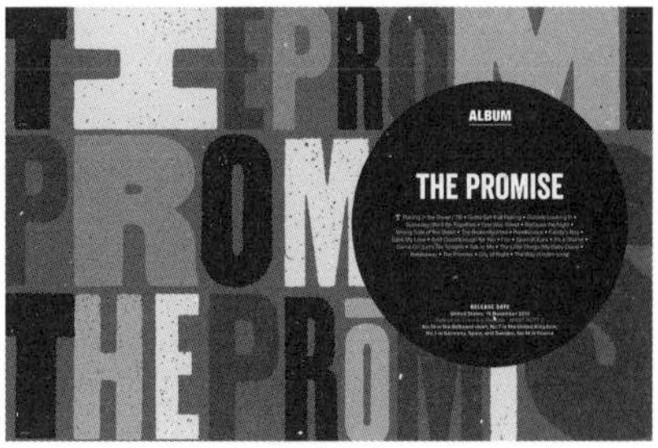

552

570

598

624

630

636

Bruce Springsteen with his mother Adele Ann (née Zerilli), onstage at Madison Square Garden, New York, in August 1978.

DUTCH ORIGINS

Springsteen is of Italian, Irish, and Dutch descent. The Boss's ancestors include Casper Springsteen and his wife Geertje, who were both born in Groningen, circa 1620, and left the United Provinces several years later for New Netherland (a Dutch colony between New England and Virginia). Interesting fact: the name Springsteen is derived from two Dutch words, *spring* and *steen*, meaning "leap" and "stone."

A NEW JERSEY BOY

New Jersey, to the south of New York State with the Atlantic Ocean to the east, has witnessed the arrival of successive waves of Europeans, starting with the first settlers from the United Provinces of the Netherlands in the 1630s. In the early 20th century, the population of the Garden State, as it is known, was 90 percent white and included large Irish and Italian Catholic communities. Bruce Springsteen belongs to both these groups, as well as to the Dutch community.

Bruce Frederick Joseph Springsteen was born on 23 September 1949 in Monmouth Medical Center, Long Branch, New Jersey, and raised in Freehold, a small town in central New Jersey. He is the son of Douglas Frederick "Dutch" Springsteen and Adele Ann Zerilli. Douglas was descended from the Dutch and the Irish on his father's side (Frederick H Springsteen, son of Anthony Springsteen and Martha Ann O'Hagan) and from the Irish on his mother's side (Alice Helena McNicolas), while Adele is of 100 percent Italian descent (her family originated from Campania and Sicily). Bruce's father was an apprentice in a rug factory and, during the Second World War, he sailed on the *Queen Mary* to Europe where he took part in the Battle of the Bulge. When the war ended, he returned to Freehold where he had a number of jobs, including as a bus driver. He also worked on the production lines in the Ford factory in Edison, and was a regular in the local bars. "I was not my father's favorite citizen,"[1] Bruce Springsteen writes in his autobiography *Born to Run,* describing their complex relationship. "He loved me but he couldn't stand me."[1] Adele, his mother, worked as a legal secretary at Lawyers Title Inc. "My mother showered me with affection," he adds. "The love I missed from my father she tried to double up on and, perhaps, find the love she missed from my dad."[1]

Bruce initially lived with his parents and younger sister Virginia (born in 1950) at his paternal grandparents' home on 87 Randolph St. In 1955, the family moved to 39 1/2 Institute St, then just before the family grew with the birth of Pamela in 1962, they moved to 68 South St. Young Bruce was educated at the St Rose of Lima Catholic school, where catechism classes were followed by English and math. "No matter how much I want to, no matter how hard I try, 'the way things are' eludes me," he writes. "I desperately want to fit in but the world I have created with the unwarranted freedom from my grandparents has turned me into an unintentional rebel, an outcast weirdo misfit sissy boy. I am alienating, alienated, and socially homeless...I am seven years old."[1]

For his grandmother's love

Springsteen's early inability to fit in can be explained by his overly intense relationship with Alice, grandmother on his

Left, a neon sign of Freehold, Springsteen's hometown; right, the St Rose of Lima school in Freehold, where the future Boss of rock 'n' roll was raised.

The house where Bruce Springsteen grew up, at 39 1/2 Institute Street in Freehold, New Jersey.

father's side. Traumatized by the loss of her daughter Virginia, who was knocked down and killed by a truck at the age of five, Alice poured all her affection into Bruce, her son's firstborn. She wanted to protect him from the world, without and within, and in so doing she gradually took the place of the boy's parents, Douglas and Adele. She was partly responsible for raising him, and let him run free and do what he wanted. So once the family had moved out of Randolph St, young Bruce would return to the sanctuary of his grandparents' house as often as he could. "It was a place where I felt an ultimate security, full license, and a horrible, unforgettable, boundary-less love. It ruined me and it made me."[1] This all-encompassing love affected other relationships within the Springsteen clan, as well as Bruce's own emotional balance. "For my grandmother's love, I abandoned my parents, my sister, and much of the world itself,"[1] he writes in his autobiography. This world collapsed in 1965 with the death of his extraordinary grandmother, and the future Boss would spend the rest of his life trying to recreate the feeling of security that had grown from the love she had lavished on him and the notion of total freedom she had inculcated in him.

The Elvis bombshell

When he was almost seven years old, Bruce Springsteen's first musical bombshell hit him right between the eyes—or rather directly in the heart. On 9 September 1956, he was glued to the TV set like sixty million other Americans, watching Elvis Presley (mistakenly introduced by the actor Charles Laughton as Elvin Presley) perform on *The Ed Sullivan Show. Don't Be Cruel, Love Me Tender, Ready Teddy, Hound Dog*—all the magic of rock 'n' roll! "It was all there in his eyes, his face, the face of a Saturday night jukebox Dionysus, the shimmying eyebrows and rocking band,"[1] Bruce writes in his autobiography. The next day, he persuaded his mother to take him to Diehl's Music on South St and, because she couldn't buy him a guitar, she rented one instead for $6 a week. New horizons beckoned: "One Saturday afternoon, I brought it home. And I sat on the living room couch. And I unlatched its full alligator case. And I slowly opened it up. And up from the green velvet lining came the sweet smell of a cherrywood cocktail of power, pleasure, salvation, dreams, dreams, dreams."[2] However, Bruce's fingers were too small to go around the neck of the guitar. Discouraged by the technical difficulties of the

Elvis Presley on the set of *The Ed Sullivan Show* on 9 September 1956. This performance had a strong impact on Springsteen.

The West Long Branch, New Jersey, high school yearbook, with a student named Bruce Springsteen.

instrument, which were insurmountable for the time being, he decided with a heavy heart to take it back to the store. But his day would come.

As more and more American teenagers fell for the charms of rock 'n' roll and R&B, Springsteen felt a growing desire to become a musician and found himself absorbing the sounds of the late 1950s and early 1960s.

The Beatles revelation

Not long after that, The Beatles entered the life of the Freehold High School student. In January 1964, *I Want To Hold Your Hand* climbed to No.1 in the *Billboard* charts; a few days later, on 9 February, the Fab Four took America by storm: 73 million viewers for their first appearance on *The Ed Sullivan Show*. Another huge bombshell: Springsteen's second musical revelation after Elvis. From then on, the four Englishmen from Liverpool occupied his every thought: "I lived for every Beatles' record release. I searched the newsstands for every magazine with a photo I hadn't seen and I dreamed...dreamed ...dreamed...that it was me."[1]

Beatlemania swept the United States at the same time as the British Invasion—The Rolling Stones, The Animals, The Dave Clark Five, Manfred Mann, and Herman's Hermits were monopolizing the top spots in the American hit parades. Representing the Americans, there was Bob Dylan. After quitting the Midwest for Greenwich Village, and following the release of his second album, *The Freewheelin' Bob Dylan* (1963) and the impact of songs like *Blowin' in the Wind*, *Masters of War*, and *A Hard Rain's A-Gonna Fall*, the songwriter had become the symbol of an America that was undergoing a profound transformation, and afforded the status of campus spokesperson.

The first bands

While still in high school, Springsteen earned some pocket money doing various domestic chores, and was able to buy a decent guitar that he would play as often as he could. This was the start of a long and hard apprenticeship on the instrument. Fingers on fire from plucking strings as thick as telephone wire, some unexpected help came in the form of his cousin Frank, an accordionist and guitar player, who taught him the secrets of tuning and guitar chords. The first rock song Bruce mastered was none other than *Twist and Shout*, a song popularized by The Beatles. Then, for Christmas 1964, his mother contributed half of the $69 he needed to buy his first electric guitar (amplifier included): a Japanese Kent Sunburst with a single microphone that he had spotted at Caiazzo's Music on Center St. As soon as Bruce got home, he plugged in the little amp: "Its tiny six-inch speaker roared to life. It sounded awful, distorted beyond all recognition. The amp had one control, a volume knob. It was about the size of a large bread box but I was in the game,"[1] he later said.

The Castiles

A few chords later, Springsteen started playing with a drummer friend, Donnie Powell, and they were soon joined by other budding Freehold musicians. The group initially called themselves The Merchants before changing their name to The Rogues in early 1965, just before their baptism of fire at the Freehold Elks Lodge on 1 February, which was followed by gigs at various high schools in town. Around June, Bruce Springsteen, on vocals and guitar, became a member of The Castiles, a band set up by George Theiss (another singer-guitarist) who had named it after his shampoo brand! The band

Ed Sullivan in conversation with The Beatles in 1964. The music of the Fab Four was a true eye-opener for the young high schooler from New Jersey.

FIRST SINGLE

Bruce Springsteen first set foot in a recording studio, Mr. Music, in Bricktown, New Jersey, in May 1966. With The Castiles—George Theiss (guitar and vocals), Curt Fluhr (bass), Vinnie Maniello (drums), and Paul Popkin (tambourine and vocals)—he recorded two Springsteen-Theiss compositions: *That's What You Get* and *Baby I*. The second song was released in September 2016 on the *Chapter and Verse* compilation to accompany the launch of his autobiography *Born to Run*.

had a string of gigs at clubs, high schools, drive-ins, and psychiatric hospitals. On 1 October 1966, the band was hired to play at the Hullabaloo Club, in Middletown, New Jersey. On the same day, Springsteen met someone that would have a decisive effect on his career: Steven Van Zandt, who became known as "Miami Steve" and later "Little Steven." He was the Shadows' guitarist (and no relation to Hank Marvin's band) at the time. Springsteen was introduced to Van Zandt while he was having a short break from performing one night. Steve knew who Springsteen was because by then The Castiles were a well-known band. They got on well, and so began a long and deep friendship between the two musicians.

Bruce Springsteen remained a member of The Castiles until August 1968 (after 30 shows at the famous Café Wha?, in Greenwich Village, and a final appearance at Le Teendezvous, in New Shrewsbury, on 10 August). Meanwhile, he had replaced his Kent guitar with a teal-blue, solid-body Epiphone.

Earth

Springsteen then formed a group called Earth with John Graham on bass and Michael Burke on drums, and shortly after, Bobby Alfano on organ. Armed with a new electric guitar, a Gibson Hollow Body, and a Danelectro amplifier, the young Springsteen decided to build on what Cream and The Jimi Hendrix Experience had been doing with psychedelic rock, with a repertoire that included Hendrix's *Purple Haze*, Moby Grape's *Omaha*, and songs by The Beatles and Rolling Stones, but also, in a completely different spirit, Leonard Cohen's *Suzanne*.

As for Springsteen's Gibson guitar, it was causing him a whole lot of trouble: he found the frets too widely spaced and the neck much longer than he was used to. But the sound it produced more than made up for these minor issues. A fortuitous encounter made him realize that he was playing a somewhat unusual instrument. After a concert, a kid came up with an explanation: "He walked up and congratulated me on the brilliant idea of stringing an old Gibson 6-string bass with guitar strings and playing it as a solo instrument. I nodded coolly while thinking, 'Holy shit...it's a 6-string bass!'"[1] It was also around this time that he bought a 12-string Ovation and started composing his first acoustic songs, this time influenced by Bob Dylan, the British troubadour Donovan, and Tim Buckley. Indeed, Springsteen was very much inspired at the time by Tim Buckley, emulating his song-writing style and vocal approach, as well as playing a 12-string guitar (because that was the instrument played by Buckley).

Child, Steel Mill, and Dr Zoom and the Sonic Boom

Springsteen scoured the clubs of New Jersey, and in February 1969 set up a band called Child with Danny Federici on organ, Vinnie Roslin on bass, and Vini Lopez on drums. The band was renamed Steel Mill in November 1969.

In the late 1960s, after successfully avoiding the draft and the horrors of Vietnam, Springsteen dropped out of graduate school at Ocean County College and decided to become a professional musician. He was 19 years old. His parents did not approve, but they had already decided to leave New Jersey to start a new life in California. At first, they had considered living in Sausalito (north of the Golden Gate Bridge), home to the hippie counterculture, but then decided to settle in San Mateo. Springsteen stayed behind in the family home in Freehold, where the other members of Steel Mill now lived (until they were evicted), and organized more gigs, notably at the Upstage Club, in Asbury Park, and the Pandemonium in Wanamassa. The group also performed outside New Jersey in Randolph-Macon College, Virginia, in November 1969, and in major venues on the Californian rock scene such as the Avalon Ballroom, the Fillmore West, and The Matrix in January 1970 (as well as the Esalen Institute in Big Sur). In February 1970, a few weeks after the West Coast Tour, Steve

Singer-songwriter Tim Buckley onstage at the Bitter End, Greenwich Village, in November 1967. He was the one who inspired Springsteen to buy a 12-string guitar.

Van Zandt replaced Vinnie Roslin on bass for Steel Mill, which became a five-man band with the arrival of singer Robbin Thompson in September. The band found a new name in the spring of 1971 (after Bruce dissolved Steel Mill in December 1970). They became Dr Zoom and the Sonic Boom as new musicians joined the core group of Springsteen, Van Zandt (who switched from bass to electic guitar), and Lopez. They were Garry Tallent on bass, David Sancious on keyboards, Southside Johnny on harmonica, Bobby Williams (also on drums), and The Zoomettes as backing singers.

The Bruce Springsteen Band

Two months later (after giving only two concerts in May 1971), Dr Zoom and the Sonic Boom was dead—long live The Bruce Springsteen Band! Featuring alongside the front man, Van Zandt, Tallent, Lopez, and Sancious were Harvey Cherlin on trumpet, Bobby Feigenbaum on sax, and backing singers Barbara Dinkins and Delores Holmes. As Springsteen explains, it was after Steel Mill that he decided to use his own name for the band and assume sole responsibility, something he says was one of the best decisions he ever made: "I didn't want to get into any more decision-making squabbles or have any confusion about who set the creative direction of my music. I wanted the freedom to follow my 'muse' without unnecessary argument."[1]

When it came to the choice of manager to take charge of the destiny of The Bruce Springsteen Band, he hired Carl Virgil West, who had managed Child, Steel Mill, and Dr Zoom and the Sonic Boom. Carl "Tinker" West was a Californian who had come to the East Coast in the early 1960s to set up a surfboard manufacturing company (Challenger Eastern Surfboards). "We needed a place to rehearse, and he said we could rehearse there [at Challenger Eastern Surfboards]," explains Bruce. "He got us two speakers and said he would be the manager. We said 'okay.' He said he'd just try and get us jobs. He said [it was] 'cause he liked the band."[3]

A decisive meeting

Tinker knew a number of artistic directors and producers in New York. One day, in 1971, he asked Springsteen to accompany him to New York to meet Mike Appel, one of the key decision-makers at the Wes Farrell Organization, which was looking for songwriters. "Mike spieled me on who he was and what he could do (publish, produce, manage), and I played him a few songs that were the precursors to the songs I'd write for *Greetings from Asbury Park*," Springsteen explains in his autobiography. "Mike expressed some interest."[1]

The young songwriter and the New York producer arranged to meet up again after a tour of California. On 14 February 1972, to be precise, Springsteen got back in touch with Mike Appel and played him some of his compositions—enough to fill a whole album—but this time in the presence of Appel's partner Jimmy Cretecos and the journalist Bob Spitz. Springsteen recalls in his autobiography how, in just a few

When Tinker discovered Springsteen in the Upstage Club, he tried to set him up with Janis Joplin's band, who were looking for a guitarist at the time. But he got nowhere.

For Springsteen Addicts

On 20 July 1969, while Springsteen and Steel Mill were getting ready to perform in the Pandemonium, a Jersey Shore club, some of the customers in the room decided that they would rather watch the TV broadcasting the historical event of the decade: the first moonwalk. The atmosphere quickly turned sour and the musicians were manhandled out of the club!

seconds, he was compared to Bob Dylan, Shakespeare, James Joyce, and even Bozo the Clown. Blown away by the extraordinary talent of this 22-year-old singer-songwriter, Appel said to him: "Bruce, I don't think you're going to find anybody who's going to love your stuff any more than I do."[3] Appel then promptly resigned from the Wes Farrell Organization in March to dedicate himself entirely to his young singer-songwriter. Shortly after, Springsteen signed a contract with Laurel Canyon Productions, the company Mike Appel set up with the producer Jimmy Cretecos on 75 East 55th Street in New York. The contract committed the company to producing Springsteen's next five albums and selling them to a major label, for which Springsteen would receive 50 percent of the royalties, but none of the publishing rights. Appel's management approach was modeled on that of Elvis and the Colonel, and it was agreed that they would split everything equally between them.

The die was cast. From then on, the artist's future would largely depend on Mike Appel and Jimmy Cretecos, whose mission was to get their protégé signed up to a major record label. Bruce Springsteen's apprenticeship was over. The phase that was now beginning would take him to the pinnacle of the rock world and earn him the well-deserved sobriquet, "the Boss."

Columbia's new Dylan

As soon as the contract between Bruce Springsteen and Laurel Canyon Productions was signed, Mike Appel began calling the New York record companies. His first stop was Atlantic Records, to no avail. The producer then tried his luck with Columbia Records (and also Elektra Records). The secretary of the famous talent scout, John Hammond, answered the phone at Columbia Records. An appointment was scheduled for Wednesday, 2 May 1972. "Appel took the chair on my left, the young man with the guitar sat down in the far corner,"[4] writes John Hammond in his autobiography. Springsteen started playing *It's Hard to Be a Saint in the City*. "He launched into an extraordinary piece filled with street imagery. I heard immediately that he was both a born poet and an extremely good guitar player. I kept a lid on my excitement; I didn't want Appel to see how impressed I was."[4]

That evening, John Hammond asked Sam Hood, the owner of the Gaslight Café, in Greenwich Village, to let Bruce Springsteen perform there; he wanted to see what he was capable of onstage. The following day, he booked Springsteen a small studio at CBS Records: Studio B on 52nd Street. In less than two hours, Springsteen recorded 14 songs. Clive Davis, the record label boss, listened to the tape and immediately shared John Hammond's enthusiasm. The producer and the record industry tycoon were firmly convinced that they had just discovered the new Bob Dylan, no less! The contract included an advance of $65,000, with a guaranteed minimum of $25,000 and $40,000 for the recording, which would only cost $11,000! Springsteen was therefore able to buy his first Fender guitar and, not long after, his first Harley-Davidson.

Mike Appel (arm raised) with Bruce Springsteen (in the foreground) and Danny Federici at the 914 Sound Studios in Blauvelt, New York State.

MIKE APPEL: THE MAN WHO DISCOVERED THE BOSS

Mike Appel had already made a name for himself on the New York music scene when he met Bruce Springsteen in November 1971. He had just had an unexpected hit with *Doesn't Somebody Want To Be Loved* (No.6 in the *Billboard* charts in February 1971), a song that he cowrote with Jimmy Cretecos and Wes Farrell for *David Cassidy and The Partridge Family.*

Mike Appel was born in Queens, New York, on 27 October 1942 and, like Bruce Springsteen, had Irish Catholic roots on his mother's side. His father was Jewish; a real estate agent who had made his fortune from the economic boom on Long Island in the 1950s. Appel converted to the new religion of rock 'n' roll, thanks mainly to Chuck Berry and Carl Perkins, and set up his first band (The Humbugs) at the age of 16, followed shortly after by his baptism of fire in a recording studio. In the following years, he continued his apprenticeship in various groups, notably The Balloon Farm (named after Andy Warhol's club) with whom he recorded *Farmer Brown's Ole Mill Pond* and *A Question of Temperature* for Laurie Records. The latter made it into the US Top 40 in February 1968.

Springsteen and Laurel Canyon Management

After a period in the Marines that left its mark on him, Mike Appel went back to the music world, not just as a songwriter but also as a producer at H&L Music, the production company founded by songwriters Hugo Peretti and Luigi Creatore (who were responsible for creating hits with the likes of Sam Cooke, The Isley Brothers, and Elvis Presley). It was around this time that Appel struck up a friendship with the songwriter Jimmy Cretecos whose song, *Lay a Little Lovin' On Me* (cowritten with Jeff Barry and Robin McNamara) was his ticket into the Wes Farrell Organization. In turn, Appel was also hired by Wes Farrell's company, where he worked with the Osmond Brothers and the pioneering heavy-metal trio Sir Lord Baltimore on the *Kingdom Come* album (December 1970).

In November 1971, almost a year after the release of *Kingdom Come*, Mike Appel received a call from Tinker, suggesting that he meet a young singer, guitarist, and songwriter. "Springsteen comes up to the writers' room of the Wes Farrell Organization," Appel recounts. "He was wearing ripped-up jeans and a T-shirt. He said he wanted to get an album deal with a major label. I remember he looked at me and said, 'I'm tired of being a big fish in a little pond.' 'Fine,' I said, 'let's hear what you've got.' So he sat down at the piano and played only two songs. The first was the most boring thing I'd ever heard in my entire life. But the second had something. It was a song about dancing with a girl who was deaf, dumb, and blind with a lyric that included, 'They danced all night to a silent band...' It was a very weird line and stuck in my head, as did the way he sang, with an intensity I couldn't believe."[3]

Nevertheless, Mike Appel suggested to Springsteen that he compose some new songs and come back to see him, which is what Springsteen did in February 1972, with *It's Hard to Be a Saint in the City*, *Henry Boy*, and *The Angel*. This time Appel was convinced, and decided to sign him. Better still, in March 1972, he quit the Wes Farrell Organization and set up Laurel Canyon Productions with Jimmy Cretecos to produce Springsteen, Laurel Canyon Management to manage him, and Sioux City Music Inc. for his songwriting.

Discord and reconciliation

In the weeks after the contract was signed between the Laurel Canyon Companies, Sioux City, and Bruce Springsteen, a meeting was set up with John Hammond. The audition was a huge success: Springsteen became a Columbia artist. Appel subsequently coproduced the first three albums, *Greetings from Asbury Park, N.J.*, *The Wild, the Innocent, and the E Street Shuffle* (with Cretecos), and *Born to Run* (with Springsteen and Jon Landau). It was during the *Born to Run* sessions that Springsteen decided to change tack and invite Jon Landau, the journalist who had previously praised Springsteen's work in his column in *The Real Paper* of Cambridge (Massachusetts), to join his team as coproducer and manager. As a result, Mike Appel lost overall control of his protégé. It was an artistic split, but also a breach of contract between the artist and Laurel Canyon-Sioux City. A long legal battle ensued (see *Toward Purity and Austerity*, page 102) before an agreement was reached in 1977 (which meant that *Darkness on the Edge of Town* could then be recorded). The two men were only reconciled in November 2009, when Bruce Springsteen invited his ex-producer to the final show of his Working on a Dream Tour. By then, Appel had long since left the music scene. He and Marc Eliot coauthored the book *Down Thunder Road: The Making of Bruce Springsteen.*

Donna Carson

ALBUM

GREETINGS FROM ASBURY PARK, N.J.

Blinded by the Light • Growin' Up • Mary Queen of Arkansas • Does This Bus Stop at 82nd Street? • Lost in the Flood • The Angel • For You • Spirit in the Night • It's Hard to Be a Saint in the City

Outtakes: *Arabian Nights • Visitation at Fort Horn • Jazz Musician • Lady and the Doctor • Cowboys of the Sea • Two Hearts in True Waltz Time • Street Queen • The Chosen*

RELEASE DATE

United States: 5 January 1973

Reference: Columbia Records – KC 31903

The New Jersey songwriter is all smiles during recording sessions for his first album.

THE WHOLE ALBUM LIVE
Springsteen and the E Street Band played the whole of *Greetings from Asbury Park, N.J.* live for the first time on 22 November 2009, at the HSBC Arena in Buffalo, New York.

THE ALBUM OF AN EVOLVING SINGER-SONGWRITER

What is the musical flavor of Bruce Springsteen's first album? Clive Davis and John Hammond heard a folk singer who sounded like Bob Dylan in his early days, or contemporary artists such as James Taylor and Jackson Browne, despite Springsteen's previous stage experiences with more rock 'n' roll-style bands. "He's much farther along, much more developed than Bobby [Dylan] was when he came to me,"[5] Hammond remarked. However, Springsteen did not want to be cast in the role of "folky" singer-songwriter that was expected of him; he wanted to work with a band. A compromise was eventually reached. "On *Greetings* I managed to bring in my homeboys Vini Lopez, Davey Sancious, and Garry Tallent," he explains in his autobiography *Born to Run*, "with a cameo performance by Steve Van Zandt shaking my Danelectro amp's reverb unit at the intro to *Lost in the Flood*. Steve was to be on the record but we opted out of electric guitar in my concession to the singer-songwriter I was signed to be."[1] In other words, *Greetings from Asbury Park, N.J.* is a record by a young rock musician transformed into a folk-rock songwriter, and not the other way round.

Springsteen began writing his album in early 1972, just after signing with Mike Appel and Jimmy Cretecos: "I went home and started to work on the songs for *Greetings from Asbury Park, N.J.*"[6] It came easily to him, as his producers were expecting a mostly acoustic record: "From the late '60s on, I always had a notebook full of acoustic songs,"[6] he explains. He found inspiration at the back of a former beauty salon under his Asbury Park apartment. "There I had an Aeolian spinet piano my aunt had given me, and amid the old hairdryers and washing sinks, I wrote the songs that comprised *Greetings*."[6] He would later state that this was the only album where he worked on the words first, then the music. "I never wrote in that style again,"[6] he said.

Nine songs: the start of the epic adventure

The nine songs on this first musical confession were largely autobiographical—a young songwriter from New Jersey expressing what was on his mind as he set out to conquer New York. "That record reflects the mood I was in at that particular time," he said in 1974. "You know, the fact of having to come into the city from where I was living, and I didn't have a band, so it all contributed to that kind of down feel. But toward the end of the record I started pulling out of it with songs like *Spirit in the Night,* which started to get into a whole different feel."[7] His still raw memories of adolescence pervade the album, from *Blinded by the Light*, to the numerous references to New Jersey, to *It's Hard to Be a Saint in the City*, where there are implicit references to his Catholic education and his love-hate relationship with the big city. *Does This Bus Stop at 82nd Street?* alludes to his difficult relationship with his father and his early days as a songwriter, as does the aforementioned *Spirit in the Night.*

However, four songs escape this introspective feel. *Mary Queen of Arkansas* may have historical connotations, while *Lost in the Flood* evokes the war in Vietnam; *For You* is both sentimental and heroic; and *The Angel* tackles for the first time

Lester Bangs (left) was the first rock critic to write a favorable review of *Greetings from Asbury Park, N.J.*

a theme that would become central to the New Jersey songwriter: the imagery of the open road and the freedom it offers. The strong imagery, notably in *Blinded by the Light* and *Mary Queen of Arkansas*, is inherited as much from the Beat Generation poets (Jack Kerouac and Allen Ginsberg) as it is from Bob Dylan.

The first album of a promising career

Greetings from Asbury Park, N.J. was available in American record stores from 5 January 1973 (outside the United States, Columbia was distributed by CBS Records). Springsteen was stunned when he first saw his record: "Somebody brought down a copy of *Greetings from Asbury Park, N.J.*, and pulled it out of the sleeve. It was on that red Columbia label and, to me, it was like an impossibility, because I pulled *Highway 61 Revisited* [by Dylan] out of that sleeve with the red label on it. Seeing my name on that red label was quite miraculous."[7] The decision to release the album after the Christmas vacation—a particularly lucrative period for the record industry—seems surprising to say the least, because no one at the record company really expected the album to succeed. So, it is all the more astonishing that Columbia actually accompanied the release of the record with a genuine promotional campaign. An article about the campaign appeared in *Rolling Stone* magazine in April 1973: "A member of the press would get a phone call from the publicity department at Columbia and be told he would receive an advance copy of a record by a new artist (not unusual), and after he had a chance to listen to it, President Clive Davis would appreciate a call to get his reaction (highly unusual). Meanwhile, visitors to the CBS Building encountered publicity personnel and suited executives alike greeting people with the question, 'Hi...have you heard Bruce Springsteen yet?'"[8] Bruce Springsteen and Columbia nevertheless had to wait several months before a favorable review appeared, once again thanks to the essential *Rolling Stone* magazine (and penned by the inimitable Lester Bangs): "He's been influenced a lot by The Band, his arrangements tend to take on a Van Morrison tinge every now and then, and he sort of catarrh-mumbles his ditties in a disgruntled mushmouth sorta like Robbie Robertson on Quaaludes with Dylan barfing down the back of his neck. It's a tuff combination, but it's only the beginning."[9]

While *Greetings from Asbury Park, N.J.* was musically promising, it initially only achieved modest commercial success, selling just 25,000 copies (or 23,000, depending on the source) in the first year of its release. It was not until 1975, thanks to the huge impact of *Born to Run,* that it entered the *Billboard* charts. It has since been certified gold in 1978, then multi-platinum in 1992.

The sleeve

Once the songs on Springsteen's first album had been recorded, Columbia Records' idea was to present him to the press and

The postcard that inspired Bruce Springsteen and Columbia Record's artistic director John Berg for the graphics of the first album.

The handwritten credits on the album insert contain some spelling mistakes: Lahav is spelled Lehav; Clemons, Clemmons; and Garry, Gary.

public as a new artist from the New York scene. However, the songwriter from Freehold was determined to emphasize his connections with New Jersey, where he had been born 23 years earlier. His idea came in the form of a postcard that he had purchased while walking along the pier in Asbury Park. Written on it were the words "Greetings from Asbury Park N.J." and inside the letters A S B U R Y P A R K were illustrations of the town, including the pier, the beaches, and the ocean. Against Mike Appel's better judgment, Bruce Springsteen presented his project to Columbia. "Like the main reason I put it on that first album (as the title) was because they were pushing for this big New York thing—this, this big town," Springsteen admitted to Ray Coleman of *Melody Maker* in November 1975. "I said, 'Wait, you guys are nuts or something. I'm from Asbury Park, New Jersey. Can you dig it? NEW JERSEY.' I wasn't too cool. I said, 'I want this on the album cover.'"[10] Finally, Columbia's artistic director John Berg took the young songwriter's side and work began on the album cover that Springsteen wanted.

On the back, a photograph of the smiling young songwriter appears inside the printed image of a stamp. The photograph was taken by Fred Lombardi. Inside, an insert made to look like a postcard features handwritten credits for the album.

The recording

Laurel Canyon received an advance of $65,000 from Columbia Records and allocated $40,000 to the production of Bruce Springsteen's first album, which ultimately cost only $11,000 to make. The studios chosen for the recording were 914 Sound Recording Studios, 34 Route 303, in the hamlet of Blauvelt, in Rockland County (whose dialing code was 914 until 2000), 30 miles (48km) from New York. Mike Appel and Jimmy Cretecos had already worked there. "We were very friendly with Brooks Arthur [the owner and recording engineer] and thought it would be a good studio, away from the New York studios where you'd have people coming in for the next session and you'd have to get out whether you were finished or not. Up there we had a kind of freedom."[3] However, the 914 Sound Recording Studios were not exactly state-of-the-art: they had been installed in an old garage with fairly mediocre acoustics and a leaking roof. A real "crapper,"[11] Springsteen would later say—a rather harsh opinion because he nevertheless recorded his song *Born to Run* there in 1974.

In *Down Thunder Road: The Making of Bruce Springsteen*, the book he wrote in collaboration with Marc Eliot, Mike Appel points out that, contrary to what people have said, the *Greetings from Asbury Park, N.J.* sessions did not begin in June 1972, but in the August, and carried on into September. Mike Appel and Jimmy Cretecos were the producers; there was a union engineer from Columbia Records and another recording engineer, Louis (sometimes spelled Luis) Lahav, who had been a paratrooper in Israel before coming to America and getting to know Appel and Cretecos. Lahav, a

Brooks Arthur (left, with songwriters Jeff Barry and Ellie Greenwich) founded 914 Sound Recording Studios, where Bruce Springsteen recorded his first album.

former assistant at A&R Studios, recalls the first time he met the future Boss: "One day, in 1973, a producer named Mike Appel brought a young and practically unknown artist to the studio, with whom I immediately fell in love. It was Bruce Springsteen and we made two records almost right on the spot."[12] Larry Alexander was also present as Lahav's assistant. Alexander would go on to have a brilliant career, working with artists such as David Bowie, Diana Ross, Steely Dan, and Paul McCartney, to name but a few. Right from the very first session, the atmosphere was tense because Columbia Records insisted on using its own recording engineer, maintaining that he absolutely must be involved in the recording process. Mike Appel saw things differently and moved heaven and earth to get Louis Lahav on the job. Finally, after many exhausting negotiations, witnessed by a perplexed Springsteen who was patiently waiting to get down to work, the decision was made to leave Lahav on the console, but pay the Columbia recording engineer his full salary to sit in a corner reading the newspapers.

A difficult delivery

Although Mike Appel has stated that recording began in August, Springsteen did start recording some solo acoustic tracks, probably on 7 June. The first versions of *Street Queen*, *Arabian Nights*, *Growin' Up*, and *Lady and the Doctor* were completed around that date. But as Springsteen felt the need to play as a band, he brought his musicians together at the end of June with his producers' approval. He subsequently carried on recording acoustic versions alone. When everyone listened to the results, two conflicting camps emerged: Hammond and Appel were determined to have a mainly acoustic album whereas Springsteen and Cretecos preferred more of a rock style. As explained earlier, they came to a compromise: half of the album would be with the band (*Growin' Up*, *Does This Bus Stop at 82nd Street?*, *Lost in the Flood*, *For You*, *It's Hard to Be a Saint in the City*) and the other half would be mostly solo (*Mary Queen of Arkansas*, *The Angel*, *Jazz Musician*, *Arabian Nights*, and *Visitation at Fort Horn*).

On 10 August, Appel and Cretecos sent a copy of the album to Columbia for approval. They were confident of the outcome. Clive Davis listened to it and, to their great surprise, the tape was immediately returned to sender. The tape was accompanied by a note explicitly stating that Davis did not think the album contained any hits or anything that could be played on the radio. There was only one thing for it: over the next few days, Springsteen composed *Spirit in the Night* and *Blinded by the Light*, which were then recorded and included with the other songs on the first album. As a result, *Jazz Musician*, *Arabian Nights*, and *Visitation at Fort Horn* were definitively excluded from the tracklisting. Although the recordings appear to have been spread out from June to October, in actual fact it took only three weeks to complete the main versions of the songs for the album over two concentrated periods in June and September (the last overdubs were done on 26 October).

Big Man and the others

For *Blinded by the Light* and *Spirit in the Night*, Springsteen called on Clarence "Big Man" Clemons, the irreplaceable sax player who would be one of the figures forever associated with what became the E Street Band.

At Columbia's request, Steve Van Zandt was not involved

Columbia Records president Clive Davis signed Bruce Springsteen, confident that he'd discovered the new Bob Dylan.

in the recording (although he had a prior commitment anyway as a sideman with The Dovells). The other musicians accompanying the future Boss in the studio were Vincent Lopez (who would become known as Vini "Mad Dog" Lopez) on drums, Garry Tallent on bass, and David Sancious on keyboards, all of whom had previously played with Dr Zoom and the Sonic Boom (Lopez had also been in Child and Steel Mill). Sancious and Tallent were not available in September, as they were busy at Alpha Sound Studios, in Richmond, Virginia, so Harold Wheeler helped out on piano for *Blinded by the Light* and *Spirit in the Night*, while Richard Davis stepped in to play double bass for *The Angel*.

Technical details

The 914 Sound Recording Studios were founded by the producer and recording engineer Brooks Arthur, in October 1970, as a subsidiary of A&R Studios. Brooks, who produced and collaborated with artists such as Van Morrison, Neil Diamond, and The Shangri-Las, set up the studios in partnership with Phil Ramone, Donald Frey, and Art Ward; he retained 50 percent of the shares and the three others held the remaining 50 percent between them. Hank Cattaneo built the studio on the site of an old garage. Besides Springsteen, other artists who worked at the studio included James Taylor, Blood, Sweat & Tears, Dusty Springfield, the Ramones, and Janis Ian—who recorded the 1974 album *Between the Lines* there (featuring the hit *At Seventeen*), which reached the top spot on the *Billboard* album chart in September 1975. The 914 Sound Recording Studios closed in 1978, after Springsteen had recorded his first two albums as well as part of *Born to Run* there.

On the technical side, the console, built by Neil Monsey, had 32 inputs and outputs, each equipped with a Melchoir equalizer. The tape recorder was a Scully 288 Series 16-track, 2-inch, connected to a DBX, while the monitors were a pair of huge Altecs. For the reverb, there were two echo chambers: an EMT 140 plate and an AKG BX-10. Brooks says that he recorded Springsteen's vocals using a Neumann U47 microphone.

The instruments

For this first album, Springsteen recorded mainly with an acoustic guitar. Given the mediocre quality of his own

Saxophonist Clarence Clemons in 1973. He was already a key part of Bruce Springsteen's sound.

A Martin D-28, similar to the model Springsteen used in *Greetings from Asbury Park, N.J.*

For Springsteen Addicts

Coincidentally, Laurel Canyon Productions, at 75 East 55th St, in Manhattan, was in the same building as the office of Albert Grossman, Bob Dylan's manager. "He was always very polite but on Mars," Mike Appel recalls. "Albert was out there somewhere. But we did have something in common: the only toilet bowl shared by Dylan and Springsteen."[3]

instrument, Larry Alexander, the assistant recording engineer, says that he lent Springsteen his own Martin D-28. As for the electric guitar used on *Blinded by the Light*, the question is whether in September 1972 Springsteen already had his Telecaster with the Esquire neck, which was the 1950s model purchased from Phil Petillo (see *The Instruments*, page 47). This is far from certain because, although in his autobiography Springsteen mentions using it in January 1973, he does not state when he purchased it. He could have used his Gibson Les Paul Gold Top which he played when he was with Steel Mill and The Bruce Springsteen Band. However, it does not sound like the Gibson. He may also have used a 12-string guitar to record *Does This Bus Stop at 82nd Street?*, probably the Ovation that he bought in 1969. As for the amplifier, he says in his autobiography that he had a Danelectro amp, the one that Steve Van Zandt shook for the intro to *Lost in the Flood*. Finally, Springsteen plays the bass on two tracks: *Blinded by the Light* and *Spirit in the Night*. The guitar is a 1963 Fender Precision Bass (Serial #L64990) which The Balloon Farm used to record their 1968 hit *A Question of Temperature*, a song composed by none other than Mike Appel who was also lead vocalist and guitarist. The guitar belonged to Jay Saks, the band's bass player.

BLINDED BY THE LIGHT

Bruce Springsteen / 5'02

Musicians

Bruce Springsteen: vocals, acoustic guitar, electric guitar, bass
Harold Wheeler: piano
Clarence Clemons: saxophone, backing vocals
Vini "Mad Dog" Lopez: drums
Unidentified musicians: organ, tambourine

Recording

914 Sound Recording Studios, Blauvelt, New York State: 11 September 1972

Technical team

Producers: Mike Appel, Jim Cretecos
Recording engineer: Louis Lahav
Assistant recording engineer: Larry Alexander

COVER

Blinded by the Light became a huge hit for the English rock group, Manfred Mann's Earth Band. Their version went to No.1 in the United States in December 1976 (and No.6 in the United Kingdom in August 1976). Was this down to a change of lyrics? "*Cut loose like a deuce [the 1932 Ford hot rod]*" in the original was replaced by Chris Hamlet Thompson singing "*revved up like a deuce,*" which many listeners heard as *douche*! Springsteen was clearly amused: "I have a feeling that that is why the song sky-rocketed to No.1."[13] But the excellent rendition by Manfred Mann should not be underestimated. A must-listen.

Genesis and lyrics

Blinded by the Light did not originally feature on *Greetings from Asbury Park, N.J.* Like *Spirit in the Night*, Bruce Springsteen wrote the song after Clive Davis rejected the album in its initial form because he felt that it did not contain any potential hits. "I [...] came home, busted out my rhyming dictionary, and wrote *Blinded by the Light*,"[1] Springsteen explains in his autobiography. The song was largely inspired by the melody of the demo track *Henry Boy* that he had recorded in June 1972 at Mediasound Studios, in New York, and which features on the 2016 *Chapter and Verse* compilation album.

This opening track of Springsteen's first album is an impassioned rereading of his own adolescence. He explains this in detail on the DVD *VH1 Storytellers—On Stage*: "So it was really a young musician's tale. Kind of a litany of adventures and it was rather on the autobiographical side."[13] He goes on to explain the title of the song: "I wanted to get blinded by the light, I wanted to do things I hadn't done and see things I hadn't seen."[13] It is obvious that the boy from New Jersey wanted to burn his bridges, sling his guitar over his shoulder, and set out to conquer New York.

The verses also draw on the songwriter's own experience. The expression "*madman drummers*" explicitly refers to Vini Lopez, the E Street Band drummer, known as "Mad Man" (then "Mad Dog"), while "*Indians in the summer*" alludes to the songwriter's favorite baseball team when he lived in Freehold. "*Teenage diplomat*" is a reference to himself, with "a boulder on my shoulder"—a symbol of oppression. He also includes memories of the YMCA and his first sexual stirrings ("the adolescent pumps his way into his hat"). Inevitably, this invites comparisons with Bob Dylan's *Bringing It All Back Home* and *Highway 61 Revisited*. "*And go-cart Mozart was checkin' out the weather chart to see if it was safe to go outside*" could have been borrowed from the couplet: "*You don't need a weather man to know which way the wind blows*" in Dylan's *Subterranean Homesick Blues*.

Blinded by the Light (in a shortened 3'58 version) was released as a single with *The Angel* on the B-side in February 1973 but did not make it into the *Billboard* charts. Why February, which is traditionally a bad month to launch a record? "Because they [the record company] didn't believe it

Composer and orchestra conductor Harold Wheeler on the piano, recording *Blinded by the Light.*

had a chance to go Top 40," explains Mike Appel. "And they were right."[3] However, that did not stop Bruce Springsteen performing the song regularly onstage—the first time was most probably at the Captain's Garter in Neptune City, New Jersey, on 30 January 1972.

Production

Jon Landau, a journalist at *Rolling Stone* magazine, was listening to his car radio when he was grabbed by a particular song: "*Blinded by the Light*, one of the cuts on *Greetings*, was on," he recounts. "I didn't know who it was, but I thought it was a great song and a great singer, an exciting record. It sounded like—a bit like The Band, the group The Band. I wondered, who was that? It was identified at the end. I made a mental note."[3] Good job too, because, thanks to this track, not that long after Landau would meet the singer in question, become his manager, and go on to coproduce many of his albums. *Blinded by the Light* unquestionably already had this immediately recognizable force and resonance that would soon become known as the Springsteen sound. Rather surprising, perhaps, because the only musicians present at the recording session on 11 September were Springsteen himself, Vincent Lopez, Clarence Clemons, and Harold Wheeler, a musician who was not part of the songwriter's inner circle. Springsteen poured all his talent and energy into this piece, showing such conviction that it left no one indifferent. Hence Jon Landau's reaction.

The introduction is structured around three guitars: the first, an electric guitar, starts with a country-rock lick; the second, an acoustic guitar (the Martin D-28); then a third, electric again, for the solo parts. Was Springsteen using his Fender Telecaster with the Esquire neck? It's hard to tell. The introduction continues with the drums, bass, piano, and saxophone coming in. This is followed by a short liaison in which the electric guitar adopts a rhythmic pattern similar to the one used on The Doobie Brothers' smash hit *Listen to the Music*, which was released in early September 1972 (listen from 0'12 onward).

Springsteen then attacks the first verse with a warm voice, not yet perfectly mastered or polished, but already unique and luminous. When the record was released, critics rushed to compare him to Bob Dylan, but the resemblance is definitely not in the voice; Springsteen was a real singer, and Dylan, without wishing to be pejorative, was more of a storyteller than a singer. However, there is an obvious Van Morrison influence, notably from the *Wild Night* track on the *Tupelo Honey* album (1971). In the chorus, Clarence Clemons supports the lead vocal with his powerful voice, and Springsteen harmonizes with him in the last line (at 1'33).

The piece continues with alternating verses/choruses, a bridge at 2'37, and a coda starting at 4'29. The overall result is positive, with Springsteen performing the three guitar parts, the bass, and the vocals himself. He is supported by a piano accompaniment that is unfortunately buried too deep in the mix. It is performed by the excellent Harold Wheeler who also worked with Burt Bacharach and Nina Simone, among others. Clemons contributes some very R&B parts on the saxophone and Vini Lopez is solid on the drum part which, sadly, sometimes sounds a bit "cardboard cutout" because the sound recording is too dry. Note: A tambourine can be heard from 3'22, while a sustained note on the organ appears from the first verse (at 0'36).

A songwriter lost in thought, photographed in 1973 in his Jersey Shore stronghold. *Growin' Up* was one of the songs that landed Bruce Springsteen a contract with Columbia.

GROWIN' UP

Bruce Springsteen / 3'05

Musicians

Bruce Springsteen: vocals, acoustic guitar
David Sancious: piano
Garry Tallent: bass
Vini "Mad Dog" Lopez: drums

Recording

914 Sound Recording Studios, Blauvelt, New York State: 7 and 27 June 1972

Technical team

Producers: Mike Appel, Jim Cretecos
Recording engineer: Louis Lahav
Assistant recording engineer: Larry Alexander

For Springsteen Addicts

Bruce Springsteen surprised the crowd when he invited a young fan up onstage to play *Growin' Up* with him at a concert in Brisbane, Australia, on 16 February 2017.

COVER

David Bowie recorded a superb version of *Growin' Up* in 1973, with Ronnie Wood on guitar, during the *Diamond Dogs* sessions. Bowie was the first artist to do a cover of a Springsteen song. The recording featured as a bonus track on the rerelease of *Pinups* in 1990.

Genesis and lyrics

Growin' Up is one of the three songs (along with *It's Hard to Be a Saint in the City* and *Mary Queen of Arkansas*) that Bruce Springsteen successfully performed for John Hammond at Columbia Records. Once again, he wrote and recorded the song under the benign influence of Bob Dylan. Like the composer of *Chimes of Freedom* and *Like a Rolling Stone*, he employed a whole range of metaphors to partially lift the veil on his adolescence. "I hid in the clouded wrath of the crowd/ But when they said, 'Sit down,' I stood up." This first refrain is probably the one that best summarizes the teenager's feelings as a high school student in Freehold—an uncontrollable but healthy need to rebel and not conform. This is indeed what he sings in the second verse: "I broke all the rules."

In fact, throughout the song, Bruce Springsteen, who claims he went straight from childhood to adulthood, expresses his refusal to fit the mold and accept the authority of his elders. He says he was the "cosmic kid" who "found the key to the universe in the engine of an old parked car." What could be more typically rock 'n' roll? Bruce Springsteen has performed *Growin' Up* around 600 times, starting with the Captain's Garter show, in Neptune City, on 30 January 1972.

Production

The first studio take was on 3 May 1972. Springsteen recorded a demo of several songs for Columbia Records (these appear on the *Tracks* box set, which was released in 1998). Then in June he traveled out to 914 Sound Recording Studios, probably for two sessions on 7 and 27 June. It is the 27 June version that features on the album, and it was probably the first song that he recorded in the 914 Studios. He brought in Garry Tallent and David Sancious, two ex-members of Dr Zoom and the Sonic Boom, and also Vini "Mad Dog" Lopez, a former member of Steel Mill, to accompany him.

Growin' Up is structured around three verses and three refrains. David Sancious on piano gets the track rolling. His lyrical playing, which was influenced by R&B, works wonders (particularly his solo at 1'42). He is accompanied by two acoustic guitars in stereo. The drum and the bass come in at the third line to provide dynamic country-rock-style support, backed by a tambourine in the first refrain (at 0'45). Bruce's rendition already displays the force that would make him one of the great singer-songwriters of his generation.

MARY QUEEN OF ARKANSAS

Bruce Springsteen / 5'20

Musician
Bruce Springsteen: vocals, guitar, harmonica
Recording
914 Sound Recording Studios, Blauvelt, New York State:
26–27 June 1972
Technical team
Producers: Mike Appel, Jim Cretecos
Recording engineer: Louis Lahav
Assistant recording engineer: Larry Alexander

For Springsteen Addicts

On 22 April 1984, a promotional disc including a live version of *Mary Queen of Arkansas,* recorded on 31 January 1973 at Springsteen's first show at Max's Kansas City in New York, was sent out to radio stations to celebrate the 500th broadcast of the radio show the King Biscuit Flower Hour.

John Hammond Sr (sitting). After Bob Dylan, the charismatic Columbia producer put Bruce Springsteen on the road to success.

Genesis and lyrics

Who was Bruce Springsteen thinking of when he wrote *Mary Queen of Arkansas*? Particularly intriguing is the sentence: "You're not man enough for me to hate or woman enough for kissing." The songwriter kept everyone wondering until 2014, when he confided that the subject of the song was the love a man felt for a transvestite. Looking at the title, the song could also have been influenced by Charles Jarrott's film *Mary, Queen of Scots*, starring Vanessa Redgrave. The movie, which Springsteen would have seen when it was first screened in New York in February 1972, recounts the dramatic destiny of the Scottish queen who was beheaded in 1587. Springsteen was raised a Catholic, so this lyric may also be a reference to Mary, the mother of Jesus, or perhaps it simply refers to a woman that the narrator once loved despite their many relationship problems: "I don't understand how you can hold me so tight and love me so damn loose," sings Springsteen at the end of the song. In one way or another, it is the story of an impossible love. A love seen as a dangerous game, with the narrator comparing himself to a "lonely acrobat" for whom "the live wire is my trade."

Production

Mary Queen of Arkansas was one of the demos recorded by Phil Giambalvo on 3 May at CBS's Studio B on 52nd St (and features on the *Tracks* box set from 1998). "Springsteen immediately impressed me," the recording engineer said. "He was cordial, friendly, and a little awed at being at the CBS studios."[14] Although John Hammond was not hugely keen on this version, it has a particular charm, probably more so than the one that Bruce produced for Louis Lahav's microphones on 26 and 27 June.

On 26 June, Springsteen laid down the vocals and the acoustic guitar. The next day, he overdubbed his superb harmonica part. He starts with an introduction on his Martin D-28, creating a rhythmic effect with the palm of his right hand (at 0'08). The harmonica heightens the atmosphere with melancholic flourishes, along with a deep reverberation from the EMT 140 plate. Springsteen's voice gently resonates warmth. He pours his heart and soul into telling his story. Springsteen was definitely talented; Appel and Hammond were not mistaken.

DOES THIS BUS STOP AT 82ND STREET?

Bruce Springsteen / 2'05

Musicians
Bruce Springsteen: vocals, acoustic guitars
David Sancious: piano
Garry Tallent: bass
Vini "Mad Dog" Lopez: drums

Recording
914 Sound Recording Studios, Blauvelt, New York State: 26–27 June, 12 July 1972

Technical team
Producers: Mike Appel, Jim Cretecos
Recording engineer: Louis Lahav
Assistant recording engineer: Larry Alexander

Actress Joan Fontaine is all smiles. The heroine from *Rebecca* played a part in the writing of *Does this Bus Stop At 82nd Street?*

Genesis and lyrics

Does This Bus Stop at 82nd Street? is another song drawn from the songwriter's personal experience. It was a memory of his father who was a bus driver and with whom he was often at odds. "There were two things that were unpopular in my house," Springsteen once mused. "One was me, the other one was my guitar."[10] There was a huge gulf between Douglas Springsteen and the young musician who dreamed of turning professional. But, beyond this family allusion, *Does This Bus Stop at 82nd Street?* also recalls the journey that Bruce Springsteen used to make from New Jersey to New York to see his girlfriend. The images roll slowly by as the bus makes its way to 82nd Street: they include the actress Joan Fontaine, the heroine of Hitchcock's *Rebecca* (on an ad in a downtown train), "Tainted women in VistaVision/[who] Perform for out-of-state kids," and "Mary Lou [who] found out how to cope." All are mini-portraits of the city world. Finally, the bus arrives at its destination and everything is wonderful because "Uptown in Harlem [the Spanish rose] throws a rose/To some lucky young matador."

Production

Does This Bus Stop at 82nd Street? was one of the demos Springsteen recorded on 3 May at CBS Studios. But, unlike *Mary Queen of Arkansas*, where the demo version was arguably better than the album version, this time the *Greetings* version achieves an unparalleled breadth. Where Bruce Springsteen struggled to keep the tempo on the demo (which features on the 1998 *Tracks* box set), on this version he keeps to the beat, surrounded by his musician buddies. Vini Lopez and Garry Tallent's rhythm section breathes welcome strength and energy into the piece, although "Mad Dog" slightly overdoes it.

David Sancious contributes to the texture of the piece with a piano accompaniment that once again has been under-mixed, while Springsteen takes on lead vocals, as well as two rhythmic acoustic guitar parts, most probably with the 12-string Ovation that he bought in 1969 and Larry Alexander's Martin D-28, a 6-string guitar.

The album version most likely emerged from the 27 June and 12 July sessions.

LOST IN THE FLOOD

Bruce Springsteen / 5'14

For Springsteen Addicts

Bruce Springsteen has played *Lost in the Flood* onstage on very few occasions. One notable performance was on the Vote for Change Tour (September to October 2004), which was organized by America Coming Together to encourage Americans to register on the electoral lists, especially in the swing states, and vote (preferably for the Democrats).

Musicians
- **Bruce Springsteen:** vocals
- **David Sancious:** keyboards
- **Garry Tallent:** bass
- **Vini "Mad Dog" Lopez:** drums
- **Steve Van Zandt:** special effects

Recording
- **914 Sound Recording Studios, Blauvelt, New York State:** 27 June, (?) July 1972

Technical team
- **Producers:** Mike Appel, Jim Cretecos
- **Recording engineer:** Louis Lahav
- **Assistant recording engineer:** Larry Alexander

Steve Van Zandt participated in the recording of *Lost in the Flood*: the thunderclap at the beginning!

Genesis and lyrics

Lost in the Flood sees Bruce Springsteen following on from the tradition of the great American singer-songwriters of the 1960s and 1970s, first and foremost of whom was Bob Dylan. Indeed, there is something dramatic about this song and its vision of society that is reminiscent of the oppressive, broken atmosphere of Dylan songs such as *My Back Pages* and *Desolation Row*. Springsteen demonstrates his originality as a songwriter here by telling three stories that come together as one. In the first part, a "ragamuffin gunner" who is back from Vietnam beholds an abandoned town on the brink of chaos with "Nuns [...] pregnant, pleadin' immaculate conception" and "everybody wrecked on Main Street from drinking unholy blood." In the second part, Springsteen introduces Jimmy the Saint (the Vietnam veteran transformed?) who is a fan of stock car racing, a passion that will eventually lead to his annihilation. Finally, the third part depicts New York city dwellers who have lost touch with reality: "Eighth Avenue sailors in satin shirts," the "Bronx's best apostle stands with his hand on his own hardware," then "five quick shots" and "the cops come up for air." What does all this mean? Did the GI escape death in Vietnam only to meet his end in the urban jungle of New York?

Production

A clap of thunder, in stereo, opens *Lost in the Flood*. The sound is created by Steve Van Zandt, in his sole contribution to the album, by shaking Springsteen's Danelectro amp to make it reverberate. While the song itself was probably recorded on 27 June, this effect seems to have been overdubbed toward the end of July.

This superb song is partly dominated by David Sancious's piano: Springsteen, with no instrument to play on this piece, was free to concentrate fully on his vocal performance. And what a performance! Instinctively, through his entire body, he expresses his emotions with conviction and sensitivity. He commands total respect with the mastery that he displays at this early stage of his career.

The rhythm section comes in around the middle of the second verse to accentuate the tension (at around 2'01), with the bass and drum injecting a somewhat heavy and aggressive sound. Besides the piano, David Sancious also lends color to the arrangements with a calliope (from 1'29), then a church organ (at 3'31).

THE ANGEL

Bruce Springsteen / 3'23

For Springsteen Addicts
At the start of the song Springsteen mentions "*Hubcap Heaven.*" This was the name of a real-life store in Howell, New Jersey. It has since been renamed Hubcap Farm.

Musicians
Bruce Springsteen: vocals
David Sancious: piano
Richard Davis: double bass

Recording
914 Sound Recording Studios, Blauvelt, New York State: 26, 27, and 29 June, 26 October 1972

Technical team
Producers: Mike Appel, Jim Cretecos
Recording engineer: Louis Lahav
Assistant recording engineer: Larry Alexander

Only three musicians were involved in recording *The Angel*. Bruce Springsteen on vocals, David Sancious on piano, and Richard Davis (above in 1984) on the double bass.

Genesis and lyrics

"The Angel is one of my great favorites—conceived, constructed, and completed inside of 15 minutes," says Bruce Springsteen. "It's the most sophisticated thing I've done."[7] When Springsteen penned the first stanzas of this song, did the songwriter have in mind Laslo Benedek's *The Wild One*, featuring Marlon Brando as the leader of a biker gang? What is certain is that Springsteen foregrounds his all-consuming passion for the open road—the ultimate freedom in the United States—as well as for the world of bikers, whose love for their machines is sometimes lethal. There are two heroes here: The Angel, a biker who regards his machine as "a lethal weapon" riding past "nomadic hordes/In Volkswagen vans," and Madison Avenue who has "eyes like rain."

Bruce Springsteen sang *The Angel* for his audition with Mike Appel and Jim Cretecos on 14 February 1972. To date, he has only performed the song onstage three times: on 6 October 1973 at Radnor, Pennsylvania; on 22 April 1996 in London; and for the first time with the E Street Band on 22 November 2009 in Buffalo, New York State.

Production

The Angel is one of the songs that Springsteen recorded on 3 May in the CBS Studios during his audition for Columbia. The album version appears to have been worked on at three sessions on 26, 27, and 29 June. One of the takes features Springsteen accompanying himself on guitar. However, in the album version, David Sancious provides invaluable backup with a delicate and lyrical piano part that replaces Springsteen's guitar. Then, at the session on the 26 October, the excellent Richard Davis further enriches the end of the piece by playing his double bass with a bow (from 2'38). Davis is an accomplished jazzman who has worked with Sarah Vaughan, Eric Dolphy, and Chet Baker, among others, and has contributed to albums by artists such as Van Morrison (*Astral Weeks*) and Paul Simon (*There Goes Rhymin' Simon*).

Bruce once again gives a remarkable performance; his rendition has an astonishing subtlety and depth, especially for a young man who was only 22 years old. His vocal mastery is perfect, his delivery totally sincere, and he holds the vibrato extremely well. His voice is drawn out and utterly compelling. Amazing artistry. *The Angel* opens the B-side of the original album.

FOR YOU

Bruce Springsteen / 4'39

Musicians
Bruce Springsteen: vocals, acoustic guitar
David Sancious: piano, organ
Garry Tallent: bass
Vini "Mad Dog" Lopez: drums

Recording
914 Sound Recording Studios, Blauvelt, New York State: 27 June, 26 October 1972

Technical team
Producers: Mike Appel, Jim Cretecos
Recording engineer: Louis Lahav
Assistant recording engineer: Larry Alexander

COVERS
For You was the second Bruce Springsteen composition covered by Manfred Mann's Earth Band. It is also worth mentioning the successful adaptation by Greg Kihn, who recorded the song for his second album *Greg Kihn Again* (1977).

Vini Lopez, in 2017, at the premier of *Just Before the Dawn*, a documentary about the Upstage Club, where Bruce Springsteen recruited the future members of the E Street Band.

Genesis and lyrics

For You is another standout moment on *Greetings from Asbury Park, N.J.* It is one of the first love songs that Springsteen recorded, inspired by his breakup with Diane Lozito—his girlfriend (see *Genesis and Lyrics*, page 56)—in late 1971. He explained the situation in June 1978: "And I remember I was breaking up with this girlfriend and I went away for a week and I came back and she'd painted all the walls in my room black...That's not true, I made that, I made that up...actually she'd painted 'em all blue."[15]

This is a deeply tragic love story because we sense that the heroine is on the edge of a precipice and has taken the irreversible step, and the narrator can do nothing to help the woman he loves. "I came for you, for you, I came for you/But you did not need my urgency/I came for you, for you, I came for you/ But your life was one long emergency,"[3] goes the chorus. The drama happens in Chelsea, London. An ambulance arrives and rushes the young woman to hospital, but it is already too late. "So you left to find a better reason than the one we were living for," Springsteen sings toward the end of the song.

This "suicide ballad" was chosen as the B-side of the second single taken from *Greetings from Asbury Park, N.J.* (with *Spirit in the Night* on the A-side). It was released in May 1973 without great success.

Production

For You is one of the songs Springsteen played for Mike Appel, Jim Cretecos, and Bob Spitz on 14 February. When Appel heard it, he was blown away: "Why me?" he wondered. "I mean, I'm sitting there in this big commercial firm knocking my brains out, banging my head against the wall when suddenly this wonderful, talented guy walks into my life."[3] He couldn't believe his luck.

For You appears to have been recorded on 27 June with the entire band, then finished on 26 October with an overdubbing session, notably involving Steve Van Zandt, who recorded a slide guitar part that was unfortunately rejected by Appel.

The piece is a gentle rock song typical of the Springsteen style. Springsteen contributes lead vocals and an acoustic guitar part, supported by an efficient rhythm section, consisting of Vini Lopez and Garry Tallent, as well as David Sancious's piano and his organ contribution from the first chorus (at 1'03).

SPIRIT IN THE NIGHT

Bruce Springsteen / 4'58

Musicians
Bruce Springsteen: vocals, bass, conga, handclaps, piano (?), organ (?)
Clarence Clemons: saxophone, backing vocals, handclaps
Vini "Mad Dog" Lopez: drums, handclaps
Harold Wheeler: piano

Recording
914 Sound Recording Studios, Blauvelt, New York State: 11 September, 26 October 1972

Technical team
Producers: Mike Appel, Jim Cretecos
Recording engineer: Louis Lahav
Assistant recording engineer: Larry Alexander

THE FIRST TIME
The first time Springsteen heard one of his songs on the radio he was about to give a concert in Connecticut in 1973. He was on a street corner when a car drew up next to him playing *Spirit in the Night*. "Your number one rock 'n' roll dream come true!" the Boss would later recount. "You never forget the first time you hear your song on the radio."[1] And that was just the start.

For Springsteen Addicts
Did Bruce Springsteen write *Spirit in the Night* with William Butler Yeats' poem *Crazy Jane Talks with the Bishop* in mind?

Genesis and lyrics

Bruce Springsteen wrote *Spirit in the Night* in August 1972 (at the same time as *Blinded by the Light*) at the request of Clive Davis, who felt there was no hit potential in the album that he had heard so far. The songwriter has said that he was inspired by Joe Cocker when composing the song: "When I wrote the song I had his kind of voice in mind which is something that I rarely do."[10]

However, the lyrics to *Spirit in the Night* are totally in keeping with the universe of the New Jersey songwriter. Mission Man, the song's main character, tells the story of a group of buddies who decide to go partying one Saturday night. Alcohol, sex, and good music are the name of the game. Mission Man is accompanied by his young girlfriend, Crazy Janey, Wild Billy, G-Man (the FBI agent), Hazy Davy, and Killer Joe. In a 1974 interview, Springsteen says that Hazy Davy's character was partly inspired by Little John, the protagonist of *The Moon Struck One*, a track from the *Cahoots* album (1971) by The Band. A man called David Hazlett has also said that Springsteen nicknamed him "Hazy" back in the days of The Castiles. Wild Billy was the boyfriend of a girl called Diane Lozito with whom Springsteen was madly in love throughout 1971 (see *Genesis and Lyrics*, page 56). She is Crazy Janey in the song.

The night's revelries take place at Greasy Lake, "about a mile down on the dark side of Route 88 [the highway that crosses Ocean County along the Jersey Shore]." This is "where the gypsy angels go" and "dance like spirits in the night." The fictional Greasy Lake is based on several real lakes: Shenandoah and Carsaljoakes, near Lakewood, and Topanemus near Freehold. It is so named because the homeless would wash themselves in lakes such as these. Dave Marsh notes that the "Greasy Lake of *Spirit in the Night* is [Springsteen's] equivalent of John Ford's Monument Valley, but he celebrates its inhabitants more than its natural splendor."[16] Interesting fact: in the United States, homeless people are also known as "gypsy angels" and "spirits in the night."

This ode to youth and New Jersey was released as the A-side (with *For You* as the B-side) of the second single taken from *Greetings from Asbury Park, N.J.*

Joe Cocker electrifies the crowd at Woodstock in 1969. *Spirit in the Night* stands somewhere between R&B and rock. Springsteen composed it thinking about Joe Cocker, the emblematic singer of blue-eyed soul.

Manfred Mann's Earth Band in concert in Berlin. The British group performed a phenomenal version of *Spirit in the Night*.

COVER

Spirit in the Night is the third song from *Greetings from Asbury Park, N.J.* to be recorded by Manfred Mann's Earth Band.

A NEW LEASE OF LIFE

The 1963 Fender Precision bass guitar originally belonged to Jay Saks of The Balloon Farm and was initially bought by the group's drummer, Don Henry. It was later sold at Guernsey's Auctions, in New York, on 2 December 2017.

Production

Like *Blinded by the Light*, this song was recorded on 11 September with the same lineup: Bruce, Clarence, Vini, and Harold. A single overdub session was added on 26 October. At the time this rapidly written version was being recorded, it would appear that a previous version may have been written the year before. Indeed, when Clarence Clemons was asked about the title of the piece being played in September 1971, when the two men first met at the Student Prince club, he replied: "It was an early version of *Spirit in the Night*."[17]

Whatever the truth of the matter, the Big Man gets the song underway with a heady riff on tenor saxophone. Springsteen wrote a sort of melancholic R&B rock for this track, the most musically accomplished on the album. When Springsteen starts singing, Van Morrison immediately comes to mind again, in particular his 1971 album *Tupelo Honey*. Although Springsteen was thinking of Joe Cocker while writing this song, he could not help but be influenced by the Irish artist, in terms of both its composition and rendition. Besides being a vocalist, Springsteen is also a very talented multi-instrumentalist. Although he does not play guitar on this piece (unless it is buried somewhere in the mix), he plays the bass part, as he did for *Blinded by the Light*. For the 11 September session, Mike Appel had been wondering who could replace Garry Tallent, as he was not available that day. Bruce suggested himself, and the four-string parts he recorded that day are of a very high quality, particularly the one on *Spirit*. He is playing a 1963 Fender Precision that once belonged to The Balloon Farm's Jay Saks, and he is a perfect match for Vini Lopez's drums.

Although not credited on the album, Springsteen was probably also on the organ (from 0'08) and the piano—leaving the talented Harold Wheeler to do the bridge (between 3'23 and 4'00). What we do know for sure is that he recorded the congas on the refrains to accompany the handclaps by Clemons and Lopez (example at 1'05). Finally, again with Clemons, he sings the backing vocals in the refrains and the choir vocals that give the instrumental bridge a rather gospel feel (at 2'35).

Despite Mike Appel's preference for an acoustic rendition, Springsteen was right to insist on recording this song with the band. *Spirit in the Night* was one of the album's successes, and a sign of the style and strength of the future Boss's albums to come.

The singer-songwriter with his Martin D-28, the guitar from *It's Hard to Be a Saint in the City.*

IT'S HARD TO BE A SAINT IN THE CITY

Bruce Springsteen / 3'13

For Springsteen Addicts

The director John Sayles used *It's Hard to Be a Saint in the City* on the original soundtrack for his movie *Baby It's You* (1983), starring Rosanna Arquette.

Musicians

Bruce Springsteen: vocals, acoustic guitar
David Sancious: piano
Garry Tallent: bass
Vini "Mad Dog" Lopez: drums

Recording

914 Sound Recording Studios, Blauvelt, New York State: 26–27 June, 26 October 1972

Technical team

Producers: Mike Appel, Jim Cretecos
Recording engineer: Louis Lahav
Assistant recording engineer: Larry Alexander

COVER

This is another song from *Greetings from Asbury Park, N.J.* that was covered by David Bowie. Bowie recorded it in 1974, but his version was only released in 1989 on the *Sound + Vision* box set.

42nd Street and its porn theaters served as backdrops for Bruce Springsteen in *It's Hard to Be a Saint in the City.*

Genesis and lyrics

It's Hard to Be a Saint in the City marks Bruce Springsteen's debut as a professional musician, as it was thanks to this song that Mike Appel became his manager and John Hammond hired him for Columbia Records. Both men sensed that Springsteen was a real songwriter, capable of reaching large audiences.

The narrator appears to be Springsteen himself, an adolescent from New Jersey who is discovering New York: "I could walk like Brando right into the sun/Then dance just like a Casanova." The author does not shy away from using witticisms, but what might sometimes be considered clichés should not be allowed to obscure the core meaning: an ambivalent feeling of being simultaneously repulsed and attracted by Manhattan and the multitude of colorful characters roaming the streets. Which impression is the strongest? Springsteen provides the answer when he sings: "I was the king of the alley, mama," "I was the prince of the paupers," and "I was the pimp's main prophet."

Production

Before the sessions at 914 Sound Recording Studios, Springsteen recorded a demo of this song at CBS Studios, in New York, on 3 May 1972 with Phil Giambalvo on console. The demo version, with Springsteen alone on guitar, inevitably makes one think of Dylan, but Springsteen's feverish rendition is very much his own, revealing the inner fire that would stay with him throughout his career (the demo version appears on the 1998 *Tracks* box set). Then, on 26 June, he recorded another acoustic take, this time with Louis Lahav at the controls. The next day, he got his musicians together for a rendition with the band.

The introduction to the piece is structured around Springsteen's Martin D-28 and David Sancious's piano, with Vini Lopez marking time on his hi-hat. It is the piano part that is astonishing: a bluesy solo that does not always match the guitar (especially in the second part). The whole band then launches in at a quick tempo, with Vini Lopez and Garry Tallent delivering an excellent rhythm section, arguably the most accomplished on the album. Sancious, meanwhile, accompanies them on his keyboard, with Springsteen on acoustic guitar. Springsteen's vocals are once again excellent; and he pushes his voice to breaking point, before resuming like a sleepwalker and continuing serenely. Listen to the phrase "And them South Side sisters sure look pretty" (at 2'25); it is very impressive.

ALBUM

THE WILD, THE INNOCENT, & THE E STREET SHUFFLE

The E Street Shuffle • 4th of July, Asbury Park (Sandy) • Kitty's Back • Wild Billy's Circus Story • Incident on 57th Street • Rosalita (Come Out Tonight) • New York City Serenade

Outtakes: *Evacuation of the West • Phantoms (or Over the Hills of St George) • Fire on the Wing • New York Song • Secret to the Blues • Angel's Blues (or She's So Fine or Ride On Sweet William) • Santa Ana • Seaside Bar Song • The Fever • Thundercrack • Zero and Blind Terry*

RELEASE DATE

United States: 5 November 1973

Reference: Columbia Records – KC 32432

David Gahr took this picture of Bruce Springsteen in Long Branch, New Jersey, during shooting for the *The Wild, the Innocent, and the E Street Shuffle* album jacket.

Artistic director Charles Koppelman (sitting on the left) was not convinced Bruce Springsteen would make it big.

BIRTH OF A GROUP

Despite the commercial failure of *Greetings from Asbury Park, N.J.*, Columbia Records hoped that Bruce Springsteen would eventually find his rightful place in the world of 1970s songwriters. A second album had to be recorded and out in stores as fast as possible, in the hope that it would establish Springsteen's reputation. "On the second album, I started slowly to find out who I am and where I wanted to be," Springsteen would later say. "It was like coming out of the shadow of various influences and trying to be yourself."[16]

For the New Jersey singer-songwriter, *The Wild, the Innocent, and the E Street Shuffle* was an album that represented both change and continuity. Continuity in the sense that it contained many of the same themes which had influenced him hugely for *Greetings from Asbury Park, N.J.* His childhood and adolescence on the Jersey Shore are portrayed in *The E Street Shuffle*, *4th of July, Asbury Park (Sandy)*, *Wild Billy's Circus Story,* and *Rosalita (Come Out Tonight)*, while the streets of New York form the backdrop to *Kitty's Back*, *Incident on 57th Street,* and *New York City Serenade.* Once again, with poetry, realism, and tenderness, Springsteen paints portraits of the first young women he loved, or who passed through his life: girls like Sandy, a more or less imaginary composite of the girls he once knew in New Jersey; Kitty, who abandons everything, lover included, for the bohemian delights of Greenwich Village; and pretty young Rosalita, whose mother disapproves of the behavior and social background of a young rock 'n' roll singer. As he did on his first album, Springsteen embellishes his songs with flamboyant characters, showing an attention to detail that invites comparisons with the great songwriters. There is an excellent example in this line from *4th of July, Asbury Park (Sandy)*: "And the boys from the casino dance with their shirts open/ Like Latin lovers on the shore."

At the same time, *The Wild, the Innocent, and the E Street Shuffle* marks a musical progression from *Greetings from Asbury Park, N.J.* It is not the album of a songwriter accompanied by a band, but an album with a real, coherent band, and a rock 'n' roll and R&B feel. "The new album was a little more what I wanted to do," Bruce Springsteen explains. "There was more of the band in there and the songs were written more in the way I wanted to write."[16] Of the seven songs, four are over seven minutes long, which is proof of the songwriter's overwhelming urge to convey his emotions and feelings about the world around him, to free himself and his musicians from the standard structure of folk and folk-rock songs, and to express himself through what could be called a new epic spirit. Although the folk-rock feel is still there throughout the album, Springsteen expands his musical palette considerably, alternating jazz, soul, funk, and pop sounds à la Tin Pan Alley/Brill Building (from George Gershwin to Burt Bacharach). As Ken Emerson rightly said in a *Rolling Stone* magazine article: "Having released two fine albums in less than a year, Springsteen is obviously a considerable new talent."[18]

However, not everyone at Columbia Records was a fan of *The Wild, The Innocent, and The E Street Shuffle.* Far from it.

1973

1973

David Gahr took this photo for the back cover of *The Wild, the Innocent, and the E Street Shuffle.* From left to right: Clarence Clemons, Bruce Springsteen, Danny Sancious, Vini Lopez, Danny Federici, and Garry Tallent.

With John Hammond retired and Clive Davis fired, the artistic director Charles Koppelman was now in charge of Bruce Springsteen. He listened to the tapes and was skeptical to say the least, particularly about the musicianship. Koppelman asked Springsteen to meet up at the Columbia Records' studio in order to show him what real musicians could do with the songs on the album. The songwriter refused to change the record in any way. However, Koppelman made it clear that if he released the record as it was, then it would be poorly promoted and unsuccessful, eventually fading into insignificance (along with Springsteen himself). The Columbia representatives would even go so far as instructing radio stations not to give the album airtime.

Koppelmann was more interested in promoting Billy Joel's career than Springsteen's. But everything changed in the weeks following the release of *The Wild, the Innocent, and the E Street Shuffle*, on 5 November 1973, when the son of Irwin Siegelstein, who had succeeded Clive Davis as the head of Columbia Records, attended a concert by Bruce Springsteen and the E Street Band. Fired with enthusiasm, he organized a dinner with his father and the songwriter. Springsteen recalls the CEO saying to him, "'How can we fix this?' He was a straight-up honest broker who realized we were of value to his company and wanted to set things right."[1] The first publicity for the album followed shortly after, along with the first positive reviews, such as the aforementioned article by Ken Emerson in *Rolling Stone*. Nevertheless, the second album was no more of a hit than *Greetings from Asbury Park, N.J.* (although it did finally make the UK charts in the mid-1980s, thanks to the impact of *Born in the U.S.A.*). In the United States, it now occupies a notable 133rd place in *Rolling Stone*'s list of the 500 Greatest Albums of All Time.

The sleeve

A close-up of Bruce Springsteen was chosen for the cover of his second album. The songwriter's head is turned slightly to one side, hand on mouth, lost in thought. The back cover is much more revealing of the new approach. It shows the whole band in front of an antiques store on Sairs Ave, in Long Branch, New Jersey: from left to right, Clarence Clemons, Bruce Springsteen, David Sancious, Vini Lopez, Danny Federici, and Garry Tallent. The photographs were taken by David Gahr, a

For Springsteen Addicts

The E Street Band only became the official name of the band in 1974, but it was already mentioned on Bruce Springsteen's second album. "E Street" is a street in Belmar, New Jersey, where David Sancious lived with his mother. *The Wild and the Innocent* is the title of a 1959 Jack Sher Western, starring Audie Murphy and Joanne Dru.

famous rock photographer (whose other notable subjects include Bob Dylan, Janis Joplin, John Lennon, and Van Morrison). The cover design is the work of Teresa Alfieri and John Berg.

The recording

The Wild, the Innocent, and the E Street Shuffle was recorded at the 914 Sound Recording Studios, in Blauvelt, New York state, as *Greetings from Asbury Park, N.J.* had been. The producers were Mike Appel and Jim Cretecos, and the recording engineer was Louis Lahav, assisted by Larry Alexander. Brooks Arthur, the studio's owner, remembers Springsteen turning up: "He'd show up in this old VW bus. There was a Carvel's [a chain of ice cream parlors famous throughout the US] right across the street; my daughters and Bruce would get ice cream together every day."[19]

The sessions took place in two stages between May and September 1973: Springsteen, accompanied by Clarence Clemons, Garry Tallent, Vini Lopez, and Danny Federici, initially recorded from 15 to 22 May, then from 17 to 20 June. When David Sancious—who had been busy at Alpha Sound Studios in Richmond, Virginia—turned up, the sessions continued from 26 June to 2 July, 4–12 August, and 10–25 September. The sessions were split up in this way because the band were still performing concerts on their first tour, unofficially called the Greetings from Asbury Park, N.J. Tour, between October 1972 and September 1973. Despite the many forays into the studio, most of the final cuts were made in late June and mid-September.

This time, unlike with the first album, Springsteen wanted to be more involved in the production: "Heading into *The Wild, The Innocent*, I was intent on taking control of the recording process,"[6] he would later explain. He wanted Mike Appel and Jim Cretecos to understand the performance aspect of his music, which they had not yet fully grasped. "Now I wanted to continue the lyrical content of my first album but add to it the physicality my music always had coming up through the clubs," he explained. "For this record, I was determined to call on my songwriting ability and my bar band experience."[6] Appel confirms his protégé's change in attitude: "I would say that [Bruce] performed more [as a producer on the second album], took a more active role on the creative side than he had previously. We were starting to think it was time that maybe he should be considered a producer, possibly on the third album."[3]

The way the sessions were run was radically different from the first album: the whole band was involved right from the outset. All the musicians played in the same room, with the exception of Vini Lopez, who was shut in a drum booth. When David Sancious joined his buddies in the studio from 22 June onward, most of the backing tracks were already in the can. The sessions were intense because they had to be slotted in between concerts, which increasingly worried Springsteen as he saw the deadline fast approaching. He and his musicians threw themselves into marathon around-the-clock sessions, and, at one point, in order to finish the last overdubs, Springsteen and Clemons even shared a tent pitched in the studio's backyard! Toward the end of the mixing, Springsteen realized he had been up for three days, the result being that he couldn't stay awake long enough to hear even one song played back and had to be shaken awake so he could listen to the rest of the mixing.

Once the recording and mixing were finished in late September, Mike Appel took the tapes to the Columbia executives. The total cost of the second album was $17,882.29, which was $6,000 more than the first.

The team

Absent from Springsteen's first album, Danny Federici, accordionist, keyboard player, and multi-instrumentalist, appears on his second album. The two men had known one another since the Child era, and Federici would be one of the most influential members of the E Street Band up until his death in 2008.

Other musicians who were not part of the E Street Band included percussionist Richard Blackwell, roadie Albany "Al" or "Albee" Tellone, who as a one-off played the baritone saxophone on *The E Street Shuffle,* and the recording engineer's

1973

wife, Suki Lahav (not credited on the album), whose pretty voice was used for the chorus singing on *4th of July, Asbury Park (Sandy)* and *Incident on 57th Street.*

The instruments

Although it is hard to pinpoint the exact date that Springsteen purchased the famous Fender Telecaster-Esquire, and especially to know whether he used it on his first album, there is no doubt that he did so on *The Wild, the Innocent, and the E Street Shuffle* because it makes a huge impression. Springsteen describes it in his autobiography *Born to Run*: "I strapped on my new guitar, a 1950s mutt with a Telecaster body and an Esquire neck I'd purchased at Phil Petillo's Belmar guitar shop for 185 dollars. With its wood body worn in like the piece of the cross it was, it became the guitar I'd play for the next 40 years. It was the best deal of my life."[1] According to some experts, the neck of this odd guitar appears to come from a 1957 Esquire. The luthier Phil Petillo said that the body came from a Telecaster which belonged to a record company, and that the guitar had been altered in order to insert four microphones with four outputs that could be plugged into four console inputs. A large hole had been cut under the black pickguard, making the guitar lighter and giving it a sound resembling an acoustic guitar. Petillo had removed all the electronics before selling it to Springsteen, and remembers the impression that Springsteen made on him when they first met: "I knew he was going to be successful. The first time I saw him play was with Dr Zoom and the Sonic Boom, and I said to myself that he was going to be great someday."[20] The luthier went on to become a friend of Springsteen's and would look after his guitar until his death in 2010. Springsteen stopped playing this particular guitar in concerts in 2005, as it was starting to show signs of serious deterioration. Today, its value is incalculable; the cost of insuring it is said to be somewhere between one and five million dollars.

As far as the acoustic guitar is concerned, Springsteen seems to have recorded with a 1972 Martin D-35. This was later stolen from the dressing rooms after a concert at Stony Brook University, New York, on 30 September 1973.

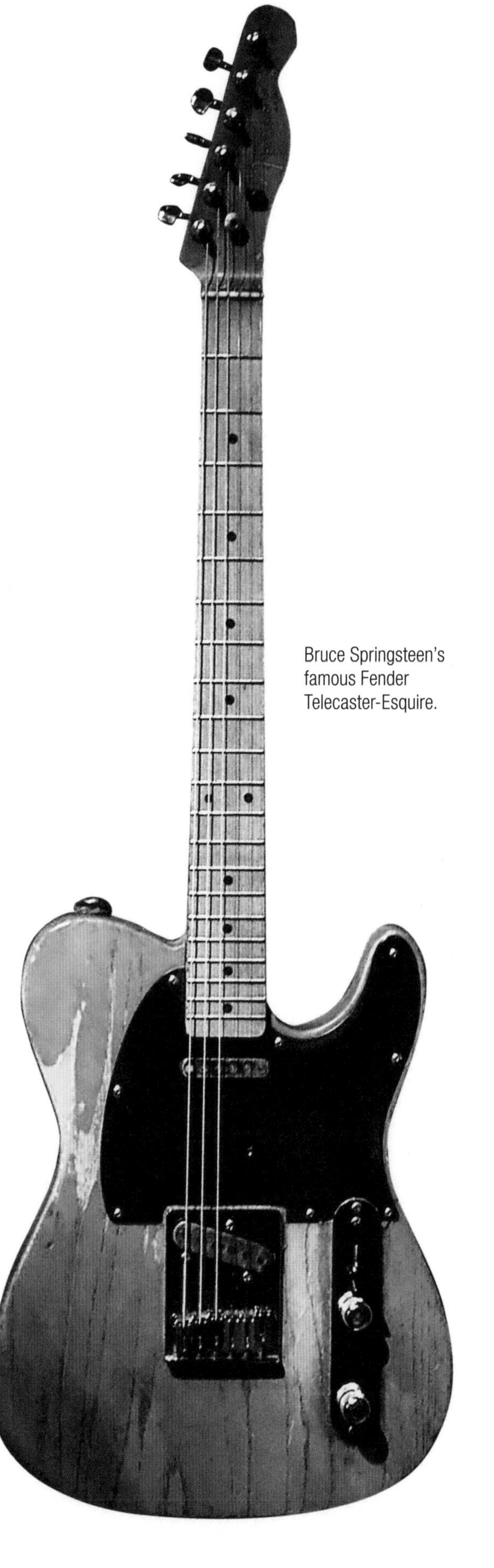

Bruce Springsteen's famous Fender Telecaster-Esquire.

THE E STREET SHUFFLE

Bruce Springsteen / 4'26

Musicians

Bruce Springsteen: vocals, guitar
Clarence Clemons: tenor saxophone, backing vocals
Danny Federici: keyboards (?), backing vocals
David Sancious: clavinet, electric piano, soprano saxophone, background vocals
Garry Tallent: bass, tuba
Vini "Mad Dog" Lopez: drums, cornet, background vocals
Richard Blackwell: percussion
Albee Tellone: baritone saxophone, background vocals

Recording

914 Sound Recording Studios, Blauvelt, New York State: May to September 1973

Technical team

Producers: Mike Appel, Jim Cretecos
Recording engineer: Louis Lahav
Assistant recording engineer: Larry Alexander

For Springsteen Addicts

Drummer of the E Street Band for 20 years (from 1974 to 1993), Max Weinberg started his own group in 1993 called The Max Weinberg 7. During shows performed with the group at the Convention Hall in Asbury Park on 4 and 8 December 2001, he revisited *The E Street Shuffle*.

Genesis and lyrics

This song marked a milestone in Bruce Springsteen's career since it was the first time that he was accompanied by the whole E Street Band. In this story about the New Jersey music scene of his teenage years, the songwriter from Freehold was hugely inspired by *The Monkey Time*—a song by the R&B singer Major Lance, written by Curtis Mayfield, which in 1963 reached No.2 and No.8 in the *Billboard* R&B and pop charts, respectively. "I wanted to describe a neighborhood, a way of life, and I wanted to invent a dance with no exact steps,"[1] Springsteen explains in his autobiography. Some of the characters in the song, such as Power Thirteen and Little Angel, were people that Springsteen had come across in Asbury Park in the days when the Upstage was one of the iconic clubs in what was a dynamic music scene. In many ways, *The E Street Shuffle* is the story of the golden age of Asbury Park, by then long since over. "The boardwalk was still operating, but the crowds were sparse," recalls Springsteen in his book *Songs*. "Many of the usual summer vacationers were now passing Asbury Park by for less troubled locations farther south along the coast."[6] Here the songwriter is alluding to the race riots that brought bloodshed to New Jersey, and Asbury Park in particular.

Bruce Springsteen played *The E Street Shuffle* onstage for the first time at The Spectrum, in Philadelphia, on 6 June 1973. His last performance of the song to date was also in Philadelphia, at the Citizens Bank Park, on 7 September 2016.

Production

If Springsteen was looking to shed his image as an acoustic singer, he could not have been more convincing than by opening his album with the supercharged *E Street Shuffle*! The entire band is gathered, ready to launch into a frenetic R&B peppered with funk, heavily inspired, it would seem, by Major Lance's hit. This is certainly what Albee Tellone, the band's roadie, felt when he heard the early drafts of the song at the house on 1107 E St, Belmar, where David Sancious lived with his mother. When Tellone pointed out the similarity between the two songs, Bruce and David shrugged their shoulders and replied: "Don't worry about it."[21] Springsteen's idea was to begin with a kind of brass-band sound, and, as Albee had briefly studied the saxophone in his youth, he was asked to

Composed by Curtis Mayfield and performed by R&B singer Major Lance (seen here in 1973), *The Monkey Time* was the New Jersey songwriter's main inspiration for *The E Street Shuffle*.

take part in the recording: "[Bruce told me] that he had rented a baritone saxophone for me to play especially for this one song. I remember him telling me that they had a 'new' model of baritone that had one low A note—lower than the traditional type [...] This low note was what he was looking for to be the 'hook' for this song called *The E Street Shuffle*."[21] This section was completed with Clarence Clemons on tenor saxophone, Garry Tallent on tuba, and Vini Lopez on cornet. The introduction begins with a prelude in which the musicians are tuning up, as Springsteen called it, and is followed by the actual motif. The Fender Telecaster-Esquire then attacks with a superb, clear-sounding, funky rhythm pattern, immediately accompanied by two clavinet parts in stereo (from 0'18), modulated on the wah-wah by the excellent Sancious in the style of Stevie Wonder's huge hit, *Superstition* (released in late 1972).

The entire band then comes in with a frenzied and funky R&B. Lopez and Tallent on the rhythm section are a real groove machine, with the two musicians making this E Street Band's shuffle soar. The basic track was obtained by recording all the musicians live in the studio (apparently on 28 June), then leaving each to rerecord his own solo part, through overdubbing (including Albee's bass note). The only exceptions were the drums and the bass, where the live take was the definitive one (Tallent was playing live into the console).

Springsteen proves here that he is not only a highly talented singer, but also a top-notch rhythm guitarist. He plays the very blues-rock licks from the second verse (listen at around 1'17). All the musicians participate in the chorus, singing in the central bridge (at 2'02) before creating a humorous atmosphere and launching into the final verse (at 2'16). An instrumental part then follows, with Bruce playing a guitar solo tinged with a short reverberation (from 3'08). This section is accompanied by voices and whistles, as Tellone explains: "[Bruce] wanted us to just start jive talking and yelling out stuff like 'Hey, what are you looking at!' and 'What is it?' It came out great and sounded like a bunch of guys out on a street corner in New York yelling at each other—hilarious!"[21]

The E Street Shuffle ends with a very rhythmic coda, at a livelier tempo, featuring the talented percussionist Richard Blackwell, who single-handedly recorded a large number of percussion instruments, including congas, cabasas, and a guiro, from a Spanish percussion kit specially rented for the occasion.

The E Street Shuffle is an incredible opening track, and it is hard to see why it was not better received at the time. It is even harder to fathom why Charles Koppelman, Springsteen's artistic director, advised him to change his musicians—hilarious, as Albee Tellone would have said.

4TH OF JULY, ASBURY PARK (SANDY)

Bruce Springsteen / 5'35

Madame Marie, the fortune-teller, was a real-life character in Asbury Park. Her real name was Marie Castello, and she operated a booth on the boardwalk called the Temple of Knowledge. Legend has it that she predicted Bruce Springsteen's success, as well as that of many other artists.

Musicians

Bruce Springsteen: vocals, acoustic guitar, electric guitar, recorder
Clarence Clemons: saxophone
Danny Federici: accordion
David Sancious: electric piano
Garry Tallent: bass
Vini "Mad Dog" Lopez: drums
Suki Lahav: choir vocals

Recording

914 Sound Recording Studios, Blauvelt, New York State:
9 August, 23 September 1973

Technical team

Producers: Mike Appel, Jim Cretecos
Recording engineer: Louis Lahav
Assistant recording engineer: Larry Alexander

Fortune-teller Madam Marie's booth on the Asbury Park boardwalk, at the heart of Bruce Springsteen's song.

1973

Genesis and lyrics

Bruce Springsteen has said that he wrote *4th of July, Asbury Park (Sandy)* in the garage apartment that he shared with his new girlfriend at Bradley Beach (next to Asbury Park): "She was Italian, funny, a beatific tomboy, with just the hint of a lazy eye, and wore a pair of glasses that made me think of the wonders of the library,"[1] he writes in his autobiography.

The second track on *The Wild, the Innocent, and the E Street Shuffle* is a beautiful ballad in the same vein as Van Morrison's *Cyprus Avenue* or *Madame George*, but imbued with a melancholic atmosphere and dotted with imagery that powerfully evokes a small, old-fashioned seaside resort on the East Coast of the United States. At a concert on 3 March 1974, Bruce Springsteen introduced the song with these words: "You travel around Nashville, Atlanta, Tennessee, and [people say], 'Hey! What's Asbury Park like?' and I play them this number."[22]

It is the 4 July, Independence Day in the United States. The narrator is whispering sweet nothings to his girlfriend as fireworks light up the ocean: "Sandy the aurora is risin', behind us/This pier lights our carnival life forever/Oh, love me tonight for I may never see you again." They are surrounded by a variety of colorful characters like the "switchblade lovers," the "wizards [who] play down on Pinball Way on the boardwalk way past dark," and "the boys from the casino [who] dance with their shirts open like Latin lovers on the shore." There are also the "greasers [who] tramp the streets," the "boys in their high heels," and Madame Marie, a fortune-teller. Springsteen writes about the heroine of the song in *Born to Run:* "Sandy was a composite of some of the girls I'd known along the Shore. I used the boardwalk and the closing down of the town as a metaphor for the end of a summer romance and the changes I was experiencing in my own life."[1]

4th of July, Asbury Park (Sandy) was a favorite song for radio presenters, who gave it plenty of airplay after the album was released. It is also one of the regulars on Bruce Springsteen's setlists, and has been performed 275 times to date.

Production

The basic track appears to have been completed on 9 August. Springsteen laid down his first vocals at this session, before

Bruce Springsteen with Danny Federici on the accordion—a key instrument in *4th of July, Asbury Park (Sandy)*—in concert during the Magic Tour in Boston on 19 November 2007.

COVERS

4th of July, Asbury Park (Sandy) has been recorded by a number of other artists, including Richard Shindell and Brian Fallon. The best-known cover version is the one by the British group The Hollies, entitled simply *Sandy*. It was the first Bruce Springsteen composition to enter the hit parades (at No.85 in the United States in 1975).

doing further takes and finalizing it during the last recording sessions on 23 September.

This second track on the album has a calmer, more acoustic atmosphere than *The E Street Shuffle*. The introduction is structured around several guitars, all played by Springsteen: the first, an acoustic guitar, placed in the middle of the stereo, provides the rhythm pattern for the piece; then, to the left and right, he recorded solo phrases on his Telecaster-Esquire that he harmonized in places through overdubbing. The whole section is carried by a deep, wide reverb. When Springsteen starts singing, he chooses to whisper to suggest intimacy (at 0'20). After the first verse, the entire band comes in to support the chorus, adding a Cajun tinge, mostly thanks to Danny Federici's accordion (from 1'12). In addition to the bass and drums, played by Garry Tallent and Vini Lopez, respectively, David Sancious is on electric piano, probably a Fender Rhodes. Springsteen, who contributes lead vocals and various guitar parts, is backed by the saxophone of Clarence Clemons for the melody.

On the next refrain, Suki Lahav, the wife of the recording engineer Louis Lahav, provides the chorus singing. As she explains: "I was only in the picture because I was Louis's wife. I remember once they invited a children's choir to record on the track *Sandy*. They didn't turn up, so Bruce decided to record me over and over, track on track, and make it sound like a choir. That was hard work, trying to sound like a choir."[23] Nonetheless, the result is convincing, despite an over-generous reverb that tends to drown out the different voices (listen from 3'01).

In the last verse, Springsteen accompanies himself on acoustic guitar, backed only by Sancious's Fender Rhodes, its crystal-clear notes moving across the stereo (at 3'48). The piece finishes with a final chorus in which the Boss plays a somewhat unexpected recorder motif (from 5'11).

KITTY'S BACK

Bruce Springsteen / 7'07

For Springsteen Addicts

Kitty's Back, which Springsteen performed for the first time in Amherst, Massachusetts, on 25 November 1973, has often led to long improvisations onstage, giving all the members of the E Street Band their moment in the limelight. The version on the *Hammersmith Odeon London '75* album (released in 2006) is over 17 minutes long and includes part of Van Morrison's *Moondance.*

Musicians

Bruce Springsteen: vocals, electric guitar
Clarence Clemons: saxophone, backing vocals
Danny Federici: organ, backing vocals
David Sancious: electric piano, organ, backing vocals
Garry Tallent: bass, backing vocals
Vini "Mad Dog" Lopez: drums, backing vocals

Recording

914 Sound Recording Studios, Blauvelt, New York State: 28 June, 24 July, and 23 September 1973

Technical team

Producers: Mike Appel, Jim Cretecos
Recording engineer: Louis Lahav
Assistant recording engineer: Larry Alexander

Orchard St, one of Manhattan's busiest streets. *Kitty's Back* is one of Bruce Springsteen's New York-themed songs.

Genesis and lyrics

Like *Incident on 57th Street* and *New York Serenade*, the backdrop to *Kitty's Back* is the Big Apple. It is a romantic and poignant vision of the city, told through the story of a young woman who has abandoned everything, boyfriend included, to join the bohemian community in Greenwich Village and live love's dream with a seductive young dude from Bleecker Street. Jack Knife, the abandoned lover, expresses his immense sadness at seeing his sweetheart go "running nightly, lightly through the jungle."

In a 1975 interview, Springsteen described this song as a "striptease number." The inspiration for the title came from an advertising sign announcing the return of a striptease show in a Jersey Shore club. "It's a strange song," he continues. "Sort of big band-y. I like it because it communicates the heat."[10]

Production

Kitty's Back is very different musically from everything Springsteen had recorded up until then, although it does have echoes of the jazzy rock that he had played now and again with a few of his early bands. But, listening to the piece, many influences can be heard, notably that of Van Morrison.

The song starts with a brilliant B.B. King-style blues intro, set alight by an extremely good solo guitar played by an inspired Springsteen, whose Telecaster-Esquire roars with added saturation and delay. He is supported by Clarence Clemons's sax parts, Danny Federici's organ, David Sancious's Fender Rhodes, and a rhythm section provided by Garry Tallent and Vini Lopez. The verses alternate between jazzy, soul, and blues-rock groove influences. Instrumentals feature heavily in this piece, in particular a second, spirited Springsteen solo (at 2'47) and an extraordinary contribution from Sancious, who launches into a superb Booker T Jones-style improvisation on his Hammond B-3 organ (from 3'34). In the only chorus of the song, backing vocals and handclaps respond to Springsteen's voice (at 4'55). A big-band atmosphere permeates the coda, with the musicians singing in unison and Clemons launching into a final saxophone solo (from 6'19).

Kitty's Back is an incredible track. In his autobiography, Springsteen comments that in 1973 he felt he needed songs that would attract audiences who did not know who he was. Listening to the result, we can safely say it is mission accomplished.

WILD BILLY'S CIRCUS STORY

Bruce Springsteen / 4'43

For Springsteen Addicts

Springsteen's work can be understood as a logical progression. The first sentence of *Wild Billy's Circus Story* is "All aboard, Nebraska's our next stop"; *Nebraska* is the title of the album that he released in 1982.

Musicians

Bruce Springsteen: vocals, guitar, harmonica, mandolin
Danny Federici: accordion
Garry Tallent: tuba
Vini "Mad Dog" Lopez: drums (?)
Unidentified musician: Mellotron (?)

Recording

914 Sound Recording Studios, Blauvelt, New York State: 25, 26, and 28 June 1973

Technical team

Producers: Mike Appel, Jim Cretecos
Recording engineer: Louis Lahav
Assistant recording engineer: Larry Alexander

Friends with Springsteen since 1971, E Street Band bassist Garry Tallent (seen here in 2012) is on the tuba recording *Wild Billy's Circus Story.*

Genesis and lyrics

Originally called just *Circus Song, Wild Billy's Circus Story* provides another striking glimpse into Bruce Springsteen's childhood on the Jersey Shore. It is "a black comedy based on my memories of the fairs and the Clyde Beatty-Cole Bros Circus that visited Freehold every summer when I was a kid,"[1] he explains in his autobiography. Throughout the song there are characters who evidently fascinated the future songwriter. They include a fire-eater, a sword-swallower, pudgy Missy Bimbo, a man-beast in his cage, Samson the strongman, and Tiny Tim, the midget. Beyond this, the song also centers around the themes of seduction and the isolation that people experience when they live on the margins of society.

Bruce Springsteen and his band performed *Wild Billy's Circus Story* for the first time at the Captain's Garter in Neptune City, New Jersey, on 30 January 1972, several months before it was recorded at the 914 Sound Recording Studios. Since then, he has only performed it relatively few times (around 50 to date), with Garry Tallent's tuba simulating the trumpeting of an elephant.

Production

Springsteen appears to have recorded an early version of *Wild Billy's Circus Story,* entitled *Circus Town,* during the sessions for his first album. But when he performed it in public in late 1972, it was called *Circus Song.* He then worked on an initial version of what was to become *Wild Billy's Circus Story* at 914 Sound Recording Studios, on 14 May 1973. The final version with the definitive title was recorded on 25, 26, and 28 June.

The song begins with Springsteen counting in: "*Ah one, two, three, four.*" He picks/strums his acoustic guitar, accompanied by Danny Federici on accordion and Garry Tallent on tuba. This creates an acoustic feel, and when Springsteen launches into the first verse, Bob Dylan immediately comes to mind. The song continues with other instruments contributing to the arrangements: the Boss plays two mandolin parts (at 1'22), and not long after (from 2'22), a snare roll can be heard, ending on a clash of the cymbal—which, according to Mike Appel, was played by a studio drummer and not Vini Lopez, who struggled to get it right. Brass and string harmonies also feature and appear to come from a Mellotron (at 2'45 and 2'55). Springsteen's harmonica resounds in the last verse (at 3'19).

INCIDENT ON 57TH STREET

Bruce Springsteen / 7'45

Musicians
Bruce Springsteen: vocals, electric guitars
Danny Federici: piano
David Sancious: piano, organ
Garry Tallent: bass
Vini "Mad Dog" Lopez: drums
Suki Lahav: vocals and chorus singing

Recording
914 Sound Recording Studios, Blauvelt, New York State: 23 September 1973

Technical team
Producers: Mike Appel, Jim Cretecos
Recording engineer: Louis Lahav
Assistant recording engineer: Larry Alexander

For Springsteen Addicts

A ten-minute version of *Incident on 57th Street* was chosen for the B-side of the European single *War,* released in 1986.

Genesis and lyrics

Incident on 57th Street was initially called *Puerto Rican Jane.* It is a rereading of *Romeo and Juliet*—not the original work by Shakespeare, but Jerome Robbins and Robert Wise's 1961 musical, *West Side Story,* starring Natalie Wood and Richard Beymer. Coincidentally, the two protagonists are Latin-American in origin, and nicknamed Spanish Johnny or Cool Romeo, and Puerto Rican Jane or Late Juliet. However, in 1975, Springsteen said that he had never seen the movie.

The story of *Incident on 57th Street* starts with Spanish Johnny quitting the salubrious backstreets and arriving in midtown Manhattan at the wheel of an old Buick. He is hoping to earn some money as a male escort, but has no success. Puerto Rican Jane then appears: "Don't cry," she says. They spend the night together, but Spanish Johnny's friends remind him who he really is. Johnny leaves Jane to join them, while Jane asks him not to leave her alone. He swears he'll be back the next day. What will Johnny do? Unlike many 1970s songwriters whose work was mostly introspective, Springsteen weaves a real New York tale here. He deliberately shrouds the events in mystery, leaving listeners to make their own interpretation of the song.

Through the character of Spanish Johnny, *Incident on 57th Street* broaches the theme of the search for redemption. Springsteen was raised a Catholic, and this is a theme that he would come back to throughout his career. This song is almost unanimously considered one of the first masterpieces by the New Jersey songwriter. In his book *Two Hearts*, Dave Marsh, the *Rolling Stone* magazine critic, writes: "There are a few precious moments in rock when you can hear a musician overcoming both his own limits and the restrictions of the form."[16] He even compares *Incident on 57th Street* to Eric Clapton's *Layla*, Dylan's *Like a Rolling Stone*, and Neil Young's *Helpless.* Bruce Springsteen sang this song for the first time at the Student Union Center Ballroom in Kent, Ohio, on 19 January 1974.

Production

Incident on 57th Street was probably finished on 23 September, which was the day Bruce celebrated his 24th birthday. The song begins with David Sancious's heavily compressed piano. Jon Landau, the Boss's future manager, later

Bruce Springsteen in concert at the Trenton War Memorial, New Jersey, on 11 November 1974. *Incident on 57th Street* earned him his true stripes as a songwriter.

explained that he couldn't bear the noise made by the piano pedal: "It irritated me no end."[3] Apparently, this was a deliberate effect, an integral part of the mixing. If an instrument is compressed, all the weak points inevitably come to the fore—which explains the pedal sound.

After four beats, Sancious adds an organ and Springsteen comes in with his Telecaster-Esquire to perform an initial guitar solo, with a very pronounced delay (on the right, at 0'15). Then the whole band comes in, and a second guitar with added saturation responds to the first (on the left). In addition to Sancious's two keyboards, Danny Federici records a second piano part. Springsteen's vocals are excellent, as always, and he particularly accentuates the "spoken" feel of his performance to make the story clearer. The first refrain is preceded by a kind of bridge (where Sancious's organ is particularly obvious), which is vaguely similar to the future *Born to Run* (from 1'38). Suki Lahav performs the chorus singing on the refrain, just as she did for the *4th of July, Asbury Park (Sandy)*, although she is not credited for that song.

In the third verse, Springsteen is accompanied only by Garry Tallent's bass—also highly compressed—and Vini Lopez's ride cymbal (from 4'00). Another refrain follows, again with a contribution from Suki Lahav, who this time responds to the lead vocal with her clear, gentle voice ("Those romantic young boys" at 4'46).

After three final refrains, Springsteen plays a saturated solo on his Fender, leaving Sancious to close the song with a kind of ritornello on the piano (from 7'18). This final, overdubbed part segues into the next track, *Rosalita (Come Out Tonight)*.

Clarence Clemons is conspicuously absent from *Incident on 57th Street* although Albee Tellone, the saxophonist roadie on *The E Street Shuffle*, refutes this: "Bruce had two weeks to do some serious recording and planned on having me play the baritone sax on *Incident on 57th Street*, but we ran out of time and Clarence did the overdub instead."[21] However, no saxophone is audible on the piece. It was either removed or buried in the mix.

ROSALITA (COME OUT TONIGHT)

Bruce Springsteen / 7'02

According to Diane Lozito, Springsteen's girlfriend in the early 1970s, the name Rosalita came from her grandmother Rose, with Rose Lozito becoming Rosalita.

Musicians

Bruce Springsteen: vocals, acoustic and electric guitars
Clarence Clemons: saxophone, vocals, backing vocals
Danny Federici: keyboards (?), backing vocals
David Sancious: organ, piano, backing vocals
Garry Tallent: bass
Vini "Mad Dog" Lopez: drums, backing vocals
Unidentified musicians: handclaps

Recording

914 Sound Recording Studios, Blauvelt, New York State: 23 September 1973

Technical team

Producers: Mike Appel, Jim Cretecos
Recording engineer: Louis Lahav
Assistant recording engineer: Larry Alexander

Rosalita was never released as a single in the United States. However, in 1979, the single was released in the Netherlands and several other European countries with *Night* (from the *Born to Run* album) on the B-side.

Genesis and lyrics

"Now, I know your mama, she don't like me 'cause I play in a rock and roll band/And I know your daddy, he don't dig me, but he never did understand," sings Springsteen in the fourth verse. *Rosalita (Come Out Tonight)* was written in a single day and is clearly autobiographical. It is about one of Springsteen's first serious relationships when he was living in Freehold. "As a teenager, I'd had a girlfriend whose mother had threatened to get a court injunction against me to keep me away from her daughter due to my low-rent beginnings and defiant (for my little town) appearance,"[1] he writes in his autobiography.

This song is therefore one of the first manifestos where Springsteen thumbs his nose at middle-class conventions and the narrow-mindedness of polite society in New Jersey. Ignoring the hostility of Rosalita's parents, he encourages her to "cut loose her mama's reins," "come out tonight and make that highway run," and enjoy the pleasures of physical love: "Rosalita, jump a little lighter/Señorita, come sit by my fire/I just want to be your lover..." The chorus could not make it any clearer. Who is the song about? It can only be Diane Lozito, a high school student who, along with her student boyfriend, met Bruce Springsteen at a concert on the Jersey Shore in the summer of 1971, and subsequently became his girlfriend, much to the displeasure of her parents. "Rosalita was the first major song that Bruce wrote after we started going out together," Diane Lozito explained. She continued: "Bruce suggested that we rented an apartment together, but he wanted my mother's permission. So, one evening, he came to dinner at the house. Mom had made an Italian meal. They got on very well together and Bruce thought that she would give her consent. But finally she said to me, 'No, you'd be better off staying with your law school boyfriend.' Bruce didn't understand. I said to him, 'My father is a musician, my mother doesn't want me ending up with a musician too.' So Bruce replied, 'If your father is a musician, he'll approve.' But my father said, 'No, musicians don't earn money, they always fool around.'"[24]

Rosalita (Come Out Tonight) is also autobiographical in the sense that Springsteen refers explicitly to his career: "Well, tell him [your father] this is his last chance to get his daughter in a fine romance/Because the record company, Rosie, just gave me a big advance."

For Springsteen Addicts
After making the cover of *Time* and *Newsweek* in October 1975, Springsteen changed some of the lyrics of *Rosalita (Come Out Tonight)*: "Tell your papa I ain't no freak, 'cause I got my picture on the cover of *Time* and *Newsweek*."

Rosalita (Come Out Tonight) was one of the first great songs Bruce Springsteen wrote that had been inspired by The Byrds and Irish singer Van Morrison (seen here in the studio in 1971).

Like all the other tracks on the album, *Rosalita (Come Out Tonight)* was never released as a single in the United States, but it was frequently played on American FM radio stations, evidently as a result of the critical acclaim it garnered. "A raucous celebration of desire,"[18] wrote Ken Emerson in *Rolling Stone* magazine. It was also, in fact primarily, used as a vehicle for Bruce Springsteen's virtuosic stage performances, and for a long time it would either be the last song or the encore in his shows—it has been performed live over 800 times to date (the first at Max's Kansas City, New York, on 1 February 1973). Today, *Rosalita (Come Out Tonight)* is one of the 500 Songs that Shaped Rock in the Rock & Roll Hall of Fame.

Production

Rosalita (Come Out Tonight) is one of the songs that was completed on 23 September during the final sessions for this album. "*Rosalita* was my musical autobiography,"[6] Springsteen confided in *Songs* (published in 1998). He could not have put this better because a whole host of musical styles light up this superb song. The electric guitar arpeggios in the intro recall the characteristic sound of The Byrds. The next passage appears to be inspired by Van Morrison's extraordinary track, *Domino*, from his 1970 album, *His Band and the Street Choir*. However, Springsteen has sufficient imagination as a songwriter to totally recreate what he borrows from others, with his own unique and powerful language. *Rosalita* exudes vitality and good humor, with Clarence Clemons's omnipresent saxophone clearly paving the way for the upcoming *Born to Run*.

After the second chorus, a surprisingly progressive rock-style instrumental bridge changes the atmosphere (at 3'18). Carried by David Sancious's organ and Springsteen's guitar solo, it is similar to the one in *Yours Is No Disgrace* by Yes (from *The Yes Album*, 1971). Then, at the end of the next verse, where Clemons's baritone can be heard alongside the Boss (at 4'45), there is a nod to 1950s rock with handclaps and *a cappella* vocals (at 4'54). In the outro, the band enters Ritchie Valens-style *La Bamba* territory to a background of impassioned battle cries and guitar reverbs (at 6'31).

Rosalita (Come Out Tonight) is a real musical mishmash that would subsequently inspire other bands, including, it would seem, the talented Blues Traveler, from New Jersey, on their superb 1995 track *Run-Around*. Springsteen now had a key ingredient for his stage performances: "With the opening chords of *Rosie*, I geared up my band and hit the road without dread."[6] Although he added: "That would come later."[6] For the time being, this penultimate track of his second album was a total success.

David Sancious, the E Street Band's pianist, playing a demo on a Steinway piano at Abbey Road Studios in February 2018.

NEW YORK CITY SERENADE

Bruce Springsteen / 9'56

Musicians
Bruce Springsteen: vocals, acoustic guitar
Clarence Clemons: saxophone, backing vocals
Danny Federici: backing vocals
David Sancious: piano, Mellotron (?)
Garry Tallent: bass, backing vocals
Vini "Mad Dog" Lopez: tambourine, conga, backing vocals
Richard Blackwell: congas
Unidentified musicians: handclaps, violins

Recording
914 Sound Recording Studios, Blauvelt, New York State: 7 August 1973

Technical team
Producers: Mike Appel, Jim Cretecos
Recording engineer: Louis Lahav
Assistant recording engineer: Larry Alexander

HEADPHONES AT THE READY

Jon Landau complained that he could hear the piano pedals grinding on the recording from 914 Sound Recording Studios. There are several examples of this in David Sancious's tremendous piano introduction: at 0'56, 1'02, 1'32, 1'37, 1'43, and so on. It was one of the reasons why the band would soon choose another studio for their future work.

Genesis and lyrics

New York City Serenade was a combination of the first drafts of two other songs, *Vibes Man* and *New York City Song*. Once again, Springsteen shines the spotlight on two East Coast antiheroes: Billy, a minor gangster with "cleats on his boots," and his girlfriend Diamond Jackie, a prostitute who "won't take corner boys, they ain't got no money." We sense that they are planning something nefarious in Manhattan. "Together they're gonna boogaloo down Broadway/And come back home with the loot," sings Springsteen in the first verse.

This final song on *The Wild, the Innocent, and the E Street Shuffle* is also primarily about how these characters from outside New York, who don't live there, view the city. For them, it is a kind of fantasy-filled romantic getaway, a frenetic city with music blaring in the streets, creating a typically jazzy atmosphere. *New York Serenade* is another Bruce Springsteen song that he first performed at Max's Kansas City, on Park Avenue South, on 30 August 1972.

Production

New York City Serenade is first and foremost the incredible piano intro by David Sancious. Indeed, Springsteen believes Sancious played amazingly on the whole album and that he has also contributed greatly to the team both when they are recording and while on tour. The piece begins with some strange sounds, which are in fact Sancious scraping his piano strings. He then launches into a breathtaking improvisation, containing elements of Frederic Chopin, Erroll Garner, and Thelonious Monk, among others. Springsteen had asked him to take his time and then signal for him to come in with his acoustic guitar, which Sancious finally does at 1'37! The two musicians then play a delicate, bluesy instrumental ballad, with the future Boss alternating licks, harmonics, bending, and strumming. There is a barely audible percussion part in the background, which was not really wanted, as Vini Lopez explains: "When the boys started to record this song, they found that the timing was off. So, they put me with a conga drum under a foot of padding so the sound wouldn't be picked up by the other instrument mikes. I was the click track. As you can hear, the sound of the conga did bleed into everything else. They couldn't get it out."[25]

Springsteen then starts singing (at 2'26). The congas, played this time by Richard Blackwell, come in strongly. You

1973

can hear the drumheads "singing" after Blackwell moistened his fingers to obtain the desired effect. Garry Tallent comes in a few bars later with a very good bass line, which is simultaneously melodic and rhythmic. He is then joined by Lopez's tambourine and some string arrangements written by Sancious (from 3'44). "It was the first time I've ever done that and it worked out beautifully,"[26] he said.

The strings theory

A "string section" appears on the album credits, but it is not clear what this is exactly. According to roadie Albee Tellone, it was played by an instrument, the Mellotron, that was commonly used in prog rock: "The new album had a song on it called *New York City Serenade* that had the Mellotron playing violins on it."[21] The Mellotron is a polyphonic keyboard that uses tape loops (listen to the intro to The Beatles' *Strawberry Fields Forever* or the *Watcher of The Skies* by Genesis). However, in 2012, Sancious said that this part was recorded by actual musicians: "And then I think the producer or the engineer found these three guys, these three violinists, who were music school teachers. They were from the local area. So the whole 'string section' actually, was three people who got overdubbed [...]"[27] For Sancious, writing the score was relentlessly hard work, and, on the day of the recording, he took charge of the three musicians: "So I'm standing there conducting these three guys who were the age of the teachers I had in high school, music teachers, and I thought, this is crazy, and it was all working so beautifully. It worked out well. I just remember everyone being really, really happy with it. I was, of course, and Bruce was thrilled."[27]

So, why did Tellone mention the Mellotron? Listening to the coda, it is obvious that no Mellotron was used in the song. It could have been added to the real strings in order to thicken the sound, a technique that is frequently used in recording studios. Or it could have been used to guide the violinists; or, quite possibly, Tellone was actually referring to *Wild Billy's Circus Story,* where the Mellotron did appear to be used.

At 5'11, Springsteen inserts a short gospel sequence with handclapping and chorus singing. The piece then takes up where it left off, with Clarence Clemons lighting up the arrangements with his brilliant saxophone contributions. As for the Boss, his performance is simply amazing, and shows an astonishing emotional power.

New York City Serenade is a magnificent fresco, dreamed up by an extraordinarily talented 24-year-old who was nevertheless happy to admit that the imprint of another musical giant hovers over the song. As Springsteen later wrote of the song in his autobiography: there would have been no *New York City Serenade* without the inspiration of Van Morrison.

Garry Tallent (seen here in 1987) worked on Bruce Springsteen's albums from 1973 to 1987, then rejoined the Boss in 1995.

GARRY TALLENT: THE BOSS'S BASSIST

Garry Wayne Tallent was the E Street Band bassist from 1972. He was born in Wayne County, Michigan, on 27 October 1949, and spent his teenage years in Neptune City, on the Jersey Shore, where he learned to play tuba and then bass. He was heavily influenced by great instrumentalists such as James Jamerson, Donald "Duck" Dunn, Paul McCartney, and Bill Wyman. While attending Neptune High School, with drummer Vini Lopez and guitarist-singer Johnny Lyon (the future Southside Johnny), Tallent began frequenting the Jersey Shore clubs (especially the Upstage Club). He played with Little Melvin & the Invaders, an Afro-American soul band, where he met saxophonist Clarence Clemons. He went on to play with the Downtown Tangiers Band and the Moment of Truth, where he found himself back with Vini Lopez and became friendly with Danny Federici.

In the early 1970s, Tallent became part of Bruce Springsteen's inner circle, and would be involved in the recording of most of the Boss's albums with the E Street Band, from *Greetings from Asbury Park, N.J.* (1973) to *Tunnel Of Love* (1987), as well as many world tours.

From the second half of the 1980s, Garry Talent also worked as a musician and/or producer with other artists, notably Gary U.S. Bonds (*Dedication*, 1981), Steve Forbert (*Streets of this Town*, 1988), his longstanding friend, Southside Johnny (*Better Days*, 1991), Sonny Burgess (on an album of the same name, 1996), and Steve Earle (*I Feel Alright*, 1996). At the time, he was living in Nashville, Tennessee, where he created his own studio, MoonDog, and his own record label, the D'Ville Record Group.

Garry Tallent reunited with Bruce Springsteen for *The Ghost of Tom Joad* sessions in 1995, and also played bass on the Bruce Springsteen and the E Street Band Reunion Tour, as well as *The Rising* (2002), *Devils & Dust* (2005), *Magic* (2007), *Working on a Dream* (2009), and *High Hopes* (2014). In 2016, Tallent recorded his first solo album: *Break Time*.

A self-taught pianist, David Sancious (seen here in 1991) joined the E Street Band in 1973 and left it during sessions for *Born to Run*. He was back at the Boss's side for *Human Touch* and, many years later, for *Western Stars*.

DAVID SANCIOUS, FROM MOZART TO THELONIOUS MONK

David Sancious is one of the musicians who played a major role in Bruce Springsteen's rise to international success. He was born in Long Branch, New Jersey, on 30 November 1953, and from the late 1960s he was a regular in the New Jersey clubs. He became a pianist at Alpha Sound Studios in Richmond, Virginia, and played for groups like Glory Road and Dr Zoom and the Sonic Boom, developing his talents alongside the big names on the Jersey Shore scene such as Southside Johnny and Bruce Springsteen. He participated in the *Greetings from Asbury Park, N.J.* sessions before becoming an official member of the E Street Band.

David Sancious is a self-taught pianist who claims that his style is influenced by both Mozart and Thelonious Monk. He has an ability to adapt to Springsteen's different musical styles, as is shown by his organ solo on *Kitty's Back* and his piano intro on *New York City Serenade* (both songs on *The Wild, the Innocent, and the E Street Shuffle* album). After recording the song *Born to Run*, he left the E Street Band, and he and Ernest Carter (who had just replaced Vini Lopez) formed a jazz rock and prog rock group called Tone that featured, among others, guitarist Patti Scialfa, singer-keyboardist Gayle Moran (a former member of Return To Forever), and the singer and guitarist Alex Ligertwood (Jeff Beck Group, Brian Auger's Oblivion Express, Santana). Their first album, *Forest of Feelings* (bearing only Sancious's name and with no mention of Tone), was produced by Billy Cobham and appeared in record stores in 1975, followed by *Transformation (The Speed of Love)* in 1976.

Tone was then dissolved, and David Sancious went on to record the albums *Just As I Thought* (1979) and *The Bridge* (1981), as well as being involved in diverse projects with Stanley Clarke, John McLaughlin, and Billy Cobham, before becoming one of Narada Michael Walden's closest collaborators. In the early 1980s, he played with Jack Bruce & Friends, alongside Cobham again, and, in 1982, he played keyboards on the *Animation* album by Yes frontman, Jon Anderson. Several years later, he joined Peter Gabriel's touring band, and recorded five albums with him between 1989 and 2003. He also worked with Youssou N'Dour (*The Lion*, 1989), Sting (*The Soul Cages*, 1991, *Ten Summoner's Tales*, 1993), and Eric Clapton (*Clapton Live at Budokan*, 2001, *One More Car, One More Rider*, 2002). It is also worth mentioning two singers that he worked with who had very different styles: the Italian rock singer Zucchero and the French easy-listening singer France Gall.

David Sancious released three solo works between 2000 and 2007: *Nine Piano Improvisations*, *Cinema*, and *Live in the Now*. Finally, many years after *Human Touch* (1992), he was reunited with Bruce Springsteen for the *Western Stars* (2019) sessions.

ALBUM

BORN TO RUN

Thunder Road • Tenth Avenue Freeze-Out • Night • Backstreets • Born to Run • She's the One • Meeting Across the River • Jungleland

Outtakes: *Walking in the Street* (aka *Lovers in the Cold*) • *Lonely Night in the Park* • *A Love So Fine* • *A Night Like This* • *Janey Needs a Shooter* • *Linda Let Me Be the One* • *So Young and in Love*

RELEASE DATE

United States: 25 August 1975

Reference: Columbia Records – PC 33795

No.1 in *Record World* magazine and No.3 in the *Billboard chart,* No.17 in the United Kingdom

Springsteen in a hat during the legendary sessions for his third album. A star is born.

Fred "Sonic" Smith, Dennis "Machine Gun" Thompson, Rob Tyner, Wayne Kramer, and Michael Davis of MC5. A certain Jon Landau produced their second album, *Back in the USA* (1970).

THE NEW JERSEY "WALL OF SOUND"

1975

On 9 May 1974, Bruce Springsteen and the E Street Band shared the billing with Bonnie Raitt at the Harvard Square Theater in Cambridge, Massachusetts. They played *New York Serenade*, *Spirit in the Night*, *Does This Bus Stop at 82nd Street?*, and *Rosalita (Come Out Tonight)*. It was a dazzling concert. The rock critic Jon Landau, who was there that night, was totally stunned. Several days later, in his column in *The Real Paper,* a Massachusetts publication that often covered the counterculture, he wrote: "I saw the rock 'n' roll future and its name is Bruce Springsteen [...], he made me feel like I was hearing music for the very first time."[28] He continued: "Springsteen does it all. He is a rock 'n' roll punk, a Latin street poet, a ballet dancer, an actor, a joker, bar band leader, hot-shit rhythm guitar player, extraordinary singer, and a truly great rock 'n' roll composer."[28] As far as praise goes, it doesn't get much better than this. Landau's words carried even more weight because he was also a regular contributor to *Rolling Stone* magazine and had a certain amount of influence in the rock world. In 1967, he had introduced American youth to a talented musician by the name of Jimi Hendrix, before going on to produce MC5's second album *Back in the USA* (1970). Jon Landau and Bruce Springsteen soon developed a musical bond and close friendship. "Jon and I related both as conspiratorial music fans and as young men in search of something," Springsteen writes in his autobiography *Born to Run*. "Jon would serve me as a friend and mentor, someone who'd been exposed to and held information I felt would augment my creativity and deepen the truth seeking I was trying to make a part of my music."[1]

Although the *Born to Run* sessions had already started (with the recording of the title track) by the time Jon Landau officially became one of the album's three producers, along with Springsteen and Mike Appel, it was really only after Landau came along that the New Jersey songwriter made decisive progress. Jon Landau had the creative vision and musical ability to channel Springsteen's proliferation of ideas and help make *Born to Run* a masterpiece of rock history.

From *Rolling Stone* to *Born to Run*

How did Jon Landau, a professional journalist, much appreciated for his laudatory reviews, manage to become so involved in Springsteen's professional and personal life? That is precisely what Mike Appel was wondering: "Jon Landau was the last guy in the world I expected to turn up during the recording of the *Born to Run* album and to wind up producing and managing Bruce Springsteen."[3] Landau's appearance on the scene coincided with Springsteen experiencing a loss of direction in his career. The young man from Freehold was exhausted from the long, tiresome sessions for the *Born to Run* song, and, by this point, was simply unable to stand back and take a good look at what he was doing in the studio. He had spent months bogged down in arrangements, endless takes, and dealing with recording equipment that was often not fit for purpose. He needed help, shrewd advice, and someone from the outside to lend a listening ear. Mike Appel was not enough; he was not right for Springsteen anymore. Jon Landau would give Springsteen what he needed, and he

Clarence Clemons, Danny Federici, Bruce Springsteen, Max Weinberg, Garry Tallent, and Steve Van Zandt during the Born to Run Tour, which passed through London in November 1975.

For Springsteen Addicts

The third studio album was initially entitled *War and Roses*, then *The Hungry and the Hunted*, *American Summer*, and *Sometimes at Night*, before the final title, *Born to Run*, was eventually chosen.

Jon Landau (seen here in 1989). After seeing the future of rock 'n' roll in Bruce Springsteen, the rock critic coproduced *Born to Run*.

would do so with such generosity and dedication that it became a genuine friendship.

Toward February 1975, Springsteen made up his mind. He wanted Landau to be involved in the production: "I remember talking to Mike and saying, 'We need this guy in. We need this guy in. Give him what he wants.'"[3] Appel did not share his enthusiasm; he saw it as an intrusion and felt unjustly sidelined. This resentment would last a long time. In 1992, for example, Appel told Marc Eliot (as quoted in the excellent book, *Down Thunder Road: The Making of Bruce Springsteen*) how Landau felt the order of the coproducers in the album credits was extremely important. When he found out that he was only third, he apparently argued his case: "Oh, Mike, please, it would really mean the world to me if my name came second. I'd really appreciate it, I want it in the worst way."[3] Whatever the truth of the matter, *Born to Run* was the end of Mike Appel's professional association with Bruce Springsteen. However, the credit for spotting that Springsteen was an exceptional artist, and for producing and coproducing his first three albums, will always be his.

1975

Movie writing

The concept behind the new album was "the feel of an endless summer night,"[29] as Springsteen explains in the Thom Zimny documentary *Wings for Wheels: The Making of Born to Run*. He goes on to explain that "it could all be taking place in the course of one evening in all these different locations [...] all these different stories on one, sort of, long summer night."[29] New Jersey and New York were no longer the only settings for his songs; in this album, Springsteen sings about the whole of America, the reality of the 1970s, and the broken American dream, which was now out of reach for many. To some degree, *Born to Run* is a song about the open road as the ultimate freedom, an escape, a last resort for social outcasts, for those who know deep down in their souls that they were "born to lose." But, like the others, this third album is still largely autobiographical. Springsteen undoubtedly sees himself in the characters depicted in his songs. "I always contend you're writing about yourself in some fashion," he says in the same documentary. "If you look at the record closely, once again it mirrors a lot of my own life, these were the kinds of things I was going through at the time."[29] To put it another way, he was guided by an insatiable need to be free, to get away, to discover other places, and to experience different sensations.

Springsteen's creative approach is even more stunning and powerful, when you understand that he draws a great deal of his inspiration from the cinema. "He is not afraid of being very cinematic in his music," Patti Scialfa points out in the Thom Zimny documentary. "You feel that inside the song, the way it just spreads out before you."[29] Steve Van Zandt also talks about "that sort of visual impact on your imagination."[29] When you listen to the eight songs on *Born to Run,* legendary Hollywood images instantly come to mind: Marlon Brando in *The Wild One*, James Dean in *Rebel Without a Cause*, and

The almost symphonic sound of *Born to Run* was derived from Phil Spector's Wall of Sound. Here is the producer with The Ronettes at the Gold Star Studios in 1963.

James Taylor and Warren Oates in *Two-Lane Blacktop*, as does the drama of the heyday of American film noir in the 1940s and 1950s, with movies like *The Big Sleep*, *The Asphalt Jungle*, and *Pickup on South Street*. Once again, the night and the city loom large in ways that are both exhilarating and threatening (*Tenth Avenue Freeze-Out*, *Backstreets*, *Meeting Across the River*), as do real or imaginary women, who are unforgettable either way (*She's the One*), the drudgery and enslavement of the working classes (*Night*), and, as always, the highway as a quest, a coming-of-age journey (*Thunder Road*, *Born to Run*, *Jungleland*).

Remarkable too is Springsteen's constant search for the right phrase, the image that catches the imagination. The introductions set up "a particularly theatrical way of writing that I really only did on that record,"[29] says Bruce Springsteen. Much ink was spilled before he hit on the core message. "I worked very very long on the lyrics to *Born to Run* because I was very aware that I was messing with classic rock 'n' roll images that easily turned into clichés,"[29] he continues. After which, he deleted all the clichés, so that the emotions were fully developed, and the characters took shape. "It was the beginning of the creation of a certain world that all my others would refer back to, resonate off of, for the next 20 or 30 years,"[29] he says.

Little symphonies with a difference

Born to Run also marks a musical turning point. The rock 'n' roll, R&B, and folk-rock fundamentals are still there, in the sense that recordings by Bo Diddley, Roy Orbison, and, even more so, Bob Dylan and The Band, come to mind, but the songs are also transcended by a spectacular sonic breadth. Bruce Springsteen has clearly learned from Phil Spector's Wall of Sound, which profoundly transformed rock 'n' roll in the early 1960s. The eight songs on *Born to Run* contain a masterful abundance of sound. The difference lies in the message: These are not "little symphonies for kids," as Phil Spector called the songs that he created in Gold Star Studios in Los Angeles (including *Da Doo Ron Ron* by The Crystals and *Be My Baby* by The Ronettes), but mini-epics for American teenagers in the post-Vietnam, post-Watergate era following the

The cover photo of *Born to Run* influenced Cheap Trick for their album *Next Position Please* (1983), as well as Tom and Ray Magliozzi for *Car Talk: Born Not to Run* (2004).

For Springsteen Addicts

On the first print run of the *Born to Run* album sleeve, Landau's first name was spelled "John" instead of "Jon." Columbia immediately had tens of thousands of stickers printed to cover over the error—up to 400,000 according to the source.

first oil crisis. "No gas no cars,"[6] writes Springsteen in his book *Songs*. In short, the carefree attitude of one era has been superseded by the realities of another.

Born to Run propelled Bruce Springsteen into the ranks of the greatest songwriters on the rock scene. He composed all eight songs chosen for the album on a small Aeolian piano, paying particular attention to the strength of the melodies, the atmosphere, and the dreamlike power of the introductions. "I was interested in setting the scene. That's why the introductions. They all set the scene. Whether it's like you think of the morning or the beginning of something,"[29] he explains in the Thom Zimny documentary.

The winners and the losers

With *Born to Run* Springsteen earned his stripes as a coproducer alongside Mike Appel and Jon Landau, who replaced Jimmy Cretecos after the latter decided to throw in the towel in early 1974 because he felt the Springsteen business was not profitable. Everyone was broke, and morale was at rock bottom, with sales of the first two albums remaining slow despite glowing reviews. Even Appel had his doubts: "I seriously considered, in January of 1974, turning all my contracts over to Bruce and saying, 'Here's the contracts, these big contracts that are worth exactly nothing. Good luck, you can have them. I'm going back to writing commercials. At least I can earn a living there.'"[3] But, just as Appel was at the point of pulling out of his commitments, Springsteen came to see him in his office to play him his latest production. "I don't remember what it was," Appel explains, "but as soon as I heard him sing it, the whole thing started for me all over again. How could anyone be this good, I wondered, and not be on the top of the charts?"[3] Appel decided to carry on, unlike Cretecos, who had lost faith; Appel brought Cretecos' shares for $1,500, making Cretecos one of the biggest losers in the history of rock 'n' roll.

Another person who was sacrificed on the altar of glory was drummer Vini Lopez. With his fiery temperament, "Mad Dog" was known for his frequently out-of-control behavior. But it was his relationship with Clarence Clemons that really caused the problem, as the two men did not get on well at all. After one particular argument, probably about money, they almost came to blows, with Clemons flying off the handle: "I went off on that motherfucker. I didn't hit him but I put him up against the wall, I threw shit all over the apartment, I think I broke down the front door [...] I was in total rage."[30] Lopez immediately went round to Springsteen's and insisted that he choose between him and Clemons. "Turned out to be the best day of Max Weinberg's life,"[30] Clemons later joked (Weinberg became the band's future long-standing drummer). So, in February 1974, Lopez was replaced by a new drummer: Ernest "Boom" Carter, who was a friend of David Sancious. Carter later recalled auditioning for the job at Garry Tallent's parents' house. Bruce liked what he played, and he got the job—see the Bibliography, source 31, if you would like to read more of this interview with Ernest Carter (although please note: it is only available in French). However, Carter only stayed for a few concerts and the recording of the song *Born to Run*. David Sancious left in August (also after recording the *Born to Run* song) to spread his wings and set up his own jazz-fusion group called Tone. Ernest "Boom" Carter left with him.

After 60 or so auditions, Sancious and Carter were replaced by Roy Bittan and Max Weinberg to record the other seven tracks on the album. As Springsteen says in the Thom Zimny documentary: "One of the musical heroes of the *Born to Run* album was Roy Bittan and his piano playing. Roy would take the intros and the themes and the melodies that I had written and turn them into something that had a kind of power that my own very basic piano playing could never match. His piano really defined the sound of that record."[29] The piano, but Springsteen's voice too, we could add.

The album

Once the sessions, which were staggered from spring 1974 to summer 1975, came to an end, *Born to Run* appeared in stores on 25 August 1975. Columbia's promotional campaign, which cost an estimated $250,000, certainly played its part, but it is first and foremost the inspired brilliance and energy of the eight songs that explain the album's huge success. In the United States, it reached No.1 and No.3 in *Record World* and *Billboard* magazines, respectively (it is now certified six times platinum), and No.17 in the United Kingdom. More significant

Irwin Segelstein (second on the right) did not appreciate the unflattering remarks Springsteen made about his record label.

still than the impact of the actual album was Bruce Springsteen making the cover of *Time* and *Newsweek* in October 1975.

As had been the case with Springsteen's first two albums, the critics were unanimous that this was a talented songwriter, now at the height of his powers. Even Greil Marcus, who had never hidden his preference for the glam/prog rock of the British band Roxy Music, made up for this opinion in some style in the *Rolling Stone* issue of 9 October 1975, saying: "No, you've never heard anything like this before, but you understand it instantly, because this music—or Springsteen crying, singing wordlessly, moaning over the last guitar lines of *Born to Run*, or the astonishing chords that follow each verse of *Jungleland*, or the opening of *Thunder Road*—is what rock 'n' roll is supposed to sound like."[32] Colin Larkin, in Virgin's *All-Time Top 1000 Albums*, wrote that "Springsteen exhumed his youth and reminded us of ours with honest tales of growing up in post-Eisenhower America."[33] Today, *Born to Run* is No.18 in *Rolling Stone*'s list of the 500 Greatest Albums of All Time. And, to date, it is the only Springsteen album chosen to appear in the National Recording Registry.

Double or quits

Yet, *Born to Run* almost failed to see the light of day. In 1973, the CBS team was hesitant about continuing with its commitment to Springsteen. The poor performance of the first two albums had undermined their confidence. They only agreed in extremis to finance a third record, and, if this failed, it would be the last. Mike Appel nevertheless managed to secure a small budgetary increase for the production: $50,000 instead of the $40,000 dollars allocated for the two previous albums. This limited budget meant that recording would take place once again at 914 Sound Recording Studios. However, after production of *Born to Run*, the first track to be completed in August 1974, the CBS team was still not convinced about Springsteen's future. As a last resort, Mike Appel made some copies of the song on audiocassettes and sent them to a few radio stations. It was an immediate hit, but the CBS bigwigs viewed this as professional misconduct, and interfering with their marketing plan, as the record was not yet available on the market.

Elsewhere, Springsteen, in an interview for the Brown University magazine (as reported by Mike Appel), was very

frank about how badly he felt his record company was treating him. This attracted the wrath of Irwin Segelstein, one of the label's directors. When the record company subsequently found out that their protégé was also about to be interviewed by *Rolling Stone* magazine, they immediately decided to organize a lunch for all parties. "And that became something of a turning point for Bruce," Appel recounts, "the precise moment when CBS began to change its attitude toward Springsteen. They agreed that day to finance the rest of the album at the Record Plant, no hassles, whatever it takes to get the next record out. And during all of this, Bruce didn't say a word. He just sat there and watched the entire thing unfold!"[3]

The sleeve

While Springsteen and his musicians were putting the finishing touches to *Born to Run*, Mike Appel contacted Eric Meola about the record sleeve. At the time, Meola was already a renowned photographer. He had created his own studio in 1971 and worked with prestigious publications such as *Life*, *Time*, and *Esquire* (before becoming associated with American Express, Porsche, and BMW). A meeting was set up—not without difficulty, given the songwriter's busy schedule. Springsteen ended up going to Meola's studio with his saxophonist Clarence Clemons. Around 900 photos were taken: Springsteen turning on a radio set, playing with his guitar. There was nothing particularly original, at least until the shot of Springsteen leaning on Clemons's shoulder, with a conspiratorial smile and his Telecaster slung over his shoulder. "We just stood there, I went into this pose," recalled Clemons in the documentary *Wings for Wheels*. "He was leaning on my shoulder and that was it."[29] Springsteen adds: "The sleeve says it all. Even before people buy the record. For me, it's a record that you want to buy, even without listening to it, just by seeing the sleeve."[29] As Jon Landau explains: "I think it's one of the great covers ever, one of the most memorable."[29] A "record about friendship,"[29] Springsteen concludes.

Eric Meola's photo, set to a white background, covers both sides of the sleeve. Printed on the front is the artist's name and the album title; the back cover features the tracklist with the names of the musicians. Inside is a portrait of the songwriter and the lyrics of the eight songs. Springsteen's Telecaster-Esquire, which appears in this legendary photo (he'd bought the guitar for $185), also features on *Human Touch*, the *Bruce Springsteen & The E Street Band Live/1975–85* box set (released in 1986), and the *Greatest Hits* compilation (1995).

The recording

The recording of Springsteen's third album began at 914 Sound Recording Studios, in Blauvelt, New York State, between May and October 1974 (according to the Sony archives). The band worked there four times over the six months: 11–22 May, in early June, 1–8 August, and, finally, on 16 and 17 October. The song *Born to Run* was recorded during this period, and accompanying Springsteen were Clarence Clemons, Danny Federici, David Sancious, Garry Tallent, and Ernest "Boom" Carter. Louis Lahav, the recording engineer for the first two records, was still at the controls. He remembers interminable sessions: "On the song *Born to Run* alone we had been working six months! Springsteen kept changing the lyrics and the song got finished only when he was pleased with the text. But we weren't working only on the vocals that entire time. We were tweaking, overdubbing, and pre-mixing until the last moment."[12]

Everything changed when Jon Landau (who was not yet the coproducer) arrived on the scene. "When I arrived, we were in the legendary 914 Studio," he recalls. "I said to Bruce: 'You're an excellent artist, you deserve an excellent recording studio.' We moved to a popular studio at the time, the Record Plant."[29] The Record Plant, in New York, which was founded

The Boss on the Sunset Strip in Los Angeles, in 1975, standing before a billboard advertising his album. The jacket photo was taken by Eric Meola.

On the back cover of the album, Springsteen is wearing a pin badge on his shirt. It is an Elvis Presley New York fan club badge, The King.

While promoting the album, Bruce Springsteen became the first rock singer to perform at the Grand Ole Opry in Nashville, on 28 April 1976. Two days later, passing through Memphis, he scaled the gates of Graceland, Elvis Presley's estate. He was caught red-handed by security guards and thrown out. The King was at Lake Tahoe at the time.

Jimmy Iovine at Electric Lady Studios. He recorded Bruce Springsteen's third album at the Record Plant.

Gary Kellgren (left) founded the Record Plant. Seen here in 1969 with Jimi Hendrix and Eddie Kramer (standing).

BETTER THAN COFFEE
To stay awake during the never-ending recording sessions, Jimmy Iovine used to chew the foil from his packs of chewing gum as the pain stopped him falling asleep.

by Gary Kellgren and Chris Stone in April 1968, was famous for producing several major albums prior to *Born to Run,* including John Lennon's *Imagine*, Alice Cooper's *Welcome to My Nightmare*, and *Electric Ladyland* by The Jimi Hendrix Experience. Housed in a former garage on 321 West 44th St, the Record Plant resembled a Greenwich Village club rather than a traditional recording studio, thanks to the inventiveness of the architect John Storyk.

However, not everyone agreed with the decision to quit the 914 Studios. "Yeah, they started to feel that 914 was getting a little old," Louis Lahav later said. "Nothing really serious, but the piano was croaking—this sort of stuff."[12] Mike Appel was worried about going over budget, as CBS had not yet really decided whether it would run with Springsteen: "[...] for a lot of reasons, we moved down to Manhattan, to the Record Plant, where we went over budget in about two seconds, money that, of course, ultimately came out of our pockets."[3]

Since Lahav was unavailable due to family commitments, and Landau wanted to change the recording engineer, a certain Jimmy Iovine took his place. This is how Springsteen saw it: "So Jimmy Iovine, brilliant impostor, young studio dog with the fastest learning curve I've ever seen (and soon to be one of the world's biggest music moguls and star of *American Idol*), became the engineer on the most important record of my life."[1] He went on to work on the other seven songs on *Born to Run* between March and July 1975.

1975

Jimmy "I-veen"

When Jimmy Iovine met Bruce Springsteen, he was still a young recording engineer who was barely 21 years old. He'd already had a few past glories, having worked on the recording of John Lennon's legendary 1974 album *Rock 'n' Roll*, which was produced by Phil Spector. Iovine still hasn't forgotten his first meeting with the man who by then was known as the Boss. Springsteen, accompanied by Mike Appel and Jon Landau, was on piano. He was playing *Thunder Road*: "I heard this guy sing—and those lyrics. I said, 'Oh, my God.' Then they played me the track they already had for *Born to Run*. Landau looked at me and said, 'Hey, I-veen'—Bruce still calls me that—'can you do this?' Absolutely. I'm 21 and I have my second client. [Grins] I'm spoiled."[35]

However, the sessions were grueling for everyone. Max Weinberg would later call it the hardest project of his career; Danny Federici said that they ate, drank, and slept *Born to Run*; Steve Van Zandt summarized the sessions as follows: "Fun's a tough word to use for those early days."[29] Springsteen's perfectionism bordered on madness. Jimmy Iovine even went so far as to say that they were all afraid of him. "This guy was broke," he later said. "You couldn't borrow him, rent him, get him to compromise. He didn't give a fuck who you were, what you were going to give him. It was him and that record. Anything else... [Shrugs his shoulders]. That's powerful."[35]

Water + rock 'n' roll don't mix

After the long months of recording, Springsteen and the band finally reached the penultimate stage: the mixing. Once again, Springsteen was demanding, piling on the pressure and refusing to compromise. As he recalls: "We had to mix *Born to Run* in, like, a week. And we didn't stop."[29] Then came the final stage, the mastering, which was done by Jimmy Iovine. With a copy of the album tucked under his arm, the recording engineer traveled by train to Baltimore, where Springsteen and Landau were relaxing in a motel with a swimming pool. He was eager for them to hear the result. "I go into Bruce's room, and he goes, 'OK, I-veen, put it on.' We're listening to it on a stereo he'd just bought, with two speakers and a turntable. When the album is over, he gets up, takes it off, walks outside—and throws it in the pool."[35] Iovine was devastated; he did not understand the Boss's reaction. Totally dissatisfied with what he had just heard, Springsteen then decided to rerecord the whole thing live. Back in New York, the recording engineer received a phone call from Landau: he had managed to reason with Springsteen, and the master copy would be used to make *Born to Run*.

Technical details

The only track on the album recorded at the 914 Sound Recording Studios, where Springsteen had recorded his two previous albums, was *Born to Run*. The tape machine was still a Scully 16-track and the console, according to Louis Lahav, was an API, although Brooks Arthur, the studio's owner, mentioned a console that was custom-built by Neil Monsey. Lahav says that they used Urei LA-2A and LA-3A compressors.

The other songs on the album were recorded and mixed in Studio A at the Record Plant in New York. The console there was a 32-input Spectra Sonic, the tape machine a modified MCI 2 inch 16-track, and the monitors were Westlake. The various effects included EMT 140 plate reverbs, Meyer and Fairchild, and also Urei LA-4 and 1176 compressors, and Pultec equalizers.

The instruments

Unfortunately, very little is known about the instruments Springsteen played while recording this album. He mainly recorded with an electric guitar, his famous Fender Telecaster-Esquire, and used a large number of amplifiers, or a "wall of amps," according to Jimmy Iovine and Mike Appel. Although the Boss later said that he could not recall the brand, it is highly likely that he used a 1959 Fender Bassman combo 4x10, among others. He played Martin acoustic guitars.

Garry Tallent played his parts on a Danelectro Longhorn bass. It was most probably plugged into a 60 W Ampeg B-15S amp for some takes, but most of the time he recorded directly into the console through a DI unit.

The Big Man (Clarence Clemons) recorded his parts on a Selmer tenor saxophone.

THUNDER ROAD

Bruce Springsteen / 4'50

Musicians
Bruce Springsteen: vocals, guitar, harmonica
Clarence Clemons: saxophone
Roy Bittan: piano, glockenspiel, backing vocals
Garry Tallent: bass
Max Weinberg: drums
Mike Appel, Steve Van Zandt: backing vocals

Recording
The Record Plant, 321 West 44th St, New York: 18, 19, and 23 April 1975

Mixing
The Record Plant, 321 West 44th St, New York: 15–16 July 1975 (?)

Technical team
Producers: Bruce Springsteen, Jon Landau, Mike Appel
Recording engineer: Jimmy Iovine
Assistant recording engineers: Thom Panunzio, Corky Stasiak, Dave Thoener, Ricke Delena, Angie Arcuri, Andy Abrams

Bruce Springsteen recorded a version of *Thunder Road* for the funeral of James Berger, who died after managing to help numerous people out of the World Trade Center on 11 September 2001. This recording is dedicated to the New York hero's son.

1975

Genesis and lyrics

Bruce Springsteen and the E Street Band played an early version of *Thunder Road,* entitled *Wings for Wheels,* at a concert at The Main Point in Bryn Mawr, Pennsylvania, on 5 February 1975. "This song kind of had a long gestation,"[13] explains Springsteen on the DVD *VH1 Storytellers—On Stage.* The songwriter was constantly reworking it. Before definitely plumping for Mary, the heroine was called Angelina, Anne, Chrissie, and Christina. The title of the song comes from a 1958 Arthur Ripley movie of the same name, starring Robert Mitchum. Springsteen had not seen the film, but was inspired by a poster in a movie theater.

What is *Thunder Road* about? In *Storytellers—On Stage*, the songwriter explains that the song is an "invitation."[13] We learn that it is an invitation to go on the long, exhilarating journey that the *Born to Run* album sets out to be. Springsteen also talks about the song in his autobiography, explaining how it introduces the main characters on the album and also the key question: are you willing to take a chance in life? The song opens with the lyrics: "The screen door slams, Mary's dress sways/Like a vision she dances across the porch as the radio plays/Roy Orbison singing for the lonely." The scene is set in the first couplet: we are plunged into a movie plot and the main characters, Mary and the narrator, appear. The narrator is in love with Mary: he begs her not to leave him alone and tells her that "there's magic in the night."

The narrator says: "So you're scared and you're thinking that maybe we ain't that young anymore." What does he mean by that? Have the couple gone from adolescence to adulthood without really realizing it? Is it a metaphor for the end of innocence? Perhaps. Springsteen wrote *Thunder Road* just after the Vietnam War, from which the North emerged victorious following the withdrawal of American troops and the deaths of over 58,000 American soldiers. An entire generation, starting with its youth, was in shock as the hoped-for utopias of the 1960s simultaneously vanished. So, there was this need to escape an oppressive, relentless reality. For the narrator, there is only one way forward: "All the redemption I can offer, girl, is beneath this dirty hood/Climb in back, heaven's waiting down on the tracks/Come take my hand/Riding out tonight to case the promised land/Thunder Road." And the song ends with a sentence that in many ways summarizes both his past and his future: "I'm pulling out of here to win." *Thunder Road*

Bruce Springsteen (Roy Bittan is on the keyboards) onstage at Alex Cooley's Electric Ballroom, in Atlanta, during the *Born to Run* promotional tour.

opens the album with the intention of showing what's at stake when you take a chance in life and then sets a high standard for the rest of the action to come.

Thunder Road is one of the most important songs in the whole of Bruce Springsteen's repertoire. Since 1975, he has performed it over 1,400 times.

Production

Thunder Road is the opening track of the album, where we discover the new E Street Band lineup, without David Sancious and Vini Lopez, but with Max Weinberg, Roy Bittan, and Steve Van Zandt—plus Jon Landau on production instead of Jimmy Cretecos. It was probably one of the first songs the band worked on some time in March 1975, with the recording completed in April. It was hugely significant for Landau, because it was following his shrewd advice that the new lineup for the band had taken shape, which definitively tied him to Springsteen's destiny.

The intro opens with piano and harmonica, or, as Springsteen describes the opening in his autobiography, with the sound of a harmonica breaking the silence of early morning. The atmosphere is calm. Roy Bittan, appearing for the first time, plays with emotion, but also huge assertiveness and structural mastery—as he will go on to prove in the rest of the piece. He is recording with an acoustic piano, probably a Steinway concert piano, and not a Fender Rhodes, as the album credits incorrectly state.

Springsteen joins him on vocals in the first two couplets. His rendition is markedly different from that of the first two albums: his phrasing is more affected, with a touch of Roy Orbison, as he himself later confirmed. As the song progresses, he unfurls all his vocal power, which is still as impressive as ever.

Roy Orbison. The New Jersey singer paid an emphatic tribute to him in *Thunder Road*.

Opposite Drummer Max Weinberg, member of the E Street Band during *Born to Run* sessions and for the eponymous tour.

For Springsteen Addicts

Springsteen makes explicit reference in the song to one of his idols, the singer Roy Orbison whose hits included *Only the Lonely* (which reached No.2 in the *Billboard* pop charts in July 1960).

1975

It is not until the second verse that the other band members come in (at 1'15). Max Weinberg's drums can be heard in stereo, decidedly less tormented and more "business-like" than Vini Lopez's playing. He is supported by Garry Tallent's bass (which was recorded directly into the console). Tallent later gave a good description of the enthusiasm the musicians felt when they were recording the song: "*Thunder Road* was one of those songs that, with the pictures that the words gave you, it was just real immediate, and we said, 'Yeah, okay! This is a great song, let's work on this. Let's make this happen!'"[36]

In the next verse/chorus, the backing vocals of Mike Appel, Steve Van Zandt, and Roy Bittan come in to support the Boss's powerful vocals (at 1'43). Another instrument, which would become part of the texture of many of the E Street Band's other pieces, also puts in an appearance: a glockenspiel. Played by Bittan, it underlines Springsteen's Phil Spector-like vision.

When it comes to the various guitars that Springsteen plays on this song, Jimmy Iovine recalls interminable sessions: "The guitar parts on *Thunder Road* were 13 hours in the studio. I fell asleep at the console in the middle of it. All [Bruce] said for 13 hours was 'Again. Again. Again.'"[35]

The song ends with an instrumental sequence (from 3'50) that was originally between two verses. But Jon Landau suggested that it would be more effective at the end of the song. It was an excellent idea, enabling the track to follow a logical progression by ending on a lively coda. It is carried by a melodic motif by Clarence Clemons on saxophone and Roy Bittan on glockenspiel, with the latter also playing a superb lyrical and rhythmic piano part.

Thunder Road defined the new Springsteen sound that would carry him to glory. The sheer magnetism of this fantastic song is down to the lyrics as much as the music and the performers. It is the emotion conveyed by a whole series of factors, and the driving force of an incredible young man, just 24 years old, who believed in his dreams and made them come true. "This is beyond all our grasps, what this guy has in his head,"[35] Jimmy Iovine would later say, quite rightly, of Springsteen.

Zildjian

TENTH AVENUE FREEZE-OUT

Bruce Springsteen / 3'11

COVERS

Tenth Avenue Freeze-Out has been adapted numerous times. Besides Max Weinberg and Little Steven and The Disciples of Soul, other versions have been performed by Southside Johnny and The Asbury Jukes, Billy Joel, Bon Jovi, and John Hiatt.

Musicians

Bruce Springsteen: vocals, guitar, brass arrangements
Clarence Clemons: tenor saxophone
Roy Bittan: piano
Garry Tallent: bass
Max Weinberg: drums
Randy Brecker: trumpet, bugle
Michael Brecker: tenor saxophone
David Sanborn: baritone saxophone
Wayne Andre: trombone
Steve Van Zandt: brass arrangements

Recording

The Record Plant, 321 West 44th St, New York: 5 and 16 May 1975

Technical team

Producers: Bruce Springsteen, Jon Landau, Mike Appel
Recording engineer: Jimmy Iovine
Assistant recording engineers: Thom Panunzio, Corky Stasiak, Dave Thoener, Ricke Delena, Angie Arcuri, Andy Abrams

Before becoming official guitarist of the E Street Band, Steve Van Zandt (seen here in 1979) wrote the brass arrangements for *Tenth Avenue Freeze-Out*.

1975

Genesis and lyrics

The Tenth Avenue on the second track of *Born to Run* could refer to 10th Avenue in Belmar, New Jersey, which runs perpendicular to the E Street after which Bruce Springsteen's band is named. Belmar was David Sancious's hometown. But it could also be 10th Avenue in Manhattan, which runs through Hell's Kitchen, a disreputable and derelict neighborhood in the mid-1970s that was mainly inhabited by working-class Italian and Irish Americans. This is the same 10th Avenue that leads to Greenwich Village, where Springsteen had played the clubs a few years earlier. The phrase, "'Cause I'm running on the bad side" therefore makes perfect sense. However, the meaning of "Freeze-Out" remains a mystery. "I have no idea what that means to this day,"[29] Springsteen says himself in the documentary *Wings for Wheels: The Making of Born to Run*.

Yet *Tenth Avenue Freeze-Out* is a song in which Springsteen is clearly singing about himself. "Bad Scooter searching for his groove," he sings at the beginning. Bad Scooter is Bruce Springsteen (the initials are the same), and when he says, "I got my back to the wall," he is referring to the relative commercial failure of his first two albums and the questions being asked by Columbia. He is "stranded in the jungle," by which we understand the city, where "the night is dark, but the sidewalk bright." For the moment, he is "all alone" and he "can't go home."

Everything changes in the third and final verse, when the "Big Man" joins the band. Big Man is Clarence Clemons who up until then had been a social worker and amateur saxophonist. Suddenly, "From the coastline to the city/All the little pretties raise their hands." In other words, the E Street Band is heading for success and international fame. In the documentary *Springsteen on Broadway*, the songwriter says: "It was a story where not only did Scooter and the Big Man bust this city in half. But we remade this city. We remade this city shaping it into the kind of place where our friendship and our love for one another wouldn't have been such an exceptional thing."[2]

Springsteen played *Tenth Avenue Freeze-Out* for the first time at the Palace Concert Theater in Providence, Rhode Island. Since then, he has performed it over a thousand times, often as the first song in concerts in the mid-1970s. It was chosen as the A-side of the second single taken from the album (with *She's the One* as the B-side), but never made it into the hit parades.

The Brecker brothers Michael (tenor sax) and Randy (trumpet) accompany the E Street Band as they record R&B song *Tenth Avenue Freeze-Out*.

Production

From the very first notes, it is hard not to think of Otis Redding or Wilson Pickett. The various brass sounds, Steve Cropper-style guitar, the bass, the piano, and the drums all contribute to a Stax sound, a Muscle Shoals Studios rhythm. Besides the undeniable quality of the song and Springsteen's excellent rendition, *Tenth Avenue Freeze-Out* stands out for its brass arrangements and the caliber of the various participants. Alongside the indispensable Clarence Clemons, the famous Brecker brothers, Randy and Michael, were invited to take part in the sessions. The brothers, who formed a partnership that became one of the most sought-after brass sections in the 1970s and 1980s, always impressed people with their skills and knowledge. With them, David Sanborn also qualified as a seasoned veteran, having participated in sessions for Stevie Wonder, Gil Evans, and David Bowie, among others. Finally, Wayne Andre, the essential trombonist who had worked with jazz giants such as Sarah Vaughan, Oscar Peterson, and Wes Montgomery, also provided precious support.

However, once all these excellent musicians had gathered in the studio, the problem was: What exactly were they were going to play? Springsteen and Bittan had tried to write the arrangements, but on the day of the recording the musicians stood there stumped in front of the stands. As Randy Brecker explained: "They didn't have the horn parts worked out. They hadn't figured out what they wanted. We spent several hours on that tune."[37] It was general panic in the control room. Mike Appel suggested postponing the session. All of a sudden, Steve Van Zandt jumped up from the corner where he had been sitting. Although not yet a member of the E Street Band, he often hung out with Springsteen, always ready to lend a hand. On this occasion, he thought he had found the solution for the brass section. Mike Appel recalls: "We played the track over and over, and finally, he comes up with that riff that's on the record. When Steve went out there, he was totally, absolutely cocky confident that he had it—and he did have it. The Brecker brothers followed him immediately. They took everything he said; he had it down in his head what they should play, and that was it."[38] Full of admiration for the skilful tour de force of his friend "Miami Steve," Springsteen more or less decided there and then to make him a member of the E Street Band. Although Van Zandt himself has never confirmed this story, he became an official member of the team on 20 July 1975 when he performed in his first concert at the Palace Concert Theater, in Providence, Rhode Island.

NIGHT

Bruce Springsteen / 3'01

Musicians
Bruce Springsteen: vocals, guitar
Clarence Clemons: saxophone
Roy Bittan: piano, harpsichord, glockenspiel
Garry Tallent: bass
Max Weinberg: drums

Recording
The Record Plant, 321 West 44th St, New York: 10 May 1975

Technical team
Producers: Bruce Springsteen, Jon Landau, Mike Appel
Recording engineer: Jimmy Iovine
Assistant recording engineers: Thom Panunzio, Corky Stasiak, Dave Thoener, Ricke Delena, Angie Arcuri, Andy Abrams

Roy Bittan (seen here at the 2012 Grammy Awards) is one of the great orchestrators of the Wall of Sound in *Night*, in which he plays the piano, glockenspiel, and harpsicord.

1975

Genesis and lyrics

During the Springsteen on Broadway concerts at the Walter Kerr Theatre in 2018, the songwriter from New Jersey confessed to audiences that he had "never held an honest job in [his] entire life." He continued, "I've never done any hard labor. I've never worked nine to five. I've never worked five days a week until right now. I don't like it. I've never seen the inside of a factory and yet it's all I've ever written about."[2] It is a curious paradox: never having been working class himself, Bruce Springsteen describes the daily life of blue-collar workers with unusual realism and, often epic, poetry.

Night is a brilliant illustration of this. The song begins with the lyrics, "Get up every morning at the sound of the bell/You get to work late and the boss man's giving you hell." It is easy to imagine the main character in *Night* as a factory worker trapped in the hellish downward spiral of Taylorism. Like Charlie Chaplin in *Modern Times*, he is the victim of what can only be called modern slavery. "And you're just a prisoner of your dreams," Springsteen continues. Some have chosen alcohol as an escape, while others have turned to drugs or tranquilizers. For the hero/antihero of *Night*, it is his love for his motorbike: he relishes the sheer exhilaration that makes him forget his work worries, putting his faith in his machine as they "scream into the night" and "the highway ignites." Once again, it is the highway that frees him from his frustrations, and from his solitude. This is a dual theme that Springsteen pursues further in his next opus, *Darkness on the Edge of Town*.

Night is the shortest track on *Born to Run*, a typically rock 'n' roll song following the lineage of Chuck Berry. Bruce Springsteen and his musicians performed it for the first time onstage at The Bottom Line in New York on 13 August 1975.

Production

Night was recorded at the Record Plant, probably in around a dozen takes, with the eighth appearing to have been chosen for the master. The very first bars of the intro immediately set the tone: the band is playing a rock song. In a strange way, it sounds like the beginning of *Venus*, the Shocking Blue hit released in 1969, but reinterpreted with added adrenaline. Clarence Clemons's roaring and impassioned saxophone quickly takes charge of operations, and the song continues with more familiar E Street Band sounds.

Clarence Clemons's saxophone elevates *Night* to its apex before bringing it to a close (seen here with Springsteen onstage at The Bottom Line, New York, on 13 August 1975).

Night is a good example of what Springsteen was aiming for with the arrangements, as a Phil Spector-style Wall of Sound can be heard with, among others, numerous Telecaster-Esquire tracks. The sound is homogenous, dense, and a little stodgy. Exactly like the Wall of Sound. "You can't really pick out what's playing," said Jimmy Iovine. "But if you listen closely, you can hear each instrument. Phil called that a 'wall.' Bruce wanted that."[35]

Another characteristic of the song is the different keyboard parts. Roy Bittan is on acoustic piano, a Baldwin electric harpsichord (which tinges the arrangements with somewhat restrained chords, as can be heard on the right of the panorama), and on glockenspiel (whose buoyant notes struggle to emerge from the mix). The band is powerfully propelled by Max Weinberg on drums and a frenetic hi-hat. Weinberg is supported by Garry Tallent on his Danelectro Longhorn bass, which adds speed and energy.

This song is structured around two verses, three other parts that serve harmonically as choruses, and a bridge (at 1'58). When Springsteen starts singing his lead vocals, he does so with Roy Orbison's voice in mind. His rendition is therefore more affected, more channeled. He called this "the Jersey-Pavarotti–via–Roy Orbison singing."[1] He performs his own harmonies throughout the song to reinforce this effect, and the result, it has to be said, is a success. Finally, Clarence Clemon's saxophone closes this third track of the album with a brief and lively solo, a red-hot sound heightened by a very short delay.

Night is an excellent song with excellent performers. If there is one slight criticism, it is the somewhat lackluster mixing that leans too heavily on the Spector model.

The first few bars of the intro to *Night* vaguely resemble *Venus* by Shocking Blue, who themselves were greatly inspired by *The Banjo Song*, which was released in 1963 by a group called The Big Three.

BACKSTREETS

Bruce Springsteen / 6'29

Musicians
Bruce Springsteen: vocals, guitar
Roy Bittan: piano, organ
Garry Tallent: bass
Max Weinberg: drums

Recording
The Record Plant, 321 West 44th St, New York: 25 April, 19 and 23 May, 6 and 18 July 1975

Technical team
Producers: Bruce Springsteen, Jon Landau, Mike Appel
Recording engineer: Jimmy Iovine
Assistant recording engineers: Thom Panunzio, Corky Stasiak, Dave Thoener, Ricke Delena, Angie Arcuri, Andy Abrams

Bruce Springsteen mentions Stockton's Wing in the second verse. The Irish musicians Paul Roche, Maurice Lennon, Tommy Hayes, Kieran Hanrahan, and Tony Callinan used this name for their group in the noble cause of folk rock and Celtic rock.

1975

For Springsteen Addicts

Backstreets was later used as the name of a magazine that was very popular with Springsteen's American fans.

Genesis and lyrics

In an interview with Brian Hiatt for *Rolling Stone* magazine, on 5 October 2016, Springsteen talked about the message he had in mind when he was writing *Backstreets.* He said that it was just a song about "youth, the beach, the night, friendships, the feeling of being an outcast and kind of living far away from things in this little outpost in New Jersey. It's also about a place of personal refuge. It wasn't a specific relationship [...]"[39] Reading the lyrics of *Backstreets*, there is nevertheless a sense that a close relationship exists between the narrator and Terry. There is no way of knowing whether it is an intimate relationship or just a friendship. Is Terry a woman? And, if so, is she real or imaginary? Perhaps the New Jersey songwriter was hinting at the end of his relationship with Diane Lozito (see *Genesis and Lyrics*, page 56). Or is Terry a man? In an interview with Roger Scott and Patrick Humphries for *Hot Press* (2 November 1984), Springsteen gave a partial explanation: "A song like *No Surrender* [on the *Born in the U.S.A.* album], or *Backstreets*, or *Bobby Jean* [also on *Born in the U.S.A.]* are just basic songs about friendship, which me and Steve [Little Steven]—we've been best friends since we were like 16, so anytime I wrote one of those, I had to be drawing on our relationship I guess to a certain degree. They're just songs about people passin' through, the rites of passage together."[40]

There are definitely some autobiographical elements in *Backstreets*, which are seen in phrases like: "Catching rides to the outskirts," "Sleeping in that old abandoned beach house," and "Hiding on the backstreets/With a love so hard and filled with defeat." The similarities with Springsteen's youth are obvious. The song then develops into a kind of full-blown movie with images rolling past—of the beach at Stockton's Wing "where desperate lovers park" and the "juke joints [...]/Where dancers scraped the tears up." The sprawling city is a place where lies have killed, and dreams have become nightmares. And there are repeated references to the cinema: "Remember all the movies, Terry, we'd go see/Trying to learn how to walk like the heroes we thought we had to be." Their dreams fade, and all they can do is hide in the backstreets.

Production

The piano intro, or at least the first six bars of *Backstreets,* sow the seeds for *Hungry Heart* on the 1980 album, *The River.* Roy

Al Kooper in 1966. Roy Bittan said he took inspiration from his music for *Highway 61 Revisited* and *Blonde on Blonde* for *Backstreets*.

Bittan, aka The Professor, takes flight on a stunningly lyrical, 50-second intro. He is accompanied by Garry Tallent's bass and some organ pads that he plays himself. His highly structured technique is one of the great strengths of Springsteen's music. Springsteen himself is perfectly aware of this, believing that 88 piano keys are just not enough for The Professor and that Bittan's piano-playing has been a key sound of his greatest records. For Springsteen, Bittan's arpeggios on the piano and his glockenspiel sounds are as immediately recognizable as Clarence Clemon's inimitable saxophone.

Yet this piano part was almost deleted from the mix. Jon Landau, ever the shrewd producer, introduced Springsteen to editing as a means of encouraging him to reduce the length of some of his pieces, and just keep what was essential. Landau explained to Springsteen that a longer song was not necessarily better, but that neither was a shorter one. However, Springsteen has admitted that he latched onto the editing process, with the result that Landau had to stop him from making drastic cuts to the classic intro and outro of *Backstreets*.

After the virtuosic piano display, the whole band come in for the second part of this long intro (from 0'49). The E Street Band provide amazing support, led by Springsteen's Telecaster-Esquire, which is tinged with a very '50s-style vibrato. Roy Bittan said he was inspired for his organ part by Al Kooper on *Blonde on Blonde*, Bob Dylan's double album that was released in 1966—although it is particularly reminiscent of the organ on *Like a Rolling Stone* (*Highway 61 Revisited*, 1965). The rhythm section, comprising Garry Tallent and Max Weinberg, is particularly efficient, with an unusual drum part: "I remember rehearsing in a little warehouse on Heck Avenue in Neptune, NJ, and Jon [Landau] came down. He wasn't at that point actively involved in terms of management or anything like that. He was Bruce's friend. We were playing *Backstreets* in a completely different way, and I think Jon just said to Bruce: *Running Scared* by Roy Orbison. And Bruce said, 'Yeah, play something like this,' and he air-drummed the tom-tom part, which became the drum part on *Backstreets*."[41]

Although Roy Orbison's influence is evident throughout the album, on this occasion Springsteen did not draw upon it for the lead vocals. With an Elvis-style slapback echo on the vocals—probably a result of John Lennon's influence on Jimmy Iovine, who worked on his *Rock 'n' Roll* album—the Boss delivers an incredible performance, alternating between gentleness and power. His way of straining his voice on the parts that serve as choruses (there are examples at 1'30 and 2'18) is quite impressive, especially as he recorded it in a hurry. As he recounts: "In a three-day, 72-hour sprint, working in three studios simultaneously, Clarence and I finishing the *Jungleland* sax solo, phrase by phrase, in one, while we mixed *Thunder Road* in another, singing *Backstreets* in a third."[1]

Springsteen performs a very good guitar solo on his Telecaster-Esquire (at 3'34), also enhanced by a slapback echo (as are the piano and tom-toms). Mike Appel helped out here by getting him to listen to the James Burton solo in Ricky Nelson's *Hello Mary Lou* (1961). The similarity is not striking, with the Boss playing more of a melodic solo, with many guitar bends.

Backstreets is one of Bruce Springsteen's greatest songs. It shines a light on the incredible Roy Bittan and his magnificent piano part. We also hear for the first time the true nature of the Boss's voice, which is somewhere between gentleness and fury, and quite different from the many voices that had influenced him.

Bruce Springsteen and Clarence Clemons in Amsterdam on 23 November 1975 during the Born to Run Tour. *Born to Run*, the thrill of rock and speed.

BORN TO RUN

Bruce Springsteen / 4'30

Musicians

Bruce Springsteen: vocals, acoustic and electric guitars
Clarence Clemons: saxophone
David Sancious: piano, Fender Rhodes, synthesizer (?)
Danny Federici: organ, glockenspiel (?)
Garry Tallent: bass
Ernest "Boom" Carter: drums
Unidentified musicians: string section, tambourines, backing vocals

Recording

914 Sound Recording Studios, Blauvelt, New York State: 21 May, 6 August 1974

Technical team

Producers: Bruce Springsteen, Mike Appel
Recording engineer: Louis Lahav

For Springsteen Addicts

A handwritten sheet with Springsteen's first draft of *Born to Run* was sold at auction for $197,000 on 5 December 2013.

Above his bed, Springsteen had a poster of Peter Pan holding hands with Wendy, the young heroine who followed him into Neverland. This is the name that the Boss used for *Born to Run*, with all the symbolism it entails.

1975

Genesis and lyrics

Born to Run is to Bruce Springsteen what *Like a Rolling Stone* is to Bob Dylan: his quintessential work. The New Jersey songwriter wrote the song in his bedroom in a cottage that he was renting in Long Branch, New Jersey. At the time, he was giving himself a crash course in the rock 'n' roll sound of the 1950s and 1960s. As he explains: "Love, work, sex, and fun. The darkly romantic visions of both Spector and Orbison felt in tune with my own sense of romance, with love itself as a risky proposition."[1] And then there is the music: *Born to Run* revisits, in a way, the raw energy of rock 'n' roll—the wind of freedom that deeply transformed the United States, followed by the rest of the Western world, in the 1950s—but it has to be listened to in the light of the singer-songwriter's experiences of the post-Vietnam era, the assassination of the Kennedy brothers and Martin Luther King, and the Watergate scandal.

The lyrics for *Born to Run* have nothing of the optimism and carefree spirit of the early 1960s. "I worked really hard getting the soul of the song and the spiritual side of the song right,"[29] explains Springsteen in the documentary *Wings for Wheels*. The first drafts of the lyrics were a lot darker than the definitive version would be. At a concert at The Bottom Line in New York, in 1974, the phrase "Of a runaway American dream" was already there at the start of the song, but Springsteen then followed it with: "At night we stop and tremble in the heat/With murder in our dreams" instead of "At night, we ride through mansions of glory in suicide machines."

Jon Landau provides further insight into *Born to Run* in the same documentary: "It's about the tension in the life of somebody, at a critical moment in their life, trying to move from one place in the world to another."[29] In some ways, it is the soundtrack for the end of a particular American dream, with a proliferation of images flashing by and a kind of intoxication with speed, which, once again, echoes cinematic images from movies like *The Wild One*, *Vanishing Point*, *Easy Rider*, and *Two-Lane Blacktop*. These images fire the listener's imagination. Throughout this Springsteen epic, the sound of fuel-injection engines can be heard roaring down Highway 9 at full power. A little later on in the song, "Beyond the Palace the hemi-powered drones/Scream down the boulevard." Springsteen then sings at the start of the fourth and final verse: "The highway's jammed with broken heroes."

Among the antiheroes are the narrator and his girlfriend Wendy. The town where they live is dragging them down. And the town in question is Asbury Park, as Springsteen reveals at the beginning of the documentary: "In 1974, Asbury Park still managed to come alive on Friday and Saturday nights. Down by the boardwalk, Kingsley and Ocean Avenue formed a sort of racetrack oval that the locals called 'The Circuit.'"[29] Since then, Asbury Park has lost its charm, and become an old-fashioned seaside resort and the scene of violent clashes between Afro-Americans and the authorities. For the narrator and Wendy, it is "a death trap." The narrator says to Wendy: "We gotta get out while we're young." It is almost an order, "'Cause tramps like us, baby we were born to run." And then comes the exhilaration of the open road, at the end of which the young lovers will walk in the sun. What message is Springsteen conveying? Probably that we can achieve our goals by confronting life head on, letting go of our past, leaving adolescence behind, and becoming adults.

Bruce Springsteen and the E Street Band played *Born to Run* in public for the first time at Swarthmore College, Pennsylvania, on 28 April 1974. According to the website Brucebase.wikidot.com, it is the song that he has performed the greatest number of times to date—on over 1,700 occasions. Some performances have left a particular mark, notably at The Spectrum in Philadelphia, on 9 December 1980, when Springsteen dedicated it to John Lennon (the day after his assassination); a charity concert for homeless children, on 13 December 1987, at Madison Square Garden; and at half-time at the 2009 Superbowl. The title track of Bruce Springsteen's third album was broadcast on the radio for the first time on 3 November 1974, on Philadelphia's WMMR station. It was released on 25 August 1975 as the A-side of the first single taken from the album, with *Meeting Across the River* on the B-side. In the October, it climbed to No.23 in the *Billboard* charts. Today, it is No.21 in *Rolling Stone*'s list of the 500 Greatest Albums of All Time.

Production

Born to Run was produced over a period of six months, probably from early 1974 up until the last overdubs on 6 August 1974. It is the only track on the album that was recorded at 914 Sound Recording Studios, and it was the last time Springsteen worked there. David Sancious, who at that point had not yet quit the band, recollects that no one was on top form when

Bruce Springsteen wrote a veritable hymn with *Born to Run*, which could easily have been a hymn to New Jersey.

For Springsteen Addicts

In 1980, the state of New Jersey adopted a resolution to make Bruce Springsteen New Jersey's ambassador to the United States federal government and *Born to Run* its unofficial rock anthem. This resolution was never passed by the New Jersey Senate.

the sessions began: "I remember that when we started the recording for that album, everybody was a little run-down physically. Clarence had tonsillitis, I had a kind of cold or something...it was a bunch of people who were just working because you had to do that, and then everybody got better, of course, and carried on."[27] The atmosphere was serious and intense, but also fairly laid-back which, according to Sancious again, would not be the case at all once they started work in the Record Plant.

Springsteen knew that he had to hit hard with this first track—Columbia Records was watching for the slightest false move to drop him. *Born to Run* had to be a smash, and Springsteen was pinning all his hopes and energy on it. The sessions were tiresome and exhausting, with Springsteen relentlessly striving for perfection: "We layered instrument upon instrument, mixing down and down, track to track, combining sections of instruments until we could fit our 72 tracks of rock 'n' roll overkill on the 16 available tracks at 914 Studios,"[1] he said.

1975

The recording

The track begins with a drum fill, a highly memorable intro: "It was Bruce's idea," Ernest "Boom" Carter later explained. "He told me what he wanted and I played it."[31] Vini Lopez's replacement suffered a strange fate: he played the intro for one of the Boss's best-known songs, but it would be the only track that he recorded with Springsteen. At the end of August, Carter followed his friend David Sancious, who had left to form Tone, his own jazz-fusion band.

The intro to *Born to Run* is dazzling and luminous, and it radiates energy and joy. The arrangements are a Phil Spector-style Wall of Sound, a kind of Holy Grail at the time for Springsteen, who was fascinated by it. His guitar riff on the Telecaster-Esquire, which is tinged with vibrato, delay, and reverb, guides the other musicians. Based on these initial notes, he had started composing *Born to Run* on the 6-string guitar, before continuing on the piano. As he points out in his autobiography, the key to the success of a song is finding a good riff. In the *Wings for Wheels* documentary, we find out that Steve Van Zandt, although not on the recording, did make a decisive contribution to the texture of the riff. He suggested to Bruce that he remove the bend he was playing on one of the notes in the riff because it was totally inaudible, brought nothing to the mix, and gave the impression that he was playing in a minor key rather than the major key required. A small detail, but it made a big difference.

Accompanying the Telecaster-Esquire (which is doubled, tripled, or more), David Sancious is on piano, the Fender Rhodes, and probably the Mellotron, adding weight to Clarence Clemons's saxophone contributions. Danny Federici—in his sole contribution to this album—is on the organ, and probably also the glockenspiel, the Spector touch par excellence. On the rhythm section, Garry Tallent and Ernest "Boom" Carter provide speed, power, and efficiency.

Several acoustic guitars, a 12-string, and a barrage of instruments embedded within one another can be heard in the verses. Louis Lahav, the recording engineer, recalls the riot of sound and the complexity of the recording process: "You've got to remember it was only 16-track, so pre-mixing and bouncing was the only way to go. There are probably thousands of parts and instruments in it, all bounced down to 16

In an episode of the fifth season of the series *The Sopranos*, Christopher Moltisanti quotes a phrase from *Born to Run* to explain why he is late for a meeting: "The highway's jammed with broken heroes on a last chance power drive." This is clearly a nod to Steve Van Zandt, who appeared in the series.

Ernest "Boom" Carter, the invincible drummer from *Born to Run*.

tracks."[12] Similarly, Clemons's superb saxophone solo was assembled from seven different takes (at 1'52).

A string section can be heard in the arrangements (there's an example from 3'05). Unfortunately, the musicians are not identified—Suki Lahav has said that she was not one of them. "Once we got the guitars on," Springsteen commented, "I think I wanted the thing to feel more...just grittier and the strings took away some of the darkness."[29]

Ernest's fault

Louis Lahav showed enormous patience achieving the required sound for the drums. He explains: "For the snare drum we used a big AKG reverb box, maybe it was a BX20, but we didn't have gates [an electronic effect that abruptly cuts the sound off] so I had to do yet another bounce, muting the reverb after each snare hit. That's the reason why the reverb on the snare sounds different throughout the song. And it took me hours punching in and out, what you can do these days in seconds."[12] It was not the only difficulty posed by Carter's drums. On the instrumental bridge, there is an incredible syncopated part that he intuitively performs with a masterful jazz feel, supported by an amazing bass line played by Garry Tallent in the style of Chris Squire from Yes (from 2'38). It is such an awe-inspiring sound that Max Weinberg, who replaced Carter, never managed to reproduce it onstage. "After a while he just gave up and did his own thing, which was great on its own,"[12] Lahav later said.

The mixing

Mixing *Born to Run* was a delicate task. The 16 tracks are so rich, some comprising several different parts, that three pairs of hands were needed to complete the job: those of Springsteen, Mike Appel, and Louis Lahav. After spending the night struggling in vain on a number of aborted attempts, it was 8 o'clock in the morning when the three men made a final attempt before having to vacate the studio for the next session. "It was all hands-on deck," writes Springsteen in his autobiography. "Our engineer, Louis Lahav, would have his left hand riding the guitar faders, his right riding the keyboards; Mike might ride the voice, the acoustic guitars in the final verse, while I'd be reaching over their shoulders to nudge the sax solo as it peaked and the guitar riff in the outro."[1] In the absence of automated consoles, which did not exist at the time, the slightest error meant that they would have to start again from the beginning. But in spite of the fatigue, stress, and the next customers shouting and banging on the studio door, the three men managed in extremis to complete the final mix. The song sounded great and Springsteen was happy to be able to return home with the recording exactly as he had wanted it (which doesn't happen very often). However, the record company asked them to do another recording in another New York studio, to try and bring the lead vocal to the fore. In vain.

Born to Run is living proof of months of effort and trial and error. The song, which opens the second side of the album, symbolizes the vision and the dream that the young singer-songwriter from New Jersey had always believed in, and makes them real. *Born to Run* is a masterclass in willpower and talent. A formidable talent.

SHE'S THE ONE

Bruce Springsteen / 4'30

The phrase "Because French cream won't soften them boots" was taken from *Santa Ana*, a song that Springsteen composed in late 1972 or early 1973. The song was an outtake from *The Wild, The Innocent, and The E Street Shuffle* and features on the *Tracks* box set (1998).

Musicians
Bruce Springsteen: vocals, guitar
Clarence Clemons: saxophone
Roy Bittan: piano, harpsichord, organ
Garry Tallent: bass
Max Weinberg: drums
Unidentified musicians: backing vocals

Recording
The Record Plant, 321 West 44th St, New York: March to May, 24–25 July 1975

Technical team
Producers: Bruce Springsteen, Jon Landau, Mike Appel
Recording engineer: Jimmy Iovine
Assistant recording engineers: Thom Panunzio, Corky Stasiak, Dave Thoener, Ricke Delena, Angie Arcuri, Andy Abrams

Bruce Springsteen with top model Karen Darvin, who could well have been the heroine in *She's the One.*

1975

Genesis and lyrics

She's the One is the definitive version of a song that was originally called *Virgin Summer Nights.* A song "written just so I could hear C blow that sax solo over the top of it,"[1] as Springsteen explains in his autobiography. However, the lyrics, which were written after the music—in an explicit homage to the Bo Diddley beat—have nothing whatsoever to do with his favorite saxophonist. Instead, they evoke a woman who has bewitching powers of seduction. A woman with "killer graces" and "that smile on her lips/Because she knows that it kills me," sings Springsteen in the intro. The narrator is utterly possessed by this creature, who may be real or a fantasy, as she appears before him, "Standing in that doorway like a dream." But it is obvious that even the most torrid of kisses (even French ones) "will not break that heart of stone." But what does it matter? With "her eyes that shine like a midnight sun/She's the one, she's the one." The narrator will never find the strength to leave her, not just because they made a "secret pact" to stay together forever, but also because of "her tenderness" and "her love [that] could save you from the bitterness."

There was plenty of speculation as to the identity of Springsteen's heroine in *She's the One.* Was she the top model Karen Darvin, who was the New Jersey songwriter's girlfriend at the time (before she got together with Todd Rundgren)? Was she Suki Lahav, the violinist in the E Street Band from September 1974 to March 1975 (before she returned to her native Israel)? When asked, she gave an enigmatic reply: "I think the only person who has the answer is Springsteen."[44] Clarence Clemons provided a possible clue: "We thought she was an angel. We all loved her, especially Bruce. She had this kind of mystical aura."[30]

Bruce Springsteen and the E Street Band performed *She's the One* for the first time onstage on 7 March 1974, in front of an exuberant crowd at the Liberty Hall in Houston, Texas. It is the B-side of the second single taken from *Born to Run*, with *Tenth Avenue Freeze-Out* on the A-side.

Production

The first version of *She's the One* seems to have been recorded in March 1975. It was over six minutes long and contained a number of phrases that Springsteen chose to recycle for the

Clarence Clemons, Bruce Springsteen, and Max Weinberg in Red Bank, New Jersey, on 11 October 1975, during the Born to Run Tour. *She's the One* has been a mainstay of setlists since the spring of 1974.

lyrics of *Backstreets*. Another basic track went into the can in around May, and the song was finished in July.

The Fender Telecaster-Esquire opens the piece. Springsteen strums with the pad of his thumb to obtain a rounder, more muted tonality. Reverberated organ arpeggios then come in to accompany him and are themselves doubled on piano in an overdub several bars later (from 0'17). Among his other contributions, Roy Bittan adds some chords played on his Baldwin Electric harpsichord. It's not surprising that Danny Federici struggled to find space during the Record Plant sessions! Bittan was absolutely everywhere. Bittan later explained that this was down to their different styles, with his being more structured and Federici's more instinctive. He also felt the need to prove himself, as he was relatively new to the band. "So, I think the architecture that I provided was maybe difficult for Danny to play with at the time. I was just being asked to play piano and then when it came time to overdub organ, I was just being asked to overdub organ [...] I would take two swipes at the organ on a song and I would pretty much have it because I knew every note I had played on the piano."[45]

Springsteen, as usual, performs excellent lead vocals, with a very pronounced slapback echo that emphasizes the Spector-style texture of the piece. The mixing was done in mono, another typical feature of the Wall of Sound. The Boss introduces the rhythm section with a powerful, lumberjack-style "Ha!" (at 1'14). On drums, Max Weinberg bashes away powerfully at his tom-toms, Garry Tallent's Danelectro Longhorn bass roars with huge conviction, and Springsteen's Fender hammers out Bo Diddley-style chords. *She's the One* is a strange mix of diverse influences: Phil Spector for the overall texture, Roy Orbison for the voice, and Bo Diddley for the rhythm.

One of the song's highlights is Clemons's superb saxophone solo (from 2'50). The phrasing is rock, brass, sensual, and powerful, with hints of Lee Allen when he played for Little Richard. Springsteen was keen to see what the Big Man could deliver, and he was not disappointed. He was supported by backing vocals vigorously chanting, *"Whoah she's the one."* After a coda, once again stamped with the Bo Diddley touch, the musicians abruptly end the piece.

Although *She's the One* is a very good song, apparently Springsteen was not sure whether to include it on the record. Luckily, he made the right decision.

MEETING ACROSS THE RIVER

Bruce Springsteen / 3'16

Musicians
Bruce Springsteen: vocals
Roy Bittan: piano
Richard Davis: double bass
Randy Brecker: trumpet
Recording
The Record Plant, 321 West 44th St, New York: 28 May, July 1975
Technical team
Producers: Bruce Springsteen, Jon Landau, Mike Appel
Recording engineer: Jimmy Iovine
Assistant recording engineers: Thom Panunzio, Corky Stasiak, Dave Thoener, Ricke Delena, Angie Arcuri, Andy Abrams

For Springsteen Addicts

A book of 21 short stories, *Meeting Across the River: Stories Inspired by the Haunting Bruce Springsteen Song,* was named after this song. It was written by Jessica Kaye, Richard Brewer, and Stefan Rudnicki, and published in 2005.

1975

Genesis and lyrics

Roy Bittan's piano and, to an even greater extent, Randy Brecker's trumpet create a film noir jazz ambience, which is perfect for the story that Bruce Springsteen is telling in *Meeting Across the River.* The narrator is clearly a small-time gangster. He asks his friend Eddie to lend him some money and give him a ride. "Got to make it through the tunnel, got a meeting with a man on the other side," sings Springsteen. We understand that the narrator lives in New Jersey and needs to get across the Hudson River to New York. "If you wanna come along [to the meeting]," he says to Eddie, he can, but also he warns him that "this guy don't dance." Worse still, if they blow it, their lives could be on the line. However, as it says in the last verse, the risk will be worth it if the operation (probably drug dealing) is successful: "And when I walk through that door/ I'm just gonna throw that money on the bed/She'll see this time I wasn't just talking."

Beyond the story of small-time gangsters, which could easily have been a movie script written by John Huston or Howard Hawks in their day, lies a theme that had inspired Bruce Springsteen since his first album *Greetings from Asbury Park, N.J.* This is the attraction of the big city for a young man from out-of-town. Springsteen talked about this in an interview with Brian Hiatt for *Rolling Stone* magazine: "There was that New York–New Jersey, big-time/small-time thing, you know? It's funny, because back then, when you lived in New Jersey, you could've been a million miles from New York City [...] By that time, I think we'd been counted out, and it probably had something to do with that, a feeling I had about myself maybe, that you'd been underestimated. Most of the folks that go into my business have had the experience of someone counting them out, or of being underestimated, of someone judging your life as being without great value. So that song grew out of, 'Hey, that guy's sort of a small-time player, but he's still got his sights set on what's across that river.'"[46]

So, for the narrator and Eddie, a new, possibly dangerous, but definitely exciting, life begins when they go through either the Lincoln or the Holland Tunnel from the state of New Jersey to New York, and then emerge "on the other side." The "other side" is awash with money for anyone who can get their hands on it. *Meeting Across the River* was played for the first time at the Hancher Auditorium in Iowa City, on 26 September 1975,

Richard Davis (seen here in 1978) on the double bass recording *Meeting Across the River.*

Randy Brecker's performance in *Meeting Across the River* brings to mind Miles Davis in the film *Ascenseur pour l'échafaud.*

but has rarely been performed since (only around 70 times). The song was chosen as the B-side of the single *Born to Run*.

Production

Randy Brecker's trumpet intro has its roots in the music composed and performed by Miles Davis for the 1958 film *Ascenseur pour l'échafaud* ("Elevator to the Gallows") by French director Louis Malle. The improvisation that Brecker delivers has a similar harmonic progression, an end-of-night feel, and a muted and melancholic mood that is bewitching and hypnotic. Especially as his trumpet, which is quite far back in the mix, is tinged by a wide reverb, just like Davis's. "It's difficult to get that kind of thing recorded these days,"[47] Brecker would later comment.

Roy Bittan provides a piano accompaniment that falls somewhere between jazz and a rock ballad, and one that is definitely less structured than in the livelier pieces. He indirectly inspired Springsteen in the composition of *The Heist*, which was the working title for *Meeting Across the River*, with a piano improvisation that he played one evening at home. The following day, the Boss was playing around with chords that had a similar feel to those Bittan had played the previous night. On double bass once again is the excellent Richard Davis, who contributed to *The Angel* in *Greetings from Asbury Park, N.J.* "Bruce Springsteen had heard my bass on the Van Morrison album [*Astral Weeks*] and he said he wanted that bass player on his album."[48] It has to be said that he delivers a top-notch performance, bringing beautiful harmonic and rhythmic support. Springsteen sticks to lead vocals only, but his performance is magnificent and far removed from Roy Orbison-style clichés. He sings with an artless, emotion-filled beauty, bringing his story to life in a stupefying way.

Oddly, this song is sometimes seen as the weak spot of the *Born to Run* album. This is possibly because its jazzy feel clashes with the other tracks. It was thanks to Mike Appel that it was included. "Bruce and Jon didn't think that *Meeting Across the River* should be in the album," he explains. "I did and fought for it like heck [...] It was only after I said, 'That's a great song, it reminds me of *Naked City*, it's a gem, we have to put it on the album,' that Bruce did."[3]

Recorded around the end of May and then finalized in July, this is the only track on *Born to Run* apart from *Tenth Avenue Freeze-Out* that was mixed by Springsteen and Landau only. The other songs on the album were mixed by either Springsteen, Lahav, and Appel working together (*Born to Run*), or Springsteen, Iovine, Appel, and Landau (all the other tracks).

JUNGLELAND

Bruce Springsteen / 9'33

Musicians

Bruce Springsteen: vocals, guitar
Clarence Clemons: tenor saxophone
Roy Bittan: piano, organ
Garry Tallent: bass
Max Weinberg: drums
Suki Lahav: violin
Charles Calello: string arrangements
Unidentified musicians: string section

Recording

The Record Plant, 321 West 44th St, New York: 18, 23, and 25 April, 14, 19, and 20 July 1975

Technical team

Producers: Bruce Springsteen, Jon Landau, Mike Appel
Recording engineer: Jimmy Iovine
Assistant recording engineers: Thom Panunzio, Corky Stasiak, Dave Thoener, Ricke Delena, Angie Arcuri, Andy Abrams

The magic of *Jungleland* largely rests on Roy Bittan's keyboards and arpeggios. Seen here in concert in London during the River Tour of 2016.

Genesis and lyrics

The "long summer night" of the *Born to Run* album ends with *Jungleland*. "From there it's all night, the city, and the spiritual battleground,"[1] Springsteen writes in his autobiography. Does Bruce Springsteen reach the heights of Dylan in the 1960s with this song? With its dramatic and poetic force, and abundance of metaphors, *Jungleland* does come close to Dylan's *Desolation Row*, even if the New Jersey songwriter is singing about being disenchanted with his town and what New Jersey has become, while his illustrious predecessor in the last track of *Highway 61 Revisited* evokes the apocalypse with a sense of irony that is impossible to top.

Jungleland is a long urban poem—a kind of poetic realism—in which Bruce portrays several characters who, once again, are irresistibly drawn to the city lights. While "the rangers had a homecoming in Harlem late last night," "Magic Rat drove his sleek machine over the Jersey state line" and Barefoot Girl was "sitting on the hood of a Dodge drinking warm beer in the soft summer rain." Magic Rat and Barefoot Girl go off to Flamingo Lane, followed by a third person, Maximum Lawman. The atmosphere described by the songwriter is dark and foreboding: "From the churches to the jails tonight all is silence in the world/As we take our stand down in Jungleland," Springsteen sings.

The description of Jungleland continues with "the midnight gang" assembling "'neath that giant Exxon sign" with a "ballet being fought out in the alley" until the "local cops, Cherry Tops, rips this holy night."

In the third verse, the music itself becomes one of the characters in this urban scene, as "Kids flash guitars just like switchblades hustling for the record machine." There are also "backstreet girls [...] dancing to the records that the deejay plays" and "lonely-hearted lovers." In the last verse, the curtain falls on Jungleland, where the "poets down here don't write nothing at all" and simply "stand back and let it all be." The message is clear: Jungleland is a symbol of despair, a place of relentless torment and desolation, where rock 'n' roll seems to be the only salvation! In a special issue of *Rolling Stone* magazine on the 100 best singers of all time, Melissa Etheridge said: "When Bruce Springsteen does those wordless wails, like at the end of *Jungleland*, that's the definition of rock 'n' roll for me. He uses his whole body when he sings, and he puts

1975

Bruce Springsteen and the "Big Man" onstage at The Bottom Line, New York, on 17 August 1975.

out this enormous amount of force and emotion and passion."[49] Bruce Springsteen and the E Street Band played *Jungleland* for the first time onstage at Liberty Hall in Houston, Texas, on 7 March 1974.

Production

Jungleland got the production of the *Born to Run* album underway. An early version of the piece was recorded on 1 August 1974 at the 914 Sound Recording Studios. But multiple equipment failures and the terrible state of the piano complicated matters for the musicians. The song was frequently on the band's setlists when performing live and they knew the song inside and out. However, they found that they just couldn't make any headway due to all the technical problems. Something was clearly amiss. According to Mike Appel, how ever, the real problem was not caused by faulty equipment, but by the songwriter himself: "The truth of the matter is, Bruce had lost his direction, his energy, and to some extent his confidence."[3] Jon Landau would come to Bruce's rescue, and, with his help, Springsteen continued the sessions at the Record Plant in New York. As Landau says: "My first visit was in February [1975]. I observed the session without comment. Bruce came over to me and sort of pulled me over to the side of one of the rooms and said, 'What do you think?' There was one particular part of one song [*Jungleland*] that was like—the drummer and the bass player kept making the same mistake every time. They were doing endless takes of the song."[3] Landau pointed this out to Springsteen, which got things moving again, to the Boss's enormous relief. *Jungleland* was finally completed after many months of procrastination and the final version emerged from the sessions in April and July 1975.

It all starts with the intro

The piece starts with a superb 30-second intro, played by Suki Lahav on violin and Roy Bittan on piano. They are progressively joined by a string section and the unobtrusive support of Garry Tallent on bass. The result is a success, with Suki's violin adding emotion and spirituality. Clarence Clemons would later explain that the intro was the same one Lahav and Bittan played together on live performances at the start of *Incident on 57th Street*, from Springsteen's second album: "When we got to that song in the studio Bruce told them to use what they'd been playing live. Turned out to be a perfect fit."[30] Elsewhere, we see in the documentary *Wings for Wheels: The Making of Born to Run* an alternative intro with castanets and tom-tom rolls that was recorded on the 16th take.

The rest of the piece is mainly carried by Springsteen's sublime rendition, as he delivers a stunning lead vocal, and by

1975

Bruce Springsteen, Clarence Clemons, and Max Weinberg at the No Nukes concert in Madison Square Garden, New York, on 21 September 1971. The program included *Jungleland.*

Roy Bittan's incredible piano accompaniment. As Jeff Kazee, keyboardist for Southside Johnny and The Asbury Jukes (and Bon Jovi), comments: "His playing on *Jungleland* moved me to tears. He helped make those brilliant songs into masterpieces."[50] It has to be said that Bittan alternates flowing arpeggios and inspired chord progressions (listen at around 6'34), as well as subtle pads and counterpoint on the Hammond B-3 organ.

The Gospel of the E Street Band

Jungleland also owes its status as a standout piece for the band to Clarence Clemons's extraordinary tenor saxophone solo, which is over two minutes long (from 3'54 to 6'12)—Springsteen has described this as Clemons's finest moment on record. The texture is rich, rough, silky, and guttural, and has an utterly astounding feel. Yet the recording took 16 hours to finalize, with the Boss dictating practically every note to the saxophonist. Mike Appel recalls: "A lot of people don't realize the degree to which Bruce Springsteen was responsible for that solo. I sat in the control room while Bruce literally stood right in front of Clarence and went through it. Bruce was guiding him: 'Hit this one...no, no, hit that one...' That kind of stuff."[51] So, Clemons was guided by Springsteen as he recorded his contribution phrase by phrase. According to Jimmy Iovine, seven or eight tenor tracks were put in the can, and in the end only the best parts were kept. According to Appel, Clemons then replayed his entire solo, reproducing exactly the result of the different edits. This recording was the peak of the Big Man's career; Max Weinberg would later declare: "It is the true gospel of the E Street Band."[29]

CLARENCE CLEMONS: THE SOUL OF THE E STREET BAND

"If I was some embodiment of Jon's [Landau] rock 'n' roll dream, Clarence was an embodiment of mine."[1] These words, taken from Springsteen's autobiography, testify to the deep bond and understanding that existed between the songwriter from New Jersey and the Afro-American saxophonist, a bond that lasted for years. The E Street Band sound largely fed off Clemons's very R&B tenor saxophone.

From football to sax

Clarence Anicholas Clemons Jr was born on 11 January 1942 in Norfolk, Virginia. He was the son of Thelma and Clarence Clemons Sr, fish wholesalers from Chesapeake Bay, and the grandson of a Baptist preacher. As a young teenager, he had a serious road accident, which left him with a severe knee injury and forced him to abandon the idea of becoming a professional American football player. The alto saxophone—which he had played since the age of nine—was initially just a stopgap. "I wanted an electric train for Christmas, but [my father] got me a saxophone. I flipped out,"[52] he told the Associated Press in 1989. Gradually, his passion for the instrument grew, notably thanks to the influence of King Curtis and the records that he made with The Coasters (*Yakety Yak*, *Charlie Brown*). Clarence soon swapped the alto sax for the baritone, then the tenor.

When he was 18 years old, Clarence Clemons took his first steps in the studio with a group from Plainfield, New Jersey, called Tyrone Ashley's Funky Music Machine (several of its members would later play with Parliament-Funkadelic). In the early 1960s, as a student at Maryland State College, Clemons started his own band, The Vibratones, whose repertoire mostly comprised James Brown covers. At the same time, and up until 1970, he worked as a counselor at the Jamesburg Training School for Boys, which specialized in the re-education of mentally disturbed children.

One night at the Student Prince

It was through Garry Tallent that Clarence Clemons met Bruce Springsteen one night in an Asbury Park club called the Student Prince. "As the Big Man approached the front of the Prince, a mighty gale blew down Ocean Avenue, ripping the club door off its hinges and down the street,"[1] Springsteen writes in his autobiography. This was "good omen." A few minutes later, Clarence Clemons climbed up onstage to the right of the singer and started playing. "[...] there was something in the chemistry between the two of us, side by side, that felt like the future being written,"[1] Springsteen continues. The piece that sealed the deal that night was the aptly named *Spirit in the Night*...

The Student Prince was the start of a wonderful adventure and a rare artistic understanding. Clarence Clemons, with the E Street Band, would participate in the recording of all the Boss's albums, from *Greetings from Asbury Park, N.J.* to *High Hopes*, with his sax parts from *Born to Run* onward becoming one of the key elements in Springsteen's approach. "Nobody captured my audience's imagination or their hearts like Clarence," Springsteen admitted as he performed *Tenth Avenue Freeze-Out* in the fascinating documentary *Springsteen on Broadway*. "Clarence was a figure out of a rock 'n' roll story book and together we told a story that was bigger than any of the ones I'd written in my songs."[2] Just listen to *Paradise by the "C"*, *Thunder Road*, *Badlands*, or *Hungry Heart*, and you'll see why.

A tenor for all occasions

Although Clarence Clemons traveled a long artistic road with Bruce Springsteen, he also worked with other artists. From 1985 to 2008, the saxophonist recorded several albums as the frontman, notably *Hero* (1985), *A Night with Mr. C* (1989), and, under the name Clarence Clemons and Temple of Soul, *Live in Asbury Park* (2002) and *Brothers in Arms* (2008). His work with other artists was unusually diverse, ranging from Gary U.S. Bonds (*Dedication*, 1981), Zucchero (*Oro Incenso & Birra*, 1989), Aretha Franklin (*Who's Zoomin' Who?*, 1985) to Ringo Starr and His All-Starr Band (on an album of the same name, 1990), Jackson Browne (*You're a Friend of Mine*, 1985), Todd Rundgren (*Nearly Human*, 1989), Joe Cocker (*Unchain My Heart*, 1987), and Lady Gaga (*The Edge of Glory* and *Hair*, 2011). That's not to forget long-standing friends Southside Johnny (*I Don't Want to Go Home*, 1976), Little Steven (*Men Without Women*, 1982), and Nils Lofgren (*Silver Lining*, 1991).

Clarence Clemons also enjoyed a parallel career as an actor, both for the cinema (*New York, New York*, 1977; *Fatal Instinct*, 1993; and *Blues Brothers 2000*, 1998) and for television (*Jake and the Fatman*, 1989; *Nash Bridges*, 1996; and *Viper*, 1998).

Clarence "Big Man" Clemons in 1975. His tenor sax resonated with exceptional sensuality in the albums Bruce Springsteen made with the E Street Band, from *Greetings from Asbury Park, N.J.* to *High Hopes*.

Throughout his life, Clemons was involved with many humanitarian causes, in particular against child abuse. He suffered a stroke on 12 June 2011 and died on 18 June at Palm Beach, Florida. He was married five times and had four sons. In 2012, his nephew Jake Clemons rose to the considerable challenge of replacing him in the E Street Band. At Clarence's funeral at the Royal Poinciana Chapel, in Palm Beach, on 21 June, a visibly emotional Bruce Springsteen delivered a speech laden with symbolism: "Clarence was big, and he made me feel, and think, and love, and dream big. How big was the Big Man? Too fucking big to die."[53]

ALBUM

DARKNESS ON THE EDGE OF TOWN

Badlands • Adam Raised a Cain • Something in the Night • Candy's Room • Racing in the Street • The Promised Land • Factory • Streets of Fire • Prove It All Night • Darkness on the Edge of Town

Outtakes (excluding those on *The Promise): Don't Look Back • Hearts of Stone • Iceman • Give the Girl a Kiss • I Wanna Be with You • Frankie • Bring on the Night • Crazy Rocker • Down by the River • Break Out • The Ballad • Preacher's Daughter • Don't Say No (I Want to Be Wild).*

RELEASE DATE

United States: 2 June 1978

Reference: Columbia Records– JC 35318

No.5 in the *Billboard* chart, No.14 in the United Kingdom

Darkness on the Edge of Town marked a new chapter for Bruce Springsteen.

The Boss's first concert in the UK at the Hammersmith Odeon, London, on 18 November 1975. The English rock scene would widen his horizons.

TOWARD PURITY AND AUSTERITY

1978

Almost three years would elapse between the release of *Born to Run* and that of *Darkness on the Edge of Town*. This long silence, which could have proved fatal to the career of the New Jersey songwriter, can be explained by the dispute between Bruce Springsteen and Mike Appel. Reeling from the emotional shock of his encounter with John Hammond and, above all, of his acceptance by as prestigious a record label as Columbia, the young Springsteen had not really paid any attention to the contracts he signed. "It all came through Mike, filtered through those Laurel Canyon production, publishing, and management agreements I'd signed so many hazy years ago,"[1] he comments in his autobiography *Born to Run*. Mike Appel, for his part, explained in the Thom Zimny documentary *Bruce Springsteen, The Promise: The Making of Darkness on the Edge of Town*: "It was customary in the business when an artist gets a record deal to give away half his publishing to EMI, Blackwood Music, Abell Blackwood Music, whoever it might be. He gave it to me and it was a good thing he did because he ended up getting it all back. That wouldn't have happened elsewhere."[54]

The first contracts, like the new ones Mike Appel wanted Springsteen to sign following the resounding success of *Born to Run*, were hardly financially advantageous for the songwriter—the lawyer Michael Mayer (who knew Jon Landau) even went so far as to say that they were the worst contracts he had seen since those of Frankie Lymon. However, musically, the situation was even worse: "With regard to the legal situation, the actual initial court order was that Bruce couldn't go in the studio with a producer not approved by Mike Appel,"[54] Jon Landau recalls in Thom Zimny's documentary. Hence Springsteen's decision not to enter a studio unless he was allowed to enjoy complete artistic freedom.

In the end, it took a lawsuit for an agreement to be reached: Appel retained 25 percent of the royalties on the first three records, and received compensation amounting to around $800,000. Springsteen could return to the studio. However, two years later, Mike Appel was forced to sell back his share of the publishing to Springsteen: "[...] after depleting my capital reserves by investing large sums of money into independent motion picture production, I sold my share of the publishing back to Bruce. I had to. I had no choice. Of course, I was over 21, I knew the business, nobody held a gun to my head. However, the reality of my situation was that as far as the music business was concerned, I was dead in the water, my reputation seriously damaged, my credibility impaired. I had a family to support and bills to pay. Practically speaking, I really had no choice but to sell my remaining rights."[3] The songwriter owns everything he has ever created and is one of only a handful of artists from that time in such as position. The other side of the coin was the traumatic—though temporary—ending of a friendship! Springsteen said: "We had come to cross-purposes—this is the world—but I could never

Bruce Springsteen on his property in Holmdel, New Jersey, in 1977. A horse-whispering rock star.

hate Mike; I can only love him. His motormouth walked me into John Hammond's office. From Asbury Park to New York City and Columbia Records, that's a long walk. When it was toughest, he made it work."[1]

1978

A samurai record

From September 1974 to March 1975—so, before the release of *Born to Run*—Bruce Springsteen performed more than 40 concerts, chiefly on the East Coast of the United States and in the Midwest (plus several in Texas). Then, as leader of the E Street Band—which now included Steve Van Zandt (guitar, backing vocals), Clarence Clemons (saxophone, backing vocals), Roy Bittan (piano), Danny Federici (keyboards), Suki Lahav (violin, backing vocals), Garry Tallent (bass guitar), and Max Weinberg (drums)—and in conjunction with The Miami Horns (August 1976, then from September 1976 to March 1977), there were no fewer than four tours in quick succession. First came the Born to Run Tour, from 20 July to 11 November 1975 and then—after four performances in Europe (London on 18 and 24 November, Stockholm on 21 November, and Amsterdam on 23 November)—from 2–31 December. Then came the Chicken Scratch Tour, from 25 March to 28 May 1976, the US Tour, from 26 September to 4 November, and finally The Lawsuit Drags On Tour, from 7 February to 25 March 1977.

Despite the long months spent on the road—210 concerts to be precise, between September 1974 and March 1977!—Bruce Springsteen composed prolifically. Some 70 songs (according to Jimmy Iovine) were ready to be recorded when he went into the studio with the E Street Band and Jon Landau on 1 June 1977. Only ten would be retained for the fourth album.

Should *Darkness on the Edge of Town* be listened to as the antithesis of *Born to Run*? Not entirely (probably). Throughout the album, as in the preceding one, there are constant references to film, be it New Hollywood or film noir; the album's (and the song's) very title could have been borrowed from a Raymond Chandler novel or a John Huston movie. Even more revealingly, the drummer of the E Street Band, Max Weinberg, described the album as "this vast cinematic landscape."[54]

In truth, if *Darkness on the Edge of Town* differs from *Born to Run* it is above all because of what Jon Landau himself called a "certain feeling of loneliness."[54] These circumstances encouraged the lovers created by Springsteen for *Born to Run*, who had been desperate to escape, to make the decision to turn around and drive back to town. Like his characters, the songwriter had changed. He drew his inspiration from the often hard and traumatic reality of his own past, from his experience of family (his parents' recurrent financial dif-

Johnny Rotten, Paul Cook, Sid Vicious, and Steve Jones of the Sex Pistols. Bruce Springsteen did not remain immune to punk energy.

Darkness on the Edge of Town also bears the mark of country-music pioneer Hank Williams.

ficulties), and also from his Catholic upbringing. It was a return to his roots, of sorts, marked by an end to romantic dreams...

"After *Born to Run*, I wanted to write about life in the close confines of the small towns I grew up in," the songwriter explained. "In 1977, I was living on a farm in Holmdel, New Jersey. It was there that I wrote most of the songs for *Darkness on the Edge of Town*."[54] Thus, it was like a movie of his own adolescence that Springsteen was showing throughout the album, and which he revealed to his audience—a father who had been a taxi driver, prison guard, bus driver, truck driver, and worker in a carpet factory, as well as daily life in a working-class neighborhood where humble people were crushed by debt and forced into grueling work in factories—but also a movie made by an artist who had since won fame and recognition for his work. As Springsteen writes in his autobiography, he felt that he owed something to the people who he had grown up with and also a need to deal with that feeling. Indeed, of the characters he introduces in the album, he added: "I wanted them to feel older, weathered, wiser but not beaten."[1] These are characters upon whom fortune has not smiled—in an America that was nevertheless prosperous—but who still had enough energy to try to defeat hostile fate: characters, one might say, who were fighting back. Those are the themes that are encountered throughout *Darkness on the Edge of Town*, from *Badlands* to the title track, as well as in *Adam Raised a Cain*, *Racing in the Street*, and *The Promised Land*.

From a musical point of view, too, *Darkness on the Edge of Town* reveals the transformation that took place in Bruce Springsteen after *Born to Run*. The Phil Spector-inspired Wall of Sound was gone. On the contrary, this fourth album was driven by raw energy and the immediacy of rock 'n' roll (even though the recording sessions dragged on for ten months). The songwriter would reveal that at the height of the creative process of *Darkness on the Edge of Town* he had discovered the white folk music tradition, especially Hank Williams and Woody Guthrie, and their social themes, while at the same time listening attentively to the new British scenes—the punk rock of the Sex Pistols and The Clash, and the new wave bearing the hallmark of Elvis Costello. "*Darkness* was also informed by the punk explosion at the time. I went out and I got all the records, all the early punk records, and I brought *Anarchy in the UK*, and *God Save the Queen*, and the Sex Pistols were so frightening. They literally shook the earth."[55]

From this explosive mix—to which should be added the folk rock that he mastered in his first two albums and also the rock blues of The Animals—Springsteen succeeded in creating a timeless, powerful album, a true reflection of the cruelty and injustice of life. In this he was totally supported by the E Street Band (including a new member called Steven Van Zandt). The actors in *Darkness on the Edge of Town* no longer sought escape on the highways of America, driving their Dodge or their Harley-Davidson; now they are forced to live as a group of people who are under attack. To use Springsteen's own words: "*Darkness* was my samurai record, all stripped down for fighting."[1]

The album

Of the album, Bruce Springsteen says: "After the year of recording, listening to all the stuff we had, I stripped the record down to its—really its barest and most austere elements, and I decided I wanted something that felt like a tone poem and I didn't want any distractions from the narrative and the stories that I was telling. And I also wanted to have a sort of apocalyptic grandeur."[54] Springsteen's fourth album went on sale on 2 June 1978, a fortnight before the start of the Darkness Tour (23 May 1978 to 1 January 1979). Though released without great publicity, as Springsteen had wished, the album nevertheless entered the *Billboard* chart at No.10 in June, climbing to No.5 on 29 July (it would remain in the chart for 167 weeks, and become a triple platinum disc to boot). In Britain, it reached No.17 on 17 June. Critical reception was on the whole approving, and even acclaimed the

Elvis Costello in concert in the late 1970s. Bruce Springsteen would become a fan of this songwriter from the new English music scene.

new turn taken by the songwriter from New Jersey. In the 27 July 1978 issue of *Rolling Stone* magazine, Dave Marsh wrote:

"Occasionally, a record appears that changes fundamentally the way we hear rock 'n' roll, the way it's recorded, the way it's played. Such records—Jimi Hendrix's *Are You Experienced*, Bob Dylan's *Like a Rolling Stone*, Van Morrison's *Astral Weeks*, *Who's Next*, *The Band*—force a response, both from the musical community and the audience. To me, these are the records justifiably called classics, and I have no doubt that Bruce Springsteen's *Darkness on the Edge of Town* will some day fit as naturally within that list as The Rolling Stones' *(I Can't Get No) Satisfaction* or Sly and the Family Stone's *Dance to the Music*."[56]

Years later, writing on the AllMusic website, William Ruhlmann would note with good reason that this fourth album "presaged even starker efforts, such as *Nebraska* and *The Ghost of Tom Joad*."[57] Today, *Darkness on the Edge of Town* is in 150th place in *Rolling Stone's* list of the 500 Greatest Albums of All Time.

The sleeve

The photographer who shot Bruce Springsteen for the sleeve of *Darkness on the Edge of Town* was Frank Stefanko. He had been recommended to Springsteen by Patti Smith, who had just recorded *Because the Night*. Patti had been photographed by Frank at the start of her career. Although he worked at a meatpacking factory during the day, he would devote his spare time to photography. Several shoots were held at Stefanko's home in Haddonfield, New Jersey. These were the first photographs that the songwriter kept—shot in the bedroom of the photographer and his wife, whose walls were covered in floral wallpaper. "I knew what his past music sounded like, but I had no idea what intention he had for *Darkness on the Edge of Town*," Frank Stefanko explained in an interview with *Pitchfork*. "I actually didn't hear it until several weeks later. So the original shoot was just done with my perception of how I *thought* he wanted to look or how I wanted him to look."[58] Stefanko added: "From what I understand, when he looked at the photograph he said, 'That's the person that I'm writing about. That's the person that is the *Darkness on the Edge of Town* character and that's what I want on my cover.'"[58] A character with tired eyes, hands in his jacket pockets, but clearly determined to defeat his difficulties. "Frank looked for your true grit and he naturally intuited the conflicts I was struggling to come to terms with,"[1] wrote Bruce Springsteen in his autobiography. On the back of the album sleeve the songwriter is featured again, wearing the same clothes (this time minus the black jacket), along with the titles of the ten songs.

The fourth solo album jacket. A determined musician poses for the camera.

Against Columbia's wishes, some radio stations in large cities such as New York, Los Angeles, San Francisco, and Detroit broadcast the album on 18 May 1978, more than a fortnight before the official release date, forcing Century Broadcasting to send them a formal notice the following day.

The recording

On the 28 May 1977, the legal dispute between Bruce Springsteen and Mike Appel came to a close. The songwriter was now free to return to the studio once again. On 1 June—barely four days after the end of the proceedings—he entered Atlantic Studios, at 1841 Broadway in Manhattan, with the E Street Band and Jon Landau. During the first session Springsteen recorded eight songs! Two long years spent away from the soft lighting of the studio had left him deeply frustrated—like the rest of the band, for that matter. Thom Panunzio, the assistant recording engineer, later said that the original plan had been to make the new album very quickly. But the band were rusty, and all had lost the hard-earned fluency they had acquired in making *Born to Run*. Moreover, Springsteen realized, after two or three weeks, that he did not like the sound at Atlantic Studios. Neither did he appreciate the lodging arrangements and the environment in which the musicians had to work. A decision was made to return to the Record Plant, New York. However, the latter had already been booked by other artists, and he could not set up there properly until September. All the songs on *Darkness on the Edge of Town* would be recorded there (except *Something in the Night*, which may well have been recorded at Atlantic, apart from the mixing).

Once back in their hideout, where they had made *Born to Run* (with the exception of the title track), the musicians found their bearings again. However, they were still not on top form: for a time, the E Street Band seemed well and truly seized up: "As with *Born to Run*, our recording process was thwarted by our seeming inability to get the most basic acceptable sounds. Days went by with the only sound emanating from Studio B at the Record Plant the dull, endless thwack of Max's drumstick on a tom-tom. 'Stiiiiiiiiiiiiiiiick!' That was our frustrated mantra, shouted day and night, over and over."[1]

However, with dogged determination, the pieces eventually materialized, with some 70 songs in the bag, according to Jimmy Iovine, and between 50 and 60 according to Springsteen. Officially, only 32 are known, which are all the result of these recording sessions: ten make up the bulk of *Darkness on the Edge of Town*, four are on the *Tracks* box set (1998), and 18 on the double album *The Promise* (2010). What happened to the other numbers? Some made their way onto the following LP, *The River*, but the majority remain unknown to this day.

In search of the absolute

In the studio, Bruce Springsteen remained true to himself: he was in search of perfection. "I've never seen anybody work so hard for so long. That's inspiring,"[59] Max Weinberg later said. He demanded total involvement from his musicians—which none of them hesitated to show, as Weinberg testified: "Bruce

Frank Stefanko shot this photo for *Darkness on the Edge of Town.* Here displayed at the exhibition *From Darkness to a Dream,* at the Morrison Hotel Gallery, New York, on 14 October 2010.

respects the people he's with [...] He leads all of us and we're right there with him. He knows that the six of us are tuned totally into him one-hundred percent of the time."[59]

Unlike with *Born to Run*, the songwriter was aiming for a rawer, more aggressive, more immediate sound. "I was after a leaner sound, a little bit of an angrier sound, I wanted to toughen up the songs,"[54] he confirmed in Thom Zimny's documentary.

The idea was to record the musicians live, in order to avoid endless overdubbing as much as possible and thus to obtain a live tone color—despite the presence of carpeting that muffled all resonance. It was a difficult task, and Springsteen was careful not to direct his musicians too much. "Bruce gives us very little direction," explained Max Weinberg. "He's got this technique—I'm sure it's not a conscious thing—but he's not constantly nitpicking over details. He lets things flow. In a lot of instances, he'll give you enough rope to hang yourself!"[59]

Jimmy Iovine and his assistant, Thom Panunzio, would spend a considerable amount of time polishing the sound. Iovine has summed up his career thus: "For me, it's still about getting the guitar sound on *Darkness*. [Grins] Which was impossible."[35] As for Panunzio, it was recording the drums that left him with a painful memory: "We put the drums every place you could put them in that building. We put the drums in the elevator. You would hear the whole reverb of this whole big stairwell which made no sense at all."[54] And to cap it all, Max Weinberg was going through a difficult time personally: "I was sick; badly ill during that whole record. It was real hard to make."[59]

In fact, Springsteen and Landau did not succeed in making the sounds they had in mind materialize: "At bottom, we were amateur producers and simply failed to understand the basic physics of getting sound to tape [...] When the drums are forceful but moderate, they leave room for a big guitar sound. When the guitars are powerful but lean, you can have drums the size of a house. But you can't feature everything, for in effect you're featuring nothing."[1]

The mixing

Recording of *Darkness on the Edge of Town* was completed in early January 1978 (although the overdubs were recorded in February and March). It was necessary to sift through the large number of songs recorded over the past seven months—especially since the end of September, when the group definitively set up at the Record Plant. Springsteen did not want to depart from a rule that had become established: each song had to remain sober and austere, so as to convey its message as effectively as possible. This led him to scrap a number of songs that he considered too removed from what he was seeking to create, too bland, or too commercial. Thus, he gifted *Because the Night* to Patti Smith and *Fire* to Robert Gordon. As a result, *Darkness on the Edge of Town* did not yield a single hit.

Forty years before winning a 2017 Grammy Award for his work as a producer, Thom Panunzio (middle) was just a simple assistant recording engineer for Springsteen.

During the mixing, different people had different views: Jon Landau wanted a highly professional, technically perfect sound, whereas Steve Van Zandt sought a more garage-band tone color. Springsteen chose a middle line, and entrusted Jimmy Iovine with the task of following it. But the recording engineer, doubtless worn out after so many months of exhausting work, found himself incapable of doing the mixing. "He lost his mojo in the middle of *Darkness* somewhere,"[54] Springsteen said. That was when Chuck Plotkin came on the scene. Following an appeal for help from Jon Landau, Plotkin, then a producer and recording engineer in Los Angeles, brought a new pair of ears to the project and, thanks to an exceptional sense for the balance of sounds, succeeded in lightening the mix and giving it a new dynamism. "He didn't tell me what to do with the music, he told me what he wanted the thing to feel like."[54] Plotkin became part of the Springsteen galaxy, and was to mix and coproduce many of the Boss's albums. As for the mastering for *Darkness*, it was done by Mike Reese at the Mastering Lab in Los Angeles.

Technical details

The album's ten songs were recorded at the Record Plant, as were those on *Born to Run* (except for the title track). The console was, again, a Spectra Sonic, and the tape recorder a modified 24-track MCI.

The instruments

Once again, Bruce favored the Fender Telecaster-Esquire in the studio. He may have used other guitars, but information on this is lacking. Steve Van Zandt, for his part, mostly recorded using a Fender Stratocaster. As for Garry Tallent, he played a Fender Precision Bass.

For Springsteen Addicts

Initially, the title of Bruce Springsteen's fourth album was to have been *Badlands*. Columbia had even worked on a sleeve bearing this title in October 1977. At one point, Springsteen had also considered *American Madness*, a reference to Frank Capra's movie on America during the Great Depression (released in 1932), or *History Is Made at Night*, which was inspired by another movie, this time directed by Frank Borzage and released in 1937.

BADLANDS

Bruce Springsteen / 4'01

Musicians

Bruce Springsteen: vocals, guitars
Steve Van Zandt: guitars, backing vocals
Clarence Clemons: saxophone, percussion, backing vocals
Roy Bittan: piano
Danny Federici: organ
Garry Tallent: bass guitar
Max Weinberg: drums

Recording

The Record Plant, 321 West 44th St, New York: 13 July, August, 4 and 12 December 1977; 22, 23, and 25 February 1978

Technical team

Producers: Jon Landau, Bruce Springsteen
Assistant producer: Steve Van Zandt
Recording engineer: Jimmy Iovine
Assistant recording engineer: Thom Panunzio
Mixing: Chuck Plotkin, Jimmy Iovine

1978

Martin Sheen and director Terrence Mallick shooting *Badlands*. The film gave its name to a song in *Darkness on the Edge of Town*.

Genesis and lyrics

Bruce Springsteen took the title of the opening track of *Darkness on the Edge of Town* from the first movie directed by Terrence Malick, starring Martin Sheen, Sissy Spacek, and Warren Oates. Released in the US in 1973, *Badlands* tells the story of two young lovers who, unable to love each other openly in a small South Dakota town, go on the run and sow death around them. The Badlands in the United States are arid regions where it is extremely difficult, even impossible, to grow anything. They include certain parts of Nebraska and, indeed, South Dakota (where there is a Badlands National Park).

As was very often the case, Springsteen composed the music for this song before writing the words. "With *Badlands*, I had the word 'badlands' and then I had chord changes and we'd go in the studio and lay the track down," he explained during an interview with Dave Herman for the show *King Biscuit Flower Hour* on 9 July 1978. "And I'd go home and I'd play the tape and write the words, but I wouldn't do it out loud, I'd write 'em in my head. So I'd go in the studio and I'd try to sing it, and I'd realize that it was hard to breathe and sing it all at once. So that was hard to sing. Some of the songs are physically harder to play than some of the other ones."[60]

Badlands was the first charge, Springsteen's first cry of revenge after a three-year silence. Since *Born to Run*, his characters had developed: having reached adulthood, they seem to have lost many of their illusions—it was a traumatic retracing of steps, in a sense. "Got a head on collision/Smashin' in my guts, man/I'm caught in a cross fire/That I don't understand," the narrator sings. He then addresses his girlfriend, manifestly in the hope that she will materialize out of his dreams and wild fantasies: "You spend your life waiting/For a moment that just don't come." Finally, a little later in the song, he reserves his fiercest attack for American society: "Poor man wanna be rich/Rich man wanna be king/And a king ain't satisfied/'Til he rules everything." This sentence, almost like a nihilist slogan that the British punks might have made their own, was in fact borrowed from *King of the Whole Wide World*, a song sung by Elvis Presley in *Kid Galahad*, a movie directed by Phil Karlson and released in 1962.

A song based on the riff of The Animals' version of *Don't Let Me Be Misunderstood* (1965), *Badlands* was first performed live at Shea's Performing Arts Center in Buffalo, New York

Bruce Springsteen and his Telecaster-Esquire onstage at The Roxy Theatre, West Hollywood, on 7 September 1978 during the Darkness Tour.

The first sentence of *Badlands* begins with the words: "Lights out tonight." Why is this? While Springsteen was working on the song in the studio, on 13 July 1977, a huge power cut dubbed the "New York City Blackout" plunged the city into darkness—at exactly 21:36. The outage lasted more than 20 hours.

For *Badlands*, Bruce Springsteen borrowed a line from *King of the Whole Wide World*, sung by Elvis Presley in the movie *Kid Galahad* in 1962.

For Springsteen Addicts

The version of *Badlands* included in the *Live/1975–85* box set, released in 1986, was recorded at the University of Arizona on 5 November 1980, the day Ronald Reagan was elected president of the United States. Bruce Springsteen commented: "I don't know what you guys thought of what happened last night, but I thought it was pretty terrifying."[71]

Bill Murray and Paul Shaffer celebrated the 25th anniversary of *Saturday Night Live* with *Badlands* (performed by Nick the Lounge Singer, the character played by Murray), because they felt it was a good description of what they had both experienced in their youth when starting out in the world of showbiz.

1978

state, on 23 May 1978. Since then, Springsteen has performed it more than 1,200 times, making it one of his great signature songs. It was chosen for the A-side of the second single from the album (on the B-side was *Streets of Fire*, *Something in the Night*, or *Candy's Room*, depending on which country the record was sold in). However, *Badlands* reached only a very modest No.42 in the *Billboard* charts.

Production

Badlands, the opening track on the Boss's fourth album, introduces us to the band's new sound quality. Sparser and simpler, the song is striking for its sense of urgency, but also for its dynamism. It is still, for sure, far from the sound of the London punks, but Springsteen has understood the message of the "no-future" generation and distilled it in his own way.

Max Weinberg opens *Badlands* with an effective drum fill that's played on his Ludwig drum kit. The band then attacks the song's riff, where Roy Bittan's piano predominates, supported and answered by the Hammond B-3 organ of Danny Federici—who is making a triumphant return after not having appeared in a single song on the *Born to Run* album. Composed on the guitar, the riff was largely inspired, as explained earlier, by that of *Don't Let Me Be Misunderstood* by The Animals, who themselves had made use of the final bars of the original song performed by Nina Simone in 1964 (listen to The Animals' version at 2'25). Springsteen jokingly confessed much later: "It's the same fucking riff, man. Listen up, listen up, youngsters, this is how successful theft is accomplished."[7]

Badlands is also the first time that Steve Van Zandt officially plays rhythm guitar. He uses a Fender Stratocaster, and

Hilton Valentine, Dave Rowberry, Eric Burdon, and Chas Chandler on set for *Ready Steady Go!* in 1965. Their riff in *Don't Let Me Be Misunderstood* inspired the one in *Badlands*.

his presence inevitably swells the song's sound texture. "Miami Steve" is a rock musician, as can be clearly heard. He also contributes to vocal harmonies, his voice blending particularly well with Springsteen's. On the rhythm side, Max Weinberg and Garry Tallent provide a generous drive, although this does not stop the drummer—who at the time had problems keeping a regular tempo—from criticizing his own failings. He later said: "There's a slowdown in *Badlands* which is just terrible."[59]

Finally, the song allows Clarence Clemons to play a very good saxophone solo, which almost did not come about at first. As Springsteen explained, "At the end of the record I didn't think we had enough saxophone on the record. Took the guitar out and Clarence played over that. Of course it would have been a terrible mistake to leave that sax solo out."[54]

In the end, as the songwriter himself would acknowledge, *Badlands* is a very fine song, but one that only truly comes into its own when played live. The acetate disc, which would be used to check the quality of the mixing before the final mastering, was made on 11 April 1978 at Sterling Sound Inc. in New York.

ADAM RAISED A CAIN

Bruce Springsteen / 4'32

Musicians
Bruce Springsteen: vocals, guitars
Steve Van Zandt: guitars, backing vocals
Clarence Clemons: percussion, backing vocals
Roy Bittan: piano
Danny Federici: organ
Garry Tallent: bass guitar
Max Weinberg: drums
The band: backing vocals

Recording
The Record Plant, 321 West 44th St, New York: 9 November, 15 December 1977; 15–17 February 1978

Technical team
Producers: Jon Landau, Bruce Springsteen
Assistant producer: Steve Van Zandt
Recording engineer: Jimmy Iovine
Assistant recording engineer: Thom Panunzio
Mixing: Chuck Plotkin, Jimmy Iovine

1978

For Springsteen Addicts

Adam Raised a Cain is on the *Baby It's You* (1983) movie soundtrack, directed by John Sayles and starring Rosanna Arquette. John Sayles later made the videos for Springsteen's *I'm on Fire* and *Born in the U.S.A.*

Adam Raised a Cain was chosen as part of the soundtrack for the seventh season of the American television series *Sons of Anarchy*, created by Kurt Sutter and broadcast from 2008 to 2014.

Genesis and lyrics

Bruce Springsteen's Catholic upbringing played a large part in this song. "I did read the Bible some," he explained to Robert Duncan of *Creem* magazine. "I tried to read it for a while about a year ago. It's fascinating. I got into it quite a ways. Great stories. Actually, what happened was, I was thinking of writing that particular song, and I went back trying to get a feeling for it."[7] In the Book of Genesis, Cain is the eldest son of Adam and Eve who, having killed his young brother, Abel, is condemned by God to be a restless wanderer.

Beyond the biblical reference, the song is above all a redemptive confession, an introspective look at the songwriter's childhood and adolescence in New Jersey, and, more specifically, at the often difficult relationship he had with his father Douglas Springsteen: "Most of my writing is emotionally autobiographical,"[6] Bruce Springsteen declares in his book *Songs*. This is especially true of *Adam Raised a Cain*. The story begins with the recollection of a baptism, the memory of a father by his son who is crying at the font. But from the end of the first verse, the essential point is made: "With the same hot blood burning in our veins/Adam raised a Cain." These words testify to the lack of understanding between a father and son, and the former's disappointment at seeing his son take a path of which he disapproves. The third verse refers directly to Scripture: "In the Bible Cain slew Abel/And East of Eden he was cast," Springsteen sings. This is what is described in Genesis 4:16 (King James Version): "And Cain went out from the presence of the LORD, and dwelt in the land of Nod, on the east of Eden." There is clearly also another reference here—this time to the movies and specifically to the Hollywood classic *East of Eden*, directed by Elia Kazan and based on John Steinbeck's eponymous novel, starring James Dean. This is the song's theme in a nutshell: the impossibility of a father and son reaching an understanding, followed by the death of the mother.

Despite everything, Springsteen sees what might be described as mitigating circumstances relating to his father, which were, above all, social: "Daddy worked his whole life, for nothing but the pain." A father whose frustration led him to find culprits in his family. Springsteen first performed *Adam Raised a Cain* on 23 May 1978 at Shea's Performing Arts Center, in Buffalo, New York State.

Max Weinberg and his powerful, cataclysmic drumming on *Adam Raised a Cain*. Seen here in concert at Seton Hall University, New Jersey, on 11 December 1975.

Production

It was under the title *Daddy Raised a Cain* that Bruce Springsteen and the E Street Band worked on the new song between October and December 1977, completing it in 1978. From the very first few bars, the listener is struck by the strong rock tone of the piece. This time, the influence of the British punk groups can be clearly felt, as can that of Steve Van Zandt, the band's real rocker. The sound is harsh, driven by a riff played simultaneously by the guitars, the bass guitar, the piano, and the organ. Springsteen launches into the first solo, which is direct and raw, but highly effective. He makes his Telecaster-Esquire (colored by a fairly short delay) roar to convincing effect. As for the drums, their beat is heavy, sparse, and powerful, Max Weinberg giving his partners a solid foundation.

From the initial phrases of the first verse, the Boss adopts a drawling, almost weary voice. But Springsteen very quickly collects himself to infuse his performance with his characteristic energy, which reaches a climax in the choruses. Here he is supported by backing vocals, probably by Clarence Clemons and Steve Van Zandt, whic heighten the song's punk-like timbre—it brings to mind The Clash.

On the keyboard side, Roy Bittan's piano is more discreet than it was in *Badlands*; in fact, it gives way to Danny Federici, who delivers an excellent accompaniment here on his Hammond B-3 organ—in certain passages you can hear the spinning of his Leslie speaker (for example, between 0'42 and 0'55). Curiously, Federici regains a place on this album, which he had lost on the previous one, unlike Clarence Clemons who, for his part, finds himself confined to backing vocals and percussion. In fact, he plays the saxophone in only three of the ten tracks on *Darkness*.

Springsteen plays a second solo after verse two—again, it is simple in structure, tense, and aggressive, with the notes bent to the maximum (from 1'51). There follows a bridge, the band singing *"yeaaahhh"* in unison and sounding rather like people at a party. Some poor editing is also audible here, at 2'34 exactly, just after the chord played by Bruce's guitar. Finally, the song ends with a coda in which the whole band once more declaims *"whooaaaaaa"* in a manner worthy of a group of sports fans, who are fairly vague as regards tuning (from 3'53).

Adam Raised a Cain is a very convincing song, but Springsteen probably overdoes his attempt to come close to the sound of the punk movement. His vocal intonation, which sometimes calls to mind that of The Clash's Joe Strummer, and the deliberately vague backing vocals in the end contribute nothing that is truly authentic. Springsteen was not to be the only musician to fall for the siren call of "no future": Paul McCartney and his album *Back to the Egg* (1979) is another example.

SOMETHING IN THE NIGHT

Bruce Springsteen / 5'12

Musicians

Bruce Springsteen: vocals, guitars
Steve Van Zandt: guitars, backing vocals (?)
Roy Bittan: piano
Danny Federici: organ, glockenspiel
Garry Tallent: bass guitar
Max Weinberg: drums

Recording

Atlantic Studios, 1841 Broadway, New York: 1, 14, and 16 June 1977
The Record Plant, 321 West 44th St, New York: September to December 1977 (?); 27 February 1978

Technical team

Producers: Jon Landau, Bruce Springsteen
Assistant producer: Steve Van Zandt
Recording engineer: Jimmy Iovine
Assistant recording engineer: Thom Panunzio
Mixing: Chuck Plotkin, Jimmy Iovine

1978

For Springsteen Addicts

Bruce Springsteen begins *Something in the Night* with the words: "I'm riding down Kingsley." Kingsley Street is in Asbury Park and, together with Ocean Avenue, forms the circuit often alluded to by the songwriter.

Genesis and lyrics

In the time between the first live performance, on 1 August 1976 at the Monmouth Arts Center in Red Bank, New Jersey, and its recording in mid-1977, the arrangements and lyrics of *Something in the Night* changed constantly. At all events, the lyrics are among the darkest Springsteen ever wrote. The central character has left the nighttime drives of *Born to Run* in favor of those of *Darkness on the Edge of Town*, but the atmosphere is markedly different. Having turned up the volume of his car radio, "So I don't have to think," the narrator plunges into the ecstasy of physical love with his girlfriend, seeking in it "a moment when the world/Seems right." His view of this world is dark. "Nothing is forgotten or forgiven," Springsteen sings in the bridge between the second and third verses (in the album version). What is he saying? Probably that we cannot escape our fate. Indeed, Springsteen expresses this unambiguously in the song's second verse: "You're born with nothing [...] Soon as you've got something they send/Someone to try and take it away." This looks very much like a cry of despair—that rage experienced and expressed by America's dispossessed. The despair is total, therefore, when we are faced with all those "things we loved" which are "crushed and dying in the dirt."

Something in the Night is an inexorable plunge into the bottom of the abyss. And here's another theory: it might be a personal reflection on Bruce Springsteen's relationship with Mike Appel and with the record industry.

Production

Four days after the court verdict of 28 May 1977, which allowed him to make a record once more, Springsteen set up with his musicians in Atlantic Studios. They recorded eight songs in one day, including a first version of *Something in the Night*. The reason the band was so prolific during this session was because, for several months, they had been trying out, live, most of the songs recorded that day.

Springsteen reworked both the lyrics and the music for the song several times. For example, in 1976, the trumpet player Steve Paraczky, a member of The Miami Horns quartet, who had accompanied the E Street Band from the first dates of the Lawsuit Tour (from 26 September 1976 to 25 March 1977), played a trumpet solo in the song's introduction (although this is absent from the definitive recording). "I'll

After a concert at the Palladium, New York, in October 1976, Bruce Springsteen and Steve Van Zandt exit through the artists' entrance.

HEADPHONES AT THE READY

Max Weinberg appears to have had some difficulty executing the drum break that follows the second verse (this can be heard between 2'56 and 3'02). It must be said that the piece's slow tempo did not make his task any easier.

never forget that first night in the Phoenix Coliseum [26 September 1976]. I had to play the intro to *Something in the Night* with Roy Bittan. I was shaking in my boots,"[61] Paraczky later said. This introduction, which is one of the song's high points, appeared in a number of different versions. The one with Paraczky on trumpet possessed a melancholy power that the Boss, however, did not want to keep. "I thought it sounded better with it in,"[61] the trumpet player commented.

Fortunately, the version on the album does not lose its appeal as a result: Roy Bittan's piano dominates the long, very expressive introduction, which is based on two chords and colored by Danni Federici's chiming glockenspiel. Springsteen's Telecaster-Esquire strings out chords, supported by Garry Tallent's bass guitar. Then the Boss's moaning voice rises from the depths of a very noticeable reverberation, surreptitiously haunting this harmonic progression, a little as it did at the end of *Jungleland*, on the *Born to Run* album. "I love the wily, lone-wolf image that I get when I hear that record,"[62] the songwriter later said. He is accompanied by a long roll on the floor tom, courtesy of Max Weinberg, who sustains it for almost 30 seconds! At the end of this superb introduction, the song takes off, with a powerful rhythmic section that is chiefly sustained by the drummer's bass drum and snare drum (from 1'07).

Springsteen provides some magnificent lead vocals, his voice full of emotion. His technical mastery commands respect, notably in the bridge, where a second voice—probably that of Steve Van Zandt—accompanies him in the vocal harmonies (at 3'03). In the last verse, he sings *a cappella*, supported only by Weinberg's bass and snare drums (from 3'29). The emotional power of the song is at its height, and the darkness of the lyrics is clearly highlighted. There is a lack of drums at 4'14 because, during the recording, Springsteen apparently asked Weinberg to stop playing, in order to heighten the drama of his performance. The piece ends with the whole band joining in again, the songwriter's voice improvising, heartbroken, amid the reverberation—with a few wrong notes, it must be said...

Something in the Night is an extraordinary song—greatly underrated, yet one of the most powerful on the album. It would benefit from being (re)discovered.

CANDY'S ROOM

Bruce Springsteen / 2'45

Musicians
Bruce Springsteen: vocals, guitars
Steve Van Zandt: guitars, backing vocals (?)
Roy Bittan: piano
Danny Federici: organ, glockenspiel
Garry Tallent: bass guitar
Max Weinberg: drums

Recording
The Record Plant, 321 West 44th St, New York: September to December 1977; 3–5 March 1978

Technical team
Producers: Jon Landau, Bruce Springsteen
Assistant producer: Steve Van Zandt
Recording engineer: Jimmy Iovine
Assistant recording engineer: Thom Panunzio
Mixing: Chuck Plotkin, Jimmy Iovine

1978

Artist Karon Bihari had a fling with Bruce Springsteen in the 1970s. Is she Candy from the song?

Genesis and lyrics

Candy's Room is the definitive version of two songs: *Candy's Boy* (see *The Promise*, page 561) and *The Fast Song*. When Brian Hiatt of *Rolling Stone* magazine asked Bruce Springsteen whether the main character in the song was a prostitute, he merely replied, smiling: "Does it really matter?"[63] What matters, in fact, lies elsewhere: it is the narrator's love for the song's heroine. "I'd give all that I got to give/All that I want, all that I live/To make Candy mine/Tonight," are the last words Springsteen sings. Earlier in the song, the songwriter has given us a fairly precise description of Candy: "There's a sadness hidden in that pretty face." She "has fancy clothes and diamond rings" and "In Candy's room, there are pictures of her heroes on the wall."

Might Candy be something of a romantic? Above all, she enjoys cultivating the gift of turning men's heads, to the point that they "give her anything she wants." The narrator, for his part, says that "the blood rushes in my veins" and "fire rushes toward the sky" when he kisses her. However, make no mistake: there is great distress in the beautiful young Candy, whose bedroom is reached via a corridor that is plunged into darkness—perhaps this is an allegory of Mary Magdalene entering Jesus's tomb? Yet two of the songwriter's ex-girlfriends recognized themselves in Candy, notably the artist Karon Bihari, with whom he had a relationship that lasted almost eight months. In 2002, Karon told the tabloid newspaper *National Enquirer*: "When his *Darkness on the Edge of Town* album came out, there was a song about us called *Candy's Room* and it just took my breath away [...] The lyrics described my little apartment, what we talked about, when we kissed [...] It was the most romantic thing anyone had ever done for me."[64]

First performed on 23 May 1978, at Shea's Performing Arts Center in Buffalo, New York state, *Candy's Room* was on the setlist of some 260 concerts given by Bruce Springsteen.

Production

Max Weinberg's hi-hat opens *Candy's Room*. The tempo is quick, and the rhythmic figure was inspired, according to the drummer, by several Barry White songs. Notably, White's 1973 hit *Never, Never Gonna Give Ya Up*, which has an introduction in a similar spirit, springs to mind. But the similarity ends

For Springsteen Addicts

Candy is one of the numerous heroines in his songs whom Bruce Springsteen mentions by their first name. There is also Wendy, Sandy, Rosalita, Sherry...

The Boss launches into a punk solo for *Candy's Room.*

there, for as soon as the Boss attacks the first sentences of the song we are far from the soul-funk disco world of the African-American baritone—except that Bruce talks (in a mournful tone) and does not sing for the first four lines of the verse. Accompanying him are Roy Bittan on piano and Danny Federici on glockenspiel. But Springsteen quickly breaks up this melancholy atmosphere by driving his song toward something closer to punk rock than to a ballad (at 0'41). The band supports his singing energetically—driven this time, not by Weinberg's hi-hat, but by his snare drum. Here the E Street Band's drummer delivers an excellent performance of metronomic regularity—providing the true backbone of the song. That is exactly how Weinberg saw his role in the band, as he explained: "My position is to keep time and be that center stripe down the road. An anchor! The best thing someone can tell me is, 'Man, that was rock steady.' You know Bernard Purdie on Aretha's *Rock Steady*? That is rock steady. That is what rock drumming is all about. Keeping that groove."[59]

As usual, Springsteen gives an excellent vocal performance (harmonized in the bridge at 1'04). But he also plays a superb solo on his Telecaster-Esquire: a solo that is punk in character, with its very pronounced bent notes and vibrato, but which displays a range of different influences, including the riff in The Yardbirds' *Heart Full of Soul* (1965). This is vaguely echoed in the first few phrases of his improvisation (at 1'28).

As we have seen, *Candy's Room* picks up on the melodic line and part of the arrangements of *The Fast Song.* However, *The Fast Song* had been worked on between June and September 1977, at Atlantic Studios, before the Boss decided to rewrite the lyrics and incorporate the first verse from *Candy's Boy*—another song—and to retain part of the third verse of *The Fast Song.* When he renamed it *New Fast Song (Candy)* he was working with the E Street Band at the Record Plant. The mixing was done in haste, between 3 and 5 March 1978, and the master came from the 42nd take.

Candy's Room is one of the album's most successful songs, in which Springsteen demonstrates, once again, that he knows how to reinvent himself and surprise by dint of inspiration that is constantly being challenged.

RACING IN THE STREET

Bruce Springsteen / 6'52

Musicians
Bruce Springsteen: vocals, guitars, backing vocals (?)
Steve Van Zandt: guitar (?), backing vocals (?)
Clarence Clemons: maracas, tambourine
Roy Bittan: piano
Danny Federici: organ
Garry Tallent: bass guitar
Max Weinberg: drums
Recording
Atlantic Studios, 1841 Broadway, New York: 2 July, August 1977
The Record Plant, 321 West 44th St, New York: August, 28–30 November, 6 and 9 December 1977; 21 and 23 March 1978
Technical team
Producers: Jon Landau, Bruce Springsteen
Assistant producer: Steve Van Zandt
Recording engineer: Jimmy Iovine
Assistant recording engineer: Thom Panunzio
Mixing: Chuck Plotkin, Jimmy Iovine

1978

Carl Wilson, Brian Wilson, Dennis Wilson, Mike Love, and Al Jardine of the Beach Boys sang *Don't Worry Baby.* Hot-rod sensations!

Genesis and lyrics

Racing in the Street is the last song on the A-side of the LP *Darkness on the Edge of Town*. It sounds like a new ode to the motor car by the New Jersey songwriter. In the second half of the 1970s, the car was still a symbol of pop culture and a certain kind of freedom. The street racers in *Racing in the Street* highlight the changes in American culture from the innocent car songs of the 1960s to the reality of America in 1978. He told *Rolling Stone* magazine (in 25 November 2010): "When you pick a song title like *Racing in the Street*, that's a hard song to write." He elaborated, "But that was sort of the local culture of Asbury in the 1970s, which was still deeply enmeshed in car culture. If you went to The Stone Pony [a famous club in Asbury Park], it was a constant circle of souped-up muscle cars on Saturday and Sunday. Once again, I sort of stood outside of it, I was hitchhiking, I didn't have a car! But I wanted one real bad."[63]

Springsteen transfer this love of the car, and of speed, to the narrator: "To make *Racing* and those other big titles personal, I had to infuse the music with my own hopes and fears,"[6] he explains in his book *Songs*. "If you don't do that, your characters ring hollow, and you're left with rhetoric, words without meaning."[6] The character in the song is at the wheel of a 1969 Chevrolet. It's a muscle car that he has completely restored with his friend Sonny. First, there are trials on the boulevard, then it's racing in the street—"From the fire roads to the interstate"—with the adrenalin running high. The central character has met a young woman who was riding "In a Camaro with this dude from LA." He "blew that Camaro off my back and drove that little girl away." They share the same temptation: to "ride to the sea/And wash these sins off our hands." In a sense, *Racing in the Street* is the Springsteen equivalent of Chuck Berry's *You Can't Catch Me*, or The Beach Boys' *Don't Worry Baby*—as the Boss himself acknowledged. It is one of the songs on *Darkness on the Edge of Town* that was first performed on 23 May 1978 at Shea's Performing Arts Center in Buffalo, New York State. Springsteen has played it regularly ever since, up to the present day.

Production

Like many of Springsteen's songs, *Racing in the Street*

A 1960 Corvette, star of the exhibition *From Asbury Park to the Promised Land: The Life and Music of Bruce Springsteen*, at the National Constitution Center, Philadelphia, on 15 February 2012.

Known as an excellent guitarist, David Lindley plays the violin in a version of *Racing in the Street* (*The Promise*, 2010).

1978

underwent many transformations before reaching its final form. At least four different versions of this song exist. The most notable of these appears on *The Promise* (released in 2010), and includes harmonica and violin solos, the latter performed by the excellent David Lindley in place of Suki Lahav. As a result, the version that features on *Darkness on the Edge of Town* is quite different in comparison—much less Dylanesque and more introspective.

From the introduction, Roy Bittan on piano plays a melodious and melancholy motif, which in no way resembles the one on *The Promise*. Springsteen joins him in singing after eight bars, and his performance is superb: emotion is always palpable, all the more so because it is reinforced by magnificent reverberation courtesy of the EMT 140 plate reverb. Then the musicians are heard, one by one. First, Max Weinberg takes the stage, playing a cross-stick rhythm on his snare drum (at 1'30). Then come Garry Tallent's bass guitar and Danny Federici's organ (at 1'54). It is worth mentioning the quality of Tallent's bass playing here—doubtless recorded live and amplified on his Fender Precision. The sound is powerful, very much to the fore, and reinforced by Weinberg's bass drum. The rhythm then reaches its cruising speed with the second chorus, Weinberg now hitting his snare drum with force (from 2'14). It is also worth noting that maracas can be heard at exactly 2'14—in all probability played by Clarence Clemons who makes a modest but welcome appearance!

The chorus is followed by an instrumental section, dominated by Federici's organ, which echoes the motif played on the piano in the introduction. During this passage (from 2'36), there is a noticeable slowing of the tempo—Weinberg's Achilles heel, at least at that point in his career. The rest of the song is sung by Springsteen, accompanied solely by Bittan's superb piano. Then, at 3'23, backing vocals progressively join the arrangement, unquestionably recorded by the songwriter

Racing in the Street was a leading song at the concert at the Nassau Veterans Memorial Coliseum in Uniondale, New York, on 3 June 1978.

and his friend Steve Van Zandt. Thanks to the magic of overdubbing, the vocal quality is ethereal and rich—the effect is reminiscent of a synth pad, but breathing can be heard again at 4'19, which seems to indicate that these are indeed real backing vocals. Finally, the song ends with a very fine, lyrical, and impassioned instrumental sequence, with each musician being heard one after the other—including Clarence Clemons on tambourine.

Racing in the Street is one of Bruce Springsteen's great successes, and indeed one of his favorite songs. It was to have an impact on numerous artists, including Emmylou Harris and Queen's Roger Taylor, and on its own justifies the making of the superb album that is *Darkness on the Edge of Town.*

For Springsteen Addicts

Racing in the Street pays tribute to *Dancing in the Street* by Martha and The Vandellas, not only because of its title but also through its lyrics. Springsteen sings: "Summer's here and the time is right/For racing in the street"; the Motown vocal group sings: "Summer's here and the time is right/For dancing in the street."

HEADPHONES AT THE READY

Roy Bittan's piano was recorded (or mixed) sometimes in mono, sometimes in stereo. Thus, it can be heard in mono during the introduction (until 0'23) and in the last two lines sung by Springsteen (from 4'29 to 4'46). Probably these were two edits made from different takes.

THE PROMISED LAND

Bruce Springsteen / 4'24

Musicians

Bruce Springsteen: vocals, guitars, harmonica
Steve Van Zandt: guitars
Clarence Clemons: saxophone
Roy Bittan: piano
Danny Federici: organ
Garry Tallent: bass guitar
Max Weinberg: drums

Recording

The Record Plant, 321 West 44th St, New York: 30 September, 27 October, 1 and 27 December 1977; May 1978 (mixing)

Technical team

Producers: Jon Landau, Bruce Springsteen
Assistant producer: Steve Van Zandt
Recording engineer: Jimmy Iovine
Assistant recording engineer: Thom Panunzio
Mixing: Chuck Plotkin, Jimmy Iovine

1978

The King Is Dead

Elvis Presley: Jan. 8, 1935 — Aug. 16, 1977

Elvis Presley was one of those rare individuals who was a true legend in his own time. He was the 'King of Rock 'n' Roll.'

Elvis Presley died at age 42 after being found unconscious in the bedroom of his mansion, Graceland, near Memphis, Tenn.

He was known as a singer, guitarist and actor with roots that ran back to the rural farming community of Tupelo, Miss., where he was born in early 1935. A Depression baby, he moved to Memphis with his family in 1948. Within seven years, he was the hottest new recording artist in the western world with a superseller titled "Heartbreak Hotel." Popular music was never the same.

Several generations knew him. "Hound Dog," one of his earliest hits in the late '50s, passed to "It's Now or Never" (1960), "Can't Help Falling In Love" (1961), and "Return To Sender" (1962).

Tupelo to Top

Long Live The King

Presley was inducted into the Army in 1958. Discharged in 1960, he was a legend at 25 and one of the best known public figures in the world.

Shunning live performances and the lure of the new mass medium, television, Presley concentrated on a string of very successful, though second rate, movies. By age 30, he was the highest-paid performer in the history of show business.

Under the brilliant aegis of his manager, Col. Tom Parker, Presley faded briefly in the mid-1960s and then knocked the world on its ear. He returned to the stage in 1969 with a record smashing engagement at Las Vegas. Singles, albums, road shows, concerts. . .nothing could miss; nothing did.

Elvis Presley died Tuesday, Aug. 16, 1977, at Baptist Hospital, Memphis, Tenn., at 3:30 p.m. (CDT). He was pronounced dead of a heart attack.

Elvis Poster

The death of Elvis Presley on the front page. Bruce Springsteen wrote *The Promised Land* shortly after the death of the King.

Genesis and lyrics

Bruce Springsteen wrote *The Promised Land* after the death of Elvis Presley (on 16 August 1977), during a road trip in the Utah desert. The desert is crossed by the Rattlesnake Speedway, a road that should lead to a "promised land" according to the songwriter. With him in the hired convertible were Steve Van Zandt and the photographer Eric Meola. The song's title was borrowed directly from one of Chuck Berry's last hits, *Promised Land* (1964), which was performed by the King himself but also by Johnny Rivers, the Grateful Dead, and, in France, by Johnny Hallyday.

In the Thom Zimny documentary *Bruce Springsteen, The Promise: The Making of Darkness on the Edge of Town*, Springsteen explains that *The Promised Land* asked the question: "'How do we honor the community and the place we came from.'"[54] The hero, whom the songwriter introduces here, says he is "Working all day in my daddy's garage" and that "I've done my best to live the right way/I get up every morning and go to work each day." But today he has had enough: he feels an urgent need first to change his life and his surroundings, and then to head for "a promised land."

The narrator is, therefore, not the only character in the song: the town, the desert, and the automobile also feature. The town is where the hero grew up, a place where the burden of society and convention has become too much for him to bear: "Sometimes I feel so weak I just want to explode/Explode and tear this old town apart," Springsteen sings. The desert, by contrast, symbolizes freedom, a place of transformation in a sense, where there's "Gonna be a twister to blow everything down," starting with "the dreams that break your heart." Finally, the automobile is what enables him to transition from enslavement to independence. Here too, as in *Adam Raised a Cain*, the biblical references are obvious: like the people of Israel, the character in the song must cross the desert to reach a promised land.

First performed in concert at Shea's Performing Arts Center in Buffalo, New York state, on 23 May 1978—and almost 1,400 times since—*The Promised Land* is one of the most important songs in Bruce Springsteen's discography, and one that elevates him to the rank of a Woody Guthrie for the 1970s. The song was released as a single (with *Streets of Fire* on the B-side) in the UK and Ireland, but never made it into the charts.

The E Street Band in rehearsal. Bruce Springsteen and Steve Van Zandt are in the foreground guiding the group toward the promised land.

Eric Meola took advantage of his road trip through Utah with Bruce Springsteen and Steve Van Zandt in August 1977 to shoot some superb photographs of the desert.

Members of the E Street Band jamming in *The Promised Land*. From left to right: Clarence Clemons, Bruce Springsteen, Garry Tallent, and Steve Van Zandt.

Production

The Promised Land is a country-rock song in the Springsteen style, with that indefinable mix of diverse influences, from Van Morrison to Bob Dylan, The Beatles to Elvis, Chuck Berry to Hank Williams—to name but a few. The tempo is relatively lively, led from the introduction by the songwriter's harmonica which, inevitably, calls Dylan to mind. But Springsteen and his E Street Band have succeeded in creating an immediately recognizable musical language, with a color all their own: the combinations of piano and organ, and of guitars and rhythm section—not to mention the saxophone—are unique, and provide an ideal framework for the Boss's creations.

With the exception of the introduction and an instrumental section, *The Promised Land* is built around three verses and three choruses. It is unusual enough to be worth highlighting that these are true choruses, repeating exactly the same words each time—which, until that point, had almost never been the case with Springsteen. They are sung by two voices, that of Steve Van Zandt harmonizing perfectly with that of the songwriter.

Another striking thing about the song is the sequence of three consecutive solos in the instrumental section (starting at 1'58). The first of these is by Miami Steve, a first on a disc since he officially joined the band. His playing style is totally rock: he makes his Stratocaster sing with well-judged vibrato and bent notes, with very powerful results. Van Zandt is not the original guitar hero, but is possessed of an ear, musicality, and feel that are impressively effective—exactly like Springsteen, in fact. It is worth mentioning that this guitar solo was rejected from the initial mixes.

Van Zandt is followed by Clarence Clemons, with his magnificent trademark sound (at 2'15). The tone of his saxophone is brilliant, warm, and infinitely clever. If he is not given pride of place on this album, it is because Springsteen wanted *Darkness* to be a collection of songs with a more rural charac-

Upon making the Rock & Roll Hall of Fame in 2005, U2 performed *The Promised Land* with the Boss (seen here with The Edge and Bono).

ter: "And so I then began to say, 'Well, how do I use this sax, which always, for me, was a very urban instrument,'" he explains in Thom Zimny's documentary. "How do I integrate, you know, what Clarence is doing into this context?"[54] Answer: only three songs out of ten would feature him. Finally, after the saxophone, it is the Boss who takes the last solo, on the harmonica, in a country-rock vein—simple, but essential (at 2'32).

The mixing was done in great haste, around mid-May, before the band were due to go on tour. Dick Wingate, who was in charge of marketing, recalled the phone call from Jon Landau: "'Dick, I couldn't tell you this this morning, but I got some bad news for ya. Bruce and I are going back to LA at six o'clock tonight to remix *The Promised Land*,'" Wingate explained. "They were going to put the guitar solo back in. I couldn't believe it."[16] As a result, the album's release was put back by a few weeks.

When the members of U2 were inducted into the Rock & Roll Hall of Fame in 2005, under the aegis of Bruce Springsteen, Bono sang a few lines from *The Promised Land*.

FACTORY

Bruce Springsteen / 2'17

Musicians
Bruce Springsteen: vocals, guitars
Steve Van Zandt: guitars, vocal harmonies (?)
Clarence Clemons: tambourine
Roy Bittan: piano
Danny Federici: organ
Garry Tallent: bass guitar
Max Weinberg: drums

Recording
The Record Plant, 321 West 44th St, New York: September to December 1977; 2 January, 10 and 14 March 1978 (mixing)

Technical team
Producers: Jon Landau, Bruce Springsteen
Assistant producer: Steve Van Zandt
Recording engineer: Jimmy Iovine
Assistant recording engineer: Thom Panunzio
Mixing: Chuck Plotkin, Jimmy Iovine

1978

COVER
For her 20th studio album, *The Ghosts of Highway 20* (2016), Lucinda Williams recorded a version of *Factory.*

Lucinda Williams (seen here in Glasgow in 2016), one of the most gifted folk musicians of our time, added *Factory* to her repertoire.

Genesis and lyrics

Factory is another foray into Springsteen's youth, through the experiences of his father who, among other jobs, was a production line worker in a factory. Above all, it is a tribute, as Springsteen explained to Dave Marsh of *Musician* magazine in February 1981: "There's people that get a chance to do the kind of work that changes the world and make things really different. And then there's the kind that just keeps the world from falling apart. And that was the kind that my dad always did. 'Cause we were always together as a family, and we grew up in a...good situation, where we had what we needed. And there was a lot of sacrifice on his part and my mother's part for that to happen..."[65] In the documentary *Bruce Springsteen, The Promise: The Making of Darkness on the Edge of Town*, he added that *Factory* asks: "How do we honor the life that our brothers or sisters and parents lived."[54]

Beyond this filial reverence in particular, and reverence for the family in general, *Factory* is a comprehensive indictment of the world of work in modern society: "Early in the morning factory whistle blows/Man rises from bed and puts on his clothes [...] It's the working, the working, just the working life," Springsteen sings. He goes on: "I see my daddy walking through them factory gates in the rain/Factory takes his hearing [a reference to factory bosses refusing to issue ear protectors to their production line workers], factory gives him life [what is meant is a meager salary that allows survival]." The third and last verse is even more pessimistic, referring to workers with "death in their eyes" who suffer injury, which is inherent in their dangerous, monotonous work. *Factory* is a protest song, which Bruce Springsteen first performed live on 21 July 1978 at the Nashville Municipal Auditorium.

Production

Factory is another song that was largely reworked and adapted during production. The first versions date from June 1977 and were tape-recorded at Atlantic Studios. The song's title at the time was *Come On (Let's Go Tonight)*, and the lyrics were different from those on the album. Only in the September did Springsteen revisit the song at the Record Plant, making its subject his father and his circumstances as a worker. David Lindley—the multi-instrumentalist who has accompanied Jackson Browne, Linda Ronstadt, and Dolly Parton, among

Accompanied by Garry Tallent and Steve Van Zandt at Madison Square Garden in 1980, Bruce Springsteen looks back on his youth with *Factory*, especially at his father, who worked in a factory.

For Springsteen Addicts

The first version of *Factory*, which can be heard under the title *Come On (Let's Go Tonight)* on *The Promise* (released in 2010), features radically different words. These describe the death of Elvis Presley, on 16 August 1977, soon after the start of the making of *Darkness*. However, Springsteen's voice does not date from that time: it was recorded in 2010, for the release of *The Promise*.

others, and who was already present in the version of *Racing in the Street* that features on *The Promise* (2010)—then recorded a violin part. Overdubbing sessions followed, in October and December, but it was not until 2 January 1978 that the song was given the title *Factory Song*, with Roy Bittan's piano replacing Lindley's violin. Finally, on 10 and 14 March, it was mixed under the definitive title of *Factory*.

Recorded live in the studio, this melancholy piece is a moderate rock song influenced by country music—the songwriter had just discovered Hank Williams. The introduction showcases Bittan's piano, supported by the precise and forthright rhythm of Max Weinberg and Garry Tallent. It is interesting to note that Tallent adopts a precise way of playing, to fit the style of the drummer he is accompanying. He explained this himself in an interview in 2017: "Vini [Lopez] had a certain style that you play a certain way together. And then we changed to Boom Carter for a while and he's more jazzy, and we played a lot together. And now Max and I have played together for 40 years. You play differently in different situations [...]"[66]

Factory is built around three verses. The first features the piano, the Telecaster-Esquire playing arpeggios, a tambourine, the bass guitar, and the drums. The second is enhanced by Danny Federici's organ and a second guitar part, colored with tremolo and reverb—in all likelihood Steve Van Zandt's Stratocaster. The third comes after an instrumental section, led initially by Bittan's piano. Bittan's country style of playing calls to mind that of Floyd Cramer (starting at 0'59). This is followed by a solo, performed on the organ by Federici, whose style is more reminiscent of Booker T. Jones (starting at 1'12). The piece ends with Springsteen humming the melody.

Factory is the shortest song on *Darkness on the Edge of Town*. By virtue of its simplicity, of both the words and the music, it possesses undeniable power and charm, which fully justify its place on the album. Bruce hit the mark.

STREETS OF FIRE

Bruce Springsteen / 4'03

Musicians
Bruce Springsteen: vocals, guitars
Steve Van Zandt: guitars, vocal harmonies (?)
Roy Bittan: piano
Danny Federici: organ
Garry Tallent: bass guitar
Max Weinberg: drums
Recording
The Record Plant, 321 West 44th St, New York: August, December 1977; 5 April 1978 (mixing)
Technical team
Producers: Jon Landau, Bruce Springsteen
Assistant producer: Steve Van Zandt
Recording engineer: Jimmy Iovine
Assistant recording engineer: Thom Panunzio
Mixing: Chuck Plotkin, Jimmy Iovine

1978

HEADPHONES AT THE READY
In all the initial bars of the introduction, snapping fingers can be heard, marking the tempo.

Genesis and lyrics

Leonard Cohen's superb novel *Beautiful Losers*, published in 1966, is in many ways a reflection of the spirit of the 1960s. Bruce Springsteen could very well have used its title for this song on *Darkness on the Edge of Town*. The narrator of *Streets of Fire* also describes himself thus: "I'm wandering, a loser down these tracks." He appears to have abandoned everything—quite obviously the city and society, symbolized all at once by the "weak lies," "cold walls," and "Streets of fire"—in order to defeat his inner demons. This is, in fact, an illusion of victory, for he admits to his girlfriend that he is a liar. He adds, "I can't go back/'Cause in the darkness I hear somebody call my name." What is this voice? Springsteen's father? God? The last verse suggests that the wanderer has passed into another world: "I live now, only with strangers/I talk to only strangers/I walk with angels that have no place..."

Streets of Fire was first performed onstage during a great concert at Shea's Performing Arts Center in Buffalo, New York state. However, after that Bruce Springsteen and the E Street Band performed the song not much more than 70 times.

Production

The gestation of *Streets Of Fire* was rather long: between initial practice runs at Atlantic Studios in June 1977, overdubs made in the fall at the Record Plant, new takes recorded on 6, 12, and 29 December, and mixing completed in April 1978, it would take 11 months. Surprising given that the recording was made virtually live in the studio, and the song does not present any special difficulties. It is a slow rock that is rather fast, with phenomenal variations in volume. The intro is misleadingly gentle, lulled by Danny Federici's organ and Springsteen's rhythm guitar and introspective voice. The break comes in the first chorus, where the band thunder in, driven by the beat of Max Weinberg (at 0'52). The bass guitar, saturated rhythm guitars, and Roy Bittan's piano bring a heaviness and dynamism that are rather unexpected.

In the second verse, the musicians draw back a little, with Weinberg playing cross-stick and Bittan ceasing his accompaniment. But, at 1'20, Springsteen launches into a harrowing vocal performance, his voice on the verge of breaking. What he succeeds in recording right up to the end of the song is quite a feat—and one that surprised even his fellow musicians

For Springsteen Addicts

Street of Fire lent its title to a 1984 movie by Walter Hill, starring Michael Paré, Diane Lane, and Willem Dafoe. The song was meant to be on the original soundtrack, but Bruce Springsteen refused permission when he learned it would be rearranged. The music for *Streets of Fire* was eventually written by Ry Cooder.

In *Streets of Fire*, the Boss is supported by a phenomenal rhythmic section, in this case Max Weinberg and Garry Tallent.

and the recording engineer. Furthermore, recording Springsteen's voice must have presented a problem because to reach such a powerful intensity, his voice would have needed warming up first. In the studio, it must have taken many attempts before they arrived at the right result. Nevertheless, the Boss would reproduce the same performance in concert without batting an eyelid, thus joining the very select ranks of singers capable of such a feat (others include Paul McCartney, Ray Charles, and Little Richard, for example).

Springsteen also takes care of the guitar solo, on his Fender Telecaster-Esquire, displaying the same ferocious intensity as his lead vocals (starting at 1'55). He makes his 6-string guitar roar, going so far as to create feedback, Hendrix-style (at 2'00). The sound quality is live, and his playing always equally intense. Springsteen does not seek technical virtuosity—that is not his aim—but rather notes filled with feeling. It must be admitted that he succeeds, with bent notes, double stopping, and vibrato.

The piece ends with a final verse/chorus and a coda. In the latter, Springsteen can be heard humming, harmonizing with himself in two parts (from 3'45)—or is that Steve Van Zandt lending a helping hand?

Although *Streets of Fire* is not the best track on the album, it gives Springsteen the chance to produce a surprising vocal performance. It is intriguing that this song was included in the tracklisting of *Darkness on the Edge of Town*, given the superior quality of other songs that were dropped from the album and which can be found on *The Promise* (released in 2010).

PROVE IT ALL NIGHT

Bruce Springsteen / 3'57

Musicians
- **Bruce Springsteen:** vocals, guitars
- **Steve Van Zandt:** guitars, vocal harmonies
- **Clarence Clemons:** saxophone
- **Roy Bittan:** piano
- **Danny Federici:** organ, glockenspiel (?)
- **Garry Tallent:** bass guitar
- **Max Weinberg:** drums

Recording
- **The Record Plant, 321 West 44th St, New York:** 12, 14, and 16 September 1977

Technical team
- **Producers:** Jon Landau, Bruce Springsteen
- **Assistant producer:** Steve Van Zandt
- **Recording engineer:** Jimmy Iovine
- **Assistant recording engineer:** Thom Panunzio
- **Mixing:** Chuck Plotkin, Jimmy Iovine

1978

Billboard on Sunset Boulevard for the album *Darkness on the Edge of Town*. Springsteen and a few friends covered it in graffiti that read *Prove It All Night*.

Genesis and lyrics

During the concert at Berkeley Community Theater, in California, on 30 June 1978, Bruce Springsteen explained that the idea for *Prove It All Night* had come to him after hearing the confessions of an exceptionally talkative New York taxi driver. "I only knew this guy was about 45 years old and he was just raving about how all day long you gotta prove it to your boss driving around in a cab, and all night you gotta go home and prove it to your wife. On weekends, you gotta prove it to your kids. It never lets up, you know," Bruce Springsteen said, adding: "Anyway, I wrote this song. Sometimes you gotta prove it all night."[72]

Prove It All Night turns the spotlight on a couple who, in all likelihood, are preparing to get married. Perhaps, incidentally, this is the same couple from *Racing in the Street*, but they have become more mature...The guy says that he has "been working real hard, trying to get my hands clean." He is on the point of buying the woman he loves "a gold ring and pretty dress of blue." What he wants is "A kiss to seal our fate." Behind this fate there appears to lie an element of Bruce Springsteen's philosophy: "Everybody's got a hunger, a hunger they can't resist/There's so much that you want, you deserve much more than this/Well if dreams came true, oh, wouldn't that be nice." Probably the message here is that to attain success and fulfilment you must first go through a period of questioning and sacrifice. Here, again, can be seen a resurgence of Springsteen's Catholic upbringing—an act of contrition, in a way...

First performed live at Shea's Performing Arts Center in Buffalo, New York state, on 23 May 1978, *Prove It All Night* was released on the A-side of the first single from *Darkness on the Edge of Town* (*Factory* was on the B-side). Despite being energetically promoted by US radio stations, it got to only No.33 in the *Billboard* charts.

Production

For the first recordings of the song, in September 1977, Springsteen used the lyrics of *Something in the Night*, with the exception of the choruses and the second verse. Only after a long writing process, which was constantly called into question, did the songwriter arrive at the definitive version, as is described in his book *Songs* (published in 1998).

For Springsteen Addicts

After the release of *Darkness on the Edge of Town*, Bruce Springsteen and several friends—including Clarence Clemons and Garry Tallent—wanted to have fun by drawing a moustache on the songwriter's huge promotional poster high on a building on Sunset Strip in LA. However, they settled for simply writing: "*Prove It All Night.*"

A promotional single destined for radio stations had been planned for the summer of 1978, with a live version on the A-side of *Prove It All Night*, recorded on 1 July at the Berkeley Community Theater, California (in the presence of the Boss's parents and younger sister). Lasting 7'45, it was meant to convey the atmosphere of a concert, while the B-side would have featured the version on the album. But Springsteen changed his mind; apparently, just a single copy went on sale, bearing only the A-side recording. One for collectors...

Bruce Springsteen (seen here at the Berkeley Community Theater, in July 1978) wrote *Prove It All Night* after a conversation he had with a New York taxi driver.

Prove It All Night is one of the many pieces that fully comes into its own in concert. Certain live versions far surpass the one that appears on the album. If you had to choose one of these, it might be the version performed on 15 August 1978 at the Capital Center in Largo, Maryland. It is 11 minutes long and features a superb introduction, dominated by Roy Bittan's piano and an incredible guitar solo by the Boss. Springsteen would willingly acknowledge that he could have reworked some of the songs on *Darkness*: "Some of that stuff I think was a little dry, like I underplayed and oversang. It would be interesting to get different versions of some of those songs, like *Badlands*, *Prove It All Night*, and *The Promised Land*."[7]

The album version starts with a riff that sounds faintly Oriental, supported by Bittan's piano, which is in turn doubled by Federici's organ and, it appears, his glockenspiel (which is present in concert). Then, the band attacks the first verse, which has a rock quality, with that tone color typical of the E Street Band, made up of interwoven rhythm guitars and

1978

The Boss brandishes his superb Telecaster-Esquire with panache at the Capital Center in Largo, Maryland, on November 1978, where he performed *Prove It All Night*.

COVERS

Prove It All Night has been performed by some ten artists, including Southside Johnny and The Asbury Jukes, and also the US-Canadian experimental pop group US Girls (on the album *Introducing*, 2008).

keyboards of all kinds. Not forgetting the Weinberg-Tallent duo, which provides that immediately recognizable rhythm: simultaneously heavy and simple, yet infinitely subtle. In the chorus, Springsteen is joined in the harmony by Steve Van Zandt (this can be heard at 0'39).

The second chorus is followed by an instrumental section which is shared by Clarence Clemons and the Boss. Clemons launches into a fine chorus on his Selmer tenor saxophone—the third and last on the album. The sound is still just as powerful and laden with feeling (at 1'42). Then the Boss follows him with an extraordinary solo on his Telecaster-Esquire (at 2'02). He reels off incandescent musical phrases, which are surprising in their technical mastery and execution. The guitar sounds almost out of phase, so unusual is its aggressiveness. This song would give Springsteen the opportunity to demonstrate, in concert, that he was also an excellent solo guitarist. Springsteen is a disconcerting musician: a talented multi-instrumentalist and a formidable perfectionist.

Prove It All Night ends with a final verse and chorus, and a coda in which the voices of Bruce and Steve harmonize to perfection (from 3'00). It is worth noting that a few very brief notes on the saxophone can be heard at the very end of the piece (at 3'52 precisely): was that deliberate, or is it the remains of a poorly deleted solo?

This penultimate song on the album, imbued with the spirit of The Animals, according to Springsteen himself, is one of the highlights of *Darkness*. Nevertheless, it is a must to hear the live version.

DARKNESS ON THE EDGE OF TOWN

Bruce Springsteen / 4'28

Musicians

Bruce Springsteen: vocals, guitars
Steve Van Zandt: guitar
Clarence Clemons: tambourine
Roy Bittan: piano
Danny Federici: organ, glockenspiel
Garry Tallent: bass guitar
Max Weinberg: drums

Recording

The Record Plant, 321 West 44th St, New York: September to December 1977 (?); 8–10 March 1978

Technical team

Producers: Jon Landau, Bruce Springsteen
Assistant producer: Steve Van Zandt
Recording engineer: Jimmy Iovine
Assistant recording engineer: Thom Panunzio
Mixing: Chuck Plotkin, Jimmy Iovine

1978

Darkness on the Edge of Town is one of the ten songs performed most often in concert by the E Street Band and its Boss.

Genesis and lyrics

Logically enough, the title track concludes Bruce Springsteen's fourth album. The final verse of this song—starting with "Tonight I'll be on that hill..."—marks a point in the lives of Springsteen's characters when they are unsure of what the future holds, but they are determined and committed to whatever that may be.

While the songwriter describes the humble folk of New Jersey—the manual workers and low-ranking employees who lived alongside him in Freehold, as well as the blue-collar workers that his father rubbed shoulders with in the bars—as opposed to the privileged classes of Manhattan, here he certainly seems to be alluding to the narrator of *Racing in the Street*, who still has the company of Sonny, but no longer of the woman he loves. "Now I hear she's got a house up in Fairview/In a style she's trying to maintain," Springsteen sings in the first verse.

Misfortune has befallen the narrator—but there is still hope: "You can tell her that I'm easily found/Tell her there's a spot out 'neath Abram's Bridge." These words express all the songwriter's spirituality: "I grew up Catholic, and I suppose I go back to that for so much imagery in my music over the years," Springsteen told *Spin* magazine's Steve Kandell (in December 2007). "I was always interested in the spiritual background; it's just what fascinates me. Like, hey, where's the place you lose your soul, and how do I get there without falling in? I was always drawn to that, and it's shot through all my music, including this record."[67]

The hero of a film noir, has the central character found refuge in the "darkness on the edge of town"? Might he have found the way to transcendence there? Bruce Springsteen touches on this in his autobiography, explaining that by the end of the *Darkness* album he felt he had found his adult voice.

Darkness on the Edge of Town has been performed more than 700 times since the concert at Shea's Performing Arts Center in Buffalo, New York state, on 23 May 1978, but the song has not been released as a single.

Production

The first recordings of *Darkness on the Edge of Town* date from June 1977, at Atlantic Studios, on 6, 8, 9, 20, and 23 June, according to Sony Music's database. But it is likely that the

Bruce Springsteen at the Fox Theater in Atlanta, Georgia, on 30 September 1978, with Max Weinberg and Garry Tallent. He has performed the title song of his fourth album more than 700 times onstage.

basic tracks and various overdubs were recorded between September and December at the Record Plant. However, the definitive version appears to have been recorded and mixed only toward the end of the album's production, on 8 and 10 March 1978, in Studio A at the Record Plant, which was then in the process of being renovated. It was then that the band found, by chance, the drum sound they had been looking for since recording started. "We'd stumbled upon this by accident at the end of *Darkness*,"[1] Springsteen explains. "The Record Plant had been tearing apart Studio A to rebuild it. We went in to cut the song *Darkness on the Edge of Town* when the room was still four bare concrete walls. That's it! That resonance, that aggression from the drums, was exactly what we'd been searching for during all our early days of 'Stiiiiiiiiiiiick' mania."[1] It must be said that Max Weinberg's Ludwig drum kit was finally able to breathe—its beats no longer sound as dry and suffocated as they do in the other songs on the album. He succeeds in providing a very good accompaniment with—as

The Boss in shadow and light onstage at Madison Square Garden in August 1978.

COVERS

Darkness on the Edge of Town has been performed by more than 20 artists, from the faithful Southside Johnny to the tribute band Blood Brothers, as well as the Felice Brothers and The No Surrender Band.

Bruce Springsteen at The Stone Pony in 1976 with two other key figures of the New Jersey sound, Steve Van Zandt (right) and Southside Johnny, who covered *Darkness on the Edge of Town.*

1978

a bonus—a raw sound, as he himself explained: "At the end of the song *Darkness on the Edge of Town* I play a quarter-note triplet and end up with one snare shot that sets up the next passage perfectly. Visually, in my mind, it sets up some guy riding out into the sun. It's like a whip crack. The perfect spot. That's what I'm talking about. I don't do it all the time but I try for it all the time."[59]

The song also rests on Roy Bittan's sumptuous piano part. From the introduction he plays a melodic phrase (or gimmick) at the keyboard, which he repeats regularly until the final bars of the fade-out. Supported by Garry Tallent's bass guitar, the result is exquisite. The other instruments join in as the song develops: Danny Federici and his organ appear in the second verse; his glockenspiel joins the dance in the following verse (beating a delicate, crystalline note—a G—which returns insistently); and a rhythm guitar comes in, probably played by Steve Van Zandt. As for Clarence Clemons, from the start he plays a metronomic tambourine that jingles in the reverb.

As regards the singing, Springsteen varies the intensity of his performance, as he likes to do, starting pianissimo, only to roar from the second verse (starting at 0'36). The phrase that functions as a chorus is harmonized by two voices; it would seem that this is his voice, overdubbed, and not his voice with Miami Steve's.

"That was a very important song to me," the songwriter once confessed. "It was my samurai song."[73] And that is indeed the impression it has on the listener. The beauty of *Darkness on the Edge of Town* lies as much in its starkness as in the alternation of melancholy passages and sudden bursts of passion.

THE RIV

ALBUM

THE RIVER

The Ties That Bind • Sherry Darling • Jackson Cage • Two Hearts • Independence Day • Hungry Heart • Out in the Street • Crush on You • You Can Look (But You Better Not Touch) • I Wanna Marry You • The River • Point Blank • Cadillac Ranch • I'm a Rocker • Fade Away • Stolen Car • Ramrod • The Price You Pay • Drive All Night • Wreck on the Highway

RELEASE DATE

United States: 17 October 1980

Reference: Columbia Records – PC2 36854

No.1 in the *Billboard* chart, No.2 in the United Kingdom, No.1 in Canada and Norway, No.2 in the Netherlands and Sweden, No.3 in France, No.5 in Spain

Bruce Springsteen's fifth album is a beautiful retrospective of American popular music.

Graham Parker and The Rumour in the late 1970s. The London musicians' pub rock made its mark on the composer of *The River.*

1980

THE LAST PART OF THE SPRINGSTEEN TRILOGY

At the end of the 1970s Bruce Springsteen was still going through an exceptionally creative phase. Since the release of *Darkness on the Edge of Town*, he had composed constantly. So much so that, as he was about to enter the studio for the recording sessions for his fifth album, several dozen songs had expanded an already extremely rich repertoire—and that's not to mention those he had discarded from the previous album.

Originally, the idea was to record an album called *The Ties That Bind.* Besides the title track, it would include *Cindy, Hungry Heart, Stolen Car, Be True, The River, You Can Look (But You Better Not Touch), The Price You Pay, I Wanna Marry You,* and *Loose Ends*—ten songs recorded at The Power Station studio by Bob Clearmountain between March and September 1979. Springsteen, however, was unsure. "As I spent time listening to it, I felt that it just wasn't enough,"[1] he writes in his autobiography *Born to Run.*

What he wanted was to follow the example of songwriters such as Bob Dylan, Van Morrison, and Marvin Gaye, "who created self-aware, self-contained worlds on their albums, and then invited fans to discover them."[1] So, Springsteen returned to the studio with the E Street Band and recorded some new songs. Thus, the single album *The Ties That Bind* became the double album *The River*, comprising the above-mentioned songs (except for *Cindy*, which was released on *The Ties That Bind: The River Collection* in 2015, as well as *Be True* and *Loose Ends*, released on the *Tracks* box set in 1998), plus some new ones: *Sherry Darling, Jackson Cage, Two Hearts, Independence Day, Out in the Street, Crush on You, Point Blank, Cadillac Ranch, I'm a Rocker, Fade Away, Ramrod, Drive All Night,* and *Wreck on the Highway.*

Chronicler of 1970s America

This fifth album can be regarded as the last of a trilogy, comprising *Born to Run* and *Darkness on the Edge of Town*—a trilogy that would elevate Springsteen to the rank of brilliant and perceptive chronicler of 1970s America, as his mentor, Bob Dylan, had been for the 1960s with *Bringing It All Back Home, Highway 61 Revisited,* and *Blonde on Blonde.* It was above all a double album that took a new approach. From a musical point of view, it sounds like the very essence of the two preceding albums, in that it often displays the energy of a band playing in a bar but with the experience and cohesion of true musicians. "This was the album where the E Street Band hit its stride, striking the perfect balance between a garage band and the professionalism required to make good records,"[1] Bruce Springsteen confirms in his autobiography.

Four sides of black vinyl packed with powerful rock 'n' roll, recorded with a dynamism worthy of live performance,

1980

The E Street Band on the roof of The Power Station, where *The River* was recorded. From left to right: Garry Tallent, Max Weinberg, Roy Bittan, Steve Van Zandt, Bruce Springsteen, Clarence Clemons, and Danny Federici.

The River also has merit for the diversity of atmosphere it contains: it's a double album of rock, R&B, folk, and country that is typically American, even though Springsteen's singing hints at a certain interest in the British punk/new wave scene embodied by The Clash, Graham Parker, and Elvis Costello. The urgency of the rock 'n' roll is magnified by songs such as *The Ties That Bind*, *Jackson Cage*, *Cadillac Ranch*, *I'm a Rocker*, and *Ramrod*, while its melancholy and romanticism achieve a sort of dark climax in *Independence Day*, *Stolen Car*, *Point Blank*, and *The River*. Finally, there are songs which, on the first hear-ing, suggest they are future classics, such as *Two Hearts*, *Hungry Heart*, *Drive All Night,* and *The River*. Some of these songs point the way to the next evolution of Springsteen's sound, seen in the album *Nebraska*.

A dark, serious album—but not all that much

The River is the first of Springsteen's albums to center tentatively around the themes of love, marriage, and family. It is

Bruce Springsteen with a fan at the Wembley Arena during The River Tour.

clear that he has turned a corner, that he has developed, along with his characters, since *Darkness on the Edge of Town*, and that he has felt a burning need to take stock of his life. All things considered, that is the approach of an artist who is not seeking himself, but reflecting both on himself and on the world around him, on solitude and, consequently, on the need to "live together" and for mutual understanding. The family—*his* family—is another central theme that has always haunted him. It is therefore not surprising that two of the best songs on this double album—*Independence Day* and *The River*—were inspired, in the former, by his relations with his father (yet again) and in the latter by the experiences of his sister. What is new, in this familial catharsis, is that he expresses his feelings in a pared-down style, and no longer necessarily through an abundance of words and images.

In fact, *The River* is, on the whole, a dark, serious work through which runs one fundamental question, like a connecting thread: at the start of the 1980s, after the Vietnam war, Watergate, recession, the Three Mile Island nuclear accident, and the Iran hostage crisis, did the American dream still exist? Or, more specifically: if this American dream still existed for some, could others escape and free themselves from their social determinism? Springsteen implicitly asks this dual question at the end of *The River*: "Now those memories come back to haunt me, they haunt me like a curse/Is a dream a lie if it don't come true," while hinting that he knows the answer, which can only be tragic.

The songwriter also wished to leave behind the austere image he had deliberately cultivated in his previous album: "Now, after the unrelenting seriousness of *Darkness*, I wanted more flexibility in the emotional range of the songs I chose. Along with 'gravitas,' our shows were always filled with fun,

The jacket for *The River* was again made by Frank Stefanko.

1980

and I wanted to make sure, this time around, that didn't get lost,"[1] he explains. It is clear that he succeeded in this, managing to balance seriousness with a light touch: songs such as *I'm a Rocker* evoke the energy and enthusiasm of the band's concerts, while others, such as *Point Blank*, echo the austerity of *Darkness*.

The album

The River was released in the United States on 17 October 1980 and met with enormous success on both sides of the Atlantic, clearly exceeding the wildest hopes of both the songwriter and the people at Columbia. It would, indeed, get to No.1 in the United States—a first for the Boss—(for four consecutive weeks!) and in Canada, No.2 in the UK and the Netherlands, No.3 in France, and so forth. Critics were equally enthusiastic about the double album, starting with Paul Nelson of *Rolling Stone* magazine, who considered it a "rock 'n' roll milestone."[74] This is a long way from the image some had painted of the songwriter from New Jersey—that of an artist from the working classes who climbed the social ladder by exalting the simple pleasures of taking to the road astride a Harley-Davidson or at the wheel of a chromed monster from Detroit.

What is certain is that *The River* was viewed by most rock critics, and a very large part of the public, as an essential part of Bruce Springsteen's work and even of the whole of rock history, up there with other legendary double albums—The Beatles' *White Album*, The Rolling Stones' *Exile on Main St*, Bob Dylan's *Blonde on Blonde*, and Stevie Wonder's *Songs in the Key of Life*. Today, it is in 253rd place in *Rolling Stone's* list of the 500 Greatest Albums of All Time.

The sleeve

The black and white photograph on the sleeve of *The River* was shot by Frank Stefanko, who had already created the visual for *Darkness on the Edge of Town*. Two years later, while the songwriter was mixing *The River* in California, he called Stefanko again. "He called me up, and he had a complete duplicate set of contact sheets from all the *Darkness* sessions," Stefanko explained to David Chiu of *Rolling Stone*. "He was looking through them [...] and just said, 'Pull out sheet 28, look at negative number four. Can we make that a little darker on the right side?' And I'd go into the darkroom all night and then FedEx everything to him. For two weeks we were going back and forth over shots until he finally settled on [a] close-up portrait shot, with the same plaid shirt that was in *Corvette Winter*, and that was the cover of *The River*."[75]

Springsteen wanted the sleeve of his fifth album to be sober and serious. He is seen in close-up, looking at the

Steve Van Zandt, coproducer of *The River* along with Springsteen and Landau. Seen here with Roger Daltrey, lead singer for The Who.

Tony Bongiovi (right at the console). He and Bob Walters cofounded The Power Station in New York.

camera, unshaven, and wearing a lumberjack shirt. This is doubtless intended to indicate, before you even put the first record on the turntable, that this is a double album from the American heartland of the countryside and small towns—and an album recorded by blue-collar musicians. The artist's name and the album title are in blue on a black background.

On the back there is a montage of various images, including five brides and a bridegroom, a bald eagle (the national bird of the United States of America), and other elements. Inside the album sleeve are several photographs of Springsteen and the E Street Band, together with the words of the 20 songs on the double album. The design is by Jimmy Wachtel.

The recording

The sessions for Bruce Springsteen's fifth album took place in two long phases. The first of these, for what was meant to be *The Ties That Bind* (which was due for release before the 1979 New Year celebrations), stretched from the end of March to the end of August 1979; the recording engineer was Bob Clearmountain. That period saw the recording of the ten songs already mentioned, as well as *Ricky Wants a Man for her Own* and *The Man Who Got Away*, which were both dropped from the tracklist in September. The first of these, *Ricky Wants a Man for her Own,* was released in 1998 on the *Tracks* box set, then together with *The Man Who Got Away* on *The Ties That Bind: The River Collection* in 2015. The second phase, which would result in the double album *The River*, ran from October 1979 to June 1980.

For these different recording sessions, the team around Bruce Springsteen was expanded: as well as Jon Landau, Steve Van Zandt also came on board as coproducer (he had only been assistant producer on the previous album). He was entrusted with the task of giving the E Street Band a more "garage" and "rugged" sound, in order to contrast as much possible with the over-production of *Born to Run*, and especially with the austerity and overly formulaic sound of *Darkness on the Edge of Town*. Neil Dorfsman was at the controls. This recording engineer, producer, and mixing engineer was to build up one of the most impressive résumés in the business, working with musicians such as Sting, Dire Straits, Paul McCartney, Bob Dylan, Kiss, Weather Report, and Jaco Pastorius, to name but a few. Chuck Plotkin and Toby Scott—a newcomer to the team—were put in charge of mixing. All these sessions were held in the same place: The Power Station, a studio at 441 West 53rd St, Manhattan, between 9th Avenue and 10th Avenue, housed in a former power station and founded in 1977 by Tony Bongiovi and Bob Walters. This recording mecca, with a legendary acoustic, welcomed within its walls the cream of the Western music scene, including David Bowie, Norah Jones, Dire Straits, Sting, and John Lennon, among many others. Bruce Springsteen set up in Studio A, which had a lovely wooden room with high ceilings that would help release the sound of the E Street Band.

However, although Springsteen had decided to leave the Record Plant in favor of The Power Station, this was essentially because his drummer, Max Weinberg, along with Garry Tallent and Roy Bittan, had taken part in 1979 in the recording of an album by Ian Hunter called *You're Never Alone with a Schizophrenic.* Hunter was the ex-leader of English rock band Mott the Hoople. This was confirmed by the studio's owner, Tony Bongiovi, who said: "When Max Weinberg came out and played drums, he said he had to record here. That's how we got Bruce Springsteen and people like that to record here."[76]

From Clearmountain to Dorfsman

The first clutch of songs, recorded from the end of March to the end of August 1979, was entrusted to one of the most celebrated recording engineers of the day: the famous Bob Clearmountain, who was resident engineer at The Power Station. Clearmountain had taken part in numerous projects with artists such as The Rolling Stones, David Bowie, Chic, Elton John, Tears for Fears, INXS, and many others. His star quality was speed. However, what he recorded and mixed with the band disconcerted him: Springsteen's pernickety side, which demanded consistency and stamina, was not something he was used to. Nevertheless, he admitted to being impressed by him due to the quality of his songs, his seriousness, and his dedication to achieving perfection— see the

For Springsteen Addicts

Three songs recorded for the album initially called *The Ties That Bind* were dropped from *The River*: *Be True* would later be used on the B-side of the single *Fade Away*, while *Loose Ends* and *Cindy* would appear on the *Tracks* box set (1998) and *The Ties That Bind: The River Collection* (2015), respectively.

Bibliography, source 77, if you would like to read more of this interview with Bob Clearmountain. Yet when the songwriter decided on a double album, he jumped ship. Springsteen believes that Bob Clearmountain did not have the time, or patience, to deal with the long creative process demanded by the E Street Band when they put an album together and so had graciously withdrawn some years before.

So it was that Neil Dorfsman took Clearmountain's place for the second stage of the album's production, in all probability from October to June 1980, although Dorfsman maintains that he was present from the start of the project: "When I heard they were coming in [to record at The Power Station], I went to the studio manager and, basically, begged to be on the date. Bob Clearmountain started the project, did a track or two, then had to leave for a prior commitment, and they gave me a shot. I was so nervous the night [Springsteen] walked in, I was shaking. I was sure the first night would be my last. Little did I know it would go on for something like 16 months."[78] Thus, Dorfsman would record the whole of *The River*, with the exception of *Hungry Heart* and *The Ties That Bind*, which were recorded by Clearmountain, and *Drive All Night*, recorded by Jimmy Iovine, who had been the recording engineer on the two previous albums.

The production process did not speed up for all that. "And in the studio, I'm slow,"[10] Springsteen admitted. One of the main reasons for those long months dragging on was the considerable number of songs that they worked on—almost 50! "We wrote and recorded about 48 songs and at one time I thought they were all gonna be on [the record],"[10] the songwriter recalled. Nevertheless, they were rather quick in the studio and didn't make too many overdubs or record too many takes. "We just recorded so much stuff,"[10] Springsteen added.

A nightmare of a mixing

The inertia surrounding the creation of the album was more a result of the mixing. Having chosen 20 songs, Springsteen traveled to Clover Studios, in Los Angeles, with Chuck Plotkin and Toby Scott in charge of operations. Unfortunately, they came up against a serious problem: what had been recorded in the huge space of The Power Station's Studio A with room mics (two Neumann U87s) to capture the premises' live sound—and thus come close to the desired garage-band sound color—would turn out to be a nightmare: "Now everything we'd recorded was bleeding into everything else (those ceiling mikes worked!),"[1] as Springsteen explains in his autobiography. The resulting sound was muddled and unclear, and no one had a solution, not even Neil Dorfsman. After weeks of fruitless trying, the Boss decided to seek Jimmy Iovine's advice. He made him listen to 80 minutes of music from different mixings, after which the E Street Band's former recording engineer gave his verdict, asking Springsteen when he was planning to record the vocals, the implication being that these couldn't be heard clearly. Springsteen was devastated—and realized that they would have to start all over again.

Work resumed at a frantic pace. Toby Scott described the difficulties that they encountered: "Neil [Dorfsman]'s recording of the room mics had been one of my problems when I mixed *The River*. There was so much cymbal in those room mics, I had to recreate [the acoustic of] the room by using the Clover studio and piping some of the drums back out over speakers into the studio to have them reverberate around [the room], while also using [electronic] reverb units."[79] Work continued: to try to restore as far as possible what had been recorded, while preserving the original garage-band sound. While the songwriter waited patiently upstairs, Toby Scott adjusted his mixing: "I can't remember which song it was, but clearly he wanted the room in there, and that was fine [...] So, I rebalanced it for the room, readjusting stuff to account for the drums sounding like they were coming from the other end of a basketball court, and when Bruce came back down and listened he went, 'That's it! Great! Good deal!'"[79]

Together with Chuck Plotkin, who helped him with the final mixing, Scott succeeded in bringing the 20 songs on *The River* to life. Begun in March 1979 and completed in June 1980, Bruce Springsteen's fifth album had required a considerable number of hours in the studio, spread over a period of 16 months and divided between The Power Station in New York, Clover Studios in LA, and Capitol Studios in Hollywood—which were used for the mastering (by Ken Perry).

Technical details

Studio A at The Power Station was equipped with a Neve 8048 console with 32 channels, a Studer A80 24-track tape recorder, and, it would appear, Altec 604 E speakers. The Boss's voice was captured with either a Neumann U67 or U87 microphone. For the musical effects, there were notably Teletronix LA-2A and UREI LA-3A leveling limiters/compressors, Pultec equalizers, and an EMT 250 digital reverb.

Mixing was carried out at Clover Studios using a digital machine, one of the first of its kind: the Sony PCM-1600 Digital Recorder (1610 according to Toby Scott), which worked with U-Matic 3⁄4-inch videotape. The console was an API 32-track and, among other effects, the studio was equipped with two EMT 140 plate reverbs, Eventide H910 harmonizers, and EMT 156 compressors.

The instruments

Bruce Springsteen remained faithful to his Fender Telecaster-Esquire, but appears to have used other 6-string guitars in the studio, which sadly have not been identified. He also recorded using a modified Fender Electric XII, a 12-string in a natural wood color that can notably be heard in *The Ties That Bind*. For amplification, according to Neil Dorfsman, in the studio he plugged into a Fender Bassman. When playing acoustic, he appears to have used 6-string and 12-string Martin and Gibson guitars.

Steve Van Zandt worked with his two Sunburst Stratocasters, one dating from 1957, one from 1967. As regards keyboards, Danny Federici always played his Hammond B-3 organ with his Leslie speaker. He also used a Farfisa Combo Compact. As for Garry Tallent, he recorded on a black Music Man StingRay bass guitar, repainted by himself.

A 1965 Fender Electric XII, similar to the model the Boss used in his album.

THE TIES THAT BIND

Bruce Springsteen / 3'33

Musicians
Bruce Springsteen: vocals, guitars
Steve Van Zandt: guitars
Clarence Clemons: saxophone
Garry Tallent: bass guitar
Max Weinberg: drums

Recording
The Power Station, 441 West 53rd St, New York: 10–11 April 1979; 10 April 1980

Technical team
Producers: Bruce Springsteen, Jon Landau, Steve Van Zandt
Recording engineer: Bob Clearmountain
Assistant recording engineers: Jeff Hendrickson, Garry Rindfuss, Dana Bisbee, Raymond Willhard, James Farber
Mixing: Chuck Plotkin, Toby Scott

1980

For Springsteen Addicts

The Ties That Bind regularly featured on the setlist of concerts during the E Street Band's Reunion Tour in 1999.

The Ties That Bind is also the title of the third documentary, released in 2015, that Thom Zimny made about Bruce Springsteen, and specifically about the making of *The River*. The first was about *Born to Run*, the second about *Darkness on the Edge of Town*.

Genesis and lyrics

Bruce Springsteen composed the first version of *The Ties That Bind* in 1978, playing it with the E Street Band during a sound check that same year, probably on 1 November at the Jadwin Gymnasium, in Princeton, New Jersey. The song bore little resemblance to the one he would record some time later at The Power Station, part of which came from another song, *The Brokenhearted*. Springsteen had dropped *The Brokenhearted* during the recording sessions for *Darkness on the Edge of Town*, but it would appear on the box set *The Promise: The Darkness on the Edge of Town Story* (released in 2010).

"Brokenhearted" is precisely the word that best describes the definitive version of *The Ties That Bind*. The narrator is addressing his girlfriend who, heartbroken, henceforth wants to live without giving a thought to other people. "You walk down the street pushing people outta your way/You packed your bags and all alone you wanna ride," Springsteen sings in the first verse. The chorus, however, sounds like a warning or, more accurately, a piece of advice: "Now you can't break the ties that bind." In other words, you should not break the ties that bind you to others: you cannot escape your destiny. So, after the splendid isolation of *Darkness on the Edge of Town*—the solitude of the hill in the dark, on the outskirts of the city—in this first track of *The River*, and in others too, the songwriter from New Jersey champions the idea that it is possible, and necessary, to live together.

Production

The Ties That Bind is one of only two songs, the other being *Hungry Heart*, that was recorded by Bob Clearmountain rather than Neil Dorfsman. Clearmountain was a new member of the team and knew how to capture the best ambience of the room. The resulting recording is very dynamic and airy, with a much warmer, bigger drum sound than on the preceding albums. The same goes for the multiple guitar tracks. The main track, which is played on none other than a modified Fender Electric XII, imbues the piece with a tone color reminiscent of The Byrds.

A snare drum opens *The Ties That Bind*. The band immediately plunges into a rather joyous rock sound, dominated by guitars—including acoustic guitars—and featuring a riff on the 12-string electric played by the Boss. Bass guitar and drums throb powerfully, and keyboards are conspicuously absent.

First performed onstage in November 1978 in Princeton, New Jersey, *The Ties That Bind* was also performed in concert on 9 October 1980 in Detroit.

There is also no piano, organ, or glockenspiel, unless they were buried during the mixing—although these instruments are nevertheless present in live versions of the song.

In the first verse, Springsteen attacks the lead vocals with his usual energy, in a rather joyous way despite the less than happy lyrics. The tessitura is fairly high, and he does not seem very comfortable with his performance, even though he completely rerecorded his voice at the end of production. Most unusually, he is out of tune in places, especially in the second line of the second verse (listen between 1'06 and 1'09). In the choruses, he is supported by vocal harmonies from Steve Van Zandt, who lends a hand in those sung at the end of the second and third verses too, but these are also barely in tune (there's an example at 1'15).

The piece is lit up by a very fine saxophone solo played by Clarence Clemons who was clearly at the top of his game, with that immediately recognizable King Curtis-like sound (starting at 2'02). For the following verse, the key changes, going up a whole tone—a device used to increase a song's intensity slightly. The final chorus follows, ending cleanly.

So, what should we make of *The Ties That Bind*, the second piece recorded for *The River* after *Roulette*? The song, which is very fine when all is said and done, does hint at the problems Springsteen and his team had to face: the overall tone of the recordings, muddled by the room mics which drowned out the perception of sounds. For sure, the band sounds live, and the drums breathe at last, but a lack of precision in the instruments and voices leads to moments of looseness that are not always necessary or successful. "Everything was splashing around," the songwriter said. "We weren't in complete control of the way everything sounded, but that was the idea."[6] A pity.

SHERRY DARLING

Bruce Springsteen / 4'02

Musicians

Bruce Springsteen: vocals, guitars
Steve Van Zandt: guitars, vocal harmonies
Clarence Clemons: saxophone, maracas
Roy Bittan: piano
Danny Federici: organ
Garry Tallent: bass guitar
Max Weinberg: drums
The band: handclaps, backing vocals, party noises

Recording

The Power Station, 441 West 53rd St, New York: 25 May 1979; 23 February, 8 March, 12 April 1980

Technical team

Producers: Bruce Springsteen, Jon Landau, Steve Van Zandt
Recording engineer: Neil Dorfsman
Assistant recording engineers: Jeff Hendrickson, Garry Rindfuss, Dana Bisbee, Raymond Willhard, James Farber
Mixing: Chuck Plotkin, Toby Scott

1980

SHERRY, DARLENE, OR DEBBY?

Before deciding on *Sherry Darling*, Springsteen toyed with *Darlene* and *Debby May*.

For Springsteen Addicts

The name Sherry has inspired various artists: a song entitled *Sherry*, written by Hank Crawford, was performed by Ray Charles in 1958; another, written by Bob Gaudio, was recorded by Frankie Valli & the Four Seasons in 1962. Finally, The Rolling Stones adapted Eric Donaldson's *Cherry Oh Baby* during the sessions for *Black and Blue* (1976).

Genesis and lyrics

In this song, Springsteen uses a light tone, full of sarcasm, before addressing the serious themes that punctuate *The River*. Recorded during the sessions for *Darkness on the Edge of Town*, but dropped from the final tracklisting, *Sherry Darling* features three characters: a man, a woman, and the latter's mother. The three are in a car, and the narrator complains to his wife about the behavior of his mother-in-law, who is "yapping in the back seat." He has had enough of driving her to the employment agency and threatens to let her take the subway back to the ghetto in the evening. What he wants is to be alone with the woman he loves, Sherry, drink some beer with her, and drive down the highway...

Behind this family conflict, which is described with humor, lies the desire of the songwriter, who is in New York—"I'm stuck in traffic down here on 53rd Street"—to return to his native New Jersey and pretty girls on the beach.

Production

Unusually, *Sherry Darling* opens with a party atmosphere (shouts, clapping, whistling). The E Street Band then launches into a cheerful rock sound, led by the burning saxophone of Clarence Clemons. You can tell the group are enjoying themselves, and we are a long way from the dark ambience of the previous album. The songwriter, himself surprised by the recreational feel of his song, observed: "How could a happy song like *Sherry Darling* coexist with *Point Blank* or *Darkness on the Edge of Town*? I couldn't face that."[16]

When Springsteen performed *Sherry Darling* in concert, notably in 1978, he declared that he had been influenced by songs such as The Kingsmen's *Louie, Louie* (1966) and the Swingin' Medallions' 1966 *Double Shot (Of My Baby's Love)*. (The clapping reinforces the song's rhythm, exactly as in the song by the Medallions.) Springsteen enjoys himself singing, supported by Danny Federici's organ, Roy Bittan's piano, Garry Tallent's bass guitar, Max Weinberg's drums, Clarence Clemons' maracas, and Steve Van Zandt's guitar (Zandt also provides vocal harmonies in the choruses). Then the Boss shares the instrumental parts with Clemons (at 2'07 and 2'22), even allowing himself the luxury of harmonizing his solo using double stopping! The whole band brings *Sherry Darling* to a close with highly animated backing vocals.

JACKSON CAGE

Bruce Springsteen / 3'04

For Springsteen Addicts
Bruce Springsteen adapted the first two sentences of *Jackson Cage*—"Driving home she grabs something to eat/Turns a corner and drives down her street"—from *Where the Bands Are*, the official version of which features on the compilation album *18 Tracks* (1999).

Musicians
Bruce Springsteen: vocals, guitars, harmonica
Steve Van Zandt: guitars, vocal harmonies
Roy Bittan: piano
Danny Federici: organ
Garry Tallent: bass guitar
Max Weinberg: drums

Recording
The Power Station, 441 West 53rd St, New York: 17 February, 10 March 1980

Technical team
Producers: Bruce Springsteen, Jon Landau, Steve Van Zandt
Recording engineer: Neil Dorfsman
Assistant recording engineers: Jeff Hendrickson, Garry Rindfuss, Dana Bisbee, Raymond Willhard, James Farber
Mixing: Chuck Plotkin, Toby Scott

Max Weinberg plays an excellent drum part in *Jackson Cage*. Seen here in Chicago, during the 2016 River Tour.

Genesis and lyrics

In an interview with Dave Marsh for *Musician* magazine, Bruce Springsteen explained the key idea behind *Jackson Cage*: "I never knew anybody who was unhappy with their job and was happy with their life. It's your sense of purpose. Now, some people can find it elsewhere. Some people can work a job and find it some place else."[65]

Jackson Cage is certainly a reflection on what those living around him could have gone through. Jackson Township, which adjoins Freehold, Bruce Springsteen's hometown, is close to Lakewood, where Virginia Springsteen (the songwriter's sister) lived. She worked in a Kmart store, which doubtless inspired some especially eloquent words: "And you can try with all your might/But you're reminded every night/That you been judged and handed life/Down in the Jackson Cage." These words need no interpretation: the song's heroine cannot escape her environment or her condition. She is excluded from the American dream.

Production

It is Max Weinberg who begins *Jackson Cage* with his snare drum, which cracks like the report from a firearm: the sound is violent, aggressive, and in the mid-range. Throughout the piece, Weinberg provides a perfect, very dynamic beat, with a few technical subtleties that are a credit to him, notably an excellent snare drum roll (at 2'04). However, although his performance is at the highest level, the same does not go for the recording: the room mics are picked up by the mics of the other musicians. Toby Scott's job in trying to master this fine mess cannot have been an easy task. Yet, in the end, *Jackson Cage* is an effective piece of rock music, its tone colored simultaneously by Danny Federici's Farfisa organ and by the multiple guitars of Springsteen and Steve Van Zandt, which call to mind, with their numerous arpeggio passages, those of The Byrds—exactly as in *The Ties That Bind*.

As regards singing, Springsteen's voice is aggressive, a powerful vocal effort—chiefly in the choruses, which are partly harmonized by the trusty "Miami Steve." Then, at 1'52, the Boss plays a harmonica solo, with phrasing that is inevitably reminiscent of Bob Dylan.

Jackson Cage is a rather raw piece of rock music, with an urgent delivery that is characteristic of British punk musicians.

TWO HEARTS

Bruce Springsteen / 2'42

Two Hearts is a song much loved by writers, composers, and musicians: it has inspired many songs, notably by Toto in 1992 (Toto), Phil Collins in 1988 (Lamont Dozier/Phil Collins), Cliff Richard in 1988 (Alan Tarney), and Chris Isaak in 1993 (Chris Isaak).

Musicians
Bruce Springsteen: vocals, guitars
Steve Van Zandt: guitars, vocal harmonies
Roy Bittan: piano
Danny Federici: organ
Garry Tallent: bass guitar
Max Weinberg: drums

Recording
The Power Station, 441 West 53rd St, New York: 23–24 February, 17 March, 9 and 26 April 1980

Technical team
Producers: Bruce Springsteen, Jon Landau, Steve Van Zandt
Recording engineer: Neil Dorfsman
Assistant recording engineers: Jeff Hendrickson, Garry Rindfuss, Dana Bisbee, Raymond Willhard, James Farber
Mixing: Chuck Plotkin, Toby Scott

1980

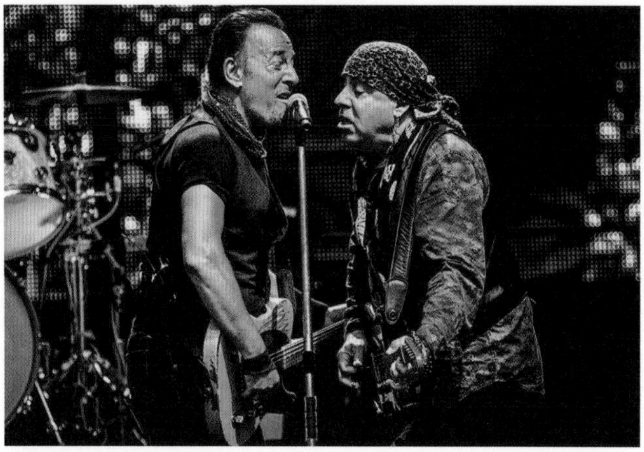

Bruce Springsteen and Steve Van Zandt on guitars and vocals, the two hearts of the E Street Band.

Genesis and lyrics

The heroine Bruce Springsteen introduces in *Two Hearts* could well be the same as the one in *The Ties That Bind*. The narrator sees her weep as she walks along: "She'd been hurt so bad, said she'd never love again." Here too, as in *The Ties That Bind*, he wants to be reassuring: "Someday your crying, girl, will end."

Springsteen continues and concludes thus: for him, there can be no salvation in solitude; it can be found only in understanding, in an emotional bond with another. And the songwriter-narrator describes his own experience: "Once I spent my time playing tough guy scenes/But I was living in a world of childish dreams." He adds that he has grown up, and becoming an adult has allowed him to dream again...

Musically, *Two Hearts* runs on the pure, corrosive energy of garage rock—the hand of Steve Van Zandt is clearly visible. As Bruce Springsteen rightly writes in his book *Songs*: "The album got its energy from *Cadillac Ranch*, *Hungry Heart*, *Two Hearts*, *Ramrod*, and the other club rockers. This was the music I wrote to provide fuel for our live show and to create a counterbalance to the ballads that began showing up more and more in my work."[6]

Production

Once again, it is Max Weinberg who starts the song, with a drum fill: it is a piece of powerful rock music, with a sound closer to punk than to that of the pioneers of rock 'n' roll. The live sound quality of the recording fits perfectly with the album's garage-band character, which doubtless made the task of mixing easier. The multiple guitar tracks form a veritable wall of saturated sound, while Danny Federici brings a more traditional touch with his organ, playing a repeating musical figure (or gimmick) until the last bar.

Above all, *Two Hearts* gives us the chance to hear Steve Van Zandt accompany Springsteen in the vocal harmonies (except in the first verse). Their two voices blend perfectly, and it is in concert, especially, that the duo takes on its full significance when they sing together into the same mic—the symbol of an unbreakable friendship. "You don't have that many friends for that length of time [...],"[80] Little Steven said after performing the song once again on the River Tour in 2016.

INDEPENDENCE DAY

Bruce Springsteen / 4'46

Musicians

Bruce Springsteen: vocals, guitars
Steve Van Zandt: guitars
Clarence Clemons: saxophone, tambourine
Roy Bittan: piano
Danny Federici: organ
Garry Tallent: bass guitar
Max Weinberg: drums

Recording

The Power Station, 441 West 53rd St, New York: 29 May, 11 October 1979; 24–25 April 1980

Technical team

Producers: Bruce Springsteen, Jon Landau, Steve Van Zandt
Recording engineer: Neil Dorfsman
Assistant recording engineers: Jeff Hendrickson, Garry Rindfuss, Dana Bisbee, Raymond Willhard, James Farber
Mixing: Chuck Plotkin, Toby Scott

HEADPHONES AT THE READY

If you listen closely you can hear the organ play a discord, at 2'08 precisely.

Genesis and lyrics

Bruce Springsteen wrote *Independence Day* in 1976. He had intended to include this song on *Darkness on the Edge of Town*, then eventually changed his mind, probably because he felt that it did not fit with the other tracks on the album. So, he rerecorded it some time later and it became one of the main songs on his fifth album. The emotional resonance of *The River* comes from the ballads—for Springsteen, *Point Blank*, *Independence Day*, *The River*, and *Stolen Car* are all songs that are driven by the narrative.

The story of *Independence Day* is only loosely connected to the US holiday celebrated on 4 July. This story is about Bruce Springsteen and his father, and their difficult relationship—a sort of mutual incomprehension. Time has since passed, but the recollections remain engraved in the songwriter's memory: a father who rose early to go off to work to feed his family; his sacrifices, his frustrations. Silences, too: "I grew up in a house where it seems nobody ever talked to each other,"[10] he revealed during the River Tour. Likewise, years later, he told Patrick Humphries: "I remember when I called and said to my pop: 'I'm going to be on the cover of *Time* and *Newsweek*.' That must have sounded insane. I had made a few records, but they hadn't done particularly well, and I remember my dad's only comment was: 'Well, better you than another picture of the President.'"[81]

With *Independence Day*, Brue Springsteen seems, despite everything, to have wanted to strengthen the bond with his father, which had been strained since his adolescence. And he puts a great deal of feeling into it. This song is perhaps the saddest on the double album. Its most original feature is role reversal: "Well Papa go to bed now, it's getting late." Although the son is looking after his father, who is old and ill, there is at the same time a profound resentment, which has only increased in a gloomy environment—the song refers to the "darkness of this house" and "a darkness in this town." The son adds: "They ain't gonna do to me what I watched them do to you." So, he has decided to leave. Also, he cannot live in the same house as his father because they are too alike. In other words, the son does not want, in his turn, to be society's victim, to become a prisoner of his social class. In a highly symbolic manner, the son asserts his independence—on Independence Day.

Bruce Springsteen supported by Clarence Clemons at the Cobo Arena, Detroit, on 9 October 1980, during the River Tour.

1980

Independence Day was released as a single, on the B-side of *The River* in several countries, and of *Sherry Darling* in others, but it did not make it into the charts.

Production

Springsteen and his musicians recorded an initial version of *Independence Day* in August 1977, at Atlantic Studios in New York. They then worked on the song until the end of the year, this time at the Record Plant. The piece nevertheless already featured on concert setlists, having first been performed on 7 July 1978 at The Roxy Theatre, in West Hollywood, with Springsteen alone at the piano. However, it was not until 1979 and 1980 that the band would record the definitive version, at The Power Station in the Big Apple, with Neil Dorfsman at the controls.

Independence Day begins with Danny Federici's organ, Springsteen's acoustic guitar, and Clarence Clemons's tambourine. The introspective atmosphere is reminiscent of an Irish ballad—doubtless a nod to the Boss's father, who was of Irish descent.

From the first notes of the vocals Springsteen sounds moved and immersed in his lyrics. The burden of his childhood and its traumas seems to emanate from his voice. The songwriter from Freehold possesses exceptional charisma and persuasive power. Like a shaman, he gently captures his audience and delivers his message with disconcerting ease.

One after the other, the musicians make their contribution, in order to support the Boss's performance as much as possible—totally devoted to his cause. Thus, Roy Bittan joins in from the first verse with a delicate piano accompaniment, which progressively develops without ever becoming invasive. Garry Tallent supports the harmony with a simple but effective bass line, always in symbiosis with Max Weinberg's drums. Weinberg, for his part, drums rather discreetly, alternately playing cross-stick and on the snare drum. As regards guitars, a 12-string acoustic can be heard, notably in the fourth verse (starting at 2'47), as well as an electric that plays arpeggios (from 1'12). Finally, Clarence Clemons, as well as having played the tambourine, delivers a very fine saxophone solo, full of feeling and melancholy (at 2'23). The piece then ends with both a reprise of the motif from the introduction, played on the organ by Federici, and a long fade-out that lasts more than 25 seconds (from 4'20).

HUNGRY HEART

Bruce Springsteen / 3'19

For Springsteen Addicts

A first in Bruce Springsteen's career: *Hungry Heart* found its way onto several movie soundtracks. Worthy of mention are Paul Brickman's *Risky Business* (1983), Kenneth Branagh's *Peter's Friends* (1992), and Frank Coraci's *The Wedding Singer* (1998).

Musicians

Bruce Springsteen: vocals, guitars (?)
Steve Van Zandt: guitars, backing vocals
Clarence Clemons: baritone saxophone
Roy Bittan: piano
Danny Federici: organ, glockenspiel
Garry Tallent: bass guitar
Max Weinberg: drums
Mark Volman, Howard Kaylan: backing vocals

Recording

The Power Station, 441 West 53rd St, New York: 14 and 21 June, 5 September 1979; 24 March, 10 April 1980

Technical team

Producers: Bruce Springsteen, Jon Landau, Steve Van Zandt
Recording engineer: Neil Dorfsman
Assistant recording engineers: Jeff Hendrickson, Garry Rindfuss, Dana Bisbee, Raymond Willhard, James Farber
Mixing: Bob Clearmountain

Bruce Springsteen, an exceptional voice singing one of his greatest hits.

Genesis and lyrics

In his book *Big Man: Real Life & Tall Tales*, Clarence Clemons revealed that Bruce Springsteen wrote *Hungry Heart* in about ten minutes, when he was extremely angry with his record label (the reason remains unknown). After an unproductive day, the songwriter and the E Street Band got back to work. "Bruce goes to take a piss," Clemons wrote, "and when he comes back, he says, 'Back in the studio, guys, I think I've got something.' And he sits down and writes the whole thing out without pausing. Boom! Just like that. I think it's still our biggest hit. One of them, anyway. 'Got a wife and kid in Baltimore Jack.' I loved that it was Baltimore and Jack. Good sounds. The perfect words. 'I went out for a ride and I never went back.' Who hasn't been there? Ten minutes. Amazing."[17]

Clarence Clemons' account of the creation of *Hungry Heart* differed somewhat from the one given by Bruce Springsteen, who said that he originally wrote the song for the Ramones at the request of Joey Ramone, whom he had met at Asbury Park. He explained that it was only after he had played the song to Jon Landau, who sensed a potential hit and persuaded him to keep it, that he recorded it for *The River*.

The song's story can be summed up in a few words: a man has decided to leave everything—his wife, his children—and, although he "took a wrong turn," "just kept going"—in other words, he has changed his life. At that point the man realizes he is not made to be alone, to live like a vagabond. The last verse expresses none other than the need to return to living as part of a couple: "Everybody needs a place to rest/ Everybody wants to have a home."

The title of the song, and the very idea of a journey, was borrowed by Springsteen from the poem *Ulysses* by the British Victorian poet Alfred, Lord Tennyson, especially its line: "For always roaming with a hungry heart." Tennyson's poem, in turn, was inspired by Homer's *Iliad* and *Odyssey*, and also by Dante's *Divine Comedy*.

Hungry Heart marks a decisive stage in Bruce Springsteen's career. Performed onstage more than 730 times, ever since the concert at Kiel Opera House in Saint-Louis, Missouri, on 18 October 1980, this song was also, and above all, his first big hit. Indeed, it reached No.5 in the *Billboard* charts, on 8 November 1980, and, with *Held up Without a Gun* on the B-side, was voted that year's best single by the readers of

At Neil and Pegi Young's first Bridge School Benefit (1986) Bruce Springsteen sang *Hungry Heart* with Crosby, Stills, Nash & Young.

Mark Volman and Howard Kaylan, backing vocalists for Frank Zappa. They participated in the recording of *Hungry Heart*.

Bob Clearmountain in the late 1970s at the Mediasound Studios in New York. He mixed *Hungry Heart*.

Rolling Stone magazine (Springsteen, for his part, was voted best artist and best singer, while *The River* was voted best album). In the UK, the song got to only No.44, on 22 November 1980, and to No.25 on its second release in 1995. Today, it is still one of Springsteen's best-loved songs, which enables him to communicate with his audience via a call and response.

Production

What better homage could Bruce Springsteen have paid to the sound of the 1950s than recording *Hungry Heart*? Moreover, he succeeded in producing the sound he had been constantly seeking, that of Elvis Presley's *Hound Dog*—his "Holy Grail," as he called it. For once, despite spill problems with The Power Station's room mics, the result came up to expectations: *Hungry Heart* is a song that combines the band's sound and that of the studio's acoustic to perfection. To be sure, it took some technical tricks to achieve this, notably during the mixing by Bob Clearmountain. Clearmountain, who found the tempo too slow, actually increased this slightly to give the song more dynamism—a common practice, introduced by The Beatles in 1966 for their album *Revolver*. When Chuck Plotkin and Toby Scott tried, several months later, to do their own mixing at Clover Studios in LA, they simply could not improve on Clearmountain's. They therefore decided to keep his mixing, while again slightly increasing the initial tempo, which now borders on parody. There is a difference of a semitone between the live versions and that on the record, which is a direct consequence of speeding up the magnetic tape.

The unique mixing by Bob Clearmountain for *The River* (he made a dozen more, which were discarded) elicited a humorous reaction from Springsteen: "We'd done it. Of course, I recollected that Bob Clearmountain had mixed *Hungry Heart*, our soon-to-be Top five (and only) smash, in 30 seconds, but we could never have worked with Bob. HE WAS TOO FUCKING FAST!"[1] This did not stop Springsteen calling on his services in the future, however.

The secrets of a hit

The success of *Hungry Heart* was due to three factors. First, the song's composition and writing, which are clear and filled with light. Second, the recording: as explained above, its live quality is, for once, a real plus, unlike that of other songs on the album. Finally, the musicians' performance, which is simply perfect: the band plays with complete unity and infectious enthusiasm.

As was often the case, Max Weinberg starts the piece, with an absolutely devastating drum fill. The sound is spectacular, and the drums beat with power and brilliance. Neil Dorfsman later explained that he recorded in conventional style, at least

The Ramones, a key band of the New York punk scene, for whom Bruce Springsteen composed *Hungry Heart*.

by the criteria of The Power Station: using an SM57 mic for the snare drum, a Sennheiser MD 421 and Electro-Voice RE20 for the bass drum, a 421 for the tom-toms, and some 451s for the hi-hat and the overheads. He confirmed the importance of these various factors to the success of the recording: "The sound was the room, the board [a Neve 8048], and the band."[78]

From the introduction, Roy Bittan's piano and Danny Federici's glockenspiel dominate the sound palette with their luminous harmonies, which are reminiscent of a certain Phil Spector. They are accompanied by an excellent riff played on the baritone saxophone by Clarence Clemons, another essential element of the song (it is doubled and recorded in stereo). An acoustic guitar, mixed very far away, supports the rhythm with its strumming (on the right). As for the duo of Max Weinberg and Garry Tallent, they contribute an irresistible groove and an irrepressible beat.

Bruce Springsteen appears to have been content to record only his own lead vocals, in all probability leaving the discreet 6-string guitar passages to Steve Van Zandt. But his performance is remarkable: he sings with infectious passion and exuberant joy. For sure, the speeding up of the mixing brings a higher pitch and delicacy to his voice, but the result is dynamic and powerful.

The end of the Boss?

Springsteen is accompanied in the choruses by Beach Boys-style backing vocals: in fact, these are the voices of Mark Volman and Howard Kaylan, better known as Flo & Eddie, a duo who would work with artists as varied as Frank Zappa, John Lennon, T. Rex, Steely Dan, Alice Cooper, Blondie, and many others. Volman and Kaylan were also the founding members of the Turtles, writing *Happy Together* and *She'd Rather Be with Me* (1967). When they recorded the backing vocals for *Hungry Heart*, they were convinced that they were taking part in a second-rate song: "We'd heard the songs that would comprise *The River* and didn't think this song would fit at all," Howard Kaylan said. "We just felt like he [Bruce] was wasting his time and thought it was a throwaway bullshit B-side [...]" When they found out the song had been earmarked as the band's next single, they could not believe it, saying: "'What are you talking about?'" Then when the record came out, Kaylan continued, they said, "'We killed him [Bruce], we ruined his career, this is horrible.' I loved the guy and now he put out this piece of crap. It went to No.1 and I was shocked."[82]

Although *Hungry Heart* only reached No.5 in the charts, the quality of this song, which is admittedly fairly atypical of Springsteen's repertoire, established his reputation interna-tion-ally—despite the rather extreme opinion of Kaylan...

OUT IN THE STREET

Bruce Springsteen / 4'17

Musicians
Bruce Springsteen: vocals, guitars
Steve Van Zandt: guitars, vocal harmonies
Clarence Clemons: saxophone, tambourine
Roy Bittan: piano
Danny Federici: organ
Garry Tallent: bass guitar
Max Weinberg: drums

Recording
The Power Station, 441 West 53rd St, New York: 21 March 1980

Technical team
Producers: Bruce Springsteen, Jon Landau, Steve Van Zandt
Recording engineer: Neil Dorfsman
Assistant recording engineers: Jeff Hendrickson, Garry Rindfuss, Dana Bisbee, Raymond Willhard, James Farber
Mixing: Chuck Plotkin, Toby Scott

1980

Bruce Springsteen and Max Weinberg at San Siro, Milan, on July 2016. The drummer struggled through the recording of *Out in the Street.*

Genesis and lyrics

Musically speaking, *Out in the Street* is the definitive version of *I'm Gonna Be There Tonight* (which never got beyond the stage of a demo, but appears on the recordings of rehearsals at Telegraph Hill). In the song, the songwriter from New Jersey celebrates the street party as the only release from tedious, depressing everyday life for America's humble, hard-working people. "Put on your best dress baby and, darling, fix your hair up right/'Cause there's a party, honey, way down beneath the neon lights," it begins. The second verse is in the first person singular. The narrator says that he slaves away five days a week, and when Monday comes and "the foreman calls time/I've already got Friday on my mind." The only thing that motivates him is to go down into the street and party again and again...

Springsteen hesitated to include *Out in the Street* on *The River* because of the optimism, even idealism, that it expresses. Eventually, he made it one of the double album's key songs. The album's energy comes from the bar band-style music and songs such as *Cadillac Ranch*, *Out in the Street*, and *Ramrod*.

Production

Out in the Street is a piece of rock in the Springsteen style: energetic, melodious, and displaying a range of different influences, from Roy Orbison to British pop, from Chuck Berry to The Byrds—but always with the sound that belongs only to the E Street Band: a blend of keyboards and guitars which is unique and devastatingly effective. *Out in the Street* also showcases the Boss's voice supported by vocal harmonies from the trusty Miami Steve, who sings a solo phrase (at 3'49).

Out in the Street marks a crucial step in the career of Max Weinberg. The E Street Band's drummer indeed struggled to keep a regular tempo during the recording sessions: "It came down to a very painful night in the studio where Bruce said that my time-keeping was a very specific problem that I should address myself to."[59] From then on, he made frantic attempts to solve the problem, notably taking lessons with Sonny Igoe, also a native of New Jersey, who was a teacher and an ex-drummer for Benny Goodman. His playing soon became irreproachable and, as a result, he remained the band's drummer for more than 40 years. Nevertheless, this did not erase the bad memory. He said: "*Out in the Street* is one of the worst bits of drumming I've ever done."[59]

CRUSH ON YOU

Bruce Springsteen / 3'10

The Hong Kong special mentioned by Springsteen exists only in his imagination.

Musicians

Bruce Springsteen: vocals, guitars
Steve Van Zandt: guitars
Clarence Clemons: saxophone, cowbell
Roy Bittan: piano
Danny Federici: organ
Garry Tallent: bass guitar
Max Weinberg: drums
The band: backing vocals, handclaps

Recording

The Power Station, 441 West 53rd St, New York: 11–12 October 1979

Technical team

Producers: Bruce Springsteen, Jon Landau, Steve Van Zandt
Recording engineer: Neil Dorfsman
Assistant recording engineers: Jeff Hendrickson, Garry Rindfuss, Dana Bisbee, Raymond Willhard, James Farber
Mixing: Chuck Plotkin, Toby Scott

Keith Richards during The Rolling Stones' 1981 American tour. His performance influenced the Boss's style for *Crush on You.*

Genesis and lyrics

Crush on You is the E Street Band Rolling Stones-style, with Steve Van Zandt playing Keith Richards. Bruce Springsteen's lyrics describe an experience he had in New Jersey, although the song is set in Los Angeles—the city where everything is possible. The girl of his dreams is at the wheel of a Hong Kong special at a stoplight. It is love at first sight. Who is this beautiful stranger, who "makes the Venus de Milo look like she's got no style"? In the heat of his emotion, and slightly amused, the songwriter gives free rein to his imagination, indulging in the wildest speculation: "Well now she might be the talk of high society/She's probably got a lousy personality/She might be a heiress to Rockefeller/She might be a waitress or a bank teller." One thing is for certain: he has a crush on her!

Production

From the first notes the comparison with the Stones is inescapable: Springsteen plays a riff that is very Keith Richards on his Telecaster-Esquire, with a sound that the king of riffs would probably not have disowned (on the left in the panorama). Steve Van Zandt answers him on his Stratocaster and plays lead guitar, in the style of Ronnie Wood (on the right). Max Weinberg does not deny himself a tribute to Charlie Watts's drumming, while Garry Tallent slips easily into the shadow of Bill Wyman's bass guitar. After this pastiche intro, the rest of the song is also inspired by Jagger's band, especially the choruses, with their distinctive backing vocals. Even the clapping in the second verse is reminiscent of The Rolling Stones (from 0'44). The same goes for Clarence Clemons's sax solo, the tone of which is very Bobby Keys (at 1'13). Only Springsteen's voice retains its personality, with a very hoarse rock timbre.

However, it is really in live performance that *Crush on You* unleashes its full power, with Springsteen wildly unchained (see the River Tour concerts in 1980). Although the song's title is practically identical to the one on the B-side of The Clash's single *1-2 Crush on You*, released in 1978, the lyrics and music have nothing in common.

YOU CAN LOOK (BUT YOU BETTER NOT TOUCH)

Bruce Springsteen / 2'36

Musicians
Bruce Springsteen: vocals, guitars
Steve Van Zandt: guitars, vocal harmonies
Roy Bittan: piano
Danny Federici: organ
Garry Tallent: bass guitar
Max Weinberg: drums

Recording
The Power Station, 441 West 53rd St, New York: 17 and 23 February, 1, 9, and 21 April 1980

Technical team
Producers: Bruce Springsteen, Jon Landau, Steve Van Zandt
Recording engineer: Neil Dorfsman
Assistant recording engineers: Jeff Hendrickson, Garry Rindfuss, Dana Bisbee, Raymond Willhard, James Farber
Mixing: Chuck Plotkin, Toby Scott

Neil Young and his wife Pegi in 1998 at the Shoreline Amphitheatre in Mountain View, California, for the Bridge School Benefit Concert.

Genesis and lyrics

After a nod to the Stones with *Crush on You*, Bruce Springsteen and the E Street Band turned the clock back a bit further into rock 'n' roll history, as *You Can Look (But You Better Not Touch)* sounds like a sort of salute to pioneers like Eddie Cochran and Duane Eddy. Although...15 years on, the frustration of the narrator of this song and that of *(I Can't Get No) Satisfaction* are more or less the same: frustration at seeing a beautiful girl on television, whom he cannot touch, frustration at not being able to satisfy his sexual desire with "Dirty Annie" at a drive-in. Although *You Can Look (But You Better Not Touch)* is a song that is not meant to be taken entirely seriously, it comes into its own onstage. It was first performed live on 7 October 1980 at the Richfield Coliseum, in Ohio.

Production

The first version of *You Can Look (But You Better Not Touch)*, recorded and mixed by Bob Clearmountain at The Power Station, was pure rockabilly and superbly performed by the quartet of Springsteen, Bittan, Weinberg, and Tallent, who took visible pleasure in playing. It might seem surprising, therefore, that the songwriter did not wish to keep that version of the song, as it was certainly superior to the one which eventually appeared on the album (they would perform that first version only once during the Tunnel of Love Express Tour in 1988). Be that as it may, the definitive version is a piece of rock music that was "[...] written very quickly [...],"[10] according to the Boss, whose only hint at rockabilly is the feeble slapback echo applied to his voice.

For the rest, the arrangement has a certain Stones-like flavor, but this is much less pronounced than in *Crush on You*. The song was probably recorded live in the studio, with very little overdubbing. Springsteen's solo thus appears to have been played when the backing track was being recorded (at 1'10). During the River Tour, in 1980, the Boss and his musicians finished the song in a rather surprising, gospel rock-like vein. It is a pity that the version on the album is, when all is said and done, the least surprising of all.

HEADPHONES AT THE READY
Danny Federici plays a wrong note on the organ at 1'17.

I WANNA MARRY YOU

Bruce Springsteen / 3'26

Musicians
Bruce Springsteen: vocals, guitars
Steve Van Zandt: guitars
Clarence Clemons: saxophone, maracas
Roy Bittan: piano
Danny Federici: organ
Garry Tallent: bass guitar
Max Weinberg: drums
Unidentified musicians: backing vocals

Recording
The Power Station, 441 West 53rd St, New York: 5, 11, and 12 July 1979; 12 April, 6–7 May 1980

Technical team
Producers: Bruce Springsteen, Jon Landau, Steve Van Zandt
Recording engineer: Neil Dorfsman
Assistant recording engineers: Jeff Hendrickson, Garry Rindfuss, Dana Bisbee, Raymond Willhard, James Farber
Mixing: Chuck Plotkin, Toby Scott

Bruce Springsteen following in the footsteps of singer Ben E King for the soul ballad *I Wanna Marry You*. Seen here in Detroit in 1980.

Genesis and lyrics

With this song, Bruce Springsteen returns to the main theme of *The River*: only life as a couple allows you to overcome the misfortunes and failures of life. In an interview with Neil Strauss of *Guitar World* (October 1995), the songwriter said: "I didn't write about relationships, probably because I didn't know much about 'em and I wasn't very good at 'em, and also it was a subject in pop music that had been written about so much and I wasn't interested in writing just your classic sort of pop love songs."[83]

Thus, with *I Wanna Marry You* he is taking the plunge; it is a story that came to him in a dream. For some time, the narrator has been watching a young woman walking down the street pushing a pram. She never smiles, never speaks—because she is bringing up her two children alone. He wants to help her, and declares that he is even prepared to marry her: "But a time comes when two people should think of these things/Having a home and a family/Facing up to their responsibilities," Springsteen sings, even though before he died the narrator's father had said to him that "true true love was just a lie."

Production

I Wanna Marry You is a fine ballad, in the same vein as songs like Ben E King's *Spanish Harlem* and the Drifters' *Save the Last Dance for Me*. After a series of supercharged rock sounds, the Boss calms things down to create a more tender ambience. From the introduction, the tone is set: the guitars are predominantly acoustics—although an electric guitar tinges the atmosphere with a strong tremolo (from the left). Max Weinberg plays cross-stick, the bass guitar is lyrical, the piano sentimental, the organ romantic, and Clemons' maracas accentuate the song's Hispanic flavor. Springsteen's strength lies in his capacity to retain credibility when playing totally different genres. When he sings the lead vocals, the emotional power he unleashes is surprising, as Steve Van Zandt remarked: "He's one of the greatest white soul singers of all time. *I Wanna Marry You* or *Fade Away* or *Drive All Night*—those real real classic soul songs that he's so great at."[80] Backing vocals come to his support from the fourth verse (at 1'30), before a highly inspired saxophone solo ends the song, supported by those same ethereal, Roy Orbison-like backing vocals (at 2'41).

THE RIVER

Bruce Springsteen / 4'59

Musicians

Bruce Springsteen: vocals, guitars, harmonica
Steve Van Zandt: guitars, vocal harmonies
Clarence Clemons: tambourine
Roy Bittan: piano
Danny Federici: organ
Garry Tallent: bass guitar
Max Weinberg: drums

Recording

The Power Station, 441 West 53rd St, New York: 26 and 29 August 1979; 21 January, 12 and 24 April 1980

Technical team

Producers: Bruce Springsteen, Jon Landau, Steve Van Zandt
Recording engineer: Neil Dorfsman
Assistant recording engineers: Jeff Hendrickson, Garry Rindfuss, Dana Bisbee, Raymond Willhard, James Farber
Mixing: Chuck Plotkin, Toby Scott

1980

Founder of the honky-tonk style, Hank Williams composed *My Bucket's Got a Hole in It,* which influenced Bruce Springsteen for *The River.*

Genesis and lyrics

In his autobiography, Bruce Springsteen reveals that he composed *The River* in a New York hotel room after singing *My Bucket's Got a Hole in It* by the country-music pioneer Hank Williams. He says, "I drove home to New Jersey and sat at a small oak table in my bedroom watching the dawn sky draw blue out of black and I imagined my story. It was just a guy in a bar talking to the stranger on the next stool."[1] In a way, this is an Edward Hopper painting set to music...

With the song *The River*, the poet returns to the role of an observer of late-1970s America: "I come from down in the valley where mister when you're young/They bring you up to do like your daddy done." What is he saying? Quite clearly it is that, for poor people in rural America, it is impossible to escape a predetermined destiny. Especially as the song's two characters, the narrator and Mary, met when they were 17 and immediately became parents. The young father has had to find work on a building site, but, as he explains: "lately there ain't been much work on account of the economy." He thinks back to his past with a touch of nostalgia and sadness; his memories "haunt [him] like a curse." The narrator asks himself: "Is a dream a lie if it don't come true"? The image speaks for itself: not so long ago, the river was a place of pleasure, somewhere to escape day-to-day reality; today, that river has dried up. These words ring all the more true, because Springsteen was inspired to write them by the experience of his sister and his brother-in-law, who, a victim of the recession, had lost his job. When Springsteen's sister first heard him perform the song at a concert, she came backstage and gave him a hug, saying that it had encapsulated her life. In his autobiography, the songwriter explains that he wrote *The River* in honor of his sister and brother-in-law.

Strangely, this superb song was not released as a single in the United States. It was, however, in Europe and Australia—with *Independence Day*, *Ramrod*, or *I'm a Rocker* on the B-side, depending on the country in which it was released. It reached No.35 in the UK, but No.5 in Norway and No.6 in Denmark. *The River* is a key song in the world of Bruce Springsteen, and the song that would ultimately lead to *Nebraska*.

Production

Although Springsteen asserted that he was inspired by Hank Williams' *My Bucket's Got a Hole in It*, only the song's words,

Pages 164–165 The Boss, the "Big Man," and "Little Steven" at the Joe Luis Arena, in Detroit, August 1981, during the River Tour.

Bruce Springsteen at the No Nukes concert in Madison Square Garden in September 1979, during which he performed *The River*.

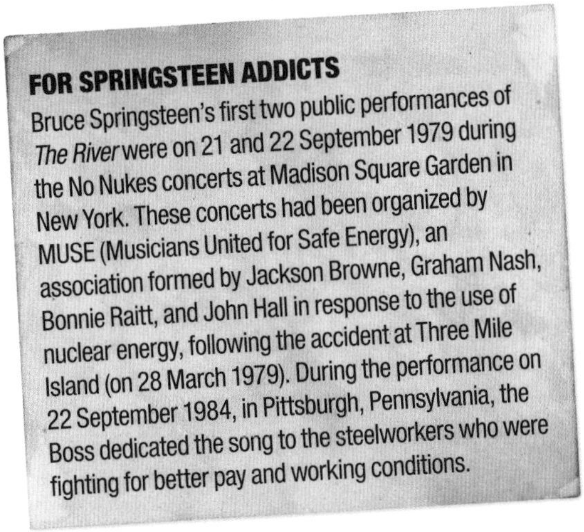

FOR SPRINGSTEEN ADDICTS

Bruce Springsteen's first two public performances of *The River* were on 21 and 22 September 1979 during the No Nukes concerts at Madison Square Garden in New York. These concerts had been organized by MUSE (Musicians United for Safe Energy), an association formed by Jackson Browne, Graham Nash, Bonnie Raitt, and John Hall in response to the use of nuclear energy, following the accident at Three Mile Island (on 28 March 1979). During the performance on 22 September 1984, in Pittsburgh, Pennsylvania, the Boss dedicated the song to the steelworkers who were fighting for better pay and working conditions.

"Well, I went upon the mountain, I looked down in the sea" actually gave him the creative spark, as he explains in his autobiography. For neither the song's music, nor its other lyrics, bear any relation to *The River*, apart from the fact that both musicians play a 12-string acoustic guitar. Indeed, it is on this instrument (a 1978 Ovation 1618 Glen Campbell?) that the songwriter starts the piece, while playing a superb (overdubbed) harmonica part, highly lyrical and melancholy, its notes imbued with sadness. He then begins to sing. And, as always, the power of his performance commands respect. Toby Scott, who was in charge of mixing, remembers being completely overwhelmed on hearing it: "I was sitting there, actually sobbing away at the console. And I was thinking, 'Geez, how am I going to do this?' Finally, it was, 'I've got to get on with the job at hand,' and I went on and mixed it. But even then, a couple of days later when I would listen back, I'd be sobbing again...it really was the most emotional song."[78]

It is true that *The River* is an exceptional piece, delivered by a magnificent writer, composer, and performer, with a no less talented group of musicians. Whether it is Roy Bittan's piano, Danny Federici's organ, the rhythm section of Max Weinberg and Garry Tallent, Clarence Clemons's tambourine, the acoustic guitar parts, or Steve Van Zandt's vocal harmonies, all contribute to making this piece poignant and unique.

Neil Dorfsman explained that he recorded several versions of *The River*, with different tempi or with more rock-like arrangements. He described how, for the album, each song required between 20 and 40 takes, sometimes as many as 50. "We had over 400 reels of tape. But I do remember, when we first heard *The River*, I looked at my assistant and went, 'Wow, this is great.' It had a special vibe and everybody—at least everybody at my end, in the control room—knew it was a special tune when we cut it."[78]

Before being given the title *The River*, the last song on the second side of the original LP was called *Oh Angelyne*. Unlike most of the other songs on the album, the songwriter struggled before completing it: "*The River* took a while. I had the verses, I never had any chorus, and I didn't have no title for a long time."[10] But the quality of the result reflects this toil, as *The River* is certainly one of the high points of the album, if not of Springsteen's career.

POINT BLANK

Bruce Springsteen / 6'05

Musicians

Bruce Springsteen: vocals, guitars
Steve Van Zandt: guitars, vocal harmonies
Clarence Clemons: triangle, güiro
Roy Bittan: piano
Danny Federici: organ
Garry Tallent: bass guitar
Max Weinberg: drums

Recording

The Power Station, 441 West 53rd St, New York: 23 and 25 August 1979 (?); 16 February 1980

Technical team

Producers: Bruce Springsteen, Jon Landau, Steve Van Zandt
Recording engineer: Neil Dorfsman
Assistant recording engineers: Jeff Hendrickson, Garry Rindfuss, Dana Bisbee, Raymond Willhard, James Farber
Mixing: Chuck Plotkin, Toby Scott

1980

ROMEO AND SPRINGSTEEN

This was the third time the Boss referenced the character of Romeo in his songs: the first was in *Incident on 57th Street* and the second in *Fire*.

Genesis and lyrics

Bruce Springsteen composed *Point Blank* just before the release of the album *Darkness on the Edge of Town*, in all probability between 29 and 31 May 1978, during the sound check at one of the three concerts he performed at the Boston Music Hall in Massachusetts. The lyrics were written later, during the Darkness Tour. The song was finally performed live for the first time on 7 July, at The Roxy Theatre in West Hollywood, with slightly different lyrics and featuring a slightly differently performance from the version on the album. Once again, the songwriter borrowed a title from a classic Hollywood movie—*Point Blank*, a thriller by John Boorman starring Lee Marvin and Angie Dickinson. The narrator tells a sad love story, which is full of pathos because the woman he loves is about to die. An early version of the lyrics explicitly states that the dying young woman is—or has been—a junkie. In the version recorded for *The River*, the songwriter leaves some lingering doubt: "You wake up and you're dying, you don't even know what from," he sings in the first verse.

One thing is certain: the narrator expresses profound sadness and pained disappointment, as he thinks back to the past and observes the wrecked life of his beloved: "And I was gonna be your Romeo, you were gonna be my Juliet." Now, though, she can count only on "that welfare check" and there are also those "little white lies you tell to ease the pain." He has even dreamed they could be together once again, but that kind of dream never comes true—or very rarely. "Well I saw you last night down on the avenue [...] You didn't answer when I called out your name." End of story!

Production

The early versions of *Point Blank* were in a rather rock vein, with guitar and glockenspiel solos. The lyrics, harmonies, and melody were markedly different. But Springsteen, an assiduous writer and composer, always in search of perfection, reworked the piece to come up with this magnificent ballad, which opens the double vinyl album's third side. In fact, he finished the song only two weeks before the end of recording at The Power Station, having rewritten the last two verses—probably the most important in the song—and inserted a bridge, which was eventually scrapped during mixing.

Point Blank is one of the darkest and saddest songs Bruce Springsteen ever wrote. He performed it in Oslo, Norway, on 28 July 2016.

From the introduction, the dense, dark, and melancholy atmosphere created by the song is striking. Roy Bittan plays a superb, typically lyrical, piano part. He is accompanied by a strummed acoustic guitar and arpeggiated chords on an electric guitar (on the left). On the rhythm side, Max Weinberg's drumming is rather restrained and Garry Tallent's bass guitar is discreet and subtle, while Clarence Clemons provides percussion on the triangle and güiro (the latter overdubbed). In the second part of the introduction, there is a countermelody, in all probability played on the Fender Telecaster-Esquire by the Boss, which is drowned in a profound reverb, Shadows-style (from 0'19).

Springsteen delivers a vocal performance that is striking and simply superb. He sings with astonishing conviction and a real sense of drama. Although there are always echoes of Van Morrison in the way he tells the story—and also of the country musician George Jones, to whom he was listening at the time—his emotional power is unique. We should also do justice to the E Street Band, which provides first-class support, with each musician putting himself at Springsteen's service to magnify his performance. Another masterstroke of the song is Danny Federici's Hammond B-3 organ. It comes in only from the first chorus (at 1'08) and Federici plays a short solo at the end of the following chorus (at 3'02). The sound of his instrument, which is enhanced by an ample, very pronounced reverb, has a hypnotic quality that is largely due to the excellent recording made by Neil Dorfsman. To do this, Dorfsman recorded his Leslie speaker in stereo with two Shure SM57 mics and one Neumann U47 mic. Finally, we must emphasize the excellent vocal harmonies provided by Steve Van Zandt, whose voice and high timbre effectively counterbalance and complement Springsteen's deeper singing—a little like Keith Richards with Mick Jagger.

For Springsteen Addicts

Bruce Springsteen repeats several lines from *Point Blank* in another song, *Party Lights*, which features on the box set *The Ties That Bind: The River Collection* (2015).

CADILLAC RANCH

Bruce Springsteen / 3'02

For Springsteen Addicts

The celebrities Bruce Springsteen mentions in *Cadillac Ranch* are interchangeable, depending on where he is performing. In Australia, he mentioned...Mad Max!

Musicians

Bruce Springsteen: vocals, guitars
Steve Van Zandt: guitars, vocal harmonies, and backing vocals
Clarence Clemons: saxophone, backing vocals
Roy Bittan: piano, backing vocals
Danny Federici: organ
Garry Tallent: bass guitar
Max Weinberg: drums

Recording

The Power Station, 441 West 53rd St, New York: 16 February, 9, 15, and 17 March, 9 and 26 April 1980

Technical team

Producers: Bruce Springsteen, Jon Landau, Steve Van Zandt
Recording engineer: Neil Dorfsman
Assistant recording engineers: Jeff Hendrickson, Garry Rindfuss, Dana Blsbee, Raymond Willhard, James Farber
Mixing: Chuck Plotkin, Toby Scott

1980

The famous buried Cadillacs at Cadillac Ranch in Amarillo, Texas, on Route 66, inspired Springsteen's song.

Genesis and lyrics

With a good old rock 'n' roll rhythm, here Bruce Springsteen truly worships the famous make of car from Detroit—this Cadillac "Tearing up the highway like a big old dinosaur"—while at the same time joyfully thumbing his nose at death. The title of this song references a creation by the architects Chip Lord, Hudson Marquez, and Douglas Michels (the Ant Farm practice): a spectacular line of ten old Cadillacs planted in the ground alongside Route 66 at Amarillo, northern Texas.

Cadillac Ranch is therefore a cemetery, and it is indeed about the Grim Reaper that the songwriter is singing here—no doubt to exorcize his fear. It is a nice metaphor, anyway. "Well buddy when I die throw my body in the back/Drive me to the junkyard in my Cadillac," he sings. And he mentions James Dean, who drives a 1949 Mercury (not a Cadillac) in the movie *Rebel Without a Cause*; Junior Johnson, a famous NASCAR driver of the 1950s; and the actor Burt Reynolds, who drives a Pontiac Trans Am in the movie *Smokey and the Bandit (1977)*.

Production

In writing *Cadillac Ranch*, Springsteen was trying to recreate the energy of bars where live music is performed—magical places that he used to frequent when first starting out. The song begins with a rather basic, but very effective, drum pattern by Max Weinberg, which is amplified by the studio's live reverberation. After two bars, the Boss's Telecaster-Esquire joins Weinberg, performing a riff in the great rock tradition. Then Roy Bittan announces, with furious glissandi on his keyboard, the arrival of the whole E Street Band (at 0'17). The band immediately delivers a blazing power, which is doubtless close to what they produce in concert—indeed, this was one of Springsteen's main concerns, as with this album he wanted finally to record that on-stage dimension which seemed to him to be missing from his first four albums. Each musician plays with force: Danny Federici on his Farfisa Combo Compact organ and Garry Tallent on his black Music Man StingRay, which he strikes with such vigor that you can hear the strings slapping against the pickups!

Cadillac Ranch is a very honest piece of rock, with a certain Chuck Berry side to it. Springsteen produces perfect lead vocals, and Clarence Clemons a solo at the end of the piece that is equally luminous.

I'M A ROCKER

Bruce Springsteen / 3'34

Musicians

Bruce Springsteen: vocals, guitars
Steve Van Zandt: guitars, backing vocals
Clarence Clemons: saxophone, backing vocals
Roy Bittan: piano, organ, backing vocals
Garry Tallent: bass guitar
Max Weinberg: drums
The band: handclaps

Recording

The Power Station, 441 West 53rd St, New York: Late 1979; early 1980

Technical team

Producers: Bruce Springsteen, Jon Landau, Steve Van Zandt
Recording engineer: Neil Dorfsman
Assistant recording engineers: Jeff Hendrickson, Garry Rindfuss, Dana Bisbee, Raymond Willhard, James Farber
Mixing: Chuck Plotkin, Toby Scott

Before Springsteen, Chuck Berry had recorded a song called *I'm a Rocker* for his 1970 album *Back Home*, on the occasion of his return to Chess Records. However, that has nothing in common with the song performed by the Boss. In France, Eddy Mitchell recorded a very good cover of the version by Berry in 1974, with the title *C'est un Rockeur* ("He's a Rocker").

Genesis and lyrics

Is this song a nod, or a reply, to *Sheena Is a Punk Rocker*, which the Ramones recorded in 1977? Whichever it is, *I'm a Rocker* has the strong flavor of supercharged rock, a sort of Eddie Cochran-style rock 'n' roll, mixed with punk. As for the lyrics, like those of the Ramones, they have a comic-book quality—no doubt the songwriter devoured such books as an adolescent. Thus, the narrator claims to possess a watch that is "a one and only," as used by agent 007, and to drive a Batmobile. A hardcore rocker, he even persuades a girl who is suffering heartache not to call James Bond or Secret Agent Man—most certainly a reference to John Drake from the British TV series *Danger Man Danger* (1960–1962), broadcast in the United States with the title *Secret Agent*—because he claims that he is better than them...and all the rest. Indeed, the girl is "hanging from a cliff" or "tied to the tracks," when "Columbo split and you can't find Kojak." He even claims that he can free her heart from "some jerk who was tall, dark and handsome" who has taken her hostage.

Production

In some takes for the song, Springsteen sang: "She's a rocker," before correcting himself at the last moment. But why record such a song, if not to dispel an image of himself that was doubtless too severe and serious, or to inject more imagination after the austere *Darkness on the Edge of Town*? However, if you listen to the song, you realize that it is not only an amusing parody, but also a well-made piece of rock music, with a top-class vocal performance—Springsteen pushes his voice to breaking point to achieve a true feat (listen at 0'40 or 1'16).

I'm a Rocker is based on a rhythm that was inspired, in all likelihood, by *Any Way You Want It* (released in 1964), a song by the British band Dave Clark Five, which Springsteen liked very much. It has the same rock vibe and rhythmic pulse; features a saxophone (baritone in Clarence Clemons's case); and has the same slapback echo for the vocals! And, as God moves in mysterious ways, *Any Way You Want It* was the very last cover played by the Ramones in the last concert of their career, performed on 6 August 1996 at the Palace in LA.

It is worth noting that for this song the Farfisa organ is played by Roy Bittan, not Danny Federici.

I'm a Rocker is without a doubt one of the best rock songs on *The River*.

For Springsteen Addicts

In an interview with *Rolling Stone* (17 March 2008) Steve Van Zandt revealed that *Fade Away* was one of his favorite Bruce Springsteen songs. Yet it has very rarely been performed live: about 60 times since the concert at the Los Angeles Memorial Sports Arena on 1 November 1980.

FADE AWAY

Bruce Springsteen / 4'40

Musicians
Bruce Springsteen: vocals, guitars
Steve Van Zandt: guitars, vocal harmonies
Clarence Clemons: tambourine, shaker
Roy Bittan: piano
Danny Federici: organ
Garry Tallent: bass guitar
Max Weinberg: drums

Recording
The Power Station, 441 West 53rd St, New York: 9, 15, 16, and 17 March, 9 and 29 April 1980

Technical team
Producers: Bruce Springsteen, Jon Landau, Steve Van Zandt
Recording engineer: Neil Dorfsman
Assistant recording engineers: Jeff Hendrickson, Garry Rindfuss, Dana Bisbee, Raymond Willhard, James Farber
Mixing: Chuck Plotkin, Toby Scott

1980

Bruce Springsteen and Steve Van Zandt. *Fade Away* has a soul feel that suits them perfectly.

Genesis and lyrics

Fade Away is a fairly traditional love song. The narrator expresses all the sadness he feels after his ex-girlfriend falls in love with another man. She can tell him as much as she likes how the time is long gone when all was well between them—he refuses to give up this lost love, to be this "other ghost out on the street to whom you stop/And politely speak." He knows that without her, he will disappear...

The lyrics of *Fade Away* are certainly not the most original Bruce Springsteen ever wrote. The song's interest lies in its musical atmosphere. Here, Springsteen has composed a pop soul song, and sings like Elvis Costello. It is doubtless for this reason that he and Columbia decided to make *Fade Away* the A-side of the second single from *The River* (with *Be True* on the B-side). This single was released in February 1981, but only in North America, Australia, and New Zealand. In the US, it reached No.20 in the *Billboard* pop charts.

Production

A soul atmosphere dominates in *Fade Away*. There are hints of various influences, from Otis Redding to Wilson Pickett, but also, in a more pop-rock register, of the Stones and songs such as *Time Is on My Side* (1964).

Danny Federici's organ gives the song its tone color. He has learned from his seniors, and with his Hammond B-3 and Leslie speaker gives the song that essential gospel touch. Several guitars are heard: two acoustics (center and right) and an electric with a strong tremolo (left). Roy Bittan plays a rather syncopated piano part (right); Clarence Clemons some maybe under-mixed percussion (tambourine and shaker); Garry Tallent a rhythmic, harmonic bass guitar; and Max Weinberg chiefly cross-stick drumming.

Springsteen's vocals are probably not the most successful on the album. His performance sometimes verges on being out of tune (listen to the second sentence of the first verse at 0'27, or at 3'39). It is a shame, especially as he has the ideal voice for this musical style: "He's one of the greatest white soul singers of all time,"[80] as Steve Van Zandt never tired of reminding people. But he would do the song justice in concert, producing a perfect performance on 26 February 2014 at the Brisbane Entertainment Center, in Australia, during the High Hopes Tour. He said that he was playing *Fade Away* "for Steve."

STOLEN CAR

Bruce Springsteen / 3'53

> **COVER**
> Elliott Murphy made an excellent cover of *Stolen Car*, with just an acoustic guitar and a harmonica, on the album *One Step Up/Two Steps Back: The Songs of Bruce Springsteen*, which was released in 1997.

Musicians
Bruce Springsteen: vocals, guitar
Roy Bittan: piano
Danny Federici: organ
Garry Tallent: bass guitar
Max Weinberg: drums

Recording
The Power Station, 441 West 53rd St, New York: 21 January, 20 February, 1 and 9 April, 9 May 1980

Technical team
Producers: Bruce Springsteen, Jon Landau, Steve Van Zandt
Recording engineer: Neil Dorfsman
Assistant recording engineers: Jeff Hendrickson, Garry Rindfuss, Dana Bisbee, Raymond Willhard, James Farber
Mixing: Chuck Plotkin, Toby Scott

Stolen Car is one of the great successes of the double album *The River*, with an effective but subtle bass line from Garry Tallent (seen here in Norway in 2016).

Genesis and lyrics

In his book *Songs*, Bruce Springsteen writes: "*Stolen Car* was the predecessor for a good deal of the music I'd be writing in the future. It was inner-directed, psychological; this was the character whose progress I'd soon be following on *Tunnel of Love*. He was the archetype for the male role in my later songs about men and women."[6] The character in question describes his marriage and very peaceful life: "In a little house out on the edge of town," but "Then little by little we drifted from each other's heart." The young woman tells him she has reread the letters he wrote to her, love letters that "made her feel one hundred years old."

Will the husband return to his wife's side? It is far from certain. It would seem that he has found the spice of life in driving a stolen car and even more in the exciting idea of being arrested by the police. Better to live briefly, but intensely, than to live as a good family man: that could be the central idea of this song. As Bruce Springsteen explains in his autobiography: "That song's character, drifting through the night, is the first to face the angels and devils that will drive him toward his love and keep him from ever reaching her."[1] He goes on to explain that this character also gives voice to his own personal conflicts.

Production

There are several recordings of *Stolen Car*; the two main ones are on *The Ties That Bind: The River Collection* box set (2015) and the *Tracks* box set (1998). The former is the version of *The River* made by Bob Clearmountain in June 1979, while the second (recorded on 26 July 1979 and almost identical) has been mixed differently. Both are in a more or less country style, similar to that of *Point Blank* or *The River*. The whole band is present, including Danny Federici on the accordion. However, although the early versions are superb, they possess neither the power nor the intensity of the definitive version. Indeed, Springsteen profoundly revised the arrangement and shortened his lyrics, and then delivers an extraordinary song with a dense, dreamlike atmosphere, filled with a superb, very ample reverb, which is similar to the sort of atmosphere created by the producer Daniel Lanois. He accompanies himself only on his Fender Telecaster-Esquire, supported by Roy Bittan's piano, Max Weinberg's tom-toms, and Garry Tallent's bass guitar (from 1'42), followed by Federici's organ (from 2'58). The result is simply dazzling.

1980

Springsteen with
Clarence Clemons,
Garry Tallent, and
"Miami Steve" onstage
at the Spectrum,
Philadelphia, on
8 December 1980.
Seized with doubt?

RAMROD

Bruce Springsteen / 4'04

Bruce Springsteen often turns to movies to come up with titles for his songs. Was this the case with *Ramrod*, whose title is also that of a 1947 movie directed by André De Toth, which was based on a novel by Luke Short (published in 1943)?

Musicians
Bruce Springsteen: vocals, guitars
Steve Van Zandt: guitars, vocal harmonies
Clarence Clemons: saxophone, tambourine
Roy Bittan: piano
Danny Federici: organ
Garry Tallent: bass guitar
Max Weinberg: drums
The band: handclaps

Recording
The Power Station, 441 West 53rd St, New York: 12 June, 27 August, 5 September 1979; 4 and 19 April 1980

Technical team
Producers: Bruce Springsteen, Jon Landau, Steve Van Zandt
Recording engineer: Neil Dorfsman
Assistant recording engineers: Jeff Hendrickson, Garry Rindfuss, Dana Bisbee, Raymond Willhard, James Farber
Mixing: Chuck Plotkin, Toby Scott

1980

The E Street Band performs at Wembley on 29 May 1981. *Ramrod* is on the setlist.

Genesis and lyrics

During the interview with Dave Marsh of *Musician* magazine, Bruce Springsteen explained *Ramrod*: "Well, it's so anachronistic, you know. The character—it's impossible, what he wants to do. One of the ideas of it, when I wrote it, it was sort of like a partner to *Cadillac Ranch* and a few things, it's got that old big engine sound. That song is a goddam gas guzzler [laughing]. And that was the sound I wanted, that big, rumbling, big engine sound. And this guy, he's there, but he's really not there no more."[65]

In fact, the central character of *Ramrod* is none other than Bruce Springsteen himself, reminiscing about his adolescence in New Jersey. The song's main character is thinking about when he would climb to the top of a hill to glimpse the lights of New York in the distance and walk with his girlfriend (he had promised to marry her in the little chapel). The years of his youth are gone, but the passions of those years endure—starting with a passion for his car: a high-performance 1932 Ford with a Hemi engine and four gears. An automobile that allows him to guarantee his girlfriend a good time.

Production

Ramrod, which opens the last side of the double album, is a muscular rock number, conventional in character and construction. Originally destined for *Darkness on the Edge of Town*, it had no chance of featuring on the Boss's samurai album.

The Boss himself starts the song, with a Chuck Berry-style riff played on his Telecaster-Esquire. The band then plunges in with a heavy beat, the bass guitar and drums strongly supporting the groove. Danny Federici's Farfisa organ makes a distinct contrast to the saturated guitar tone, as well as to Clarence Clemons's tenor sax, which roars in the mass of sound. Springsteen has no difficulty in performing this rather traditional rock song, accompanied by appropriate vocal harmonies from the piercing voice of Miami Steve (from 1'39). The Boss gets Clemons's solo going by cheerfully calling out "Big Man!" (at 1'59), leaving him to deliver some fine musical phrases on the saxophone, supported by clapping from his fellow band members.

It would appear that the master tape was speeded up at the time of mixing, as the live versions of *Ramrod* are a semitone lower than the one on the album.

THE PRICE YOU PAY

Bruce Springsteen / 5'27

COVER

The singer and guitarist Emmylou Harris, who has always appreciated Bruce Springsteen's musical approach, recorded a very beautiful version of *The Price You Pay* during the sessions for the album *Cimarron* (1981).

Musicians

Bruce Springsteen: vocals, guitars, harmonica
Steve Van Zandt: guitars, vocal harmonies (?)
Clarence Clemons: tambourine
Roy Bittan: piano
Danny Federici: organ, accordion
Garry Tallent: bass guitar
Max Weinberg: drums

Recording

The Power Station, 441 West 53rd St, New York: 15, 18, 19, and 21 June 1979; 4 April 1980

Technical team

Producers: Bruce Springsteen, Jon Landau, Steve Van Zandt
Recording engineer: Neil Dorfsman
Assistant recording engineers: Jeff Hendrickson, Garry Rindfuss, Dana Bisbee, Raymond Willhard, James Farber
Mixing: Chuck Plotkin, Toby Scott

Singer Emmylou Harris added *The Price You Pay* to her repertoire while recording her album *Cimarron*, which came out in 1981.

Genesis and lyrics

The Price You Pay is a highly poetic evocation of one of the chapters of the Old Testament: "Little girl down on the strand with that pretty little baby in your hands/Do you remember the story of the promised land/How he crossed the desert sands," Bruce Springsteen sings in the third verse.

The songwriter is referring to Moses, to whom God gave the mission of freeing the Israelites from the Egyptian yoke and taking them to Canaan, the Promised Land. Having grumbled about Moses' authority, and even that of God, and gone so far as to miss their condition of slavery in Egypt and to worship an idol in the form of a golden calf, the Israelites were condemned to wander in the wilderness for 40 years. That was the price to be paid for challenging God's supreme mission.

Beyond this reference to the Old Testament, doubtless Bruce Springsteen is emphasizing the fact that every decision has consequences and, for this reason, it is important to follow the path one believes to be right. The desert is perhaps a symbol of solitude, and the open skies of transcendence, of going beyond the self.

Production

The Price You Pay is a well-made rock ballad with a moderate tempo, whose arrangement chiefly hinges on a multiplicity of guitars, especially 12-string electrics and acoustics. Springsteen performed it using a 12-string Custom Telecaster Sunburst on the River Tour in 2016.

Max Weinberg opens the song with a descending sequence on the tom-toms, generously supplemented with reverb. The introduction is energetic, with Roy Bittan's piano underlying the melody played on the Fender Electric XII. Clarence Clemons marks the tempo with his tambourine, while the duo of Garry Tallent and Max Weinberg supplies the main groove. On the vocals side, it seems that the Boss doubles himself in the harmonies in place of Miami Steve—unlike in the version mixed by Bob Clearmountain in October 1979. He also plays the song's only solo on the harmonica (at 2'46). In the fourth verse, Danny Federici returns to his accordion, together with his organ (from 3'19).

It is worth noting that the third verse of the Clearmountain version was different to the one that features on the double album; that is how the Boss sang it on the River Tour in 1980.

DRIVE ALL NIGHT

Bruce Springsteen / 8'26

Musicians

Bruce Springsteen: vocals, guitars, piano
Steve Van Zandt: backing vocals
Clarence Clemons: saxophone
Roy Bittan: organ, synthesizer (?)
Danny Federici: glockenspiel (?), synthesizer (?)
Garry Tallent: bass guitar
Max Weinberg: drums

Recording

Atlantic Studios 1841 Broadway, New York: 16 June 1977
The Record Plant, 321 West 44th St, New York: 24 August 1977
The Power Station, 441 West 53rd St, New York: 24 February, 8 and 16 March, 10 April 1980

Technical team

Producers: Bruce Springsteen, Jon Landau, Steve Van Zandt
Recording engineer: Jimmy Iovine
Assistant recording engineers: Jeff Hendrickson, Garry Rindfuss, Dana Bisbee, Raymond Willhard, James Farber
Mixing: Chuck Plotkin, Toby Scott

1980

Jimmy Iovine, the recording engineer for *Drive All Night*, with Doug Morris, president of Universal Music Group.

Genesis and lyrics

Drive All Night was written at the time *Darkness on the Edge of Town* was being made. The song was dropped, however, perhaps because of its length, but more probably because of its musical atmosphere, which would have contrasted markedly with that of the other songs on the earlier album. Did Bruce Springsteen compose *Drive All Night* under the beneficial influence of Van Morrison's *Madame George* (on the 1968 album *Astral Weeks*)? It is not impossible.

Also, the words "There's machines and there's fire/Baby, waiting on the edge of town/Out there for hire/But, baby, they can't hurt us now" are almost the same as those of *Candy's Boy* (on *The Promise*): "Well, there's machines and there's fire/Waiting for us on the edge of town/And there's some roughboys for hire/And they're waiting to blow me and Candy down/It's all right 'cause they can't touch us now."

Driven by a dark romanticism, in *Drive All Night* Springsteen describes all the pain felt by a man whose beloved has left him. Perhaps she has passed away, as the narrator invokes God and mentions fallen angels. Perhaps she has decided to go and live a different life. Without a doubt, what he wants more than anything is to hold her tight, sleep in her arms again, drive all night to taste her tender charm, and defeat the elements—wind, rain, snow—for her: in short, to brave all dangers, those machines and fire waiting on the edge of town...

Production

It was in September 1976, at the start of the Lawsuit Tour, that the first ideas which would eventually produce *Drive All Night* began to take shape. The band was playing an interlude, which they introduced at the end of *Backstreets* (see *Born to Run*, page 84), dubbed the *Sad Eyes Interlude* (nothing to do with the outtake included on the *Tracks* box set released in 1998). As one concert followed another, this developed into the basis for *Drive All Night*, which was first performed live on 31 December 1977 at the Capitol Theatre, in Passaic, New Jersey.

Yet the piece had been recorded some months earlier at Atlantic Studios and the Record Plant in New York, between 16 June and 24 August 1977, because it was initially destined for the album *Darkness on the Edge of Town*, as explained above. Jimmy Iovine was the recording engineer, and in early 1980 at The Power Station some overdubs of Springsteen's

For Springsteen Addicts

Many musicians have composed their own *Drive All Night*, such as Elliott Murphy (on the 1977 album *Just a Story from America*). As for Roy Orbison, he missed the boat when he let Cyndi Lauper record *I Drove All Night* before he did. It was a song written for him by Billy Steinberg and Tom Kelly in 1987. Cyndi Lauper took it to No.6 in the charts in 1989; Orbison did not release it until 1992.

Bruce Springsteen and Clarence Clemons at the Oakland Coliseum on 28 October 1980. They'd only been performing *Drive All Night* for a few days.

voice were added to the backing track—which had been recorded in all likelihood at the Record Plant. The songwriter did not finish writing the definitive lyrics until just three weeks before the album was wrapped up, as he confirmed: "Those songs [*Point Blank* and *Drive All Night*] didn't exist, in the form that they're on the record, until the last few weeks we were in the studio."[10]

However, the main reason that led Springsteen to keep the recording made by Jimmy Iovine was the inability of the musicians to reproduce such a satisfactory basic track. Everyone was in favor of preserving the magic of the initial takes, recorded in 1977.

Drive All Night is essentially based on three instruments: Max Weinberg's drums, Garry Tallent's bass guitar, and the piano, played—an exception, this—by the Boss himself. The tempo is slow and the harmony simple (there are no more than three chords). The three musicians make a pattern, which becomes richer as the piece develops. First, Springsteen adds a second piano part (the instrument is not very well tuned...), in order to strengthen the first chorus (at 1'22). Then the sound of the glockenspiel against the background of the Farfisa organ chimes in to create an instrumental bridge: are these real instruments or a synthesizer (perhaps a Prophet-5 or Yamaha CS-80)? It is hard to say. Roy Bittan then records a Hammond B-3 organ in the second verse (at 2'10). An electric guitar strumming spread chords, colored with a chorus effect, enriches the following chorus (at 3'08).

There follows a fabulous saxophone solo by Clarence Clemons, probably one of the best on the album (at 3'40). To support it, the sound of strings is played on the synthesizer (it sounds like an ARP Solina); this is one of the first appearances of such an instrument on a recording by the E Street Band.

In the last part of the song, backing vocals answer the lead vocal, probably courtesy of Springsteen and Van Zandt (from 6'48). Boss's performance is deeply moving, technically stunning—with surprising vibrato and changes of texture (despite some tuning issues)—and filled with a feeling worthy of a great soul singer. Steve Van Zandt commented: "Unfortunately he takes that part of his talent for granted, which is criminal if you ask me because that part of his thing is my favorite part."[80]

WRECK ON THE HIGHWAY

Bruce Springsteen / 3'53

Musicians

Bruce Springsteen: vocals, guitars
Steve Van Zandt: guitars
Clarence Clemons: tambourine
Roy Bittan: piano
Danny Federici: organ
Garry Tallent: bass guitar
Max Weinberg: drums

Recording

The Power Station, 441 West 53rd St, New York: 10, 11, and 12 April 1980

Technical team

Producers: Bruce Springsteen, Jon Landau, Steve Van Zandt
Recording engineer: Neil Dorfsman
Assistant recording engineers: Jeff Hendrickson, Garry Rindfuss, Dana Bisbee, Raymond Willhard, James Farber
Mixing: Chuck Plotkin, Toby Scott

Poster for *Night Train to Memphis*, starring country-music singer Roy Acuff. He sang *Wreck on the Highway* in 1942.

Genesis and lyrics

Wreck on the Highway brings down the curtain on *The River* double album. Springsteen borrowed the song's title from the country-music singer and violinist Roy Acuff. "That was a funny song," he told journalist Dave Marsh. "I wrote that song real fast, in one night. We came in and played a few takes of it and that's pretty much what's on the album, I think. That's an automatic song, a song that you don't really think about, or work on."[65]

The central character in *Wreck on the Highway* is the same person who features in *Ramrod* and *Drive All Night*. As he returns home at the end of a day's work, he witnesses a car accident. A young man is lying by the side of the road; an ambulance arrives and takes him to hospital. The narrator's thoughts then turn to the victim's wife or girlfriend, and her distress when the police knock on her door. Sometimes, thinking back to the accident, he looks at his sleeping wife, climbs into bed, and holds her tight. "He realizes you have a limited number of opportunities to love someone, to do your work, to be a part of something, to parent your children, to do something good,"[1] the songwriter concludes in his autobiography.

"I just lay there awake in the middle of the night/Thinking 'bout the wreck on the highway." These are the last words of the song—and of *The River*.

Production

The last song on the album—and the last to be recorded—*Wreck on the Highway* is a country-style ballad that bears the imprint and color of the E Street Band. The tone of Danny Federici's organ is dominant. Springsteen and Van Zandt play very fine arpeggiated acoustic guitar parts, supported by the rather discreet presence of the piano and the delicate rhythm of the duo of Max Weinberg and Garry Tallent. It is worth noting the excellent recording of the bass guitar, especially in the song's coda (from 3'12). Neil Dorfsman has explained that he recorded it simultaneously direct (that is, via a DI box plugged into the recording console) and from the amplifier, using a Sennheiser MD421 or Neumann U47 microphone.

On the Thom Zimny documentary *The Ties That Bind* (2015), Springsteen says this song was written without anyone knowing what to do with it. He explains that, while the song was viewed as unimportant, it actually turned out to be a little gem which came along at just the right time to end the album.

Bruce Springsteen and Garry Tallent greet the audience at Sportpaleis Ahoy in Rotterdam on 29 April 1981, where the group performed *Wreck on the Highway*.

For Springsteen Addicts

Although *Wreck on the Highway* is also a song by Roy Acuff, which he recorded in 1942, it is, in fact, an adaptation of *Didn't Hear Nobody Pray*, written by Dorsey Dixon in 1937.

Danny Federici, the E Street Band keyboardist, during the last concert of The Rising Tour at Shea Stadium, New York, on 4 October 2003.

DANNY FEDERICI: A FRIENDLY PHANTOM

Born on 23 January 1950 in Flemington, New York, Daniel Paul Federici learned the accordion and classical piano before getting into jazz and blues. In the late 1960s, he began frequenting the clubs on the Jersey Shore. It was during this period that he met Bruce Springsteen. The two of them, along with Vini "Mad Dog" Lopez, formed the band Child, which was later renamed Steel Mill. They then went on to play together in other bands, notably Dr Zoom and the Sonic Boom and The Bruce Springsteen Band.

Danny Federici became part of the great E Street Band adventure from *The Wild, the Innocent, and The E Street Shuffle* (1973) onward, and, of course, the world tours until the second half of the 2000s. During the Magic Tour in 2007, the musician publicly announced that he was suffering from skin cancer (melanoma). He died from the disease on 17 April 2008 in New York, at the age of 58. His last appearance with the E Street Band was on 20 March 2008 in Indianapolis.

When Bruce Springsteen was inducted into the Rock & Roll Hall of Fame in 1999, he said that Danny Federici was "the most instinctive and natural musician that he had ever met."[104]

Federici also played with Gary U.S. Bonds, Graham Parker, Garland Jeffreys, and his old friends Steve Van Zandt in Little Steven and The Disciples of Soul. He recorded four solo albums: *Flemington* (1997), *Danny Federici* (2001), *Sweet* (2004), and *Out of a Dream* (2005).

His nickname, the Phantom, harked back to an incident at the start of his career, when he accidentally injured a police officer and had to go incognito for a while.

Max Weinberg became the drummer for the E Street Band in 1974. Twenty years later, he started his own group. Seen here at Castello Sforzesco, Milan, on 19 July 2019.

MAX WEINBERG: MIGHTY MAX, A DRUMMER WITH A HIGHLY NUANCED STYLE

Another musician from New Jersey—born in Newark, 13 April 1951—Max Weinberg learned to play drums at a very young age. Initially a member of the Jim Marino Band, he joined the E Street Band in 1974—at the same time as Roy Bittan—as the successor to Vini "Mad Dog" Lopez, and he took part in the *Born to Run* sessions (1975). This was the start of a long partnership.

In 1986 Max Weinberg was named best rock drummer by *Rolling Stone* magazine.

In 1993, Mighty Max formed his own band, The Max Weinberg 7, and began working with Conan O'Brien on the NBC show *Late Night with Conan O'Brien*, and then, from 2009, on the *Tonight Show with Conan O'Brien*, this time as leader of the Max Weinberg Big Band.

In the meantime, the drummer reported for duty when Bruce Springsteen reformed the E Street Band. He is behind the drums on *The Rising* (2002), and on all albums from *Magic* (2007) to *High Hopes* (2014).

Worth noting: in 2009, when his schedule didn't allow him to join the E Street Band, his son, Jay Weinberg, took his place on drums alongside the Boss.

SIDE B

HELD UP WITHOUT A GUN

Bruce Springsteen / 1'15

Single: *Hungry Heart/Held Up Without a Gun* **Reference:** Columbia Records – 11-11391 **Release date:** United States, 21 October 1980

Musicians
Bruce Springsteen: vocals, guitar
Steve Van Zandt: guitar, vocal harmonies
Clarence Clemons: saxophone
Roy Bittan: piano (?)
Danny Federici: organ
Garry Tallent: bass guitar
Max Weinberg: drums

Recording
The Power Station, 441 West 53rd St, New York: 23 February, 1, 9, 20, and 21 April 1980

Technical team
Producers: Bruce Springsteen, Jon Landau, Steve Van Zandt
Recording engineer: Neil Dorfsman
Assistant recording engineers: Jeff Hendrickson, Garry Rindfuss, Dana Bisbee, Raymond Willhard, James Farber
Mixing: Chuck Plotkin, Toby Scott

Genesis and lyrics

This song, which is very short—it lasts less than 80 seconds—dates from the sessions for *The River*. Like *Crush on You* and *Cadillac Ranch*, it is a true rock number, such as Bruce Springsteen and the E Street Band clearly took pleasure in playing throughout the double album. The story told in the song is in the same recreational vein, so to speak. The narrator stops at a gas station to fill up, and there is a dramatic turn of events: "Held up without a gun," Springsteen sings by way of a chorus. Then, "Some damn fool with a guitar walks in off the street/Ain't got nowhere to go, ain't got nothing to eat/Man with a cigar says 'sign here, son.'" Is this a nod to his manager, Mike Appel? Perhaps. And, again, Springsteen sings, "Held up without a gun." The songwriter provides the moral of the song at the very end: it is not as easy as people might think to "make a living" and "have a little fun."

Dropped from the tracklisting for *The River*, *Held Up Without a Gun* was chosen for the B-side of the single *Hungry Heart*. It also features on the maxi single *I'm Goin' Down*, released in 1985 (along with *Janey, Don't Lose Your Heart*), as well as on the box set *The Ties That Bind: The River Collection* (2015).

Production

The garage-band sound and the song's brevity clearly hint at the influence of the punk movement, as is the case with other songs. Max Weinberg launches *Held Up Without a Gun*, counting in the band at the top of his lungs and shouting off mic. The band launches at full throttle, with a ferocious, hearty, contagious energy. Weinberg beats his Ludwig drum kit like

Bruce Springsteen and Max Weinberg in Hamburg, on 21 June 2008. The drummer's role is paramount in *Held Up Without a Gun*, which came out on the B-side of *Hungry Heart* in 1980.

a lumberjack and Garry Tallent supports him with a white-hot bass guitar; Danny Federici literally smashes down the keys of his Farfisa organ; Clarence Clemons threatens to burst his carotid arteries on the saxophone (which is nevertheless almost inaudible); and the guitars of Steve Van Zandt and Springsteen produce enough voltage to light up a city the size of Los Angeles. On the vocals side, the two of them share the singing, "Miami Steve" always providing the harmonies; the Boss can be heard encouraging him in the introduction (at 0'07): *"Come on Steve!"* In rock numbers as punchy as this one, their duo never fails to bring to mind Jagger and Richards. *Held Up Without a Gun* is an excellent B-side, which might have found a place on *The River*.

For Springsteen Addicts

It was only at the last moment that Bruce Springsteen dropped *Held Up Without a Gun* from *The River*. As a result, Columbia Records had to reprint the sleeve of the record's first pressing.

SIDE B

BE TRUE

Bruce Springsteen / 3'39

Single: *Fade Away/Be True* **Reference:** Columbia Records – 11-11431 **Release date:** United States, 22 January 1981

Musicians
- **Bruce Springsteen:** vocals, guitars
- **Steve Van Zandt:** guitars
- **Clarence Clemons:** saxophone, tambourine
- **Roy Bittan:** piano
- **Danny Federici:** organ, glockenspiel
- **Garry Tallent:** bass guitar
- **Max Weinberg:** drums

Recording
- **The Power Station, 441 West 53rd St, New York:** 18 and 21 July 1979; 22 April 1980

Technical team
- **Producers:** Bruce Springsteen, Jon Landau, Steve Van Zandt
- **Recording engineer:** Neil Dorfsman
- **Assistant recording engineers:** Jeff Hendrickson, Garry Rindfuss, Dana Bisbee, Raymond Willhard, James Farber, Bill Sheniman
- **Mixing:** Chuck Plotkin, Toby Scott

Genesis and lyrics

In *Be True*, Bruce Springsteen addresses tender-hearted young girls who to a degree live vicariously through the lives of their idols. Thus, the heroine of this song has a scrapbook in which she has placed photographs of her favorite actors. Her (presumed) boyfriend asks her not to add his photograph to the collection: "Don't make us some little girl's dream that can't ever come true," he explains, because if that fails to materialize, the disappointment will be bitter.

There is more disappointment in the second verse: we learn that the heroine, who is addicted to romantic movies, returns home with her head full of movie heroes, but that these cannot take away her loneliness. "You deserve better than this, little girl," the narrator assures her. At the end of the song, it is clear that this romantic young woman cannot really experience what she sees on the screen and, her head "filled [...] with pretty lies," she is "gonna go broken-hearted looking for that happy ending." Therefore, the message of the song is that it is best to be sincere under all circumstances.

This version of *Be True* is on the B-side of *Fade Away*, and also features on the box set *Tracks* (1998). There is a second version on the box set *The Ties That Bind: The River Collection* (2015).

Production

The sleeve notes to *Tracks* state that *Be True* was recorded on 21 July 1979 at The Power Station. The Sony database has 18 July. Since there are two versions of this song, it is likely that one was recorded on 18 July and the other three days later. Be that as it may, the first version of *Be True* was entitled *Mary Lou*, and fea-

Be True, a rock song where the sound of the guitars blends in perfectly with the saxophone.

tured different music. *Be True* is a very fine rock number with a moderate tempo. The version on *Tracks* is more energetic, faster, and better mixed than on *The Ties That Bind: The River Collection*. The piece is rich in instrumentation, with several electric and acoustic guitar tracks, a Hammond B-3 organ, glockenspiel, bass guitar, and drums. Springsteen doubles himself in the vocal harmonies, while Clarence Clemons provides a tambourine part and a very fine saxophone motif in the coda.

For Springsteen Addicts

Be True was originally on the tracklisting for the album *The Ties That Bind* mixed by Bob Clearmountain in October 1979.

NEBRA

ALBUM

NEBRASKA

Nebraska • Atlantic City • Mansion on the Hill • Johnny 99 • Highway Patrolman • State Trooper • Used Cars • Open All Night • My Father's House • Reason to Believe

RELEASE DATE

United States: 30 September 1982

Reference: Columbia Records – TC 38358

No.3 in the *Billboard* charts, No.3 in the United Kingdom, Canada, and Norway, No.2 in Sweden, No.18 in France, No.7 in the Netherlands

With *Nebraska*, Bruce Springsteen made a definitive mark as one of the most brilliant songwriters of his generation.

For Springsteen Addicts

Mike Batlan and Doug Sutphin (a roadie) sued Bruce Springsteen in 1985, seeking $6 million in damages and interest after being relieved of their duties. When their claim was dismissed, they sued again, claiming payment from Springsteen for hundreds of thousands of unpaid hours (less the cost of the Boss's canoe, which they admitted to having unfortunately lost). Following a six-year legal battle, the dispute was resolved amicably.

A GUITAR, A PORTASTUDIO, BUT NO E STREET SHUFFLE

On 3 October 1980, a fortnight after *The River* went on sale, Bruce Springsteen and the E Street Band began a tour that took them all over North America, from Detroit to Los Angeles, Philadelphia, Montreal, and New York, as well as to several European cities, including Berlin, Munich, Paris, Lyon, Barcelona, and London. A total of 140 concerts spread over 11 months, performed in front of thousands of passionate fans...

As soon as the last concert—at the Riverfront Coliseum, in Cincinnati, on 14 September 1981—was over, Bruce Springsteen headed back to his native New Jersey. There, he rented a ranch of some 375 acres (150 hectares) by the shore of a lake in Colts Neck, after he had been evicted from his farm at Holmdel. This quiet village, set in protected countryside and moreover not far from the Jersey Shore, was a haven of peace for the songwriter, but also a place that was conducive to reflection—on himself, and on the America of yesterday and today. The *Nebraska* album began as an unconscious reflection on Springsteen's own childhood and its various mysteries. His childhood in New Jersey was about his parents, of course, but also about his grandparents' house, where he had lived until he was six years old. In short, a humble life lived in a modest neighborhood. Springsteen points out in his autobiography that the remains of this world were only ten miles or so from where he was living at the time and that the ghosts of *Nebraska* were inspired by his many explorations of the streets of the small town in which he'd grown up.

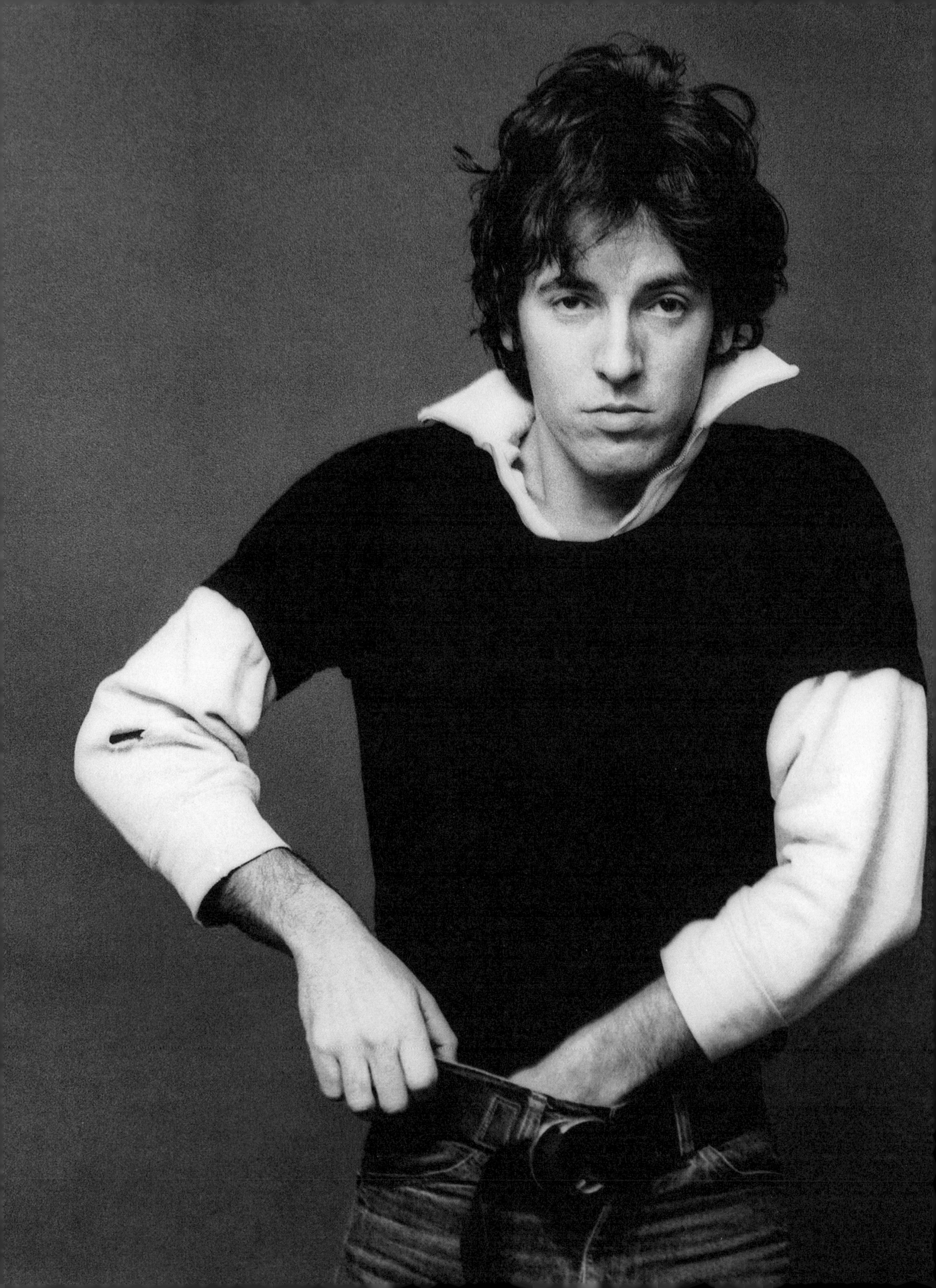

Writer Flannery O'Connor, whose vision of America (especially of the South) and Catholic faith, inspired Bruce Springsteen.

1982

For Springsteen Addicts

The works of Flannery O'Connor (1925–1964) had a significant influence on Bruce Springsteen's songwriting. Born in Savannah, Georgia, and a devout Catholic, she wrote two novels, including *Wise Blood*, and about 30 short stories in the Gothic genre—specifically, Southern Gothic, as her characters, whose behavior is extraordinary, inhabit the world of the American South.

Songs of quiet power

The songs Bruce Springsteen began to write in his ranch at Colts Neck could not, however, be confined to introspection, however profound. On the River Tour he had met Ron Kovic, a Vietnam veteran who had returned from the war paralysed and written his autobiography, *Born on the Fourth of July* (later adapted into a movie by Oliver Stone in 1989). The two became friends and, at Kovic's suggestion, Springsteen went to meet some Vietnam veterans in Venice, Los Angeles. "Some of the guys were homeless, had drug problems, were dealing with post-traumatic stress or life-changing physical injury,"[1] he writes in his autobiography *Born to Run*. This deeply moving meeting left a permanent mark on Springsteen and, inevitably, made him see America in a darker light than he had ever imagined—something that would be reflected in the various songs on *Nebraska*. The *romans noirs* of James M Cain and Jim Thompson, as well as the Gothic short stories of Flannery O'Connor, which he had either read or was reading, also played a part in the development of *Nebraska*. So, too, did his musical mentors, who had guided him along the difficult path of the songwriter—above all, Bob Dylan, Hank Williams, and the father of the American folk song, Woody Guthrie.

So, in the autumn of 1981, having started as a simple retreat from the demands of show business, Colts Neck was transformed into a veritable creative sanctuary. Springsteen recorded the songs he wrote there—the ones on *Nebraska*, but also some of those on *Born in the U.S.A.*, and a dozen more—on a simple, cassette-based Teac Tascam Portastudio 144, bought by his guitar technician, Mike Batlan. The idea was to record demos before playing them to the band, thus saving time in the studio. This is what happened, until Springsteen realized that the versions made with the band at The Hit Factory in New York, in April and May 1982, sounded much less authentic than the acoustic recordings he had made on his own, with guitar and harmonica in a room at Colts Neck. Having abandoned his plan for a double album—comprising an acoustic first disc, *Nebraska*, and a second, electric one, *Born in the U.S.A.*— Springsteen managed to overcome reluctance on the part of Columbia Records, who finally agreed to release the record as it was (after mastering by Chuck Plotkin at Atlantic Studios, nonetheless).

A minimalist, folk-inspired album, *Nebraska* marks a radical stylistic rethink by the songwriter, after the sympho-

Vietnam veteran Ron Kovic (in the wheelchair) at a peace protest in Los Angeles in 1972.

Folk singer Woody Guthrie displays his sticker on his guitar: "This machine kills fascists."

nies of *Born to Run*, the punk inspiration of *Darkness on the Edge of Town*, and the rock 'n' roll elation of *The River* (even though *Stolen Car*, *Wreck on the Highway*, and *The River* contain the seeds of the songs on this sixth album). It is a record of quiet power, sometimes of rebellion. Within this album, Springsteen alternates between fatalism and determination, singing of the dark everyday life of blue-collar and itinerant workers, and the suffering of America's rural poor. He also tells stories that had recently hit the headlines—of criminals of the worst kind, or losers at the hands of the modern world who had fallen into a life of crime through weakness or paranoia. Inevitably, this brings to mind Bob Dylan in the 1960s, and even Johnny Cash, but also Jack Kcrouac's *On the Road*, the book that was emblematic of the Beat Generation and counterculture. Without a doubt, the ten songs on *Nebraska* played a major part in Springsteen's elevation to the very select ranks of the best singers in American popular music, thanks to the emotion he conveys to his listeners. And this just as the Republican president Ronald Reagan was preparing to unleash a conservative revolution in the United States.

The album

Released on 30 September 1982, Bruce Springsteen's sixth studio album reached No.29 in the *Billboard* charts on 9 October, climbing to No.3 on 30 October (it is now a certified platinum disc, with more than one million copies sold). Yet Springsteen complained of receiving almost no support from radio stations. In the UK, Canada, and Norway, the album met with considerable commercial success, even reaching No.3 in the charts. In Sweden, it climbed even higher, reaching No.2. In the Netherlands, it got to No.7, and in France to No.18. As for the reception by the press, overall it was excellent. "*Nebraska* is an acoustic triumph, a basic folk album on which Springsteen has stripped his art down to the core,"[85] Steve Pond wrote in *Rolling Stone* magazine. More recently, in the British magazine *Mojo*, Sylvie Simmons wrote of "that nakedness and willingness to face the darkness head-on that made Nebraska a touchstone for a whole new wave of young American bands."[86] Bruce Springsteen's sixth (heartfelt) record is now ranked 226th in *Rolling Stone's* 2012 list of the 500 Greatest Albums of All Time.

The *Nebraska* album cover, dark like the ten songs on the album.

On the record sleeve, the name of Mike Batlan is misspelled—"Batlin." A Freudian slip?

1982

The sleeve

"I wanted black bedtime stories. I thought of the records of John Lee Hooker and Robert Johnson, music that sounded so good with the lights out,"[1] Bruce Springsteen writes of *Nebraska* in his autobiography. The album sleeve expresses this intention eloquently: it features a black and white photograph of a desolate landscape (in Nebraska?) under a cloudy sky, crossed by a road that seems to stretch to infinity. It was shot by David Michael Kennedy: "from the window of an old pickup truck in the dead of winter,"[87] the photographer explained—hence the snow visible on the hood. "When Bruce was working on the *Nebraska* album, he had an idea for a landscape in mind for the cover. He was working with Andy Klein as the art director on the cover. Andy was familiar with my portraits and she also was aware of my landscape work, so she asked me to put together some of my landscapes to show to Bruce. He fell in love with the image (that became the cover)."[87] The words "Bruce Springsteen" and "Nebraska," in red capital letters, appear above and below this image, respectively. On the back of the sleeve is a photograph of the songwriter, in a room lit by a powerful light source. Inside are the lyrics of the ten songs.

The recording

Bruce Springsteen recorded the songs for his sixth album in one of the rooms at his house in Colts Neck. The idea behind this was simple, as he explains in his autobiography: "Frustrated at blowing all my money on studio time, I sent my guitar tech out to get a recorder, a little less lo-fi than the cassette recorder I usually used to lay down my new song ideas. I needed a better and less expensive way to tell if my new material was record-worthy."[1] Mike Batlan went to the nearest music store and bought the first cassette-based, multitrack recorder ever made, the famous Teac Tascam Portastudio 144—which the assistant warmly recommended. He also bought two Shure SM57 microphones, along with their stands. Back at Colts Neck, the equipment was immediately set up in the room. "I was real lucky because I wrote almost all the *Nebraska* songs in about two months. Which is really fast for me,"[10] he said. The time had now come to record all his ideas on cassette.

Homemade magic

When Springsteen reached the recording stage, the year 1981 was coming to an end: "[...] I think I recorded those right around New Year, in a couple of days,"[10] he explained. The

David Michael Kennedy (seen here in Santa Fe, New Mexico, in 2015) took the photo for *Nebraska* in 1982 out of the window of a pickup truck.

The Teac Tascam Portastudio 144, the first multitrack cassette recorder.

recordings are generally believed to have been made between 17 December and 3 January. But there was a problem: who was to be the recording engineer? Although Mike Batlan was a guitar technician, and not really comfortable with studio methods, he was stuck with the task—by default. He adjusted the levels as best he could, in order to avoid saturation as much as possible. Toby Scott, the recording engineer who, with Chuck Plotkin, had taken care of the mixing for *The River*, tried to work out how Batlan had recorded the songs: "It seems also that during the recording process, Mike had never really figured out what that little round knob next to the transport controls was for, and had left it at around the two o'clock position. So they'd ended up recording everything with the varispeed set fast. Then he thought well, maybe it shouldn't be in that position, so he turned it back to twelve o'clock for mixdown."[88] This approach had the effect of slightly lowering the general pitch of what had been recorded.

To mix the whole, Batlan initially plugged the Portastudio's output into a Maestro Echoplex, a tape-delay effect for guitar (the EP-3 model). Then he used Springsteen's Boombox, a large Panasonic portable radio cassette player, to do the final mix on an audio cassette, which the Boss then carried around in the front pocket of his jeans for weeks. Toward the end of April, he met up with the E Street Band, to rerecord the contents of his demo under professional conditions.

Electric *Nebraska*

Before reserving an actual recording studio, Springsteen prudently rehearsed the songs with the group first, as Roy Bittan confirmed: "I think we actually rehearsed those songs in the living room of my house. I had a really high-ceilinged living room with lots of glass and wood, and it actually sounded great in there."[45] Then, between 27 April and 3 May, they all set up in The Power Station. Springsteen was nonetheless disappointed with the results, being unable to hear the beauty of his demo: "[...] it just didn't work out, didn't sound as good, but we did end up recording about half of the *Born in the U.S.A.* album."[10] However, to date, none of these electric versions of *Nebraska* has reappeared. "I'd like to hear it, too. There may be a tape around somewhere. I'm not sure,"[45] Bittan later said.

Mastering

Springsteen quickly realized that he would not be able to recreate the magic of his demo at The Power Station or, what

Fans have a picnic while waiting for their favorite singer to appear in concert. A Boombox in the open trunk.

is more, with the E Street Band. All the technical errors—such as the varispeed, the recording, and the playback heads of the two cassette recorders, which had never been cleaned—along with the confined space of the room had contributed to creating an authentic and unique atmosphere, to which the songwriter was especially attached. One day, Springsteen pulled the tape out of his jeans' pocket and asked Toby Scott whether he could make a master from it. Determined to help him in his artistic approach, the recording engineer agreed. He had the cassette transferred onto tape, but, unfortunately, the poor quality of the recordings made it impossible to produce a record with them. "We went to Bob Ludwig, Steve Marcussen at Precision, Sterling Sound, CBS," the recording engineer explained. "Finally, we ended up at Atlantic in New York, and Dennis King tried one time and also couldn't get it onto disc. So we had him try a different technique, putting it onto disc at a much lower level, and that seemed to work. In the end we ended up having Bob Ludwig use his EQ and his mastering facility, but with Dennis' mastering parameters. And that's the master we ended up using."[88] The result was as good as Springsteen expected: simple, magical, and totally authentic. "I had no intention of recording *Nebraska* in that fashion, whatsoever," he said. "It was—not a mistake—an accident."[10] His sixth album cost him, in the end, only around $1,000. Not a bad investment...

Mono or stereo?

Since the songs recorded by Springsteen on his Portastudio were all in mono, an attempt was made to produce a stereo version of *Nebraska* in 1982: the stereo effect was created by remixing the original versions with a stereo reverb. Although Springsteen did not want to keep the results, someone sent the stereo tapes by mistake to Japan in 1985, for the launch of *Nebraska* on CD. Several records of these were made until 1995, including in Europe and the United States, and described as a "Japanese import," but eventually they were all taken off the market.

The instruments

Establishing which acoustic guitar Springsteen used to record the vast majority of his songs is, as ever, difficult because the Boss has given little information on this subject—apparently, since he did not think it mattered. He may have used two models: a Gibson J-200 and, more probably, an old 1950s Gibson Southern Jumbo SJ-200 Sunburst. He has supposedly said himself that he used the Sunburst and it appears in many photographs of him, especially in his book *Songs* (published in 1998). Among other instruments, he also used his Fender Telecaster-Esquire, a mandolin, harmonicas, a glockenspiel, a keyboard, a tambourine, and probably a 12-string acoustic—sadly unidentified.

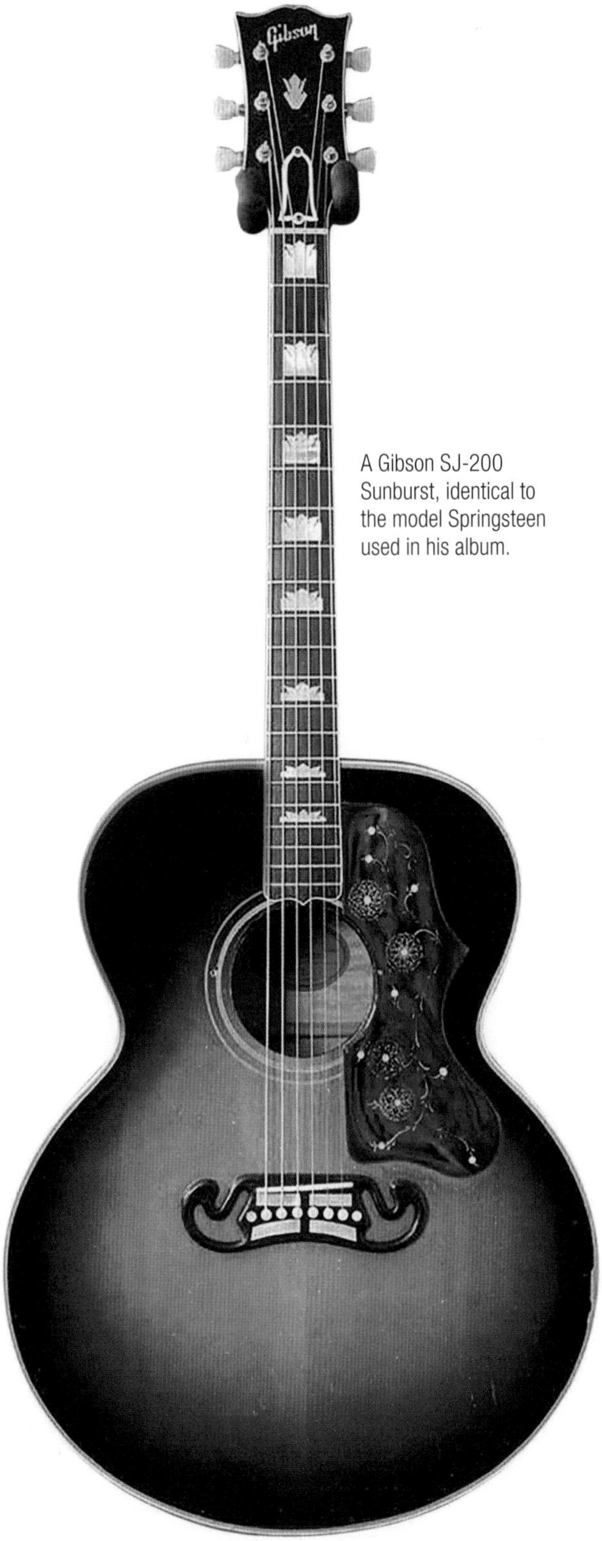

A Gibson SJ-200 Sunburst, identical to the model Springsteen used in his album.

A DISCONCERTING RESURRECTION

The Boombox used in the mixing of *Nebraska* fell out of Springsteen's canoe in the summer of 1981, during a short trip on the river near his home. He managed to retrieve the Boombox from the mud, and then left it to dry on his veranda, believing it to be beyond rescue. But a few days later, while reading the newspaper, the songwriter was surprised to hear his Boombox come back to life all on its own...It hadn't yet had the last word!

Springsteen tells the story of Charles Starkweather and Caril Ann Fugate's murder spree in *Nebraska*. Here, the singer in Rotterdam in 1996.

NEBRASKA

Bruce Springsteen / 4'27

1982

Musician
Bruce Springsteen: vocals, guitar, harmonica, mandolin, glockenspiel
Recording
Thrill Hill East, Bruce Springsteen's room at Colts Neck, New Jersey: 17 December 1981 to 3 January 1982
Technical team
Producer: Bruce Springsteen
Recording engineer: Mike Batlan
Mastering: Dennis King (Atlantic Studios)

For Springsteen Addicts

As well as Terrence Malick, other movie directors also took an interest in the bloody journey of Charles Starkweather and Caril Ann Fugate, notably Oliver Stone, who made *Natural Born Killers* (1994), and Peter Jackson, who directed *The Frighteners* (1996).

Caril Ann Fugate, Charles Starkweather's girlfriend, leaving her cell to be fingerprinted (30 January 1958).

Genesis and lyrics

In writing the song that gave its title to his sixth album, "one of the early examples of my narrative song writing,"[13] as Bruce Springsteen explains on the DVD *VH1 Storytellers—On Stage,* he drew inspiration from a true story: that of Charles Starkweather and his girlfriend, Caril Ann Fugate. Starkweather was born in Lincoln, Nebraska, in 1938. His horrific journey began on 30 November 1957, when he murdered a gas station attendant who had refused to sell him a stuffed animal for young Caril Ann . A few months later, he killed Caril Ann 's mother, stepfather, and half-sister. There followed an even more murderous road trip in Nebraska and Wyoming, which ended with the arrest of the fiendish couple. Starkweather was executed in the electric chair in Nebraska State Penitentiary on 25 June 1959. Caril Ann Fugate was sentenced to life in jail but released in 1976.

Starkweather and Fugate were viewed with morbid fascination in late 1950s America. Some 20 years later, Terrence Malick brought the Nebraska couple's bloody saga to the big screen with the movie *Badlands*, starring Sissy Spacek and Martin Sheen. It was just after having seen the film, and read the book, *Caril*, which tells the story of Caril Ann Fugate's life, that Bruce Springsteen composed *Nebraska*. As he explains: "You can put together a lot of detail, but unless you pull something up out of yourself it's just gonna lay flat on the page. You've got to find what you have in common with that character, no matter who they are or what they did."[13] This is why Springsteen sings *Nebraska* in the first person singular, on the principle that "everyone knows what it is like to be condemned."[13] He sings: "I saw her standing on her front lawn/Just twirling her baton/Me and her went for a ride, sir/And ten innocent people died." Springsteen adds in *Storytellers—On Stage,* "I was interested in an oral projection of, I don't know if you're familiar with the Robert Mitchum film *Night of the Hunter*, which is kind of this horror story told through a child's perspective."[13]

In an interview with Kurt Loder of *Rolling Stone* magazine, in December 1984, the songwriter revealed the message of his song: "*Nebraska* was about that American isolation: what happens to people when they're alienated from their friends and their community and their government and their job. Because those are the things that keep you sane, that give

Fans surround their idol at a concert at the Royal Albert Hall, London, on 27 May 2005. *Nebraska* is among the 25 songs on the setlist.

meaning to life in some fashion. And if they slip away, and you start to exist in some void where the basic constraints of society are a joke, then life becomes kind of a joke. And anything can happen."[89]

Production

In the handwritten letter Bruce Springsteen sent Jon Landau with the demos for *Nebraska*, he said that for the title track he had made four different mixes: the first with a 12-string guitar, the second ending with a more hasty fade-out, the third with a harmonica part that did not work, and the last with a glockenspiel. The Boss had four tracks at his disposal on his Portastudio 144. The first two he used to record his voice, harmonica, and guitar, using a pair of Shure SM57 mics. The other two allowed him to add overdubs, namely a mandolin, which is heard from the second verse (at 1'03), and a glockenspiel, from the fifth verse (at 2'47)—which leads to the conclusion that the version on the album is the fourth mix, as it is the only one that features this instrument.

From the first few seconds of the song, the recording displays a striking creative inspiration. Doubtless Springsteen wanted to highlight his innovative approach and alert the listener to his new album's atypical quality. Then the plaintive harmonica emerges from this analog fog, introduced by the delay of his Echoplex. The guitar is discreet, but sufficiently present to support the songwriter's somber, infinitely touching voice. It calls to mind Woody Guthrie's *This Land Is Your Land*, but also Dave Van Ronk's *He Was a Friend of Mine*. The voice has such deep resonance, in part because of the tape speed which had accidentally been reduced by Mike Batlan during mixing. The instruments and voice are at a slightly lower pitch than Springsteen's original recording. But the result, although due to pure chance, is incredibly powerful. *Nebraska* is a little masterpiece and heralds an album that is out of the ordinary.

COVER

Chrissie Hynde recorded a version of *Nebraska* for the album *Badlands* (2000), which consists precisely of covers of the songs on Bruce Springsteen's album.

ATLANTIC CITY

Bruce Springsteen / 3'54

Musician
Bruce Springsteen: vocals, guitar, harmonica, mandolin
Recording
Thrill Hill East, Bruce Springsteen's room at Colts Neck, New Jersey: 17 December 1981 to 3 January 1982
Technical team
Producer: Bruce Springsteen
Recording engineer: Mike Batlan
Mastering: Dennis King (Atlantic Studios)

For Springsteen Addicts

The Philadelphia Mafia boss Philip Testa, or "Chicken Man" as he was known, was so nicknamed on account of his pock-marked face, which was the result of a serious bout of chicken pox. He was murdered with a nail bomb planted at his home.

In *Atlantic City*, Bruce Springsteen makes an explicit reference to mobster Philip Testa (seen here flanked by two FBI agents in 1963).

Genesis and lyrics

Atlantic City, on the coast of New Jersey in the south of the state, owes its reputation as "the Las Vegas of the East Coast" to the many casinos that sprang up under the protection of the Mafia boss Enoch L Johnson during the Roaring Twenties, as well as the alcohol that flowed liberally there despite Prohibition. As the decades passed, the city continued to make money from gambling premises, which not only attracted compulsive heavy gamblers, but also adventurers of all kinds and criminals—both small- and big-time.

In this song, which is the definitive version of a demo entitled *Fistful of Dollars*—a title inspired by Sergio Leone's 1964 Spaghetti Western starring Clint Eastwood—Bruce Springsteen evokes Atlantic City in the early 1980s, the narrator explicitly referring to the Mafia boss Chicken Man, who was killed in Philadelphia on 15 March 1981. Although the city finally hoped to achieve a certain respectability, with the legalization of gambling, it was, on the contrary, a veritable theater of war between gangs from other states. "Gonna be a rumble out on the promenade," Springsteen sings in the second verse.

Despite the city's highly dangerous nature, the narrator seems to have no choice but to go there with his girlfriend, with the aim of paying his debts. However, even in the city where "the sand's turning to gold," it is not easy to find a job. "Well I'm tired of coming out on this losing end/So honey last night I met this guy and I'm gonna do a little favor for him," the narrator explains to his partner: it is clear that he has finally joined the ranks of small-time Mafiosi and that, from that moment, he has made a pact with the devil—and with death.

Atlantic City was chosen to be on the A-side (*Mansion on the Hill* was on the B-side) of the first single from *Nebraska*, which was released in 1982, although only in Europe and Japan. This single was used for a videoclip made by Arnold Levine—although neither the Boss nor any other band member makes an appearance.

Production

Springsteen made three different mixes of *Atlantic City*, each with slight changes to the lyrics; the third mix was chosen for the album. In a note to Jon Landau, Springsteen explained that "This song should probably be done with the whole band and

Springsteen first submitted the songs for *Nebraska* to his loyal friend Jon Landau, expecting his critiques. Here, the two buddies in 2011.

1982

really rockin' out."[6] However, having tried to record it at The Power Station with the E Street Band, from 26 to 28 April 1982, he gave up, as Landau confirmed. "I remember the main one we kept whackin' away at was *Atlantic City*, which was a song that sounded like it was gonna really lend itself to the band," said Landau. "That was one song that seemed like it wasn't gonna be any problem. And that was goin' nowhere. No way was it as good as what he had goin' on that demo tape."[16] Only live performances did the song justice, with the band bringing to it a rock dimension and an Irish folk music flavor that were highly effective.

Springsteen's demo does indeed have incomparable power: the listener is immediately gripped by its dense atmosphere and the performance's feeling of urgency. Yet he accompanies himself only on the guitar for the first three verses—probably his old 1950s Gibson SJ-200. He is heard singing backing vocals in the distance, in the depths of the Echoplex (at 0'18). The recording also features a mandolin, clearly heard from the fourth verse, and much less after the choruses, when he plays an Irish riff (for example, at 1'39), which fortunately was highlighted by the band in concert performances (see the Born in the U.S.A. Tour of 1984 to 1985). Once again, Springsteen is heard on the harmonica, his phrasing more reminiscent of Neil Young than of Dylan (for example, at 0'54). He then harmonizes with himself in the choruses, thus attaining the maximum number of overdubs possible on the four-track Portastudio 144.

Springsteen (and Clarence Clemons) at Slane Castle, Ireland, on 1 June 1985. The harmonica at the center of the theatrics in *Atlantic City*.

MANSION ON THE HILL

Bruce Springsteen / 4'03

Musician
Bruce Springsteen: vocals, guitar, harmonica, mandolin
Recording
Thrill Hill East, Bruce Springsteen's room at Colts Neck, New Jersey: 17 December 1981 to 3 January 1982
Technical team
Producer: Bruce Springsteen
Recording engineer: Mike Batlan
Mastering: Dennis King (Atlantic Studios)

Poster for Robert Mulligan's famous movie, which sparked the songwriter's imagination while writing *Mansion on the Hill.*

Genesis and lyrics

Bruce Springsteen started work on this song at the time of *Darkness on the Edge of Town*. He then gave the song its final shape when he echoed the title of a song by one of his mentors, Hank Williams. "*Mansion on the Hill,* which I had the beginning of for some time, was the first song I finished,"[6] he writes in his book *Songs*. Once again, he evokes his childhood in New Jersey, remembering the house at the top of a hill that aroused his curiosity and also his trips in the car with his father, which, more often than not, passed close to that strange mansion... "At night my daddy'd take me and we'd ride/Through the streets of a town so silent and still/Park on a back road along the highway side/Look up at that mansion on the hill," Springsteen sings. Here there is a reference, as in so many of his lyrics, to the movies. "I was thinking in a way of [Robert Mulligan's 1963 movie] *To Kill a Mockingbird*, because in that movie there was a child's-eye view," he explained to *Musician* magazine's Chet Flippo. "And [Charles Laughton's 1955 movie] *Night of the Hunter* also had that—I'm not sure if surrealistic is the right view. But that was poetic when the little girl was running through the woods. I was thinking of scenes like that."[90]

Bruce Springsteen also touches a nostalgic nerve when he thinks back to that time: "There'd be music playing, people laughing all the time." It is clear that times have changed: the mansion still overlooks the town, but the factories have closed and many jobs have gone. Springsteen is talking about Linden, a town in New Jersey not far from New York, where a large General Motors factory and a refinery were built.

Mansion on the Hill is on the B-side of a single (with *Atlantic City* on the A-side) that was destined for the European market in 1982.

Production

Bruce Springsteen made three mixes of *Mansion on the Hill*: according to his notes, "One and two mixes are a little dirty."[6] The third was of good quality. And, yet again, the electric versions tried with the band on 27, 28, and 30 April 1982 at The Power Station came to nothing: "I wouldn't even say that the stuff didn't come out beautifully. But the big thing was gone. The stillness was gone, the intimacy was gone. It was being scaled incorrectly,"[16] Chuck Plotkin commented.

Bruce Springsteen borrowed the title *Mansion on the Hill* from a Hank Williams' (shown here) song.

For Springsteen Addicts

A Mansion on the Hill is a song that Hank Williams wrote with Fred Rose. Recorded in November 1947, it went to No.12 in the country charts in 1948. It was subsequently adapted by several performers, including George Jones, Willie Nelson, Roy Orbison, and Waylon Jennings.

The "mansion on the hill" that the songwriter would go and look at as a child with his father inspired a superb song with a spellbinding, hypnotic atmosphere, filled with emotion and restraint. The piece begins with a harmonica, the Boss accompanying himself on the 6-string guitar. Then comes the first verse: his voice, borne by the Echoplex's delay, resounds with a remarkable magnetism. Springsteen sings almost confidentially, his words practically whispered, and images succeed each other throughout the performance with palpable nostalgia. It is obvious that he could not recreate such fragility, such emotional power, with the whole band. This is a trap with which singer-songwriters are frequently confronted: in the studio they cannot recapture the magic of a demo made at home, in an intimate setting, using more or less amateur equipment. Nevertheless, the public performances Springsteen would give of this song with the E Street Band were of a good quality; on those occasions, he was accompanied on the accordion by Danny Federici (as on the Born in the U.S.A. Tour of 1984 to 1985) or on the steel guitar by Nils Lofgren (as on the Reunion Tour of 1999 to 2000).

Among the other instruments the Boss recorded on his four-track recorder we can hear a mandolin from the third verse onward (at 1'33). But it is also possible that he added a 12-string acoustic guitar to double his Gibson SJ-200—this can be heard in the song's final chord (at around 3'58).

JOHNNY 99

Bruce Springsteen / 3'38

Musician
Bruce Springsteen: vocals, guitars, harmonica
Recording
Thrill Hill East, Bruce Springsteen's room at Colts Neck, New Jersey: 17 December 1981 to 3 January 1982
Technical team
Producer: Bruce Springsteen
Recording engineer: Mike Batlan
Mastering: Dennis King (Atlantic Studios)

1982

Genesis and lyrics

After recording the songs for *Nebraska* (and others) on his Tascam Portastudio 144, Bruce Springsteen sent several notes to Jon Landau. Regarding *Johnny 99,* he wrote: "These words are not completely worked out or finished so the singing is occasionally awkward. I don't know if this song is a keeper or not but I thought you'd get a kick out of it."[6]

Johnny 99 is a topical song. After the closure of a car factory in Mahwah, northern New Jersey—a real event, for it was a Ford assembly plant that was shut down after 35 years of operation—many workers and employees found themselves unemployed. One, named Ralph, while drunk on a cocktail of gin and wine, shot and killed a night clerk. He was arrested and then defended by a court-appointed lawyer before a pitiless judge, "Mean John Brown," who sentenced him to 99 years in jail—hence his nickname, Johnny 99. There was astonishment, anger, and then rebellion in the courtroom. While Johnny's fiancée had to be dragged away, his mother begged: "Judge, don't take my boy this way." Then it was Johnny's turn to express himself and try to explain: he had debts he could not pay and his house was going to be repossessed. The hellish downward spiral had already begun.

Ford assembly lines in Mahaw, New Jersey. The real-life environment that provided the backdrop to *Johnny 99*.

Production

Johnny 99 is one of the songs that persuaded Bruce Springsteen to release *Nebraska* as it was originally recorded. "Like *Johnny 99*—I thought 'Oh, that'd be great if we could do a rock version,'" he explained to Roger Scott and Patrick Humphries of the Irish magazine *Hot Press.* "But when you did that, the song disappeared. A lot of its content was in its style, in the treatment of it. It needed that really kinda austere, echoey sound, just one guitar—one guy telling his story. That's what made the record work, the sound of real conversation...like you were meeting different people, and they just told you what had happened to them, or what was happening to them."[40]

It is true that the recording of *Johnny 99* is one of the most spare on the album: Springsteen launches into his song with a sort of wail, which owes as much to Elvis-style rock as it does to a Jimmie Rodgers' blue yodel. His voice is strongly colored by the delay of the Maestro Echoplex EP-3—the slapback echo that is typical of rockabilly. The words

For Springsteen Addicts

During the concert at the Civic Arena in Pittsburgh, Pennsylvania, on 21 September 1984, Springsteen addressed the audience in order to reply to Ronald Reagan, who had complimented him during a meeting in Hammonton two days earlier. "Well, the President was mentioning my name in his speech the other day, and I kind of got to wondering what his favorite album of mine must've been...I don't think it was the *Nebraska* album, I don't think he's been listening to this one."[9] And he launched into *Johnny 99*...

The E Street Band played *Johnny 99* during the Born in the U.S.A. Tour in 1985, notably with Nils Lofgren on the acoustic guitar.

rebound with a percussive effect, while the Gibson SJ-200 plays a pure rock 'n' roll rhythm. Springsteen is in search of a particular ambience, atmosphere, sound—that of the records that left a permanent mark on him. This is doubtless one of the reasons that led him to prolong the sessions for the making of his previous albums so interminably: he was never completely happy with the excessively "clean" recordings of professional studios. It is the chief reason that convinced him to make his demo into the master of his new album. Feeling, intention, and sound: these were the three criteria that led him to be musically demanding.

The other instruments that occupy the four tracks of *Johnny 99* are a harmonica and another acoustic guitar: the former plays two solos after the third verse and at the start of the coda (at 1'30 and at 3'10), while the latter is used to add force to the first take played on the Gibson SJ-200 (from 1'30).

The E Street Band did try to record *Johnny 99* at The Power Station, on 27 and 28 April, and 3 May 1982. Although the results were not satisfactory, this did not stop Springsteen and his band returning to the song onstage, with totally different instrumental lineups. The version closest to the spirit of *Nebraska* was notably played on the Born to Run Tour in 1985, with only the guitar of Nils Lofgren supporting the Boss's vocals and harmonica. Other, later performances, such as those during the Working on a Dream Tour in 2009, involved group rock performances that totally distorted the song's original feeling, with solos by a lap steel guitar, violin, and saxophone, as well as backing vocals.

For Springsteen Addicts

Sean Penn was living with Pamela Springsteen, Bruce's younger sister, when he made *The Indian Runner.* He also made the video for *Highway Patrolman.*

HIGHWAY PATROLMAN

Bruce Springsteen / 5'39

Musician

Bruce Springsteen: vocals, guitar, harmonica, mandolin

Recording

Thrill Hill East, Bruce Springsteen's room at Colts Neck, New Jersey: 17 December 1981 to 3 January 1982

Technical team

Producer: Bruce Springsteen

Recording engineer: Mike Batlan

Mastering: Dennis King (Atlantic Studios)

1982

Sean Penn and Robin Wright on the set of *The Indian Runner.* This superb film was based on Bruce Springsteen's *Highway Patrolman.*

Genesis and lyrics

Highway Patrolman is certainly one of the most revealing examples of Springsteen's talent as a storyteller. Here he lends his voice to Sergeant Joe Roberts, a traffic police officer based in a small US town, who has always been as honest as he could. The same is not true, however, of his brother, Franky, who does not observe the law. "Now ever since we was young kids, it's been the same comedown/I get a call on the shortwave, Franky's in trouble downtown/Well if it was any other man, I'd put him straight away/But when it's your brother sometimes you look the other way," he sings in the second verse, adding: "[...] nothin' feels better than blood on blood."

The policeman describes his past, and that of his brother. Joe got a draft deferment to run his farm, married Maria, and then faced a drop in wheat prices; Franky "went in the army" and probably fought in Vietnam from 1965 to 1968. Joe also reminisces about the time he received a call from Michigan after Franky started a fight that went wrong. Joe immediately drove at breakneck speed toward the scene. In the distance, he caught sight of his brother's car, a Buick with Ohio plates, and chased it—then gave up the chase and let him flee toward the Canadian border...

Highway Patrolman is one of the most moving songs Bruce Springsteen wrote; it had a profound effect on a young movie director named Sean Penn. Indeed, the story of *Highway Patrolman*, and a Native American legend, formed the basis for his first feature-length movie, *The Indian Runner* (1991), starring David Morse, Viggo Mortensen, Valeria Golino, and Patricia Arquette.

Production

It took just one take for Springsteen to record *Highway Patrolman*, and four mixes to finally sort the recording out—the last of these featuring on *Nebraska*. However, the writing of this song, which was initially entitled *Deputy*, posed some difficulties, as he explains in his letter to Jon Landau: "worked very long on this and always had the feeling I was comin' up short. Not really finished but is about as good as I can get it at the time. Don't think the ending was quite strong enough."[6]

As with all the songs on the album, the power of *Highway Patrolman* lies in the simplicity of the recording, but also in its pared-down arrangements. Indeed, in the first two verses

Johnny Cash covered *Highway Patrolman* in 1983 for the album *Johnny 99*. It did not come out well.

and the pseudo-chorus (at 1'18, where the opening words of the chorus differ slightly), Springsteen accompanies himself only on the guitar, thus bringing his voice out exceptionally. The tone is resigned: it is the tone of a storyteller and, as always, his charisma is astonishing. He sings with a slight delay that colors his performance, and his vocal technique has become soft and calm, as in the other songs on the album, which is something new for him. He strums arpeggiated chords on his Gibson in a highly regular fashion, which suggests he was probably using the click of a drum machine to help him keep time. The third verse and second chorus (at 1'55 and 2'33) are the only parts of the song where the songwriter adds other instruments: he has recorded a harmonica part to enrich the harmony, as well as a mandolin accompaniment (from 1'55). The two are mixed discreetly, their presence serving only to change the overall atmosphere. They then disappear in the fourth verse, to allow the drama of the lyrics to be brought out.

It is worth noting that the song Springsteen refers to in his chorus, *Night of the Johnstown Flood*, is a traditional song recounting the catastrophic flood which engulfed Johnstown after the failure of the South Fork Dam in 1889, killing more than 2,000 people.

The end of the song is moving: the austerity and fragility of the songwriter's performance command admiration. Springsteen pulls off a real feat in rendering credible a text that is nothing more than a fiction created by his imagination. "I was real happy with it," he said. "It just felt real. I didn't know I was gonna do that, but I knew I was going somewhere in that direction."[10]

In *Highway Patrolman*, Bruce Springsteen mentions the town of Perrineville, New Jersey. But it is unlikely that the protagonist, Joe Roberts, drives from New Jersey to Michigan. It is more plausible that the town in question is Perronville, which is indeed in Michigan.

STATE TROOPER

Bruce Springsteen / 3'15

Musician

Bruce Springsteen: vocals, guitar

Recording

Thrill Hill East, Bruce Springsteen's room at Colts Neck, New Jersey: 17 December 1981 to 3 January 1982

Technical team

Producer: Bruce Springsteen

Recording engineer: Mike Batlan

Mastering: Dennis King (Atlantic Studios)

1982

State Trooper can be heard at the end of the last episode of the first season of *The Sopranos*, an HBO production in which Steve Van Zandt plays Silvio Dante, one of Tony Soprano's inner circle.

Tony Soprano's merry crew in the series *The Sopranos*, with Steve Van Zandt (second on the left) in the role of Silvio Dante.

Genesis and lyrics

In the notes sent to Jon Landau after the recordings were made at Colts Neck, Bruce Springsteen wrote about *State Trooper*: "I dreamed this one up coming back from New York one night. I don't know if it's even really a song or not [...] It's a weird song."[6] The story begins as the narrator is leaving New York. After going through the Holland Tunnel, the driver-narrator heads onto the New Jersey Turnpike, the famous toll road that crosses the whole of New Jersey. Who is he? We know that he is driving without a license or registration document, and it is clear that he has committed a crime—perhaps a murder. Does he fear committing some irrevocable act if he is arrested by a police officer (perhaps a father, married to a pretty wife)? It is a mystery. The state trooper never appears in the flesh.

It would seem that everything takes place in the narrator's imagination, as his mind wanders with what looks like a paranoia which grows with every passing mile. Those he is fleeing from do not wear a uniform, for they are his inner demons, a loneliness symbolized by the rainy night and by this road that seems to lead to the middle of nowhere, and, more tragically still, his headlong plunge into madness. The last lines of the song, in this regard, require no comment: "Hey, somebody out there, listen to my last prayer/Hi ho silver-o deliver me from nowhere."

Musically, *State Trooper* can be described as lo-fi folk. In this particular case, Springsteen was influenced by Alan Vega's avant-garde protopunk band Suicide, especially by the song *Frankie Teardrop*. In an interview in 2014 with the *New York Post* (quoted by Jeff Tericho on treblezine.com), Alan Vega recalled, "We first met Springsteen in 1980." He continued: "He was recording *The River* and we were recording our second album in New York...Then we had a playback meeting for our album. There were three or four big shots from our label, and Bruce was there, too. After we played the album, there was deathly silence...except for Bruce, who said, 'That was fucking great.' He made a point of telling us how much he loved us."[92] Later in that interview, Alan Vega explained his reaction to hearing *State Trooper* for the first time: "I remember walking into my label just after it came out," and he added, "I thought it was one of my albums that I had forgotten about. But it was Bruce!"[92]

Before Bruce Springsteen did so with *State Trooper*, Simon and Garfunkel immortalized the New Jersey Turnpike in the song *America* (on the album *Bookends*, 1968).

Bruce Springsteen performing a poignant solo of *State Trooper* in June 2005 in Rome, during the Devils & Dust Tour.

Production

It is certain that Springsteen was influenced by the minimalism and dark side of the band Suicide, and specifically by the song *Frankie Teardrop*. He would emulate the song's use of a synthesizer in live versions of *State Trooper* (this can be heard in the performance given on 18 September 1984 at the Spectrum, in Philadelphia).

Recorded in a single take, *State Trooper* is probably the most austere song on *Nebraska*, and also the most incomplete—all that can be heard is the guitar and the songwriter's voice, and no other instrument. The atmosphere and tempo of the song, which is the last on the vinyl album's A-side, are those of a moderate rock piece, based on two chords that are played only on two strings. Incidentally, this rather thin harmony caused Springsteen some problems: there is a lack of reference points for adjusting his voice, as can be heard in the first verse. However, he quickly rectifies this problem, to deliver a very fine performance. He sings with a very pronounced and distinct delay from the Echoplex, in a drawling tone, his voice weary and soft. The result is quite remarkable: he succeeds in creating a heavy, oppressive atmosphere, punctuating the song with shrill cries, which inevitably saturate the inputs of the Portastudio (listen at 2'29 and 3'03).

It is a pity that Springsteen did not complete or repeat *State Trooper* as a studio version because the song has a stealthy, but marvelous strength—which, incidentally, made an impact in the world of movies, as the French director Jacques Audiard used it on the soundtrack for his movie *De rouille et d'os* ("Rust and Bone"), which was released in 2012 and starred Marion Cotillard and Matthias Schoenaerts.

USED CARS

Bruce Springsteen / 3'06

Musician
Bruce Springsteen: vocals, guitar, harmonica, glockenspiel
Recording
Thrill Hill East, Bruce Springsteen's room at Colts Neck, New Jersey: 17 December 1981 to 3 January 1982
Technical team
Producer: Bruce Springsteen
Recording engineer: Mike Batlan
Mastering: Dennis King (Atlantic Studios)

1982

COVER
For the album *Badlands*, on which various artists revisit the songs on *Nebraska*, there is a recording of *Used Cars* by Ani DiFranco.

Singer Ani DiFranco in Chicago in 1997. She recorded a version of *Used Cars* for *Badlands*.

Genesis and lyrics

Used Cars is another plunge back into Bruce Springsteen's childhood. "The exciting story of my own personal life,"[6] was how the songwriter ironically put it to Jon Landau. Memories of his family come back to him: "My little sister's in the front seat with an ice cream cone/My ma's in the back seat sitting all alone/As my pa steers her slow out of the lot for a test drive down Michigan Avenue." Then there are negotiations—or rather attempted negotiations—with the car-lot salesman. At the time, the future songwriter's parents were of rather modest means: the purchase of a new car was beyond them. Bruce Springsteen sings: "Now mister the day the lottery I win I ain't ever gonna ride in no used car again."

Tedium at work, condescending looks from the neighbors, and a depressing environment—in *Used Cars* Bruce Springsteen is not only describing his father's day-to-day life but, all things considered, that of the most vulnerable social classes in 1950s and 1960s America. The songwriter is asking himself: is the American dream within reach of blue-collar workers? It is a question that has often come up, ever since *The River*.

Production

Used Cars is the first song on the second side of the vinyl *Nebraska* album. Springsteen recorded it in two takes, the second being the better of the two. This is yet another gem recorded by the Boss. The atmosphere of this recording is magical. To be sure, the sound quality is not up to professional standards, but what does that matter? The emotion that makes itself felt throughout the song's three minutes is unique and would have been difficult to reproduce in the setting of The Power Station. A version with the band was indeed made on 30 April—but, as with the other songs on the album, to no avail.

Springsteen sings in a soft, plaintive, almost childlike voice, accompanying himself on his Gibson acoustic with arpeggiated chords. In the second verse, a harmonica very discreetly heightens the piece's harmony, in the manner of an accordion. He then launches into a first solo after the third verse, and into a second in the coda (at 1'39 and 2'28). A glockenspiel also features in the recording, the crystalline tone of its notes resonating in the Echoplex's delay. *Used Cars* is one of the highlights of *Nebraska*.

Bruce Springsteen at a Barack Obama rally in Ypsilanti, Michigan, on 6 October 2008. *Used Cars* is one of eight songs on the setlist.

OPEN ALL NIGHT

Bruce Springsteen / 2'58

Musician
Bruce Springsteen: vocals, guitar
Recording
Thrill Hill East, Bruce Springsteen's room at Colts Neck, New Jersey: 17 December 1981 to 3 January 1982
Technical team
Producer: Bruce Springsteen
Recording engineer: Mike Batlan
Mastering: Dennis King (Atlantic Studios)

1982

For Springsteen Addicts

William Price Fox (1926–2015) is known for his collections of short stories, one of the most famous of which is *Southern Fried*, and for his work for many newspapers, notably *USA Today*, *the Los Angeles Times*, and the *Village Voice*.

HEADPHONES AT THE READY

While the Boss has difficulty singing all his phrases in time at such a fast tempo, he is also audibly short of breath at 0'42, at the beginning of the phrase "Gotta hit the gas."

Genesis and lyrics

In an interview with Chet Flippo for *Musician* magazine, Bruce Springsteen declared that he had discovered the works of William Price Fox more or less at the same time as he was recording *Nebraska* at Colts Neck. "He's just great with detail," he said. "In *Open All Night* I remember he had some short story that inspired me. I forgot what it was. But I was just interested in maintaining a real line through the thing. If you look just beneath the immediate surface, it's usually right there. So I like the girls and cars idea."[90]

A girl and a car are indeed the essence of what *Open All Night* is about. It is a song "in which the hero braves snow, sleet, rain, and the highway patrol for a kiss from his baby's lips."[6] That is how Springsteen described the song to Jon Landau. The narrator says he has taken great care of his car—a Cobra Jet that is fully prepped. He is driving along the turnpike, which is "spooky at night when you're all alone," across a New Jersey that is "in the morning like a lunar landscape," with his foot to the floor, risking being chased by the police. His ultimate goal is to find the woman with whom he has fallen in love. Her name is Wanda. She "was employed/Behind the counter at Route 60 Bob's Big Boy Fried Chicken" when he met her. A wonderful girl, "With them big brown eyes that make your heart stand still." The hours pass too slowly for the lovelorn narrator, who says, "I got three more hours." While the radio stations are playing only gospel, he wants rock 'n' roll to "deliver me from nowhere." There is a lot going on in this song...

Open All Night was released on the A-side of the second single from *Nebraska*, on 22 November 1982, with *The Big Payback* on the B-side. It was another single destined for a European audience.

The lyrics of *Open All Night* are essentially taken from a song entitled *Living on the Edge of the World*, recorded on 7 December 1979. Dropped from the tracklisting for *The River*, the song made a reappearance on the *Tracks* box set (1998) and *The Ties That Bind: The River Collection* box set (2015). Other lyrics can be found in *State Trooper*.

Production

Springsteen recorded this song under its working title of *Wanda (Open All Night)*. It is a rock number in the finest tradition of the genre. He made two takes, with the second

Bruce Springsteen and the Pete Seeger Sessions orchestra played a completely new version of *Open All Night* at the New Orleans Jazz & Heritage Festival on 30 April 2006.

one featuring on *Nebraska*. And, most unusually for this album, he does not play his Gibson acoustic but his Fender Telecaster-Esquire, apparently plugged directly into his Portastudio, via his Maestro Echoplex EB-3. It does not appear to be accompanied by any other instrument. The tempo is quick, and the Boss needs to make an effort to keep time without any rhythmic support. He begins the song with a short Chuck Berry-style introduction played on his Fender, in which the slapback echo is very marked. As regards vocals, he struggles to enunciate all his phrases in time—the difficulty arising as a result of the speed of the delivery: "This song is very hard to perform,"[6] he wrote to Landau.

If there is a song on the album that could have been improved in a truly electric version, it is certainly this one. There was an attempt to make such a version with the E Street Band, at The Power Station on 27 April, but nothing survives of this today.

However, the song's power can be experienced through its live performances, in totally reworked versions—notably during the 2006 Seeger Sessions Band Tour, with Springsteen accompanied by The Sessions Band. The concert that took place at the New Orleans Jazz & Heritage Festival, on 30 April 2006, is a wonderful example of this, with *Open All Night* being revisited in the form of a boogie, with backing vocals, a brass section, and steel guitar, as well as piano, trumpet, and violin solos. As for the Boss's vocal performance, it is quite simply superb.

MY FATHER'S HOUSE

Bruce Springsteen / 5'03

Musician
Bruce Springsteen: vocals, guitars, harmonica, synthesizer
Recording
Thrill Hill East, Bruce Springsteen's room at Colts Neck, New Jersey: 25 May 1982
Technical team
Producer: Bruce Springsteen
Recording engineer: Mike Batlan
Mastering: Dennis King (Atlantic Studios)

1982

The legend of the Jersey Devil dates back to the 18th century. In 1735, Deborah Leeds gave birth to her 13th child—a monster with the head of a horse (or a goat, according to some sources), the wings of a bat, horns, and a forked tail. After killing its mother, the beast fled into the forest of the Pine Barrens. What became of it? In the early 20th century, several people claimed to have been attacked by this evil creature.

Genesis and lyrics

My Father's House is one of the songs that describes Bruce Springsteen's childhood, along with *Mansion on the Hill* and *Used Cars* on *Nebraska*, and, before them, *Adam Raised a Cain* and *Factory* (on *Darkness on the Edge of Town*) and *Independence Day* (on *The River*). The song's uniqueness lies in the way in which Springsteen wrote it, blending the reality of childhood with dreams and myths. "Last night I dreamed that I was a child," the song begins: everything, therefore, starts with a dream. The songwriter then mentions a pine forest which he must cross in order to return home, hearing "ghostly voices" and "With the devil snapping at my heels." There are two references here: to the movie *Night of the Hunter* (see *Mansion on the Hill*) and to the legend of the fiend of New Jersey (the Jersey Devil). The narrator makes it to his father's house, which "stood shining hard and bright," but there he encounters a cruel disappointment, shock even: a woman is now living in this house. "She said 'I'm sorry son but no one by that name lives here anymore.'" The narrator is thus abruptly jolted out of his dream and out of the hope he had harbored: to atone for his sins; that is, to make peace with his father, after so many years of misunderstanding and strife.

Production

This is the only song on the album to have been finished five months after all the rest. Springsteen kept the same equipment and recorded the song in the same way, at home at Colts Neck. He accompanies himself on his Gibson acoustic, with a kind of finger-picking that suits the folk atmosphere perfectly, and he is certainly influenced by Woody Guthrie. His voice is different: its tone is more gravelly and less soft. The mood is sad, introverted, and moving. A tambourine joins in to support the rhythm from the third verse. The Boss plays two solos on his harmonica, and also a keyboard, very probably a synthesizer (between 3'09 and 4'20). There is, incidentally, a long version of *My Father's House* that includes a coda played on a synthesizer, which was cut from the official version. However, a problem arose in 1985: the master that was destined for the Japanese market accidentally included this longer version with the synthesizer coda. Several records got into circulation there, as well as in Europe and the USA, until they were all taken off the market in 1995.

REASON TO BELIEVE

Bruce Springsteen / 4'11

For Springsteen Addicts

In 1966, the folk singer Tim Hardin had already recorded a song called *Reason to Believe* (revisited in 1971 by Rod Stewart). Bruce Springsteen's song, however, bears no relation to it. The Boss incidentally pointed this out in his letter to Landau: "No not the Tim Hardin song but a completely original tune by the same name."[6]

Musician

Bruce Springsteen: vocals, guitars, harmonica

Recording

Thrill Hill East, Bruce Springsteen's room at Colts Neck, New Jersey: 17 December 1981 to 3 January 1982

Technical team

Producer: Bruce Springsteen
Recording engineer: Mike Batlan
Mastering: Dennis King (Atlantic Studios)

Folk singer Tim Hardin at Piccadilly Circus, London, in 1968. He wrote a song called *Reason to Believe*, which had no relation to Springsteen's song.

Genesis and lyrics

The majestic shadow of Flannery O'Connor was surely hovering over Springsteen when he wrote the lyrics for *Reason to Believe*. The song's characters could very well have been created by the author of *Wise Blood* (even though the place described in the song is in New Jersey, not in the former Confederate States). There is this man on Route 31 who seems to want to bring a dead dog back to life, using a stick. There is Mary Lou, who said she was prepared to work for the man she loves and continues to wait for him after he abandoned her to her sad fate. There is this baby, Kyle William, who is taken to the river to be cleansed of his sins, and this old man who is taken to the cemetery. Finally, at the church, there is the bridegroom, waiting in vain for his chosen one.

What is Springsteen trying to say? The answer lies in the song's title: we need a reason to believe, for without one life is only a series of bitter disappointments—in particular, waiting for someone who will never come—until we are plunged into eternal nothingness. The songwriter explained that the inspiration for the song came to him as he was driving down Highway 33 on his way to Millstone.[6]

Production

Springsteen brings *Nebraska* to a close with a rather hopeless song, which has a heavy feel and a rock rhythm with a moderate tempo. His performance gives the impression of sorrow and fatalism, especially in the final verse, where his voice drops to a murmur to emphasize the realism of his words. He accompanies himself on his Gibson acoustic, adds a harmonica, and punctuates the piece with sparse notes, very probably played on his Fender Telecaster-Esquire (from 1'00).

There exist two takes of *Reason to Believe*, with the second of these containing an extra verse. However, the first version was chosen for the album. Electric versions were also recorded at The Power Station, on 27 and 28 April.

It is clear from this final confession on *Nebraska*—as it is from the other songs on the album—that Springsteen was right to prefer his demos to "professional" versions. They have an emotional power that he could not achieve in the studio. What is more, his writing has acquired a new dimension—an intensity and maturity to match those of the greatest songwriters in American popular music.

SIDE B

THE BIG PAYBACK

Bruce Springsteen / 1'58

Single: *Open All Night/The Big Payback* **Reference:** CBS – A2969 **Release date:** Europe, 21 October 1980

Musician
Bruce Springsteen: vocals, guitar, harmonica

Recording
Thrill Hill East, Bruce Springsteen's room at Colts Neck, New Jersey: Between March and April 1982

Technical team
Producer: Bruce Springsteen
Recording engineer: Mike Batlan
Mastering: Dennis King (Atlantic Studios)

Genesis and lyrics

The Big Payback was recorded at Colts Neck in March or April 1982, just after the songs that feature on the album *Nebraska*, as the songwriter explains in the sleeve notes to the compilation album *The Essential Bruce Springsteen*, released in November 2003 (this song is on the bonus CD).

Against a background of music that calls to mind the golden age of rockabilly—Carl Perkins, Warren Smith, and Roy Orbison—Bruce Springsteen once again excoriates the working conditions that manual workers and employees have to put up with every day. "I work so long that I'm a-losing track/ Waiting waiting on the big payback," he sings. The narrator then lashes out at his foreman: "He just throws me a shovel and yells 'Go, Bobby, Go.'" He ends up quitting, and in an alley, armed with a knife, decides to get his hands on the money he cannot earn by honest means. There is no way he will have his neck in a noose any more.

Production

The song begins with a Chuck Berry-style intro and indeed proceeds with a rock rhythm worthy of the inventor of the duckwalk. Yet *The Big Payback* could not have featured on the tracklisting for *Nebraska*. Although the Boss recorded it under similar conditions to those of the other songs on his sixth album, this one possesses none of their power.

Springsteen accompanies himself on his Telecaster-Esquire, exactly as he does in *Open All Night*, with both voice and guitar generously colored by his Echoplex—to produce the rockabilly feel. He adds two harmonica solos, but the magic is not there. Springsteen no doubt did not believe in the

James Brown recorded a song called *The Big Payback* in 1973. The godfather of soul and the boss of rock 'n' roll—were they fighting the same fight?

song himself, for neither the music nor the lyrics are of any real appeal. You might ask yourself, in fact, why he chose this song for the B-side of the single *Open All Night*.

The Big Payback sounds more like a track that was discarded in the studio than a finished song. Perhaps Springsteen should have returned to the song and recorded it in The Power Station with the whole E Street Band?

In 1973, James Brown recorded *The Payback*, an album that contains a song with the same title, written by Brown, Wesley, and Starks. In the lyrics, Brown mentions "the big payback," words that are echoed by the backing vocals. Is this where the Boss got his inspiration?

ALBUM

BORN IN THE U.S.A.

Born in the U.S.A. • Cover Me • Darlington County • Working on the Highway • Downbound Train • I'm on Fire • No Surrender • Bobby Jean • I'm Goin' Down • Glory Days • Dancing in the Dark • My Hometown

Outtakes: *100 Miles from Jackson •A Good Man Is Hard to Find (Pittsburgh) • Baby I'm So Cold • Bad Boy • Bells of San Salvador • Betty Jean • Body and Soul • Brothers Under the Bridges • Car Wash • Child Bridge • Common Ground (Stay Hungry) • County Fair • Cynthia • Delivery Man • Don't Back Down • Follow that Dream • Frankie • Fugitive's Dream • Glory of Love • Gone, Gone, Gone • Gun in Every Home • Hold on (To What You Got) • Ida Rose (No One Knows) • I Don't Care • Invitation to Your Party • Johnny Go Down • Just Around the Corner to the Light Of Day • King's Highway • Little Girl (Like You) • Love's on the Line • Man at the Top • Murder Incorporated • My Love Will Not Let You Down • None But the Brave • One Love • On the Prowl • Out of Work • Pink Cadillac • Protection • Refrigerator Blues • Richfield Whistle • Rockaway the Days • Roll Away the Stone • Savin' Up • Seven Tears • Shut Down • Stand On It • Stop the War • Sugarland • Swoop Man • The Klansman • The Money We Didn't Make • This Hard Land • True Love is Hard to Come By • TV Movie • Under the Big Sky • Unsatisfied Heart • Wages of Sin • Workin' on it • Your Love is All Around Me*

RELEASE DATE

United States: 4 June 1984

Reference: Columbia Records – QC 38653

No.1 in the United States, United Kingdom, Australia, Canada, Netherlands, West Germany, Norway, Sweden, and Switzerland, No.2 in France, Italy, and Spain

Leather jacket, jeans, vest, and bandana, Bruce Springsteen chronicled a certain vision of America throughout *Born in the U.S.A.*

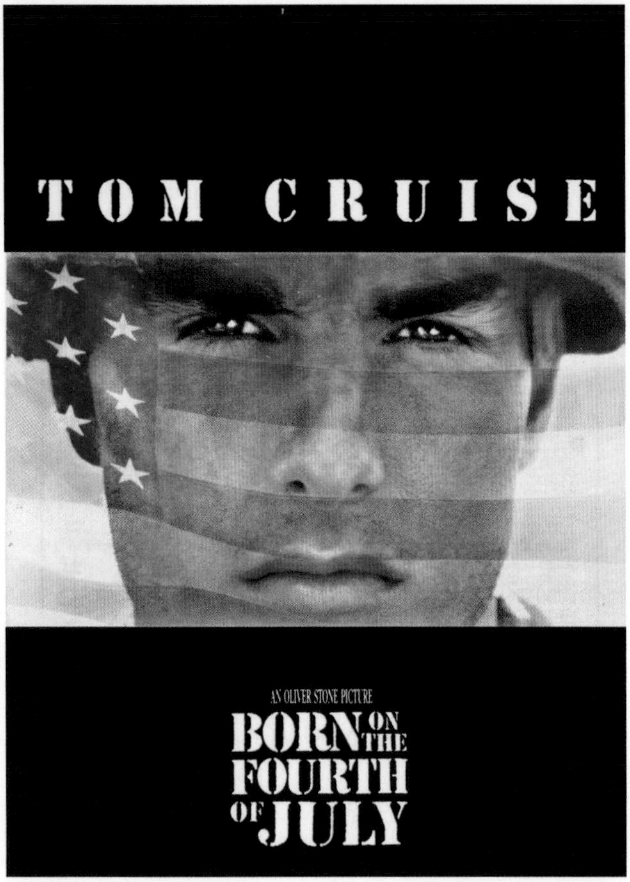

Poster of Oliver Stone's film adapted from the memoir by Ron Kovic, himself an inspiration for Bruce Springsteen.

BETWEEN DOUBT AND SUCCESS

Nebraska and *Born in the U.S.A.* make an unlikely pair in Bruce Springsteen's discography: a "pair" because they were written at the same time; "unlikely" because musically they're very different from each other. *Nebraska* can be considered an acoustic solo album, while *Born in the U.S.A.* is an electronic album recorded with the E Street Band.

Bruce Springsteen's seventh studio album was created in the fall of 1981, when he rented a ranch at Colts Neck, New Jersey, not far from his hometown. There, he wrote the tracks that would become *Nebraska*, as well as several other songs which he would later include on *Born in the U.S.A.* The songwriter had just read *Born on the Fourth of July* (during the River Tour) and had also met the book's author, Ron Kovic, who had been paralysed in the Vietnam War. Kovic's account, and Springsteen's meeting of Vietnam War veterans living in Los Angeles, affected him deeply (see *Songs of Quiet Power*, page 192). These experiences probably reinforced his pacifist ideals and led him to participate, in his own way, in the national political debate. Thus, *Born in the U.S.A.* was born.

A songwriter at his best

Born in the U.S.A. is one of the most important songs in Bruce Springsteen's repertoire. The strength of its lyrics comes from the depiction of the end of the American dream through a Vietnam veteran who watched his comrades die by his side, but who was ignored and even hated after returning to the land of Uncle Sam. These same lyrics were widely misunderstood and became controversial. By then, Springsteen's audience—which had grown considerably since *Born to Run*—had been calling him "The Boss" for about ten years, and this song only served to confirm his writing talent for them. The other 11 songs on the album are also fine reflections of Springsteen's authenticity. The songs *No Surrender* and *Bobby Jean* are in essence tributes to how the power of rock can help form bonds and to Springsteen's close friendship with Steve Van Zandt. *My Hometown* is about the racial riots that took place in New Jersey in the 1960s, *Glory Days* is highly autobiographical, *Downbound Train* very nostalgic, and *I'm on Fire* downright erotic. The other songs are *Cover Me*, which was originally written for Donna Summer; *Darlington County*, which is about the trials and tribulations

During the Born in the U.S.A. Tour Springsteen starts his show with the eponymous song.

Born in the U.S.A. was nominated in the category of "Best Album of the Year" at the 27th Grammy Awards (on 26 February 1985), but had to cede victory to *Can't Slow Down* by Lionel Richie.

1984

of two New York friends traveling south; *Working on the Highway*, another glimpse into the daily lives of blue-collar workers; *I'm Goin' Down*, on the troubles of a couple; and *Dancing in the Dark*, on Springsteen's blank-page syndrome caused by physical and emotional dejection.

A long time coming

Although *Born in the U.S.A.* and *Nebraska* explore similar themes, their musical styles are very different. For the album following *Nebraska* (which features some of his strongest songs), Springsteen wanted to draw on the same themes, but to electrify them. Thus, *Born in the U.S.A.* became Springsteen's seventh studio album. It took several stages to create. The first stage, as previously mentioned, took place at Colts Neck at the beginning of 1982, when Springsteen composed *Born in the U.S.A., Working on the Highway, Downbound Train*, and the songs for *Nebraska* on his acoustic guitar. Springsteen then held recording sessions with the E Street Band, and after a solo recording of *Nebraska* at Colts Neck, he rejoined the group in the studio to record the final versions of *Born in the U.S.A., Working on the Highway, Downbound Train, Darlington County, Glory Days, I'm on Fire*, and *Cover Me.*

In his autobiography *Born to Run*, Bruce Springsteen talks about what happened next: "Then brain freeze settled in. I was uncomfortable with the pop aspect of my finished material and wanted something deeper, heavier, and more serious."[1] He then sat down to write again, this time in a small house he'd bought close to the Navesink River in New Jersey. There, he wrote *Bobby Jean, No Surrender, Dancing in the Dark*, and many other songs (which are available on the 1998 *Tracks* box set). Springsteen goes on to say that it was worth waiting for those last songs because they are such important elements in the final shape of the record. Two more stages, which took place between May and June 1983, and then between September and February 1984, would finally allow him to wrap up the album.

The E Street Band musicians together as never before during the Born in the U.S.A Tour. From left to right: Clarence Clemons, Bruce Springsteen, Nils Lofgren, Garry Tallent, and Patti Scialfa.

A rock orchestration

Born in the U.S.A. boasts a distinct rock orchestration characterized by slamming guitars, keyboards, a bass, and drums that hammer out, with each beat, the rage and disenchantment of the songwriter. Examples include the title song, *Cover Me*, and the highly provocative R&B sax performance (in *I'm Goin' Down*) performed by Clarence Clemons. For the first time, Bruce Springsteen's style was turning toward rock FM (known as Adult Contemporary in the United States), as is clearly seen in *Dancing in the Dark* and *My Hometown*.

The Boss, however, had not forgotten his roots. His intimate folk style remained intact in *Downbound Train*, while rockabilly still loomed large in *Working on the Highway*. He was still writing superb melodies that went straight to the hearts of his fans, like those in *Darlington County, No Surrender, Bobby Jean*, or *Dancing in the Dark*. *Born in the U.S.A.* allowed Bruce Springsteen to reach even greater heights in his career as a singer and songwriter than he had with *Born to Run* or *Darkness on the Edge of Town*, drawing on Bob Dylan and The Rolling Stones for ultimate inspiration. "*Born in the U.S.A.* changed my life, gave me my largest audience, forced me to think harder about the way I presented my music, and set me briefly at the center of the pop world,"[1] he writes in his autobiography.

The album

That was for sure. *Born in the U.S.A.* came out on 4 June 1984. Three weeks later it reached No.9 in the *Billboard* charts, after which it climbed to No.3 and, finally, No.1 on 7 July (for almost a month). To date, some 15 million copies have been sold in the United States alone (the album went platinum 15 times). Springsteen's commercial success was equally colossal outside his home country, with the album reaching No.1 in a dozen countries, including the United Kingdom, Australia, Canada, the Netherlands, West Germany, Norway, and Switzerland. It also reached No.2 in France, Italy, and Spain. With seven singles hitting the Top 10 charts, *Born in the U.S.A.* became a bestselling album (about 30 million copies).

The tour that followed the album's release began in Saint Paul, Minnesota, on 29 June 1984 and ended on 2 October the following year in Los Angeles (for a total of 156 concerts, eight of which were in Asia and 18 in Europe). The tour clearly contributed to the global success of the album, but it couldn't explain everything. As Ronald Reagan launched his neoliberal revolution in the United States and Margaret Thatcher implemented it in the United Kingdom, Bruce Springsteen's album looked like an act of resistance. It was at once a critique of American society and an impassioned declaration of love to those marginalized by this very society. As Keith Cameron wrote in *Mojo* magazine, "Behind the bluster and the '80s

In 1982, Steve Van Zandt left the Boss to play his own music with The Disciples of Soul (photographed here at the Kabuki Theater, San Francisco, in 1984).

production of *Born in the U.S.A.* lies a genuine cry of blue-collar political protest."[93]

Mio Fratello

Although *Born in the U.S.A.* was a monumental success for Bruce Springsteen, it came at a very painful price: Steve Van Zandt decided to leave the E Street Band in June 1982. "I've always felt a combination of personal frustration, internal politics, and unhappiness with some of my decisions led to Steve's departure," explained the Boss. "That along with my closeness to Jon Landau left my friend feeling distant from his pal and the direction my work had taken me."[1] In fact, Steve, aka "Miami Steve" and later "Little Steven"—to emphasize his transformation—was feeling more or less trapped in the E Street Band. He knew that if he couldn't be Springsteen's eternal right-hand man, he could not hope for anything else. The only solution that would allow him to set off on his own was to start a band, go on tour, and record his own songs. In June 1982, that's exactly what he did. He founded The Disciples of Soul and immediately took to the road. He also took advantage of the summer to finish his first album, *Men Without Women*. Van Zandt would, however, remain a coproducer of *Born in the U.S.A.* and sometimes participated in recording sessions even after leaving the group.

Springsteen and Van Zandt's friendship remained strong as their professional paths continued to cross; they met again on the concert circuit in the 2000s with the E Street Band. Springsteen marked his friend's departure (which, incidentally, was not made official until 1984 on the release of the album) and expressed his gratitude by writing a few words in Italian on the sleeve of *Born in the U.S.A.*: *"Buon viaggio, mio fratello, Little Steven"* ("Safe travels, my brother, Little Steven").

The sleeve

Annie Leibovitz was the photographer for the *Born in the U.S.A.* album sleeve. She had worked for *Rolling Stone* magazine between 1970 and 1983, and for *Vanity Fair* magazine from 1983. She took particularly striking portraits of rock stars, including members of The Rolling Stones and The Beach Boys, Marvin Gaye, and John Lennon and Yoko Ono (Annie Leibovitz took the famous shot of the couple embracing just a few hours before the former Beatle was assassinated). On both sides of the sleeve, Bruce Springsteen is standing with his back to the camera in front of the stripes of the American flag. He is wearing a white T-shirt and jeans, and a red baseball cap is tucked into his right back pocket. The cap, which belonged to the recently deceased father of his old friend, Lance Larson, matches the three colors of the flag.

As with the title song, this photograph provoked strong emotional responses, including outright anger. Firebrand Republicans believed it to be the ultimate sacrilege: the songwriter was clearly pissing on the sacred Star-Spangled

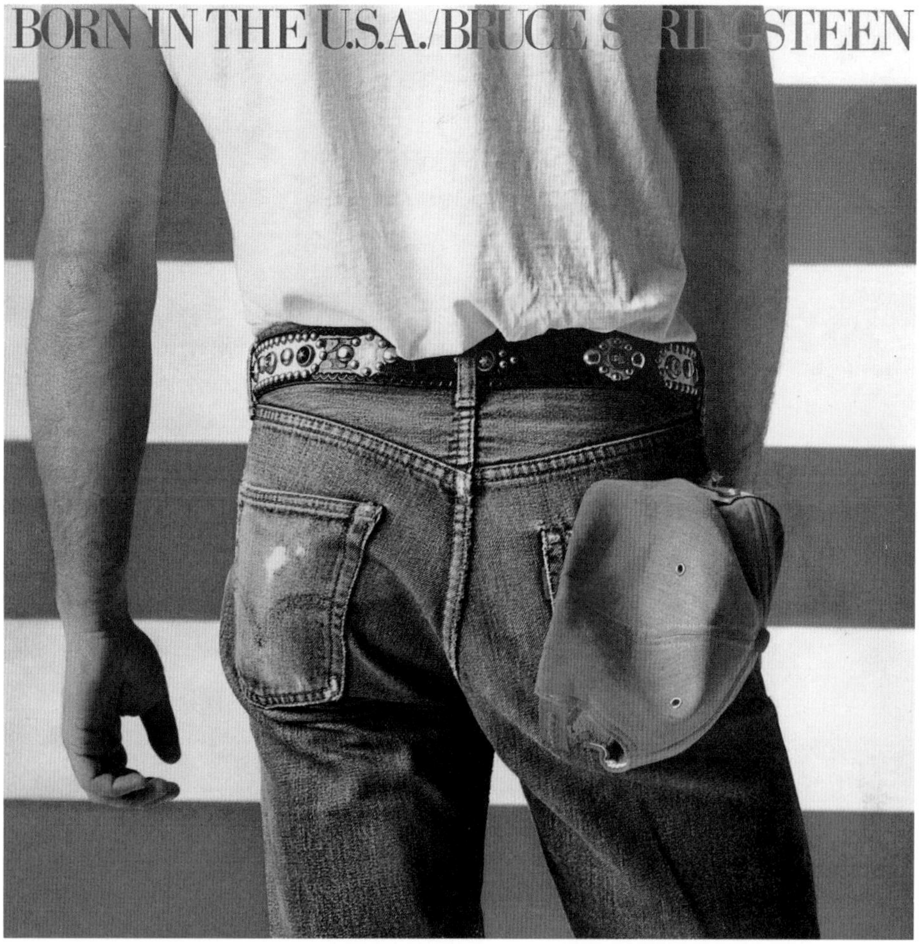

Annie Leibovitz took the controversial photo used for the *Born in the U.S.A.* jacket

Banner. This was not the case, as Springsteen assured Kurt Loder of *Rolling Stone* magazine: "That was unintentional. We took a lot of different types of pictures, and in the end, the picture of my ass looked better than the picture of my face, so that's what went on the cover. I didn't have any secret message."[89] Likewise, regarding the "Stars and Stripes," he said, "Well, we had the flag on the cover because the first song was called *Born in the U.S.A.*, and the theme of the record kind of follows from the themes I've been writing about for at least the last six or seven years."[89]

The inside of the sleeve contained a black and white photo of Bruce Springsteen (taken in front of his old house at 391/2 Institute Street in Freehold), another of the songwriter with the E Street Band, and the lyrics to the 12 songs.

The recording

Funnily enough, *Born in the U.S.A.*, Springsteen's bestselling album and the biggest success of his career, was also the most time-consuming and tortuous to make: it was created over the course of two years and in four separate stages.

During the first stage, from December 1981 to May 1982, Springsteen composed and recorded the material for *Nebraska* along with a few songs for *Born to Run*. Then, between April and May, he recorded the electric versions of *Nebraska* and the tracks for the first side of *Born in the U.S.A.* at The Power Station. Springsteen was still thinking of dropping a double album before reconsidering and opting to release *Nebraska* on its own in the September of that year.

The second phase took place between January and April 1983 in the garage of his new house in Los Angeles, where he'd had Mike Batlan install another home studio. He recorded a series of songs that he had hoped, at one point, to release as a follow-up to Nebraska. Only two of those songs would make their way onto the B-side of two singles released in 1984: *Shut Out the Light* and *Johnny Bye-Bye*.

During the third phase, from May to July 1983, the E Street Band got back together and stormed The Hit Factory in New York. During the fourth phase, from September 1984 to March 1984, the last songs of the album were recorded and the whole thing was mixed and mastered.

According to the estimates of Springsteen himself, Max Weinberg, and Chuck Plotkin, a total of 70 to 90 songs—including the *Nebraska* tracks—were recorded during this time. This was a testament to Springsteen's creativity, even though writer's block had momentarily slowed him down.

In addition to Jon Landau and Steve Van Zandt, Chuck Plotkin had come to the rescue, joining the team as a coproducer rather than as a mixer. The loyal Toby Scott got stuck with the job of recording engineer at The Power Station and at The Hit Factory, even though he knew he would also be working on Steve Van Zandt's first solo album in the summer of 1982.

Bob Clearmountain (in New York in 2010). His mixing contributions helped *Born in the U.S.A.* succeed as an album.

For Springsteen Addicts

Born in the U.S.A. was the first CD to be made in the United States. CBS and Sony made it at their appliance factory in Terre Haute, Indiana, which opened in 1984.

Discontent

Not for lack of songs, the production of *Born in the U.S.A.* revealed cracks in the group's dynamic and in the Boss's creative process. The release of *Nebraska*, which was his first real solo album, had shaken his artistic vision to the core. He had taken so much pleasure in its creation and had been so satisfied with the result that he subconsciously—or consciously—wanted to repeat the operation with a *Nebraska II*. Hence, his home studio in Los Angeles. However, the E Street Band had literally been unemployed since the recording sessions of April and May 1982. The group wouldn't return to a studio until the following year, at The Hit Factory in New York, and without Steve Van Zandt who'd left to launch his own solo career. Chuck Plotkin, who was by then a coproducer, described the discontent Springsteen was feeling when he said, "Bruce would ask me what I thought about a guitar solo, and I'd say, 'I don't know. I don't know what the song's about. I don't know whether the guitar solo's the right guitar solo, because I'm not getting any hit off the song.' He'd say, 'Well, all right then, I'll just do this guitar solo.' After two or three of those responses, he just stopped asking me what I thought. I went through a period for about two months where we hardly talked."[16]

Meanwhile, the songwriter was having a nervous breakdown that would come to haunt him for more than 30 years. His strength wavered and his childhood frustrations began to weigh on him heavily. Dr Wayne Myers eventually helped him confront his personal challenges and keep his head above water. But for the time being, he was hiding his problems from those closest to him. This was the context in which he completed *Born in the U.S.A.*, whose phenomenal success would only deepen his neurosis.

A painful delivery

Before deciding on a final tracklisting, Springsteen and his team fought over the best choices for this seventh album. Faced with a considerable number of songs, Springsteen struggled to define the character of the album. He considered scrapping the songs recorded during the Electric Nebraska Sessions between April and May 1982, including *Born in the U.S.A.* Landau and Plotkin fought this decision. Springsteen ended up giving in, despite his desire to incorporate more material recorded in 1983. "By that time, I'd recorded a lot of music (see Disc three of *Tracks*)," he explains in his autobiography. "But in the end, I circled back to my original group of songs. There I found a naturalism and aliveness that couldn't be argued with. They weren't exactly what I'd been looking for, but they were what I had."[1]

Mixing began in late 1983. Chuck Plotkin, who was too closely involved in the production of the album, didn't have the distance needed to take the lead on it. So, the team recruited Bob Clearmountain, who'd already worked on *The River*, including *Hungry Heart*. However, toward the end of mixing, in February 1984, Landau thought the album was

The Yamaha CS-80—one of the star synthesizers of the 1980s—lent its idiosyncratic sound to *Born in the U.S.A.*

missing a hit for the radio stations. He managed to convince Springsteen to go back to work, but this was not without some agony. This is how the songwriter came to compose *Dancing in the Dark*, which went on to become the bestselling song of his career, in only one night.

Technical details

The equipment in Studio A, at The Power Station, was pretty much the same as that used for *The River* except for the console, which, according to Toby Scott, was a 44-input Neve 8048. To record the group, which was basically playing live in the studio, the recording engineer placed each member in a separate part of the room: Max Weinberg and Garry Tallent were together in the main area, with the bass on live input and connected to an amp (taken with an Electro-Voice RE20), and Steve Van Zandt, Springsteen, Danny Federici, and Roy Bittan were each in an isolated booth. Meanwhile, Clarence Clemons was playing both the saxophone and percussion in the recording room, all while remaining in visual contact with his band mates through the porthole in the front door.

Springsteen's voice was recorded with Neuman U87s and U67 microphones, a dual capsule Sanken CU-41, and a superb Telefunken ELA M 251E. Scott chose to use an AKG 451 microphone for his acoustic guitar. Finally, the recording engineer got his hands on the famous Yamaha NS-10 loudspeakers that would become the quintessential speakers for the majority of studios around the world.

Bob Clearmountain used the Digital Delay Line AMS DMX 15-80, particularly for its digital sampling option and to successfully sample the snare drum in *Born in the U.S.A.*

The Boss's home studio that Mike Batlan had installed in the garage of his home in Los Angeles was equipped with a Teac Tascam 38 eight-track tape recorder and an 8-voice console, likely the eight input Teac Model 3, Pro series.

The instruments

In addition to his usual instrument, Roy Bittan played the Yamaha CS-80, one of the first digital synthesizers with FM synthesis. It was a heavy synthesizer—it weighed 220lb (100kg)! Vangelis was one of its most famous users; he used one to compose the soundtrack for *Chariots of Fire* (1981) and *Blade Runner* (1982). It would later become world famous during the 1980s. Bittan also appears to have used a Yamaha DX7 for *Dancing in the Dark*.

BORN IN THE U.S.A.

Bruce Springsteen / 4'39

1984

Musicians

Bruce Springsteen: vocals, guitars
Steve Van Zandt: guitars
Clarence Clemons: maracas
Roy Bittan: keyboards
Danny Federici: glockenspiel, piano
Garry Tallent: bass
Max Weinberg: drums

Recording

The Power Station, 441 West 53rd St, New York: 27–28 April, 3 May 1982

Technical team

Producers: Bruce Springsteen, Jon Landau, Chuck Plotkin, Steve Van Zandt
Recording engineer: Toby Scott
Assistant recording engineers: John Davenport, Jeff Hendrickson, Bruce Lampcov, Billy Straus, Zoë Yanakas
Mixing: Bob Clearmountain
Mastering: Bob Ludwig

Director Paul Schrader. Bruce Springsteen named one of his songs after a script that was sent to him.

Genesis and lyrics

Bruce Springsteen wrote *Born in the U.S.A.* in Colts Neck alongside the acoustic songs in *Nebraska*. The director Paul Schrader had sent him a screenplay and had asked him to write the music for it. It was the story of a brother and sister who try, with some difficulty, to make a name for themselves on the Cleveland rock scene. "I strummed a few chords on my Sunburst Gibson J-200, paged through my notebook, stopped and murmured a verse of a song I had under way about returning Vietnam vets. I glanced over at the unread script's cover page and sang out its title; I was *Born in the U.S.A.*"[1] Something had clicked for the songwriter. As he admits in his autobiography, the song *Born in the U.S.A.* was taken straight from the title page of that script by Paul Schrader. He goes on to note: "The film would later be released as *Light of Day*, featuring my song of the same name, my polite attempt at paying Paul back for my fortuitous and career-boosting theft."[1]

Born in the U.S.A. is a protest song. In a sense, it is the musical version of the book *Born on the Fourth of July*, in which Ron Kovic, who would later be wheelchair-bound, bore witness to the events of the Vietnam War. The main character is a former soldier from a forgotten corner of the American heartland. They "put a gun in his hand" and "sent him off to a foreign land to go and kill the yellow man." Once home in the land of Uncle Sam, he returns to his job at a refinery. Kovic came out alive from this war, unlike one of his friends, who was "fighting off the Viet Cong" and died at Khe Sanh, leaving behind "a woman he loved in Saigon." Meanwhile, the communist fighters are still there, living, but ignored—even hated, abandoned to memories that will haunt them forever, and to emotional scars with which they will have to live until their dying day. However, he was "born in the U.S.A." and was defending the free world...

The essence of this song lies in the duality between the verses—which express the somber reality of a soldier—and the chorus, which loudly and proudly proclaims the glory of American civilization. Springsteen remembers giving the first recording of this rock rhythm duality to Bobby Muller, then president of the Vietnam Veterans of America. Muller apparently listened to the song and then gave a huge smile.

"A songwriter writes to be understood,"[1] affirms Bruce Springsteen in his autobiography. He must therefore have been

The Boss sings *Born in the U.S.A.* dressed in leather and with his fist in the air.

pretty surprised when some Americans understood *Born in the U.S.A.* to be a patriotic song, a sort of glorification of American pride. Ronald Reagan himself, during a rally in Hammonton, New Jersey, during his 1984 presidential campaign, made sure to bring up Springsteen's greatness: "America's future rests in a thousand dreams inside your hearts; it rests in the message of hope in songs of a man so many young Americans admire: New Jersey's own, Bruce Springsteen."[94]

Was it all a misunderstanding? By all accounts, yes. Although Bruce Springsteen hadn't wanted to write a particularly antipatriotic or anti-nationalist song, he had taken the side of rural American blue-collar workers who had been raised to respect the ideals of the founding fathers and had gone to fight a war that, if not already lost from the start, was at least illegitimate for many. These were the people who now bore the burden of this injustice. Springsteen, however, was very kind, or resigned, when the Republicans, or Grand Old Party, tried to claim the author of *Born in the U.S.A.* for themselves. In an interview with Terry Gross, he confessed: "My music, it's often been a football...where I'd occasionally have folks from the far left to the right wanting to use it as 'this represents us and our ideas.'"[95] He added, "But people use pop music in a lot of different ways. So it's an ongoing struggle, what can I say?"[95]

Born in the U.S.A. was chosen for the A-side of the third single from this album (with *Shut Out the Light* on the B-side). It came out on 30 October 1984. While the song only reached No.8 in the United States, it climbed to the top of the charts in Ireland and New Zealand, reaching No.2 in Australia and No.5 in the United Kingdom. Today, it is 275th in *Rolling Stone's* list of the 500 Greatest Songs of All Time and 59th on the American record industry's (Recording Industry Association of America) list of songs of the century. Since the concert at The Stone Pony in Asbury Park on 8 June 1984, Springsteen has performed this song close to a thousand times.

Production

Born in the U.S.A. came from a song that was originally called *Vietnam*, written and recorded by Springsteen at Colts Neck in the fall of 1981. After receiving Paul Schrader's script from Jon Landau, he gave it a different spin and changed its title. In a letter to Landau containing the demo of the piece (as well as all the pieces from *Nebraska*), he specified that, "This song should be done very hard rockin..."[6] And added, "It might have

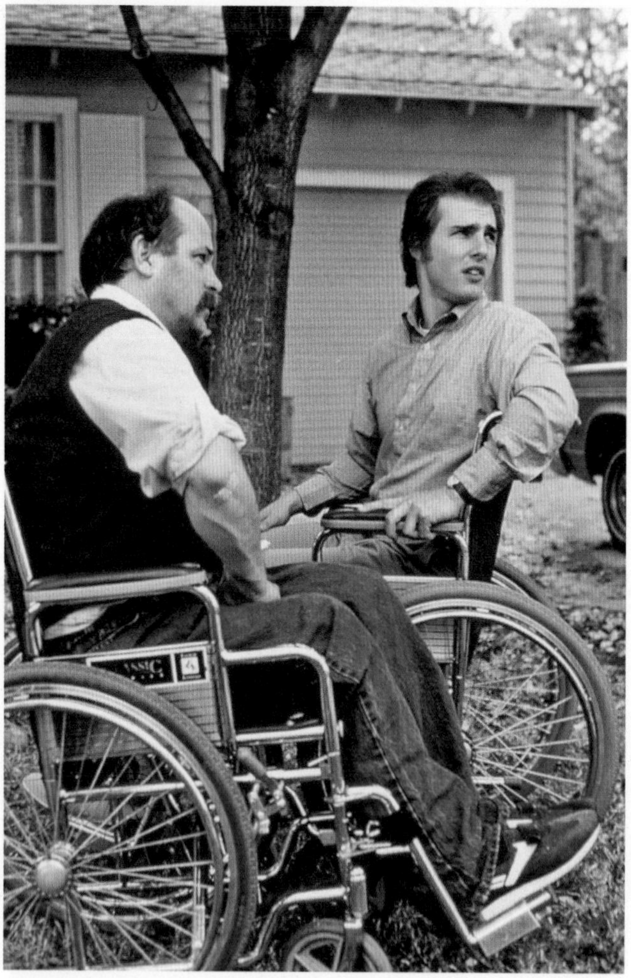

Tom Cruise plays Ron Kovic in *Born on the Fourth of July*, directed by Oliver Stone. A pacifist film.

John Sayles shot the music video for *Born in the U.S.A.* He was the scriptwriter for *Piranha* (1978) and *Battle Beyond the Stars* (1980), as well as the director, among other feature films, of *Eight Men Out* (1988), with John Cusak, and *Sunshine State* (2002) with Angela Bassett.

For Springsteen Addicts

Chrysler offered Bruce Springsteen $12 million to use *Born in the U.S.A.* for an ad campaign. The songwriter refused. On the other hand, he allowed the rap group The 2 Live Crew to repurpose the song for *Banned in the USA* (1990).

1984

potential."[6] This version is completely different from the one on the album. The style is rockabilly, and the melody is something else altogether—only the lyrics are practically the same. During the April 1982 sessions, known as the Electric Nebraska Sessions, Springsteen presented the song to the group after having modified it. No one, not even Landau, remembers having heard it on the demo. "To me, it was a dead song. It was one of the lesser songs on the *Nebraska* tape. Clearly the words and the music didn't go together,"[16] said Landau. But Springsteen knew there was something special about it, and that, unlike the other pieces in his demo, it would take all his energy to make an electronic version of this song with the group. He explained their respective parts to the musicians, and, as was his usual approach, kept them from over-rehearsing in order to preserve their spontaneity. "We just kinda did it off the cuff," Bruce remembered. "I went in and said, 'Roy, get this riff.' And he just pulled out that sound, played the riff on the synthesizer. We played it two times and our second take is the record. That's why the guys are really on the edge. You can hear Max—to me, he was right up there with the best of them on that song. There was no arrangement. I said, 'When I stop, keep the drums going.' That thing in the end with all the drums, that just kinda happened."[16]

The piece was recorded at The Power Station recording studio, in New York, on 27 and 28 April, and completed on 3 May. There were reportedly four recordings, only two of which were completed (the first ended with a long coda, bringing the length of the piece to more than eight minutes). However, on the session sheet it says: "Take 9." Whatever the case, the recording was done at lightning speed.

How to make a hit

Born in the U.S.A. is composed of two sounds: the synthesizer and the snare drum. The piece starts off with a bass note on Roy Bittan's synthesizer and on Danny Federici's piano. Then the half-brassy, half-Oriental riff of the Yamaha CS-80 literally illuminates the extraordinary introduction. According to Bittan, this riff came to him after hearing the melody of the chorus as he was trying to find a sound that was both warlike and Oriental. But why feature a tonality that was so different from Springsteen's style? "I think Bruce was looking, even at that time, for more color other than just classic instrumentation," he explained. "At that particular moment, synthesizers were in vogue. I, of course, was interested for obvious reasons. There was a backlash against synthesizers for not really being a rock 'n' roll thing and 'it's not this and not that,' but I always recognized it as a tool to paint other colors."[45]

Another important feature is Max Weinberg's snare drum. Multiple factors combined to create this sound: the extraordi-

Bruce Springsteen inveighs against warmongers in *Born in the U.S.A.* under the supportive eye of Max Weinberg, whose snare drum cracks like a gunshot.

narily powerful beat of the drummer, the incredible acoustics of The Power Station's Studio A, and a happy series of accidents. Toby Scott, the recording engineer, had found a faulty EMT reverb unit. After troubleshooting it with his assistant, he wrote: "Perfect, I'll take it!" He continued: "'Put my name on it for the duration of this project!' I wanted stuff that nobody else was going to screw with."[79] This is how, after plugging the first snare drum mic into a Valley People Kepex—the only noise gate available at the time—and the second into the faulty reverb unit, he obtained an incredible sound that literally cracked like a gunshot.

One last element adds to the magic of this snare drum, even though it more or less contradicts Toby Scott's version. Bob Clearmountain brought it to the final mixing session: "What I did for a few songs on that album—and I think that was one of them—was to use the great sound I'd got from the stereo overhead mics. The snare sound was amazing, for one thing because Max [Weinberg] tunes his drums really well. The snare drum mic itself wasn't happening, maybe because it was too close, but the overhead mics were picking up this 'Glyn Johns' kind of snare sound. So I just sampled that into an AMS, and it became the predominant snare drum sound, although it is mixed in with the original snare drum track. It was easy to do because there are no other drums playing during the intro part."[96]

The rest of the song is characterized by the extraordinary vocals of Springsteen, who always pushed his voice to breaking point, and the formidable performance of the other musicians: Danny Federici on the piano, Steve Van Zandt (probably on the 12-string guitar), the Boss on both the 6-string acoustic guitar and the electric guitar, Garry Tallent on an absolutely superb bass line, and Clarence Clemons on the maracas.

As explained earlier, Springsteen had asked Max Weinberg to continue drumming on his signal, while he himself would stop. But the message was misunderstood: Weinberg stopped playing, and the other musicians, who hadn't been warned, continued to play (starting from 3'58). Some confusion ensued, but the Boss quickly intervened to set the group back on track with a well-timed count (at 4'09).

Born in the U.S.A., the first song recorded for Springsteen's seventh album, was also one of the most successful from a production standpoint, in terms of artistic value, and because of the notoriety that it brought him. That's art.

COVER ME

Bruce Springsteen / 3'26

1984

Musicians

Bruce Springsteen: vocals, guitars
Steve Van Zandt: guitars (?), backing vocals (?)
Clarence Clemons: maracas
Roy Bittan: piano
Danny Federici: organ
Garry Tallent: bass
Max Weinberg: drums
Richie "La Bamba" Rosenberg: backing vocals

Recording

The Hit Factory, 421 West 54th St, New York: 25 January 1982

Technical team

Producers: Bruce Springsteen, Jon Landau, Chuck Plotkin, Steve Van Zandt
Recording engineers: Bill Sheniman (?), Neil Dorfsman (?)
Mixing: Bob Clearmountain
Mastering: Bob Ludwig

David Geffen, founder of Geffen Records and friend of Jon Landau. Bruce Springsteen wrote *Cover Me* at his request.

Genesis and lyrics

The narrator of *Cover Me* could very well be the main character in *Born in the U.S.A.*; that is, a Vietnam veteran who has returned home with some serious problems. Clearly afflicted by what's known as post-traumatic stress disorder, he asks his girlfriend, almost begs her, to protect him: "Promise me, baby, you won't let them find us." Who is he hiding from? It must be a flashback, in which case, it would be the Viet Cong, or the soldiers of the North Vietnamese People's Army. What is for sure, is that he has fallen, or is in the process of falling, into acute paranoia. He wants his girlfriend to turn off the light and lock the door to the house as a wild wind has picked up and "this whole world is out there just trying to score."

David Geffen, Jon Landau's friend and the founder of Geffen Records, had asked Bruce Springsteen to write *Cover Me* (a song that originated from another of the Boss's compositions called *Drop On Down and Cover Me*) for disco queen Donna Summer—whom Geffen had just signed. "She could really sing and I disliked the veiled racism of the anti-disco movement,"[6] Springsteen explains in his book *Songs*. "When I cut the demo, it came out so good that I held on to it. I later wrote another song, *Protection*, and recorded it with Donna and Quincy Jones in LA."[6] It would seem that Jon Landau was really the one to convince Bruce Springsteen to include it in *Born in the U.S.A.*

Cover Me is on the A-side of the second single from the album (with *Jersey Girl* on the B-side). It became available in stores on 31 July 1984 and would reach No.7 in the *Billboard* Hot 100, but No.2 in the *Billboard* US Mainstream Rock chart.

Production

The making of *Cover Me* was somewhat atypical of Bruce Springsteen's discography: while at The Hit Factory in New York to produce Gary U.S. Bonds' next album, *On the Line*, with Steve Van Zandt on 25 January 1982, he recorded the demo for *Cover Me*, a new piece he'd just written. Since the entire E Street Band was present in the studio, it was easy enough to record the song, which included one of the best guitar solos the Boss had ever played. This was the song David Geffen had asked him to reserve for Donna Summer. After hearing the hit, Landau convinced him to keep it. Bill Sheniman, Neil Dorfsman's assistant, who was then in charge

Clarence Clemons and Bruce Springsteen at the Giants Stadium, East Rutherford, New Jersey, on 21 August 1985. A Telecaster-Esquire and percussion instruments for *Cover Me*.

of *On the Line*, would have been at the controls, but Dorfsman would later claim that it was more him, and that a mistake had crept into the credits of *Born in the U.S.A.*

Cover Me starts off with a very good introduction carried by Springsteen's Telecaster-Esquire, with which he delivers a solo reminiscent of David Gilmour. The rhythm is a mix of rock, disco, and funk. It is impressive in its efficiency, to say the least. The Weinberg-Tallent duo provides an excellent groove, even though the drummer would later say he was not satisfied with his performance. The guitars of Van Zandt and the Boss rival the masters of the genre and are supported by Roy Bittan's excellent and perfectly syncopated piano. Clarence Clemons is once again at the maracas, while Danny Federici has picked up his Hammond B-3 again, to bring that crucial touch of soul.

Springsteen's vocals are excellent, as are Richie "La Bamba" Rosenberg's backing vocals, which can be heard at the end of the chorus (for example, at 0'25). Steve Van Zandt did not appear to participate. "La Bamba," a trombonist by trade, was also working on the latter's first solo album, *Men Without Women*, during this time. He would cross paths with Springsteen over the course of his career, and even more so with Max Weinberg, as he would later join the Max Weinberg and The Tonight Show Band in 2009.

Cover Me is most notable for Springsteen's superb guitar solo (at 1'37). He plays with surprising motivation and technique, his Telecaster-Esquire roaring with elegance and emotion. Although he is not a "guitar hero" of the level of Jimmy Page, Hendrix, or Clapton, his feeling for the instrument is just as deep. He has the instinct for that killer note and delivers a more than honorable performance. Springsteen astonishes, once again, with his many talents.

On 12 May 1982, the Boss would try to rerecord *Cover Me* at The Power Station, but he wouldn't be able to beat the version made at The Hit Factory. This excellent song, performed by incredible musicians, is among the album's greatest successes.

Bruce Springsteen wasn't the only one to name a song *Cover Me*: others have done it both before and after him, including Percy Sledge in 1968 (in *Take Time to Know Her*), Björk in 1995 (in *Post*), or, more recently, Depeche Mode in 2017 (in *Spirit*).

DARLINGTON COUNTY

Bruce Springsteen / 4'48

1984

Musicians
Bruce Springsteen: vocals, guitars
Steve Van Zandt: guitars, backing vocals
Clarence Clemons: saxophone, cowbell, maracas, backing vocals
Roy Bittan: piano, backing vocals
Danny Federici: organ
Garry Tallent: bass, backing vocals
Max Weinberg: drums, backing vocals
Recording
The Power Station, 441 West 53rd St, New York: 13 May 1982
Technical team
Producers: Bruce Springsteen, Jon Landau, Chuck Plotkin, Steve Van Zandt
Recording engineer: Toby Scott
Assistant recording engineers: John Davenport, Jeff Hendrickson, Bruce Lampcov, Billy Straus, Zoë Yanakas
Mixing: Bob Clearmountain
Mastering: Bob Ludwig

Clarence Clemons at the Oakland Coliseum Arena in October 1984. The saxophonist plays a passionate solo of *Darlington County*.

Genesis and lyrics

Bruce Springsteen wrote *Darlington County* at the end of the 1970s during the recording sessions for *Darkness on the Edge of Town*. He recorded a version of it with the E Street Band in April 1982. Using music that pays tribute to John Fogerty of Creedence Clearwater Revival, the songwriter tells the story of two New York friends on a road trip. The narrator and his friend Wayne set out on 4 July, a day of national celebration, toward the southern United States. They think they can find work there, thanks to Wayne's uncle, who seems to have some sway in a union. However, when they arrive in Darlington, South Carolina, after having covered some 800 miles (1,300km) while listening to good rock 'n' roll on the radio, they're more interested in girls than in anything else. They have so much money in their pockets that, as they say with a good dose of humor, their "pas each own one of the world trade centers." In short, they plan to seduce these sweet teens with the mighty dollar.

The journey south, however, doesn't turn out as they'd hoped. The narrator stops hiding his concern when he hasn't seen his friend in seven days. As he gets ready to leave Darlington with a "young and pretty" girl, he sees Wayne handcuffed to the bumper of a state police Ford. What could he have done to get himself arrested? Bruce Springsteen doesn't tell us. One can only hazard a guess. To get to South Carolina, the two friends would have had to take I-95, which connects Florida to Canada (New Brunswick) through big East Coast cities. I-95 is a strategic route for drug traffickers who supply networks in Philadelphia, Newark, or New York from Miami. One can also assume that the uncle in question, the head of a large-scale drug operation, had entrusted Wayne, his nephew, with a dangerous mission, and that the latter had finally been caught. But that's just a theory. What's certain is that Bruce Springsteen and the E Street Band loved performing *Darlington County* live, which they did at The Stone Pony, in Asbury Park, on 8 June 1984.

Production

Darlington County was recorded in two takes at The Power Station on 13 May 1982, with a few extra overdubs to complete the track. It was among the first songs recorded during the Electric Nebraska Sessions. Springsteen would return to this

The E Street Band during the Born in the U.S.A. Tour. *Darlington County* is a rock song with an infectious seductive power and a very "Stonian" riff.

studio after many months of wandering to complete *Born in the U.S.A.*

During this time, the group displayed impressive style and effectiveness. Most of the musicians had participated in the recording of Gary U.S. Bonds' album *On the Line* and also Steve Van Zandt's *Men Without Women*. The E Street Band machine was therefore perfectly oiled to record the Boss's new songs, especially since Springsteen used psychological tricks to get as much spontaneity as possible out of them. As he explains: "But the first two takes when they're learnin' it, they're worried about just hangin' on. So they're playing right at the edge, and they're playing very intuitively, which is in general how our best stuff happens right now."[10]

This is what happens with *Darlington County*, which is an upbeat rock over very cryptic lyrics. The piece starts off with Clarence Clemons's cowbells and is immediately followed by a riff in the style of The Rolling Stones (a "Stonian" riff) performed by Springsteen on his Telecaster-Esquire. The strings crack and are backed up by the booming sound of Max Weinberg's snare drum, which he plays liberally. After a few measures, the group joins in in the purest tradition of the genre. There is nothing new under the sun here, which is rather surprising. *Born in the U.S.A.* and *Cover Me* had taken the album in a direction that conformed to its era.

The musicians clearly enjoyed playing this musical style, which was so close to their common roots. Clarence Clemons, previously on percussion, finally dives into a very good saxophone solo after the second chorus (at 2'34). He reappears in the coda after the Boss has, for the second time, introduced him with an enthusiastic shout of "Big Man!" (at 2'33 and 3'41). The piece concludes with the laughs and shouts that can be heard at the end of the fade-out (from 4'42).

Bruce Springsteen also played *Darlington County* as an acoustic version, with him on vocals, harmonica, and 6-string guitar, Nils Lofgren on 12-string guitar, and Danny Federici on accordion. He performed this excellent version at the first Bridge School Benefit Concert, a nonprofit organization run by Neil and Pegi Young, at the Shoreline Amphitheatre in Mountain View, California, on 13 October 1986.

COVER

Jeff Stevens and The Bullets recorded a version of *Darlington County* for their first album, *Bolt Out of the Blue* (1986). This version reached No.69 in the *Billboard* charts for country music the following year.

WORKING ON THE HIGHWAY

Bruce Springsteen / 3'13

1984

Musicians

Bruce Springsteen: vocals, guitars
Steve Van Zandt: guitars
Danny Federici: organ
Garry Tallent: bass
Max Weinberg: drums
The group: handclaps

Recording

The Power Station, 441 West 53rd St, New York: 30 April, 6 May 1982

Technical team

Producers: Bruce Springsteen, Jon Landau, Chuck Plotkin, Steve Van Zandt
Recording engineer: Toby Scott
Assistant recording engineers: John Davenport, Jeff Hendrickson, Bruce Lampcov, Billy Straus, Zoë Yanakas
Mixing: Bob Clearmountain
Mastering: Bob Ludwig

For Springsteen Addicts

The story behind *Working on the Highway* is similar to that of *I Fought the Law*, written by Sonny Curtis and recorded by Bobby Fuller in 1966, and later by The Clash in 1977. The main character splits rocks under an unforgiving sun because he "fought the law, and the law won."

Genesis and lyrics

Originally called *Child Bride*, *Working on the Highway* was created in 1982 at Colts Neck. It was another song dedicated to blue-collar workers whom Bruce Springsteen knew well (for want of sharing their day-to-day experiences). His character is a roadside worker on I-95 (a nod to *Darlington County*?). He says, "I hold a red flag and watch the traffic pass me by," while "laying down the blacktop" all day long. But his mind is elsewhere. He obsesses over the image of a young woman he wants to marry. He ends up running away to Florida with his girlfriend against her father's wishes. That's where the troubles start: first, the brothers of the innocent fugitive set off to take her home, then a judge sends him straight to prison. This is when he is sentenced to forced labor. "Me and my warden go swinging on the Charlotte County road gang," sings Springsteen at the end of the song. The downtrodden working-class hero now leads a life where he and his fellow roadside workers must wait for payday before they can go for a few drinks and leave their shovel, pickax, and asphalt behind.

Production

Working on the Highway is an excellent rockabilly tune marked by the expert hand of Max Weinberg and his irresistible drums. The drummer had come a long way. During the production of *The River*, the Boss had told him that his beat was off. Feeling that his position in the band was precarious, he immediately signed up for classes with Sonny Igoe, a master of rhythm. *Working on the Highway* is a testament to the progress he made.

The familiar atmosphere of the song leaves no doubt as to its association with *Nebraska*, especially with songs such as *Johnny 99*. The rhythm revolves around the riff of the Telecaster-Esquire—accompanied by Danny Federici's Farfisa organ from the third chorus—Garry Tallent's excellent bass line, the two acoustic guitar parts, and, of course, Weinberg's drums as well as the handclaps, a key rockabilly element. Springsteen's voice is exemplary, colored by a slapback echo that Elvis himself would have envied. Despite its '50s-revival feel, *Working on the Highway* sounds strikingly modern—no doubt thanks to Clearmountain's expert mixing.

DOWNBOUND TRAIN

Bruce Springsteen / 3'35

The Downbound Train is a song by Chuck Berry, released by Chess Records on the B-side of *No Money Down* in 1956. While it has nothing in common with Springsteen's song, it also deserves to be (re)discovered.

Musicians

Bruce Springsteen: vocals, guitars
Steve Van Zandt: guitars (?)
Roy Bittan: keyboards
Garry Tallent: bass
Max Weinberg: drums

Recording

The Power Station, 441 West 53rd St, New York: 27–28 April, 3, 5, and 6 May 1982

Technical team

Producers: Bruce Springsteen, Jon Landau, Chuck Plotkin, Steve Van Zandt
Recording engineer: Toby Scott
Assistant recording engineers: John Davenport, Jeff Hendrickson, Bruce Lampcov, Billy Straus, Zoë Yanakas
Mixing: Bob Clearmountain
Mastering: Bob Ludwig

Bruce Springsteen, a born performer and passionate defender of a forgotten America, as evidenced by *Downbound Train*.

Genesis and lyrics

Bruce Springsteen recorded an acoustic demo of *Downbound Train* in early 1982, along with the songs that would make up *Nebraska*. Again, the song portrays the life of the American lay person, more specifically a sawmill worker who has just lost his job. He barely makes ends meet, thanks to a small job at a car wash. What's worse, the woman he loves has left him. One evening, "she bought a ticket on the Central Line" and "I feel her kiss in the misty rain," sings Springsteen, who then adds, "I feel like I'm a rider on a downbound train."

The narrator is so distressed, that in his dreams he thinks he hears the voice of his ex-wife, who is crying and saying she is waiting for him at home. But after running back to his "wedding house," he finds that no one is there. "The room was dark, our bed was empty." The only real thing is his job, no longer at the car wash, but on the railroad. And always that dripping water, a persistent symbol of bitter disillusionment and loss. A song in the tradition of Bob Dylan.

Production

"An uptempo rocker for full effect needs band/could be exciting."[6] This is what Springsteen said in his letter to Jon Landau that he included with the *Nebraska* demo, which contained *Downbound Train*. He and the E Street Band put his plan into action in April, during the Electric Nebraska Sessions. However, the rhythm of the recorded version was more moderate than expected, and, while he hoped the group would bring more power, the second part of *Downbound Train*—aside from the coda—is only accompanied by a synthesizer and an acoustic guitar (between 1'35 and 2'33). He may have been hesitating between acoustic and electric methods.

Whatever the case, *Downbound Train* is a very good rock song with a minimalist approach. It is mainly harmonized by the synth pads and sounds of Roy Bitten's Yamaha CS-80, the superb drums of Max Weinberg—whose ambience mics were added during mixing—and the moving voice of the songwriter. *Downbound Train* was a new foray into the sounds of the early 1980s.

On 30 June 2013, Springsteen and his band electrify a London audience with an incandescent version of *I'm on Fire.*

Many American radio stations stopped playing *I'm on Fire* after September 11 because the words were thought to be too sensitive.

I'M ON FIRE

Bruce Springsteen / 2'36

1984

Musicians
Bruce Springsteen: vocals, guitar
Roy Bittan: keyboard
Max Weinberg: drums

Recording
The Power Station, 441 West 53rd St, New York: 11 May 1982

Technical team
Producers: Bruce Springsteen, Jon Landau, Chuck Plotkin, Steve Van Zandt
Recording engineer: Toby Scott
Assistant recording engineers: John Davenport, Jeff Hendrickson, Bruce Lampcov, Billy Straus, Zoë Yanakas
Mixing: Bob Clearmountain
Mastering: Bob Ludwig

Johnny Cash (seen here backstage at Carnegie Hall, in July 1965). *I'm on Fire* is a tribute to the "man in black".

Genesis and lyrics

In his book *Songs*, Bruce Springsteen reveals the context in which this song was born in May 1982 during the electric phase of *Nebraska*: "*I'm on Fire* came to me one night in the studio when I was just goofing around with a Johnny Cash and The Tennessee Three rhythm."[6] Roy Bittan and Max Weinberg were on the keyboard and drums, respectively.

While "the man in black" inspired the rhythm, its lyrics were among the most erotic the New Jersey songwriter had ever written. He sings: "Hey, little girl, is your daddy home?" and "Tell me now, baby, is he good to you?/And can he do to you the things that I do?" Adding: "I'm on fire." (The "daddy" in question is not the father of the young woman, but her boyfriend.) The heroine provokes an uncontrollable desire in the narrator, who that night "[wakes] up with the sheet soaking wet and a freight train running through the middle of my head."

I'm on Fire is on the A-side of the fourth single from *Born in the U.S.A.* (with *Bye Bye Johnny* by Chuck Berry on the B-side). The song reached No.7 in the *Billboard* chart on 2 March 1985, then No.5 in the British charts on 15 June the following year (on a double A-side single with *Born in the U.S.A.*). It was a big success, thanks in part to the music video directed by John Sayles. Bruce Springsteen plays the role of a mechanic who becomes captivated by a young woman in a white dress even though he can only see her legs, at first. She then speaks to him in a sensual voice and hands him the keys to her car. It won "Best Video for a Male Artist" at the second MTV Video Music Awards (1985).

Production

During a break in the studio one evening, Springsteen was having some fun with a rhythmic pattern inspired by a Johnny Cash song, *Ring of Fire*. Did this song provide twofold inspiration, with its rhythm and title? Regardless, after hearing Springsteen, Jon Landau, who was at the controls, pushed him to continue. Max Weinberg and Roy Bittan chimed in after taking their places at their respective instruments: the first at his drums, and the second at his Yamaha CS-80. As soon as they got a feel for the song, they began to accompany the Boss as best they could, and, after nine takes, *I'm on Fire* was successfully recorded. The trio had just achieved a masterstroke: there were no other musicians present—there was no bass, no

For Springsteen Addicts

The voice of the faceless young woman in the video is that of Maggie Renzi, the producer of the video and an associate of John Sayles. She was also an actress in her time, notably in *Eight Men Out* (1988) and *City of Hope* (1991), which were both directed by the very same John Sayles. The woman whose legs and hands we see is probably Cybill Shepherd (*Taxi Driver* [1976], *Chances Are* [1989], and the series *Moonlighting* [1985–1989]).

I'm on Fire is on the original score of *Fifty Shades of Grey* (2015), directed by Sam Taylor-Johnson. This is not Springsteen's original recording, but the version by the electronic rock group Awolnation.

organ, no percussion. "That album was more minimalist than most people realize," explained Roy Bitten. "In many ways, less is really more. Often, we'd think we were making it big by piling on overdubs, but it works better and sounds larger when there's space between what people are playing."[50]

As for the arrangements, *I'm on Fire* relies on three instruments. First, Weinberg's superb drum performance using both cross-stick and broomstick (on the left of the stereo), and the bass drum punctuating the tempo with precise regularity. The result is simple, the groove exemplar, the effectiveness total. Then there is Springsteen's Telecaster-Esquire (on the right), on which he plays a rhythmic and melodic tune in palm mute, more or less stifling his cords. The sound is carried by a delay, which is probably created by his Echoplex. The perfect regularity of the chords is also notable. Finally, the last essential element of this piece: Bittan's Yamaha CS-80 is both soaring and harmonious, encircled by extraordinary, space-like reverberations that bring an almost dreamlike dimension to the arrangements.

I'm on Fire would be nothing without the voice of the Boss. As soon as he starts to sing, he immediately fills the entire sound space with a sweet, sensual, and almost weary tone. This is no doubt one of the shortest songs he's ever written, and he performs it masterfully.

One last important factor ensures the success of this song: the mixing. Bob Clearmountain explains how he did it: "[...] that song was an exception. Most of the album is set up so it's like watching Bruce while he's playing onstage. If your stereo is wired correctly, the organ is on the left, and the piano is on the right, lead guitar is off to the right a bit, because that's how they set up. But on moody songs like *I'm on Fire*, I'll put the drums outside, and have the spotlight on Bruce as if he was standing alone with his guitar."[96]

The result is simply astounding, and the combination of all these elements is what makes *I'm on Fire* such a resounding success.

NO SURRENDER

Bruce Springsteen / 4'01

1984

Musicians

Bruce Springsteen: vocals, guitars
Clarence Clemons: backing vocals (?)
Roy Bittan: piano, backing vocals (?)
Danny Federici: organ
Garry Tallent: bass
Max Weinberg: drums
Richie "La Bamba" Rosenberg: backing vocals and vocal harmonies

Recording

The Hit Factory, 421 West 54th St, New York: 25–27 October 1983

Technical team

Producers: Bruce Springsteen, Jon Landau, Chuck Plotkin, Steve Van Zandt
Recording engineer: Toby Scott
Assistant recording engineers: John Davenport, Jeff Hendrickson, Bruce Lampcov, Billy Straus, Zoë Yanakas
Mixing: Bob Clearmountain
Mastering: Bob Ludwig

Although primarily known as a trombonist, Richie "La Bamba" Rosenberg participated in the recording of *No Surrender* as a backup singer.

Genesis and lyrics

No Surrender is the final version of a song originally called *Brothers Under the Bridges* (which came out later in the 1998 *Tracks* box set), to which it bears a vague musical resemblance. It starts with a slogan that likely resonated with many teenagers: "We learned more from a three-minute record than we ever learned from school." It was not so much an attack on education—Bruce Springsteen is no Roger Waters, of Pink Floyd—as a call to friendship. Which is exactly how the songwriter explained it to Roger Scott and Patrick Humphries of *Hot Press* magazine: "A song like that, or *Backstreets*, or *Bobby Jean*, are just basic songs about friendship, which me and Steve—we've been best friends since we were like 16 [...]"[40]

It was a call to freedom, rock music, and adolescence. A call to rock, when Springsteen says his heart begins to pound when he hears "the neighborhood drummer sound." A call to adolescence, when he alludes to the birth of his group, "Well, maybe we could cut someplace of our own with these drums and these guitars," and when, in thinking about the past, he boasts with pride that these "blood brothers" never looked back, never surrendered. Behind this impassioned declaration, Bruce Springsteen expresses immense gratitude for the chance he was given to realize his childhood dreams.

Nevertheless, when it was time to choose the tracks for *Born in the U.S.A.*, Springsteen wanted to discard *No Surrender*. "But Steve Van Zandt convinced me otherwise," he explains in his book *Songs*. "It was a song I was uncomfortable with. You don't hold out and triumph all the time in life. You compromise, you suffer defeat, you slip into life's gray areas. But Steve talked me into putting the song on the album in the eleventh hour. He argued that the portrait of friendship and the song's expression of the inspirational power of rock music was an important part of the picture."[6]

Production

No Surrender was the first song on the album that was recorded at The Hit Factory and the first song on the B-side of the original vinyl album. Its style of rock was typical of the E Street Band. After the minimalism of *I'm on Fire*, Springsteen and his band returned to a dense, rich, and heavy sound, not unlike the one they had created for *Born to Run*. During the sessions on 25 and 27 October, the group started working with-

During one of her concerts, Taylor Swift scribbled the key lyrics to *No Surrender* on her left arm: "We learned more from a three-minute record than we ever learned from school."

No Surrender was one of John Kerry's theme songs during his 2004 presidential campaign.

out Jon Landau, Chuck Plotkin, and Steve Van Zandt (who was busy with his solo career). Nevertheless, the shadow of Little Steven—as he was by then known—makes itself felt in the lyrics and musical inflection of *No Surrender*. We know that he insisted the song be included on the album. The style of rock, with its '50s and '60s feel, had appealed to him.

Max Weinberg starts off the song, first on the bass drum, then with a drum fill. The group then dives right in, launching into a swift rock sequence with arrangements that mimic the Wall of Sound (see *Little Symphonies with a Difference*, page 69) so dear to Springsteen. The sound is powerful and, strangely, the absence of Van Zandt's guitar does not stand out—maybe this is a sign of his lack of involvement in the production, which he would later come to regret and which ultimately caused him to leave the group. The introduction is dominated, once again, by the chorus of Richie "La Bamba" Rosenberg, who'd already worked on *Cover Me*. Garry Tallent delivers an excellent bass line throughout the piece, revealing his considerable talent for the first time. Danny Federici is on the Farfisa organ, Roy Bittan on the piano, and Springsteen on the various rhythm guitars and also on the lead guitar for a few solo passages toward the end of the song (around 2'09). He clearly takes charge of the vocals, harmonizing over Rosenberg's, but the absence of Little Steven is felt more keenly here than anywhere else: his very high voice, à la Keith Richards, is the ideal complement to that of the Boss.

No Surrender is a good song, though maybe not the best on *Born in the U.S.A.*, as its "retro" feel does not really match the more modern sounds of the other songs. This is what Springsteen must have been thinking before Van Zandt changed his mind, even suggesting that he leave out *Dancing in the Dark* to make room in the tracklisting. Luckily, at the last moment, Landau was able to include both songs. Springsteen performed a very good version of *No Surrender* on 26 July 1984, in Toronto, where he was alone on the acoustic guitar and the harmonica. In his introduction, he dedicated the song to "one of my best dreamin' partners": Little Steven.

Bruce Springsteen watches Clarence Clemons admiringly during a concert at the Rupp Arena in Lexington, Kentucky, in December 1984. A very assertive tenor for *Bobby Jean*.

BOBBY JEAN

Bruce Springsteen / 3'48

Musicians

Bruce Springsteen: Vocals, guitar
Clarence Clemons: saxophone, tambourine
Roy Bittan: synthesizer, piano
Danny Federici: glockenspiel
Garry Tallent: bass
Max Weinberg: drums

Recording

The Hit Factory, 421 West 54th St, New York: 28 July, 10 October 1983

Technical team

Producers: Bruce Springsteen, Jon Landau, Chuck Plotkin, Steve Van Zandt
Recording engineer: Toby Scott
Assistant recording engineers: John Davenport, Jeff Hendrickson, Bruce Lampcov, Billy Straus, Zoë Yanakas
Mixing: Bob Clearmountain
Mastering: Bob Ludwig

Steve Van Zandt in concert in San Bernardino, California, in 1983. *Bobby Jean* is a celebration of Springsteen's friendship with the guitarist.

Genesis and lyrics

The narrator visits Bobby Jean, who has left the city some time ago, causing his memories to come back to him with a hint of nostalgia: "You hung with me when all the others turned away, turned up their nose/We liked the same music, we liked the same bands, we liked the same clothes." Who is Bruce Springsteen referring to here? A teenage love from his time in Freehold or Asbury Park? No. The songwriter provides a clue in his book *Songs*: "*Bobby Jean* is a good song about youthful friendship,"[6] he writes. It would seem that, like *No Surrender*, *Bobby Jean* was dedicated to Steve Van Zandt. "Now there ain't nobody nowhere nohow gonna ever understand me the way you did." This line, which Springsteen sings in the bridge, is loaded with real emotion. In all probability, he wrote it during sessions for *Born in the U.S.A.*, after the guitarist had decided to leave the E Street Band. Van Zandt was frustrated that he did not have the role he wanted—that of the Boss's right-hand man (which had always been filled by Jon Landau)—and needing, above all, to see his projects through as the head of The Disciples of Soul.

One thing was for sure: the friendship and musical bond between Bruce Springsteen and Steve Van Zandt would survive life's twists and turns, as the pair would get back together in the 1990s for new adventures onstage and in the studio.

Bruce Springsteen and the E Street Band performed *Bobby Jean* onstage for the first time at a concert in Saint Paul, Minnesota, on 29 June 1984.

Production

Before returning to The Hit Factory with the E Street Band in July 1983 to record *Bobby Jean*, Bruce Springsteen lost the thread of his next album. Although he'd recorded most of the songs for the A-side of *Born in the U.S.A.* in the spring of 1982, as he worked alone in his new home studio in Los Angeles, in early 1983 he still didn't know what kind of character to give to his seventh album. The poppiness of some of the songs, like *Cover Me* or *I'm on Fire*, were not completely to his liking. Chuck Plotkin, at that point a coproducer, had tried to explain to him that his strength was in rock, but the Boss was doubtful and did not know where to turn. A heated discussion left Plotkin feeling uncertain of his position. Then, a miracle: "Two nights later, we went into the studio and he said, 'I have a song

For Springsteen Addicts

In *High Fidelity* (1995), the British novelist (and fan of Bruce Springsteen) Nick Hornby makes his main character, who works in a music store in London, say that Bobby Jean is a woman who has left without leaving an address. There is a brilliant nod to this in the Stephen Frears' film adaptation of Hornby's novel (2000): the main character (played by John Cusak) dreams of being in deep conversation with Bruce Springsteen. This just happens to be the Boss's first appearance on the big screen!

HEADPHONES AT THE READY

On the "two," which is the first number we hear on the Boss's countdown (the "one" having probably been cut during production), you can hear an accidental hit of the cowbells.

I want to cut.' We cut *Bobby Jean* and it was like the fever had broken."[16] From that moment on, the songwriter knew what character to give to *Born in the U.S.A.*: it would be rock. This did not prevent him, at the time, from disliking the songs from the Electric Nebraska Sessions. Landau and Plotkin would still have to fight hard to change his mind.

Even more so than *No Surrender*, *Bobby Jean* has hints of *Born to Run*, with a tight and powerful sound distinguished by Danny Federici's persistent glockenspiel, Clarence Clemons's tenor sax, and Max Weinberg's assertive drum performance. Aside from the bridge (at 1'57), the entire song revolves around the same four chords. Springsteen never tires, always delivers a gripping performance, and persuades with feeling and sincerity. Two musicians stand out in particular: Garry Tallent, who, once again, delivers a superb bass line, and Clarence Clemons, who, for the second time on the album (after *Darlington County*), launches into an excellent saxophone solo in the coda (starting from 2'48).

Not to be outdone, Roy Bittan uses his Yamaha CS-80 to create sounds befitting of his time—brassy sounds that bring an upbeat feel to the harmony. His piano accompaniment is also essential to the song, particularly in the last verse, where his lyrical flights add to the emotion expressed in Bruce Springsteen's lyrics.

Bobby Jean, which was mixed by Bob Clearmountain on 10 October 1983, is one of the key songs of *Born in the U.S.A.*

I'M GOIN' DOWN

Bruce Springsteen / 3'30

1984

Musicians

Bruce Springsteen: vocals, guitars
Steve Van Zandt: guitars
Clarence Clemons: saxophone, tambourine
Roy Bittan: piano
Danny Federici: organ
Garry Tallent: bass
Max Weinberg: drums
The group: handclaps

Recording

The Power Station, 441 West 53rd St, New York: 12–13 May 1982

Technical team

Producers: Bruce Springsteen, Jon Landau, Chuck Plotkin, Steve Van Zandt
Recording engineer: Toby Scott
Assistant recording engineers: John Davenport, Jeff Hendrickson, Bruce Lampcov, Billy Straus, Zoë Yanakas
Mixing: Bob Clearmountain
Mastering: Bob Ludwig

COVERS

I'm Goin' Down was recorded by Frank Black and the Catholics (on the single *Dog Gone* [1998] and the compilation *The Complete Recordings* [2015]). Florence Welch (Florence and the Machine) and Kid Harpoon's adaptation for the BBC is also noteworthy.

Genesis and lyrics

I'm Goin' Down was one of the songs created during the spring of 1982 at The Power Station, but which were then discarded to make way for the acoustic album *Nebraska*. Bruce Springsteen revisits a theme that had inspired him since his very first album: that of a love story which takes place on a road trip. A love story that seems to be about to end. While the narrator appears to be a bit too eager, his girlfriend lets "out one of [her] bored sighs." Then, early one morning, there's a fight. The narrator feels humiliated and he goes "down, down, down." The years pass by and the heroine feels that her former passion has slowly died and turned to indifference, even a need for revenge. Does she regret the life she has led with her partner? One can only guess.

Chosen as the A-side of the sixth single from *Born in the U.S.A.*, with *Janey, Don't You Lose Heart* on the B-side, *I'm Goin' Down* would go far in the *Billboard* charts. The song reached No.9 in September 1985. It didn't place in the United Kingdom, but reached No.13 and No.29 in Sweden and Italy, respectively.

Production

I'm Goin' Down was clearly recorded with the other songs from the Electric Nebraska Sessions: its rock sound starts off with a strong introduction, giving prominence to the guitars (notably the two string guitar phrases). This is followed by a strong rhythm section led by Max Weinberg and Garry Tallent, who are both on top form. The snare drum bears the "Clearmountain" signature because of the way it cracks like a whip. He has clearly achieved a great mixing feat by creating an atmosphere typical of the times. At the keyboards, Danny Federici performs an excellent part on the Hammond B-3, the Leslie performing beautifully, and Roy Bittan accompanies his band mates with an equally astonishing piano. Clarence Clemons launches into a superb tenor saxophone solo, carried by a generous and space-like delay. The Boss and Miami Steve are on the guitars, proving, if there ever was a need to, that both are excellent guitarists and too often underrated.

Bruce Springsteen and the E Street Band in September 1984 at the Spectrum Stadium in Philadelphia, during the Born in the U.S.A. Tour.

For Springsteen Addicts

Bruce Springsteen almost didn't include *I'm Goin' Down* on *Born in the U.S.A.*, as he preferred *Pink Cadillac*. In the end, the latter song made its way onto the B-side of *Dancing in the Dark*.

GLORY DAYS

Bruce Springsteen / 4'15

1984

Musicians

Bruce Springsteen: vocals, guitars
Steve Van Zandt: guitars, mandolin, vocal harmonies, vocals
Clarence Clemons: tambourine
Roy Bittan: keyboard
Danny Federici: organ
Garry Tallent: bass
Max Weinberg: drums

Recording

The Power Station, 441 West 53rd St, New York: 5 May 1982

Technical team

Producers: Bruce Springsteen, Jon Landau, Chuck Plotkin, Steve Van Zandt
Recording engineer: Toby Scott
Assistant recording engineers: John Davenport, Jeff Hendrickson, Bruce Lampcov, Billy Straus, Zoë Yanakas
Mixing: Bob Clearmountain
Mastering: Bob Ludwig

For Springsteen Addicts

At the end of the video for *Glory Days*, Julianne Phillips, who was then married to Bruce Springsteen, makes a brief appearance (she comes to pick up Springsteen and their son at the baseball field). We also see Patti Scialfa, then backing vocalist with the E Street Band and the future wife of the songwriter.

Genesis and lyrics

Glory Days is the story of a chance meeting between Bruce Springsteen and an old friend of his who could have become a great baseball player. Springsteen took this meeting, which occurred one evening in the summer of 1973 in a bar on the Jersey Shore, and built a story based on his teenage years: his "glory days." As he wrote in his booklet *Greatest Hits*: "The first verse actually happened, the second verse mostly happened, the third verse, of course, is happening now."[97]

"Saw him the other night at this roadside bar/I was walking in, he was walking out," sings Bruce Springsteen in the first verse. The baseball player in question is Joe DePugh. He and Springsteen were friends at the St Rose of Lima School, in Freehold, at the start of the 1960s. Their paths then diverged: one toward sport, the other toward music. In the second verse, the heroine is a girl from the high school years, who "could turn all the boys' heads." Now, she's divorced. The narrator/Springsteen goes for a few drinks with her, to talk about "old times," not without a certain sense of nostalgia, even sadness. The third verse, finally, takes place in the present day—there's a bar, alcohol, stories of irony and disappointment.

When interviewed by Chet Flippo for *Musician* magazine, Bruce Springsteen explained the narrative arc he used in this song: "In *Glory Days*, it sounds like you're just talking to somebody; that's what I wanted to do. Wanted to make it feel like you meet somebody. The *Nebraska* stuff was like that: you meet somebody and you walk a little while in their shoes and see what their life is like. And then what does that mean to you? That's kind of the direction my writing's going in and in general it's just the thing I end up finding most satisfying. Just saying what somebody had to say and not making a big deal out of it."[90]

Initially, *Glory Days* contained a fourth verse that mentioned Bruce Springsteen's father when he was working on an assembly line at Ford Motors.

Glory Days was on the A-side of the fifth single that Columbia Records took from *Born in the U.S.A.*, with *Stand On It* on the B-side. It reached No.5 in the *Billboard* charts in June 1985, then No.17 in August in the United Kingdom. Springsteen has played this song regularly since the concert at The Stone Pony, in Asbury Park, on 8 June 1984.

Bruce Springsteen and Julianne Phillips in the late 1980s. The actress and first wife of the Boss makes an appearance in the *Glory Days* video.

Joe DePugh was an excellent pitcher, but he was not able to have the career he had hoped for. He later turned to coaching. Thanks to a former pupil of the St Rose of Lima School, Springsteen and DePugh were able to have dinner together in 2005 and reminisce about the good old days.

OFF THE BEAT

In addition to Patti Scialfa, Nils Lofgren and Steve Van Zandt also appear in the 1985 video. The irony of the situation comes from the fact that neither Scialfa nor Lofgren, the two new recruits of the E Street Band, were involved in recording *Glory Days*, and that Steve Van Zandt had not been part of the group for more than two years. In the clip, however, they're all at a New Jersey night club: Maxwell's in Hoboken.

Production

Glory Days is one of the merriest, most humorous songs Springsteen has ever written and performed. It was recorded during the Electric Nebraska Sessions, and has the same freshness and energy that the group gave off at the time, before Springsteen gradually started to lose his bearings. *Glory Days* is also one of the last songs recorded with Steve Van Zandt, whose enthusiasm and dynamism likely contributed to making the song so musically festive.

Springsteen starts the piece by playing a "Stonian" riff on the Telecaster-Esquire. Max Weinberg supports him with a powerful beat on the snare drum, which Bob Clearmountain would sample for use in other songs on the album. The group then joins in to deliver an exhilarating rock accompaniment. The song is primarily characterized by Danny Federici's riff on the Farfisa organ, highlighted by Garry Tallent's very effective bass line. What's funny is that at the same time (1985), Dire Straits was releasing *Walk of Life*, a single from the album *Brothers in Arms*. Its tones and sounds were not that different from those of *Glory Days*, particularly since Neil Dorfsman, the recording engineer for *The River*, had coproduced it with Mark Knopfler.

In the chorus, Steve Van Zandt harmonizes with the Boss's lead vocals in his very high voice, one of the musical characteristics of the E Street Band at that time. Miami Steve—not yet Little Steven—is present throughout the piece with his guitar parts and various vocal contributions, notably in the coda, where he responds to Springsteen in a bantering spirit (starting from 3'05). He also chimes in with the mandolin, giving an improvised solo during the recording (at 1'55) and an accompaniment that lasts until the end of the song. At the time, rumors were circulating that he'd had an argument with Springsteen and that the latter had deleted some of his tracks. Van Zandt reacted by denouncing these allegations as absurd, saying: "I did the mandolin solo on *Glory Days* into my vocal mike. How you gonna wipe that?"[16]

Glory Days does very well in concert. The group clearly enjoys playing it, and Springsteen can literally let himself go, jumping from joke to joke, as he did at the concert at La Courneuve, in France, on 29 June 1985.

DANCING IN THE DARK

Bruce Springsteen / 4'04

Musicians

Bruce Springsteen: vocals, guitars
Clarence Clemons: saxophone
Roy Bittan: keyboards
Danny Federici: keyboards (?)
Garry Tallent: bass
Max Weinberg: drums

Recording

The Hit Factory, 421 West 54th St, New York: 14 February 1984

Technical team

Producers: Bruce Springsteen, Jon Landau, Chuck Plotkin, Steve Van Zandt
Recording engineer: Toby Scott
Assistant recording engineers: John Davenport, Jeff Hendrickson, Bruce Lampcov, Billy Straus, Zoë Yanakas
Mixing: Bob Clearmountain
Mastering: Bob Ludwig

In the center of the photo, Danny Federici plays an excellent organ part for *Dancing in the Dark*.

Genesis and lyrics

As strange as it may seem today, *Dancing in the Dark* was not supposed to be on *Born in the U.S.A.* Jon Landau had asked Bruce Springsteen to write it because, after listening to the album tapes, he felt that it did not contain a strong enough song to constitute a hit. A dispute ensued: "Look," grumbled the songwriter, "I've written 70 songs. You want another one, you write it."[16] Back in his hotel room, Springsteen finally sat down to work. Inspiration eventually came: "My song about my own alienation, fatigue, and desire to get out from inside the studio, my room, my record, my head,"[1] writes Bruce Springsteen in his autobiography.

Dancing in the Dark goes back to 1984, when the songwriter was going through a depression. This is exactly what he expresses throughout the song: an immense physical and emotional weariness. "I'm just tired and bored with myself"; "I ain't getting nowhere, I'm just living in a dump with myself," he confesses to his girlfriend in the second verse. He's calling for help to free himself from the daily grind and find a spark to light his way, something that could once again stimulate his imagination. "I'm sick of sitting 'round here trying to write this book." This sentence from the third verse alludes to the previously mentioned fight between Springsteen and Jon Landau, and to how hard it is to create something, though instead of the "book," he means "album." In order for the writing to come, there has to be a spark, but for the moment, the narrator (who is none other than Bruce Springsteen) and his partner are just "dancing in the dark"; that is, they are living without a purpose, impervious to the passing of time.

While it was the last song to be recorded for *Born in the U.S.A.*, *Dancing in the Dark* was chosen as the A-side of the first single, which came out on 4 May 1984 (one month to the day before the album), with *Pink Cadillac* on the B-side. Success soon came knocking. This was the songwriter's biggest hit to date, reaching No.2 in the *Billboard* charts on 26 May 1984 and No.1 in Canada, the Netherlands, and Belgium. In the United Kingdom, the song initially reached No.28, on 26 May 1984, then No.4 on 15 January 1985. Bruce Springsteen has performed it more than a thousand times since the famous concert at The Stone Pony in Asbury Park on 8 June 1984.

Bruce Springsteen and a young fan named Courteney Cox in the video for *Dancing in the Dark*. The *Friends* years are yet to come.

Production

Dancing in the Dark is a contradiction in terms: while the lyrics are not very light-hearted, the music is upbeat, lively, and danceable. It was almost as if Springsteen were trying to downplay his feelings. The mysteries of his subconscious led him to compose a catchy pop piece for the charts and give it that atmosphere popular in the 1980s, the very one that made him feel uncomfortable.

Dancing in the Dark was recorded on 14 February at The Hit Factory, the day after the fateful fight between Springsteen and Landau. It was the last song to be adapted for the album—two years separate this song from the first pieces. *Dancing in the Dark*, as with most of the other songs on the album, was recorded practically live in the studio. Aside from a few overdubs, including voice—except for Springsteen's—this hit only needed six takes. The mixing, skillfully done by Bob Clearmountain, was finalized in March.

Dancing in the Dark is primarily characterized by Roy Bittan's synthesizer. He reportedly used Yamaha's latest novelty, the DX7, which was the first digital synthesizer to use FM technology and a future favorite among musicians: it would soon become an essential piece of technology that was used in endless numbers of productions in the 1980s. The brassy sound Bittan uses for the riff literally dominates the other instruments, not in an aggressive way, but with its majestic yet subtle presence. He also plays a bass line that is nothing more than a pulsing sound, which Garry Tallent backs up with his own bass line. Then there is Max Weinberg's drum, whose very simple sound mimics, almost exactly, that of a drum machine. Jon Landau, once again very shrewdly, advised Springsteen to play in the style of Jeff Porcaro, the drummer for *Beat It*, the Michael Jackson hit that came out in 1983. Weinberg only uses his bass drum, snare drum, and his hi-hat, which was mixed remotely.

Springsteen recorded very lively lead vocals, which contrasted with his lyrics. The contrast is obvious in the video for the song, where he can be seen smiling, dancing, and showing off. However, his performance belies an unmistakable depth and sincerity, as Springsteen remains an exceptional singer-songwriter and performer.

Lastly, Clarence Clemons enters in the coda with a subtle and slightly jazzy solo sax performance.

Arthur Baker made some radio and dance club remixes in May 1984 at The Power Station, including a "dub" mix. These versions exemplify all the clichés of the time: Rototom drums, bland female choruses, typical DX-7 sounds, and so on. Nothing could beat Bob Clearmountain's original mix.

Dancing in the Dark won Bruce Springsteen his first Grammy Award (in 1985) for "Best Rock Singer."

For Springsteen Addicts

The *Dancing in the Dark* video was directed by Brian De Palma during a Bruce Springsteen and E Street Band concert at the St Paul Civic Center, in Minnesota, on 29 June 1984. The young fan who the singer invites onto the stage is none other than Courteney Cox, the future Monica from *Friends*.

COVERS

U2 played a version of *My Hometown* during the Unforgettable Fire Tour of 1985. Neil Young also recorded it for his album *A Letter Home* (2014).

MY HOMETOWN

Bruce Springsteen / 4'34

1984

Musicians

Bruce Springsteen: vocals, guitars
Clarence Clemons: tambourine
Roy Bittan: keyboards
Danny Federici: organ
Garry Tallent: bass
Max Weinberg: drums
Ruth Jackson: backing vocals

Recording

The Hit Factory, 421 West 54th St, New York: 29 June 1983

Technical team

Producers: Bruce Springsteen, Jon Landau, Chuck Plotkin, Steve Van Zandt
Recording engineer: Toby Scott
Assistant recording engineers: John Davenport, Jeff Hendrickson, Bruce Lampcov, Billy Straus, Zoë Yanakas
Mixing: Bob Clearmountain
Mastering: Bob Ludwig

A giant of folk and rock, and also an extraordinary composer, Neil Young recorded *My Hometown* for his album *A Letter Home*, released in 2014.

Genesis and lyrics

Bruce Springsteen ended *Born in the U.S.A.* with another throwback to his childhood in Freehold. A therapeutic throwback, perhaps? He's eight years old and running to the bus stop to buy his father a newspaper. Memories flood back when he sings: "I'd sit on his lap in that big old Buick." Then comes adolescence, the 1960s, and racial tensions that did not spare the songwriter's hometown. "Words were passed in a shotgun blast." This sentence alludes to the sad events that took place in Freehold on 19 May 1969: the city center was devastated by riots after the town prevented a group of African-Americans from holding a protest march. That night, a white man shot into a car occupied by African-Americans, severely wounding two of them. More memories unfold in the third verse: Springsteen mentions his town and how it was practically abandoned after the closure of "the textile mill across the railroad tracks." This was terrible news for dozens of workers and employees who became victims of Ronald Reagan's neoliberal policies and of a post-industrial society. The song continues: "Foreman says 'These jobs are going, boys, and they ain't coming back.'" In the fourth verse, the narrator decides to leave with his wife and child. He looks back on his hometown one last time before heading south.

My Hometown is on the A-side of the seventh and last single from *Born in the U.S.A.* It came out on 21 November 1985, with *Santa Claus is Comin' to Town* on the B-side. The song climbed to a respectable No.6 in the *Billboard* charts, on 21 December 1985, and to No.9 in the United Kingdom on 14 December.

Production

My Hometown is one of three songs on the album that were recorded in 1983, along with *Bobby Jean* and *No Surrender*. Springsteen, who'd been facing writer's block since the release of *Nebraska*, had found new inspiration and creativity along with his way back to the studios, in this case The Hit Factory.

It was also one of the pieces from *Born in the U.S.A.* in which Steve Van Zandt did not participate. In a possible attempt to make up for his absence, Roy Bittan and his synthesizer, probably the Yamaha CS-80, dominate the arrangements. He starts the introduction with some slightly brassy, rather trippy synth pads. The only accompaniments are Max Weinberg's drums, who plays again in a simple register—bass

Michael Stipe (REM), Tracy Chapman, Bruce Springsteen, and the E Street Band sing *My Hometown* together at the Concert for Change in support of John Kerry on 8 October 2004.

drum and hi-hat—and Clarence Clemons's tambourine. The feeling is nostalgic, almost country in spirit, despite the Yamaha's electronic sounds.

Springsteen is clearly overwhelmed with emotion as he launches into the lead vocals. His voice is sweet, probably overcome with memories. Unlike his rendering of *Dancing in the Dark*, this performance is in perfect harmony with the lyrics. As for the arrangements, he adds some strumming on his acoustic guitar, entering in the second verse with Garry Tallent's bass. Then, for the bridge, he records another 6-string guitar, played in arpeggios toward the top of the neck (on the left, at 2'03). Weinberg accompanies him with cross-stick drumming. The hi-hat, which was by now being mixed remotely, was replaced with the tambourine, which therefore became more noticeable. In the last verse, Bittan's sounds are complemented by Ruth Jackson's backing vocals. He is joined in the coda by Danny Federici's Hammond B-3.

My Hometown ends the album on a high note, and it is no doubt one of the songs that most affected his compatriots, all of whom were "born in the U.S.A." The Boss sang a superb version of this song on 8 October 2004 at the TD Waterhouse Centre in Orlando, Florida, in a duet with Tracy Chapman.

For Springsteen Addicts

Shot at the end of the Born in the U.S.A. Tour, the video for *My Hometown* was directed by Arthur Rosato. Also a New Jersey native, in addition to Bruce Springsteen, he had worked most notably with Bob Dylan, George Harrison, Carlos Santana, and Crosby, Stills, Nash & Young.

The long-standing friendship between Steve Van Zandt (here, in 1985) and Bruce Springsteen was apparent in the recording of one of the biggest albums in rock history.

STEVE VAN ZANDT: THE E STREET BAND'S PIRATE

Steve Van Zandt's name is forever associated with that of Bruce Springsteen. The friendship between the two Jersey Shore musicians goes back to the 1960s when the future boss of American rock went to the Hullabaloo Club in Middletown Township where he heard a singer-guitarist launch into a flamboyant version of *Happy Together* by The Turtles. Shortly after, Van Zandt went on to play with Springsteen in Steel Mill (as a bassist) and The Bruce Springsteen Band (as a guitarist). Then, in 1975, Steve became a fully paid-up member of the E Street Band. He remained with the band until the early 1980s, briefly returning when the band was reformed in 1995 and then on a permanent basis from 1999.

A guitar and a bandana

Steve Van Zandt's career has been a lot more than just the E Street Band, although his close collaboration with Bruce Springsteen has produced some absolute masterpieces. He was born Steven Lento in Winthrop, Massachusetts, on 22 November 1950, the son of Mary, a young woman of Italian descent who married William Brewster Van Zandt in the second half of the 1950s. Steve spent his childhood in Middletown Township, New Jersey.

Everything clicked into place for him when he saw The Beatles and The Rolling Stones performing on TV. He learned to play the guitar and went on to form The Whirlwinds in 1964, followed by Mates, before joining the Shadows (not the Hank Marvin band) in May 1965. After his fortuitous encounter with Bruce Springsteen, he became part of Steel Mill followed by The Bruce Springsteen Band. By then, he was already sporting either a hat or a bandana as a result of a car accident that had left him with scars on his head.

Jersey Shore Sound

Affectionately nicknamed "Little Steven" or "Miami Steve"—because of the Hawaiian shirts he wears all year round—the guitarist founded The Asbury Jukes in 1975 with Southside Johnny and the brass section, The Miami Horns. He produced the first three albums for Southside Johnny and The Asbury Jukes, which combine rock 'n' roll and R&B, and perfectly define the Jersey Shore Sound: *I Don't Want To Go Home* (1976), *This Time It's For Real* (1977), and *Hearts of Stone* (1978).

He also worked as a producer for Gary U.S. Bonds in the first half of the 1980s, producing *Dedication* (1981), *On the Line* (1982), and *Standing in the Line of Fire* (1984), as well as with the Pittsburgh band Iron City Houserockers on several songs from the album *Have a Good Time but Get Out Alive!* (1980). He also composed *While You Were Looking at Me* for Michael Monroe (*Not Fakin' It*, 1989), *All Alone On Christmas* for the 1992 Chris Columbus film, *Home Alone 2: Lost in New York*, and *Baby Please Don't Go* (2004) for Nancy Sinatra's homonymous album.

From The Disciples of Soul to *The Sopranos*

After the first adventure with the E Street Band, Steve Van Zandt set up The Disciples of Soul, with, among others, the bassist Jean Beauvoir, the drummer Dino Danelli, and The Miami Horns, and recorded *Men without Women* in 1982. This album was followed by six others, including *Voice of America* (1984), *Freedom—No Compromise* (1987), and *Summer of Sorcery* (2019). Van Zandt is a politically committed artist, as is evident from many of the songs on his albums, and he created Artists United Against Apartheid in which musicians, including Bruce Springsteen, Pete Townshend, and the members of U2, came together to record the anti-apartheid anthem *Sun City* in 1985.

Since the late 1990s, Steve Van Zandt has pursued a dual career as a musician and actor. In the TV series *The Sopranos*, he played Silvio Dante, a close friend of Tony Soprano (James Gandolfini), the boss of a criminal organization in New Jersey. He then starred in the Norwegian-American series, *Lilyhammer*, in which he played Frank Tagliano, an ex-Mafioso from New York. He also appeared as the singer Jerry Vale in Martin Scorsese's *The Irishman*. Since the early 2000s, he has presented a radio show about garage rock called *Underground Garage*, while in 2005 he founded the Wicked Cool Records label. He also created the Rock and Roll Forever Foundation and the TeachRock project, an online multimedia educational concept.

Steve Van Zandt has been married to the actress Maureen Santoro since 31 December 1982. She plays his onscreen wife in *The Sopranos*. The wedding took place in New York and was presided over by the "Reverend" Little Richard!

SIDE B

PINK CADILLAC

Bruce Springsteen / 3'33

Single: *Dancing in the Dark/Pink Cadillac* **Reference:** Columbia Records – 38-04463 **Release date:** United States, 4 May 1984
Musicians: Bruce Springsteen: vocals, guitar / Clarence Clemons: saxophone / Garry Tallent: bass / Max Weinberg: drums **Recording:** The Hit Factory, 421 West 54th St, New York: 31 May 1983 **Technical team:** Producers: Bruce Springsteen, Chuck Plotkin, Jon Landau, Steve Van Zandt / Recording engineer: Toby Scott / Mixing: Bob Clearmountain

Genesis and lyrics

Pink Cadillac originates from a song called *Love is a Dangerous Thing*, which was recorded in December 1981. Bruce Springsteen then changed almost all the lyrics, except for the line: "Eve tempted Adam with an apple," for an acoustic version in January 1982, around the time of *Nebraska*. The rhythm of the final version is pure rock 'n' roll, which inevitably brings to mind Elvis Presley, who was already talking about his favorite car in 1954 with *Baby Let's Play House*. Thirty years later, the New Jersey songwriter indulged in his own take on this prestigious vehicle. His girlfriend seems to be a piece of work, starting with her special talent for getting on his nerves, but her faults magically vanish at the sight of his pink Cadillac with crushed-velvet seats.

Pink Cadillac is the B-side of *Dancing in the Dark*—the first single from *Born in the U.S.A.*—and can also be found on the *Tracks* (1998) and *18 Tracks* (1999) compilations.

Production

Pink Cadillac's main riff is strangely reminiscent of the *Peter Gunn Theme*, which was composed in 1958 by Henry Mancini for the TV series *Peter Gunn*, produced by Blake Edwards. It's a rockabilly song. A slapback echo enhances Springsteen's voice and Telecaster-Esquire; the saxophone of Clarence Clemons clearly highlights the similarities to the Peter Gunn Theme (at 2'08); the bass of Garry Tallent faithfully accompanies Springsteen's guitar; and Max Weinberg's drums carry a plain and simple rhythm. The spirit of the song also resembles that of the 1980 hit *Runaway Boys*, by the Stray Cats.

Chuck Plotkin, then the producer for Bette Midler, offered her *Pink Cadillac* for her album *No Frills* (1983)—with Springsteen's permission, as he did not want to record it himself at the time. However, as soon as he heard the song, the Boss vetoed the move, though he allowed Midler to sing it onstage out of courtesy. Bette Midler was annoyed, and in an interview would call him "Another stiff."[161]

Brue Springsteen finally recorded *Pink Cadillac* in May 1983, but it's not among his best songs, as it lacks originality and conviction.

COVERS

While Bette Midler could not meet the Boss's requirements, Natalie Cole was able to record *Pink Cadillac* for her album *Everlasting* (1987). Her version reached No.5 in March 1988. Jerry Lee Lewis' version (with the Boss) for the album *Last Man Standing* (2006) was also remarkable.

SIDE B

JERSEY GIRL

Tom Waits / 6'10

Single: *Cover Me/Jersey Girl* **Reference:** Columbia Records – 13-08409 **Release date:** United States, 31 July 1984
Musicians: Bruce Springsteen: vocals, guitar / Steve Van Zandt: guitar, backing vocals / Clarence Clemons: maracas, saxophone, backing vocals / Roy Bittan: piano, backing vocals / Danny Federici: organ, glockenspiel / Garry Tallent: bass / Max Weinberg: drums **Recording:** Brendan Byrne Arena, East Rutherford, New Jersey: 9 July 1981 **Technical team:** Producers: Bruce Springsteen, Jon Landau, Chuck Plotkin / Recording engineers: Bruce Jackson, Toby Scott / Mixing: Bob Clearmountain

Genesis and lyrics

Tom Waits composed *Jersey Girl* during a pivotal time in his life, right after his breakup with Rickie Lee Jones and after meeting songwriter, producer, and actress Kathleen Brennan. The song is, in fact, dedicated to Kathleen, his future wife: "Tonight I'm gonna take that ride/Across the river to the Jersey side/Take my baby to the carnival." The song was recorded during sessions for the album *Heartattack and Vine* (1980).

Bruce Springsteen was intrigued by this love story, written by one of the most original and whacky songwriters of rock, and started recording it in concert in 1981. The version on the B-side of *Cover Me* was recorded during the last of six concerts of the River Tour, at the Brendan Byrne Arena, in East Rutherford, New Jersey, on 9 July 1981. The Boss added a verse and a few lines from *Party Lights*, an outtake of *The River*. The same recording can be found on the *Live 1975–85* box set (1986), with an added spoken introduction that brings the total length of the song to 6'30.

Production

This cover is just as good as the original version, allowing Springsteen to pay a superb tribute to the brilliant Tom Waits. It helps that the voices of the two songwriters are quite similar, even though the Boss has a somewhat clearer timbre and a wider vocal range. The E Street Band provides the ideal accompaniment, with each musician backing the lead vocals with the best possible support. Steve Van Zandt, who is still with the group, plays the rhythm guitar alongside Springsteen's arpeggios. Synth pads and organ pads complete the harmonies, supported by Garry Tallent and Max Weinberg's subtle, but effective, rhythm. Clarence Clemons is on the maracas, saxophone, and, it would appear, backing vocals—alongside Roy Bittan and Miami Steve. There's also a glockenspiel in the chorus (for example, at 1'40), likely recorded as an overdub during post-production (as with the backing vocals, which seem to have been boosted).

For Springsteen Addicts

In addition to adding a verse and a few lines to *Jersey Girl*, Bruce Springsteen replaced the line, "Don't want no whore on Eighth Avenue" with something much more polite: "The girls out on the avenue."

SIDE B

SHUT OUT THE LIGHT

Bruce Springsteen / 3'52

Single: *Born in the U.S.A./Shut Out the Light* **Reference:** Columbia Records – 38-04680 **Release date:** United States, 30 October 1984
Musicians: Bruce Springsteen: vocals, guitars, harmonica, tambourine / Soozie Tyrell: violin **Recording:** Thrill Hill Recording, Beverly Hills, Los Angeles, California: 19 January 1983, The Hit Factory, 421 West 54th St, New York: May 1983 (?) **Technical team:** Producer: Bruce Springsteen / Recording engineers: Mike Batlan, Toby Scott / Mixing: Ed Thacker

Genesis and lyrics

Bruce Springsteen and the staff at Columbia Records couldn't have chosen a better B-side for *Born in the U.S.A.* than *Shut Out the Light*. It's another song about Vietnam, specifically about a soldier named Johnson Leneir, known as Johnny, who returns home to his family. He lands at the airport, gets into a taxi, then stops for a drink on Main Street. Meanwhile, his wife is getting ready for his return. The emotional peak comes when they meet: "I've got the shakes and I'm gonna be sick/Throw your arms around me in the cold dark night/Hey now mama don't shut out the light." His parents are there, too: his mother is, "so glad to have [him] back with [her]" and his father says that he's "sure they'd give him his job back down at the factory," while Bobby (perhaps his younger brother) has polished up the chrome on the Ford.

But Johnny isn't really there—at least not mentally. Alone again in a Maryland pine forest, by the black waters of a river, "He stares across the lights of the city" and thinks about where he has been. Is he contemplating suicide? In any case, Johnny will not have an easy time finding his place back in the land of Uncle Sam.

Production

Shut Out the Light is one of the two songs—along with *Johnny Bye-Bye* (the B-side of *I'm on Fire*)—that survived Springsteen's early 1983 recordings in the garage of his home studio in Los Angeles. At the time, the songwriter was thinking of making a follow-up to *Nebraska*, but he abandoned the idea to focus on *Born in the U.S.A.*

Shut Out the Light is a folk song, with Springsteen playing two acoustic guitar parts, each placed at either end in stereo. He sings with restraint, harmonizing with himself in the choruses. He also adds a tambourine to mark the tempo (from 0'35). The novelty of the piece comes from Soozie Tyrell's first contribution on the violin. She would later play in many other songs for the Boss (starting from the 1992 album *Lucky Town*). Her style is both simple and subtle, especially in the last verse, where she performs a few notes in treble (from 2'24), and in the elegant harmonica solo at the end of the song.

Shut Out the Light was a success, but it's clear that the songwriter wasn't completely satisfied with his project, wracked as he was in early 1983 with personal and professional doubts.

For Springsteen Addicts

Soozie Tyrell, who in a way stepped into Suki Lahav's shoes, was introduced to the Springsteen galaxy in the late 1970s when she founded Trickster, a street group whose members included Lisa Lowell and a certain Patti Scialfa.

SIDE B

JOHNNY BYE-BYE

Bruce Springsteen, Chuck Berry / 1'50

Single: *I'm on Fire/Johnny Bye-Bye* **Reference:** Columbia Records – 38-04772 **Release date:** United States, 6 February 1985
Musicians: Bruce Springsteen: vocals, guitars, bass synthesizer / Max Weinberg: drums, tambourine **Recording:** Thrill Hill Recording, Beverly Hills, Los Angeles, California: January, 9, 24 March 1983 **Technical team:** Producers: Bruce Springsteen, Jon Landau, Chuck Plotkin (single)/Bruce Springsteen (*Tracks*) / Recording engineers: Toby Scott (single)/Mike Batlan (*Tracks*) / Mixing: Bob Clearmountain (single)/Ed Thacker (*Tracks*)

Genesis and lyrics

Bruce Springsteen recorded three versions of a song called *Come On (Let's Go Tonight)*. The first (unofficial studio recording) and the second (official studio recording) took place in 1977. The third was a demo recorded in March or April 1981. *Come On (Let's Go Tonight)* led to *Johnny Bye-Bye*, especially the demo version, to which Springsteen added two verses (two lines of which he borrowed from *Bye Bye Johnny* by Chuck Berry)—the title is a respectful nod.

Incidentally, the lyrics of this B-side to *I'm on Fire* are especially good, as they pay tribute to Elvis Presley. A young woman sends her "little boy" off in a Greyhound with his guitar, headed to the Promised Land. On her way to a party in Memphis, she hears about the death of the King on the radio. The sky above Memphis is "hard and black," sings Springsteen, then he adds, "Up over the ridge came a white Cadillac/They [drew] out all his money and they laid him in the back/A woman cried from the roadside, 'Ah he's gone, he's gone.'" America mourned their king.

Production

The making of *Johnny Bye-Bye* goes back to when Springsteen wanted to make a sequel to *Nebraska*. Mike Batlan recorded the piece at the Boss's home studio, in Los Angeles, and Ed Thacker mixed it, at least for the 1998 *Tracks* box set version. The credits on the CD say that Toby Scott recorded the version on the B-side of *I'm on Fire* and Bob Clearmountain mixed it. It's more likely that the two simply retouched the original version just for the single, unless it was a mistake and the credits for *Tracks* are correct. Whatever the case, *Johnny Bye-Bye* is a very good song, which musically has nothing to do with Chuck Berry's version, aside from its rock vibe. Springsteen most likely played all the instruments (synthesizer, acoustic and electric guitars, and bass), except for the tambourine and drums, which fell to Max Weinberg. The sound quality is good, except for Weinberg's drum set, which almost sounds like a drum machine. *Johnny Bye-Bye* could have appeared on *Born in the U.S.A.*

JOHNNY GRILLON

There's another version of *Johnny Bye-Bye* called *Bye Bye Johnny*. It has a much more folky sound, with the Boss accompanying himself on the synthesizer and picking his acoustic guitar. The sound of crickets can be heard, giving the song a unique quality.

SIDE B

STAND ON IT

Bruce Springsteen / 2'30

Single: *Glory Days/Stand On It* **Reference:** Columbia Records – 38-04924 **Release date:** United States, 31 May 1985

Musicians:
Bruce Springsteen: vocals, guitars
Roy Bittan: piano
Garry Tallent: bass
Max Weinberg: drums
Recording:
The Hit Factory, 421 West 54th St, New York: 16 June 1983
Technical team:
Producers: Bruce Springsteen, Chuck Plotkin, Jon Landau, Steve Van Zandt
Recording engineer: Toby Scott
Mixing: Bob Clearmountain (single), Ed Thacker (Tracks)

Genesis and lyrics

Neither Jerry Lee Lewis nor Little Richard composed this song. It was Bruce Springsteen himself, once again declaring his love for rock and rockabilly. The lyrics glorify risky behavior at the wheel of a speeding car: Jimmy Lee wants to beat all speed records on a dirt track in Florida, while Mary Beth drives at breakneck speed down Florida 39 (State Road 39) past an admiring hitchhiker who yells, "Stand on it, go 'head baby, stand on it!" The songwriter even mentions Christopher Columbus, who "discovered America even though he hadn't planned on it" and "wouldn't have got out of Italy [...]/Without Queen Isabella standing on the shore shouting 'Stand on it!'"

A lively B-side to *Glory Days, Stand On It* also features on the third CD of the *Tracks* box set (1998).

Production

Springsteen created *Stand On It* there and then in The Hit Factory recording studio, as the musicians were getting ready to leave. Max Weinberg remembers that the songwriter was sitting in a corner of the room with his acoustic guitar when he suddenly started writing down several rockabilly songs. "We'd been recording all night and were dead tired, but they had to open up the cases and set up the equipment so that we could start recording again at five in the morning. That's when we got *Pink Cadillac, Stand On It*, and a song called *TV Movie*. Bruce got on a roll, and when that happens, you just hold on for dear life."[102] It would seem only preliminary versions were created that evening, as the final recording dates don't match up: 31 May for *Pink Cadillac*, 13 June for *TV Movie*, and 16 June for *Stand On It*.

Stand On It shows that rockabilly holds no secrets for Bruce Springsteen. Here, with Patti Scialfa at De Kuip, Rotterdam, on 29 June 1988.

In any case, *Stand On It* is a raging rockabilly number: Roy Bittan plays a glowing piano part to rival that of "The Killer" himself, Max Weinberg and Garry Tallent carry the beat with power and groove, and the Boss delivers very good lead vocals as well as an excellent solo on his Telecaster-Esquire (at 1'08). Notably, the last verse of this single version is cut off and starts to fade out sooner than the version on *Tracks*.

For Springsteen Addicts

A typewritten piece of paper with annotations in red in Springsteen's handwriting was sold on eBay in March 2016. These were the last corrections he made before recording the *Tracks* box set (1998).

SIDE B

JANEY, DON'T YOU LOSE HEART

Bruce Springsteen / 3'23

Single: *I'm Goin' Down/Janey, Don't You Lose Heart* **Reference:** Columbia Records – 38-05603 **Release date:** United States, August 1985
Musicians: Bruce Springsteen: vocals, guitars / Steve Van Zandt: guitar / Nils Lofgren: vocal harmonies / Clarence Clemons: saxophone, percussion instruments / Roy Bittan: piano, synthesizer / Garry Tallent: bass / Max Weinberg: drums **Recording:** The Hit Factory, 421 West 54th St, New York: 16 June 1983 **Technical team:** Producers: Bruce Springsteen, Chuck Plotkin, Jon Landau, Steve Van Zandt / Recording engineer: Toby Scott / Mixing: Bob Clearmountain

Genesis and lyrics

Janey, Don't You Lose Heart is a beautiful love song, one of the best Bruce Springsteen ever wrote. The young woman's sorrow runs deep: "You say you got no more dreams to touch" and that "you feel like a stranger babe who knows too much." The man who loves the unhappy heroine says that he'll do anything for her and begs her to not "lose heart." He's the only one who can fill the immense void she feels and help her overcome her fears. "'Til every river baby it runs dry [...]/Listen to me," sings Springsteen at the end of the song.

Initially chosen as the B-side of *Born in the U.S.A.*, *Janey, Don't You Lose Heart* was ultimately released on the *I'm Goin' Down* single. It's also on the third CD of the *Tracks* box set (1998).

Production

Janey, Don't You Lose Heart was composed in early 1979 and originally called *Every Day and Every Night.* The songwriter renamed and reworked it before recording it at The Hit Factory in June 1983. The arrangements resemble those from songs like *Bobby Jean* or even *Glory Days* despite the absence of a glockenspiel or Farfisa. With its catchy chorus, this song is firmly in the realm of pop. According to Chuck Plotkin, Springsteen wrote it for Stevie Nicks of Fleetwood Mac, but when she turned it down, he made it the B-side of *I'm Goin' Down.* The song's individuality comes from Nils Lofgren's vocal harmonies—his first as a future member of the E Street Band: this recording was his studio debut with the group. Contrary to what's indicated in the credits on the *Tracks* box set, Clarence Clemons is definitely present on the saxophone, performing a solo at 1'33, as is Roy Bittan, who holds his own on the piano and synth—he plays the riff of the piece, among other things.

For Springsteen Addicts

Bruce Springsteen used this song to make a thoughtful gesture. During a concert in Albany, New York, on 16 April 2012, he told the audience that he would play *Janey, Don't Lose Heart* for Molly, a young woman who'd recently lost her mother, who was nicknamed Janey.

SIDE B

SANTA CLAUS IS COMIN' TO TOWN

Haven Gillespie, John Frederick Coots / 4'27

Single: *My Hometown/Santa Claus is Comin' to Town* **Reference:** Columbia Records – 38-05728 **Release date:** United States, 21 November 1985
Musicians: Bruce Springsteen: vocals, guitar / Steve Van Zandt: guitar, backing vocals / Clarence Clemons: vocals, saxophone, bells / Roy Bittan: piano, backing vocals / Danny Federici: organ, glockenspiel / Garry Tallent: bass / Max Weinberg: drums **Recording:** C W Post College, Greenvale, New York (live): 12 December 1975 **Technical team:** Producers: Bruce Springsteen, Jimmy Iovine, Mike Appel / Recording engineers: Jimmy Iovine, Thom Panunzio

Genesis and lyrics

Santa Claus is Comin' to Town is a Christmas song written by Haven Gillespie and John Frederick Coots during the economic crisis that struck the United States after the October 1929 stock market crash. "You better watch out, you better not cry/ You better not pout, I'm telling you why/Santa Claus is coming to town." A call to fortitude, this song has a double reference: Christmas time and the start of the Great Depression.

Eddie Cantor was among the first to sing *Santa Claus is Comin' to Town*, during a radio broadcast in November 1934. The song was later performed many times, including by The Crystals, Mariah Carey, Frank Sinatra, and the Jackson 5. Bruce Springsteen first sang it for his audience in 1973. He recorded the version on the B-side of *My Hometown* on 12 December 1975 at C W Post College, in Greenvale, New York, during the Born to Run tour.

Production

This is clearly a far cry from the first version that Harry Reser and His Orchestra recorded in 1934, with Tom Stacks on vocals. Springsteen and the E Street Band turned what was originally a foxtrot into an upbeat rock frenzy. The piece starts off with a spoken part, the Boss talking to his band mates to announce the upcoming arrival of Santa Claus against a backdrop of bells, piano, and laughs. Then the group starts jamming, initially with Phil Spector-style arrangements, and then with more punch and swing (from 1'56). The one-and-only Clarence Clemons stands out in this performance, lending his baritone to a call and response with Springsteen (listen, for example, at 1'52 and 2'51, or in the coda). He also delivers an excellent saxophone solo (at 2'16). It sounds like the musicians are having fun, and their high spirits are infectious.

Roy Bittan ends this superb cover with a short take on *Jingle Bells*. In the United States, this *Santa Claus is Comin' to Town* is one of the most popular versions of the Christmas season and one of Springsteen's most downloaded songs.

For Springsteen Addicts

Bruce Springsteen sang other versions of *Santa Claus is Comin' to Town*. Five, to be precise: on 20 September 1978, 8 December 1978, 31 December 1980, 18 May 2014, and 19 December 2015.

TUNNE
TUNNEL

ALBUM

TUNNEL OF LOVE

Ain't Got You • Tougher Than the Rest • All That Heaven Will Allow • Spare Parts • Cautious Man • Walk Like a Man • Tunnel of Love • Two Faces • Brilliant Disguise • One Step Up • When You're Alone • Valentine's Day

Outtakes: *Part Man, Part Monkey • Walking Through Midnight • When You Need Me • The Wish • The Honeymooners • Lucky Man • Two for the Road*

RELEASE DATE

United States: 9 October 1987

Reference: Columbia Records – OC 40999

No.1 in the United States, United Kingdom, Italy, Norway, Spain, and Sweden, No.2 in Switzerland, No.5 in France

Springsteen during a photoshoot in 1988. His album *Tunnel of Love* reflected his failing relationship with Julianne Phillips.

1987

THE DIVORCE ALBUM

After the huge success of *Born in the U.S.A.* and the resulting tour—156 concerts between 29 June 1984 and 2 October 1985, with more than four million tickets sold and an estimated $90 million in gross profits—Bruce Springsteen became the next great rock icon on both sides of the Atlantic, in Japan, and in Australia.

Back in Rumson, New Jersey, in the house he'd bought just before going on tour, Springsteen was already thinking about his next album. The idea for a second *Born in the U.S.A.* album was quickly scrapped; it would have been an easy way out and most likely a failure compared to the first album—he was not likely to replicate a success of that caliber. The new challenge, then, was to return to something a bit more personal, like *Nebraska* after *The River*. He planned to draw on the E Street Band—though only up to a point (as by then, Steve Van Zandt had already left the band)—and, most importantly, to explore a new topic. Springsteen had recently started writing new material that took a different direction, focusing on the concerns of the man at home rather than those of the man on the road. In other words, the man who is done giving in to wild abandon on America's open roads and is ready to find meaning in his life by getting married and starting a family. "My first full record about men and women in love would be a pretty rough affair,"[1] he adds.

Love is, in fact, one of the main themes of *Tunnel of Love*, love with all its pleasures and dreams, its regrets and frustrations. "I wanted to write a different kind of romantic song, one that took in the different types of emotional experiences of any relationship,"[98] Springsteen told the journalist Steve Pond, adding, "I wanted to make a record about what I felt, about really letting another person in your life and trying to be a part of someone else's life. That's a frightening thing, something that's always filled with shadows and doubts and also wonderful things and beautiful things."[98]

Bruce Springsteen married actress and top model Julianne Phillips on 13 May 1985, seven months after meeting her in Los Angeles. Their romantic bond, however, began to weaken within a matter of months. Even though the

Poster for the Tunnel of Love Express Tour that kicked off on 25 February 1988 in Worcester, Massachusetts, and ended in Barcelona on 4 August.

songwriter had made sure to thank his wife on the album sleeve, the gesture seemed to bear the deep mark of a failing relationship at a time when Patti Scialfa was becoming a part of Springsteen's life as more than just a backing vocalist for the E Street Band. "When Julie was filming on location, I'd be at home in New Jersey, slowly slipping back to my old ways, the bars, the late nights—nothing serious, just my usual drifting—but it wasn't the married life,"[1] admits Springsteen in his autobiography *Born to Run*. He goes on to say that on one of the occasions when Julie was away, he and Patti used the excuse that they had to work on their duets to get together.

Much like the songwriter himself, the characters in *Tunnel of Love* had grown and matured—distancing themselves from the world of adolescence—only to realize that they were not immortal. The moment had come for a reckoning; it was time to find out whether they'd made the right choices in life. Springsteen asks himself this fundamental question throughout *Tunnel of Love*, mostly with intimate, modest, and poetic ballads that were probably influenced by his Catholic upbringing.

As Springsteen says in his autobiography, this new confessional style came from one of the songs on a previous album. "The beginnings of this new music went back to *Stolen Car* from *The River*," he explains. "That song's character, drifting through the night, is the first to face the angels and devils that will drive him toward his love and keep him from ever reaching her. This was the voice that embodied my own conflicts."[1]

As Springsteen's marriage to Julianne Phillips floundered, the singer Patti Scialfa became part of his professional and personal life.

After the release of the album, Bruce Springsteen asked Patti Scialfa to join him on his Tunnel of Love Express Tour. She was initially hesitant because of the recording schedule for her first album, but, in the end, she accepted, putting her solo career on the backburner for nonartistic reasons.

The album

Tunnel of Love was Bruce Springsteen's eighth studio album. It was released worldwide on 9 October 1987. It was a considerable commercial success, though not to the same level as the previous album. In the United States, it reached No.3 during the week of 31 October, then No.1 the week of 7 November (it is now a triple platinum disc). It was also No.1 in Canada and in several European countries, including the United Kingdom, Italy, Spain, Sweden, and Norway. It was No.3, 4, and 5 in West Germany, the Netherlands, and France, respectively. The song won a Grammy Award for the best vocal performance in rock music and is today 467th in *Rolling Stone's* list of the 500 Greatest Albums of All Time (and No.25 on the list of most important albums of the 1980s).

The sleeve

As with the previous album, Annie Leibovitz took the sleeve photo. However, its atmosphere is completely different. The blue-collar image of *Born in the U.S.A.* was replaced by that of a 1980s man about town. We see the Boss wearing a black suit with a white shirt and bolo tie. His head is slightly tilted as he stares into the camera and leans against a white convertible limo. The picture on the back is almost the same, except that Springsteen is no longer wearing the jacket.

The recording

Springsteen recorded most of this eighth album in his home studio. This was in a large room over the guest garage in his Georgian mansion, in Rumson. The studio had been installed by Toby Scott because Mike Batlan could no longer handle the

The cover image by Annie Leibovitz for the *Tunnel of Love* album is radically different in style from the one she shot for the *Born in the U.S.A.* album.

work, as he usually did, having been in a legal conflict with his former boss since 1985. Springsteen had used basic equipment to record *Nebraska* and the second phase of *Born in the U.S.A.* in early 1983. But now, thanks to the sound advice of his recording engineer, he had access to more sturdy equipment, including a 24-track digital tape recorder—he had come a long way since the 8-track Portastudio!

Springsteen began recording in the summer of 1986, but CBS asked him to put this on pause and work on the *Live/1975–85* box set which covered ten years of concerts with the E Street Band. The project was due for release in November and took up all of the summer and fall. It met with enormous success: more than 4.5 million box sets were sold around the world, one of the biggest sales to date for that type of product.

Released from his duties, the songwriter returned to his new album in January 1987. Recording would take place between 20 January and the end of May.

The beginning of the end of the E Street Band

Springsteen approximated the process he used for *Nebraska* by recording most of the instruments alone with his recording engineer, in this case Toby Scott. The only difference was that the members of the E Street Band only added a few overdubs without participating in real sessions, as in the past, with the whole group together in the studio for live takes. All they had to do was list how many of the 12 songs they had participated in: one for Garry Tallent and Clarence Clemons—the latter again on backing vocals, not the saxophone—two for Roy Bittan and Nils Lofgren, three for Patti Scialfa and Danny Federici, and eight for Max Weinberg, the big winner of this record. But make no mistake: Weinberg featured more prominently than the others as Springsteen wanted to do away with using the drum machine as a guide, and also because the drums were one of the few instruments he did not play well. "At the same time," said the drummer, "it obviously was the beginning of the end of the E Street Band, and I didn't realize that until the first rehearsal for The Tunnel of Love Tour."[99]

What happened next?

Recording took place in short sessions at the A&M Studios and the Kren Studio, both in Los Angeles, between May and July 1987. Except for *One Step Up*, these sessions yielded few new songs. Other songs were recorded, probably with a few members of the E Street Band, but definitely with three musicians from outside the group: James "Jimmie" Wood on the harmonica, Jay Dee Maness on the pedal steel guitar, and Richard Greene on the fiddle. The only song to make the

The Yamaha DX-7, one of the most popular synthesizers of the 1980s.

Pages 272–273 The members of the E Street Band leaping above the Boss at the Giants Stadium, in East Rutherford, in 1986.

album and be recorded at Rumson would be the one with the harmonicist: *Spare Parts*. In the end, it would take 18 sessions and about three weeks of work to record *Tunnel of Love*. A true speed record for the Boss!

Once again Bob Clearmountain was in charge of mixing the 12 songs on *Tunnel of Love*. He mixed all of them at A&M Studios, except for the title song which he did at The Hit Factory in New York. As with *Born in the U.S.A.*, Bob Ludwig was in charge of the mastering, which he did at Masterdisk in New York. CBS received the master recording in August 1987.

The instruments

In addition to his Fender Telecaster-Esquire, his Fender Bandmaster amp, and his various 6-string and 12-string guitars, Springsteen used, among others, a Kurzweil 250 synthesizer, a Yamaha DX7, probably a Roland D-50, a LinnDrum drum machine, and a Guild bass guitar. Toby Scott likely programmed the LinnDrum—as he would assert in various interviews—while Bob Clearmountain replaced some of its sounds with something rawer and more authentic, namely the snare drum, which gave the drum machine a much more realistic sound.

Lastly, the songwriter added a slew of other instruments, such as claves, maracas, the tambourine, the harmonica, and the mandolin.

Technical details

Bruce Springsteen used a 24-track digital tape recorder and a Sony PCM-3324 to record himself and a Yamaha NS-10M to listen. Bob Clearmountain used one of the first digital reverbs, an Ursa Major Space Station. "It came out around 1979 or 1980," explained Clearmountain in an interview. "It was one of the first digital reverbs. I mean, it's a horrible-sounding thing on its own, but used suddenly combined with other effects is quite effective, and in Springsteen's *Tunnel of Love* album I've used it quite a bit on vocals and guitars."[77]

For Springsteen Addicts

Even though Danny Federici, Garry Tallent, and Max Weinberg participated in the recording, *Tunnel of Love* is not considered an album by Springsteen with the E Street Band. According to Shore Fire Media, the Boss's public relations firm, *The Rising*, which came out in 2002, should be considered the first album made with the E Street Band since *Born in the U.S.A.*

Ain't Got You centers on the Bo Diddley beat. Bo Diddley in 1957 with his famous Gretsch guitar.

AIN'T GOT YOU

Bruce Springsteen / 2'11

Musician
Bruce Springsteen: vocals, guitar, harmonica, claves, maracas
Recording
Thrill Hill East, Rumson, New Jersey: January to April 1987
Technical team
Producers: Bruce Springsteen, Jon Landau, Chuck Plotkin
Recording engineer: Toby Scott
Mixing
A&M Recording Studios, Los Angeles: May to July 1987
Recording engineer: Bob Clearmountain
Assistant recording engineer: Mark McKenna
Mastering
Masterdisk, New York: August 1987
Recording engineer: Bob Ludwig
Mastering assistant: Heidi Cron

For Springsteen Addicts

"'Cause I got more good luck, honey, than old King Farouk," sings Bruce Springsteen. Here he's referring to Farouk (1920–1965), the second to last king of Egypt. Forced to abdicate the throne for his son Fouad, he was exiled to Monaco and then Italy.

Genesis and lyrics

Ain't Got You starts off *a cappella* before launching into a Bo Diddley rhythm (the famous Bo Diddley beat). The lyrics relay a true sense of frustration. The narrator is swimming in money. He has bonds, "houses 'cross the country," "Rembrandt and priceless art," can eat a "pound of caviar" whenever he wants to, and he's been "all across the seven seas," not to mention having a "hundred pretty women knocking down my door." But he's missing the best part: a woman who loves him. Is there a hidden message in this song of dissatisfaction? Maybe his regret at being married despite having fallen in love with someone else? It's just a theory.

To date, Bruce Springsteen has only performed this song about 50 times onstage, the first time at a concert in the Rupp Arena, in Lexington, Kentucky, on 26 March 1988.

Production

The first song in *Tunnel of Love* is surprising: Springsteen effectively sings the whole first verse *a cappella*, supported only by snapping fingers. Then, for the rest of the song, he plays all the other instruments in his home studio in Rumson (starting from 0'30): the acoustic guitar, which he plays practically in palm mute to better highlight the instrument's rhythmic strengths; the harmonica, for additional rhythmic and harmonic support; the claves and the maracas. After the instrumental fullness and meticulous production of *Born in the U.S.A.*, the contrast is striking. The Boss has returned to his roots, those of a simple songwriter far from the glamour of celebrity life and the spotlights of show business. It's a return to the spirit of *Nebraska* and to his love of rockabilly: he enhances his voice and arrangements with a slapback echo, a key characteristic of the genre.

The idea for the song most likely came from *I Ain't Got You* by Calvin Carter, which was made popular by Jimmy Reed and Billy Boy Arnold toward the mid-1950s. But the music—if not its rock and blue spirit—is very different. On the other hand, the shadow of Bo Diddley is everywhere in the rhythmic beat, guitar performance, and percussion.

TOUGHER THAN THE REST

Bruce Springsteen / 4'35

COVER
Country singer Emmylou Harris recorded *Tougher Than the Rest* during sessions for *Brand New Dance*, released in October 1990.

Musicians
Bruce Springsteen: vocals, guitars, harmonica, drum-machine programming (with Toby Scott), synthesizers
Danny Federici: organ
Max Weinberg: snare drum, cymbals, maracas, tambourine
Recording
Thrill Hill East, Rumson, New Jersey: January to May 1987
Technical team
Producers: Bruce Springsteen, Jon Landau, Chuck Plotkin
Recording engineer: Toby Scott
Mixing
A&M Recording Studios, Los Angeles: May to July 1987
Recording engineer: Bob Clearmountain
Assistant recording engineer: Mark McKenna
Mastering
Masterdisk, New York: August 1987
Recording engineer: Bob Ludwig
Mastering assistant: Heidi Cron

The Irish filmmaker Meiert Avis directed the music video for *Tougher Than the Rest.*

Genesis and lyrics

The character in *Tougher Than the Rest* is noticeably less rich than the one from *Ain't Got You*, but he has other wily ways for winning over the young woman he loves. It's Saturday evening in a small town on the Jersey Shore (one can easily picture it). The heroine is "all dressed up in blue" and the narrator is telling her that if she's looking for love—meaning Love with a capital L—he's tougher than the others. Tougher than "handsome Dan" or "some good-looking Joe" or a "sweet-talking Romeo." It's an invitation to dance, and it's meant to make her understand that he would do anything for her, even if "the road is dark" or full of unforeseen events.

It's clear that the narrator, who has been through (likely very recently) a traumatizing breakup, does not want to have his heart broken again, so he asks the young woman to be strong, too. In short, Bruce Springsteen's heart is no longer hesitating between Julianne Phillips and Patti Scialfa. In fact, when *Tougher Than the Rest* premiered onstage at Sea Bright, New Jersey, on 31 October 1987, Patti Scialfa and Bruce Springsteen sang the chorus together with an obvious affinity.

Tougher Than the Rest is the A-side of the fourth single from *Tunnel of Love* (with *Roulette* on the B-side). It came out on 23 June 1988, not in the United States, but in Europe, Australia, and Japan. It reached No.3 and No.13 in Switzerland and the United Kingdom, respectively. The single came out with a video directed by Meiert Avis.

Production

In spite of the songwriter's original intention to write a rockabilly song, and despite an opening line borrowed from *Rip It Up* by Little Richard ("Well it's Saturday night"), *Tougher Than the Rest* has a distinctive 1980s sound, with an atmosphere of disillusionment and melancholy. Springsteen sings with an almost disappointed tone, one that expresses his inner conflicts, as he would say. There is no need to sing forcefully here: the performance is sweet and airy, carried by an ever-present delay. Aside from the first verse, there are harmonies throughout the song, especially in the bridge (starting from 1'39).

Springsteen recorded the groundwork for *Tougher Than the Rest* in his home studio. He also played two acoustic guitars in rhythm (the first can be heard from the beginning, the

Tougher Than the Rest can be regarded as Bruce Springsteen's declaration of love for Patti Scialfa, particularly as they later sung it together onstage.

second enters sporadically, starting from the second verse, at 1'02); an arpeggio on the electric guitar (enhanced with a chorus on the right); a synthesizer, on which he played a brassy-sounding melody that he maintained throughout the song (Yamaha DX7? Kurzweil 150?); and a second synthesizer, which allowed him to overlay some held chords (at 1'02). He also played two solo parts, the first of which was on his Telecaster-Esquire, the sound warped by a sort of flanging and supported by a reverb (from 2'16). When Bob Clearmountain began to mix the song, he found two different versions of this solo and decided, against the Boss's wishes, to keep the more serious one, which made it onto the album. The other instrumental section, on the harmonica, is in the coda (at 3'41).

To set the rhythm, Springsteen—and most likely Toby Scott—programmed a drum pattern on his drum machine, the famous LinnDrum, which was big in the early 1980s. But to add spark and power, he asked Max Weinberg to record overdubs of a new snare drum, a cymbal (two clashes: at 3'41 and 4'18), a tambourine, and two maracas parts in stereo. He then asked Danny Federici to record an organ part, which he likely played on one of the two synths he had at his home studio (from 1'39).

While this version of *Tunnel of Love* was of perfectly good quality, the live performances were far superior, with or without the E Street Band, or even as a duo with Patti Scialfa. This song came into its own once its idiosyncratic 1980s sounds were removed and it was given a slightly slower tempo.

ALL THAT HEAVEN WILL ALLOW

Bruce Springsteen / 2'38

Musicians
Bruce Springsteen: vocals, guitars, synthesizers, percussion instruments (?)
Max Weinberg: drums, percussion (?)

Recording
Thrill Hill East, Rumson, New Jersey: January to May 1987

Technical team
Producers: Bruce Springsteen, Jon Landau, Chuck Plotkin
Recording engineer: Toby Scott

Mixing
A&M Recording Studios, Los Angeles: May to July 1987
Recording engineer: Bob Clearmountain
Assistant recording engineer: Mark McKenna

Mastering
Masterdisk, New York: August 1987
Recording engineer: Bob Ludwig
Mastering assistant: Heidi Cron

COVER
The Mavericks recorded a version of *All That Heaven Will Allow* during sessions for their third album, *What a Crying Shame* (1994), which has since been certified double platinum.

Raul Malo and Robert Reynolds from the country-rock band The Mavericks ventured into the Springsteenian universe with their cover version of *All That Heaven Will Allow*.

Genesis and lyrics

Bruce Springsteen's inspiration for the title of this love song was the Douglas Sirk film that came out in 1955 (*All That Heaven Allows*). Jane Wyman plays a rich widow who falls in love with a much younger man, the modest son of a gardener (Rock Hudson), and has to face the ignorance of her two children and the contempt of East Coast society. Like Rock Hudson's character, Bruce Springsteen comes from a modest social class. He's the worker who "left [his] wallet back home in [his] working pants." The one the bouncer doesn't want to let into the club. But his social status doesn't really matter to him, as he's in love with a woman who loves him back. "I got a picture in a locket that says 'baby, I love you,'" sings Springsteen at the end of the first verse. The young woman even wants to "wear [his] ring." His happiness is complete. It's a happiness that makes him say, "some may wanna die young, man, young and gloriously/Get it straight now, mister, hey buddy that ain't me." This is a line that Springsteen revived from *City of Night* (that song was scrapped from *Darkness on the Edge of Town* and only released on *The Promise*).

Production

The absence of the E Street Band from *All That Heaven Will Allow* is apparent, as is the reason for it: Springsteen now has full command of the ins and outs of his home studio, and his talent as a multi-instrumentalist allows him to record songs practically on his own, with minimal effort. Although he does not have the know-how or the talent of his partners, at least not in their respective domains, for this type of relatively simple song, it's enough. That is not to say his technique has suffered. Quite the contrary.

Springsteen plays two electric guitar parts enhanced by a short delay (on the left, a rhythm in palm mute; on the right, a few arpeggios), an acoustic guitar, a bass guitar (likely for the first time on the album), synth pads starting from the introduction, and a second keyboard part in the second chorus (on the left), the last two very likely played on a Yamaha DX7. He then adds a counterpoint on his Telecaster-Esquire, making liberal use of reverberations (at 1'44), and his lead vocals, which he harmonizes, starting from the third verse.

Max Weinberg would be the only one to come to his aid by playing the drums. He recorded a bass drum and some

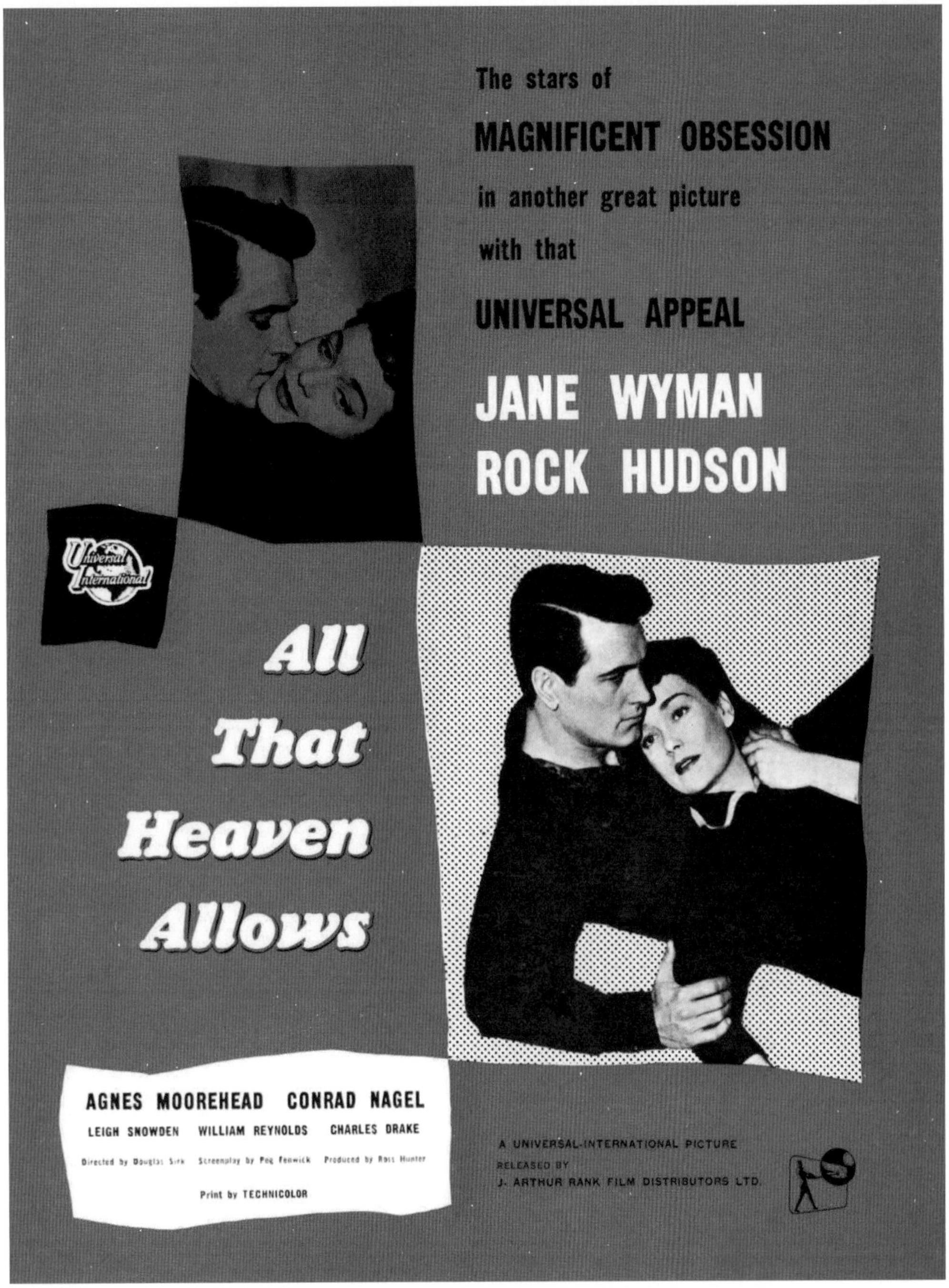

The poster for the Douglas Sirk movie from which Bruce Springsteen took the title of his song.

drumstick beats (which gave off a "bathroom"-style reverberation), to set the tempo. He also seems to have taken on various other percussion instruments: a cabasa (on the right), maracas (from 1'14, on the left), and a tambourine in the last verse (at 1'44). But, since he is not credited for these instruments in the album notes, it's possible the Boss played them himself.

Thanks to the mixing, typical 1980s sounds are less pronounced in *All That Heaven Will Allow*: Bob Clearmountain found the perfect balance between the various tones. Nevertheless, even though this is a good song, the absence of the other members of the E Street Band is glaring. Springsteen was already distancing himself from the musical language they'd built together over the course of a dozen years. This pattern, which started with *Nebraska*, would inevitably lead to the dissolution of the group, an event that finally took place in 1989. However, the live versions of *All That Heaven Will Allow* from the Tunnel of Love Tour in 1988 gave the musicians ample opportunity to play, especially Clarence Clemons, who performed the piece alone with a saxophone improvisation of almost two minutes! But, by all accounts, it was just a swan song.

1987

SPARE PARTS

Bruce Springsteen / 3'39

Musicians
Bruce Springsteen: vocals, guitars, drum-machine programming (with Toby Scott)
Danny Federici: organ
Garry Tallent: bass
Max Weinberg: percussion instruments
James Wood: harmonica

Recording
Thrill Hill East, Rumson, New Jersey: 20 January 1987
A&M Recording Studios, Los Angeles: May to July 1987
Kren Studios, Hollywood: May to July 1987 (?)

Technical team
Producers: Bruce Springsteen, Jon Landau, Chuck Plotkin
Recording engineer: Toby Scott
Assistant recording engineers: Rob Jacobs (A&M), Squeek Stone (Kren)

Mixing
A&M Recording Studios, Los Angeles: May to July 1987
Recording engineer: Bob Clearmountain
Assistant recording engineer: Mark McKenna

Mastering
Masterdisk, New York: August 1987
Recording engineer: Bob Ludwig
Assistant mastering: Heidi Cron

For Springsteen Addicts

James Wood plays the harmonica in this song even though he wasn't a member of the E Street Band. Coproducer Chuck Plotkin, his childhood friend, had asked him to come. In addition to Springsteen, James Wood has recorded with Etta James and Bruce Hornsby, but also Johnny Rotten and Megadeth. He is the front man for the Imperial Crowns.

Genesis and lyrics

Spare Parts is among the darkest songs Bruce Springsteen has ever written. It makes one think of James M Cain, master of crime novels, or Bob Dylan in the 1960s, when he sang about a down-and-out America.

Spare Parts is about two broken hearts, those of Bobby and Janey. Bobby "got scared and he ran away" when his girlfriend became pregnant. Janey went to live with her mother. The baby was born. But the young mother was not ready to raise a child, so she decided to follow the example of a woman who "put her baby in the river." At the last minute, however, when the water was up to her waist, "she lifted him in her arms and carried him home." She then wrapped her engagement ring in the sash of her wedding gown and went to sell her it to a pawnbroker. The implication is that she will use the money to raise her son.

The main character of *Spare Parts* is a woman. Initially, she tries to escape her past and take full advantage of the few years of youth she has left. Then she realizes that there is nothing more important than the life of a child, and that it is her child who gives real meaning to her life. "Spare parts and broken hearts keep the world turning around"—Springsteen's chorus, in all its wisdom, becomes clear.

Spare Parts was chosen as the A-side of the fifth and last single from *Tunnel of Love*. It came out on 18 October 1988 in many countries (with either *Pink Cadillac*, a live version of *Spare Parts*, or a live version of *Chimes of Freedom*, by Bob Dylan), but not in the United States. It reached No.32 in the United Kingdom in September 1988.

Production

Spare Parts was one of the first songs recorded for the album. It seems to have been recorded in two takes on 20 January 1987, in the Boss's home studio. As for the other instrumental parts, Springsteen probably prepared the foundation for the song in advance (notably the programming of the drum machine and a harmonic guide). Still, this was the first song from *Tunnel of Love* that saw three members of the E Street Band working together.

The only typically 1980s sound that made it into the song was that of the bass drum, which was programmed on the LinnDrum and which starts off the song unaccompanied.

Garry Tallent onstage at the Olympic Stadium, Barcelona, on 17 May 2012. The bassist only played on *Spare Parts* for the *Tunnel of Love* album.

Other than that, the spirit and tonality of the arrangements are blues rock with garage-band accents. After a few beats from the bass drum comes the plaint of a harp, its saturated sound mimicking the style of Little Walter. This was the work of the talented James "Jimmie" Wood, who recorded it as an overdub at A&M Studios between May and July. Springsteen soon joins in with a superb acoustic guitar accompaniment in country-rock style. Max Weinberg keeps the rhythm on the cabasa (on the left), supported by a hi-hat that was obviously programmed on the LinnDrum (on the right). Then he adds other percussion instruments, a tambourine (at 1'45) and the maracas (at 2'00). It's unclear whether the snare drum sound comes from the drummer or the drum machine (from 1'09).

The songwriter dusted off his rock voice for the lead vocals, giving it a sharp edge and impressive power, harmonizing through the various choruses (for example, at 0'45). He also recorded additional guitar parts, including scales on his Telecaster-Esquire, which he doubled in stereo, and a highly saturated accompaniment on the right (for example, at 0'29).

Then, for the second time in this album, Danny Federici enters with a highly inspired blues-like organ part (from 1'25). Meanwhile, Gary Tallent recorded a very good bass line, which is forceful and assertive—his only contribution to *Tunnel of Love*. He must have been very frustrated when he realized how minimal his role would be in the creation of this album.

The piece ends with a guitar/harmonica duel between Springsteen and Wood, which creates some excellent blues phrasing (from 3'05). *Spare Parts* is one of the best songs on the Boss's eighth album.

CAUTIOUS MAN

1987

Bruce Springsteen / 3'56

> **For Springsteen Addicts**
> On 2 May 2005, at the Pantages Theatre in Hollywood, Bruce Springsteen dedicated *Cautious Man* to Sean Penn.

Musician
Bruce Springsteen: vocals, guitars, mandolin, synthesizer
Recording
Thrill Hill East, Rumson, New Jersey: January to May 1987
Technical team
Producers: Bruce Springsteen, Jon Landau, Chuck Plotkin
Recording engineer: Toby Scott
Mixing
A&M Recording Studios, Los Angeles: May to July 1987
Recording engineer: Bob Clearmountain
Assistant recording engineer: Mark McKenna
Mastering
Masterdisk, New York: August 1987
Recording engineer: Bob Ludwig
Mastering assistant: Heidi Cron

Robert Mitchum in Charles Laughton's *The Night of the Hunter*, another movie that inspired Bruce Springsteen.

Genesis and lyrics

Cautious Man tells the story of Bill Horton, a man much like the Reverend Harry Powell in *The Night of the Hunter*, the 1955 masterpiece of filmmaking directed by Charles Laughton and starring Robert Mitchum. Like the hero of the film, Horton, a serial killer who pretends to have found Jesus, gets a one-word tattoo on each hand: "love" and "fear" instead of Powell's "love" and "hate." For the Reverend, the biblical reference is clear: the eternal fight between good and evil. With Bill Horton, these two words express what he's feeling, the internal conflict that governs him: on the one hand, his love for the woman he married and for whom he built "a great house down by the riverside" and, on the other, the fear of what settling down means for a wanderer like him. This cautious man prays because he knows that "in a restless heart the seed of betrayal lay." Despite his best efforts to remain with his wife, the call of the road continues to haunt him. One night, he is tempted to leave, but ends up returning to his wife. Since the release of the album in 1987, Bruce Springsteen has performed *Cautious Man* only ten times onstage. The first was at the Met Center in Bloomington, Minnesota, in May 1988. The most recent performance took place at the Continental Airlines Arena in East Rutherford, New Jersey, in November 2015.

Production

Cautious Man is the second song of the album that Springsteen recorded and performed on his own. The result is absolutely superb, surprising in its simplicity and emotion. The songwriter has recorded a folk song using his acoustic guitar as a guide, strumming with infinite sweetness. The tempo is slow, the tenor is collected. His singing is both confident and vulnerable, and he is completely immersed in the lyrics. He adds a mandolin overdub (at 0'19), most likely a 12-string, what sounds like an autoharp (at 1'29), a few synth pads after the third verse (at 1'45), and a second keyboard at the end of the following verse (at 3'07).

At the Devils & Dust Solo and Acoustic Tour of 20 May 2005, at the Orpheum Theater in Boston, Springsteen named *Cautious Man* as one of his favorite songs. It is clear why.

WALK LIKE A MAN

Bruce Springsteen / 3'37

Musicians

Bruce Springsteen: vocals, guitars, bass, synthesizers, drum-machine programming (with Toby Scott)
Max Weinberg: percussion instruments

Recording

Thrill Hill East, Rumson, New Jersey: January to May 1988

Technical team

Producers: Bruce Springsteen, Jon Landau, Chuck Plotkin
Recording engineer: Toby Scott

Mixing

A&M Recording Studios, Los Angeles: May to July 1987
Recording engineer: Bob Clearmountain
Assistant recording engineer: Mark McKenna

Mastering

Masterdisk, New York: August 1987
Recording engineer: Bob Ludwig
Mastering assistant: Heidi Cron

On 2 May 1988, at the Shoreline Amphitheatre in Mountain View, California, Bruce Springsteen dedicated *Walk Like a Man* to his "Pops," who was in the audience. What might Doug Springsteen have thought of such a tender tribute?

For Springsteen Addicts

During the Tunnel of Love Tour of 1988, the group played a superb instrumental introduction to *Walk Like a Man*. In reality, the only instrument was the keyboards, played in a slightly Oriental tone. Unfortunately, this song would only be performed twice: on 25 and 29 February.

Genesis and lyrics

Springsteen uses *Walk Like a Man* to look back on his childhood and the figure of the authoritative father. On his wedding day, the narrator remembers, "All I can think of is being five years old following behind you at the beach tracing your footprints in the sand, trying to walk like a man."

Then come the memories of a Catholic upbringing, "Well by Our Lady of the Roses we lived in the shadow of the elms/I remember ma dragging me and my sister up the street to the church whenever she heard those wedding bells." Finally, the narrator returns to the harsh reality of the present when, once again, he recalls his life with his father. "Well I was young and I didn't know what to do when I saw your best steps stolen away from you." The message is clear: always keep your chin up and walk like a man. As for marriage, it is like "a mystery ride" for the New Jersey songwriter. This is most likely another autobiographical allusion.

Production

Walk Like a Man closes the A-side of the original vinyl. Springsteen obviously thought this the perfect place to show the tenderness he felt for his father. Symbolically, this was also the first song he recorded for the album, on 20 January 1987.

An electric piano dominates the song. The Boss played it himself on the Yamaha DX7—as he did all the other instruments except for the percussion: the rhythm guitar on his Telecaster-Esquire, a 12-string acoustic guitar (from 2'58), a bass line, a second keyboard with typical 1980s sounds (like the DX7), and the LinnDrum. The latter created some programming problems, as it wasn't very effective in its performance, but neither Springsteen nor Toby Scott—who helped with the programming—could fix it. The live version would rectify this slight problem while also giving the piece a bigger sound, especially thanks to Danny Federici's Hammond B-3.

Lastly, Max Weinberg would give the songwriter a hand, probably in January, by recording overdubs with what appear to be a shaker (from 1'00, far in the background) and a tambourine (at 1'43).

A standout passage on the title track of Bruce Springsteen's eighth studio album is the superb solo from Nils Lofgren (here, in concert with the E Street Band in Washington in 2007).

1987

TUNNEL OF LOVE

Bruce Springsteen / 5'12

Musicians
Bruce Springsteen: vocals, guitars, special effects, bass, drum-machine programming (with Toby Scott)
Nils Lofgren: lead guitar
Roy Bittan: synthesizers
Max Weinberg: percussion instruments
Patti Scialfa: vocals
The Schiffer Family; roller coasters, Pleasant Beach, New Jersey: sound effects
Recording
Thrill Hill East, Rumson, New Jersey: January to May 1987
Technical team
Producers: Bruce Springsteen, Jon Landau, Chuck Plotkin
Recording engineer: Toby Scott
Mixing
The Hit Factory, New York: May to July 1987
Recording engineer: Bob Clearmountain
Assistant recording engineer: Jay Healy
Mastering
Masterdisk, New York: August 1987
Recording engineer: Bob Ludwig
Mastering assistant: Heidi Cron

Cover for Dire Straits' single. Same title as the Boss's, but a different song. Roy Bittan plays on both.

Genesis and lyrics

The memory of funfairs in Asbury Park, where Bruce Springsteen loved to go as a teenager, was the most likely inspiration for this song. It is a funfair ride that lends its name to this eighth album. The metaphor, in any case, is apt: a merry-go-round as a symbol of marriage, or more precisely, of the two-sided journey that is marriage.

A couple climbs into a carnival ride. When the lights go out, "it's just the three of us/Yeah, you me and all that stuff we're so scared of." This "stuff" is not just the ride—called tunnel of love, in this case—it's life as a couple with all its joys, but also its questions, worries, and sorrows. "There's a room of shadows that gets so dark brother/It's easy for two people to lose each other in this tunnel of love," sings Springsteen. Or, "man meets woman and they fall in love/But this house is haunted and the ride gets rough." Is Springsteen referring to his marriage with Julianne Phillips? It seems reasonable.

Tunnel of Love is the A-side of the second single of the eponymous album. It came out on 17 October 1987 with *Two for the Road* on the B-side, reaching No.9 in the United States in December 1987, before being named single of the year, 1987, by *Rolling Stone* magazine. In the United Kingdom, on the other hand, this song would never do better than No.45. It came with a video directed by Meiert Avis that was nominated in the category of "Video of the Year" at the MTV Video Music Awards. *Tunnel of Love* premiered onstage in Worcester, Massachusetts, on 25 February 1988, but since then it has not been performed very often (fewer than a hundred times).

Production

Tunnel of Love is certainly one of the most ambitious songs of the album, a true break from Springsteen's usual writing. The songwriter composed a piece that conformed to the sounds and spirit of the times, which were primarily marked by synthesizers and drum machines. Hearing it in the Boss's home studio, Nils Lofgren couldn't believe his ears. "I was shocked at the song: It was so different sounding and radical and beautiful, and just out of the box—in my eyes—from what Bruce normally did."[101]

The introduction is built around several sounds and special effects from the synthesizers (Yamaha DX7, Kurzweil 250, Roland D-50). They're carried by the LinnDrum—with a

particularly uncharacteristic half-hip-hop, half-jazz rock bass drum—and the Telecaster-Esquire. Roy Bittan enters on the keyboards with majestic flights, giving his first and second-to-last performance of the album and playing the main riff of the track, which evokes that of *Chest Fever* by The Band (from *Music from Big Pink*, 1968). Max Weinberg is on the percussion instruments, which are, truth be told, undermixed. Patti Scialfa sings some very beautiful gospel-style vocals (toward 2'18 or 2'46). Meanwhile, Springsteen provides lead vocals, vocal harmonies, electric rhythm guitars, and the bass line.

A remarkable solo

The highlight of the track is Nils Lofgren's guitar solo (from 2'01). Springsteen had asked him to record something new and surprising, so he hooked up his 6-string guitar to several effects pedals. "I asked him what key we were in and he said C," explained the guitarist. "So I just started picking out some hammered notes—something I usually don't do in my style [...] We just kept plugging in foot pedals and choruses and flangers and messing around with the sound, and we got a couple of different takes that felt great under his instruction. Then I went to writing one of my one-note-with-a-rhythm, bouncing harmonic thing under the singing, and came up with a solo that he wanted to use, which I was honored by and still love playing that live."[101]

The piece ends with the sound of screams and speeding carts from a roller coaster (at 4'59). Toby Scott recorded them at Point Pleasant, New Jersey.

This song, which opens the B-side of the original vinyl, is the definite turning point of *Tunnel of Love*.

Springsteen was not the first artist to choose *Tunnel of Love* as the theme and title of a song. In 1981, Mark Knopfler, of Dire Straits, had released a single of the same name from the album *Making Movies* (1980). Small detail: Roy Bittan was at the keyboards.

1987

TWO FACES

Bruce Springsteen / 3'00

COVER
Just this once, French artist Nicola Sirkis, singer for the group Indochine, made an excellent cover of Springsteen's *Two Faces* for his 1992 album *Dans la Lune* ("In the Moon").

Musicians
Bruce Springsteen: vocals, guitars, bass, synthesizers, drum-machine programming (with Toby Scott)
Max Weinberg: percussion instruments
Recording
Thrill Hill East, Rumson, New Jersey: January to May 1987
Technical team
Producers: Bruce Springsteen, Jon Landau, Chuck Plotkin
Recording engineer: Toby Scott
Mixing
A&M Recording Studios, Los Angeles: May to July 1987
Recording engineer: Bob Clearmountain
Assistant recording engineer: Mark McKenna
Mastering
Masterdisk, New York: August 1987
Recording engineer: Bob Ludwig
Mastering assistant: Heidi Cron

Lou Christie and his 1963 song *Two Faces Have I* were probably one of the inspirations for Springsteen's song.

Genesis and lyrics

Two Faces is another song about the end of a marriage, this time caused by the ambivalence of the narrator. An encounter, the flight of two lovers, then confessions in the form of repentance. "I swore I'd make her happy every day/And now I made her cry" or "Lord I love to see my baby smile/Then dark clouds come rolling by." The narrator says that he has "two faces": "one that laughs, one that cries." Lost to a deep manic-depressive state, he even prays for his dark side—the one that makes his lover suffer—to disappear. It's all in vain. His dark side continues to undermine their love and he says, "our life was just a lie" and claims it can even make his baby stop loving him. Will his happy side regain the upper hand? One can only hope.

Two Faces recounts a troubled love story. As such, it could have been inspired by the works of poet and intellectual Robert Bly, who believed the identity crisis and lethargy of Western men in the 1980s were largely due to a loss of traditions and rituals, and a denial of the myths that had previously sparked their imagination and strength to succeed. Bly published his *Little Book on the Human Shadow* in 1988. The theories he explores are quite similar to those of the Swiss psychoanalyst Carl Jung. Perhaps Bruce Springsteen had read this seminal text.

Production

Springsteen starts off *Two Faces* alone, with an almost 20-second introduction on the acoustic guitar. He strums a melody that he repeats in the vocals and plays all the instruments except for the percussions, which fall to Max Weinberg: claves, cabasa (all on the left), and maracas.

The songwriter plays the guitar and sings along in the first verse, his voice carried by a long delay. He then adds an electric rhythm with his Telecaster-Esquire (on the right), a bass line, and some synth pads. He enhances the texture of the sound as the song develops: vocal harmonies followed by an organ at the end of the fourth verse; then saturated guitars double-tracked in stereo (at 1'31); and, finally, a second organ for a solo in the coda, a Farfisa organ that sounds strangely like Danny Federici's. The construction and arrangements of *Two Faces* are simple, but terribly effective.

BRILLIANT DISGUISE

Bruce Springsteen / 4'15

Musicians
Bruce Springsteen: vocals, guitars, bass, synthesizers, drum-machine programming (with Toby Scott)
Roy Bittan: piano
Danny Federici: organ
Max Weinberg: percussion instruments, tom-tom drum

Recording
Thrill Hill East, Rumson, New Jersey: January to May 1987

Technical team
Producers: Bruce Springsteen, Jon Landau, Chuck Plotkin
Recording engineer: Toby Scott

Mixing
A&M Recording Studios, Los Angeles: May to July 1987
Recording engineer: Bob Clearmountain
Assistant recording engineer: Mark McKenna

Mastering
Masterdisk, New York: August 1987
Recording engineer: Bob Ludwig
Mastering assistant: Heidi Cron

Bruce Springsteen at Madison Square Garden, New York, on 19 May 1988. *Brillant Disguise* is the key song on *Tunnel of Love.*

Genesis and lyrics

Bruce Springsteen reveals in his book *Songs* that "the center of *Tunnel of Love* is *Brilliant Disguise*."[6] "Trust is a fragile thing," he adds. "It requires allowing others to see as much of ourselves as we have the courage to reveal. But you drop one mask and find another behind it, until you begin to doubt your own feelings about who you are. It's the twin issues of love and identity that form the core of *Tunnel of Love*."[6]

"So tell me what I see when I look in your eyes/Is that you, baby, or just a brilliant disguise?" As the chorus points out, the narrator is no longer sure of his partner's true feelings. "I saw something tucked in shame underneath your pillow." Was she having an affair with another man? One thing's for sure, "It all falls apart, oh, when out go the lights." In other words, they no longer satisfy each other sexually. Who's to blame? Again, the narrator wonders, "I want to know if it's you I don't trust 'cause I damn sure don't trust myself." And he prays to God, "God have mercy on the man who doubts what he's sure of."

The theme of *Brilliant Disguise* is more than a simple lack of loyalty, or even betrayal, but that of a lack of trust in himself as well as in his partner. As Springsteen explains in the DVD *VH1 Storytellers—On Stage*, the song stems, in part, from the mystery of love. "Songs shift their meanings when you sing them," he says. "They shift their meanings in time, they shift their meanings with who you sing them with. When you sing this song with somebody you love, it turns into something else, I think. It becomes a song of...kind of a reaffirmation of the world's mysteries. Its shadows, our frailties, and the acceptance of those frailties, without which there is no love."[13]

This is the precise moment in which Patti Scialfa came into his life. In other words, yesterday's questions with Julianne Phillips disappeared with the affirmation of the real feelings he shared with Patti Scialfa. *Brilliant Disguise* was released on 3 October 1987 on the A-side of the first single of *Tunnel of Love* (with *Lucky Man* on the B-side), along with a video directed by Meiert Avis. It climbed to No.5 in the *Billboard* charts in October 1987 and to No.20 in the United Kingdom in the same month. It would place in the Top 20 in Canada, Australia, the Netherlands, and Ireland. It was nominated in the category of "Best Performance" at the 1988 Grammy Awards.

For Springsteen Addicts
The black and white photograph of Bruce Springsteen on the sleeve of the *Brilliant Disguise* single was taken by Pamela Springsteen, the songwriter's sister.

Carlo Di Palma, Woody Allen's director of photography, was involved in the filming of the music video for *Brillant Disguise* (here, in 2003).

Production

Brilliant Disguise is another song that incorporates both the sounds and spirit of the 1980s, but with a more moderate use of synthesizers and the characteristic sounds of the famous Yamaha DX7—found in practically every production of the time—or the Roland D-50. Bruce Springsteen's songs were less marked by the 1980s, which allows them to stand the test of time without too many problems. One small exception to the rule was the sound of the LinnDrum at the start of *Brilliant Disguise*.

Springsteen sought the support of three members of the E Street Band: Roy Bittan on the piano (from 1'23), Danny Federici on the organ (from 1'37), and the incomparable Max Weinberg on percussions (claves, maracas, cabasa, and even the castanets, toward 1'58). The drummer confessed that the Boss had flown him in just to record a simple tom-tom part, which starts at 1'57.

The first session likely took place on 5 February, with the working title of *Is that You*. Springsteen had predictably laid the foundations for the piece before his three band mates arrived. Aside from the programming of the LinnDrum (which he did with the help of Toby Scott), he played all the various guitar parts on his Telecaster-Esquire, the bass, and the synth pads. And, of course, he sang the vocals and backing vocals with his usual ease. For once, Bob Clearmountain remained conservative on the reverb and other delays that he generally applied to Springsteen's voice.

A simple but problematic video

When Jon Landau reached out to Meiert Avis to talk about a video for *Brilliant Disguise*, the director knew of Springsteen's aversion to any type of ambitious cinematography. So, he came up with an idea that was both simple and effective, that of filming in a modest kitchen with a retro style. What's more, when he suggested Springsteen sing live instead of on playback, the singer immediately agreed. Meiert ended up finding the perfect kitchen in New Jersey. Unfortunately, the night before the shoot was due to take place, the owner went back on the agreement his wife had negotiated in his absence, leaving the director without a location. After moving heaven and earth, he managed, at the last minute, to dig up a new kitchen, which belonged to an officer in the New York National Guard who was on leave. Carlo Di Palma, Woody Allen's photography director, was at hand, as was Toby Scott. After 24 live takes, only four or five were kept, with the Boss singing the entire song live each time. The video met with resounding success on MTV and paved the way for more artistic videos.

ONE STEP UP

Bruce Springsteen / 4'21

For Springsteen Addicts

Despite his reluctance to record the songs of other artists, Kenny Chesney did a cover of *One Step Up* for the album *No Shoes, No Shirt, No Problem* (2002). After hearing the recording, Springsteen told him he liked it.

Musicians

Bruce Springsteen: vocals, guitars, bass, synthesizers, percussion instruments, drum-machine programming (with Toby Scott)
Patti Scialfa: backing vocals

Recording

A&M Recording Studios, Los Angeles: May to July 1987
Kren Studios, Hollywood: May to July 1987 (?)

Technical team

Producers: Bruce Springsteen, Jon Landau, Chuck Plotkin
Recording engineer: Toby Scott
Assistant recording engineers: Rob Jacobs (A&M), Squeek Stone (?) (Kren)

Mixing

A&M Recording Studios, Los Angeles: May to July 1987
Recording engineer: Bob Clearmountain
Assistant recording engineer: Mark McKenna

Mastering

Masterdisk, New York: August 1987
Recording engineer: Bob Ludwig
Mastering assistant: Heidi Cron

Bruce Springsteen and Julianne Phillips at London's Heathrow Airport in 1985. Two years later, *One Step Up* is about the end of a relationship.

Genesis and lyrics

One Step Up may be the song that most explicitly refers to Bruce Springsteen's first marriage to Julianne Phillips, which went down the drain. "We're the same sad story" and "in our dirty little war," he sings. He litters the verses with negative images, like the cold house, the bird that has stopped singing, the church bells that no longer ring for the bride. He asks himself, "who's wrong, baby, who's right?" and confesses that he's not "the man [he] wanted to be/Somewhere along the line [he] slipped off track."

The narrator is now in a bar looking at a girl who doesn't seem to be married—and he pretends he's not either. The last verse, however, is like a wish. "Last night I dreamed I held you in my arms." It is "One step up and two steps back." The title itself hints that this wish will not be granted.

One Step Up is the A-side of the third single from *Tunnel of Love*. It was released in Europe, North America, and Japan on 27 February 1988. It reached No.13 in the US charts on 19 March. Meiert Avis directed the music video.

Production

One Step Up was among the songs recorded at the A&M Studios, in Los Angeles, between May and July, instead of in Springsteen's home studio. To make it, three musicians from outside the E Street band came to his aid: Jay Dee Maness on the pedal steel guitar (The Byrds, Buck Owens, Eric Clapton, Ray Charles), Richard Greene on the fiddle (James Taylor, Taj Mahal, Emmylou Harris), and James Wood on the harmonica. Only Wood would make it to the album, in *Spare Parts*, which was recorded in Ramrod, not at A&M Studios. To date, no song other than *One Step Up* came of these sessions.

Springsteen played all the instruments in this rock ballad, whose intro sounds a bit like *Every Little Thing She Does is Magic* by the Police (1981), with its synth pads, bass line (likely also on the synth), guitars, percussion instruments, LinnDrum, and vocals. For the second time on this album, Patti Scialfa lent the Boss a hand with backing vocals, her beautiful voice enhanced by a very loud reverb (from 3'14).

WHEN YOU'RE ALONE

1987

Bruce Springsteen / 3'20

Musicians
Bruce Springsteen: vocals, guitars, bass, synthesizers, drum-machine programming (with Toby Scott), percussion instruments (?)
Patty Scialfa, Nils Lofgren, Clarence Clemons: backing vocals
Max Weinberg: drums, percussion instruments (?)
Recording
Thrill Hill East, Rumson, New Jersey: January to May 1987
Technical team
Producers: Bruce Springsteen, Jon Landau, Chuck Plotkin
Recording engineer: Toby Scott
Mixing
A&M Recording Studios, Los Angeles: May to July 1987
Recording engineer: Bob Clearmountain
Assistant recording engineer: Mark McKenna
Mastering
Masterdisk, New York: August 1987
Recording engineer: Bob Ludwig
Mastering assistant: Heidi Cron

Clarence Clemons provides backing vocals on *When You're Alone*. Here, at the 30th Annual Grammy Awards in 1988.

Genesis and lyrics

Love can't last forever. Johnny, the narrator of *When You're Alone*, learns this the hard way. His wife leaves him in the first verse. Why? Maybe because of a lack of money—"Times were tough, love was not enough." One can guess, anyway, that the young woman had no trouble finding a new lover, as she had a "pretty form" to work with. But looks aren't everything. "You're gonna find out someday honey, that when you're alone you're alone," he warns. He's certain that she'll come back to him after remembering the fun they had when times were good. Is this wishful thinking? While awaiting that fateful day, tossing his hard feelings into the river, all he knows is that when love is gone, it's gone.

Production

The only contribution of Clarence Clemons to *When You're Alone* serves to highlight his absence from the rest of the album. What's most disappointing is that he's not even on the saxophone, but on backing vocals with Patti Scialfa and Nils Lofgren. You can theoretically hear him in the coda (at 2'51), but Patti's voice stands out the most. Is he the one harmonizing with the Boss at the start of the third verse (at 1'55) or in the last chorus (at 2'31)? It's not clear; it's a high-pitched male voice, likely Nils'.

When You're Alone is a light ballad with a melodious tune that contrasts with the meaning behind the lyrics. Springsteen, again, is the only instrumentalist in the room, playing everything but the drums, which he entrusted to Max Weinberg, along with the percussion instruments (claves, maracas, and tambourine), even though the drummer wasn't credited for this role. The songwriter is on the keyboards (synth pads, electric piano), at the guitars (electric and acoustic), on the bass guitar, and on the LinnDrum.

When You're Alone is a good song, but definitely a bit too "smooth" to be interesting. The live versions that Springsteen would perform alone on the electric piano are far better than this one, especially the one he performed for the last time in concert in Worcester, Massachusetts, on 20 October 2005.

VALENTINE'S DAY

Bruce Springsteen / 5'10

For Springsteen Addicts

The reference to fatherhood in the second verse of *Valentine's Day* is an explicit reference to Jon Landau, who became father to little Kate in 1985 (she would also become a manager some day).

Musicians

Bruce Springsteen: vocals, guitars, mandolin, bass, synthesizers, drum-machine programming (with Toby Scott), percussion instruments

Recording

Thrill Hill East, Rumson, New Jersey: January to May 1987

Technical team

Producers: Bruce Springsteen, Jon Landau, Chuck Plotkin

Recording engineer: Toby Scott

Mixing

A&M Recording Studios, Los Angeles: May to July 1987

Recording engineer: Bob Clearmountain

Assistant recording engineer: Mark McKenna

Mastering

Masterdisk, New York: August 1987

Recording engineer: Bob Ludwig

Mastering assistant: Heidi Cron

A pensive Bruce Springsteen sitting on a sidewalk. *Valentine's Day* is a song about solitude.

Genesis and lyrics

Valentine is the name of three Catholic martyrs who are remembered on 14 February, now a day dedicated to lovers. This double reference was the spark that pushed Bruce Springsteen to write the last song on *Tunnel of Love*. The narrator says that he's driving along "the highway in the dark." Loneliness weighs down on him. He wants to be back with the one he loves as soon as possible. There is another desire: that of becoming a father, like one of his friends, who's been deeply changed by the experience.

Will the narrator get what he wants? Who knows. "They say if you die in your dreams you really die in your bed," sings Springsteen. Is he thinking about death? Or rebirth? Or metamorphosis? On the one hand, he's using dark metaphors, such as "this spooky old highway," "the timberwolf in the pines," "the cold river bottom," and "the gray fields." On the other hand, there is "God's light," a divine light that guides the traveler to the love of his life, the woman of his dreams, the mysterious Valentine. Indeed, we can hear the sweet sound of love's triumph in the last words of *Valentine's Day*: "So hold me close honey say you're forever mine/And tell me you'll be my lonely Valentine."

Production

Valentine's Day is the last song of *Tunnel of Love* and the last song to be recorded by Springsteen alone, without the help of anyone from the E Street Band. What a success! The Boss repeats two chord patters from start to finish (except in the bridge, at 1'47), each a hypnotic motif he enhances with different synth and mandolin sounds. He uses his Telecaster to build structure, playing it as an acoustic guitar surrounded by a minimalist LinnDrum and an excellent bass line. The atmosphere is intimate, simple, and collected, a bit like *Harvest Moon* by Neil Young (1992). The Boss sings with gentleness, restraint, and his signature magnetic force.

Valentine's Day could have been included in *The River* had it not been for the synthesizers and drum machine. Bruce Springsteen is a great writer and composer. With this song he proved himself yet again.

Roy Bittan, one of the musicians who crafted the Springsteen sound from the mid-1970s. Here, the pianist performs with the E Street Band at the 29th Annual Rock & Roll Hall of Fame Induction Ceremony on 10 April 2014.

ROY BITTAN: THE PROFESSOR WITH MAGIC FINGERS

Originally from Queens in New York, where he was born on 2 July 1949, Roy J Bittan joined the E Street Band in August 1974, after answering an advert in the *Village Voice* for a pianist who could play classical music as well as Jerry Lee Lewis. Before Patti Scialfa joined, he was the only member of the band to hold a music degree, hence his nickname, The Professor. Both on keyboards and backing vocals, he has contributed to most of Bruce Springsteen's albums from *Born to Run* (1975), including *Human Touch* (1992) and *Lucky Town* (1992), which were recorded without the E Street Band. He is an important part of the Springsteenian sound, as exemplified by his outstanding intro to *Jungleland*, and he is the only E Streeter to have cowritten songs with the Boss.

Roy Bittan has brought his musical sensibilities to other big names on the rock scene: Meat Loaf for *Bat Out of Hell* (1977), David Bowie for *Station to Station* (1976) and *Scary Monster* (1980), and Dire Straits for *Making Movies* (1980), as well as Lucinda Williams for *Car Wheels on a Gravel Road* (1998), an album that he coproduced and on which he plays the accordion. He has also worked with artists such as Jackson Browne, Bob Dylan, and Peter Gabriel.

The guitarist Nils Lofgren (here in London, 1975) played with Neil Young before joining the E Street Band.

NILS LOFGREN: A TALENTED GUITARIST WHO SHUNS THE LIMELIGHT

Italian on his mother's side and Swedish on his father's side, Nils Lofgren was born in Chicago on 21 June 1951, but spent his childhood in Bethesda, Maryland, in the suburbs of Washington DC. By the time he replaced Steve Van Zandt as the E Street Band guitarist in 1984, he could boast an impressive résumé. He had formed Grin with George Daly (bass) and Bob Berberich (drums) in 1968 ; he had played on Neil Young's legendary albums, *After the Gold Rush* (1970) and *Tonight's the Night* (1975) and accompanied him on tour as the Crazy Horse guitarist; he had recorded a dozen albums as a solo artist, including the successful *Nils Lofgren* (1975) and *Cry Tough* (1976); and he had played with Lou Reed during the recording sessions for *The Bells* (1979).

Nils Lofgren first studio recording with the E Street Band was on guitar for the title track for the *Tunnel of Love* album, and backing vocals for *When You're Alone* from the same album. He then played a key role in the recording sessions for *The Rising* (2002), for which he played guitar, slide guitar, Dobro, and banjo. He is also omnipresent on *Magic* (2007), despite the return of Steve Van Zandt, and then again on *Working on a Dream* (2009). Finally, he is also on guitar, pedal steel guitar, and mandolin for several songs on *High Hopes*.

Over the years, Nils Lofgren has carried on recording albums in his own name—a total of 17 between 1985 and 2019, including *Flip* (1985). In 2019, he was back playing with Neil Young and Crazy Horse on the recording sessions for *Colorado*.

SIDE B

LUCKY MAN

Bruce Springsteen / 3'30

Single: *Brilliant Disguise/Lucky Man* **Reference:** Columbia Records – 38-07595 **Release date:** United States, 3 October 1987
Musician: Bruce Springsteen: vocals, guitars, bass, synthesizers, drum-machine programming, cabasa **Recording:** Thrill Hill East, Rumson, New Jersey: 4 April 1987 **Technical team:** Producers: Bruce Springsteen, Jon Landau, Chuck Plotkin / Recording engineer: Toby Scott / Mixing: Bob Clearmountain

Genesis and lyrics

The sound of Louisiana blues permeates this song about a very lucky truck driver. A gypsy has read his palm and told him, "You're a lucky man." A lucky man compared to those around him, like his Pa who came back from the army to work in a factory; a lucky man because he left his girlfriend in Calgary in order to avoid emotional attachments. He has no shortage of girls and no need of a home. What he wants is to travel for life, and so he travels alone.

Although *Lucky Man* was recorded during sessions for *Tunnel of Love,* it was not included on that album. This was not so much because it is a tribute to freedom and lone travel, but as a result of its sound, which contrasts sharply with the other songs on this eighth album. However, it was chosen as the B-side of *Brilliant Disguise*, the first single from *Tunnel of Love*, and for the third CD of the *Tracks* box set (1998).

Production

Lucky Man clashes with the other songs on *Tunnel of Love*: the piece is centered around a low, hypnotic bass line that develops into a bluesy, dark, and intense atmosphere. It had initially been intended for the album instead of the song *Tunnel of Love*, but Springsteen changed his mind at the last moment, no doubt to preserve a consistency of sound.

The Boss is alone at the controls, taking on the various guitars, the bass, the LinnDrum programming, the synthesizers, and the only percussion part in the song (a cabasa from 1'37). Two elements in particular give *Lucky Man* its bluesy feel: first, the songwriter's properly rough voice, with its hints of Louisiana Red; then, his Telecaster-Esquire, which is played sparingly and surrounded by a deep reverberation, creating long phrasing in the arrangements (on the left). Only the LinnDrum (which runs in the same pattern throughout) and the synth pads tie *Lucky Man* to its era. An excellent B-side.

Springsteen was not the only one to call a song *Lucky Man*: Emerson, Lake & Palmer and The Verge did so as well, in 1970 and 1997, respectively.

SIDE B

TWO FOR THE ROAD

Bruce Springsteen / 1'59

Single: *Tunnel of Love/Two for the Road* **Reference:** Columbia Records – 38-07663 **Release date:** United States, 17 October 1987 **Musician:** Bruce Springsteen: vocals, guitars, synthesizer **Recording:** Thrill Hill East, Rumson, New Jersey: February 1987 **Technical team:** Producers: Bruce Springsteen, Jon Landau, Chuck Plotkin / Recording engineer: Toby Scott / Mixing: Bob Clearmountain

Genesis and lyrics

Two for the Road and *Lucky Man* convey opposing messages: where solitude is the ultimate expression of freedom in *Lucky Man*, in this song the happiness of being in a couple is what gives meaning to life. "One thousand dreams whispered in the dark/But a dream's just a dream in one empty heart," sings Springsteen in the second verse. By the same token, two are better than one when it comes to facing the hardships and difficulties of life. This is exactly what the narrator tells his partner when he says, "I'll stand beside you, we're two for the road."

As with *Lucky Man, Two for the Road* was recorded during sessions for *Tunnel of Love*. It was released as the B-side of the *Tunnel of Love* single, then it was revived for the *Tracks* box set (1998). Bruce Springsteen sang it four times during the Devils & Dust Tour.

Production

Although the first line of *Two for the Road* is an adaptation of the lyrics to *Blue Suede Shoes*, one of the greatest rock songs of all time, written by Carl Perkins in 1955 and immortalized by Elvis the following year, this B-side is a sweet and vaguely country-and-western song, sung by a Bruce Springsteen gushing with tenderness and romanticism.

Springsteen is once again the only musician in the recording room: he accompanies himself on the acoustic guitar, adding an electric guitar (on the left, at 0'17) and an electric piano to the synthesizer, a Yamaha DX7 or Roland D-50 (on the right). He harmonizes his vocals with a second vocal part in the second verse and performs a solo on his Telecaster-Esquire (enhanced by a chorus/flanger and a reverb), which he doubles with whistling (from 0'46).

Although likeable, *Two for the Road* could never be on the tracklisting for *Tunnel of Love*.

Two for the Road is also a 1967 British film directed by Stanley Donen and starring Audrey Hepburn and Albert Finney. The score, by the same name, was composed by Henry Mancini.

Onstage at Madison Square Garden for the No Nukes concert. *Roulette* is a song about atomic anxiety.

For Springsteen Addicts

On 21 and 22 September 1979, six months after the accident at Three Mile Island, Bruce Springsteen and the E Street Band—along with Jackson Browne, Bonnie Raitt, and Tom Petty—performed at the two No Nukes antinuclear concerts held at Madison Square Garden in New York.

SIDE B

ROULETTE

Bruce Springsteen / 3'46

Single: *One Step Up/Roulette* **Reference:** Columbia Records – 38-07726 **Release date:** United States, 27 February 1988

Musicians
Bruce Springsteen: vocals, guitars
Steve Van Zandt: guitars, vocal harmonies
Roy Bittan: piano
Danny Federici: organ
Garry Tallent: bass
Max Weinberg: drums

Recording
The Power Station, 441 West 53rd St, New York: 3 April 1979

Technical team
Producers: Bruce Springsteen, Jon Landau, Steve Van Zandt
Recording engineer: Neil Dorfsman
Assistant recording engineers: Jeff Hendrickson, Garry Rindfuss, Dana Bisbee, Raymond Willhard, James Farber
Mixing: Bob Clearmountain (single), Ed Thacker (*Tracks*)

Genesis and lyrics

The accident at the Three Mile Island nuclear power plant, near Harrisburg, Pennsylvania, on 28 March 1979, sparked some of the most legitimate and harrowing questions in the United States and the world as a whole. In some cases, it even provoked panic. Bruce Springsteen himself was shocked when he heard about the accident and then of the Pennsylvania governor's order to evacuate young children and pregnant woman at least 5 miles (8km) from the plant to avoid radioactive contamination after the meltdown of reactor number 2. He wrote *Roulette* in the wake of the incident.

Springsteen sings: "I want some answers, mister, I need to know" and "I hear all the talk but I don't know what you're saying." The songwriter apparently did not believe the official version of events. That is, in any case, the opinion of the narrator, a fireman who tries to save his family from a possible catastrophe. He explains: "I grew up on this street/Where nothing moves, just a strange breeze" and "I've got a house full of things that I can't touch."

The images are disquieting and evoke a sense of paranoia. As he searches for a safe place, the character in the song is stopped by police. "They said they just want to ask me a few questions but I think they had other plans/Now I don't know who to trust and I don't know what I can believe." The only thing he knows for sure is that the authorities are playing roulette with people's lives.

With an energy to rival that of the English punk scene (the Sex Pistols come to mind, and The Jam even more so), *Roulette* was the first song recorded during sessions for *The River*. It was then scrapped from that album. Springsteen fans only learned of the official version in February 1988, when Springsteen and

Columbia Records released it on the B-side of *One Step Up*, which is the third single from *Tunnel of Love*. That same month, Springsteen premiered it onstage at the Centrum, in Worcester, Massachusetts (on 25 February). It's also on the B-side of the fourth single from the same album, with *Tougher Than the Rest* as the A-side; on the second CD of the *Tracks* box set (1998); and on *The Ties That Bind: The River Collection* box set (2015).

Production

Springsteen recorded a first draft of *Roulette* the day after the Three Mile Island catastrophe, and by the sixth day after the accident, on 3 April, the E Street Band had recorded the song in full at The Power Station. The musicians couldn't have found a better fit to launch the making of *The River* than this supercharged rock song, which was ideal for uniting the group and for trying out the acoustics in the enormous Studio A. After the excessively sterile feel of *Darkness on the Edge of Town*, Springsteen was looking for more authentic sounds. As he explains in his autobiography *Born to Run*: "We wanted the sound of less control. This was how many of our favorite records from the early days of rock 'n' roll had been recorded. You miked the band and the room. You heard the band and the room. The sonic characteristics of the room were essential in the quality and personality of your recording. The room brought the messiness, the realness, the can't-get-out-of-each-other's-way."[1] However, at the conclusion of sessions for *The River*, the Boss and his team were disappointed to find that the ambient mics had recaptured the sound from the headphones during recording, seriously complicating the mixing. Nevertheless, *Roulette* seems to have come out on top, and the garage band-like power that emerges from it perfectly conforms to the desired effect.

In the introductory measures, one is hit with a surprising rhythm played by a brilliant Max Weinberg. He executes a highly effective drum fill, primarily with his tom-tom drums. The rest of his drumming is excellent, in the style of Rick Buckler, the drummer from The Jam, in songs such as *The Eton Rifles* (1979). The Boss follows it up with his Telecaster-Esquire, producing a melody reminiscent of Magazine's 1978 hit *Shot by Both Sides* (for example, at 0'12).

Each musician helps to create a very English punk sound in the verses and refrains, especially Garry Tallent, with his very good bass line; Danny Federici and Roy Bittan on the keyboards (the second one playing rich arpeggios after the second chorus, at 2'40); and even Steve Van Zandt, on both the rhythm guitar and vocal harmonies. Springsteen sings remarkable lead vocals, rough and cutting, and gives a very tight performance.

It's rather unbelievable that *Roulette* only made it to the B-side of a single, and that it wasn't included on *The River*. As Springsteen explained: "It was the first song we cut for that record and maybe later on I thought it was too specific [...] It would have been one of the best things on the record and it was just a mistake at the time—you get oversensitive when you're going to release the things."[10]

CHIMES OF FREEDOM (LIVE)

Bob Dylan / 7'18

Maxi single: *Spare Parts/Pink Cadillac/Spare Parts* (live)/*Chimes of Freedom* (live) **Reference:** CBS – 652962 6 **Release date:** Europe, 18 October 1988

Musicians
Bruce Springsteen: vocals, guitar
Nils Lofgren: guitar
Patti Scialfa: guitar, backing vocals
Roy Bittan: keyboards
Clarence Clemons: tambourine
Danny Federici: organ
Garry Tallent: bass
Max Weinberg: drums

Recording
Stockholms Olympiastadion: 3 July 1988

Technical team
Producers: Bruce Springsteen, Jon Landau, Chuck Plotkin
Recording engineer: Toby Scott
Mixing: Bob Clearmountain

Genesis and lyrics

The *Chimes of Freedom* EP is a charity work for the NGO Amnesty International. It was recorded in Stockholm during the Human Rights Now! Tour on 3 July 1988. *Chimes of Freedom* came out alongside original songs *Tougher Than the Rest* and *Born to Run*, which date back to the concert in Los Angeles on 27 April 1998, and *Be True*, from the concert in Detroit on 28 March 1998. It's a poignant tribute to Bob Dylan, without whom Bruce Springsteen wouldn't have become who he is today.

Dylan wrote *Chimes of Freedom* at the start of 1964 and released it on the album *Another Side of Bob Dylan* on 8 August of that same year. He was already at the peak of his inspiration. Two friends are strolling along when a storm forces them to take shelter under a porch. The lightning looks like "the chimes of freedom." There's a clear biblical reference—the Sermon on the Mount, where Jesus Christ defined Christian philosophy—as well as a reference to the hallucinatory poetry of William Blake and the symbolism of the poet Rimbaud, using the harmony of words to create "striking visions" that exalt the humanity of the common person. *Chimes of Freedom* made Bob Dylan America's poet of the 1960s, a step that would pave the way for Bruce Springsteen a few years later.

Fans in East Berlin at the fifth Berlin Rock Summer (1988). Bruce Springsteen's performance of Bob Dylan's *Chimes of Freedom* was seen as highly symbolic.

Production

When Springsteen and the E Street Band performed *Chimes of Freedom* in Stockholm on 3 July 1988, their performance was broadcast on various international radio stations. This superb Dylan cover closed the first part of their show, which had started with *Tunnel of Love*. The group, on the road since the start of the year (for the last time before the Boss would announce its dissolution in October 1989), was bursting with energy and confidence. Clearly, the cover done by the Boss and his acolytes had lost the intimacy and intensity of the troubadour of Duluth's version. But the assertive performance they gave on this Swedish evening was first-rate and did justice to the song's creator. It was only a flicker away from perfection. Of note: the song was shortened to fit onto the CD—this can be heard at 4'05, when Nils Lofgren's guitar solo is suddenly cut off just as it starts to take off.

For Springsteen Addicts

Bruce Springsteen sang *Chimes of Freedom* for the first time on 1 September 1978, in Detroit, during the Darkness on the Edge of Town Tour. He played it again during the Tunnel of Love Express Tour, notably in East Berlin on 19 July 1988 before more than 200,000 people (maybe even 300,000). He'd been advised to replace the word "wall" with the word "barrier" in his speech. One year and almost four months later, on 9 November 1989, the "wall of shame" came down, finally letting the chimes of freedom ring in the East.

ALBUM

HUMAN TOUCH

Human Touch • Soul Driver • 57 Channels (And Nothin' On) • Cross My Heart • Gloria's Eyes • With Every Wish • Roll of the Dice • Real World • All or Nothin' at All • Man's Job • I Wish I Were Blind • The Long Goodbye • Real Man • Pony Boy

Outtakes: *30 Days Out • All the Way Home • Chicken Lips and Lizard Hips • Gave It a Name • Goin' Cali • Leavin' Train • Loose Change • My Lover Man • Over the Rise • Part Man, Part Monkey • Red Headed Woman • Sad Eyes • Seven Angel • Trouble in Paradise • Trouble River • Viva Las Vegas • When the Lights Go Out*

RELEASE DATE

United States: 31 March 1992

Reference: Columbia Records – 471423 1

No.1 in the United Kingdom, Austria, Spain, Italy, Norway, Sweden, and Switzerland, No.2 in the United States and Canada, No.3 in France, the Netherlands, and Germany

1992

Bruce Springsteen at Wembley, London, in July 1992 during the Human Touch Tour.

Youssou N'Dour, Peter Gabriel, Bruce Springsteen, Tracy Chapman, and Sting before the Amnesty International Human Rights Now! concert at Wembley on 2 September 1988.

DISILLUSIONMENT POP

After less than four years of marriage, Bruce Springsteen and Julianne Phillips divorced. It was March 1989. The songwriter had performed for Amnesty International's Human Rights Now! Tour with the E Street Band not long before then (2 September to 15 October 1988). They'd shared the stage with Sting, Peter Gabriel, Youssou N'Dour, and Tracy Chapman. Once back in the United States, Springsteen left his native New Jersey for southern California—moving to a small house in Malibu, on the Pacific Ocean. Patti Scialfa was with him. On 25 July 1990, Evan James Springsteen was born. Bruce and Patti married on 8 June 1991. The young family moved to a stylish home on Sunset Boulevard in Hollywood. On 30 December 1991, Jessica Rae Springsteen was born.

Between his new life as a family man and the long motorcycle drives that he took across the vast desert expanses between California and Arizona, Bruce Springsteen didn't really have the time—or inclination—to pick up his guitar and start writing again. Even the E Street Band seemed like a distant memory. Roy Bittan, who had also moved to California and started composing music, was the only one connecting him to his recent past. He played two of his recordings for Springsteen, enticing him into writing the lyrics. The two demos—which would become *Roll of the Dice* and *Real World*—were behind the concept for *Human Touch*. "He was searching for something new, whether it was in writing or recording,"[45] explained Roy Bittan to Andy Greene for *Rolling Stone* magazine. Once again, Bruce Springsteen was thrust into the harsh but exhilarating labor of creation. As he explains in his book *Songs*, "I wrote a variety of music in genre that I always liked: soul, rock, pop, R&B."[6] Moreover, with the exception of Roy Bittan and David Sancious for two of the tracks, and, of course, of Patti Scialfa, this was his first time working with musicians and singers outside of the E Street Band: two session musicians in Los Angeles, Randy Jackson (bass) and Jeff Porcaro (drums), as well as Sam Moore and Bobby King (backing vocals), Tim Pierce (guitar), Ian McLagan (piano), Douglas Lunn (bass), and Kurt Wortman (also on drums). The subject, in a sense, was an extension of the one from *Tunnel of Love*: being unlucky in love, but having the strength to face it. "To receive what love delivers, they have to surrender themselves to each other and accept fate,"[6] Springsteen further explains in *Songs*. "This tension is at the heart of *Human Touch*."[6]

After the E Street Band broke up, Clarence Clemons and Nils Lofgren joined the All-Starr Band fronted by Ringo Starr (middle). Other members included Billy Preston, Joe Walsh, and Rick Danko.

The E Street Band's momentary setback

The E Street Band's musicians took the news of Springsteen's departure from the group with a deep sense of abandonment and sadness. Clarence Clemons spoke of this key moment in his career in his book *Big Man: Real Life & Tall Tales*, which was released in 2009. He and Ringo Starr were in a hotel suite in Japan, where they were on the All-Starr Band Tour of 1989 (with Nils Lofgren on the guitar). The phone rang. The Beatles drummer picked up. After exchanging a few words with the person on the other end, he turned to the "Big Man" and told him the call was for him. "Me?" asked Clemons, surprised. "No, nobody knows I'm here!"[17] But Ringo handed him the receiver. "Hey, Daddy-o," replied the saxophonist upon recognizing Springsteen's voice. "What's going on? How are you, man?"[17] The Boss gave him the bad news. "No shit? I mean, I don't know what to say, Bruce. I don't know how to respond. You know I only want what's best for you. You know if that's what it's going to take to make you happy, then that's what it's going to take. No, no, I'm fine. I'll be fine."[17] But it was a hard blow. Clemons hung up. "Shit, this has been my whole life. I mean everything has been about Bruce for so long. Fuck. This is going to require a period of adjustment. And vodka, I suspect."[17]

After Clarence Clemons and Nils Lofgren, Springsteen called the other musicians. Roy Bittan was distraught, as were his band mates. "That was a tremendously emotional time for everybody [...] I got the same phone call everybody did, and for a couple of months I was cut loose also. So at that point, we all had feelings. It was impossible to not have feelings about things."[45] Nevertheless, he was the only musician from the E Street Band who would work with the Boss again, not just on the keyboards, but as a composer and producer. It was a delicate situation, especially with regards to his band mates.

Springsteen later asked Roy Bittan to participate in a new project, but this was not intended as a deliberate slight of the other members of the group. What might they have thought of that? "I think that some guys may have had feelings about me in particular," Bittan would later say. "I think it was misguided. Again, there was no grand conspiracy. But I think whatever they felt, they were entitled to feel. It was a harsh situation at that particular moment. I kind of always described it to myself like there was a plane crash and I was the only survivor."[45] Springsteen remembers sympathetic reactions from the other musicians, writing in his autobiography that everyone in the band was disappointed but accepted the news graciously. Springsteen wished them all well, as they did him.

The album

After a long time in the making, from September 1989 to March 1991, Bruce Springsteen's ninth studio album became available in stores on 31 March 1992, the same day as *Lucky*

All the musicians have left, except for one:
Roy Bittan, on keyboards behind the Boss.

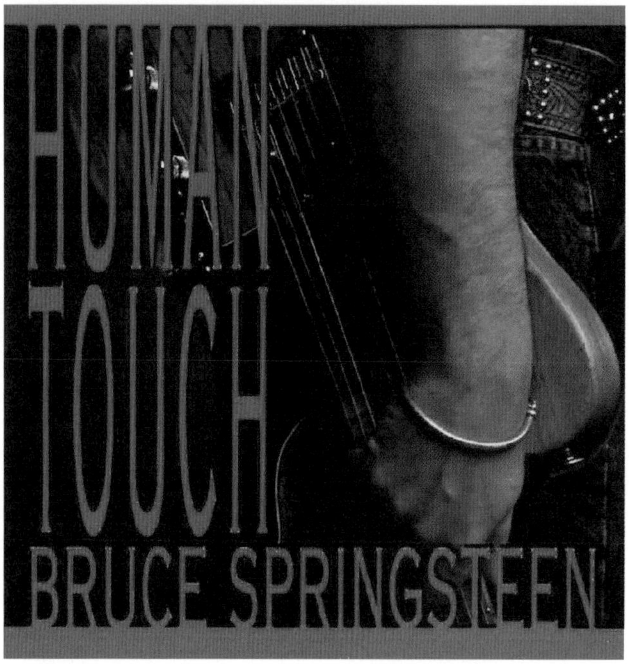

Sleeve from *Human Touch*: Red letters on a dark background mark a turning point in the songwriter's career.

Town. Were his new family life and status as a rock icon since *Born in the U.S.A.* stifling his inspiration? While *Human Touch* would never be a match for the rock masterpieces that are *Born to Run* and *Darkness on the Edge of Town*, or the introspective *Nebraska* (readers of *Nerve* magazine even voted it the Boss's least successful album), it nonetheless encapsulates the essence of what has made Springsteen so magical since the beginning: a voice that transmits powerful emotions and music that sums up the social, emotional, and musical spirit of America.

In this sense, the title song is the best on the album, but *57 Channels (And Nothin' On)* and the cover of Sonny Boy Williamson's (Rice Miller) *Cross My Heart* are also notable. In any case, the public remained loyal to the songwriter's musical style, as the album reached No.1 in various European countries, including the United Kingdom, Italy, Switzerland, Spain, and Sweden, and No.2 in the *Billboard* charts in the United States (the week of 18 April 1992), before falling to No.3 at the beginning of May and to No.12 on the 12 May.

The sleeve

The cover photo is a close-up of Bruce Springsteen's wrist firmly holding his Fender Telecaster-Esquire. He's wearing a bracelet and black jeans with a nail-studded belt. The title of the album and the name of the artist are written in big red letters against a dark background. On the back, we only see the torso of the songwriter, again holding the neck of his Fender. He's wearing a black T-shirt and a cross around his neck.

With these two photos by David Rose, Bruce Springsteen may have wanted to deliver a message and make his audience understand that he'd arrived at a turning point in his career: the E Street Band had stepped aside and made way for new experiences in California. "In Los Angeles, we were working on the *Human Touch* and *Lucky Town* album covers," Rose remembers of the shot. "We woke up in the morning and it was pouring rain. We couldn't go to the location. So I grabbed a little studio in LA. I had a lot of stuff set up in the main studio, and then I went to go get him and he was sitting against the mirror just playing. 'Don't move!' And I ran and grabbed lights and got this nice moment of Bruce just doing what he does. It's pretty much what he looks like before a show too—getting in the groove."[103]

The recording

Springsteen seems to have lost his inspiration between October 1988 and August 1989. The songwriter was enjoying the family life he'd created with Patti Scialfa, a cocoon he'd long been yearning for. "At first, I had nothing to say. Throughout '88 and '89, every time I sat down to write, I was just sort of rehashing. I didn't have a new song to sing, I just ended up rehashing *Tunnel of Love*, except not as good."[10]

The spark came when he heard Roy Bittan's two compositions. His creative process was stimulated once again. Determined to get back in the game, he fought for several months to record his ninth album, between September 1989 and March 1991, a period of 19 months (except for *Pony Boy*, which was likely recorded between June and September 1989). Of some 30 songs recorded, only 14 made it onto *Human Touch*. The others are on the 1998 *Tracks* box set (*Trouble in Paradise* or *Sad Eyes*, for example), in compilations (like *Secret Garden* on *Greatest Hits* in 1995), on the

NO SPLITTING HAIRS

When Clarence Clemons heard about the dissolution of the E Street Band in 1989, he promised—in front of Ringo Starr—never to get his hair cut again. As he said in his book *Big Man: Real Life & Tall Tales*, "Since then many things have happened. But I never cut my hair."[17]

Clarence Clemons at a book signing in the Hard Rock Café in Times Square, New York, for the launch of his book *Big Man: Real Life & Tall Tales* (November 2009).

B-side of singles (like *30 Days Out*), or added to other original albums (*All the Way Home* on *Devils & Dust* in 2005).

So, Springsteen got to work, this time with Roy Bittan. The home studio in his garage had all the equipment he needed to bring his new songs to life, as he'd done for *Nebraska* and *Tunnel of Love*. Bittan remembers the atmosphere that prevailed during these sessions: "We were experimenting with computer recording. I had an early Pro Tools system in the studio that was incredibly archaic when you look back at it. [Springsteen] was searching for something new, whether it was in writing or recording. He wanted a new direction. The interesting thing is that it was the prototype, so to speak, for the recording method that he's been using ever since. He uses a computer. He may cut some things live, but it goes into the computer [...] We overdub with the computer. It's been our method of recording ever since then. So, it really was the first time that our so-called modern technique of recording was used."[45]

In addition to the Boss's home studio, other studios were needed to complete the album, mainly A&M Studios, which would also be used for the mixing, as well as Soundworks West, Ocean Way Studios, Westlake Studios, and the Record Plant—all in the Los Angeles area. "We worked for about a year, and at the end I tried to put it together," explained Springsteen. "Some albums come out full-blown: *Tunnel of Love, Nebraska, Lucky Town*—they just came out all at once. *Human Touch* was definitely something that I struggled to put together. It was like a job. I'd work at it every day. But at the end, I felt like it was good, but it was about me trying to get to a place. It sort of chronicled the post-*Tunnel of Love* period. So when we finished it, I just sat on it for a couple of months."[10]

Technical details

The Pro Tools system Roy Bittan mentions seems to be a Sound Tools system sold by Digidesign in 1989. Along with the Mac II, this first model computer-based editing system would set the standard for studios around the world. The famous Pro Tools workstation didn't come out until 1991, far too late to have been used in the making of *Human Touch*.

The instruments

Among the many instruments that Springsteen used in his studio, there was an acoustic 1951 Gibson J-45 that Toby Scott had

For Springsteen Addicts

Bruce Springsteen was not the first American rock musician to have released two albums on the same day: a few months before, on 17 September 1991, *Use Your Illusion I* and *Use Your Illusion II*, by Guns N' Roses, hit the shelves.

Model of a Gibson J-45, similar to the one Toby Scott gave Springsteen in 1988.

given him as a Christmas present in 1988. This guitar, which the recording engineer had bought in 1972 from a pawn shop in Santa Monica, California, would act as the "house" guitar for Clover Studios. Ronnie Wood, Steve Cropper, Danny Kortchmar, Fred Tackett, and Waddy Wachtel are just some of the musicians who have used it.

As for the electric guitar, Springsteen wanted to reinvent himself, so tried his hand at several 6-string guitars, including Gibsons, Stratocasters, and others—he did the same for the amps—but each time, he would subconsciously look to recreate the sounds of his Fender Telecaster-Esquire and Fender Bandmaster amp.

1992

HUMAN TOUCH

Bruce Springsteen / 6'31

Musicians

Bruce Springsteen: vocals, guitars
Patti Scialfa: backing vocals
Roy Bittan: keyboards
Randy Jackson: bass
Jeff Porcaro: drums, tambourine

Recording

Thrill Hill West, Los Angeles/A&M Recording Studios, Hollywood/ Soundworks West, Burbank/Ocean Way Studios, Burbank/ Westlake Studios, Los Angeles/The Record Plant, Los Angeles: September 1989 to March 1991

Technical team

Producers: Bruce Springsteen, Jon Landau, Chuck Plotkin, Roy Bittan
Recording engineer: Toby Scott
Assistant recording engineers: Robert "RJ" Jaczko, Greg Goldman, Randy Wine, Dave Collins (digital editing) [A&M]/Tom Hardisty (Soundworks)/Clif Norrell (Ocean Way)/Craig Johnson (Westlake)/ Buzz Burrows (Record Plant)
Mixing: Bob Clearmountain (A&M)
Mastering: Bob Ludwig

For Springsteen Addicts

In 1992 there was a rumor going around that Springsteen had offered Jeff Porcaro a million dollars to go on tour with him. The drummer had turned it down, preferring to remain loyal to his group, Toto, and help promote his new album, *Kingdom of Desire* (1993). But it was only a rumor.

Genesis and lyrics

"In *Human Touch, Soul Driver*, and *Real World*, people search to find some emotional contact, some modest communion, some physical and sexual connection,"[6] explains Bruce Springsteen in his book *Songs*. The title song of his ninth work is about the difficult, even impossible, task of communicating with others. "In the end what you don't surrender/Well the world just strips away," sings Springsteen in the first verse. Then he adds, "Ain't no kindness in the face of strangers" and "Ain't no mercy on the streets of this town." In other words, salvation can't come from others. In the end, it can only come from within.

In any case, the narrator harbors no illusions about human nature, no more so than the woman he addresses, who's been "broken" and "hurt." What he wants is "a little of that human touch." The songwriter's dark side is expressing itself here, probably because he is still affected by his divorce from Julianne Phillips.

Bruce Springsteen performed *Human Touch* for the first time onstage at The Bottom Line, in New York, on 6 May 1992, with Roy Bittan (keyboards), Shane Fontayne (guitar), Tommy Sims (bass), and Zack Alford (drums), as well as Bobby King (for this song only). It was chosen as the A-side of the first single from the album (with *Better Days* on the double A-side for the United States and Europe, and, for Europe only, with *Souls of the Departed* on the B-side). It reached No.1 in the *Billboard* chart in the United States, in the Mainstream Rock category, as well as in Italy, Spain, and Norway. A music video was made, with the loyal Meiert Avis at the controls, as always. He landed a nomination for the MTV Video Music Awards in 1992 in the category of "Best Male Video."

Production

Human Touch was the first song Springsteen performed without the E Street Band—though obviously still with Roy Bittan. Instead, he recorded it (at least in part) with session musicians, who give it a very different sound—definitely more sterile, less warm, and more anonymous. The songwriter couldn't have hoped, or even wanted, to return to the same unity and spirit that came from working with the same band mates over many years, climbing the stairs of success one step at a time. However, Randy Jackson and Jeff Porcaro did not prove

Randy Jackson is not only a talented bass player, but was also a judge on *American Idol* from 2002 to 2013, and the producer of *America's Best Dance Crew*, which aired on MTV between 2012 and 2015.

Bruce Springsteen at Paris-Bercy on 29 June 1992. The Parisian fans loved *Human Touch*. The Boss is accompanied by Randy Jackson on bass.

unworthy, far from it. The former, who boasts such diverse collaborations as Jean-Luc Ponty, Zucchero, Whitney Houston, Journey, Bob Dylan, and Aretha Franklin, is a versatile bass player, with an incomparable style. The latter is one of the best drummers of his generation. He was a member of Toto, but was also in high demand among other artists, including Michael Jackson, Paul McCartney, Steely Dan, Donald Fagen, Pink Floyd, Paul Simon, and Lionel Richie, among others. His contribution to *Human Touch* was one of the last of his short career—he died of a heart attack at just 38 years of age, in 1993.

Although very well done, *Human Touch* suffers from an excessively smooth production. Roy Bittan's synth pads lack texture in the introduction—the sounds are too clinical, and neither the bass nor the drums can rescue the song from its apathy. This flaw intensifies in the second verse with the second keyboard, whose tone lacks character (at 0'26). Springsteen had written a medium-tempo song that intensifies as it goes along, especially during the two instrumental parts at the middle and end of the piece (at 2'36 and in the coda, from 4'35). The Boss is on the various guitar parts (rhythm electric guitar in the intro, saturated during the instrumental interludes and solos, and acoustic from 1'29), and delivers some very good lead vocals, which he initially sings with a soft voice before raising it louder and louder. Patti Scialfa supports him on backing vocals, their two voices mixing harmoniously (at 1'17). Jackson and Porcaro's style is obviously very different from that of Garry Tallent and Max Weinberg, mainly in the groove, which is much more pronounced: this is clear when listening to how the drummer plays the hi-hat at 4'00.

But what are we to make of *Human Touch*, which, as with other songs, only takes on its full scale in concert? Bob Clearmountain once said that Springsteen's decision to change his musical direction after leaving the E Street Band made sense because to "do" the E Street Band without the band would not have made any sense and, in a way, the fact that he distanced himself from their sound might be regarded as a sort of tribute to the band—see the Bibliography, source 77, if you would like to read more of this interview with Bob Clearmountain.

1992

SOUL DRIVER

Bruce Springsteen / 4'39

Musicians

Bruce Springsteen: vocals, guitar
Tim Pierce: guitar
David Sancious: organ
Randy Jackson: bass
Jeff Porcaro: drums
Michael Fisher: percussion instruments
Sam Moore: backing vocals

Recording

Thrill Hill West, Los Angeles/A&M Recording Studios, Hollywood/ Soundworks West, Burbank/Ocean Way Studios, Burbank/ Westlake Studios, Los Angeles/The Record Plant, Los Angeles: November 1989 to March 1991

Technical team

Producers: Bruce Springsteen, Jon Landau, Chuck Plotkin, Roy Bittan
Recording engineer: Toby Scott
Assistant recording engineers: Robert "RJ" Jaczko, Greg Goldman, Randy Wine, Dave Collins (digital editing) [A&M]/Tom Hardisty (Soundworks)/Clif Norrell (Ocean Way)/Craig Johnson (Westlake)/ Buzz Burrows (Record Plant)
Mixing: Bob Clearmountain (A&M)
Mastering: Bob Ludwig

For Springsteen Addicts

Michael Fisher is an extraordinary percussionist whose collaborations are as numerous as they are diverse: Larry Carlton, Maurice Jarre, Cher, Hans Zimmer, Manu Dibango, Phil Collins, and Linda Ronstadt, to name but a few. His collaboration with Toto is probably what opened the door for him to work on *Human Touch* with Jeff Porcaro.

Genesis and lyrics

The central theme of *Soul Driver* is an honest conversation between a man and a woman. The narrator wants to protect the woman he loves. "Baby let me be your soul driver," he tells her. There can't be happiness without real emotional connection. "This love potion's all we got," apparently, to escape "this black hand of fate" and avoid "destruction."

"Rode through forty nights of the gospels' rain," sings Springsteen. This is a reference to the great deluge in the Book of Genesis, during which it rained for 40 days and 40 nights. Guided by the Lord, Noah built an ark in order to save his family and all the species of animals. Another reference to the Old Testament is the "black sky pouring snakes, frogs, and love in vain." These are the Ten Plagues of Egypt, in the Book of Exodus, which God inflicted upon the Pharaoh to make him free the Jews.

Production

Soul Driver was drafted and developed in the home studio of Thrill Hill West in November 1989. It seems to have been composed by Roy Bittan, even though the album credits mistakenly attribute the song to Springsteen. This may be due to the melody, which Springsteen apparently rewrote. If this is true, it strongly resembles the melody from *Doolin-Dalton*, the opening song of the Eagles' tenth album *Desperado*, released in 1973. Whatever the case, *Soul Driver* starts with the synthesized sounds of pan flutes, which are rather dated and highly unusual for Springsteen. The remainder of the song is a blend of rock and light reggae performed by excellent musicians, most notably David Sancious, who plays two superb Hammond B-3 organ solos (at 1'49 and 3'43). He'd left the E Street Band in 1974, and his return was unexpected. Also of note: Randy Jackson and Jeff Porcaro set a respectable rhythm supported by Michael Fisher on percussions.

Springsteen was reportedly less than satisfied with the arrangements in *Soul Driver*. This is why the versions he performed in concert were stripped down and accompanied either by simple keyboard chords or the acoustic guitar.

57 CHANNELS (AND NOTHIN' ON)

Bruce Springsteen / 2'28

Musicians
Bruce Springsteen: vocals, bass
Roy Bittan: keyboards
Jeff Porcaro: drums, percussion instruments

Recording
Thrill Hill West, Los Angeles/The Record Plant, Los Angeles: December 1990 to March 1991

Technical team
Producers: Bruce Springsteen, Jon Landau, Chuck Plotkin, Roy Bittan
Recording engineer: Toby Scott
Assistant recording engineers: Buzz Burrows (Record Plant)
Mixing: Bob Clearmountain (A&M Studios)
Mastering: Bob Ludwig

For Springsteen Addicts

Bruce Springsteen struck a line from the lyrics during the studio recording: "So I went down to the porn shop next to the Pussycat Theater on Santa Monica." However, he sang it during his acoustic solo concert at the Shrine Auditorium, in Los Angeles, on 16 November 1990.

Before recording *57 Channels (And Nothin' On)*, the songwriter had tried it out onstage at the Shrine Auditorium, in Los Angeles, on 16 and 17 November 1990, for a Christic Institute charity event.

Genesis and lyrics

57 Channels (And Nothin' On) targets the merchants of illusion and entertainment, all purveyors of dreams through the satellite dish, and more broadly, the venerated consumer culture. Is it an autobiographical account? The narrator buys "a bourgeois house in the Hollywood Hills," where a "man came by to hook up [his] cable TV." Happiness on demand, in a way, except that there are "fifty-seven channels and nothin' on." It's a big dose of dark humor: the quality of the programs and the relevance of their content are as mediocre as the choices are vast. What's worse, television interferes with the harmony of the couple. In this case, the woman, who was the one who'd wanted cable, ends up leaving. The narrator, who is a fan of Elvis Presley, buys a .44 Magnum and takes it out on the television set before being arrested for "disturbin' the almighty peace." In a way, *57 Channels (And Nothin' On)* is also a song about loneliness in the country of mass entertainment.

57 Channels (And Nothin' On) is the A-side of the second single from *Human Touch,* with *Part Man, Part Monkey* on the B-side in the United States and *Stand On It* in Europe. It reached No.6 in the *Billboard* chart for Hot Mainstream Rock Tracks and No.32 in the United Kingdom. A music video was made to promote the single: Springsteen is playing the bass with various television shows on in the background. It ends with a vehicle slamming into a wall of TV sets (more than 60?) stacked on top of each other, causing them to explode. In 2014, the Boss admitted that he couldn't really explain the guiding principle of this video.

Production

Before recording this song, Springsteen had written various tracks using one bass guitar, "where you had a note and you had your idea," he explained. "I wrote about half or more of a record. The only one that made it to release was *57 Channels (And Nothin' On)*."[10] But why compose with a simple bass, which is an unusual instrument for this type of exercise? Quite simply, to purify the writing and get to the point. This is exactly how the song turns out. It was recorded in December 1990, probably at the Record Plant in Los Angeles.

The song revolves around Springsteen's very good bass line. Jeff Porcaro's bass drum supports him from start to finish, accentuating the beat. The spirit is rock, almost

Bruce Springsteen, Patti Scialfa, and Steve Van Zandt photographed in New York—they represent an alternative to the purveyors of light entertainment that the Boss sings about in *57 Channels (And Nothin' On)*.

Opposite Bruce Springsteen singing onstage in Rotterdam. *57 Channels (And Nothin' On)* was on the setlist for the 1992–1993 World Tour.

rockabilly, and the arrangements are kept to a minimum: there is no guitar, which is rare for the Boss. Only Roy Bittan's synth pads enrich the harmony from the second verse (at 0'45), and a few percussion effects enter every so often to enhance the sound texture.

Springsteen sings with a soft, restrained voice, which he doubles in the chorus (for example, at 0'25, with the two voices in stereo) and harmonizes in the coda (from 2'05).

It's interesting to note that the live versions of *57 Channels (And Nothin' On)* are quite different from the album versions. Onstage, Springsteen and his musicians perform with surprising energy and fury. The result is savage, but a total success. The percussion instruments, spoken words, choralists, saturated guitars, the insanely groovy drum and bass lines, the Hendrix-style solos, and even a conga solo all combine to create a very high-quality performance, with the Boss letting loose on the lead vocals. This interpretation didn't come out of nowhere: it was inspired by a superb remix done by "Little Steven"—aka Steve Van Zandt—in 1992. At 5'56 long, it has all the ingredients of a Springsteen concert. It is well worth discovering or rediscovering (especially since Little Steven made a total of three different remixes).

The hard crack at 1'36 corresponds to the moment in the video where a bullet hits the screen, causing it to explode.

1992

CROSS MY HEART

Bruce Springsteen, Sonny Boy Williamson / 3'51

Originally from Mississippi, Sonny Boy Williamson II played the harmonica with the pioneers of Delta blues (Robert Johnson, Robert Nighthawk, Elmore James) before going to Chicago and signing with Chess/Checker for a few giants of modern blues, such as *Nine Below Zero* and *Bring It On Home*. He added "Rice Miller" (Miller was the name of his stepfather, who raised him) to his stage name to set himself apart from another blues harmonica player called John Lee Sonny Boy Williamson.

Musicians
Bruce Springsteen: vocals, guitars, harmonica
Roy Bittan: keyboards
Randy Jackson: bass
Jeff Porcaro: drums, tambourine

Recording
Thrill Hill West, Los Angeles/A&M Recording Studios, Hollywood/Soundworks West, Burbank/Ocean Way Studios, Burbank/Westlake Studios, Los Angeles/The Record Plant, Los Angeles: September 1989 to March 1991

Technical team
Producers: Bruce Springsteen, Jon Landau, Chuck Plotkin, Roy Bittan
Recording engineer: Toby Scott
Assistant recording engineer: Robert "RJ" Jaczko, Greg Goldman, Randy Wine, Dave Collins (digital editing) [A&M]/Tom Hardisty (Soundworks)/Clif Norrell (Ocean Way)/Craig Johnson (Westlake)/Buzz Burrows (Record Plant)
Mixing: Bob Clearmountain (A&M)
Mastering: Bob Ludwig

Cross My Heart recalls the blues song of the same name recorded by the harmonica player Sonny Boy Williamson (Rice Miller) in 1957.

Genesis and lyrics

For this fourth song on *Human Touch*, Bruce Springsteen took inspiration from the homonymous blues song that Sonny Boy Williamson (Rice Miller) recorded in 1958 for Checker Records (a subsidiary of Chess Records). He borrowed its title and a few lines (notably, "First time I crossed my heart"). But the overall feel is pure Springsteen: when you give your word, you have to be sure of yourself and your feelings—in short, you must reject lies and hypocrisies. "You may think the world's black and white/And you're dirty or you're clean, son/You better watch out you don't slip/Through them spaces in between." The narrator rejects all forms of Manichaeism, wanting to protect the woman who is most likely his girlfriend. He reminds her that "little boys, little girls/Yeah they know their wrongs from their rights." He also tells her that "life ain't nothing but a cold hard ride." What are we to make of this? That life isn't worth living without true love.

Production

Musically, there's no reason to compare Sonny Boy Williamson's *Cross My Heart* with Springsteen's version, as the two pieces are radically different: the first is pure blues, the second a mid-tempo rock song. The Boss composed a very good song, with rather spare arrangements in the vein of *57 Channels (And Nothin'On),* but not as minimalist.

Randy Jackson and Jeff Porcaro's beat is excellent and boasts an impressive groove. Roy Bittan plays some very airy piano chords that contribute to the value of the piece. He also plays the synth, adding layers and sounds with an arpeggiator (listen at 1'16 to hear an example). Springsteen shines in the lead vocals and on the various guitar parts: he also plays harmonic notes (for example, at 0'12) and a very good double-tracked solo (at 1'45).

The live versions of *Cross my Heart* are rather spare. The Boss accompanies himself on the guitar and harmonica, barely supported by a bass line, synth pads, and drums, all of which are very subtle. He performed a very good version on 10 November 1992 at the Nassau Veterans Memorial Coliseum, in Uniondale, New York.

GLORIA'S EYES

Bruce Springsteen / 3'46

Musicians
Bruce Springsteen: vocals, guitars
Roy Bittan: keyboards
Randy Jackson: bass
Jeff Porcaro: drums, shaker
Recording
Thrill Hill West, Los Angeles/A&M Recording Studios, Hollywood/ Soundworks West, Burbank/Ocean Way Studios, Burbank/ Westlake Studios, Los Angeles/The Record Plant, Los Angeles: September 1989 to March 1991
Technical team
Producers: Bruce Springsteen, Jon Landau, Chuck Plotkin, Roy Bittan
Recording engineer: Toby Scott
Assistant recording engineers: Robert "RJ" Jaczko, Greg Goldman, Randy Wine, Dave Collins (digital editing) [A&M]/Tom Hardisty (Soundworks)/Clif Norrell (Ocean Way)/Craig Johnson (Westlake)/ Buzz Burrows (Record Plant)
Mixing: Bob Clearmountain (A&M)
Mastering: Bob Ludwig

A talented studio musician and cofounder of the band Toto, Jeff Porcaro plays drums on a number of tracks on *Human Touch*, including *Gloria's Eyes*.

Genesis and lyrics

Gloria's Eyes is marked by a sense of suffering, or at least a sense of incompleteness, that had haunted Bruce Springsteen since the end of his marriage to Julianne Phillips. This is where the *mea culpa* comes from at the beginning of the song: he knows that he's sunk low. "I tried to trick you yeah but baby you got wise," he sings. In this song, the relationship fails, and the young woman leaves. Sure, she comes back, but this is no victory for the narrator: "There was somethin' gone in Gloria's eyes." Her smile belies resentment and vanished dreams. How can he win back his love? "Now I work hard to prove my love is true" and "at night I pray as silently you lie," sings Bruce Springsteen. These are words that come from deep within.

Bruce Springsteen only performed *Gloria's Eyes* onstage some 40 times, between June 1992 and April 1993. The first time was at the Stockholm Globe Arena on 15 June 1992.

Production

Gloria's Eyes is an energetic rock song, sung in a rough tone by a spirited Springsteen, his voice carried by a long and persistent delay. The song is based on a simple but effective guitar riff that the Boss doubles in stereo for greater density and magnitude. He maintains the riff throughout the song, adjusting it during the various harmonic changes. Roy Bittan makes himself scarce, playing simple chords on his keyboard. Although slightly undermixed, Randy Jackson's bass line is incredibly supportive and effective, as are Jeff Porcaro's drums, which provide the driving force behind the beat and groove. A sustained shaker part reinforces the effect.

But what to make of *Gloria's Eyes*? Springsteen wrote a rock song that was halfway between the spirit of the 1950s and that of the early 1990s, without managing to be convincing in either sphere. His voice is strong, he delivers some very good guitar solos (at 1'13 and 2'52), and the rhythm is powerful, but the piece never manages to take off. Too bad.

1992

WITH EVERY WISH

Bruce Springsteen / 4'39

Musicians
Bruce Springsteen: vocals, guitar
Roy Bittan: keyboards
Mark Isham: muted trumpet
Douglas Lunn: bass
Kurt Wortman: drums, dumbek drum, cabasa

Recording
Thrill Hill West, Los Angeles/A&M Recording Studios, Hollywood/ Soundworks West, Burbank/Ocean Way Studios, Burbank/ Westlake Studios, Los Angeles/The Record Plant, Los Angeles: September 1989 to March 1991

Technical team
Producers: Bruce Springsteen, Jon Landau, Chuck Plotkin, Roy Bittan
Recording engineer: Toby Scott
Assistant recording engineers: Robert "RJ" Jaczko, Greg Goldman, Randy Wine, Dave Collins (digital editing) [A&M]/Tom Hardisty (Soundworks)/Clif Norrell (Ocean Way)/Craig Johnson (Westlake)/ Buzz Burrows (Record Plant)
Mixing: Bob Clearmountain (A&M)
Mastering: Bob Ludwig

Douglas Lunn plays fretless bass on *With Every Wish* (here, in 2013).

Genesis and lyrics

With Every Wish is a sort of continuation of *Gloria's Eyes*. Bobby, the narrator, who could very well be Bruce Springsteen himself, remembers his adolescence. He skipped church to go fishing in the lake. One day, he fell in love with the beautiful Doreen, who was "the prettiest thing this old town'd ever seen." Bobby won her over, but jealousy soon made him mean, "whenever another man'd come walking down the line." And the young woman would say, "Don't you know before you choose your wish, you better think first/'Cause with every wish there comes a curse?"

The last verse returns us to the present. Bobby remembers many rivers he's crossed—in other words, relationship difficulties he's managed to overcome, guided by "love's bluebird." A dream come true, in a way.

This is a very beautiful acoustic song in the spirit of *Meeting Across the River*, from the album *Born to Run*. *With Every Wish*, however, has only been performed onstage three times, the first being at a concert at the Stockholm Globe Arena on 15 June 1992.

Production

With Every Wish was one of the very first songs recorded for the album. This time, Springsteen surrounded himself with different musicians, with the exception of the incomparable Roy Bittan, who plays some very beautiful chords on the synths (from 1'12). The three new musicians were habitual collaborators at the time: Douglas Lunn (Brand X, Andy Summers, and so on) on the fretless bass; Kurt Wortman (Van Morrison, Jean-Luc Ponty) on the drums (which he plays with brushes), cabasa, and dumbek drum (which is also known as a darbouka); and Mark Isham, a trumpeter by profession and also an experienced composer of many film scores (notably *Point Break* and *Black Dahlia*).

With Every Wish is a superb song. It's rather folky in spirit despite Isham's muted trumpet. The introduction is somewhat reminiscent of Harry Nilsson's *Everybody's Talkin'* (1969), especially the arpeggio Springsteen plays on his Gibson J-45 and the characteristic rhythmic pulse (initially led by the cabasa, then the brushes). The rest is pure Springsteen.

Mark Isham, a jazz musician and composer, mainly known for composing music for films, plays a muted trumpet on *With Every Wish*.

The three musicians knew each other well: Douglas Lunn and Kurt Wortman had both contributed to several of Mark Isham's solo albums (notably *Tibet* in 1989, *Little Man Tate* in 1991, and *Blue Sun* in 1995).

1992

ROLL OF THE DICE

Bruce Springsteen, Roy Bittan / 4'17

For Springsteen Addicts

For this song, Bobby King is on the backing vocals. Known for founding a duo with Terry Evans in the early 1970s, this soul and gospel singer has also worked with numerous rock stars, including Bob Dylan, John Fogerty, and Boz Scaggs.

Musicians
- **Bruce Springsteen:** vocals, guitars
- **Bobby King:** backing vocals
- **Tim Pierce:** guitars
- **Roy Bittan:** keyboards
- **Randy Jackson:** bass
- **Jeff Porcaro:** drums, tambourine

Recording
- **Thrill Hill West, Los Angeles/A&M Recording Studios, Hollywood/ Soundworks West, Burbank:** December 1989 to March 1991

Technical team
- **Producers:** Bruce Springsteen, Jon Landau, Chuck Plotkin, Roy Bittan
- **Recording engineer:** Toby Scott
- **Assistant recording engineers:** Robert "RJ" Jaczko, Greg Goldman, Randy Wine, Dave Collins (digital editing) [A&M]/Tom Hardisty (Soundworks)
- **Mixing:** Bob Clearmountain (A&M)
- **Mastering:** Bob Ludwig

Among Tim Pierce's many studio appearances, one stands out in particular: the one that allowed him to participate in the recording of *Black or White* by Michael Jackson, in 1991. The king of pop had wanted to include a Mötley Crüe-style passage in his song. It was inspired by one of their hits, *Dr Feelgood* (1989), which he particularly liked. The guitarist jumped at the chance: the guitar roaring in the bridge is his.

Genesis and lyrics

The idea for *Human Touch* took shape after Bruce Springsteen heard two pieces Roy Bittan had composed. "I liked them and told him I'd be interested in writing lyrics to them," recalls the Boss in his book *Songs*. "One of them became *Roll of the Dice*, the other became *Real World*."[6] He adds, "I was looking for something to get me going. Roy was enthusiastic and had good ideas."[6] *Roll of the Dice* enjoys a special place within Bruce Springsteen's reportoire, as it was the first album song he recorded that he did not compose (aside from covers).

Springsteen tells of the misadventures of a gambler who thinks he can make a comeback each time he rolls the dice. Up until then, he's never had any luck, either in craps or in love: he either couldn't throw "snake eyes" or all his "elevens and sevens been coming up sixes and nines." But after meeting this woman, he thinks his luck will change. Between the two of them, and "lady luck," he could finally win, "celebrating/And drinking champagne on ice." A simple roll of the dice would be enough to make him happy, and make him rise to paradise...even a fake one.

Bruce Springsteen played *Roll of the Dice* for the first time onstage at the concert at The Bottom Line, in New York, on 6 May 1992. The song was chosen as the A-side of the third single from the album, with a live version of *Leap of Faith* and the never-before-heard *30 Days Out*, but only for the Japanese market.

Production

This last song on the A-side of the original vinyl is surprising because of its very E Street Band vibe, the only one on the album with that sound. What's even more surprising is that it was composed by Roy Bittan and not Springsteen. Those long years alongside the Boss must have had an impact on the keyboardist's subconscious. Whatever the case, *Roll of the Dice* is a good song, played by superb musicians, starting with its author, who, for the only time on this album, provides an excellent piano part—Springsteen had wanted to avoid any semblance of his past. Bittan then doubles it with sounds resembling a glockenspiel, an instrument emblematic of the E Street Band, along with its piano motifs, which are typical of its unique style (at 1'41 and 2'39). The rhythmic section is

Randy Jackson, known as an eclectic bass player, has played with a diverse range of musicians, from Journey and Aretha Franklin to Jean-Luc Ponty. He contributed to the *Human Touch* album, notably on *Roll of the Dice*.

equally remarkable: Randy Jackson delivers a superb bass line, bringing depth, swing, and funk to the piece, while Jeff Porcaro puts all his energy into a stellar groove, proving his strength as a drummer and demonstrating an impressive sense for arrangements. He adds a tambourine to complement his drumming.

To support the Boss on the guitar, Tim Pierce makes another appearance on the album after *Soul Driver*. Pierce is an excellent guitarist, comfortable on the acoustic as well as the electric guitars. His collaborations are as prestigious as they are eclectic: Roger Waters, Terence Trent D'Arby, Joe Cocker, Meat Loaf, Alice Cooper, Phil Collins, Santana, and even Johnny Hallyday. The talented singer Bobby King also came to the rescue, joining Springsteen in vocal harmonies and a call and response, as in the coda (from 3'00). He would later explain how he was contacted in January 1990 to come and add his voice as an overdub, as most of the song had already been recorded. As for the songwriter himself, he delivers a superb and inspired vocal performance, his voice rough and immensely powerful.

To fully appreciate *Roll of the Dice*, you have to watch and listen to the Boss's stage performances, especially the *MTV Plugged* concert at Warner Hollywood Studios, in Los Angeles, on 22 September 1992 (released on the *DVD In Concert/MTV Plugged* in 1993 as a bonus track). There's an absolutely incredible version of about 11 minutes with a never-before-heard introduction and a mind-boggling finale, Springsteen sharing the vocals with many choralists, including the formidable Bobby King, with whom he engages in a gospel-fueled duel. The other musicians accompanying them, including Roy Bittan, are exceptional. A special mention goes to drummer Zack Alford.

1992

REAL WORLD

Bruce Springsteen, Roy Bittan / 5'26

For Springsteen Addicts

Bruce Springsteen sings this song with Sam Moore, of the legendary Sam & Dave. This soul duo gave Southern soul two beautiful songs in the 1960s: *Hold On, I'm Comin'* and *Soul Man.*

Musicians

Bruce Springsteen: vocals, guitars
Sam Moore: backing vocals
Roy Bittan: keyboards
Randy Jackson: bass
Jeff Porcaro: drums, tambourine

Recording

Thrill Hill West, Los Angeles/A&M Recording Studios, Hollywood/ Soundworks West, Burbank: December 1989 to March 1991

Technical team

Producers: Bruce Springsteen, Jon Landau, Chuck Plotkin, Roy Bittan
Recording engineer: Toby Scott
Assistant recording engineers: Robert "RJ" Jaczko, Greg Goldman, Randy Wine, Dave Collins (digital editing) [A&M]/Tom Hardisty (Soundworks)
Mixing: Bob Clearmountain (A&M)
Mastering: Bob Ludwig

Sam Moore (left), with Dan Aykroyd in the John Landis film *The Blues Brothers*, provides backing vocals for the soul song *Real World.*

Genesis and lyrics

Real World is the second song on the album composed by Roy Bittan. Bruce Springsteen's lyrics fit in with the spirit of *Human Touch* and *Soul Driver*: personal fulfillment can only be achieved through relationships with others. This "real world" is "just me and you and the love [or trust, or hope, depending on the chorus] we're bringing," sings Bruce Springsteen in the chorus. Maybe this is a response, or a tribute to, *In the Real World*, performed by one of his idols, Roy Orbison (on the posthumous album *Mystery Girl*, released in January 1989).

The narrator has left "heartbreak city" to start over. After building "a shrine in [his] heart," he heads "over the rise." He's found love, it would seem. But to be sure, "I wanna find some answers, I wanna ask for some help" and "I'm tired of running scared," so he suggests that he and the woman he loves go wherever chance takes them, either to heaven or to hell.

Bruce Springsteen sang *Real World* for the first time in public at an acoustic concert on 16 November 1990 at the Shrine Auditorium, in Los Angeles, during the first Christic Show, a charity event organized by the Christic Institute.

Production

Real World is an energetic rock-soul song, but even though it's well made, it's a far cry from *Roll of the Dice*, also composed by Roy Bittan. A very effective rhythm led by Randy Jackson and Jeff Porcaro—with an especially superb bass line—highlights the multiple electric rhythm guitars of the Boss (strummed as an acoustic) and Roy Bittan's various synths, which is not necessarily the best idea, except for during the tubular bells he plays at the beginning. Springsteen's excellent performance is the real backbone of *Real World.* The talented Sam Moore, who had already worked on *Soul Driver,* backs him up on the vocal harmonies. He also contributes to one of the best passages of the song, in this case the coda, where he launches into a superb vocal duel with the Boss, in the best of all gospel traditions (from 4'39). The second key moment in the song: a very good guitar solo performed by an inspired Springsteen (at 2'49).

ALL OR NOTHIN' AT ALL

Bruce Springsteen / 3'23

All or Nothing at All is also a jazz standard written and composed in 1939 by Arthur Altman and Jack Lawrence. It has been covered countless numbers of times since it first came out, notably by Frank Sinatra, Sarah Vaughan, Billie Holiday, Chet Baker, Ella Fitzgerald, Diana Krall, and John Coltrane. Al Jarreau also used the title in 1988 for an original song written for Bobby Caldwell and Dennis Matkosky.

Musicians
Bruce Springsteen: vocals, guitars
Roy Bittan: keyboards (?)
Randy Jackson: bass
Jeff Porcaro: drums, maracas, tambourine

Recording
Thrill Hill West, Los Angeles/A&M Recording Studios, Hollywood/ Soundworks West, Burbank/Ocean Way Studios, Burbank/ Westlake Studios, Los Angeles/The Record Plant, Los Angeles: September 1989 to March 1991

Technical team
Producers: Bruce Springsteen, Jon Landau, Chuck Plotkin, Roy Bittan
Recording engineer: Toby Scott
Assistant recording engineers: Robert "RJ" Jaczko, Greg Goldman, Randy Wine, Dave Collins (digital editing) [A&M]/Tom Hardisty (Soundworks)/Clif Norrell (Ocean Way)/Craig Johnson (Westlake)/ Buzz Burrows (Record Plant)
Mixing: Bob Clearmountain (A&M)
Mastering: Bob Ludwig

Jeff Porcaro, a wizard on drums, contributes a powerful and subtle drum section to *All or Nothin' at All* (here, in concert in Rotterdam, 1988).

Genesis and lyrics

All or Nothin' at All is another song about love's desires and frustrations. The chorus says it all: "I want it all or nothing at all." The song's central character is bursting with love and wants everyone to know it: "Said you'd give me just a little kiss/ And you'd rock me for a little while." The young woman also tells him she'll save him a dance. But it's clear that the narrators is finding this burning passion somewhat troubling. He's determined to fulfill he desire for love, and justifies his insistence with the idea that, in love, fortune favors the brave: "You just ain't gonna get what you want/With one foot in and one foot out."

Bruce Springsteen performed *All or Nothin' at All* for the first time in public at the Stockholm Globe Arena on 17 June 1993. Since then, he's only sung it eight times, the last time on 6 May 2014 at the Cynthia Woods Mitchell Pavilion, in The Woodlands, Texas.

Production

All or Nothin' at All is pure Springsteen rock, the type of song he could write by the million. But it sounds like more of an exercise in style than a real song, at least musically speaking. The song starts off with Jeff Porcaro banging forcefully on a lone drum, the Gretsch set very likely outfitted with a Ludwig Black Beauty snare drum. He adds some maracas to support his drumming, as the Boss enters on the rhythm electric guitar (the two instruments are on the left, at 0'04). There is neither bass nor keyboard in the first verse, only a very subtle second guitar that reinforces the groove on the right. Then Randy Jackson enters in the chorus, bringing power and depth (at 0'22). On vocals, Springsteen provides a very good performance, although maybe a little too conventional. He doubles himself on the vocal harmonies and choruses, and even improvises a few calls and responses with Bobby King in the coda (from 2'59). Also noteworthy is the rock-like solo he launches into at 1'42. He then follows it up with some vocals in scat. Roy Bittan does not seem to have been involved in the piece, unless his contributions were lost in the mix.

While *All or Nothin' at All* is not among Springsteen's finest work, it does take on greater breadth and depth onstage.

1992

MAN'S JOB

Bruce Springsteen / 4'37

Musicians
Bruce Springsteen: vocals, guitars
Bobby King, Sam Moore: backing vocals
Roy Bittan: keyboards
Randy Jackson: bass
Jeff Porcaro: drums, tambourine, triangle
Recording
Thrill Hill West, Los Angeles/A&M Recording Studios, Hollywood/ Soundworks West, Burbank: December 1989 to March 1991
Technical team
Producers: Bruce Springsteen, Jon Landau, Chuck Plotkin, Roy Bittan
Recording engineer: Toby Scott
Assistant recording engineers: Robert "RJ" Jaczko, Greg Goldman, Randy Wine, Dave Collins (digital editing) [A&M]/Tom Hardisty (Soundworks)
Mixing: Bob Clearmountain (A&M)
Mastering: Bob Ludwig

Bruce Springsteen at the Palais Omnisports in Bercy, Paris, on 29 June 1992. *Man's Job* was particularly popular with the fans.

Genesis and lyrics

In a *Man's Job*, the narrator warns his love against the risks of associating with a man who clearly lacks integrity and whose pickup lines are below a real woman like her: "There's something in your soul that he's gonna rob" and "His kisses may thrill those other girls that he likes," "But loving you's a man's job baby." However, he doesn't stand a chance with her. As she holds her partner close, while dancing to a slow song, "All [his] illusions slip away," unless he can find the courage to stop being a stick in the mud and save the day.

Man's Job premiered onstage at The Bottom Line, in New York, on 6 May 1992.

Production

Man's Job is a nice pop-rock song with a touch of soul, courtesy of the excellent Bobby King and Sam Moore. Springsteen recorded very good, sophisticated lead vocals that alternate softness in the verses and choruses with fury in the bridge (at 1'53). The two singers accompanying him—most likely recorded as overdubs in January 1990—support him on vocal harmonies and in the lead vocals, notably at the start of each chorus, in the coda, and for the traditional calls and responses that set gospel music apart (from 4'00).

Man's Job boasts a superb rhythm provided by the Jackson-Porcaro powerhouse, the two musicians bringing a remarkable energy to the piece. Porcaro's drum set is not enough for him: he also plays the tambourine and a triangle part in the bridge (on the right, at 1'53). Roy Bittan is on the synths, enhancing the arrangements with some very beautiful chords on the keyboards. As for the various guitars, they're all excellent, especially the solo, which the Boss performs first on the acoustic guitar with a subtle quaver—carried by a rich and persistent reverberation—then, for the first time, as a slide with a saturated sound. This is a very effective instrumental sequence (from 2'23).

I WISH I WERE BLIND

Bruce Springsteen / 4'48

Bobby Hatfield, who sings the backing vocals for *I Wish I Were Blind*, is a renowned member of the Righteous Brothers, the duo he founded in the 1960s with Bill Medley. *You've Lost That Lovin' Feelin'*, *Unchained Melody*, and *(You're My) Soul and Inspiration* are just a few of their big hits.

Musicians

Bruce Springsteen: vocals, guitars
Bobby Hatfield: backing vocals
Roy Bittan: keyboards
Randy Jackson: bass
Jeff Porcaro: drums, tambourine

Recording

Thrill Hill West, Los Angeles/A&M Recording Studios, Hollywood/Soundworks West, Burbank/Ocean Way Studios, Burbank/Westlake Studios, Los Angeles/The Record Plant, Los Angeles: September 1989 to March 1991

Technical team

Producers: Bruce Springsteen, Jon Landau, Chuck Plotkin, Roy Bittan
Recording engineer: Toby Scott
Assistant recording engineers: Robert "RJ" Jaczko, Greg Goldman, Randy Wine, Dave Collins (digital editing) [A&M]/Tom Hardisty (Soundworks)/Clif Norrell (Ocean Way)/Craig Johnson (Westlake)/Buzz Burrows (Record Plant)
Mixing: Bob Clearmountain (A&M)
Mastering: Bob Ludwig

Bobby Hatfield sang with Bruce Springsteen on *I Wish I Were Blind* (here, with Bill Medley from the Righteous Brothers in Gardena, 1989).

Genesis and lyrics

The theme from *I Wish I Were Blind* is roughly the same as the one from *Man's Job*. The narrator is still deeply in love with a woman. But this love also turns into an obsession when his ex-girlfriend leaves him to his sad fate so she can be with a man who fulfills her. He watches this man take her hand and touch it as they dance. The sight breaks his heart: "I wish I were blind when I see you with your man." Then he compares the beauty of the woman he loves to the beauty of nature: "I love to see your hair shining in the long summer's light." He also loves "to watch the stars fill the sky on a summer night." A beauty that was a source of immense joy not long ago has now become a terrible torture. The end of the song is filled with hopelessness: "We struggle here but all our love's in vain."

Springsteen played *I Wish I Were Blind* for the first time onstage at The Bottom Line, in New York, on 6 May 1992. He's only performed it about 20 times since.

Production

I Wish I Were Blind is a country-rock song. Its marked synth pads lend it a certain modernity. Roy Bittan, who wrote the song, juxtaposed some trippy sounds with more unusual tones by recording a keyboard part with a harpsicord starting from the second verse (at 0'45 on the right). The rhythm is guided by an imposing bass line and by Jeff Porcaro's excellent drumming—Porcaro chose to use cross-stick for the first verses. Springsteen is on the various guitars: acoustic in the beginning, then the rhythm electric guitar in the second verse, saturated guitars in the chorus, and a very good garage-rock solo at 2'15. His vocals are soft, even disillusioned, and supported by the talented Bobby Hatfield. Bittan adds an accompaniment on the Farfisa and some chords in the last chorus, giving the piece a somewhat saccharine tone.

The live versions either enrich the song with tighter and more rock-like arrangements, or completely pare it down, with the Boss alone on the guitar or keyboards (as on 16 May 2013 in Herning, Denmark, for example).

1992

THE LONG GOODBYE

Bruce Springsteen / 3'30

Musicians
Bruce Springsteen: vocals, guitars
Roy Bittan: keyboards
Randy Jackson: bass
Jeff Porcaro: drums, maracas

Recording
Thrill Hill West, Los Angeles/A&M Recording Studios, Hollywood/ Soundworks West, Burbank: April/May 1990 to March 1991

Technical team
Producers: Bruce Springsteen, Jon Landau, Chuck Plotkin, Roy Bittan
Recording engineer: Toby Scott
Assistant recording engineer: Robert "RJ" Jaczko, Greg Goldman, Randy Wine, Dave Collins (digital editing) [A&M]/Tom Hardisty (Soundworks)
Mixing: Bob Clearmountain (A&M)
Mastering: Bob Ludwig

The Rockman, the first real amp simulator providing multiple effects for guitars—likely used by Springsteen—was invented by Tom Scholz, of the group Boston. In 1980, he had founded Scholz Research & Development, Inc., in Massachusetts, to create various effects for guitarists. The Rockman Ultralight, the Soloist, the X100, and the Bass Rockman were among the many products they sold. The name Rockman was chosen to piggy-back off the recent success of the Sony Walkman (1979).

Genesis and lyrics

Since his debut as a singer-songwriter, Springsteen has been influenced by the Golden Age of Hollywood, which inspired him to revive the title of a famous mystery novel written by the greatest author of the genre, Raymond Chandler. This song is not about Chandler's fictional private eye, Philip Marlow, but about a man who has been a prisoner of his "own lies" until he decides to take control of his destiny, climb the wall, and say his goodbyes to the "same old faces" and "same old town." "Ain't no words of mercy coming from on high," sings Springsteen in the chorus. This line says it all: you can achieve freedom or a fresh start by yourself, and only by yourself.

This "long goodbye" seems to be a metaphor for the songwriter's past. "I went to leave 20 years ago." These words likely refer to his desire to leave New Jersey to mark the end of his innocence and adolescence. Unless they refer to his parents' departure to California when he was a budding musician.

Bruce Springsteen has only performed *The Long Goodbye* onstage four times, and only during the world tour that followed the release of *Human Touch* and *Lucky Town*. The first was at a concert in Frankfurt, Germany, on 26 June 1992.

Production

The Long Goodbye was likely recorded between April and May 1990 at the Soundworks West studios, in Burbank, California. The songwriter had again composed a rock song, but this time with sounds that were more 1990s than 1970s. Why? The guitar sounds diverge from the Boss's usual style. The tone is reminiscent of groups like Boston, Def Leppard, or ZZ Top. According to Toby Scott, Springsteen used a Rockman, the first headphone guitar amplifier, which was created by Tom Scholz from Boston.

Jeff Porcaro launches the piece with a drum fill. His drumming is very effective—a new preview of his exceptional versatility. He's supported by Randy Jackson's powerful bass line, which shows that he learned a thing or two when he was with Journey. Roy Bittan and his keyboards are subtle, unlike Springsteen, who delivers several saturated guitar parts, the lead vocals, and vocal harmonies. Unfortunately, the song falls short because of its patent lack of originality.

REAL MAN

Bruce Springsteen / 4'33

For Springsteen Addicts

The name of the pianist who accompanies Bruce Springsteen in *Real Man* is spelled "McLagen" on the CD jacket for *Human Touch*. But, in reality, this is British musician Ian McLagan, a member of the Small Faces and Faces, then the New Barbarians with Keith Richards and Ronnie Wood. He's also worked with some of the biggest names in rock, including The Rolling Stones, Joe Cocker, and Bob Dylan.

Musicians

Bruce Springsteen: vocals, guitars
Roy Bittan: synthesizers
David Sancious: organ
Ian McLagan: piano
Randy Jackson: bass
Jeff Porcaro: drums, tambourine

Recording

Thrill Hill West, Los Angeles/A&M Recording Studios, Hollywood/ Soundworks West, Burbank: January/February 1990 to March 1991

Technical team

Producers: Bruce Springsteen, Jon Landau, Chuck Plotkin, Roy Bittan
Recording engineer: Toby Scott
Assistant recording engineers: Robert "RJ" Jaczko, Greg Goldman, Randy Wine, Dave Collins (digital editing) [A&M]/Tom Hardisty (Soundworks)
Mixing: Bob Clearmountain (A&M)
Mastering: Bob Ludwig

Former pianist for the Small Faces, Ian McLagan worked with Bruce Springsteen as a studio musician.

Genesis and lyrics

You don't have to show your muscles or "beat on your chest/ Hell any monkey can" to really feel like a man. What you need, is to love and be loved in return. This is Bruce Springsteen's point in *Real Man*.

A couple goes to the movies to see the exploits of Rambo. Then, on TV, they follow the investigations of a private detective for whom "the girls were dropping, they're dropping like flies." The narrator doesn't have nerves of steel or an aggressive disposition, nor is he an exceptional lover. But he believes that he has something even more important: "When the lights go down and you pull me close [...] there's one thing I know [...] I'll be tough enough/If I can find the guts to give you all my love/Then I'll be feeling like a real man," sings Springsteen.

A beautiful declaration, no doubt addressed to Patti Scialfa, but one that Bruce Springsteen has only rarely performed onstage: only a dozen times, in fact, the first of which was at a concert in Stockholm on 17 June 1992.

Production

Real Man will definitely not make it to the annals of rock, and it can certainly not be counted among the songwriter's masterpieces. The song is dominated by intrusive, impersonal, and tiresome synth sounds. It's especially unfortunate that David Sancious and Ian McLagan are sidelined by Roy Bittan. The first recorded an excellent organ part (at 1'46); the second, a piano accompaniment that is, unfortunately, completely lost in the mix, except for at the end of the song, where it finally shines (toward 3'29). One wonders what might have driven the production team to make such a choice. As for Springsteen's performance, it poses a problem: his vocals are often inaccurate, and they also lack the harmonic support needed in the arrangements to attempt the dangerous melodic acrobatics he indulges in (for example, at 0'32 and 2'13). Live performances of the song do not fix the problem either, far from it (watch and listen to the premiere in Stockholm on 17 June 1992). Only the flawless quality of the musicians saves this song from disaster.

1992

PONY BOY

Popular song / 2'14

Musicians
Bruce Springsteen: vocals, guitar, tambourine, synthesizer (?)
Patti Scialfa: backing vocals
Roy Bittan: synthesizer (?)
Recording
Thrill Hill West, Los Angeles: June to September 1990
Technical team
Producers: Bruce Springsteen, Jon Landau, Chuck Plotkin, Roy Bittan
Recording engineer: Toby Scott
Mixing: Bob Clearmountain (A&M Studios)
Mastering: Bob Ludwig

Lillian Lorraine (above) performed the song *Pony Boy* in the musical *Miss Innocence* in 1909.

Genesis and lyrics

My Pony Boy is a popular song written by Bobby Heath and composed by Charley O'Donnell. Broadway audiences first heard it in 1909 in the musical comedy *Miss Innocence*, sung by Lillian Lorraine. That same year, Ada Jones recorded it for Victor Records and the Peerless Quartet recorded it for Columbia Records. Then it was Bing Crosby's turn to add it to his repertoire in 1962, during recording for *On the Happy Side*. Finally, Springsteen used it to close *Human Touch*.

A "pony boy" is an elegant and seductive figure who has no trouble making women's heads turn. One of these women asks him if he'd like to be her pony boy and take a ride "under the starry sky," "over the hills and through the trees," and "down into the valley deep." Bruce Springsteen and Patti Scialfa sang this sweet and innocent song to Evan, their eldest son, who was born on 24 July 1990: "My grandmother sang it to me when I was young," explained the songwriter. "I made up a lot of the words for the verses; I'm sure there are real words, but I'm not sure they're the ones I used. It was the song that I used to sing to my little boy when he was still inside of Patti. And when he came out, he knew it."[10]

Production

Recorded between June and September 1990 in his home studio, in Los Angeles, *Pony Boy* is a sweet song that Springsteen plays by picking his acoustic Gibson J-45. He clearly excels at this type of simple folk music, especially when playing alone on the guitar. Patti Scialfa lends him a hand in the vocal harmonies in the choruses (except for the first chorus), as does Roy Bittan, who records the synth pads in the last verse (at 1'27)—unless the Boss did it himself. Lastly, Springsteen adds a tambourine, which resonates in the reverb at the end of the song (listen at 1'54). *Pony Boy* came out well, which is surprising on an album such as *Human Touch*, as this is not oriented toward an acoustic style of rock.

For Springsteen Addicts

Springsteen had originally considered using *Pony Boy* on the album *For Our Children*, a charity compilation edited by Walt Disney Records in 1991. Many singers, including Bob Dylan, Sting, Paul McCartney, Brian Wilson, and others also contributed. But he changed his mind at the last minute and instead chose a cover of *Chicken Lips and Lizard Hips*, by John and Nancy Cassidy.

Bruce Springsteen with his daughter Jessica and his son Evan in New York in 2002. The Boss had originally recorded *Pony Boy* for a Disney charity album.

SIDE B

PART MAN, PART MONKEY

Bruce Springsteen / 4'29

Single: *57 Channels (And Nothin' On)/Part Man, Part Monkey* **Reference:** Columbia Records – 38K 74354 **Release date:** United States, 10 July 1992
Musicians: Bruce Springsteen: vocals, guitars, bass / Roy Bittan: keyboards / David Sancious: organ / Omar Hakim: drums / Michael Fisher: percussion instruments **Recording:** Soundworks West, Burbank, California: January 1990 **Technical team:** Producers: Bruce Springsteen, Jon Landau, Chuck Plotin, Roy Bittan / Recording engineer: Toby Scott / Assistant recording engineer: Tom Hardisty / Mixing: Bob Clearmountain (A&M Studios) / Mastering: Bob Ludwig

Genesis and lyrics

Bruce Springsteen wrote *Part Man, Part Monkey* in 1986, not long before the start of recording for *Tunnel of Love*. The recording, however, was hidden away. The version chosen as the B-side of *57 Channels (And Nothin' On)*, released as a single in July 1992, dates back to January 1990 and was recorded at the Soundworks West studios in Burbank, California. It's important to note that this same version is also on the *Tracks* box set (1998) and the *18 Tracks* compilation (1999).

Did the New Jersey songwriter have a bone to pick with church dogma? He clearly stands firm on the side of evolutionists (Darwinists), who believe that animals have been evolving since the dawn of time, and against creationists, for whom God is responsible for all life on Earth. He sings: "They prosecuted some poor sucker in the United States/For teaching that man descended from the apes." The first words of this song have an unmistakable meaning: the "truth" lies in science and deceit lies with the church. "Did God make man in a breath of holy fire/Or did he crawl on up out of the muck and mire," wonders the narrator, whose behavior is proof that he is part man, part monkey. He then turns his sights on the priests, whom he believes are nothing but "soul-suckers."

Production

In support of evolutionist theories, the songwriter chose to compose a reggae song. The choice was ideal because the piece was a success. Springsteen sings very good lead vocals and is not afraid to add some funny monkey sounds. He's particularly brilliant on the guitars (and bass), especially after the bridge, where he performs two solos, first in slide, then in fingerstyle (from 2'22). David Sancious and his Hammond B-3 are back in the swing of things, supported by the percussion sounds of Roy Bittan's synthesizers (on the right). Michael Fisher, who also worked on *Soul Driver* (*Human Touch*), is on the tambourine and timbales, while Oman Hakim provides some excellent drumming.

It's a shame that the divergent style of *Part Man, Part Monkey* prevented the piece from appearing on an original album, even though it's a better song than others on *Human Touch*.

Omar Hakim is one of the best drummers of his generation, and his jazz, soul, and rock styles have allowed him to perform at countless numbers of recording sessions. Notably, he has recorded with Weather Report, Sting (*The Dream of the Blue Turtles*), David Bowie (*Let's Dance*), Dire Straits (*Money for Nothing*), and Miles Davis (*Tutu*).

SIDE B

30 DAYS OUT

Bruce Springsteen / 4'42

Single: *Leap of Faith/Leap of Faith* (live)/*30 Days Out* **Reference:** Columbia Records – 658369 2 **Release date:** United States, 1992
Musicians: Bruce Springsteen: vocals, guitars / Roy Bittan: keyboards / Randy Jackson: bass / Jeff Porcaro: drums, shaker **Recording:** A&M Recording Studios, Los Angeles, California: March to April 1990 **Technical team:** Producers: Bruce Springsteen, Jon Landau, Chuck Plotkin, Roy Bittan / Recording engineer: Toby Scott / Assistant recording engineers: Robert "RJ" Jaczko, Greg Goldman, Randy Wine, Dave Collins (digital editing) [A&M] / Mixing: Bob Clearmountain (A&M) / Mastering: Bob Ludwig

Genesis and lyrics

30 Days Out is about the end of a love story. As with other songs, it fits directly into what the songwriter might have lived through with Julianne Phillips some time before. After experiencing an intense passion, the couple in the song slowly start to grow apart. The narrator tries everything to make his girlfriend happy, but the more he tries to get close to her, the more she pulls away. He says: "I'm six days running but I'm thirty days out." This literally means that he ran for six days but is still 30 days out from his objective—the more he runs, the farther away it gets. It is the woman's feelings that have changed. Behind "every kiss [she leaves] a little shadow of doubt," sings Springsteen. The narrator asks her to tell him what's wrong, but she only responds with a smile—a smile that seems to say: you still have hundreds of miles to go.

Bruce Springsteen recorded *30 Days Out* in Los Angeles, in March or April 1990, during sessions for *Human Touch*. Although he cut it from the album, he chose it for the EP that went to various European countries and Australia, as was the case with the studio and live versions of *Leap of Faith,* or with *Lucky Town* and the live version of *Leap of Faith*. In Japan, *30 Days Out* was released with *Roll of the Dice* and the live version of *Leap of Faith*.

Production

30 Days Out is a good pop-rock song with an infectious energy, which is driven by Jeff Porcaro and Randy Jackson's excellent rhythm. Jackson plays a very good bass line that runs until the last measure, as if it were a sequencer. The drummer tops off his performance with a shaker that has a contagious groove. Springsteen plays some superb guitar parts with very good solos, notably in the introduction and in the coda, where he imitates the style of The Edge (at 2'51). On a rhythmic level, he uses several 6-string guitars to build a veritable wall of saturated sound, which he enhances with a reverb and a delay. He ends the piece with strong power chords (from 4'12). On the vocals, he doesn't push himself, and instead sings in the style of Roy Orbison. Roy Bittan does the keyboards full justice, flooding the piece with a variety of chords and sumptuous piano parts. *30 Days Out* could easily have made it onto the tracklisting for *Human Touch* in place of some far less interesting songs.

For Springsteen Addicts

A different mix of *30 Days Out* can be found on the *The Gospel's Rain* and *Human Demos 1989–1992* bootlegs.

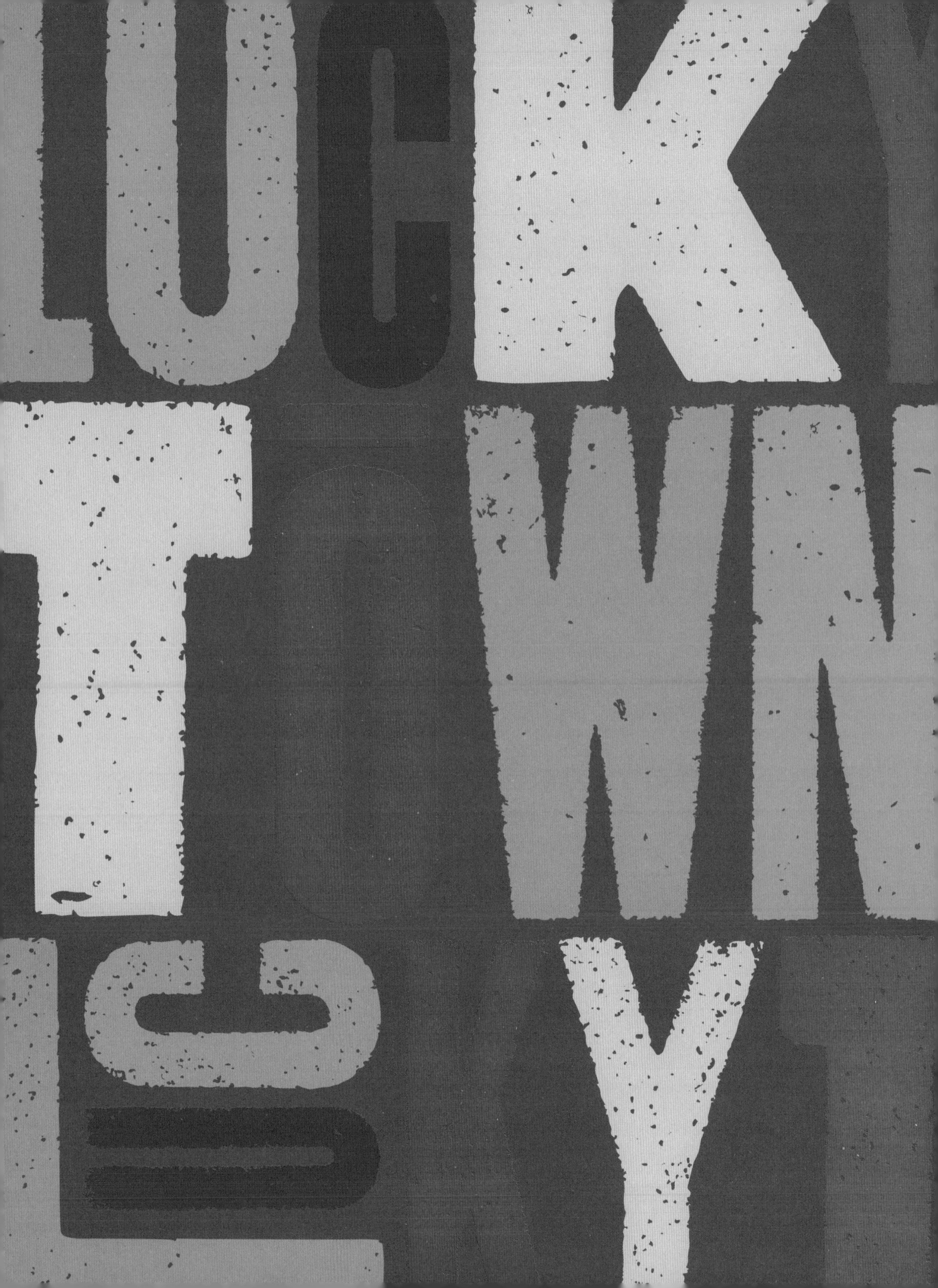

ALBUM

LUCKY TOWN

Better Days • Lucky Town • Local Hero • If I Should Fall Behind • Leap of Faith • The Big Muddy • Living Proof • Books of Dreams • Souls of the Departed • My Beautiful Reward

Outtake: *Happy*

RELEASE DATE

United States: 31 March 1992

Reference: Columbia Records – CK 53001

No. 2 in the United Kingdom, Austria, and Switzerland, No. 3 in the United States, France, Canada, and Sweden, No. 4 in Germany

Photo of Bruce Springsteen taken in the early 1990s.

Gary Mallaber is a studio drummer who provided backing for Springsteen during the recording sessions of *Lucky Town.*

THE ALBUM OF A LOCAL HERO LIKE NO OTHER

The same-day release in stores of *Lucky Town* and *Human Touch* can be explained by the proliferation of new ideas in Springsteen's mind. As the sessions for his previous opus were coming to an end, the songwriter had already started composing *Living Proof.* This song then quickly led him down other creative paths. "Once I had written *Living Proof,* over the next three weeks I wrote and recorded an entirely new record," he says in his book *Songs.* "It was a release from the long process of making *Human Touch.* I set up the home recording equipment and everything came together very quickly, as on *Nebraska* and *Tunnel of Love.*"[6]

The album

However, *Lucky Town* is not a clone of *Human Touch.* With the exception of *Souls of the Departed,* which is set to a backdrop of the Gulf War and Los Angeles gang violence, the album is largely autobiographical, a kind of introspective look at the present, rather than the past. It radiates a gentle optimism, which has much to do with the writer's lifestyle at the time: the joy he had found following his marriage to Patti Scialfa, with whom he had two children by then (with a third to come later). However, he also recognizes that happiness is fragile, and the power of love is not eternal. He knows you have to fully savor the moments of contentment that fate deals you. *Better Days* and the title track are shining examples of this: Springsteen describes how Patti's love has transformed and redeemed him. Their marriage is a meeting of minds, but also of physical love, as is shown, for example, in *Leap of Faith,* where the narrator compares his lover's body to the "promised land." Other successes on the album include *Local Hero*—a humorous reflection on his entry into the very restricted circle of 1980s/1990s rock stars—and the aforementioned *Living Proof,* which was composed after the birth of his first son.

Lucky Town shares few musical similarities with *Human Touch* either. Although Springsteen is sometimes accompanied on this record, notably by the drummer Gary Mallaber, who had previously worked with Van Morrison, the Steve Miller Band, and Bonnie Raitt, he plays most of the other instruments himself: guitars, of course, as well as bass, harmonica, and keyboards. It is an album with both folk and blues-rock accents, enriched (to a greater extent than *Human Touch*) by very soul-sounding choral vocals. It is also a Californian album, in the sense that Springsteen's vocals,

Poster for the last concert on the British leg of the 1992–1993 World Tour, at Milton Keynes on 22 May 1993.

Sleeve for the tenth studio album. The photo was taken by David Rose, as was the one for *Human Touch*.

guitar, harmonica, and melodies seem to sweep the listener along with him on his road trip to the West Coast.

Lucky Town was released on 31 March 1992, the same day as *Human Touch* (which is why some people consider it Springsteen's ninth album and others, his tenth). "I would have written just happy songs—and I tried it in the early '90s and it didn't work," he said seven years later when he was inducted into the Rock & Roll Hall of Fame. "The public didn't like it."[104] In fact, Springsteen himself doesn't appear to be a huge fan of *Lucky Town* (nor to some extent of *Human Touch*), as he barely mentions it in his autobiography *Born to Run*. Although the album wasn't a smash hit with his fans, they didn't exactly snub it either. In the United States, the album made it all the way to No.3 in the *Billboard* charts (just behind *Human Touch*) in the week of 18 April 1992, before dropping to No.4 the following week, then to No.11 in early May (it has since gone platinum). On the other side of the pond, Springsteen still attracted a large, unconditional following, notably in the United Kingdom, Austria, Italy, and Switzerland, where the album hit the No.2 spot, and in France and Sweden, where it reached No.3.

Paradoxically, *Lucky Town* was less successful worldwide than *Human Touch*, which is baffling because the melodies, lyrics, and minimalist, almost "homemade," production make the songs on *Lucky Town* largely superior to those on *Human Touch*. Taking the 24 tracks on the two albums as a whole, there are two main points to note: although these songs occupy a relatively minor place in the New Jersey songwriter's overall body of work, they still set out to seek answers to the questions that everyone asks, as was the case with his masterpieces, such as *Born to Run* and *Darkness on the Edge of Town*. "*Human Touch* and *Lucky Town* were both about the blessings and the unanswerable questions that come with adult life, mortality, and human love,"[6] as Bruce Springsteen says himself.

The sleeve

The graphic design on the sleeves of *Lucky Town* and *Human Touch* is identical: red letters in the same font and type size for the album title and artist's name. Only the photograph is different: the one on *Lucky Town*, once again taken by David Rose, shows the songwriter sporting black jeans and an unbuttoned, light-colored shirt, with a heavy chain and medallion, sunglasses, and a hint of a smile—capturing, in a way, the feel of the album. The back cover features a desert mural with a cactus in the foreground, a typically American landscape that could be Monument Valley in the middle ground, and a mountain range in the background. The booklet contains photos of Springsteen, mainly with Patti Scialfa, the song lyrics, and the sleeves of previous albums.

The recording

After the lengthy production of *Human Touch*, staggered over almost 19 months from September 1989 to March 1991, Springsteen produced *Lucky Town* in five months, from September 1991 to January 1992 (although he most probably began preproduction work in July). He mainly recorded in his home studio in Los Angeles, in parallel with extra sessions at A&M Studios. The production team was exactly the same as for the previous album: Springsteen, Jon Landau, and Chuck

Bruce Springsteen playing to the crowd at the Halle Tony Garnier, Lyon, on 13 April 1993. A world tour that more than lived up to expectations.

Plotkin. However, Roy Bittan only appears on three tracks: *Leap of Faith*, *The Big Muddy,* and *Living Proof.* He was not involved in any of the songwriting with the Boss, as he had been on *Human Touch*, for which he cowrote two tracks. He was not even aware that *Lucky Town* was being recorded until quite late on, well after the first sessions had started, in fact.

In total, 15 songs were put in the can. Other than the ten official tracks, only one outtake has so far emerged: *Happy*. Four tracks have therefore not yet been released.

The handful of musicians involved in the recording sessions, besides Roy Bittan and Gary Mallaber, include Randy Jackson on bass in *Better Days*, Ian McLagan back on the organ for *My Beautiful Reward*, and the three vocalists, Patti Scialfa, Lisa Lowell, and Soozie Tyrell, on backing vocals for *Better Days*, *Local Hero,* and *Leap of Faith*.

The recording engineer was once again Toby Scott. Springsteen asked him to install on his property (in the guesthouse next to the pool) the digital mobile studio equipment that he used for live takes. Finally, as always, Bob Clearmountain did the mixing and Bob Ludwig, the mastering.

For Springsteen Addicts

Despite good sales in the days immediately after the release of *Human Touch* and *Lucky Town*, some critics were evidently not hugely enthusiastic about the two albums. The headline in *Entertainment Weekly* was: "Whatever happened to Bruce?"[10]

Graham Nash, one of the vocalists in Crosby, Stills & Nash, also wrote and composed a song entitled *Better Days* for his first solo album, *Songs for Beginners* (1971). Finally, there are other *Better Days* on Supertramp's album *Brother Where You Bound* (1985).

BETTER DAYS

Bruce Springsteen / 4'08

Musicians
Bruce Springsteen: vocals, guitar
Lisa Lowell, Patti Scialfa, Soozie Tyrell: backing vocals
Randy Jackson: bass
Gary Mallaber: drums, tambourine (?)
Recording
Thrill Hill Recording, Beverley Hills, Los Angeles, California: September 1991 to January 1992
A&M Recording Studios, Los Angeles: September 1991 to January 1992
Technical team
Producers: Bruce Springsteen, Jon Landau, Chuck Plotkin
Recording engineer: Toby Scott
Assistant recording engineers: Greg Goldman, Robert "RJ" Jaczko, Randy Wine, Dave Collins (digital editing/assembly)
Mixing: Bob Clearmountain (A&M)
Mastering: Bob Ludwig

Early August 1992, Bruce Springsteen gets up close and personal with the crowd in East Rutherford, New Jersey.

Genesis and lyrics

In his book *Songs*, Bruce Springsteen explains that *Better Days*, along with *Book of Dreams* and *Leap of Faith*, two other tracks that feature on *Lucky Town*, are songs about second chances. "The characters return from broken love affairs and self-doubt and find the tempered optimism to take another shot,"[6] he says.

The narrator recalls a time in the recent past when nothing was going his way. He was "tired of waiting for tomorrow to come" and his "life to begin." Now he has a "pretty red rose," a "woman [he] can call [his] friend," and better days are here. "Tonight I'm lying in your arms carving lucky charms yeah out of these hard luck bones," sings Springsteen. The image speaks for itself. The narrator, who initially felt that "Every fool's got a reason to feel sorry for himself," has now been profoundly transformed by love and is "halfway to heaven and just a mile outta hell."

Like the majority of Springsteen's compositions, *Better Days* is largely autobiographical. "With a young son and about to get married (for the last time) I was feelin' like a happy guy who has his rough days rather than vice versa,"[97] he writes in the booklet accompanying the *Greatest Hits* compilation. It is a song about time passing and everything happening, and about becoming a new man with Patti Scialfa by his side.

Better Days was released in different formats in March 1991, as a single with a live version of *Tougher Than the Rest* (recorded at the Los Angeles Memorial Sports Arena on 27 April 1988) and as a CD single, also with *Tougher Than the Rest* and *Part Man, Part Monkey* as a bonus track. In the United States, the song reached No.2 in the US Mainstream Rock chart and No.16 in the *Billboard* Hot 100 (March 1992), and No.34 in the United Kingdom (May 1992). *Better Days* was also made into a music video, where the excellent relationship between the various band members and Springsteen shines through.

Production

Better Days sets the tone for the rest of Springsteen's new album: it has more of a soul feel than previous albums and is much less dominated by synthesized sound, which tended to be overdone on *Human Touch*. His new drummer, Gary Mallaber, takes us back to the roots of rock drumming, delivering a sound that is less smooth than Jeff Porcaro's—who is

Besides being a talented musician (drummer, vibraphonist, percussionist, keyboardist, singer, composer, arranger, producer, and recording engineer!), Gary Mallaber is also an actor. He has appeared in many films, series, and documentaries, notably Brian de Palma's 1974 movie *Phantom of the Paradise*, where he played a band member.

Bruce Springsteen and Patti Scialfa. These were better days for the performer from New Jersey after falling in love with his backing singer.

nevertheless an undeniably talented drummer—and his previous work with Van Morrison was probably one of the reasons the Boss hired him. Randy Jackson, who contributed to most of the tracks on *Human Touch*, plays alongside him here on bass, but sadly this is his sole participation on the record. The duo brings energy and a warm groove to the piece, providing particularly effective support for the Boss. Springsteen takes on the other instruments: various electric and acoustic rhythm guitars—a real 6-string wall of sound—the organ, with a very soul register, comes in at the first chorus (at 0'40), and some solo electric guitar parts that are more blues rock than his usual style (listen at 1'49). As far as lead vocals are concerned, there is nothing new here: Springsteen's voice is as powerful and passionate as ever. However, what is new, is the trio of backing vocalists comprising Patti Scialfa, Lisa Lowell, and Soozie Tyrell, with Tyrell already having recorded a violin part for Springsteen on *Shut Out the Light*, the B-side of the *Born in The U.S.A.* single, released on 30 October 1984. The three singers provide backing vocals on all the choruses, lending a gospel texture to the piece.

Better Days is a luminous, shimmering, and pleasantly energetic piece, and Springsteen could not have chosen a better song as the opening track of *Lucky Town*. The recorded version is so effective that it has never been surpassed by any of the live performances.

LUCKY TOWN

Bruce Springsteen / 3'27

Musicians

Bruce Springsteen: vocals, guitars, bass, keyboards
Gary Mallaber: drums, tambourine (?)

Recording

Thrill Hill Recording, Beverley Hills, Los Angeles, California: September 1991 to January 1992
A&M Recording Studios, Los Angeles: September 1991 to January 1992

Technical team

Producers: Bruce Springsteen, Jon Landau, Chuck Plotkin
Recording engineer: Toby Scott
Assistant recording engineers: Greg Goldman, Robert "RJ" Jaczko, Randy Wine, Dave Collins (digital editing)
Mixing: Bob Clearmountain (A&M)
Mastering: Bob Ludwig

For Springsteen Addicts

Lucky Town was used in the 2007 Curtis Hanson film *Lucky You*, which is set in Las Vegas and stars Eric Bana, Drew Barrymore, and Robert Duvall.

Genesis and lyrics

This song could easily have been composed after some long motorbike rides from Death Valley to Monument Valley, with a musical nod to the unlikely encounter between country rock and punk. The lyrics also express this powerful feeling of freedom. A house that "got too crowded," "clothes [that] got too tight," and the narrator on the road that leads to "Lucky Town"—by which we understand the town where he met the love of his life on the top of a hill. The days when he experienced "victory that was just failure in deceit" are over, as he is now "stepping lightly and feeling no pain." It is time for good fortune and enjoying the present. The moral of the song appears in the last verse: "When it comes to luck you make your own."

Lucky Town was released as a single in several European countries (with a live version of *Leap of Faith* on the B-side) in 1992. In the United Kingdom, the live recording entered the charts at No.48 in April 1993. Bruce Springsteen performed it onstage for the first time at The Bottom Line, in New York, on 6 May 1992.

Production

Lucky Town is a very solid song, carried by the many excellent 6-string tracks recorded by Springsteen with the clean-cutting, twangy sound characteristic of Telecasters. The song has a high-energy, country-rock style, driven by the powerful throb of Gary Mallaber's drums and the vigorous tambourine part, probably also played by Mallaber (at 0'34). Springsteen handles all the other instruments: bass, which he plays more effectively on each successive album, and fairly discreet synth pads (on the left). His clear, precise solo on his Telecaster-Esquire is highly successful (at 1'49). As for his lead vocal, the tone is somewhat unrecognizable, and the voice a little tight.

The live versions serve the song well, especially when played by the reformed E Street Band. At one particular concert with the band in Melbourne, on 16 February 2014, the boss began the song with a capo that had accidentally been put on the second fret of his guitar, before realizing there was a problem and hurriedly moving it onto the first fret where it should have been.

LOCAL HERO

Bruce Springsteen / 4'04

For Springsteen Addicts

Despite what the song claims, Bruce Springsteen did not go into the store where his portrait was displayed. He sent Patti Scialfa instead. The store in question was a Newberry Five and Dime discount store.

Musicians

Bruce Springsteen: vocals, guitar, harmonica, bass
Lisa Lowell, Patti Scialfa, Soozie Tyrell: backing vocals
Gary Mallaber: drums, tambourine (?), maracas (?)

Recording

Thrill Hill Recording, Beverley Hills, Los Angeles, California: September 1991 to January 1992
A&M Recording Studios, Los Angeles: September 1991 to January 1992

Technical team

Producers: Bruce Springsteen, Jon Landau, Chuck Plotkin
Recording engineer: Toby Scott
Assistant recording engineers: Greg Goldman, Robert "RJ" Jaczko, Randy Wine, Dave Collins (digital editing)
Mixing: Bob Clearmountain (A&M)
Mastering: Bob Ludwig

Patti Scialfa and Soozie Tyrell, friends in real life, shown here together onstage providing backing vocals for *Local Hero.*

Genesis and lyrics

At a concert in Los Angeles, on 22 September 1992, Bruce Springsteen revealed that *Local Hero* was based on real life. As he was driving through the streets of his hometown one day, he caught sight of a stylized portrait of himself in a store window next to a photo of Bruce Lee, positioned so that it looked like the actor and martial arts expert was kicking the rock star. Springsteen asked the salesgirl who was in the painting, and she answered: "Just a local hero." These four words relegated Bruce Springsteen to the status of an unknown in his own town of Freehold. This inspired a few slightly ironic and disgruntled phrases in the lyrics: "First they made me the king then they made me pope/Well then they brought the rope." And again: "These days I'm feeling all right except I can't tell my courage from my desperation." *Local Hero* is "an ironic look at the slings and arrows of outrageous fortune,"[6] as Bruce Springsteen explains in *Songs*. The song was played onstage for the first time at The Bottom Line, in New York, on 6 May 1992.

Production

Local Hero is a sort of rock-country mix with an Irish and gospel flavor. The intro opens with the drums, acoustic guitar, and harmonica (one of the predominant textures in the arrangements). The guitars gradually come in, enriching the general harmony, first the bass, then the rhythm guitars, and, finally, the saturated 6-strings, with the sound suggesting Gibson Les Paul guitars (from 0'54). One of *Local Hero's* strengths is the superb backing vocals from Lisa Lowell, Patti Scialfa, and Soozie Tyrell. The gospel texture of their voices adds warmth to Springsteen's lead vocal, which is once again excellent. Gary Mallaber's drumming, a wonderful groove that is full of feeling, is essential to the piece. Mallaber also appears to have played tambourine and maracas, notably in the choruses (for example, at 0'40).

Local Hero is one of the album's successes, and the song radiates an authenticity that is often lacking on *Human Touch.*

IF I SHOULD FALL BEHIND

Bruce Springsteen / 2'57

Musicians
Bruce Springsteen: vocals, guitar, bass, keyboards
Gary Mallaber: drums, tambourine (?), shaker (?)
Recording
Thrill Hill Recording, Beverley Hills, Los Angeles, California: September 1991 to January 1992
A&M Recording Studios, Los Angeles: September 1991 to January 1992
Technical team
Producers: Bruce Springsteen, Jon Landau, Chuck Plotkin
Recording engineer: Toby Scott
Assistant recording engineers: Greg Goldman, Robert "RJ" Jaczko, Randy Wine, Dave Collins (digital editing)
Mixing: Bob Clearmountain (A&M)
Mastering: Bob Ludwig

For Springsteen Addicts

On 3 March 1991, after a long police pursuit for speeding, the African-American Rodney King was arrested and beaten by Los Angeles police officers. The four white officers subsequently appeared in court charged with using excessive force, and their acquittal (by a jury with no African-Americans) provoked mass rioting, fires, and homicides in Los Angeles, from 29 April to 4 May 1992, leaving over 50 people dead. In 1993, the four officers stood trial again and two were sentenced to 30 months in prison.

Genesis and lyrics

"One of my best songs about the dedication to one another that comes with love,"[6] writes Springsteen in his autobiography. "We swore we'd travel, darling, side by side/We'd help each other stay in stride," he sings in the second verse. *If I Should Fall Behind* is the story of a couple who have promised to be faithful and wait for one another whatever life may bring.

However, there is another message in this superb ballad. Bruce Springsteen wrote *If I Should Fall Behind* in 1992, very probably in his home on Sunset Boulevard, Hollywood, immediately after the major riots in late April/early May 1992 which were sparked by the Rodney King affair. Springsteen felt that in America at the time the solutions for many of society's problems, including healthcare, day care for children, employment, and education, were there but that it would take an effort on the part of society on the scale of the Marshall Plan to override the destruction that generations of poor social policy had wrought.

"You and I know what this world can do/So let's make our steps clear that the other may see." These words in the third verse sound like a plea for tolerance, calling on us to help our fellow humans in a hostile world. It is a humanist manifesto that was performed in public for the first time at The Bottom Line, in New York, on 6 May 1992.

Production

If I Should Fall Behind is, without doubt, one of the big successes of *Lucky Town*. Springsteen has composed a melancholic, gentle folk ballad. He plays all the instruments, except for the drums, and probably percussion (tambourine and shaker, the latter from the second verse, at 0'43). From the intro, the acoustic feel of the arrangements gives the song its introspective atmosphere: the Boss's Gibson J-45, his bass part, and Gary Mallaber's simultaneously spirited and steady drumming draw the listener in. The quality of the recording is remarkable, with Toby Scott achieving an exceptional presence and mellowness in the sound. When Springsteen launches into the lead vocals, his tone is surprisingly different from his usual voice: it has more of a nasal twang, as if the master has been put through a varispeed, which doesn't seem to have been the case. Whatever the truth of the matter, he deli-

Riots in Los Angeles following the acquittal of the police officers accused of beating Afro-American, Rodney King. The subject of *If I Should Fall Behind.*

vers a quality rendition, as by now he has long since mastered the art of conveying the full range of emotions. He provides his own harmonies for some phrases, notably at the ends of the verses (there's an example at 1'11). He chooses to keep the arrangements simple, adding just one discreet electric rhythm guitar from the second verse (positioned on the left and colored by a very obvious tremolo), buoyant synth pads (from 0'43), and a solo acoustic guitar part in the third verse (on the right, at 1'17). The result is superb, as the songwriter is particularly comfortable with clean, direct arrangements.

The music video was filmed with some of the E Street Band at a soundcheck in September 1999, before one of the six concerts that the band gave at the First Union Center in Philadelphia (probably the one on the 25th). The musicians take turns to sing, accompanied by a single electric rhythm guitar, a bass, and a tambourine. It is an incredible performance, featuring solos from Springsteen, Steve Van Zandt, Nils Lofgren, Patti Scialfa, and Clarence Clemons—who is on saxophone, then vocals—before the finale brings them all together around the same microphone. Directed by Jonathan Demme—with whom the songwriter had already worked on the music video for *Streets of Philadelphia* in 1994—it is an incredibly moving performance.

Dion DiMucci, better known as Dion, whose 1960s hits include *Runaround Sue* and *The Wanderer* (1961), recorded an utterly irresistible doo-wop cover version of *If I Should Fall Behind* in 1992. Several years later, on 23 November 2002, he sang it onstage with Springsteen at the American Airlines Arena in Miami, Florida.

For Springsteen Addicts

"I grabbed you, baby, like a wild pitch." A wild pitch is a bad throw in baseball that the person on the receiving end is unlikely to catch.

LEAP OF FAITH

Bruce Springsteen / 3'27

Musicians

Bruce Springsteen: vocals, guitar, bass
Roy Bittan: keyboards
Lisa Lowell, Patti Scialfa, Soozie Tyrell: backing vocals
Gary Mallaber: drums, tambourine (?)

Recording

Thrill Hill Recording, Beverley Hills, Los Angeles, California: September 1991 to January 1992
A&M Recording Studios, Los Angeles: September 1991 to January 1992

Technical team

Producers: Bruce Springsteen, Jon Landau, Chuck Plotkin, Roy Bittan
Recording engineer: Toby Scott
Assistant recording engineers: Greg Goldman, Robert "RJ" Jaczko, Randy Wine, Dave Collins (digital editing)
Mixing: Bob Clearmountain (A&M)
Mastering: Bob Ludwig

Bruce Springsteen wrote *Leap of Faith* as a song about second chances and love rediscovered.

Genesis and lyrics

Love, sex, and faith are at the heart of this song, as this phrase from the chorus shows: "It takes a leap of faith to get things going." It is another song about second chances, "a sexually humorous glimpse at love and resilience,"[6] as Bruce Springsteen explains in his book *Songs*.

Following a disappointment in love, the narrator is enjoying life again after meeting another woman. "Now your legs were heaven your breasts were the altar/Your body was the holy land," "Now you were the Red Sea I was Moses/I kissed you and slipped into a bed of roses." The lyrics couldn't be more explicit. Love, which is physical here rather than cerebral, is a return to the fires of youth. "And in your love I'm born again," Springsteen concludes in the song. It is an impassioned declaration of his love for Patti Scialfa and, like other tracks on the album, was performed in public for the first time at The Bottom Line, in New York, on 6 May 1992.

Production

Leap of Faith is a pleasant little rock number, written by Springsteen when he probably wasn't feeling particularly inspired musically. The piece is largely occupied by guitars, which Springsteen recorded himself: at least three different 6-strings can be heard, two for the rhythm section and one for the solo parts. He also plays bass, which is somewhat undermixed, as are Roy Bittan's synth pads in his first contribution to the album, as both musician and coproducer. You could be forgiven for wondering if a team of four producers was slightly overdoing it for this type of song. The trio of vocalists, consisting of Lisa Lowell, Patti Scialfa, and Soozie Tyrell, proves a real asset to the song, as their contributions literally light up the piece. In 2012, Lisa Lowell describes what they felt about the Boss's songs: "Bruce's music sometimes has that really dense quality where it's almost like you're just a little fleck in the painting."[105] It is a shame that this was their last contribution to the album. Worth noting: The fade-out is exceptionally long—it starts at 2'33 and continues in stages until 3'23, lasting a total of 50 seconds. Almost a quarter of the song!

For Springsteen Addicts

"Poison snake bites you and you're poison too." Springsteen borrowed this phrase in *The Big Muddy* from Pete Dexter's novel *Paris Trout*, which was published in 1988 and adapted in 1991 as a screenplay, starring Dennis Hopper, by Stephen Gyllenhaal. It's worth noting that Springsteen used the same Dexter quote in *Gave It a Name*, an outtake from *Human Touch*.

THE BIG MUDDY

Bruce Springsteen / 4'05

Musicians

Bruce Springsteen: vocals, guitar
Roy Bittan: keyboard bass
Gary Mallaber: drums

Recording

Thrill Hill Recording, Beverley Hills, Los Angeles, California: September 1991 to January 1992
A&M Recording Studios, Los Angeles: September 1991 to January 1992

Technical team

Producers: Bruce Springsteen, Jon Landau, Chuck Plotkin, Roy Bittan
Recording engineer: Toby Scott
Assistant recording engineers: Greg Goldman, Robert "RJ" Jaczko, Randy Wine, Dave Collins (digital editing)
Mixing: Bob Clearmountain (A&M)
Mastering: Bob Ludwig

The folk singer Pete Seeger recorded *Waist Deep in the Big Muddy* in 1967 when the Vietnam War was at its height. *The Big Muddy* is to some extent the sequel.

Genesis and lyrics

"The Big Muddy" is one of the names given to the Mississippi River because its muddy waters sometimes cause spectacular flooding in the Southern states. It is also a name that refers back to the blues music which was and continues to be played from New Orleans through Clarksdale to Memphis. The folk singer Pete Seeger wrote and recorded a topical song called *Waist Deep in the Big Muddy*, which was censored on American television because it roundly condemned Washington's warmongering politics in Vietnam.

Bruce Springsteen took these diverse references and composed a song with a very low-down feel—a term used to describe the raw, unadorned sound of the blues of the Mississippi Delta—that "explores human frailty and the morally ambiguous territory that comes with adulthood."[6] Billy is the hero of the song. He has a lover whom he takes wading in *The Big Muddy* one afternoon. He has some problems and asks for help from an old friend, who has a not-entirely-legal plan to get him out of trouble. And, as Springsteen sings, "Sooner or later it all comes down to money." Compared to "how beautiful the river flows and the birds they sing," "you and I," sings Springsteen, "we're messier things." And he adds: "There ain't no one leaving this world buddy/Without their shirttail dirty or hands a little bloody." In other words, this world is not made for innocents.

Production

In this second piece coproduced by Roy Bittan, the role of the E Street Band's red-hot keyboardist is reduced to almost nothing, with Bittan merely providing the bass line on keyboards (from 1'01). *The Big Muddy* is more of a guitarist's song, with Springsteen opting for his various excellent 6-strings, starting with a slide guitar that sounds like a dobro (on the left). He then delivers an electric rhythm part that he strums in arpeggios, adding some virtuosic solo passages from 2'39, probably played with a violin bow or a volume pedal. His lead vocal is perfect, his voice wrapped in a swampy reverb, bluesy to a tee (like the guitars). Gary Mallaber's drum contribution is limited to a fairly simple pattern that sounds like a drum machine. While *Leap of Faith* could be accused of lacking in originality, this is not at all the case with *The Big Muddy*, which is a success from every angle.

LIVING PROOF

Bruce Springsteen / 4'49

Musicians
Bruce Springsteen: vocals, guitar, bass, harmonica
Roy Bittan: keyboards
Gary Mallaber: drums, tambourine (?), shaker (?)
Recording
Thrill Hill Recording, Beverley Hills, Los Angeles, California: September 1991 to January 1992
A&M Recording Studios, Los Angeles: September 1991 to January 1992
Technical team
Producers: Bruce Springsteen, Jon Landau, Chuck Plotkin, Roy Bittan
Recording engineer: Toby Scott
Assistant recording engineers: Greg Goldman, Robert "RJ" Jaczko, Randy Wine, Dave Collins (digital editing)
Mixing: Bob Clearmountain (A&M)
Mastering: Bob Ludwig

Evan Springsteen (at the Ralph Lauren show, New York, in September 2016) is the "living proof" of a couple's love for one another.

Genesis and lyrics

Living Proof is the last song that Bruce Springsteen wrote for *Human Touch*, before choosing it for *Lucky Town*, along with the other tracks composed immediately afterward. The theme is "the common strength it takes to constitute a family,"[6] as Springsteen explains in his book *Songs*, adding, "Children are the 'living proof' of our belief in one another that love is real."[6]

Living Proof makes explicit reference to the birth of Evan Springsteen on 24 July 1990 in Los Angeles. "The truth of your partner's love sings brightly before you,"[1] as Springsteen wrote of the birth of his first son. "Your love, the love you've worked so hard to show, to hide, has been ripped from you and its presence shames your lack of faith while raining light upon the good you've created."[1] Hence the words in the first verse: "Well now on a summer night oh in a dusky room/Come a little piece of the Lord's undying light." *Living Proof* is about how fatherhood changes a man and makes him aware of life's fragility: "Life is just a house of cards," sings Springsteen.

Production

When you listen to *Living Proof*, what is surprising is the sheer energy it exudes. You would expect Springsteen to approach such a sensitive subject in a gentler, more intimate fashion. But that is where this unique songwriter's real talent lies. He has chosen, on the contrary, to express his feelings with genuinely moving force and conviction. Just listen to his incredible, very rock-style lead vocals, often pushed to breaking point, which display unequivocal depth. "That's how I feel,"[10] he would say simply in 1992. Gary Mallaber accentuates this message by delivering an efficient drumming part with a very audible groove (although the bass drum is somewhat overcooked). Roy Bittan—on the last piece that he coproduced—supports the harmonies with atmospheric pads and the Boss records buoyant and powerful guitar parts, including the bass, in a garage-rock style. He finishes *Living Proof* with a 6-string solo and harmonica (at 4'35).

Listening to this wonderful piece, you can understand why Springsteen wanted to continue the *Human Touch* adventure by composing new tracks for a second chapter, which became the *Lucky Town* album.

BOOK OF DREAMS

Bruce Springsteen / 4'24

COVER
After his amazing cover of *If I Should Fall Behind* in 1992, Dion, the doo-wop and R&B singer (Dion and the Belmonts), recorded his own version of *Book of Dreams* during the sessions for the album *Déjà Nu* (2000).

Musicians
Bruce Springsteen: vocals, guitars, bass, keyboards
Gary Mallaber: drums
Recording
Thrill Hill Recording, Beverley Hills, Los Angeles, California: September 1991 to January 1992
A&M Recording Studios, Los Angeles: September 1991 to January 1992
Technical team
Producers: Bruce Springsteen, Jon Landau, Chuck Plotkin
Recording engineer: Toby Scott
Assistant recording engineers: Greg Goldman, Robert "RJ" Jaczko, Randy Wine, Dave Collins (digital editing)
Mixing: Bob Clearmountain (A&M)
Mastering: Bob Ludwig

The singer Dion often performs Bruce Springsteen's songs. He recorded a cover version of *Book of Dreams* for the *Déjà Nu* album, released in 2000.

Genesis and lyrics

Alongside *Better Days* and *Leap of Faith*, *Book of Dreams* is the third song on *Lucky Town* that centers around the theme of what Bruce Springsteen has called "the second chance"—which is also a kind of rebirth. There's a wedding, a party in full swing, and memories follow in quick succession. "The scars we carry remain but the pain slips away it seems," the narrator confides. Both he and his young wife have experienced disappointment in love. This is a new start for them, a new story that they must write together.

"In the darkness my fingers slip across your skin, I feel your sweet reply." And the narrator asks his new bride: "Oh won't you baby be in my book of dreams?" The couple then lead out the traditional dance in front of both their families, who we imagine to be full of joy. "We dance out 'neath the stars' ancient light into the darkening trees," sings Springsteen, thinking no doubt of his wedding to Patti Scialfa, and of happiness rediscovered.

Production

Book of Dreams is a country folk ballad, with an ethereal, almost New Age, synth accompaniment. Once again, Springsteen is the main instrumentalist on the piece, alongside Gary Mallaber on drums. In the first bars, the Boss plunges us into a serene, peaceful atmosphere, with his Gibson J-45 acoustic sprinkling melancholic arpeggios. He records a bass line, supported by the bass drum and some very buoyant synth pads. His lead vocal is calm and his voice gentle, and he whispers his words with infinite sensitivity. He brings in an electric guitar for the second verse, which he plays with a mix of picking and licks, all colored by a fairly audible tremolo (on the right).

While the keyboard parts recorded by Roy Bittan for this album are fairly discreet and sparse, the ones with Springsteen at the helm, notably in *Book of Dreams*, are much less so. Besides the atmospheric pads in the intro, the songwriter also plays an electric piano from the second verse onward and creates a melodic theme with a string sound on the instrumental part traditionally reserved for the guitar solo (at 1'23). He finishes the piece in the same way (from 3'24).

SOULS OF THE DEPARTED

Bruce Springsteen / 4'17

Musicians
Bruce Springsteen: vocals, guitar, bass, organ, harmonica
Gary Mallaber: drums

Recording
Thrill Hill Recording, Beverley Hills, Los Angeles, California: September 1991 to January 1992
A&M Recording Studios, Los Angeles: September 1991 to January 1992

Technical team
Producers: Bruce Springsteen, Jon Landau, Chuck Plotkin
Recording engineer: Toby Scott
Assistant recording engineers: Greg Goldman, Robert "RJ" Jaczko, Randy Wine, Dave Collins (digital editing)
Mixing: Bob Clearmountain (A&M)
Mastering: Bob Ludwig

For Springsteen Addicts

"Shot down in a schoolyard by some East Compton Cholos," sings Bruce Springsteen in the second verse. The word "cholo" is American slang for a person of Latin-American origin from a disadvantaged background and/or gang member. The Californian town of Compton, mentioned in the song, became notorious for its gang violence and the rise of gangsta rap.

Genesis and lyrics

Along with *Souls of the Departed*, *If I Should Fall Behind* is the only political song on *Lucky Town*. The first verse looks back at the Gulf War (August 1990 to February 1991) between Iraq (following the invasion of Kuwait) and a coalition of 35 countries led by the United States under President George Bush. The songwriter creates a character called Jimmy Bly, a young lieutenant on the road to Basra, the main gateway into Iraq that was the scene of fierce fighting. Jimmy's job is to sort through the clothes of the soldiers who have died in action. Jimmy is left permanently traumatized by this experience: "At night in dreams he sees their souls rise/Yeah like dark geese into the Oklahoma skies."

The second verse takes us back to the United States. A seven-year-old boy called Raphael Rodriguez has been gunned down in his school playground by a gang of Latinos from East Compton (an area in Los Angeles County). His mother cries in despair, but the indifference of others reveals an uncaring, lawless society. As Springsteen (who is the narrator of the story) tucks his son up in bed, he thinks that little Raphael could have been his own child instead and how he wants to "build me a wall so high nothing can burn it down." In his book *Songs*, he explains that the father "wrestles with his own hypocrisies about the choices he has made for his family in contrast to his beliefs."[6] And this song is his answer to the conundrum. As a musician in the country where the dollar is king, and silence is golden, Springsteen rises up against the so-called right-thinking people that write the history books exactly as they choose, and spares an almost fraternal thought for the victims, "the souls of the departed."

Souls of the Departed was performed in public for the first time at the Stockholm Globe Arena, on 15 June 1992, and subsequently played around a hundred times between 1992 and 2008, more than most other songs on *Lucky Town*.

Production

Springsteen has always liked the raw, minimalist sound of garage rock. *Souls of the Departed*, with its emphasis on "dirty," saturated guitars, has something of this feel, as well as the live quality that Springsteen was looking for on *The River* in 1980 with the E Street Band. But this piece is primarily blues rock, fairly dark and aggressive, despite the medium tempo.

During the Vote For Change Tour in 2004, Bruce Springsteen and Neil Young played *Souls of the Departed* together. Here, the two musicians are with Patti Scialfa at the Annual Rock & Roll Hall of Fame Induction Ceremony in 2011.

The Boss, who once again handles all the instruments apart from the drum, opens hostilities by recording a 6-string rhythm part. Gary Mallaber supports him with powerful drumming, and a short reverb on the snare drum. Then several slightly saturated harmonica notes come in to reinforce this dominant blues texture. A second slide guitar appears several bars later (on the right), with a heavily distorted sound. The bass then joins in, along with an organ accompaniment. Springsteen drawls his lead vocals, carried by a slight delay. He provides his own discreet but effective harmonies for the choruses (there's an example at 1'45). He performs a first very short and fairly restrained slide solo at 2'02, then launches into a second improvisation on the coda, dueling with the harmonica (from 3'07). He finishes the piece, still on slide guitar, with Jimi Hendrix-style effects, with the guitar panning from left to right to a background of acoustic feedback (listen from 3'50).

Souls of the Departed is a very solid piece which Springsteen manages to make sound live, as if a band were playing directly in the studio, instead of just him, Gary Mallaber, and abundant overdubbing.

A superb concert version, performed with the full E Street Band on the Vote for Change Tour, on 5 October 2004, at the Xcel Energy Center, in Saint Paul, Minnesota, featured the Boss sharing the stage with Neil Young. The musicians launched into a performance of *Souls of the Departed* that was over eight minutes long, with the Canadian unleashing a three-minute-long, supercharged guitar solo with plenty of delay and saturation!

MY BEAUTIFUL REWARD

Bruce Springsteen / 3'55

Musicians
Bruce Springsteen: vocals, guitar, bass, harmonica
Ian McLagan: organ
Gary Mallaber: drums

Recording
Thrill Hill Recording, Beverley Hills, Los Angeles, California: September 1991 to January 1992
A&M Recording Studios, Los Angeles: September 1991 to January 1992

Technical team
Producers: Bruce Springsteen, Jon Landau, Chuck Plotkin
Recording engineer: Toby Scott
Assistant recording engineers: Greg Goldman, Robert "RJ" Jaczko, Randy Wine, Dave Collins (digital editing)
Mixing: Bob Clearmountain (A&M)
Mastering: Bob Ludwig

Genesis and lyrics

The *Lucky Town* album concludes with *My Beautiful Reward*. The central character in the song is "a man [who] searches for something unnameable, then, slipping between life and death, transforms into a bird flying over gray fields with 'the cold wind at [his] back,'"[6] explains Bruce Springsteen.

In the first verse, the hero claims to have "Walked from the mountain to the valley floor," looking for gold and diamond rings. In vain. In the second verse, he finds himself in a house on a hill where a sacred light is shining. Then comes the aforementioned transformation. He imagines himself as a black bird flying "Down along the river's silent edge," still "Searching for [his] beautiful reward." Is it a metaphor for solitude, or for madness? Above all else, it is probably a kind of coming-of-age quest that will lead him to paradise (the house on the hill).

My Beautiful Reward is another song that Bruce Springsteen played onstage for the first time at The Bottom Line, in New York, on 6 May 1992. It was performed frequently on the Human Touch-Lucky Town Tour, and then again in 2014 in Pittsburgh.

Production

The Boss's tenth opus concludes with a very successful and gentle folk ballad. *My Beautiful Reward* is carried by two wonderful acoustic guitar parts: arpeggios followed by a solo (on the right). Gary Mallaber's masterful rhythm section gives the piece a refreshing groove and supports the songwriter's efficient bass accompanied by Ian McLagan's Hammond B-3 organ—back after his contribution to *Real Man* for the *Human Touch* album. Listening to McLagan's keyboard part, you're left wondering why the Boss did not give him more scope to improvise, as all he does is methodically follow the chords. Shame.

My Beautiful Reward finishes with a few harmonica phrases, in true Bob-Dylan style. On the live version of the song, recorded on 22 September 1992 at the Warner Hollywood Studios, in Los Angeles, for *MTV Plugged* (released on the 1993 DVD *In Concert/MTV Plugged*), Springsteen performs an inspired and magnificent harmonica solo.

For Springsteen Addicts

Springsteen reused the phrase, "Then I came crashing down like a drunk on a bar room floor" on *All the Way Home*, a song from the 2005 album, *Devils & Dust*.

Ian McLagan, a member of Faces, in concert in London in 1974. Two decades later, he was playing alongside Bruce Springsteen. He is on the organ for *My Beautiful Reward*.

GREATE
IS
GREA

ALBUM

GREATEST HITS

Born to Run • Thunder Road • Badlands • The River • Hungry Heart • Atlantic City • Dancing in the Dark • Born in the U.S.A. • My Hometown • Glory Days • Brilliant Disguise • Human Touch • Better Days • Streets of Philadelphia • Secret Garden • Murder Incorporated • Blood Brothers • This Hard Land

RELEASE DATE

United States: 27 February 1995

Reference: Columbia Records – C2 67060

No.1 in the United States, United Kingdom, Australia, Austria, Belgium, Canada, France, Germany, Italy, Spain, and Sweden

Bruce Springsteen in 1995, the year *Greatest Hits* was released, an album that features five tracks previously unreleased.

Sleeve for the *Greatest Hits* compilation. A leather jacket and Fender Telecaster are *de rigueur* in this photo taken by Eric Meola.

BEST SONGS AND NEW SONGS

Greatest Hits was Bruce Springsteen's first compilation. It contains some of his greatest songs, not counting his early work (Columbia Records did not include *Greetings from Asbury Park, N.J.* or *The Wild, The Innocent, and The E Street Shuffle*). It includes songs from *Born to Run, Lucky Town, Darkness on the Edge of Town, The River, Nebraska, Born in the U.S.A., Tunnel of Love*, and *Human Touch*. A total of 15 songs spanning some 17 years of Springsteen's career are collected here to attest the global popularity of the composer of *Badlands, Hungry Heart,* and *Dancing in the Dark*.

The most interesting part, at least for fans, is the release of five new songs. The most famous of them—and one of the most famous in all of Bruce Springsteen's discography—is *Streets of Philadelphia*. It was composed for *Philadelphia*, the Jonathan Demme film starring Tom Hanks and Denzel Washington. The four other songs were polished off and performed by the E Street Band, who'd reunited for the occasion. While *Murder Incorporated* and the first version of *This Hard Land* date back to recording sessions for *Born in the U.S.A.* in 1982, *Secret Garden*, *Blood Brothers,* and the second version of *This Hard Land* mark Springsteen's reunion with his band, as they were recorded at The Hit Factory and The Power Station between January and April (or May) 1995. Of note: the *Blood Brothers* EP, released in 1996, contains alternative versions of *Blood Brothers* and *Secret Garden* (as well as a live version of *Murder Incorporated*).

Greatest Hits became available in stores on 27 February 1995, at the same time as the *Streets of Philadelphia/If I*

Poster for film-maker Ernie Fritz's rockumentary about the E Street Band and previously unreleased tracks on *Greatest Hits*.

Tom Hanks and Jonathan Demme at the fifth GLAAD Media Awards in 1994. *Philadelphia* was the first Hollywood motion picture about AIDS.

Should Fall Behind single, and a few days before the 37th Grammy Awards. The media was quick to criticize the compilation, saying it was no more than a commercial endeavor. Parke Puterbaugh of *Rolling Stone* magazine wrote that the new songs recorded with the E Street Band "sound more like a final coda than a new beginning."[106] The public at large went into a veritable frenzy. The compilation went to No.1 in some 15 countries, including the United States, the United Kingdom, Belgium, France, Germany, Spain, and Italy. To date, it has sold almost ten million copies on both sides of the Atlantic.

The E Street Band's short-lived reunion

For the *Greatest Hits* album, Springsteen decided to gather the E Street Band together for a brief, intense, and emotional reunion. It had been ten years since the band had all worked together in a recording studio—although it had been only seven years since the recording of the *Tunnel of Love* album, only a few band members were involved at that time. Springsteen called each of his former band mates, explaining what he had in mind, but also emphasizing that the reunion was a one-off. So, on 2 January 1995, they all met up in Studio A at The Hit Factory to work on some of Springsteen's new songs. Only one key figure of the E Street Band was missing: Steve Van Zandt, who showed up soon after hearing about the reunion. Springsteen had actually hesitated to tell him, as he was nervous about seeing him again after 15 years. But "Little Steven" effortlessly jumped back into the formidable war machine that was the E Street Band. He only contributed to one song, *This Hard Land*. He also played for *Murder Incorporated*, but as an outtake recorded during *Born in the U.S.A.* sessions.

The group dissolved again after this short period—of about ten days—and wouldn't get back together again until 1999 for the Bruce Springsteen and E Street Band Reunion Tour.

Blood Brothers

Director Ernie Fritz would capture on film the reunion of the E Street Band and the studio recordings of the various new songs for *Greatest Hits*. The result was a superb documentary called *Blood Brothers*, produced in 1996 and nominated for the 1997 Grammy Awards in the category of "Best Long Form Music Video."

In the end, an EP of the same name was also released, in March 1996. It included five songs: *Blood Brothers*, *High Hopes*, *Murder Incorporated*, *Secret Garden*, and *Without You*. It was released again in January 2014, this time for downloading, then remastered and included in *The Album Collection Vol. 2, 1987–1996* (released on 18 May 2018).

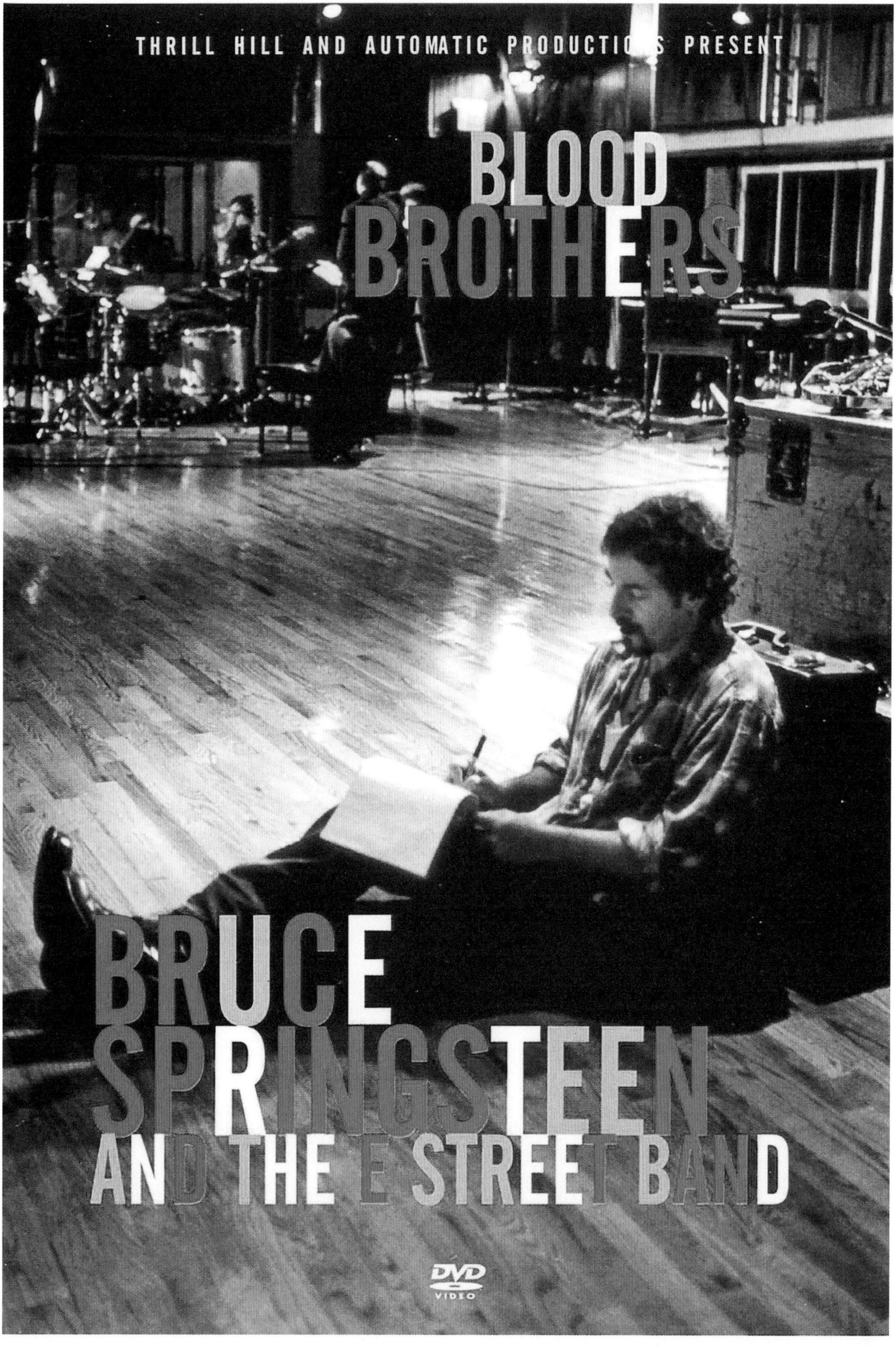
THRILL HILL AND AUTOMATIC PRODUCTIONS PRESENT
BLOOD BROTHERS
BRUCE SPRINGSTEEN
AND THE E STREET BAND
DVD VIDEO

A still image from Jonathan Demme's music video. Springsteen started working on *Streets of Philadelphia* in his home studio in Rumson.

STREETS OF PHILADELPHIA

Bruce Springsteen / 3'15 (Greatest Hits version)

Musicians
Bruce Springsteen: vocals, keyboards, bass, drum machine, tambourine
Tommy Sims: backing vocals
Recording
Thrill Hill West, Los Angeles, California: 1993
Technical team
Producers: Bruce Springsteen, Chuck Plotkin
Recording engineer: Toby Scott
Mixing: Bob Clearmountain

For Springsteen Addicts

The "close friend" that Springsteen mentions in his autobiography, and whose death inspired the lyrics for *Streets of Philadelphia*, was Kristen Ann Carr, the daughter of his co-manager Barbara Carr and biographer Dave Marsh. She died in January 1993 at the age of 21 after battling a rare form of cancer. Upon receiving the Grammy Award for "Best Song of the Year" in 1994, the songwriter thanked Kristen, "whose spirit is in this song."[16]

VARIATIONS IN TIME

There are various versions of *Streets of Philadelphia*, all of different lengths: 3'15 for the *Greatest Hits* compilation, about 3'50 for the singles and the EPs, 2'53 for the video of Springsteen's live performance, and about 4'15 for the version on the soundtrack.

Genesis and lyrics

In 1993, Bruce Springsteen received a phone call from Jonathan Demme, who was directing *Philadelphia*. The script, written by Ron Nyswaner, tells the tragic story of Andrew Beckett (played by Tom Hanks), a young gay lawyer who is fired for professional misconduct by Charles Wheeler (Jason Robards), the powerful director of a Philadelphia law form. Convinced his dismissal was actually due to his health—he is infected with the HIV virus—Beckett decides to sue Wheeler & Associates for wrongful termination. After many refusals, Joseph Miller (Denzel Washington), a hitherto homophobic, African-American lawyer, ultimately takes on his case.

Springsteen's studio was set up at his home in Rumson, New Jersey, and, over the course of a few afternoons, he worked on some lyrics that had already been partly written following the death of a close friend. A few days later, the song was ready, and the tape was sent to Jonathan Demme. "At night I could hear the blood in my veins/Just as black and whispering as the rain/On the streets of Philadelphia" and "The night has fallen, I'm lying awake/I can feel myself fading away." Bruce Springsteen's lyrics express with uncommon accuracy Andrew Beckett's desperation and loneliness in the face of an illness that would inevitably lead to his death.

Streets of Philadelphia was released on the *Greatest Hits* album-compilation and on the A-side of a 1994 single (with *If I Should Fall Behind* on the B-side). Springsteen believes that *Streets of Philadelphia* became a Top 10 hit as a result of the film and also because it deals with a sensitive topic that the country was trying to understand at the time. In fact, the song met with huge success in the United States, reaching No.9 in the *Billboard* charts, in March 1994, and winning four Grammy Awards ("Song of the Year," "Best Rock Song," "Best Vocal Rock Performance," and "Best Original Song Written for Visual Media"), as well as an Oscar for "Best Original Song." It did especially well in Europe, where it reached No.1 in the hit parades in France, Germany, Austria, and Norway, and No.2 in the United Kingdom. This worldwide recognition also stemmed from the video that Jonathan Demme had directed with his nephew Ted Demme (which features Bruce Springsteen walking along the streets of Philadelphia and includes several scenes from the feature film). It won "Best Video from a Film" at the MTV Video Music Awards.

Bruce Springsteen recorded the lead vocal and all the instruments for *Streets of Philadelphia*. Tommy Sims (above, at the Grammy Awards in 2010) provided backing vocals.

For a testosterone-fueled audience

Before reaching out to Springsteen, Jonathan Demme had asked Neil Young to write the music for his opening credits. The director had a particular rock song in mind, *Southern Man*, from the 1970 album *After the Gold Rush*. He wanted the Canadian to draw heavily on it, "'cause that will send such a strong, reassuring message to testosterone-fueled men, which is our target audience. It's like, 'Well if Neil's down with it,' you know?"[107] Three weeks later, he received a tape with the song *Philadelphia*. The director rushed to listen to it in his car with his wife. He couldn't hold back the tears as he listened to this beautiful and moving song. However, although he thought it was perfect for the ending credits, he didn't think it was strong enough for the introduction: he wanted a rock hymn. He immediately contacted Jon Landau, who'd already worked with him and Springsteen on the video for *If I Should Fall Behind* (*Lucky Town* in 1992). He repeated his request to Springsteen: "Would you consider maybe looking at the movie and seeing if you want to give us a rousing song to open the picture with?"[107] asked Demme. The Boss wrote it, and a few days later sent him the fruits of his labor. The director quickly went to listen to it, again with his wife and again in his car. He was deeply moved. However, it was not the rock song he'd been hoping for. Weary of his waffling, his wife intervened and ended up convincing him. "You know, it seems like these people trust your film more than you do. Why don't you just shut up about *Southern Man*?"[107]

Production

Writing a song for a film is a different process than it is for writing one for a record. Images, timing, style, and a slew of other parameters all come into play, each one more constraining than the other. Above all, one has to bend to the will of the director. So, when Jonathan Demme sent scenes from his film to Springsteen after failing to get what he wanted from Neil Young, he specified that he wanted a rock song, a guitar hymn, as explained above. "I spent a day or so trying to accommodate," explains the songwriter in his autobiography *Born to Run*. "But the lyrics I had seemed to resist being put to rock music. I began to fiddle with the synthesizer, playing over a light hip-hop beat I programmed on the drum machine. As soon as I slowed the rhythm down over some basic minor chords, the lyrics fell into place and the voice I was looking for came forward. I finished the song in a few hours and sent the tape off to Jonathan, feeling like I hadn't gotten it."[1] What happened next would prove him wrong.

A masterstroke

Springsteen's music is simple, refined, and, in his own words, "very linear, there's not a lot of musical development."[10] That's

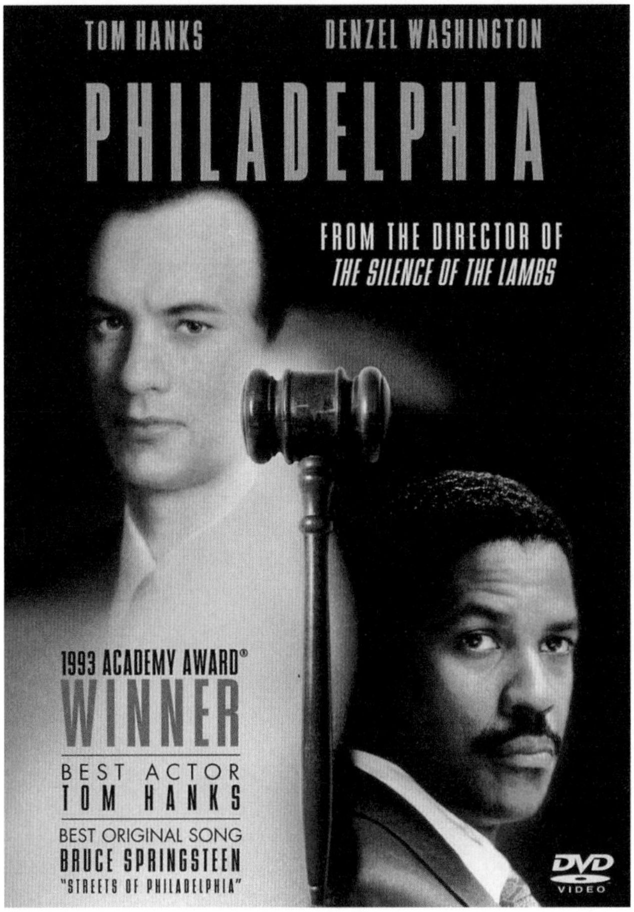

Poster for Jonathan Demme's feature-length film that won three Oscars, including "Best Original Song" for *Streets of Philadelphia* and "Best Male Rock Vocal Performance" for Bruce Springsteen.

For Springsteen Addicts

Neil Young's beautiful song, *Philadelphia*, was nominated for "Best Original Song" at the 66th Academy Awards ceremony, but it lost to Springsteen's *Streets of Philadelphia*.

THE FORGOTTEN

If anyone went completely unnoticed, it was the unfortunate composer of the film score for *Philadelphia*, who was a victim of the phenomenal success of the Boss's song. It's time to give him his due: it was composed by the very talented Howard Shore, who also wrote the music for Peter Jackson's *The Lord of the Rings* trilogy, among others.

exactly what makes it so powerful—the apparent simplicity fits the film and literally brings the scenes to life. *Streets of Philadelphia* starts with a drum pattern (LinnDrum, Roland SPD-8?). After four measures, a synthesizer floods the space with a majestic, soaring sound: likely the Yamaha CS-80, the same one used for *Born in the U.S.A*, even though, in some interviews, Springsteen speaks of a "little synthesizer." Some sources mention a Korg 01/W. A refined bass line accompanies him, providing minimal support. Springsteen built this song primarily around these three instruments, aside from the tambourine—which is heard in the distance after each verse—and other synth tracks that enrich the arrangements as the song advances (for example, at 1'13 and 1'53). Springsteen's lead vocals are magnificent. His voice is superb and charged with emotion. There is some disenchantment or fatalism in his voice, but also dignity. The Boss doesn't just sing, he embodies his character. Great art.

Back to the start

When Springsteen recorded this version at his home studio, in Los Angeles, in August 1993, he only thought of it as a draft. Chuck Plotkin then helped him rerecord it in a studio in a more conventional way, but they both soon realized that they wouldn't be able to replicate the magic of the demo. Of these lackluster attempts, only the voice of Tommy Sims—the bassist who accompanied Springsteen on his 1992–1993 World Tour—would make it onto the final version, added during the mid-October sessions that probably took place at A&M Studios in Los Angeles (his voice can be heard in the reverb toward 2'09 or 2'48). "That's the only thing that Bruce didn't actually do himself that survived,"[108] Plotkin would later confirm.

In addition to Tommy Sims, Little Jimmy Scott accompanies Springsteen in this final version, also providing backing vocals. What's even more surprising is the presence of free jazz saxophonist Ornette Coleman. This version would remain unreleased after being scrapped at the very last minute, in early December (a music video was even made for it with Little Jimmy Scott). There is a short extract of it in the film, toward 28'30, where Scott improvises on vocals (unfortunately, nothing of Ornette Coleman's made it through). In the end, the version the Boss recorded in his home studio in August was chosen for the film's official soundtrack. It can also be found on the *Music from the Motion Picture Philadelphia* compilation (which also contains songs by Peter Gabriel, Pauletta Washington, RAM, Sade, Spin Doctors, Indigo Girls, Maria Callas, Howard Shore, and, of course, Neil Young).

SECRET GARDEN

Bruce Springsteen / 4'27

Musicians
Bruce Springsteen: vocals, guitar
Patti Scialfa: vocal harmonies
Clarence Clemons: saxophone, triangle
Nils Lofgren: guitar
Roy Bittan: piano
Danny Federici: synthesizers
Garry Tallent: bass
Max Weinberg: drums
David Kahne: arrangements (EP)

Recording
The Hit Factory, 421 West 54th St, New York: January 1995
The Power Station, New York, 441 West 53rd St, New York: January 1995

Technical team
Producers: Bruce Springsteen, Jon Landau, Chuck Plotkin
Recording engineer: Toby Scott
Assistant recording engineers: Jeff Hendrickson, Zoë Yanakas

Mixing
The Hit Factory and Right Track, New York: January 1995
Recording engineer: Bob Clearmountain
Assistant recording engineers: Ryan Freeland, Jay Militscher, Tony Duino-Black
Mastering: Bob Ludwig

For Springsteen Addicts

Secret Garden is part of the original soundtrack for *Jerry Maguire* (1996), directed by Cameron Crowe and starring Tom Cruise and Renée Zellweger. It's also on the soundtrack for *A Night at the Roxbury* (1998), directed by John Fortenberry, and starring Steve Koren and Will Ferrell.

Genesis and lyrics

Bruce Springsteen reveals in his book *Songs* that he composed and recorded *Secret Garden* in 1994 for a solo album that never saw the light of day. The song then took its final shape the following year with the E Street Band. The songwriter is once again concerned with relationships between men and women, but this time, with a good dose of eroticism: "She'll let you in her mouth/If the words you say are right/If you pay the price/She'll let you deep inside." The imagery speaks volumes. The bottom line, however, is another: no one will ever venture into her secret garden. The point is that no couple will last unless each person retains a bit of mystery. The Boss would clarify this point in 1995, to Robert Hilburn of the *Los Angeles Times*: "I wrote it very quickly, one of my men-and-women [relationship] songs. It's about the unknowability of people in general. The [solo] record I was working on (last year) touched on that...how difficult it is to know even ourselves. We live with a very limited scope of our own identities unless we are pushed or pressed into moments when we surprise ourselves either pleasantly or shockingly in some fashion."[109]

Secret Garden was recorded during sessions for *Greatest Hits* and released as a single (with a live version of *Thunder Road* on the B-side) on 11 April 1995. It reached No.19 in the *Billboard* charts, No.17 in the United Kingdom, and even No.1 in Ireland. Two years later, Sony would release *Secret Garden*, again on CD, with *Missing, High Hopes, and The Ghost of Tom Joad.*

Production

Secret Garden is one of the best songs Bruce Springsteen ever wrote. It emits an incredibly delicate feeling, with a musical tone similar to the one in *Streets of Philadelphia*, due to the liberal use of synthesizers and simple and refined arrangements, despite the presence of the E Street Band. This was the first time the five musicians had gathered together in a studio, in this case Studio A at The Hit Factory, since recording *Born in the U.S.A* in 1984. Nils Lofgren and Patti Scialfa—who had not been part of the group in 1984—were also present now.

Danny Federici's synthesizer opens the song with a soaring introduction, complemented by Roy Bittan's airy piano chords, the deep bass of Garry Tallent, Max Weinberg's

The composer David Kahne did the string arrangements (on the EP) for *Secret Garden*.

Peter Care made a very good music video for *Secret Garden*, in Los Angeles, in March 1995. It stars a sublime vision of female beauty.

WITH OR WITHOUT CHORDS

Springsteen hesitated to include chord progressions in the recording for *Secret Garden*. He was worried they would overshadow his performance. It must be said that he asked the talented arranger and composer David Kahne to help him write the song. The result, played on the synthesizer, was sublime. He then put his decision to a vote, asking the musicians and Bob Clearmountain to weigh in, as seen in the documentary. Although rejected for *Greatest Hits*, these arrangements were added to the version released on the *Blood Brothers* EP in 1996 (with the mixing done by David Kahne and Michael Brauer).

rhythm (which he plays with the brushes), and the Boss's rhythm guitar, in this case his Gibson J-45. Built around four chords, this sequence expresses a strong sense of serenity and lightness that would later inspire other artists, such as Taylor Swift in *You Are in Love*, released in 2014 (on the Deluxe version of her album *1989*).

Springsteen seems to have borrowed a trick from *The Boys of Summer* by Don Henley—the singer and drummer for the Eagles—released in 1984 (on his LP *Building the Perfect Beast*). *Secret Garden* follows the same principle of using a synthesizer to run the same three notes on a loop. The effect is hypnotic. It contributes very much to the power of this wonderful song.

The songwriter sings with infinite emotion, sweetness, and even elegance. He almost whispers the words and sings in perfect harmony with his lyrics, which he never makes light of, despite the erotic tenor of certain phrases. Patti Scialfa's luminous voice supports him on the vocal harmonies. Nils Lofgren, on the lead guitar, accompanies him with delicate lines which he delivers by violining—a method of quickly raising the volume on the guitar to mimic the sound of a violin (for example, at 1'07 and 1'49). Clarence Clemons closes the song with a superb saxophone solo carried by a reverb and a lengthy delay (from 3'19). "You know," he explained in the 1996 documentary *Blood Brothers*. "A song like this, I just pick the horn up, I stand in front of the mike, and it comes out. You can make a plan. It's something that's been written many years ago, and it's just floating in the atmosphere. And it just comes together right now because the time is right, the rhythm is right, the harmonics are right, everything's right, and it just flows. You get that cosmic flow, and that's what's going to happen with the solo."[110]

MURDER INCORPORATED

Bruce Springsteen / 3'57

Musicians

Bruce Springsteen: vocals, guitar
Steve Van Zandt: guitar, backing vocals
Clarence Clemons: saxophone, cowbell (?), backing vocals
Roy Bittan: piano
Danny Federici: organ, backing vocals
Garry Tallent: bass, backing vocals
Max Weinberg: drums, backing vocals
The band: handclaps

Recording

The Power Station, 441 West 53rd St, New York: 3–4 May 1982

Technical team

Producers: Bruce Springsteen, Jon Landau, Chuck Plotkin, Steve Van Zandt
Recording engineer: Toby Scott
Assistant recording engineers: Jeff Hendrickson, Zoë Yanakas

Mixing

The Hit Factory 421 West 54th St, New York: January 1995
Right Track, New York: January 1995
Recording engineer: Bob Clearmountain
Assistant recording engineers: Ryan Freeland, Jay Militscher, Tony Duino-Black
Mastering: Bob Ludwig

THE BOOT IS ON THE OTHER FOOT

Jonathan Demme, who directed the music video for *Streets of Philadelphia*, shot a video for *Murder Incorporated* in February 1995 onstage at Tramps, in New York, before an audience of 300 people. The E Street Band was there in full for a very successful live performance. Little tidbit: as the director was filming, he was being filmed in turn by Ernie Fritz, which is how he ended up in the *Blood Brothers* documentary.

Genesis and lyrics

Murder Incorporated was recorded in 1982 during sessions for *Born in the U.S.A*, but it was cut from the tracklist in order to release it on the B-side of a single instead. It wasn't officially released until 1995, on *Greatest Hits* (even though bootleg versions kept fans busy during those 13 years).

Murder Incorporated is about Bobby, who's got "a gun that he keeps beneath his pillow" and "checks over [his] shoulder everywhere that [he goes]." He's a petty crook running from the criminal world he used to be a part of—the ubiquitous criminal world that even the police seem to tolerate. "It dealt with the paranoia and compounded violence of life in America," writes Springsteen in *Songs*. "Gated Communities, the loss of freedom, and the mistrust of your own neighbor are the price we pay for writing off generations of young people to poverty, drug dependency, and severely limited hopes and dreams."[6] *Murder Incorporated* is a dark take on 1980s America.

In an interview with French magazine *Rock & Roll*, Springsteen revealed why it took him so long to perform *Murder Incorporated* onstage: "During one of my tours, I have this very clear memory of a fan who followed us from town to town. He was always standing there, in the first row, with a big cardboard sign saying, 'Play Murder Inc.!' We actually never played it in public, but the image stayed with me, and I pulled it out at the last moment."[111]

Production

Murder Incorporated is a pretty atypical piece for Springsteen: it sounds more like British than American rock, despite its R&B backdrop. It contains a mix of different influences, including The Rolling Stones, the Kinks, and The Who. The songwriter would later explain that over the course of his career, he recorded a great many pastiches that remained in the form of outtakes: "It might be fun at some point to throw together some sort of collection of stuff like my attempts at other genres—from the bubblegum sort of thing to more pop-oriented material to the British Invasion things. We used to go in the studio [for example] and say, 'Tonight is Beatles night,' and we'd put things together that had all these influences either just for fun or because we thought they were going to work out at the time."[10] However, *Murder*

DETECTIVE DIVISION
CIRCULAR NO. 11
AUGUST 8, 1939

POLICE DEPARTMENT
CITY OF NEW YORK

CLASSIFICATION

$25,000 REWARD

DEAD OR ALIVE

TWENTY-FIVE THOUSAND DOLLARS will be paid by the City of New York for Information leading to the capture of "LEPKE" BUCHALTER, aliases LOUIS BUCHALTER, LOUIS BUCKHOUSE, LOUIS KAWAR, LOUIS KAUVAR, LOUIS COHEN, LOUIS SAFFER, LOUIS BRODSKY.

WANTED FOR CONSPIRACY AND EXTORTION

The Person or Persons who give Information Leading to the Arrest of "LEPKE" will be fully protected, his or her identity will never be revealed. The information will be received in absolute confidence.

RIGHT HAND

LEFT HAND

DESCRIPTION — Age, 42 years; white; Jewish; height, 5 feet, 5½ inches; weight, 170 pounds; build, medium; black hair; brown eyes; complexion dark; married, one son Harold, age about 18 years.

PECULARITIES—Eyes, piercing and shifting; nose, large, somewhat blunt at nostrils; ears, prominent and close to head; mouth, large, slight dimple left side; right-handed; suffering from kidney ailment.

Frequents baseball games.

Is wealthy; has connections with all important mobs in the United States. Involved in racketeering in Unions and Fur Industry, uses Strong-arm methods. Influential.

This Department holds indictment warrant charging Conspiracy and Extortion, issued by the Supreme Court, Extraordinary Special and Trial Terms, New York County.

Kindly search your Prison Records as this man may be serving a Prison sentence for some minor offense.

If located, arrest and hold as a fugitive and advise the THE DETECTIVE DIVISION, POLICE DEPARTMENT, NEW YORK CITY, by wire.

Information may be communicated in Person or by Telephone or Telegraph, Collect to the undersigned, or may be forwarded direct to the DETECTIVE DIVISION, POLICE DEPARTMENT, NEW YORK CITY.

LEWIS J. VALENTINE, Police Commissioner

TELEPHONE: SPring 7-3100, SPring 7-2722, SPring 7-1366 or CAnal 6-2000

515869

A 25,000-dollar reward, dead or alive, for Louis "Lepke" Buchalter, one of the heads of Murder Incorporated.

For Springsteen Addicts

Murder Incorporated is the name the American press gave to a 1930s Mafia organization known for internally punishing offending members of the Italian Mafia and the Yiddish Connection. It was led by the ruthless Louis "Lepke" Buchalter, Albert Anastasia, and Bugsy Siegel.

Incorporated is more than a simple nod to his British colleagues: the hand of Steve Van Zandt is noticeable, especially in the sound of the guitars in the intro (particularly "Stonian," from the *Aftermath* era of 1966), and in the choral parts.

The song opens with Max Weinberg's drums: he's alone on the bass drum and snare drum. Then Springsteen and "Little Steven" launch into the introductory chords, each on a 6-string guitar (Telecaster-Esquire for the former and likely an acoustic Gibson J-200 for the latter). The sound is both clear and "dirty." Then the whole group joins in against a backdrop of the Hammond B-3, handclaps, and a bass line. Springsteen sings the lead vocals in his rock and raspy voice which he records with the incredible intensity he's known for. Roy Bittan's piano shows up in the first refrain with a very tight sound and the feel of a tack piano (from 0'50, on the left). Clarence Clemons is also at hand with an excellent saxophone solo, again with his King Curtis-style phrasing (at 1'40). The Boss follows with a guitar solo that is simple, saturated, and aggressive, but incredibly effective (at 1'58).

The guitars in the introduction and the absolutely irresistible backing vocals (for example, at 3'09) are far and away the catchiest elements of this song. The entire group sings the vocals, except for Roy Bittan, bringing an undeniably British feel to the song. The result is a real success and makes *Murder Incorporated* a high-quality rock song. Nevertheless, the song did not make it onto the tracklist for *Born in the U.S.A*, no doubt because it was very different to the other songs on the album.

Once again, the live versions of the song are better than the studio version. This much is clear from the performance of 1 July 2000, the last in a series of ten concerts given at Madison Square Garden in New York. The musicians are fabulous, the three guitarists (Springsteen, Lofgren, and Van Zandt) each performing a memorable solo on their 6-string guitars. These versions are not to be missed, especially the one from the HBO concert film, or the DVD and CD *Bruce Springsteen and The E Street Band: Live In New York City* (released in 2001).

BLOOD BROTHERS

Bruce Springsteen / 4'34

Musicians

Bruce Springsteen: vocals, guitar, harmonica
Clarence Clemons: saxophone
Nils Lofgren: guitar
Roy Bittan: piano
Danny Federici: synthesizer, organ
Garry Tallent: bass
Max Weinberg: drums
Frank Pagano: percussion instruments

Recording

The Hit Factory, 421 West 54th St, New York: January 1995

Technical team

Producers: Bruce Springsteen, Jon Landau, Chuck Plotkin
Recording engineer: Toby Scott
Assistant recording engineers: Jeff Hendrickson, Zoë Yanakas

Mixing

The Hit Factory, 421 West 54th St, New York: January 1995
Right Track, New York: January 1995
Recording engineer: Bob Clearmountain
Assistant recording engineers: Ryan Freeland, Jay Militscher, Tony Duino-Black
Mastering: Bob Ludwig

For Springsteen Addicts

The EP version of *Blood Brothers* (released in March 1996) is radically different from the one on *Greatest Hits*: not only are there slight variations in the lyrics, but the music is also punchy rock, with Springsteen singing a slightly Celtic-sounding *a cappella* in the first verse. Meanwhile, Toby Scott did the mixing instead of Bob Clearmountain.

Genesis and lyrics

"I wrote *Blood Brothers* on the eve of recording with the E Street Band again," writes Springsteen in *Songs*. "The song is filled with the ambivalence and deep affection of revisiting a relationship spanning 25-plus years."[6] When he sings, "We stood side by side each one fighting for the other/And we said until we died we'd always be blood brothers," Springsteen is referring to, and also paying tribute to, the members of the E Street Band. He then sings, "I don't know why I made this call," meaning to the members of the group. In *Songs*, he explains himself by saying, "We walked into The Hit Factory, got behind our instruments, and had a great time."[6]

Production

As depicted in Ernie Fritz's documentary, *Blood Brothers* required a lot of work before it was considered finished. This was the song that reunited the group after many years of separation. The first sessions didn't meet the Boss's expectations. He called them "too hard."[110] The musicians had not yet found their bearings, but, after a few tries, they finally delivered the remarkable version found on *Greatest Hits*. The song was played and recorded live, as with all the other previously unreleased songs on this album. It starts with Springsteen alone on his guitar, the Gibson J-45, arpeggioing delicately with his pick. Max Weinberg marks the tempo with nothing but a hi-hat. The songwriter sings softly, radiating pure tenderness. Remarkably, he takes on the acoustic guitar, lead vocals, and the harmonica solos at the middle and end of the song by himself—without being phased in the least by the open mics and the running tape recorder.

Roy Bittan joins him on the piano after the first four verses. This incredible musician is just as good at playing rich and intense music as he is at pulling back to let a piece breathe. He applies this method in this song by supporting the harmony with simple and restrained chords. The other instruments enter in the second verse, bringing power and depth to the song. Garry Tallent and Max Weinberg's rhythmic section gives the piece its driving force, mainly due to the drummer's use of brushes. It seems that Danny Federici's keyboards and Nils Lofgren's guitar were later added as overdubs. In Ernie Fritz's documentary, the latter can be seen playing saturated chords on his electric guitar, which he controls with the

Bruce Springsteen, Max Weinberg, Garry Tallent, and Nils Lofgren performing at the Rock & Roll Hall Of Fame Induction Ceremony in 1995. *Blood Brothers* reunited the E Street Band.

volume knob. In the *Greatest Hits* version, he plays the rhythm with an added delay and a thumb tab. The same for Federici, who seems to be playing the Hammond B-3 synth pads on this album. His organ part doesn't come in until the last verse, from 2'43. The "C," as the songwriter affectionately called him, doesn't come in on the saxophone until the end of the song, with some delicate phrasing that seems to float above the harmony (at 3'15). Lastly, percussionist Frank Pagano, who's played with a considerable number of artists, including Blondie, Donald Fagen, Al Green, and The Smashing Pumpkins, adds to the song with a tambourine and güiro overdub (at 1'54 for the former and 3'29 for the latter). *Blood Brothers* is a terrific song, and Springsteen obviously could never have made it without the E Street Band. As he would later tell Neil Strauss of *Guitar World* in 1995 (for *Talk About a Dream*), "*Blood Brothers* was about trying to understand the meaning of friendship as you grow older."[10]

The recording of *This Hard Land* marked Steve Van Zandt's return to the E Street Band.

THIS HARD LAND

Bruce Springsteen / 4'50

Musicians
Bruce Springsteen: vocals, guitar, harmonica
Steve Van Zandt: mandolin
Nils Lofgren: guitar
Roy Bittan: piano
Danny Federici: organ, accordion
Garry Tallent: bass
Max Weinberg: drums
Frank Pagano: percussion instruments
Recording
The Hit Factory, 421 West 54th St, New York: January 1995
Technical team
Producers: Bruce Springsteen, Jon Landau, Chuck Plotkin
Recording engineer: Toby Scott
Assistant recording engineers: Jeff Hendrickson, Zoë Yanakas
Mixing
The Hit Factory, 421 West 54th St, New York: January 1995
Right Track, New York: January 1995
Recording engineer: Bob Clearmountain
Assistant recording engineers: Ryan Freeland, Jay Militscher, Tony Duino-Black
Mastering: Bob Ludwig

For Springsteen Addicts

Bruce Springsteen sings, "I can hear a tape deck blastin' Home on the Range," a song that is emblematic of the American West. It originated from *My Western Home*, a poem written by Dr Brewster M Higley, who'd settled in Kansas after the Homestead Act. It became Kansas' official anthem in 1947.

Genesis and lyrics

This Hard Land is about the daily challenges of down-and-out farmers in America. Frank, the narrator, says that he and his sister left Philadelphia's Germantown neighborhood for a new life, but all they found "way down south of the Rio Grande" was a "hard land," an arid land where "even the rain it don't come around" and where the wind is "slamming that back porch door." Then the sister starts talking. "Hey Frank, won't you pack your bags and meet me tonight down at Liberty Hall" (a 1771 Georgian building in Union, New Jersey, later turned into a museum). "We'll sleep in the fields, we'll sleep by the rivers," she continues. As Bruce Springsteen notes, the song is "about friendship and survival and ends the album with a shot of idealism."[6] It's about friendship, a bond between brother and sister.

An initial version of *This Hard Land* dates back to *Born in the U.S.A* sessions from 11 May 1982. It wasn't made at The Hit Factory in New York, as indicated on the *Tracks* box set (1998), but at The Power Station in New York. The version on *Greatest Hits* was recorded in January 1995.

Production

The 1982 version of *This Hard Land* is not unlike the 1995 version. The main difference lies perhaps in Springsteen's vocal power, which is much more impressive on *Greatest Hits*. There is also the conspicuous presence of Nils Lofgren, whose excellent slide guitar accompaniment brings a touch of rock to the song as he rests his instrument on his knees, as seen in Ernie Fritz's documentary. Danny Federici plays the organ and the accordion, blending in with the Boss' harmonica solos. But, above all, *This Hard Land* enabled the group to reunite with Steve Van Zandt, as Springsteen explains in his own words: "It had been 15 years, but a few nights later Steve sat on a stool in the studio with the same Groucho Marx-like, big-eyed, soft grin I'd loved and missed, plucking the mandolin for *This Hard Land*."[1] Clarence Clemons doesn't seem to have participated in this very nice folk-rock song. Frank Pagano is again on the tambourine and maracas.

TOM
GHOST

ALBUM

THE GHOST OF TOM JOAD

The Ghost of Tom Joad • Straight Time • Highway 29 • Youngstown • Sinaloa Cowboys • The Line • Balboa Park • Dry Lightning • The New Timer • Across the Border • Galveston Bay • My Best Was Never Good Enough

Outtakes: *Cynthia • Tiger Rose • I'm Turning Into Elvis • It's the Little Things That Count • Idiot's Delight • I'm Not Sleeping • 1945 • Cheap Motel • Dead Man Walkin' • Brothers Under the Bridge*

RELEASE DATE

United States: 21 November 1995

Reference: Columbia Records – CK 67484

No.1 in Denmark, No.4 in Norway, No.11 in the United States, No.16 in the United Kingdom

The poster for *Grapes of Wrath*, John Ford's masterpiece starring Henry Fonda.

Fifty-five years on, Springsteen brings John Steinbeck's character Tom Joad back to life.

A LOOK AT THE FORGOTTEN AMERICANS

Where was Bruce Springsteen in his life and career in the 1990s? He could be justifiably proud of the road that he had traveled since *Greetings from Asbury Park, N.J.*, *Born to Run*, and *Darkness on the Edge of Town*, followed by *Nebraska* and *Born in the U.S.A.*, all albums that had made him one of the most popular and talented artists on the rock scene. But the New Jersey songwriter had not forgotten where he came from. He had always felt an affinity with his fans, the blue-collar and farm workers who had helped him achieve fame and fortune, people like the Vietnam veterans, the bikers, the homeless, and the jailbirds, or "heavenly angels" (to borrow Jack Kerouac's term). In other words, the marginalized who, then as now, are excluded from the American dream.

This is the theme of his eleventh album. "*The Ghost of Tom Joad* was the result of a decade-long inner debate I'd been having with myself after the success of *Born in the U.S.A.*,"[1] Bruce Springsteen writes in his autobiography *Born to Run*. He continues: "Where does a rich man belong?"[1] To put it another way, what role should he play in a 1990s America that was experiencing profound change? While the title song explicitly refers to the main character in *The Grapes of Wrath*—John Steinbeck's cult novel about the disastrous consequences of the Great Depression, which was adapted for the big screen by John Ford in 1940 (the movie was Springsteen's real source of inspiration)—the themes that Springsteen develops in the other songs, such as deindustrialization, delocalization, and the resulting unemployment, as well as racism and the question of American identity, are both tragic and still highly relevant today. "*The Ghost of Tom Joad* chronicled the effects of the increasing economic division of the '80s and '90s,"[1] he writes. Taken as a whole, this is an album as dark and relentless as a Truman Capote or Jim Thompson novel. It offers no escape, neither through the sensual pleasures of love nor the exhilaration of speed on the highways.

"I'd pick up where I'd left off with *Nebraska*, set the stories in the mid-'90s and in the land of my current residence, California,"[1] Springsteen explains. *The Ghost of Tom Joad* is an album about contemporary America on the cusp of a new millennium. Musically, it is fairly similar to *Nebraska*. The songwriter's acoustic guitar and vocals are the predominant instruments and carry the dramatic narrative of the songs with deliberately simple melodies. There are two major differences to note: on some tracks, Springsteen is accompanied by a handful of musicians, including Danny Federici (keyboards), Garry Tallent (bass), Jim Hanson (bass), Jennifer Condos (bass), Gary Mallaber (drums), Marty Rifkin (pedal steel guitar), Patti Scialfa (backing vocals), Lisa Lowell (backing vocals), and Soozie Tyrell (backing vocals and violin), not forgetting Chuck Plotkin, who, unusually, plays the keyboards on one track. The album was recorded on a digital multitrack, which was a far cry from the modest Portastudio used for *Nebraska*. Both the lyrics and the music in *The Ghost of Tom Joad* are to Springsteen what *Dust Bowl Ballads* (1940) was for Woody Guthrie, or the first folk albums were for Bob Dylan (*The Freewheelin' Bob Dylan*, 1963, and *The Times They Are A Changin'*, 1964), namely "chronicles about forgotten Americans," as a sticker on the CD released in France states.

The album

Bruce Springsteen's eleventh original studio album was released on 21 November 1995, just nine months after *Greatest Hits*. "I'm convinced it's Springsteen's best album in ten years, and I also think it's among the bravest work that anyone has given us this decade,"[112] wrote Mikal Gilmore in *Rolling Stone* magazine.

Despite other very favorable reviews in the American press, *The Ghost of Tom Joad* only reached No.11 in the *Billboard* charts, although it sold 107,000 copies in the first week. Similarly, in the United Kingdom, it only reached No.16 (in November 1995), lagging way behind *(What's the Story) Morning Glory?* by Oasis, Pulp's *Different Class*, and *Stripped* by The Rolling Stones. Bruce Springsteen was not really surprised by this comparative commercial failure. As he explains in his book *Songs*, "I knew that *The Ghost of Tom Joad* wouldn't attract my largest audience. But I was sure the songs on it added up to be a reaffirmation of the best of what I do. The record was something new, but it was also a reference point to the things I tried to stand for and be about as a songwriter."[6] In fact, it was in Scandinavia, Denmark, and Norway, to be precise, that the album attracted the most fans, soaring to the No.1 and No.4 spots, respectively. In 1995, it won the *Grand Prix de l'Académie Charles Cros*, in France, and then two years later, the Grammy Award for "Best Contemporary Folk Album."

1995

The sleeve

Is it Bruce Springsteen transfigured or the ghost of John Steinbeck's hero on the cover of *The Ghost of Tom Joad*? It's a mystery. Eric Dinyer's spectral illustration, along with the typography chosen for the words "Bruce Springsteen" and "The Ghost of Tom Joad" are definitely disturbing. This is no invite into a dream world, but rather a journey into the heart of a postmodern America, where our guide will be the Ghost of Tom Joad, who has come back to show us where injustices still exist or have got worse. The booklet contains the song lyrics and black and white photographs of the songwriter taken by his sister, Pamela Springsteen.

The recording

For the first time since *Born to Run*, which was recorded 20 years earlier in 1975, Jon Landau was not involved in the production. He retained his role as manager, alongside Barbara Carr and Jan Stabile, but the album was produced by Springsteen and Chuck Plotkin. In the booklet, there is a warm acknowledgment of his contribution: "Thanks always to Jon Landau."

After the *Greatest Hits* episode and the short-lived reformation of the E Street Band in January 1995, the songwriter was once again following his muse, and over several months he wrote the equivalent of two albums. "I cut *The Ghost of Tom Joad* record while also cutting an entire album that was also a little more country-like at the same time," he said in

The folk singer Pete Seeger was a strong influence on Bruce Springsteen, especially for *The Ghost of Tom Joad* album.

Eric Dinyer's disturbing cover image for *The Ghost of Tom Joad.*

2014. "That became *Devils & Dust*. A lot of that album was cut alongside *Tom Joad*."[113] However, thus far very little information has filtered out about his writing and recording process; what we do know is that production took place from March to September, once again in his home studio at Thrill Hill West, in Los Angeles, with Toby Scott at the controls.

Springsteen explains in his autobiography that he and his family would spend the first six months of the year in New Jersey and the last six months in California. "It was during our California stay that I began to think about my new record. Working once again on my home equipment in our guesthouse, I began to record a variety of acoustic and country-rock songs I had recently written."[1] And, as mentioned above, he recorded some of the songs solo—an approach that he had developed a taste for since *Nebraska*—and others (five out of twelve) with the band, probably over two or three sessions between April and June. At the recordings, the musicians all played in the library, except for drummer Gary Mallaber (already present on *Lucky Town*), who was in a separate room connected to the others via video link. The guesthouse that had been converted into a recording studio (equipped with a Euphonix console, probably the CS2000) had excellent acoustics, partly due to its raised ceilings.

The approach to the mixing was different in the sense that Springsteen wanted to mix his songs as soon as they had been recorded, to retain as much of the spontaneity and raw aspect as possible. "That record was never really mastered," he explained to Brian Hiatt of *Rolling Stone* in 2016. "And we used the rough mixes we did on the day of the recordings and so it was never fucked with after that. It was this sort of very plain-sounding thing. But that's why the stories ring true on it. I didn't want to dress it at all, similar to *Nebraska*, you know. These were records that were made at the very moment the music was made."[115]

The easiest way to achieve this was to ask Toby Scott to do the mixing as well, particularly as he had already done so for the three songs on the *Blood Brothers* EP that emerged from the *Greatest Hits* sessions. The result is quite simply astonishing, with an extraordinary purity and quality that make this album a captivating sonic odyssey. The highly technical, polished work of Bob Clearmountain, who was once solely in charge of the mixing, was out. For the mastering, Bob Ludwig was replaced by Dave Collins at A&M Studios in Los Angeles.

For Springsteen Addicts

While Springsteen's recordings, at least until the 1990s, have always been considered average in sound quality, even today some audiophiles still use *The Ghost of Tom Joad* to test their audio equipment.

In the great tradition of folk singers, Bruce Springsteen glorifies noble losers in *The Ghost of Tom Joad.*

THE GHOST OF TOM JOAD

Bruce Springsteen / 4'23

Musicians

Bruce Springsteen: vocals, guitar, harmonica
Marty Rifkin: pedal steel guitar
Danny Federici: keyboard
Garry Tallent: bass
Gary Mallaber: drums

Recording and mixing

Thrill Hill West, Los Angeles, California: May 1995

Technical team

Producers: Bruce Springsteen, Chuck Plotkin
Recording engineer: Toby Scott
Assistant recording engineer: Greg Goldman
Mixing: Toby Scott
Mastering: Dave Collins (A&M Mastering Studios, Los Angeles)

After contributing to *Lucky Town*, Gary Mallaber, with his exceptional flair for drums, is back supporting Springsteen.

1995

Genesis and lyrics

Bruce Springsteen says that he composed *The Ghost of Tom Joad* for the *Greatest Hits* compilation with the E Street Band: "It started out as a rock song. But it didn't feel right, so I set it aside. I returned to it some months later, while still unsure of what I wanted to work on next."[6]

Here, Springsteen becomes the chronicler of 1990s America. He harshly criticizes the "new world order," namely the economic globalization spearheaded by the United States after the fall of the Berlin Wall and the end of the Cold War. While this invites comparisons with Woody Guthrie and Bob Dylan, who had both spoken out against injustices before him, Springsteen's main frame of reference was John Steinbeck, specifically John Ford's 1940 film adaptation of *The Grapes of Wrath*: "Yeah, that picture I guess I saw in the late '70s and it had a really deep effect on me," the songwriter explains. "I think I'd read some John Steinbeck, probably earlier than that, in high school, and there was something about the film that sort of crystallized the story for me. And it always stayed with me after that; there was something in that picture that always resonated throughout almost all of my other work. It was just an image that popped out as I was sitting around on the couch messing around with the guitar."[10]

Tom Joad (played on screen by Henry Fonda) is the main character in the film. A sharecropper on a small Oklahoma farm, Joad, along with his family, has been forced to leave for the West Coast due to the Dust Bowl (severe dust storms) that ruined the harvests. Exploited by the rich owners of orchards and cotton fields in California, he is wanted by the police for killing the murderer of his friend Jim Casy.

The "ghost of Tom Joad" reappears here half a century later, in a California where the living conditions of the underprivileged classes appear to have changed very little. This time, it is neither the Dust Bowl nor the Great Depression, but neoliberalism, as Bruce Springsteen sings, that has led to "Men walkin' 'long the railroad tracks" and "Families sleepin' in their cars in the Southwest/No home no job no peace no rest." The songwriter even evokes the "Preacher [who] lights up a butt and takes a drag/Waitin' for when the last shall be first and the first shall be last." (This is Jim Casy who, in Steinbeck's novel, is killed by the police and avenged by Tom Joad.) "Wherever somebody's strugglin' to

Springsteen and Tom Morello (from RATM) performing a spectacular version of *The Ghost of Tom Joad* at the Rock & Roll Hall of Fame Induction Ceremony in 2009.

For Springsteen Addicts

Bruce Springsteen sang *The Ghost of Tom Joad* with Tom Morello from Rage Against the Machine (there is a live recording), then again with the singer-guitarist of RATM for the *High Hopes* album (2014).

COVERS

There have been diverse cover versions of *The Ghost of Tom Joad*, notably by Rage Against the Machine (*Renegades*, 2000), Junip (*Black Refuge* EP, 2006), and Pete Seeger, alongside Springsteen himself (*Sowing the Seeds—The 10th Anniversary*, 2007).

be free/Look in their eyes Mom you'll see me"—words that paraphrase those written by Steinbeck.

The song was performed for the first time onstage at the Bridge School Benefit in Mountain View, California, on 28 October 1995, and then regularly as the opener to concerts on The Ghost of Tom Joad Tour (from 22 November 1995 to 26 May 1997). *The Ghost of Tom Joad* was released as a single in Europe (with a live version of *Straight Time* on the B-side).

Production

From the very first notes of *The Ghost of Tom Joad*, the listener is struck by the dense, contemplative, somber ambience emanating from the howl of the harmonica and from the Gibson J-45 that Springsteen fingerpicks as well as playing with a plectrum. In just a few seconds, this captures our full attention, and the story can begin. His voice is gentle and fragile, and it is reinforced by Toby Scott's superb sound recording as well as by the reverb and delay. It is hard to avoid drawing parallels with *Nebraska*, the opening track on the album of the same name: same ambience, same vocal performance, same howl of the harmonica. However, there is a marked difference: 13 years separate the two records, and Springsteen has matured massively.

The Ghost of Tom Joad is one of the five pieces that the Boss recorded with a band. When the four musicians come in at the second verse, the song suddenly takes on a majestic dimension. Garry Tallent and Danny Federici, who had been present for the recording of the previously unreleased tracks on *Greatest Hits* in January 1995, were once again called in, the first man on bass and the second providing the mellow pads on the keyboards. Gary Mallaber, the drummer on *Lucky Town*, was also brought in; Max Weinberg had initially been earmarked for these sessions, but was unavailable. Mallaber

is a fantastic drummer, and his contribution is outstanding, mostly using brushes to provide a subtle rhythm which, although further back in the mix, gives an incredible impression of speed and swing. Finally, Marty Rifkin, a new arrival in the Springsteen universe, delivers a great, nuanced performance on pedal steel guitar, which imperceptibly colors the arrangements (for example, at 1'16, on the left). This excellent musician, who has played for Tom Petty, Hans Zimmer, and Eric Clapton, to name but a few artists, later joined The Sessions Band that toured with the Boss in 2006.

The Ghost of Tom Joad is definitely one of Springsteen's best songs and also one of his biggest successes. It is excellently served by talented musicians as well as a remarkable sound recording.

Jim Hanson is an excellent bassist who has played with a diverse range of artists, including Vonda Shepard, Mark O'Connor, Rosanne Cash, and even Danny Federici, in 1997, on his album *Flemington*.

STRAIGHT TIME

Bruce Springsteen / 3'25

Musicians
- **Bruce Springsteen:** vocals, guitar
- **Marty Rifkin:** pedal steel guitar
- **Soozie Tyrell:** violin
- **Danny Federici:** keyboards
- **Jim Hanson:** bass
- **Gary Mallaber:** drums, percussion

Recording and Mixing
- **Thrill Hill West, Los Angeles, California:** April to June 1995

Technical team
- **Producers:** Bruce Springsteen, Chuck Plotkin
- **Recording engineer:** Toby Scott
- **Assistant recording engineer:** Greg Goldman
- **Mixing:** Toby Scott
- **Mastering:** Dave Collins (A&M Mastering Studios, Los Angeles)

Springsteen in acoustic mode in Rotterdam on 25 February 1996. *Straight Time* was the second song on the setlist.

1995

Genesis and lyrics

Once again, this song alludes to Tom Joad, the protagonist of *The Grapes of Wrath*, who, after being released from prison, heads westward to California along Route 66, in the hope of finding a better life. Charlie, the hero of *Straight Time*, is an ex-con. After eight years behind bars, he got out of prison in 1986 to walk the straight and narrow. He now has a wife and children, and has also found "a job at the rendering plant."

However, Charlie is only partially free because the life he's leading seems to weigh him down more each day. "Lay my head down on the pillow/And go driftin' off into foreign lands," the narrator confides. When he thinks of his recent past, he feels the itch. Especially as his uncle, who flouts the law and "makes his living runnin' hot cars," says to him, "Charlie you best remember who your friends are," as he slips him a hundred-dollar bill. Charlie is faced with a choice: sticking with a dead-end job and an honest life or going for the easy money, but a return to crime.

Production

Straight Time is one of the three songs, along with *Highway 29* and *The Ghost of Tom Joad*, that Springsteen wrote before he had decided on the tone of the album. And it was almost rejected: "I played it once, I put it away, and basically, I threw it away. And Jon [Landau] came out, and he has a tendency... he always asks my engineer, 'What's laying around that hasn't been played or I haven't heard?' I think my engineer pulled that one out, and [Jon] came back and said, 'Hey, wait a minute.'"[10] And that was how this superb ballad was saved in extremis from oblivion. Because *Straight Time* is a really subtle little gem: Springsteen's rendition is fantastic; Gary Mallaber delivers a barely audible, but extremely subtle, rhythm section with brushes and cabasa; Jim Hanson's bass is deep and sober; Danny Federici contributes mellow synth pads; Marty Rifkin colors the spaces with ghostly touches on the pedal steel guitar; and, right from the intro, Soozie Tyrell plays the violin with great finesse. *Straight Time*, or the communion between six musicians, their recording engineer, and a talented songwriter. Brilliant.

HIGHWAY 29

Bruce Springsteen / 3'39

Musicians
Bruce Springsteen: vocals, guitar, keyboard
Recording and mixing
Thrill Hill West, Los Angeles, California: March to September 1995
Technical team
Producers: Bruce Springsteen, Chuck Plotkin
Recording engineer: Toby Scott
Assistant recording engineer: Greg Goldman
Mixing: Toby Scott
Mastering: Dave Collins (A&M Mastering Studios, Los Angeles)

The Highway 29 in the song is California State Route 29 between Vallejo in San Francisco Bay and Upper Lake.

Bruce Springsteen surrounded by the American press in the mid-1990s, when he was at the height of his fame as a folk and rock singer.

Genesis and lyrics

"The ex-con of *Straight Time* became the shoe salesman of *Highway 29*,"[6] writes Bruce Springsteen in his book *Songs*. The characters in *The Ghost of Tom Joad* resemble one another: they are the dispossessed of American society in the 1990s, the unruly mob. In this particular case, the narrator's life changes dramatically after he meets a woman in a shoe store and gets on the wrong side of the law.

"My hand slipped up her skirt," and that is how it all began. He then robs "a small town bank" and there was "Money on the floorboards" and his "shirt was covered in blood." The woman "was cryin'" as they both fled the scene and holed up in a motel on Highway 29 on their way south to Sierra Madre in Mexico. It is an epic tale reminiscent of the novels of James M Cain (*The Postman Always Rings Twice*) and the bloody saga of Bonnie Parker and Clyde Barrow in the 1930s.

"I told myself it was all something in her/But as we drove I knew it was something in me." This is the key phrase in *Highway 29*. The young woman has simply been the trigger, so to speak: the character in this song turns to crime because he feels something pushing him deep down inside, the need to prove what he is really capable of. The end of the song lends itself to various interpretations. What is Springsteen suggesting when he mentions "a dream"? That the whole story is just a dream? Or that the character has simply imagined the young woman? Or has he imagined the bank robbery? Or the accident?

Production

Once again, with *Highway 29* Springsteen's amazing talent as a songwriter and composer stands out, alongside his outstanding ability as a performer. This is the first track on the album that he recorded entirely alone, at his home in Los Angeles. Accompanied only by fingerpicking on his Gibson J-45, his deeply moving vocals draw us into the story that unfolds like a film noir. He uses synth pads to add density to the atmosphere before the bridge (at 0'54), removing them in the last verse to emphasize the end of the tale, before bringing them back for the fade-out. Simple, but effective. Enhanced by Toby Scott's as-ever sublime recording, Springsteen commands respect.

YOUNGSTOWN

Bruce Springsteen / 3'52

For Springsteen Addicts
Springsteen wrote the preface for the 1996 edition of *Journey to Nowhere: The Saga of the New Underclass.*

Musicians
Bruce Springsteen: vocals, guitar
Marty Rifkin: pedal steel guitar
Soozie Tyrell: violin
Chuck Plotkin: keyboards
Jim Hanson: bass
Gary Mallaber: drums, percussion

Recording and mixing
Thrill Hill West, Los Angeles, California: April to June 1995

Technical team
Producers: Bruce Springsteen, Chuck Plotkin
Recording engineer: Toby Scott
Assistant recording engineer: Greg Goldman
Mixing: Toby Scott
Mastering: Dave Collins (A&M Mastering Studios, Los Angeles)

The book *Journey to Nowhere: The Saga of the New Underclass* inspired Bruce Springsteen when he wrote *Youngstown.*

1995

Genesis and lyrics

Bruce Springsteen had already composed all the songs for *The Ghost of Tom Joad* by the time he wrote *Youngstown* (and *The New Timer*); he then started reading the book *Journey to Nowhere: The Saga of the New Underclass*, in which the author Dale Maharidge and the photographer Michael Williamson show that neoliberalism and globalization inevitably lead to deindustrialization and the delocalization of companies, with the consequent risk of unemployment from which no social class is protected.

After coming home from Vietnam, the song's protagonist gets a job as a scarfer in a blast furnace in Youngstown, Ohio—a job that his daddy did before him and one "that'd suit the devil as well." It was tough work, but all for a good cause. In the mills "they built the tanks and bombs that won this country's wars." But times have changed. Youngstown, the heart of the American steel industry, fell into decline, with tens of thousands of workers laid off and abandoned to their fate.

Around the period of *The Ghost of Tom Joad*, Bruce Springsteen went to Youngstown and saw the devastation for himself and also the profound effect that the rise of the financial economy had had on the town. In his autobiography, Springsteen draws a parallel between Youngstown and his home town, Freehold, "[...] when the Karagheusian Rug Mill, based in Freehold, rather than settle a labor dispute with its workers, closed up shop and shipped south for cheaper, nonunionized labor."[1] And, as he says: "The jobs were gone."[1] He explains that his own musical life began and his first group, The Castiles, was formed a short distance away from the chimneys of the Karagheusian Rug Mill. So, it was perhaps a twist of fate that over 30 years later he found himself recording a song indirectly inspired by it.

Production

Youngstown begins with a single acoustic guitar and Springsteen's vocals. He strums his guitar and sings in a restrained voice. The atmosphere is austere and somber, and it's hard not to hear some similarity with *Turn the Page*, Bob Seger's superb song, which was released on his 1973 album *Back In '72*.

After the first chorus, the musicians suddenly come in, their instruments reinforcing the Appalachian ambience of

In *Journey to Nowhere: The Saga of the New Underclass*, the photographer Michael Williamson (on the left) and the author Dale Maharidge showed the devastating effects of neoliberalism on America.

the piece (from 0'43). This musical flavor is further emphasized by Soozie Tyrell's violin with its Gaelic intonations. "This is one of my favorite records," she explained. "Tears well every time I listen to it. Each song is like a novelette...so rich in storytelling yet so concise. The album takes me on a journey."[114] The rhythm section is provided by the excellent Gary Mallaber, once again using the drum brushes, and the equally talented Jim Hanson, on bass again after his contribution on *Straight Time*. This was the final bass line that Hanson played on the recording of *The Ghost of Tom Joad*. Marty Rifkin brings an indispensable country touch with his pedal steel guitar. For the first time on a recording, Chuck Plotkin swaps his producer hat for the keyboards, contributing synth pads alongside Tyrell's violin and Hanson's bass, producing a kind of drone effect that works really well.

Springsteen's rendition is typically dense and driven by an undeniable talent for storytelling. Although he has never experienced such situations himself, he manages to render the anguish of the characters in the song in an astonishingly convincing way. This is one of the songs that he sang alone, accompanying himself on guitar, at the Stambaugh Auditorium, in Youngstown, Ohio, on 12 January 1996, to an enthusiastic audience who gave him a standing ovation.

"My sweet Jenny I'm sinkin' down," Springsteen sings in the chorus. Sweet Jenny was the name of one of the furnaces in Youngstown, first commissioned in September 1918. It was named after Jeanette, the daughter of the president of the Brier Hill Steel Company. The furnace ceased operating in September 1977 and was demolished 20 years later.

SINALOA COWBOYS

Bruce Springsteen / 3'51

Musician
Bruce Springsteen: vocals, guitar, keyboard
Recording and mixing
Thrill Hill West, Los Angeles, California: March to September 1995
Technical team
Producers: Bruce Springsteen, Chuck Plotkin
Recording engineer: Toby Scott
Assistant recording engineer: Greg Goldman
Mixing: Toby Scott
Mastering: Dave Collins (A&M Mastering Studios, Los Angeles)

The methamphetamine that the two Mexican brothers are making is more potent than amphetamine. The drug is sold in various forms: crystals, capsules, tablets, and powder.

Mexicans attempting to cross the Rio Grande into the United States. This is the indirect theme of *Sinaloa Cowboys*.

1995

Genesis and lyrics

It was partly an article written by Mark Arax and Tom Gorman in the *Los Angeles Times*, on 13 March 1995, entitled "California's Illicit Farm Belt Export" and partly a chance encounter with two Mexicans in a small hotel on the California-Arizona border that gave Bruce Springsteen the idea for *Sinaloa Cowboys*. The song has a dual theme: drug-trafficking in California and the appalling living conditions of Mexican emigrants.

Sinaloa is a Mexican state on the Gulf of California, famous for one of the most powerful Mexican drug cartels, known as the Sinaloa (or Pacific) Cartel. In the song, Springsteen recounts the story of two Mexican brothers, Miguel and Luis, who have earned a few dollars picking fruit in the orchards of San Joaquin County in California. They are press-ganged into the Sinaloa Cartel and start making methamphetamine in a deserted ranch, work that is obviously far more lucrative than picking fruit. Then disaster strikes: Luis dies in an explosion in their tin shack. Miguel goes "To where the morning sunlight fell on a eucalyptus/There in the dirt he dug up ten thousand dollars all that they'd saved/Kissed his brother's lips and placed him in the grave."

Production

Sinaloa Cowboys was the second track on the album that was performed and recorded by Springsteen on his own, and it is a folk song in the pure tradition of the genre, despite the synth accompaniment, which gives it a texture more appropriate to its era. The Boss is alone on his acoustic Gibson J-45, which he strums as he sings in a gentle, melancholic voice. This song could not be more sober if it tried: apart from the 6-string and the synth pads that come in progressively from the second verse (from 0'54), no other instrument lends color to the arrangements, with the song built simply around three chords. It is reminiscent of Woody Guthrie or Bob Dylan. Nevertheless, by this stage of his career, Springsteen has an immediately recognizable musical language and identity that clearly distinguishes him from his predecessors.

THE LINE

Bruce Springsteen / 5'14

Musician
Bruce Springsteen: vocals, guitar, keyboard
Recording and mixing
Thrill Hill West, Los Angeles, California: March to September 1995
Technical team
Producers: Bruce Springsteen, Chuck Plotkin
Recording engineer: Toby Scott
Assistant recording engineer: Greg Goldman
Mixing: Toby Scott
Mastering: Dave Collins (A&M Mastering Studios, Los Angeles)

For Springsteen Addicts

Springsteen probably drew inspiration for this song from Tony Richardson's 1982 film *The Border*, starring Jack Nicholson. It is the story of a police officer who requests a transfer to the Mexican border where he finds himself having to deal with the problems of illegal immigration, and then ends up helping a young Mexican woman whose baby has been abducted.

HEADPHONES AT THE READY

Twelve seconds into the track, a plosive "p" can be heard in the first sentence of the song, a palpable popping sound in the microphone when the Boss sings the word "place."

Genesis and lyrics

It was more or less with the melody of Bob Dylan's *Love Minus Zero/No Limit* in mind that Bruce Springsteen wrote the story for *The Line*. The main character is an ex-soldier from Fort Irwin National Training Center in the Mojave Desert, California. Widowed the previous year, he now works for the Immigration and Naturalization Service. His job is to patrol the line, in other words the border between the United States and Mexico (in this particular case, between Baja California, in Mexico, and California in the United States) and to chase off anyone trying to enter the United States illegally, whether they are "Drug runners, farmers with their families, young women with little children by their sides." In other words, all the migrants who "risk death in the deserts and mountains," as Bobby Ramirez, another border guard with Mexican origins, tells him.

One day, in a migrant holding pen, the narrator spots a pretty Mexican woman, Louisa, who came from Sonora and had hair "as black as coal" with "a young child cryin' in her arms." He helps her and also her brother to join other family members in Madera County. Some time later, he decides to leave the line and go in search of his Louisa.

If there's a moral to this song, it could be that love is stronger than duty. It is a song that is still highly topical decades later.

Production

The Line is one of the songs that Springsteen recorded independently in his Los Angeles studio. He sticks to his preferred arrangements, strumming his Gibson J-45 and heightening the drama of his story with synth pads (mixed a bit further forward in each successive verse, before disappearing entirely in the last verse, then reappearing in the coda). His lead vocal has the same gentle, fragile, and intimate tone as the previous songs on the album. The emotional impact of his vocals is incredibly powerful and magnetic, and it's hard not to get swept away by them. However, it has to be said that the live versions of *The Line* are probably even more intense than the studio version, if only because no synthesizers are used, something that since the start of the album has become almost too systematic.

BALBOA PARK

Bruce Springsteen / 3'19

Musician
Bruce Springsteen: vocals, guitar, keyboard
Recording and mixing
Thrill Hill West, Los Angeles, California: March to September 1995
Technical team
Producers: Bruce Springsteen, Chuck Plotkin
Recording engineer: Toby Scott
Assistant recording engineer: Greg Goldman
Mixing: Toby Scott
Mastering: Dave Collins (A&M Mastering Studios, Los Angeles)

Balboa Park was created in 1868 and is one of the oldest parks in San Diego, California. It is named after the Spanish conquistador Vasco Núñez de Balboa. There is also a Balboa Park in San Francisco.

An article by the journalist Sebastian Rotella (here, in 2016) inspired Springsteen to write *Balbao Park*.

1995

Genesis and lyrics

As with *Sinaloa Cowboys*, *Balboa Park* was inspired by an article in the *Los Angeles Times* written by journalist Sebastian Rotella on 3 April 1993: *Children of the Border: Caught in a Makeshift Life—Immigrant Youths eke out a living in San Diego's Balboa Park. Drugs, prostitution are means of survival.* The title already says a great deal about the living conditions of Mexican migrants.

Here, Springsteen points the spotlight at a young Mexican, The Spider, a native of the Zona Norte (one of the dangerous neighborhoods in Tijuana), who prostitutes himself in Balboa Park for a few dollars that he either sends to his family or uses to buy high-top sneakers and jeans. His clients are well-off men in their Mercedes. The rest of the time, he hides in a shelter "'cross the train tracks [...] 'neath the freeway" to avoid the border patrol. But sometimes that's not enough, especially when the border patrol sweeps Twelfth Street. One night, Little Spider is hit by a car and drags himself limping back to his hiding place. He then lay "there tasting his own blood on his tongue, closed his eyes and listened to the cars rushing by so fast."

Production

Springsteen approaches *Balboa Park* almost like a recital. His voice is close to a whisper and his tone disillusioned. He plays delicate arpeggios on the guitar, supported from the intro by a very discreet synth pad. A second synth comes in to reinforce the harmony from the end of the first verse and, like all the other tracks that he recorded solo, these are the only accompanying instruments. But the result is magnificent, the emotional power of this austere, sober rendition being captivating. One might wonder about the songwriter's state of mind during the production of *Tom Joad*, as the overall atmosphere is neither light nor joyful. His chronic depression probably contributed significantly to the feel of this extraordinary album, but clearly this was to its advantage.

DRY LIGHTNING

Bruce Springsteen / 3'30

Musicians
Bruce Springsteen: vocals, guitar
Danny Federici: keyboards
Soozie Tyrell: violin
Garry Tallent: bass
Gary Mallaber: drums, percussion
Recording and mixing
Thrill Hill West, Los Angeles, California: April to June 1995
Technical team
Producers: Bruce Springsteen, Chuck Plotkin
Recording engineer: Toby Scott
Assistant recording engineer: Greg Goldman
Mixing: Toby Scott
Mastering: Dave Collins (A&M Mastering Studios, Los Angeles)

The violinist Soozie Tyrell. Her successful collaboration with Bruce Springsteen began on *Lucky Town* in 1992 and continues to this day.

Genesis and lyrics

With *Dry Lightning*, Bruce Springsteen sets aside for a moment the social dimension that is predominant in the lyrics of other songs on *The Ghost of Tom Joad* to tell the tale of a lost love. The narrator has not forgotten the woman that he loved and still loves. "I chased the heat of her blood like it was the Holy Grail/Descend beautiful spirit into the evening pale." These few words seem to imply that he has raised his sweetheart to the status of a goddess. In the fifth verse, we find out that the young woman dances in clubs on Alvarado Street to make ends meet. "Ain't nobody can give nobody what they really need," she says.

However, the narrator is still under the spell of this enigmatic and fatalistic dancer, who is probably also a hostess, saying: "But I can't lose your memory and the sweet smell of your skin." He is totally enamored. Hence his immense sadness. The metaphor in the chorus explains it perfectly: "Just dry lightning and you on my mind." The obvious interpretation here is that his pain is so unbearable that he cannot even shed tears.

Production

Dry Lightning reunites Springsteen with his musicians, who provide invaluable and elegant support. However, with the exception of Danny Federici's synth pads in the second verse (at 1'05), they only come in halfway through the song, after the second verse (from 1'58). From that moment, they bring an undeniable depth to the song, which is sometimes lacking on some of the other tracks. The rhythm section comprising Gary Mallaber and Garry Tallent—once again on bass—is incredibly graceful with a subtle groove, as are the violin contributions (two tracks, from 2'33) from Soozie Tyrell. Springsteen handles rhythm and solo guitar (on the left, from the intro), which are both played on his Gibson J-45.

Similarities in the melody inevitably bring to mind *Jersey Girl* by Tom Waits, but that doesn't detract from the fact that *Dry Lightning* is one of the album's successes. Willie Nelson certainly picked right when he recorded a cover version as a duet with Emmylou Harris in 2013 for his album *To All the Girls*.

> **HEADPHONES AT THE READY**
> In the final verse, Springsteen's voice sticks slightly on two occasions: on the word "my" at 5'10 and then again on "sorry" immediately after (at 5'18). But these minor discordant notes in no way detract from the extraordinary quality of his rendition; on the contrary, they are proof of his unique authenticity.

THE NEW TIMER

Bruce Springsteen / 5'45

Musician
Bruce Springsteen: vocals, guitar
Recording and mixing
Thrill Hill West, Los Angeles, California: March to September 1995
Technical team
Producers: Bruce Springsteen, Chuck Plotkin
Recording engineer: Toby Scott
Assistant recording engineer: Greg Goldman
Mixing: Toby Scott
Mastering: Dave Collins (A&M Mastering Studios, Los Angeles)

Bruce Springsteen during the Ghost of Tom Joad Tour. He performed *The New Timer* onstage for the first time at Berkeley on 30 November 1995.

1995

Genesis and lyrics

The New Timer shares the same origins as *Youngstown*, namely the book *Journey to Nowhere: The Saga of the New Underclass* by Dale Maharidge and Michael Williamson. The narrator is a casualty of the iron law of wages in a globalized world. He tells us that he has "Left [his] family in Pennsylvania, searching for work [...] in East Texas." It is there that he meets Frank, who has led the life of a hobo since the Great Depression of the 1930s. The narrator continues his story, or rather his journey, across America "From New Mexico Colorado/California to the sea." He has worked in the sugar beet fields outside Firebaugh and, like Tom Joad in John Steinbeck's novel, in the orchards of Marysville. But he is crushed more by the impossibility of seeing his wife and son than his appalling working conditions. And then there's Frank, who is found shot dead in the muddy hills of Stockton, California. Jesus' gracious love and mercy could do nothing this time to fill the narrator's heart. The final mission for the hero of *The New Timer* (like Tom Joad before him) is to kill Frank's murderer.

Bruce Springsteen performed *The New Timer* for the first time onstage at a concert at the Berkeley Community Theater, on 30 November 1995, but has since only performed it around 20 times.

Production

At around 5'50, *The New Timer* is the longest song on the album, but also the starkest. Springsteen does not even record keyboard pads here, as he has generally done elsewhere. This time, only his Gibson J-45 accompanies his lead vocal, although there is a second guitar track that can be heard quite far back in the mix, on the right of the stereo, starting in the third verse (at 1'04). Once again, Woody Guthrie comes to mind, as does the song *Nebraska*. One thing is clear: It is all a far cry from the Wall of Sound in *Born to Run*. Like a Zen master, Springsteen has divested himself of everything superfluous and kept just the essentials.

Springsteen performed *The New Timer* on his 2005 concert tour, accompanying himself on autoharp rather than acoustic guitar. The first performance took place on 12 October 2005 at the Northrop Auditorium in Minneapolis, Minnesota. Well worth a listen.

ACROSS THE BORDER

Bruce Springsteen / 5'24

Jennifer Condos began her career as the bassist for the Chicano rock group Tito & Tarantula, and then went on to work with a diverse range of musicians from Stevie Nicks to Ray LaMontagne, Sam Phillips, Jackson Browne, and Graham Nash, among many others.

Musicians

Bruce Springsteen: vocals, guitar, harmonica
Marty Rifkin: pedal steel guitar
Soozie Tyrell: violin, backing vocals
Danny Federici: keyboard, accordion
Jennifer Condos: bass
Gary Mallaber: drums
Patti Scialfa, Lisa Lowell: backing vocals

Recording and mixing

Thrill Hill West, Los Angeles, California: April to June 1995

Technical team

Producers: Bruce Springsteen, Chuck Plotkin
Recording engineer: Toby Scott
Assistant recording engineer: Greg Goldman
Mixing: Toby Scott
Mastering: Dave Collins (A&M Mastering Studios, Los Angeles)

Linda Ronstadt and Emmylou Harris (here, in 2019) recorded a cover version of *Across the Border* in 1999 for their superb album *Western Wall: The Tucson Sessions.*

Genesis and lyrics

Bruce Springsteen explains that he wrote *Across the Border* "like a prayer or dream you have the night before you're going to take a dangerous journey."[6] He adds: "The singer seeks a home where his love will be rewarded, his faith restored, where a tenuous peace and hope maybe exist."[6]

The main character in *Across the Border* is Mexican. He and his wife are preparing to cross the border illegally. They are the "wetbacks" who attempt to cross the Rio Bravo (or Rio Grande) in the hope of a better life in the US of A. "For you I'll build a house high upon a grassy hill," he tells his wife. "I'll kiss the sorrow from your eyes." God is with them and they have the blessing and grace of the saints. On the other side of the Rio Bravo are the American states of Texas and New Mexico, the promised land, or so they hope, a place where migrants can live.

Perhaps *Across the Border* should also be seen as a metaphor, where it is understood that the narrator is preparing for a very long journey. The river would then symbolize the journey from life to death, and the other side of the border would be heaven. But that's just speculation.

Production

Across the Border is the last song on *The Ghost of Tom Joad* that Springsteen recorded with the band. The first four verses are played on acoustic guitar, with the songwriter singing extremely softly. For the first time on this album, his tone is light and calm. The musicians come in at the fifth verse: Gary Mallaber plays drums, once again with his brushes; Jennifer Condos, a new recruit, is on bass; Marty Rifkin brings color to the harmony with his pedal steel guitar; and Danny Federici handles the synth pads. After a first harmonica solo from the Boss (at 1'56), the E Street Band keyboardist records a graceful accompaniment on accordion. Then it's over to Soozie Tyrell who lays down multiple violin tracks (around ten) that originally were not all going to be kept. But Springsteen decided otherwise, and so a wave of violins engulfs the song, creating an entertaining phasing effect (listen from 2'47). Finally, Soozie Tyrell adds her vocal harmonies alongside Patti Scialfa and Lisa Lowell (at 3'53). This wonderful song ends with a combination of harmonica, violin, and backing vocals (from 3'40).

GALVESTON BAY

Bruce Springsteen / 5'04

Musician
Bruce Springsteen: vocals, guitar, keyboard
Recording and mixing
Thrill Hill West, Los Angeles, California: March to September 1995
Technical team
Producers: Bruce Springsteen, Chuck Plotkin
Recording engineer: Toby Scott
Assistant recording engineer: Greg Goldman
Mixing: Toby Scott
Mastering: Dave Collins (A&M Mastering Studios, Los Angeles)

The events at Galveston Bay are also the theme of *Alamo Bay*, a 1985 film directed by Louis Malle, starring Amy Madigan and Ed Harris, with a soundtrack by Ry Cooder.

Members of the Klu Klux Klan burn a cross to intimidate the black community. Racism lies at the heart of the song *Galveston Bay*.

1995

Genesis and lyrics

Galveston Bay is inspired by a bloody incident that plunged Texas into mourning in the early 1980s. As a tragic consequence of the American withdrawal from Vietnam and the triumphant entry of the communists in Saigon, many southern Vietnamese quit their homeland for various countries (the United States, France, Canada, and Australia). Around 30,000 of them settled along the Gulf of Mexico where they took up shrimp fishing; this infuriated the Texans, who accused the new immigrants of not respecting the basic rules of fishing. Racial tensions grew in the early 1970s when several Vietnamese boats were set ablaze in Galveston Bay and, more particularly, when two Vietnamese who had killed a Texan fisherman were acquitted by a jury on the grounds of self-defense. Some of the more extremist Texans turned to the Ku Klux Klan, who organized a major anti-migrant rally. The lawyer and human rights activist Morris Dees defended the Vietnamese Fishermen's Association and called for an end to the Klan's intimidation. Dees wrote about these tragic events in detail in his book *A Season for Justice* (1991).

Springsteen appears to have used this as the basis for *Galveston Bay*. He tells the tale of a southern Vietnamese man who saved up and bought a shrimp boat, and the Texan Billy Sutter, who fought in Vietnam before returning home to work the coast on his father's fishing boat. "I wanted a character who is driven to do the wrong thing, but does not,"[6] Springsteen explains in his book *Songs*. "He instinctively refuses to add to the violence in the world around him. With great difficulty and against his own grain he transcends his circumstances."[6]

Production

Springsteen uses the same instrumentation for *Galveston Bay* as the other solo recordings on the album, namely his Gibson acoustic J-45 and synth pads to reinforce the harmony (from 1'17). His lead vocal therefore comes to the forefront and resonates with palpable force and emotion, making for a unique and captivating performance. We may sometimes regret that his musicians do not accompany him more often on this album, but the result is nevertheless magnificent.

MY BEST WAS NEVER GOOD ENOUGH

Bruce Springsteen / 2'00

Could there be a nod to *Forrest Gump* here? The expressions "Now life's like a box of chocolates, you never know what you're going to get" and "Stupid is as stupid does" are taken from the 1994 cult film directed by Robert Zemeckis, with Tom Hanks in the title role.

Musician

Bruce Springsteen: vocals, guitar, keyboard

Recording and mixing

Thrill Hill West, Los Angeles, California: March to September 1995

Technical team

Producers: Bruce Springsteen, Chuck Plotkin
Recording engineer: Toby Scott
Assistant recording engineer: Greg Goldman
Mixing: Toby Scott
Mastering: Dave Collins (A&M Mastering Studios, Los Angeles)

Jim Thompson, cat-lover and writer of dark crime novels. His protagonist Inspector Lou Ford is back on the case in *My Best Was Never Good Enough*

Genesis and lyrics

In *Songs*, Springsteen explains that the main character in *My Best Was Never Good Enough* was inspired by the sheriff in *The Killer Inside Me*, by noir author Jim Thompson. In Thompson's book, Lou Ford is deputy sheriff in Central City, a small town in Texas. At first glance, he is a good man who respects the law and wants others to do the same. In actual fact, he is a total psychopath who, despite being in a relationship with a young woman, pursues a sadomasochistic relationship with a prostitute. We later discover that Ford once raped a girl, a crime for which he accused his own brother in order to avoid prison.

Like Lou Ford, the character in *My Best Was Never Good Enough* has few illusions about the world and those who live in it, and even fewer about the woman with whom he shares his life. This is seen in the title of the song and in all the hackneyed clichés throughout the lyrics: "A quitter never wins," "the early bird catches the fuckin' worm," "Rome wasn't built in a day," and so on.

Production

The Ghost of Tom Joad closes on *My Best Was Never Good Enough,* the last song that Springsteen recorded alone in his Los Angeles studio. At just two minutes long, it is also the shortest track on the album. It was originally planned as the B-side of a future single, but the Boss decided otherwise at the last minute.

Rather than simply sticking to acoustic guitar and synth pads, as he does for the other solo songs, here Springsteen adds an innovative touch right from the intro—a high-pitched, percussive counterpoint played on a second synth.

On vocals, his tone remains restrained and intimate, with sections that are more spoken than sung, but the dark drama of most of his other songs gives way to a more light-hearted and carefree attitude. A way of ending the album on a lighter note. However, the song is probably the least successful piece on the album and perhaps—without overstating it—the roughest and least well mixed.

TRACKS

BOX SET

TRACKS

Disc 1: Mary Queen of Arkansas • It's Hard to Be a Saint in the City • Growin' Up • Does This Bus Stop at 82nd Street? • Bishop Danced • Santa Ana • Seaside Bar Song • Zero and Blind Terry • Linda Let Me Be the One • Thundercrack • Rendezvous • Give the Girl a Kiss • Iceman • Bring on the Night • So Young and in Love • Hearts of Stone • Don't Look Back

Disc 2: Restless Nights • A Good Man is Hard to Find (Pittsburgh) • Roulette • Dollhouse • Where the Bands Are • Loose Ends • Living on the Edge of the World • Wages of Sin • Take 'Em As They Come • Be True • Ricky Wants a Man of Her Own • I Wanna Be with You • Mary Lou • Stolen Car • Born in the U.S.A. • Johnny Bye-Bye • Shut Out the Light

Disc 3: Cynthia • My Love Will Not Let You Down • This Hard Land • Frankie • TV Movie • Stand On It • Lion's Den • Car Wash • Rockaway the Days • Brothers Under the Bridges ('83) • Man at the Top • Pink Cadillac • Two for the Road • Janey Don't You Lose Heart • When You Need Me • The Wish • The Honeymooners • Lucky Man

Disc 4: Leavin' Train • Seven Angels • Gave It a Name • Sad Eyes • My Lover Man • Over the Rise • When the Lights Go Out • Loose Change • Trouble in Paradise • Happy • Part Man, Part Monkey • Goin' Cali • Back in Your Arms • Brothers Under the Bridge

RELEASE DATE

United States: 10 November 1998

Reference: Columbia Records – CXK69475

No.27 in the United States, No.50 in the United Kingdom

Springsteen's *Tracks* offers a new musical journey along the highways and byways of his three-decade-long career.

A BOX SET AS JOURNEY

It was about time someone opened the Boss's and E Street Band's Pandora's Box. Bruce Springsteen came up with the idea for *Tracks* after realizing how many songs he'd written that had never made it onto an album—almost 250. With the help of recording engineer Toby Scott, he began to gather all the material at his disposal, mostly unreleased songs but also live performances, demos, alternative versions, and B-sides from singles. "So it began just with that idea and we listened to about 250 songs, maybe more," he explained. "I made quick notes in a notebook and put it away."[10]

Springsteen then moved on to other projects, such as the Tom Joad Tour and the writing of new songs. The future *Tracks* box set became yesterday's news. But, one fine day, he finally decided to devote some time to it, and with the much-needed help of Chuck Plotkin, he revisited his archives and began a more drastic selection process, ending up with some 100 songs. He was delighted with the result, as the songs fitted in nicely with each other. He asked Jon Landau for his opinion. "Yes it's great," said Landau, "but I think it needs to be mixed."[10] The songwriter was flabbergasted. "'Mixed,' I said, 'Oh my God, there are 100 mixes or 80 mixes, has anybody ever done 80 mixes?' We had, like, two months to go [before submitting the tape]. I said, 'It will just screw the whole thing, let's just not bother.'"[10] However, a mix was attempted on a B-side of a single and the result surprised Springsteen. "It just sounded a lot better, had more focus and impact."[10] So, he decided to mix all 80 songs. But how to pull this off in such a short amount of time? The answer came swiftly: "Charlie [Plotkin] came in and we had three studios going at once: we had a studio in the other room, a truck out in the yard, and we had Bob Clearmountain on the phone—there was a system where he can mix in California and it just plays out your stereo speakers just like you were sitting in the studio! That's basically how the things got mixed. There was a fella named Ed Thacker who took the rough mixes, basically remained very true to that [basic] sound picture and enhanced it greatly."[10]

1998

Released on 10 November 1998, more than three years after *Greatest Hits*, *Tracks* is a superb box set, almost like a four-CD and 66-song invitation to visit Bruce Springsteen's country. The journey starts at the beginning of the songwriter's career: it covers the years from 1972 to 1980, including song demos, his first masterpiece, *Greetings from Asbury Park, N.J.*, and goes all the way up to *Rendez-Vous*, which was recorded live in Nassau, in the Bahamas, on 31 December 1980. The journey continues with outtakes from *The River*, *Born in the U.S.A.*, and *Nebraska*. Then come other outtakes from *Born in the U.S.A.*, followed by outtakes from *Tunnel of Love* recorded in 1987. The final stage gathers outtakes from *Human Touch* and *Lucky Town* as well as *Brothers under the Bridge*, an outtake from *The Ghost of Tom Joad* from the spring of 1995.

Tracks comes with a booklet full of song lyrics, some beautiful pictures, and various pieces of valuable information (musicians, studios, recording dates, and so on). However, its success doesn't compare to that of the original albums, as the box set would only reach No.27 and No.50 in the United States (where it would be certified gold anyway) and the United Kingdom, respectively.

The following year, on 13 April 1999 exactly, Columbia Records would pitch a variation of *Tracks*: a CD with 18 songs, 15 of which would come from the box set and three would be the previously unreleased *Trouble River* (an outtake from *Human Touch*), *The Fever*, and *The Promise*. This CD, understandably titled *18 Tracks*, would reach No.64 in the United States and No.23 in the United Kingdom.

Some of the songs that feature on *Tracks* have already been discussed elsewhere in the book, either on original albums or compilations, or even as singles. Here, we look more closely at a few unpublished songs.

For Springsteen Addicts

One period was not covered by *Tracks*: that of the recording of *Greetings from Asbury Park, N.J.*, which was released in 1973. This is because a related legal dispute (see page 102) had not yet been resolved ahead of the box set's production.

BISHOP DANCED

Bruce Springsteen / 4:18

Musicians: Bruce Springsteen: vocals, guitar, harmonica / Danny Federici: accordion **Recording:** Max's Kansas City (live), New York: 19 February 1973 **Technical team:** producer: Bruce Springsteen (?) / recording engineer: Thom Panunzio (mixing)

Bishop Danced was recorded onstage at the famous New York club, Max's Kansas City, on 19 February 1973. During a different performance in Berkeley on 2 March 1973, Bruce Springsteen revealed that it was "a song about a bishop, his wife, and a violin player in West Virginia, how they lost their daughter to mathematics while on a business trip in Detroit."[125] The comment was followed by widespread laughter and British-style banter, but the song is also a tribute to the pioneers of old-time music of the Appalachian tradition.

The ambience of *Bishop Danced* is acoustic, with the Boss on the lead vocals, harmonica, and the 6-string guitar, joined only by Danny Federici on the accordion, including with a solo (at 2'01).

SANTA ANA

Bruce Springsteen / 4'35

Musicians: Bruce Springsteen: vocals, guitars / David Sancious: piano / Danny Federici: organ / Garry Tallent: bass / Vini "Mad Dog" Lopez: drums **Recording:** 914 Sound Recording Studios, Blauvelt, New York State: 28 June 1973 **Technical Team:** producers: Mike Appel, Jim Cretecos / recording engineers: Louis Lahav, Ed Thacker (mixing)

Written in the winter of 1972–1973, *Santa Ana*, which is also known as *My Contessa* and *The Guns of Kid Cole*, was recorded during sessions for *The Wild, the Innocent, and the E Street Shuffle*. The song's title refers to Mexican general Antonio López de Santa Ana, who defeated Texas at the Alamo (23 February to 6 March 1863), and to Sam Houston, a key figure in Texan history for leading the Texan revolution against Mexico in the 1830s. Springsteen had the idea for the song after traveling to Mexico with his father. Of note: Bruce Springsteen later reused the lines: "French cream won't soften those boots" and "Baby French kisses will not break your heart" in *She's the One* (on the *Born to Run* album). Musically, the Boss plays several acoustic and electric guitar parts, using a Leslie cabinet for one of them.

SEASIDE BAR SONG

Bruce Springsteen / 3'33

Musicians: Bruce Springsteen: vocals, guitars / Clarence Clemons: saxophone, cowbell, backing vocals (?) / David Sancious: piano (?) / Danny Federici: organ / Garry Tallent: bass, backing vocals (?) / Vini "Mad Dog" Lopez: drums **Recording:** 914 Sound Recording Studios, Blauvelt, New York State: 28 June 1973 **Technical team:** producers: Mike Appel, Jim Cretecos / recording engineers: Louis Lahav, Ed Thacker (mixing)

Also known as *Coupe De Luxe*, *Seaside Bar Song* is another outtake from *The Wild, the Innocent, and the E Street Shuffle*. It embodies the universe of the young songwriter from New Jersey: pretty girls with long hair falling down their backs, Chevrolets and Cadillacs, the road, space, freedom, and Bo Diddley. However, the song lacks musical tone; it's more of a prototype, as if Springsteen were about to develop it more with the Farfisa, Telecaster, and saxophone. Bruce Springsteen performed *Seaside Bar Song* some 20 times between 1973 and 2014. The French rock group Little Bob Story covered it for a single released in 1978.

Bruce Springsteen in New Jersey in 1973, the year that some of the songs on the *Tracks* box set were recorded.

ZERO AND BLIND TERRY

Bruce Springsteen / 5'58

Musicians: Bruce Springsteen: vocals, guitars / Clarence Clemons: saxophone, backing vocals (?) / David Sancious: piano / Danny Federici: organ, backing vocals (?) / Garry Tallent: bass, backing vocals (?) / Vini "Mad Dog" Lopez: drums / Suki Lahav: vocals **Recording:** 914 Sound Recording Studios, Blauvelt, New York State: 28 June 1973 **Technical team:** producers: Mike Appel, Jim Cretecos / recording engineers: Louis Lahav, Ed Thacker (mixing)

In all likelihood, this song was written in June 1973 before being discarded during the tracklist selection for *The Wild, the Innocent, and the E Street Shuffle. Zero and Blind Terry* debuted onstage at Max's Kansas City, in New York, on 18 July 1973. With New York as a backdrop, this song tells the story of a love between Terry and a bad boy named Zero, the leader of a gang known as the Pythons. The father of the young woman is far from happy about this. The title of the song, on the other hand, pleased Bruce Springsteen, who even considered it as a possible album title. The songwriter recycled the melody from *Phantoms*, an outtake from the same album. Of note: Suki Lahav's voice comes in at 2'19, even though her name does not appear in the credits for *Tracks*.

LINDA LET ME BE THE ONE

Bruce Springsteen / 4'24

Musicians: Bruce Springsteen: vocals, guitar / Clarence Clemons: saxophone, tambourine, backing vocals (?) / Roy Bittan: piano / Danny Federici: organ / Garry Tallent: bass / Max Weinberg: drums **Recording:** The Record Plant, New York: 28 June 1975 **Technical team:** producer: Bruce Springsteen, Jon Landau / recording engineer: Jimmy Iovine, Ed Thacker (mixing)

Linda Let Me Be the One has a strange story. Recorded for *Born to Run*, then scrapped, this song didn't reach Bruce Springsteen's fans until *Tracks* was released, and it wasn't performed onstage until 29 April 2014! The melody is a real success, just like the improbable love story between Eddie, the bad boy, and Linda. Eddie is so in love that he sneaks into Linda's room in the dead of night and throws himself at her feet, crying: "will you let me be the one?" Springsteen's sound is well established at this point—though Mike Appel hated the song, which explains his absence from *Born to Run*—notably with Clarence Clemons's omnipresent saxophone, Roy Bittan's piano, Danny Federici's organ, and Max Weinberg's drums, not to mention the Boss's unique voice.

THUNDERCRACK

Bruce Springsteen / 8'25

Musicians: Bruce Springsteen: vocals, guitars / Clarence Clemons: saxophone / David Sancious: piano / Danny Federici: organ / Garry Tallent: bass / Vini "Mad Dog" Lopez: drums / The group: backing vocals **Recording:** 914 Sound Recording Studios, Blauvelt, New York State: 28 June 1973 **Technical team:** producers: Mike Appel, Jim Cretecos / recording engineers: Louis Lahav, Ed Thacker (mixing)

Written in 1972, then developed during the first sessions for *The Wild, the Innocent, and the E Street Shuffle*, *Thundercrack* was later meant for *Born to Run*. It was then retracted as well, since it only came out on the *Tracks* box set.

It's the story of a young woman who loves a man as much as he can take, but who loves dancing even more. "She's got the heart of a ballerina" straight out of the Bronx.

Bruce Springsteen started playing this song in 1973 and again in 1974, then he rehashed it in 2001, notably for the Devils & Dust Tour (2005), playing it alone on the piano. Before *Rosalita* came along, this piece was one of the high points of his early shows. In fact, it's rather extraordinary, with some wonderful choral parts, an excellent rhythmic guitar section, a spirited Telecaster-Esquire solo, a powerful funk rhythm played by Vini Lopez and Garry Tallent, some very rhythm and soul keyboards, and a superb performance from Clarence Clemons. Lasting more than eight minutes, this song is a must. Of note: the Boss called Vini Lopez in to complete the backing vocals for *Tracks*. They'd remained unfinished since 1973!

RENDEZVOUS

Bruce Springsteen / 2'48

Musicians: Bruce Springsteen: vocals, guitar / Clarence Clemons: backing vocals, tambourine / Steve Van Zandt: guitar, backing vocals / Roy Bittan: piano / Danny Federici: glockenspiel / Garry Tallent: bass / Max Weinberg: drums **Recording:** The Record Plant Mobile, Los Angeles, California: 31 December 1980 **Technical team:** producer: Bruce Springsteen, Jon Landau, Mike Appel / recording engineers: Toby Scott, Ed Thacker (mixing)

Bruce Springsteen recorded *Rendezvous* during sessions for *Darkness on the Edge of Town*. Although discarded from the album, it inspired an initial adaptation by The Greg Kihn Band (for the album *With the Naked Eye*, in 1979) and another by Gary US Bonds (for the album *On the Line*, in 1982). For *Tracks*, Bruce Springsteen chose the live version—recorded in 1980 on the evening of Saint-Sylvester—over the studio version, which is on the *The Promise* box set. "I had a dream our love would last forever." This is the first line of the song (the word "rendezvous," in English-speaking countries implies a lovers' rendezvous). Musically, it's a Springsteen-style rock song, with a glockenspiel, a wall of guitars, and a dash of pop. It's a shame there's no Clarence Clemons solo.

GIVE THE GIRL A KISS

Bruce Springsteen / 3'51

Musicians: Bruce Springsteen: vocals, guitar / Clarence Clemons: saxophone, backing vocals / Steve Van Zandt: guitar, backing vocals / Roy Bittan: piano, keyboards / Danny Federici: organ / Garry Tallent: bass / Max Weinberg: drums / Eddie Manion: baritone saxophone / Mark Pender, Mike Spengler: trumpet /Richie "La Bamba" Rosenberg: trombone / Jerry Vivino: tenor saxophone **Recording:** The Record Plant, New York: 10 November 1977 **Technical team:** producers: Bruce Springsteen, Jon Landau / recording engineers: Jimmy Iovine, Bob Clearmountain (mixing)

Bruce Springsteen recorded this song at the Record Plant, in New York, on 10 November 1977 (a contested date), then he set it aside or even forgot about it until he started working on *Tracks*. He only performed it onstage four times, the first at the Convention Hall in Asbury Park on 19 March 1999.

It's a romantic song about the need to declare one's love. Recorded during sessions for *Darkness on the Edge of Town, Give the Girl a Kiss* clashes with the general ambience of the album, which is rather dark. It's an R&B-tinged rock song, a bit in the style of Randy Newman, with Hammond B-3 and Telecaster-Esquire solos. Brass overdubs played by the Horns of Love were added in 1998 for *Tracks*, Jerry Vivino—from the Max Weinberg 7—having replaced Mario Cruz.

ICEMAN

Bruce Springsteen / 3'17

Musicians: Bruce Springsteen: vocals, guitar / Steve Van Zandt: guitar / Roy Bittan: piano, keyboards / Danny Federici: glockenspiel / Garry Tallent: bass / Max Weinberg: drums **Recording:** The Record Plant, New York: 27 October 1977 **Technical team:** producers: Bruce Springsteen, Jon Landau / recording engineers: Jimmy Iovine, Thom Panunzio (mixing)

Iceman is another song that Bruce Springsteen recorded in 1977, at the time of *Darkness on the Edge of Town*, and that, like *Give the Girl a Kiss*, he'd forgotten about until Bob Benjamin made him listen to several bootlegs during the initial track selection for *Tracks*: one of them was *Iceman*, whose character seems to be in deep despair, making him feel like an iceman.

Also known as *The New Ballad*, this pretty song could very well have been part of the tracklisting for *Darkness*. Roy

Bittan's piano stands out, as do Danny Federici's glockenspiels and Garry Tallent's superb bass line. It seems that Bittan also gave the synth pads some brassy sounds.

BRING ON THE NIGHT

Bruce Springsteen / 2'36

Musicians: Bruce Springsteen: vocals, guitar / Clarence Clemons: saxophone, tambourine / Steve Van Zandt: guitar / Roy Bittan: piano, keyboards / Danny Federici: organ / Garry Tallent: bass / Max Weinberg: drums **Recording:** The Power Station, New York: 13 June 1979 **Technical team:** producers: Bruce Springsteen, Jon Landau / recording engineers: Neil Dorfsman, Ed Thacker (mixing)

Recorded in 1979, but scrapped during the song selection for *The River, Bring on the Night* remained locked away until *Tracks*. It has also never been performed onstage. The narrator is literally obsessed with a young woman called Mary, who always appears to him in a dream. It even goes beyond obsession, to the point where he eagerly awaits nighttime so that he can be with Mary again.

It's important to note that this is the only reference, in Bruce Springsteen's words, to 1970s disco. But the song has nothing to do with disco: it's more of a rock song with saxophone and Farfisa organ solos.

Of note: *Bring on the Night* is also the name of a song by The Police.

SO YOUNG AND IN LOVE

Bruce Springsteen / 3'47

Musicians: Bruce Springsteen: vocals, guitar / Clarence Clemons: saxophone / Roy Bittan: piano, keyboards / Danny Federici: organ / Garry Tallent: bass / Max Weinberg: drums / The group: backing vocals **Recording:** 914 Sound Recording Studios, Blauvelt, New York State: 1974 **Technical team:** producers: Bruce Springsteen, Jon Landau / recording engineers: Louis Lahav, Ed Thacker (mixing)

This song is a reinterpretation of *A Love So Fine* by the Chiffons. Bruce Springsteen regularly performed the latter between September 1974 and September 1975, then *So Young and in Love* some 15 times between 2000 and 2013. Teenage emotions loom large in this soulful song. The songwriter reused the line "Rat traps filled with soul crusaders" from *Night* (on *Born to Run*).

The *Tracks* booklet places the recording date at 6 June 1974 at the Record Plant, which is wrong, since this furious rock song was more likely recorded in October 1974 with an uninhibited Clarence Clemons and two brand-new members of the E Street Band, Max Weinberg and Roy Bittan.

HEARTS OF STONE

Bruce Springsteen / 4'29

Musicians: Bruce Springsteen: vocals, guitar / Clarence Clemons: saxophone / Steve Van Zandt: guitar, backing vocals / Roy Bittan: piano, keyboards / Danny Federici: organ / Garry Tallent: bass / Max Weinberg: drums / Mario Cruz: tenor saxophone / Eddie Manion: baritone saxophone / Mark Pender, Mike Spengler: trumpet / Richie "La Bamba" Rosenberg: trombone **Recording:** The Record Plant, New York: 14 October 1977 **Technical team:** producers: Bruce Springsteen, Jon Landau / recording engineers: Jimmy Iovine, Bob Clearmountain (mixing)

Audiences learned of this song thanks to Southside Johnny and The Asbury Jukes, who recorded it during sessions for their third album, *Hearts of Stone* (1978). Bruce Springsteen's version likely dates to 14 October 1977, but it didn't come out until 1998 on *Tracks*. This failing emotional relationship between two hearts of stone is carried by Clarence Clemons's excellent saxophone solo, which is supported by the very good arrangements played by the Horns of Love brass section, added in 1998 for *Tracks*. As for the Boss, he excels in this type of slow blues.

DON'T LOOK BACK

Bruce Springsteen / 3'00

Musicians: Bruce Springsteen: vocals, guitar / Steve Van Zandt: guitar / Roy Bittan: piano / Danny Federici: organ, glockenspiel / Garry Tallent: bass / Max Weinberg: drums **Recording:** Atlantic Studios, New York: 2 July 1977 / The Record Plant, New York: February to March 1978 (?) **Technical team:** producers: Bruce Springsteen, Jon Landau / recording engineers: Jimmy Iovine, Chuck Plotkin (mixing)

Don't Look Back was recorded on 2 July 1977. It was even included in promotional material for *Darkness on the Edge of Town* before Bruce Springsteen decided to drop it at the last moment. Although he performed it onstage in San Francisco on 26 November 1988, the public heard it for the first time on disc thanks to the Los Angeles-based group The Knack, who included it on their album *One Step Up/Two Steps Back: The Songs of Bruce Springsteen*. "There's nothing to lose, it's a heartbreak, the deck's stacked," the narrator says to a woman. He tells her not to look back—in other words, to live in the moment.

Once again, the booklet's information is incorrect. The group didn't record the song on 2 July 1977 at the Record Plant, as indicated, but at Atlantic Studios in New York. However, it was no doubt finished at the Record Plant in early 1978.

This is a good-quality, energetic rock song, but it lacked the power and originality of the other *Darkness* songs.

1998

Photo of the Boss taken on 17 October 1979 at his home in Holmdel, New Jersey.

RESTLESS NIGHTS

Bruce Springsteen / 3'44

Musicians: Bruce Springsteen: vocals, guitar / Steve Van Zandt: guitar, backing vocals / Roy Bittan: piano, keyboards / Danny Federici: organ / Garry Tallent: bass / Max Weinberg: drums **Recording:** The Power Station, New York: 11 April 1980 **Technical team:** producers: Bruce Springsteen, Jon Landau, Steve Van Zandt / recording engineers: Neil Dorfsman, Ed Thacker (mixing)

Restless Nights was one of the many songs Bruce Springsteen wrote for *The Ties That Bind*, which became a double album called *The River*, but later scrapped. Bruce Springsteen and the E Street Band recorded it on 11 April 1980. In this nostalgic song, the narrator compares the present day to the happy days of yore: "Now outside the streets are gray and the childhood games we played/Faded away."

Restless Nights opens Disc 2 of *Tracks*, but it also appears on Disc 4 of *The Ties That Bind: The River Collection* box set, released in 2015. This medium rock song is an excellent piece, with superb backing vocals—no doubt a collaboration between Springsteen and Steve Van Zandt—two blazing Farfisa organ and lead guitar solos, and a remarkable performance by the Boss.

A GOOD MAN IS HARD TO FIND (PITTSBURGH)

Bruce Springsteen / 3'15

Musicians: Bruce Springsteen: vocals, guitar / Clarence Clemons: percussion instruments / Roy Bittan: piano / Danny Federici: organ / Garry Tallent: bass / Max Weinberg: drums **Recording:** The Power Station, New York: 5 May 1982 **Technical team:** producers: Bruce Springsteen, Jon Landau, Chuck Plotkin, Steve Van Zandt / recording engineers: Toby Scott, Ed Thacker (mixing)

While its musical tone is close to *The River*, *A Good Man is Hard to Find (Pittsburgh)* dates back to the first sessions for *Born in the U.S.A.* It's another song about the Vietnam War, in which a young woman from Pittsburgh thinks about her husband who is deployed in combat. A photo sits by the bed: "Him in his dress greens her in her wedding white" and now there's "a little girl asleep in the back room." Bruce Springsteen wrote *A Good Man is Hard to Find (Pittsburgh)* after reading *Born on the 4th of July* by Ron Kovic and seeing the movie *Who'll Stop the Rain* (1978) by Karel Reisz, starring Nick Nolte.

This very pretty country-rock song highlights the Telecaster-Esquire and the Boss's voice—which lacks accuracy in some places—with its characteristic grit. Although four names appear in the production credits, the song resembles a demo rather than a completed song. Of note: Clarence Clemons was probably on the bongos.

DOLLHOUSE

Bruce Springsteen / 3'31

Musicians: Bruce Springsteen: vocals, guitar / Steve Van Zandt: guitar, backing vocals / Clarence Clemons: saxophone, backing vocals / Roy Bittan: piano / Danny Federici: glockenspiel / Garry Tallent: bass / Max Weinberg: drums **Recording:** The Power Station, New York: 21 August 1979 **Technical team:** producers: Bruce Springsteen, Jon Landau, Steve Van Zandt / recording engineers: Neil Dorfsman, Ed Thacker (mixing)

Dollhouse is an outtake from *The River* and dates to August 1978. The narrator is talking to his partner, who behaves as if the years haven't passed. She continues to play games, setting rules to fit her own little world. The narrator starts to think that he's just another one of her toys. And wonders: is their love real? What he sees is all the sadness of the world on the face of the woman he loves as her dollhouse continues to crumble.

Springsteen starts this song as a nursey rhyme on the glockenspiel and piano before diving into a powerful rock led by Max Weinberg and Garry Tallent's very effective rhythmic section. Clarence Clemons dials up the heat with an incandescent sax solo. As for the Boss, his lead vocals are simply superb: it's a veritable lesson in rock music.

The E Street Band in 1979. Standing, left to right: Max Weinberg, Roy Bittan, Clarence Clemons, Steve Van Zandt, and Garry Tallent. Sitting: Danny Federici and the Boss.

WHERE THE BANDS ARE

Bruce Springsteen / 3'43

Musicians: Bruce Springsteen: vocals, guitar / Steve Van Zandt: guitar / Clarence Clemons: saxophone / Garry Tallent: bass / Max Weinberg: drums / The group: backing vocals **Recording:** The Power Station, New York: 9 October 1979 **Technical team:** producers: Bruce Springsteen, Jon Landau, Steve Van Zandt / recording engineers: Neil Dorfsman, Ed Thacker (mixing)

Bruce Springsteen scrapped *Where the Bands Are* from *The River* tracklist, which didn't prevent him from playing it onstage several times between 1999 and 2012. The E Street Band and their fans shine in this song—"I wanna be where the bands are"—with full-on rock 'n' roll energy. The song also resembles *Dollhouse*: having exactly the same energy, the same vocal power (still not very accurate, however), the same blazing sax solo, and, as a bonus, a superb guitar solo by Steve Van Zandt and some supercharged backing vocals.

LOOSE ENDS

Bruce Springsteen / 4'04

Musicians: Bruce Springsteen: vocals, guitar / Steve Van Zandt: guitar, backing vocals / Clarence Clemons: saxophone, tambourine, handbells, backing vocals / Roy Bittan: piano / Danny Federici: organ / Garry Tallent: bass / Max Weinberg: drums **Recording:** The Power Station, New York: 18 July 1979 **Technical team:** producers: Bruce Springsteen, Jon Landau, Steve Van Zandt / recording engineers: Neil Dorfsman, Ed Thacker (mixing)

Bruce Springsteen wanted to close *The Ties That Bind* with *Loose Ends* (originally spelled without an "s"), which was recorded in July 1979. Then he scrapped it from *The River* (against Steve Van Zandt's advice), perhaps because the theme of this song—a failing love story—had already been widely covered by the New Jersey songwriter. *Loose Ends* is a rock song in the mold of *Born to Run*. The musical dynamic is similar, as are the arrangements. It contains numerous percussion parts, notably the handbells in the style of Brian Wilson (a superfan of Phil Spector and his Wall of Sound, see page 69). Only the glockenspiels are missing. The work on the backing vocals and on the Boss's voice is excellent.

LIVING ON THE EDGE OF THE WORLD

Bruce Springsteen / 4'17

Musicians: Bruce Springsteen: vocals, guitar, harmonica / Steve Van Zandt: guitar, backing vocals / Clarence Clemons: tambourine, backing vocals / Roy Bittan: keyboards (?) / Danny Federici: organ / Garry Tallent: bass / Max Weinberg: drums / The group: claps **Recording:** The Power Station, New York: 7 December 1979 **Technical team:** producers: Bruce Springsteen, Jon Landau, Steve Van Zandt / recording engineers: Neil Dorfsman, Ed Thacker (mixing)

Living on the edge means to live dangerously. In this song, recorded at the time of *The River*, the expression applies to the economic situation in the United States. "New Jersey in the morning like a lunar landscape," sings Bruce Springsteen in the second verse. But it also reflects the narrator's day-to-day life. He's at the wheel of his car trying to get back to the woman he loves. Gospel and rock songs are playing on the radio. This song paved the way for *Nebraska*, especially *Open All Night*, at least for some of the lyrics. Musically, it's a rock song with a distinctly punk dynamism, dominated by guitars, the Farfisa organ, and some excellent backing vocals. As a bonus, Springsteen performs a very good harmonica solo.

WAGES OF SIN

Bruce Springsteen / 4'51

Musicians: Bruce Springsteen: vocals, guitar / Clarence Clemons: percussion instruments / Roy Bittan: piano, synthesizer (?) / Danny

Federici: glockenspiel, synthesizer (?) / Garry Tallent: bass / Max Weinberg: drums **Recording:** The Power Station, New York: 10 May 1982 **Technical team:** producers: Bruce Springsteen, Jon Landau, Chuck Plotkin, Steve Van Zandt / recording engineers: Toby Scott, Ed Thacker (mixing)

Wages of Sin is an outtake from *Born in the U.S.A.* (the first electronic version of the album). It's one of the many songs Bruce Springsteen had forgotten about, at least until *Tracks*. "What happens is very often you have your own personal sensitivities about a particular piece of music or you may be uncomfortable with the way you've sung or what the song is about and you steer away from that a little bit," the songwriter told *Billboard*. "I think that's what happened on that one."[145] Sinful wages are a reference to the letter Saint Paul the Apostle wrote to the Romans: "For the wages of sin is death: but the gift of God is eternal life through Jesus Christ our Lord."

This beautiful and nostalgic song opens with a superb acoustic Telecaster-Esquire intro, supported by delicate drumming primarily played on Max Weinberg's tom-tom drum. Congas, a synth, glockenspiels, and a piano complete the arrangements, which also include Garry Tallent's subtle bass line and the songwriter's phenomenal performance. *Wages of Sin* is a gem plucked from oblivion.

RICKY WANTS A MAN OF HER OWN

Bruce Springsteen / 2'44

Musicians: Bruce Springsteen: vocals, guitar / Steve Van Zandt: guitar, backing vocals / Clarence Clemons: tambourine, backing vocals (?) / Roy Bittan: piano / Danny Federici: orgue / Garry Tallent: bass / Max Weinberg: drums **Recording:** The Power Station, New York: 16 July 1979 **Technical team:** producers: Bruce Springsteen, Jon Landau, Steve Van Zandt / recording engineers: Neil Dorfsman, Ed Thacker (mixing)

Ricky Wants a Man of Her Own also dates back to the prolific era of *The River*. It's about Ricky, a teenager who has grown up and wants her independence, but her parents still think of her as their little girl. It's the eternal generational conflict, especially since the songwriter used his own sister Pamela as inspiration.

Yet another mistake in the *Tracks* booklet: the song was recorded in 1979, not in 1977. The Boss composed a light pop-rock song that is unpretentious, but delightful. Danny Federici's Farfisa and Steve Van Zandt's vocal harmonies came out particularly well, and the piece as a whole is supported by the excellent Weinberg-Tallent team.

I WANNA BE WITH YOU

Bruce Springsteen / 3'21

Musicians
Bruce Springsteen: vocals, guitar
Steve Van Zandt: guitar, backing vocals (?)
Clarence Clemons: saxophone, backing vocals (?)
Roy Bittan: keyboards
Danny Federici: organ
Garry Tallent: bass
Max Weinberg: drums

Recording
The Power Station, New York: 31 May 1979

Technical team
Producers: Bruce Springsteen, Jon Landau, Steve Van Zandt
Recording engineer: Neil Dorfsman
Mixing: Ed Thacker

First performance in Belgium of *I Wanna Be With You*, on 27 May 1999, with Nils Lofgren who is not on the studio version.

1998

Genesis and lyrics

Bruce Springsteen wrote *I Wanna Be with You* in the late 1970s. There are several versions of this song, the first of which was recorded at Atlantic Studios, in New York, on 1 June 1977. The fifth and last recording, created during the sessions for *Darkness on the Edge of Town*, is the only one to have made it into Bruce Springsteen's official discography with the release of the *Tracks* box set in 1998.

The story is as old as history. A man falls hopelessly in love with a woman. He sings: "That's every day, every night/I wanna be with you." The narrator is so head over heels in love that he's willing to do anything to win over the woman of his dreams and fantasies, the one he obsesses over, which he can't even explain, since she's not even that pretty. The consequences soon catch up with him: he loses his job at the gas station and earns a bad reputation that he just can't shake off. But he doesn't care. The world can fall apart as long as he's with the woman he loves.

I Wanna Be with You came out as a single in Europe and Japan a year after the release of *Tracks*, but without making the charts. To this day, Bruce Springsteen has performed it onstage some 15 times, the first time in Milan, Italy, on 20 April 1999.

Production

Springsteen and his band had a hard time recording *I Wanna Be with You*. In addition to the first versions made in 1977 (one in July and the other in September)—although excellent—other versions were recorded in May 1979 and again a month later, but with less satisfying results.

The Boss starts off the piece with a loud countdown enhanced by a pronounced slapback echo. Vigorously strummed guitar chords ring out in the style of garage rock. Then enter the piano, organ, and drums. Springsteen then launches into the lead vocals with power and euphoria, supported by the E Street Band at its best, especially by the superb bass line of Gary Tallent. The choruses are harmonized with two voices (Litte Steven?) and the backing vocals respond to the songwriter (for example, at 1'00). Clarence Clemons is also present, providing a very good saxophone part and a short solo after the second chorus (at 1'53). Even though this version did not meet the Boss's expectations, it came out pretty well and deserved an official release.

MARY LOU

Bruce Springsteen / 3'21

Musicians: Bruce Springsteen: vocals, guitar / Steve Van Zandt: guitar, backing vocals / Clarence Clemons: saxophone, backing vocals (?) / Roy Bittan: piano / Danny Federici: organ / Garry Tallent: bass / Max Weinberg: drums **Recording:** The Power Station, New York: 30 May 1979 **Technical team:** producers: Bruce Springsteen, Jon Landau, Steve Van Zandt / recording engineers: Neil Dorfsman, Ed Thacker (mixing)

Mary Lou did not make the cut for *The River*, no doubt because Bruce Springsteen preferred *Be True*, which tells the same story: Mary Lou is a young woman who can only think about the romantic movie actors she venerates and about perfect but artificial love. Of note: *Be True* didn't make it onto the double album either. It's on the B-side of the single *Fade Away* (1981) and the box set *The Ties That Bind: The River Collection*. The song revolves around a prominent piano part, allowing Roy Bittan to shine, especially on the rhythmic element. Clarence Clemons performs a warm tenor sax solo. The arrangements and construction of the piece are nevertheless a bit too incoherent to be convincing.

CYNTHIA

Bruce Springsteen / 4'13

Musicians: Bruce Springsteen: vocals, guitars / Steve Van Zandt: guitars, backing vocals / Clarence Clemons: cowbell, tambourine / Roy Bittan: piano, keyboards / Garry Tallent: bass / Max Weinberg: drums **Recording:** The Hit Factory, New York: 15 June 1983 **Technical team:** producers: Bruce Springsteen, Jon Landau, Chuck Plotkin, Steve Van Zandt / recording engineers: Toby Scott, Ed Thacker (mixing)

There are two versions of *Cynthia*. Bruce Springsteen recorded the first one as a solo at his place, in Los Angeles, in April 1983; the second, which appears in *Tracks*, dates back to the following June (the date given in the *Tracks* booklet, 20 April 1983, is incorrect), this time recorded with the E Street Band. Cynthia doesn't smile or say hello, but when she appears, all eyes are on her, starting with those of the narrator. "I gotta be pretty naïve to believe in you." He knows that she'll never be his, but this doesn't matter. This song takes on its full strength onstage. Bruce Springsteen performed it at the Giants Stadium in East Rutherford, New Jersey, on 31 August 2003.

MY LOVE WILL NOT LET YOU DOWN

Bruce Springsteen / 4'24

Musicians: Bruce Springsteen: vocals, guitar / Steve Van Zandt: guitar / Roy Bittan: keyboards / Danny Federici: keyboards / Garry Tallent: bass / Max Weinberg: drums **Recording:** The Power Station, New York: 5–7 May 1982 **Technical team:** producers: Bruce Springsteen, Jon Landau, Chuck Plotkin, Steve Van Zandt / recording engineers: Toby Scott, Ed Thacker (mixing)

This is another song Bruce Springsteen recorded for the legendary *Born in the U.S.A* album. Its rock style and lyrics are typical of the Boss and the E Street Band. The narrator can't sleep; in the silence, his heart starts to pound as he thinks of the woman he loves: "I keep searching for you darling, searching everywhere I go." Bruce Springsteen has played this song onstage more than 40 times since March 1999.

The *Tracks* booklet says that the song was recorded at The Hit Factory, but this is another error: this actually happened at The Power Station on 5 May 1982, the same day as *Glory Days*. *My Love Will Not Let You Down* is a good song, the Boss indulging in an excellent guitar solo. A few criticisms, however: the acoustic guitar (likely that of Steve Van Zandt) does not always hit the right notes and the keyboards are a bit too prominent.

Clarence Clemons and Steve Van Zandt backstage in 1982, the year *Frankie* was recorded.

FRANKIE

Bruce Springsteen / 7'22

Musicians: Bruce Springsteen: vocals, guitars, harmonica / Steve Van Zandt: guitar / Clarence Clemons: saxophone, tambourine, backing vocals / Roy Bittan: piano, keyboards / Danny Federici: organ / Garry Tallent: bass / Max Weinberg: drums **Recording:** The Power Station, New York: 14 May 1982 **Technical team:** producers: Bruce Springsteen, Jon Landau, Chuck Plotkin, Steve Van Zandt / recording engineers: Toby Scott, Ed Thacker (mixing)

Frankie dates back to 1976. Bruce Springsteen sang it for the first time in Atlanta, Georgia, on 26 March. It's among the songs written for his fourth album, not *Darkness on the Edge of Town*, but an album that never came to fruition called *The Lost Album*. He later reworked it in May 1982 for *Born in the U.S.A.* before discarding it from the tracklist. Frankie looks like the young and pretty queens of the night who check their makeup before heading onto the dance floor. The narrator is by her side and Frankie captivates him. She's an enigmatic young woman.

Lasting more than seven minutes, *Frankie* was one of the epic songs of the Boss's 1976 concerts. The *Tracks* version perhaps doesn't have the spirit of the live performances, but it is no less phenomenal, with the E Street Band and its excellent musicians shooting from the hip. Clarence Clemons's saxophone solo and Springsteen's two harmonica solos are exceptional. The Boss's vocals are superb.

TV MOVIE

Bruce Springsteen / 2'45

Musicians: Bruce Springsteen: vocals, guitar / Roy Bittan: piano / Garry Tallent: bass / Max Weinberg: drums **Recording:** The Hit Factory, New York: 13 June 1983 **Technical team:** producers: Bruce Springsteen, Jon Landau, Chuck Plotkin, Steve Van Zandt / recording engineers: Toby Scott, Ed Thacker (mixing)

Bruce Springsteen wrote *TV Movie* at the end of a session and immediately recorded it with the E Street Band on 13 June 1983, in New York, for *Born in the U.S.A.* The songwriter fights mockery with fine art set to a rockabilly rhythm: the narrator wakes up from a bad dream to hear his wife tell him that his life will be immortalized, not in a feature film, or in a great American novel, but in a TV movie. The writers could change his story, turn him into an African-American or a Chinese person—he doesn't care. In reality, the songwriter was inspired in part by a running joke within his group: someone had once said that he would one day be the subject of a TV movie. *TV Movie* is above all a great rockabilly song, recorded in quartet and enhanced by Roy Bittan's piano, which is as flamboyant as Jerry Lee Lewis's.

LION'S DEN

Bruce Springsteen / 2'18

For Springsteen Addicts
The brass quintet of Mario Cruz, Eddie Manion, Mark Pender, Mike Spengler, and Richie "La Bamba" Rosenberg was a part of The Miami Horns, which accompanied Springsteen on numerous occasions, starting in 1976.

Musicians
Bruce Springsteen: vocals, guitars
Roy Bittan: keyboards
Danny Federici: organ
Garry Tallent: bass
Max Weinberg: drums
Mario Cruz: tenor saxophone
Eddie Manion: baritone saxophone
Mark Pender, Mike Spengler: trumpet
Richie "La Bamba" Rosenberg: trombone
The group: backing vocals

Recording
The Power Station, New York: 25 January 1982

Technical team
Producers: Bruce Springsteen, Jon Landau, Chuck Plotkin, Steve Van Zandt
Recording engineer: Neil Dorfsman
Mixing: Ed Thacker

Lion's Den was recorded at The Power Station at the same time as Gary U.S. Bonds' *On the Line*. Above, Springsteen and Bonds in 1975.

Genesis and lyrics

Bruce Springsteen started working on *Lion's Den* in the early 1980s, as attested by an acoustic demo recorded in his home at Colts Neck, New Jersey, in 1981. The version released on *Tracks* was produced on 25 January 1982 at The Power Station in New York at the start of sessions for *Born in the U.S.A.* and *On the Line*, the Gary U.S. Bonds album produced by Bruce Springsteen and Steve Van Zandt, which included performances by the E Street Band.

"You broke my heart, tore it apart," but "I'm Daniel waiting in the lion's den," sings Bruce Springsteen. He's referring to a story from the Bible, in the Book of Daniel: Daniel, a prophet from the Old Testament, falls out of favor in Babylon and is thrown into the lion's den twice, once by Darius II, then by his son Cyrus the Young, but on both occasions he comes out unscathed. This metaphor illustrates the discontent of an injured man who is deeply in love with a woman who behaves like a wild beast with men, but decides to face her anyway.

Upon the release of *Tracks*, Bruce Springsteen confessed that he regretted not releasing *Lion's Den*, even as a single, as it could have been a global success. He has performed it several times onstage, notably in Paris on 3 June 1999.

Production

Lion's Den is a good rock song, with a clear break in the melody of the chorus. Not all members of the E Street Band performed in this version, as Clarence Clemons and Steve Van Zandt were not present during the recording. Max Weinberg and Garry Tallent's rhythmic section—supported by the Boss's Telecaster-Esquire, Roy Bittan's keyboards, and Danny Federici's organ—infuses an infectious energy into the song. After digging it up, Springsteen decided to add a brass section in 1998, notably with a trombone part by Richie "La Bamba" Rosenberg. It's a good thing he did, since the five brass musicians are excellent and bring both power and enthusiasm to the piece. The tenor saxophone seems to have been played by Clarence Clemons, even though the album jacket doesn't credit him for this. As for the songwriter, his performance is remarkable. He's clearly enjoying his performance, all the more so due to the support of enthusiastic backing vocals. As so often happens, the song really comes into its own in concert.

CAR WASH

Bruce Springsteen / 2'06

Musicians: Bruce Springsteen: vocals, guitar / Roy Bittan: piano / Danny Federici: organ / Garry Tallent: bass / Max Weinberg: drums **Recording:** The Hit Factory, New York: 31 May 1983 **Technical team:** producers: Bruce Springsteen, Jon Landau, Chuck Plotkin, Steve Van Zandt / recording engineers: Toby Scott, Ed Thacker (mixing)

Car Wash is an outtake from *Born in the U.S.A.* and was recorded on 31 May 1983. It's about the day-to-day life of Catherine LeFevre, a car washer who works on Sunset Boulevard and Vine Street in Los Angeles and who says she hates her boss. She dreams of singing in nightclubs and earning a million dollars and hopes one day to see a handsome man walk toward her with a contract in his hands. But it's all just a dream—we're in Hollywood. Bruce Springsteen chose to illustrate this story with a more classic rock song initially called *Small Town Girl*. It's funny to hear him play the role of a woman, but aside from the anecdote, the song lacks flavor.

ROCKAWAY THE DAYS

Bruce Springsteen / 4'40

Musicians: Bruce Springsteen: vocals, guitars / Roy Bittan: piano / Danny Federici: organ / Garry Tallent: bass / Max Weinberg: drums **Recording:** The Hit Factory, New York: 12 January 1984 **Technical team:** producers: Bruce Springsteen, Jon Landau, Chuck Plotkin, Steve Van Zandt / recording engineers: Toby Scott, Ed Thacker (mixing)

Another song recorded for *Born in the U.S.A.*, *Rockaway the Days* focuses on Billy, who has just been released from prison—Billy loves to fight. Then, one day, he meets Mary and marries her. But happiness is not for him. A brawl at a roadside bar puts him back in. The *Tracks* booklet says that this song was recorded on 3 February 1984, but according to a Sony database, it was actually 12 January. *Rockaway the Days* is a good rock song, with Springsteen on his acoustic guitar. His bandmates support him with efficacy and aplomb—the mark of great musicians.

BROTHERS UNDER THE BRIDGES ('83)

Bruce Springsteen / 5'08

Musicians: Bruce Springsteen: vocals, guitar / Clarence Clemons: saxophone, backing vocals (?) / Roy Bittan: piano, backing vocals (?) / Danny Federici: organ, glockenspiel / Garry Tallent: bass / Max Weinberg: drums **Recording:** The Hit Factory, New York: 4 September 1983 **Technical team:** producers: Bruce Springsteen, Jon Landau, Chuck Plotkin, Steve Van Zandt / recording engineers: Toby Scott, Ed Thacker (mixing)

Musically, *Brothers Under the Bridges ('83)* was a trial run for *No Surrender*, on the *Born in the U.S.A.* album. It has the same rock 'n' roll energy, identical verses (the "la, la, la" is in both songs, serving as the intro in one and bridge in the other), and the backing vocals are similar. The story, on the other hand, is somewhat different from the one in *Brothers Under the Bridge*, which is also on *Tracks* (see page 412). From all of his 14 years of age, the narrator watches and admires the guys who, come spring, converge on the town at the wheels of their souped-up cars after being on their farms all winter. They race or just have fun together. He envies their sense of camaraderie and hopes to become a part of it.

WHEN YOU NEED ME

Bruce Springsteen / 2'58

Musicians: Bruce Springsteen: vocals, guitar, keyboards, harmonica, tambourine / Soozie Tyrell: violin, vocal harmonies (?)/ Gary Mallaber: drums **Recording:** Thrill Hill Recording, New Jersey: 20 January 1987 **Technical team:** producers: Bruce Springsteen, Jon Landau, Chuck Plotkin, Steve Van Zandt / recording engineers: Toby Scott, Bob Clearmountain (mixing)

When You Need Me is an outtake of *Tunnel of Love* recorded on 20 January 1987.

In this love song, a man tells the woman he loves that she can count on him, on his support and protection any time and in any circumstance, "'Cause without you my life just wouldn't be the same." The Boss wrote this country pop-style song with acoustic guitars, a tambourine, synth pads, and a harmonica solo. Gary Mallaber recorded a drum part in 1998 for *Tracks*. Soozie Tyrell is credited for the violin, but the instrument is inaudible in the mix. Is that her voice in the vocal harmonies?

THE WISH

Bruce Springsteen / 5'14

Musicians: Bruce Springsteen: vocals, guitar, bass, keyboards, tambourine, maracas / Gary Mallaber: drums **Recording:** Thrill Hill Recording, New Jersey: 22 February 1987 **Technical team:** producers: Bruce Springsteen, Jon Landau, Chuck Plotkin, Steve Van Zandt / recording engineers: Toby Scott, Bob Clearmountain (mixing)

In an interview with the *Los Angeles Times* in 1998, Bruce Springsteen said of *The Wish*: "That's a song I wrote for *Tunnel of Love*, and it's probably as directly autobiographical as I've ever gotten. That may be why it didn't get on the record."[146] This song is about the happiness surrounding his recent wedding, but mostly about his childhood memories with his mother: "I remember in the morning, ma, hearing your alarm clock ring/I'd lie in bed and listen to you get ready for work." Memories of Christmas, too, and of a really great present: a brand-new Japanese guitar. The songwriter's mother had been waiting for this song for a long time, as he'd only written about his father until then.

The Wish is another country-style song, with an acoustic Telecaster-Esquire solo and a Mark Marvin-style reverberation. The keyboards are not ideal—they sound a bit like elevator music. Of note: the contribution of Gary Mallaber, who recorded a drum part in 1998 for *Tracks*.

THE HONEYMOONERS

Bruce Springsteen / 2'04

Musician: Bruce Springsteen: vocals, guitars, keyboards, harmonica **Recording:** Thrill Hill Recording, New Jersey: 22 February 1987 **Technical team:** producers: Bruce Springsteen, Jon Landau, Chuck Plotkin, Steve Van Zandt / recording engineers: Toby Scott, Bob Clearmountain (mixing)

This folk song was recorded during sessions for *Tunnel of Love*, on the same day as *The Wish*. Bruce Springsteen sings accompanied by two acoustic guitars, some synth pads, and a few harmonica lines. He once again took inspiration from his recent marriage. It's the wedding day of the two characters in the song: their families congratulate them as the church bell rings. Then come the ceremony, the much-awaited wedding night, the next morning, and the continuing celebrations.

The sound of barking and a passing car can be heard at the end of the song, from 1'51. The Boss said in an interview that he recorded the song with the window open without external noises interfering with the sound. The sound of this dog and car, in fact, do not conform to the acoustic quality of the recordings, nor to the volume they should have (normally weaker). These noises must have been added later in the mixing stage.

LEAVIN' TRAIN

Bruce Springsteen / 4'05

Musicians: Bruce Springsteen: vocals, guitar / Ian McLagan: organ / Bob Glaub: bass / Jeff Porcaro: drums, percussion instruments / Unidentified musician: piano **Recording:** Oceanway Studios, Burbank, Los Angeles: 27 February 1990 **Technical team:** producers: Bruce Springsteen, Jon Landau, Chuck Plotkin, Roy Bittan / recording engineers: Toby Scott, Bob Clearmountain (mixing)

Leavin' Train comes from sessions for the *Human Touch* album and was recorded on 27 February 1990.

The song tackles a difficult relationship. "When I ask you if everything is alright/You whisper 'don't worry' and you shut out the light." A whispered sentence, doubts left hanging in a dark room.

The Boss recorded this rock song with the same three musicians from *Viva Las Vegas*, which appeared on the 1990 tribute album to the King, *The Last Temptation of Elvis*. The sound brings to mind ZZ Top, the rhythmic section providing a powerful support to the beat and the lead guitar howling incandescent lines. Small comment: a piano can be heard throughout the piece, even though Roy Bittan isn't credited in the *Tracks* booklet. An oversight? Or is the Boss playing it? Or even Ian McLagan? Bruce Springsteen played *Leavin' Train* twice in public, on 22 and 23 May 2014, at the Soldiers & Sailors Memorial Hall & Museum in Pittsburgh, Pennsylvania.

Springsteen in concert in New York in 1990, the same year that he recorded *Seven Angels*, an outtake from *Human Touch*.

SEVEN ANGELS

Bruce Springsteen / 3'26

Musicians: Bruce Springsteen: vocals, guitar, bass / Roy Bittan: keyboards / Shawn Pelton: drums **Recording:** Ocean Way Studios, Burbank, California: 29 June 1990 **Technical team:** producers: Bruce Springsteen, Jon Landau, Chuck Plotkin, Roy Bittan / recording engineers: Toby Scott, Bob Clearmountain (mixing)

This outtake from *Human Touch* was recorded on 29 June 1990.

Seven angels have been protecting the narrator since he fell in love. Each of them takes their turn giving him advice, but sometimes it's contradictory. The irony plays out in full: "Fifth angel says 'Don't worry/Love's waiting 'round the corner for you, son,'" while the sixth warns that "'You better hurry/It don't take long for the good to get gone.'"

The intro, Shawn Pelton's excellent drum line (his artistic collaborations abound, including with Billy Joel and Sheryl Crow), and the Boss's riff bring to mind *Should I Stay or Should I Go*, by The Clash, and maybe *Let Me Know* by John's Children even more. The rest of the song is different—it's a very good rock song, with clear potential, which could have benefited from more attention from its creator in order to make the tracklist of an official album.

GAVE IT A NAME

Bruce Springsteen / 2'50

Musicians: Bruce Springsteen: vocals, guitar, bass, tambourine / Roy Bittan: keyboards **Recording:** Thrill Hill Recording, New Jersey: 24 August 1998 **Technical team:** producers: Bruce Springsteen, Chuck Plotkin / recording engineers: Toby Scott, Ed Thacker (mixing)

Gave It a Name was recorded for the first time in December 1999 or January 1991, during sessions for *Human Touch*. But when Bruce Springsteen started to work on *Tracks*, he couldn't find the old demo, so he recorded it again on 24 August 1998. Twenty years after *Adam Raised a Cain* (on the *Darkness on the Edge of Town* album), the songwriter is again inspired by the biblical characters of Cain—the first murderer of humanity—and his younger brother Abel. He borrowed the line "Poison snake bites you, you're poison too," already in the lyrics for *The Big Muddy* on the *Lucky Town* album, from the 1988 novel *Paris Trout* by Pete Dexter.

The arrangements are similar to those from the Boss's songs from 1996 to 1997, meaning they include a guitar, a bass, and some synth pads. He plays his Telecaster-Esquire in rhythm, the sound enhanced by a choral effect. His performance is understated, a long way from the furor of *Seven Angels*, the song before *Gave It a Name*.

MY LOVER MAN

Bruce Springsteen / 3'56

Musicians: Bruce Springsteen: vocals, guitars, bass, keyboards / Roy Bittan: keyboards (?) / Jeff Porcaro: drums, percussion instruments **Recording:** Soundworks West, Burbank, California: 4 December 1990 **Technical team:** producers: Bruce Springsteen, Jon Landau, Chuck Plotkin, Roy Bittan / recording engineers: Toby Scott, Bob Clearmountain (mixing)

My Lover Man is an outtake from *Human Touch*. Did Bruce Springsteen write it for Patti Scialfa's solo album *Rumble Doll* (1993)? It's just a theory. While he wrote the song in the first person and from the point of view of a woman, the relationship in question—"You treated me hard and made my heart ache"—has nothing to do with Bruce and Patti's. Musically, *My Lover Man* is similar to *Brilliant Disguise* (from the *Tunnel of Love* album), especially in its rhythm. Speaking of which, the talented Jeff Porcaro is on the drums, as usual adding percussion parts to complement his drumming, notably the shakers, tambourines, and other instruments of his own device. The Boss is on the various guitars and on the keyboards. Roy Bittan is also credited with this instrument, even though his contribution can't be clearly heard.

OVER THE RISE

Bruce Springsteen / 2'38

Musicians: Bruce Springsteen: vocals, bass, drum-machine programming / Roy Bittan: keyboards **Recording:** Soundworks West, Burbank, California: 7 December 1990 **Technical team:** producers: Bruce Springsteen, Jon Landau, Chuck Plotkin, Roy Bittan / recording engineers: Toby Scott, Bob Clearmountain (mixing)

Another outtake from *Human Touch, Over the Rise* was recorded in December 1990. It was composed on a bass guitar, which gives it a dark and mysterious atmosphere. Mysterious like the meeting between the narrator and a gypsy: "He looked into my palm, then looked me in the eye/Told me you were gone, gone over the rise." "Over the rise," by the way, appears in many songs of this period, such as *Lucky Town, Real World*, and *Roll of the Dice*. What's new is that the songwriter borrowed the phrase "Is a promise that love couldn't keep same as a promise broken" from film critic Pauline Kael, which was found in her collection of essays *I Lost It at the Movies*.

The mood in *Over the Rise* is mainly created by Springsteen's bass, as is the case with *57 Channels (And Nothin' On)* from *Human Touch*. The Boss makes the most of this economy of instruments by letting his lead vocals take over the space and be carried by an ample reverberation. There is no 6-string guitar. Only keyboards and a drum machine complete the arrangements. The result is superb.

WHEN THE LIGHTS GO OUT

Bruce Springsteen / 3'05

Musicians: Bruce Springsteen: vocals, bass / Roy Bittan: keyboards / Jeff Porcaro: drums, percussion instruments **Recording:** The Record Plant, Los Angeles, California: 6 December 1990 **Technical team:** producers: Bruce Springsteen, Jon Landau, Chuck Plotkin, Roy Bittan / recording engineers: Toby Scott, Bob Clearmountain (mixing)

Bruce Springsteen performed *When the Lights Go Out* onstage at a benefit concert at the Shrine Auditorium, in Los Angeles, on 16 November 1990, dedicating the song to "the people at the Christic Institute, who watch what's going on when the lights go out."[147] He recorded it three weeks later, on 6 December, but strangely enough, didn't include it in *Human Touch*. It's strange because this song is remarkable. The message is a call to vigilance: no one can be trusted, not even a best friend.

As with *Over the Rise, When the Lights Go Out* was composed on a bass guitar, with the 4-string guitar calling the shots from beginning to end. The result is another success, especially thanks to Jeff Porcaro's very good drumming and numerous percussions. Roy Bittan's keyboards are discreet and subtle, which further highlights the Boss's excellent lead vocals.

LOOSE CHANGE

Bruce Springsteen / 4'19

Musicians: Bruce Springsteen: vocals, drum-machine programming / Roy Bittan: keyboards **Recording:** The Record Plant, Los Angeles: 31 January 1991 **Technical team:** producers: Bruce Springsteen, Jon Landau, Chuck Plotkin, Roy Bittan / recording engineers: Toby Scott, Bob Clearmountain (mixing)

This outtake from *Human Touch* is about a meeting: a man and a woman (whose birthday it is) meet in a bar, have a few drinks, and there is a brief spark. But aside from this meeting, the man wants to change scenery, to leave, without knowing exactly why. Might this be the same character from *Stolen Car* (on *The River*)? *Loose Change* was a new song composed on the bass guitar. This tactic was likely a powerful stimulus for the songwriter's inspiration, as the result was always superb. The song starts with a rhythmic bass line supported by keyboard pads and a subtle drum machine. The guitars are again absent. A refined sound texture gives the Boss's voice a whole new dimension that is both more moving and more surreal.

TROUBLE IN PARADISE

Bruce Springsteen, Roy Bittan / 3'37

Musicians: Bruce Springsteen: vocals / Roy Bittan: keyboards / Randy Jackson: bass / Jeff Porcaro: drums, percussion instruments **Recording:** Soundworks West, Burbank, California: 1 December 1989 **Technical team:** producers: Bruce Springsteen, Jon Landau, Chuck Plotkin, Roy Bittan / recording engineers: Toby Scott, Bob Clearmountain (mixing)

Trouble in Paradise is the third song from Roy Bittan and Bruce Springsteen's collaboration. But unlike *Roll of the Dice* and *Real World*, the song wasn't included on *Human Touch*. Springsteen refers to "an old black and white movie." Is this *Trouble in Paradise*, Ernst Lubitsch's romantic comedy masterpiece in which a gentleman burglar teams up with a seductive pickpocket?

What's for sure, is that the music Bittan composed is a pop song perfectly suited to radio. It's enhanced by the superb voice of the Boss (who, in an unusual move, is not playing an instrument), and by the Porcaro-Jackson duo and their unstoppable groove. Bittan's arrangements are good, and the aggregate makes up a very good sound.

HAPPY

Bruce Springsteen / 4'51

Musicians: Bruce Springsteen: vocals, guitar, bass / Roy Bittan: keyboards / Shawn Pelton: drums **Recording:** A&M Recording Studios, Los Angeles, California: 18 January 1992 (?) **Technical team:** producers: Bruce Springsteen, Jon Landau, Chuck Plotkin, Roy Bittan / recording engineers: Toby Scott, Bob Clearmountain (mixing)

According to the *Tracks* booklet, *Happy* was recorded in January 1992. If that's correct, it might have been too late to include the song on *Lucky Town*. Some sources date this recording to January 1991. Nevertheless, if the Boss was happy in January 1992, it was probably because of the birth of his daughter Jessica on 30 December 1991. Whatever the case, it's a very romantic and anti-materialistic song. The narrator says that he doesn't need gold or a diamond ring, or drugs to withstand the pain of living. All he needs is to be in the arms of his beloved. (The first two lines of *Happy* are practically the same as those from *My Beautiful Reward* on the *Lucky Town* album.)

Musically, this is the second time Shawn Pelton is at the drums in a Springsteen song, after *Seven Angels*, on the same album. His drumming supports a delicate song, primarily led by the Boss's acoustic guitar, the sound of the strings, and Roy Bittan's keyboard pads. The songwriter expresses his happiness with tenderness and coyness, unlike Keith Richards' *Happy*, recorded with the Stones in 1972, which is a rather extroverted rock song (*Exile on Main St.*)!

GOIN' CALI

Bruce Springsteen / 2'59

Musicians: Bruce Springsteen: vocals, guitar, bass, keyboards / Roy Bittan: keyboards (?) **Recording:** A&M Recording Studios, Los Angeles, California: 29 January 1991 **Technical team:** producers: Bruce Springsteen, Jon Landau, Chuck Plotkin, Roy Bittan / recording engineers: Toby Scott, Bob Clearmountain (mixing)

Recorded during sessions for *Human Touch, Goin' Cali* is autobiographical, as the narrator tells the story of his departure (from New Jersey) and his arrival on the West Coast (in Los Angeles) where "a man can really feel his success." As Springsteen explained to *Mojo* magazine in 1988: "*Goin' Cali*, I suppose, was just an experimental thing I laid down in the studio one day." He went on: "I don't even remember recording it or how it came about, but it traces, ironically, my journey at that time out West."[148]

Once again, Springsteen wrote the song on the bass. He plays a very good riff on his 4-string guitar amid a dreamlike, meditative atmosphere dotted with voices and various effects. The sound of a synth pad grows alongside harmonies that at times sound oriental, and everything is enhanced by an ample and deep reverberation. As for the Boss, he talks more than he sings. *Goin' Cali* is a gem of a song that deserves to be longer.

BACK IN YOUR ARMS

Bruce Springsteen / 4'43

Musicians: Bruce Springsteen: vocals, guitar / Clarence Clemons: saxophone / Steve Van Zandt: guitar / Roy Bittan: keyboards / Danny Federici: organ / Garry Tallent: bass / Max Weinberg: drums / Frank Pagano: congas, shaker, triangle **Recording:** The Hit Factory, New York: 12 January 1995 **Technical team:** producers: Bruce Springsteen, Jon Landau, Chuck Plotkin, Roy Bittan / recording engineers: Toby Scott, Bob Clearmountain (mixing)

Back in Your Arms dates to 12 January 1995. It was recorded for the *Greatest Hits* album but was then scrapped. Bruce Springsteen and the E Street Band performed it for the documentary *Blood Brothers* under the name *Back in Your Arms Again*. In this love song, the narrator dreams that he's lost his love and wants nothing more than to be in her arms once more. Was the songwriter thinking of Patti Scialfa when he wrote these lyrics? Or is it a metaphor for the ties that bind him to the E Street Band?

One thing's for sure: Bruce Springsteen and his favorite group shared a true bond while performing this song onstage at the Continental Airlines Arena in East Rutherford, New Jersey, on 4 August 1999. It's a beautiful soul song, with a superb vocal part from the Boss, a captivating organ part, an inspired saxophone solo, a lyrical piano part, subtle but essential acoustic and guitar parts, and a rhythmic section with a subtle groove. A falsetto voice supports Springsteen in places, likely his own voice recorded as an overdub.

Brothers Under the Bridge is another Springsteen composition about the trauma caused by the Vietnam War.

BROTHERS UNDER THE BRIDGE

Bruce Springsteen / 4'55

Musicians
Bruce Springsteen: vocals, guitar
Danny Federici: keyboards
Marty Rifkin: pedal steel guitar, dobro
Garry Tallent: bass
Gary Mallaber: drums
Soozie Tyrell: violin

Recording
Thrill Hill Recording, Beverley Hills, Los Angeles, California: 22 May 1995

Technical team
Producers: Bruce Springsteen, Chuck Plotkin
Recording engineer: Toby Scott
Mixing: Bob Clearmountain

Genesis and lyrics

The *Tracks* box set includes two songs called *Brothers Under the Bridge*. The first, *Brothers Under the Bridges ('83)*, dates back to sessions for *Born in the U.S.A.* in 1983 (it would later evolve into *No Surrender*, on the same album). The second, *Brothers Under the Bridge*, was scrapped from *The Ghost of Tom Joad* tracklisting in 1995.

Brothers Under the Bridge is another song about Vietnam, a war that deeply affected Bruce Springsteen, as well as the rest of America. It's the story of a veteran who lives—or, rather, survives—in a California canyon with some other former soldiers, far from the dangers of the city and the streets. They do, however, face one enemy there: the Santa Ana, the deadly wind that lights up the undergrowth. The character tells his daughter about his return from Vietnam in 1972, his love for his wife, and about Veterans' Day. But "One minute you're right there, and something slips..."

Bruce Springsteen regularly performed *Brothers Under the Bridge* during the Ghost of Tom Joad Solo Acoustic Tour, then on 11 April 1999 in Barcelona for the Reunion Tour and on 1 May 2014 in Tampa, Florida, during the High Hopes Tour.

Production

The 1983 version of *Brothers Under the Bridges* clearly has nothing to do with the one from 1995, aside from the title (give or take the extra "s" in "Bridges"). While the first is an assertive rock song, the second is a sweet folk-rock piece, similar in style to the great hits from *The Ghost of Tom Joad*. The atmosphere is soothing, Springsteen singing his lyrics with care and eloquence. The musicians who accompany him are all absolutely brilliant: Gary Mallaber with his fabulous brushes, Danny Federici on the keyboards (at 0'49), Gary Tallent on the bass, Marty Rifkin on that spectral-sounding pedal steel guitar (at 1'30) and on the dobro (mixed far behind the Boss's guitar), and, lastly, Soozie Tyrell, who never overdoes it on the violin (at 2'14 and 3'38). Most notable of all are Springsteen himself, who sings while picking his acoustic Gibson J-45, and Toby Scott, with his exceptional sound recording. A little gem.

TRA
CKS
18
8TRA

ALBUM

18 TRACKS

Growin' Up • Seaside Bar Song • Rendezvous • Hearts of Stone • Where the Bands Are • Loose Ends • I Wanna Be with You • Born in the U.S.A. • My Love Will Not Let You Down • Lion's Den • Pink Cadillac • Janey, Don't Lose Heart • Sad Eyes • Part Man, Part Monkey • Trouble River • Brothers Under the Bridge • The Fever • The Promise

RELEASE DATE

United States: 13 April 1999

Reference: Columbia Records – 494200 9

Springsteen and the E Street Band performing at Bercy, Paris, in 1999. *18 Tracks* came out the same year.

AN 18-CARAT GOLDEN NUGGET

The *18 Tracks* compilation is a selection of 15 songs that were already available on the 1998 *Tracks* box set, to which were added two unreleased tracks: *Trouble River* and *The Fever*. *The Promise*, for its part, is covered in the album *The Promise*, see page 566.

Released in April 1999, only five months after *Tracks*, *18 Tracks* was not as successful and only reached No.64 in the *Billboard* charts.

TROUBLE RIVER

Bruce Springsteen / 4'16

Musicians: Bruce Springsteen: vocals, guitars / Roy Bittan: keyboards / Randy Jackson: bass / Jeff Porcaro: drums **Recording:** Soundworks West, Burbank, California: 6 April 1990 **Technical team:** producers: Bruce Springsteen, Jon Landau, Chuck Plotkin / recording engineers: Toby Scott, Bob Clearmountain (mixing)

1999

Along with *The Fever* and *The Promise*, *Trouble River* is one of the three songs on *18 Tracks* that was not taken from *Tracks*.

Bruce Springsteen tells the story of a depressed man emerging from a nightmare in which "smiling faces [are] smiling back [at him]." The river, which is the other character in the song, doesn't seem to be the narrator's final destination, but more likely, the representation of his troubles, a river that is "cold and deep and black." You may notice that the line in *Trouble River* printed on the booklet that accompanies the box set—"Tonight I'm gonna shed this skin and I'll be breathin'"—is different from the one Bruce Springsteen sings: "Tonight I'm gonna shed this skin 'cause water's rising and I'm going down too."

Musically, this is an assertive rock song carried by Jeff Porcaro's powerful drums and Randy Jackson's bass, while Roy Bittan plays excellent piano and organ accompaniments. But the Boss is the one who dominates: he delivers a very good minute-long solo with a riff on the Telecaster and superb lead vocals, which sometimes take on a John Fogerty intonation.

THE FEVER

Bruce Springsteen / 7'41

Musicians: Bruce Springsteen: vocals, piano / Clarence Clemons: saxophone, backing vocals / Danny Federici: organ, backing vocals (?) / Garry Tallent: bass, backing vocals (?)/ Vini Lopez: drums, backing vocals **Recording:** 914 Sound Recording Studios, Blauvelt, New York State: 16 May 1973 **Technical team:** producers: Mike Appel, Jim Cretecos / recording engineers: Louis Lahav, Thom Panunzio (mixing at the Record Plant Remote Truck)

Bruce Springsteen wrote this song in 1971 under the name *(I Got) Fever for the Girl* and performed it for the first time onstage in Boston, in March 1973. The lyrics he sang in May of that same year, during sessions for *The Wild, the Innocent, and the E Street Shuffle*, portray a man who is literally obsessed with a woman: he can't watch TV or listen to the radio because the only thing he can hear—the only thing he cares about—are the words she spoke into his ear, words that make him more and more feverish every day.

After *The Fever* failed to make the cut for Bruce Springsteen's second album, Mike Appel decided to send the recording to underground radio stations. The song became an almost-hit on the non-mainstream circuit. Southside Johnny and The Asbury Jukes covered this song during sessions for *I Don't Want to Go Home* (1976), as did the Pointer Sisters under the name *(She's Got) The Fever* (1979).

The Fever is an excellent jazzy song, a cross between blues and rock. It was produced in a single take. Strangely, Springsteen never liked it. An effective Vini Lopez provides a ternary rhythm that is more convincing than that of many other performances. The Boss is not on the guitar but on the piano, accompanied by numerous backing vocals, including Clarence Clemons's baritone, which provides the responses in the chorus. The latter also plays two or three good saxophone solos.

EYES

EP

SAD EYES

Sad Eyes • Missing • Man at the Top •
Take 'Em as They Come

RELEASE DATE
United States: 1999
Reference: Columbia Records – COL 666884 2

SAD EYES

Bruce Springsteen / 3'47

WARNING: SEXUAL CONTENT

It was thanks to Springsteen's former recording engineer, Jimmy Iovine, that *Sad Eyes* was covered by Enrique Iglesias. Iovine was aware of the Spanish singer's interest in and admiration for the Boss, and recommended the song to him. The music video was directed by David LaChapelle; unfortunately, its explicit content, with scenes hinting at masturbation, may have ruined its chances of success.

Musicians
- **Bruce Springsteen:** vocals, guitar
- **Roy Bittan:** keyboards
- **David Sancious:** keyboards
- **Danny Federici:** organ
- **Randy Jackson:** bass
- **Jeff Porcaro:** drums
- **Michael Fisher:** percussion

Recording
- **Soundworks West, Los Angeles, California:** 25 January 1990

Technical team
- **Producers:** Chuck Plotkin, Jon Landau, Roy Bittan
- **Recording engineer:** Toby Scott
- **Mixing:** Bob Clearmountain

Michael Fisher (here, in 2004), the highly talented percussionist on *Sad Eyes*. He previously played with Joni Mitchell and Larry Carlton.

Genesis and lyrics

Sad Eyes was one of the songs recorded in the *Human Touch* and *Lucky Town* period that was dropped when the definitive tracklists for the two albums were chosen. It's nevertheless a great pop song that would probably have appealed to DJs on FM radio stations on both sides of the Atlantic, and rightly so. It is a love song directed at a rather enigmatic heroine. She claims that she is happy and all is good in her life. But her eyes cannot hide the fact that this is not true. Meanwhile, the narrator senses that his love for her is either not reciprocated or impossible, but he doesn't care. Neither of the characters in the song has the courage to reveal their true feelings, or maybe he is waiting for her to be ready. Perhaps she is married or just shy. The question is, will he wait for her?

In 1996, six years after *Sad Eyes* was recorded, Springsteen fans discovered the song when it was released on a four-track CD. Two years later, it was included on the *Tracks* box set (1998).

Production

Springsteen was venturing into mainstream pop when he wrote *Sad Eyes*, something that was quite unusual for him. So it comes as no surprise that Enrique Iglesias recorded a cover version in 2000, adapted for a younger audience. Mainstream or not, the song still contains plenty of interest. It opens with the clear, buoyant notes of the Boss's Telecaster-Esquire, underpinned by Jeff Porcaro and Randy Jackson's very efficient rhythm section (oddly, the intro has a slight Cyndi Lauper feel), multiple keyboard parts from the Bittan-Sancious-Federici trio, and Michael Fisher's various percussion parts (triangle, shaker, tambourine, woodblock, etc). But the main attraction of *Sad Eyes* is the Boss's falsetto in the chorus. This is a major event, not just because it is one of the first times that he has used this vocal technique, but also because he has a natural talent for it, and it makes the catchy melody of the song stand out all the more.

Sad Eyes is a very strong track that to a certain extent paves the way for pieces like *Secret Garden*, but it did not have the right musical texture for *Human Touch*.

MISSING

Bruce Springsteen / 5'07

Musician

Bruce Springsteen: vocals, programming, guitars, synthesizers, bass

Recording

Thrill Hill West, Los Angeles, California: Autumn 1994

Technical team

Producer: Bruce Springsteen

Recording engineer: Toby Scott

Mixing: Bob Clearmountain

For Springsteen Addicts

Another possible source of inspiration for the title, the use of drum loops, and the "house" texture of the music is *Missing* by the music duo Everything But the Girl, released in August 1994, just before the Boss wrote his song.

Sean Penn on the set of *The Crossing Guard*. After hearing *Missing*, he decided to use it on the soundtrack of his second full-length feature film.

Genesis and lyrics

Bruce Springsteen has often been inspired by masterpieces from the Golden Age of Hollywood, which have enriched his own creative universe. Likewise, he has always enjoyed writing for movies. *Streets of Philadelphia*, written for Jonathan Demme's movie *Philadelphia*, is a good example (see page 356).

The song that would be called *Missing*, dating from the mid-1990s, was not originally composed for the movies. It was only after the songwriter played it to Sean Penn that it was chosen for Penn's second full-length motion picture as a director. First screened in American movie theaters in November 1995, *The Crossing Guard* tells the tragic story of a father (Jack Nicholson) who becomes obsessed by his quest for vengeance after his daughter is killed by a drunk driver (David Morse).

Springsteen's melody and lyrics convey the father's distress perfectly. This is a man for whom nothing else matters in life. He dreams that he sees his daughter drifting across a black sky, far from home; he tries to reach her. In vain. And when he wakes up, he is gripped by an unbearable feeling of emptiness. He misses his daughter terribly.

Missing was released on a four-track CD in 1996, then again on *The Essential Bruce Springsteen* box set in 2003.

Production

This song was intended as part of a solo project that Springsteen began in 1994, but only *Secret Garden* came out of it (see *Greatest Hits*, page 360), and the rest was abandoned. *Missing* has a similar mood to *Streets of Philadelphia*: electro ambience, various loops, and omnipresent synths. The Boss handles all the instruments himself, and does so with obvious talent. The piece is based on a percussion loop on the left (tambourine, bongos, maracas), a very percussive bass drum (or tom-toms?), and a synth for modulation on the right. It feels like a combination of Massive Attack and Isaac Hayes, and it's reminiscent of the *Joe Bell* theme tune that Hayes composed for the movie *Three Tough Guys* (1974). The similarities become even more striking when the songwriter introduces a rhythmic wah-wah (from 1'50). As far as the arrangements are concerned, he introduces a second drum loop with bass on the second verse, and then adds color and texture to the sound with various saturated guitar parts. His lead vocal displays the emotion and conviction that make him an exceptional singer. *Missing* is a success.

MAN AT THE TOP

Bruce Springsteen / 3'19

Musicians
Bruce Springsteen: vocals, guitar
Garry Tallent: bass
Clarence Clemons: sax, percussion (?)
Roy Bittan: piano
Danny Federici: organ
Max Weinberg: drums, percussion (?)
The band: backing vocals
Recording
The Hit Factory, New York: 12 January 1984
Technical team
Producers: Bruce Springsteen, Jon Landau, Chuck Plotkin, Steve Van Zandt
Recording engineer: Toby Scott
Mixing: Bob Clearmountain

The saxophonist Clarence Clemons backstage in 1985, shortly after recording the aptly named *Man at the Top*.

Genesis and lyrics

With typically country-rock rhythm and orchestration (a homage to Bakersfield Sound perhaps?), Springsteen declares that whether he's a rich man, poor man, fireman, beggar, thief, doctor, lawyer, banker, businessman, Indian chief, or "a kid with a guitar in his hand/Dreaming of his record in the number one spot," everyone wants to reach the top. It has always been thus, and will never change, even if the man who is already there says that it's lonely at the top.

Man at the Top dates back to the *Born in the U.S.A.* sessions. It was one of 19 outtakes from the album and was probably not chosen due to its overtly country-rock atmosphere. However, Bruce Springsteen and Columbia Records decided to include it on a four-track CD released in 1996, then on the third disc of the *Tracks* box set (1998). To date, Springsteen has only performed it three times. It's worth noting, however, that the song is one of Nils Lofgren's favorite compositions.

Production

Man at the Top is an enjoyable country-rock number, with fairly conventional orchestration and a standard rhythm section—with Max Weinberg playing cross-stick—Floyd Cramer-style piano contributions, accompaniment on soul organ, skillfully overlapping acoustic and electric guitars, and, most of all, lavish backing vocals from what appears to be the entire band. The latter come in after the second verse (at 1'17) and throughout the coda (at 2'25). The baritone of Clarence Clemons can be heard, and he is also on saxophone (at 1'17 and 3'05). The Boss's singing voice here is rather unusual and light, almost juvenile, a little Ricky Nelson in style; he sings his own harmonies for the choruses (there's an example at 1'00). Finally, there is some percussion, probably claves, in the instrumental parts, positioned on the left of the stereo (listen at around 1'17).

The Boss performed a pared-down guitar and vocals version of *Man at the Top* at the RFK Stadium in Washington DC, on 5 August 1985, supported only by the backing vocals of Patti Scialfa, Clarence Clemons, and Nils Lofgren.

TAKE 'EM AS THEY COME

Bruce Springsteen / 4'28

For Springsteen Addicts

At a concert on 14 July 2012 in Hyde Park, in London, Springsteen grabbed a Spanish fan's poster that listed all the Spanish cities (as well as Paris) where the boss had not performed *Take 'Em as They Come*. So for the first time on British soil, and to the obvious delight of this fan, Springsteen and his band played it in front of a wildly enthusiastic crowd.

Musicians

Bruce Springsteen: vocals, guitar
Steve Van Zandt: guitar, vocal harmonies (?)
Roy Bittan: piano
Danny Federici: organ
Garry Tallent: bass
Max Weinberg: drums

Recording

The Power Station, New York: 10 April 1980

Technical team

Producers: Bruce Springsteen, Jon Landau, Steve Van Zandt
Recording engineer: Neil Dorfsman
Mixing: Ed Thacker

Bruce Springsteen and the E Street Band in London in 2012. *Take 'Em As They Come* evokes the supercharged atmosphere of *Born To Run*.

Genesis and lyrics

Take 'Em as They Come is one of the many songs written by Bruce Springsteen in the first half of his career that revolve around the essential "girlfriend-car-night out" triptych. Here, however, he has added a touch of mystery, even suspense.

At the start of the song, he recounts a dream. A couple are driving across a deserted region, far from town. In his trembling hand the man holds a weapon belonging to his fiancee's father. The girl is wearing her best dress and carrying a switchblade. We understand that the narrator has ventured into dangerous territory with his companion, but he is prepared for all eventualities; he wants to be able to comfort and protect her when the inevitable stranger comes along to pick a fight. There is nothing subliminal about the message in *Take 'Em as They Come*: whatever happens, take life as it comes.

The song was originally recorded during the prolific sessions for *The River*, but Springsteen did not feel that it was worth keeping. This is a little surprising perhaps, because it perfectly matches the spirit of this double album: raw energy drawn directly from the origins of rock 'n' roll. When *The Ties That Bind: The River Collection* was released in 2015, Robert Loss wrote in *PopMatters* that he was convinced the song "would have been a Top 40 hit."[100]

Take 'Em as They Come was released a long time before that, on a four-track CD in 1996, then on the *Tracks* box set in 1998.

Production

The backing track for *Take 'Em as They Come* appears to have been recorded in December 1979, before the Boss laid down his final vocals at The Power Station, in New York, on 10 April 1980. It is a lively rock piece which, oddly enough, is somewhat reminiscent of the musical texture of *Born to Run*. This is down to the Boss's energetic vocal performance, fairly high-pitched voice, and characteristic rasp. In any case, it is an excellent song, carried by a Byrds-style guitar duo, heavy riffs on piano and Farfisa (there's an example at 0'21), and a powerful, pulsing rhythm section from Max Weinberg and Garry Tallent. Steve Van Zandt most likely provided vocal harmonies for Springsteen, although this is not specified in the credits of *Tracks*. *Take 'Em as They Come* would have definitely merited inclusion on *The River*.

WITHOUT YOU

Bruce Springsteen / 3'59

EP: *Blood Brothers/High Hopes/Murder Incorporated* (live)/*Secret Garden* (string version)/*Without You* **Reference:** Columbia Records – CDNK 1195 **Release date:** United States, 3 March 1996 **Musicians** Bruce Springsteen: vocals, guitar / Clarence Clemons: saxophone, backing vocals / Nils Lofgren: guitar, backing vocals / Patti Scialfa: backing vocals / Roy Bittan: piano, backing vocals / Danny Federici: organ, backing vocals / Garry Tallent: bass, backing vocals / Max Weinberg: drums, backing vocals / Chuck Plotkin: backing vocals / Frank Pagano: percussion instruments **Recording:** The Hit Factory, New York: January 1995 **Technical team:** Producers: Bruce Springsteen, Jon Landau, Chuck Plotkin / Recording engineer: Toby Scott / Assistant recording engineers: Jeff Hendrickson, Zoë Yanakas / Mixing: Toby Scott

Genesis and lyrics

Without You dates back to Bruce Springsteen's reunion with the E Street Band, during the sessions for the *Greatest Hits* album in the mid-1990s. The narrator lists the days of the week, each one associated with a different mood, from the start of work on Monday to Friday and the weekends when, he says, he's "out of [his] mind." Although "everything's fine" by Thursday, Wednesday is actually the hardest day for him: he's down in the dumps, miserable that the woman he loves is not by his side.

Without You should really figure among the Boss's lesser works, which is why it didn't number among the never-before-released songs of *Greatest Hits*. Instead, it was released on the *Blood Brothers* EP, which came out in March 1996.

Production

By choosing *Without You* as the song title, Springsteen immediately ran into stiff competition: Badfinger had written a song with exactly the same name in 1970, which became a huge global hit. It was made famous first by Harry Nilsson in 1972, then by Mariah Carey in 1994. Meanwhile, Springsteen's song is nothing more than a bit of fun, unpretentious and infinitely joyful and dynamic. As depicted in Ernie Fritz's 1996 documentary *Blood Brothers*, the E Street Band lets loose on their instruments and on backing vocals, following a somewhat tropical rock rhythm led by Max Weinberg's superb drums. With the sole exception of Steve Van Zandt, they're all gathered around a microphone in The Hit Factory's Studio A, singing in a cheerful and enthusiastic atmosphere. As for "C," the inimitable Claremence Clemons, he's on his saxophone playing the song's only solo.

This song is in a category of its own among the Boss's discography, but it's refreshing and sweet.

A graduate of the Manhattan School of Music, drummer and percussionist Frank Pagano performed in various Broadway musicals, including *Smokey Joe's Cafe* and *Tommy*. In addition to working with Bruce Springsteen, he has recorded with Blondie and the Temptations. He also founded—along with singer and guitarist Jon Herington—a group that was deeply influenced by the music of Jimi Hendrix and Cream.

SIDE A

The soundtrack for *Dead Man Walking* also includes songs by Johnny Cash, Patti Smith, Suzanne Vega, Tom Waits, Steve Earle, and Eddie Vedder with Nusrat Fateh Ali Khan.

DEAD MAN WALKIN'

Bruce Springsteen / 2'43

Single: *Dead Man Walkin'* **Reference:** Columbia Records – CSK 7905 **Release date:** United States 1996 **Musicians:** Bruce Springsteen: vocals, guitar / Danny Federici: keyboards / Jim Hanson: bass / Gary Mallaber: drums, percussion **Recording:** Thrill Hill Recording, Los Angeles, California: April to May 1995 **Technical team:** Producers: Bruce Springsteen, Chuck Plotkin / Recording engineer: Toby Scott / Mixing: Toby Scott

Genesis and lyrics

Dead Man Walking is a 1995 drama directed by Tim Robbins. Susan Sarandon plays Sister Helen Prejean, who befriends Matthew Poncelet, imprisoned for murdering two teenagers, and accompanies him to his execution in the Louisiana State Penitentiary.

After attending a screening of the movie in a New York theater, Bruce Springsteen agreed to compose the title track (which is heard at the start of the movie). In pure folk tradition, *Dead Man Walkin'* is sung in the first person. Matthew Poncelet has been sentenced to die by lethal injection and is looking back on what happened. He was just a normal man with a girl and a job until drugs and guns entered his life. As the first glimmer of dawn appears over the horizon, he knows that he will not live to see another day.

Dead Man Walkin' was released on the CD of the original soundtrack at the same time as Tim Robbins' movie in December 1995. Several singles were subsequently released in early 1996 on both sides of the Atlantic and in Australia. The song also features on *The Essential Bruce Springsteen* box set (2003). The songwriter performed it for the first time on 21 November 1995 at the State Theatre in New Brunswick, New Jersey, during rehearsals for the Ghost of Tom Joad Solo Acoustic Tour.

Production

Nominated for an Oscar in the "Best Original Song" category in 1995, *Dead Man Walkin'* is a dark and somber track, carried by Springsteen's deep vocals. The song begins with a rhythm section played on two strings of his Gibson J-45, the E chord a tone lower, which is the drop D tuning favored by folk and heavy metal guitarists (D, A, D, G, B, E). Danny Federici comes in at the second verse with string sounds, and Gary Mallaber and Jim Hanson join in a verse later on drums (played with brushes) and bass, respectively (from 1'17). The rhythm section is dense, with tom-toms and percussion instruments, notably maracas (in the intro, on the right, at 0'05) and a tambourine, all played by the drummer. The result is a minor masterpiece: austere, uncluttered, and in perfect harmony with the motion picture.

David Bowie also composed a song called *Dead Man Walking*, cowritten with Reeves Gabrels and released on his 1997 album, *Earthling*.

THE
RIS
ING

ALBUM

THE RISING

Lonesome Day • Into the Fire • Waitin' on a Sunny Day • Nothing Man • Countin' on a Miracle • Empty Sky • Worlds Apart • Let's Be Friends (Skin to Skin) • Further On (Up the Road) • The Fuse • Mary's Place • You're Missing • The Rising • Paradise • My City of Ruins

RELEASE DATE

United States: 30 July 2002

Reference: Columbia Records – CK 86600

No.1 in the United States, United Kingdom, Canada, Netherlands, Germany, Spain, and Italy, No.2 in Belgium, No.3 in France

Bruce Springsteen in 2002, a few months after the September 11 attacks.

It was after seeing Van Morrison on stage (shown here in 1977) with Bob Dylan and Joni Mitchell that Bruce Springsteen decided to reform the E Street Band.

2002

THE E STREET BAND RISES FROM THE ASHES OF SEPTEMBER 11

At the end of the 1990s, Bruce Springsteen unexpectedly decided to get the E Street Band back together. In his mind, this was not a nostalgic step back, but a fresh start. As he explains in his autobiography, two events precipitated this decision: firstly, two fans leaving a restaurant told him that they were too young to have seen the E Street Band onstage and, secondly, a joint concert with Bob Dylan, Joni Mitchell, and Van Morrison in San Jose, California. "Van Morrison has always been one of my great, great heroes and an enormous source of inspiration for everything I've done," he writes. "Van put the white soul into our early E Street records."[1]

Fourteen years after *Born in the U.S.A.* (Springsteen's last album with the E Street Band), the entire group welcomed the Boss's call with open arms, especially Steve Van Zandt (although he had already started shooting the first episodes of *The Sopranos*). Rehearsals took place in March 1999 at the Asbury Park Convention Hall. The aptly named Bruce Springsteen and the E Street Band Reunion Tour launched in Barcelona on 9 April and continued until the tenth concert on 1 July 2000, at Madison Square Garden in New York. From start to finish, the group performed 131 shows all over Europe, including France, the United Kingdom, Germany, Belgium, and the Netherlands. They also performed in Canada and the United States. "The first E Street revival was over," said Springsteen. "I'd regained my confidence in the band, and with *Land of Hope and Dreams* and *American Skin* I found I was able to write material that stood with the songs of our past. Now we needed to make a great modern record."[1]

The album

Following this epic world tour, Bruce Springsteen and the E Street Band recorded several songs, including *Land of Hope and Dreams* (rerecorded for the *Wrecking Ball* album) and *American Skin* (for the album *High Hopes*). But the Boss was not enamored with the results. "It all lay flat on the tape like nothing was happening,"[1] he remembers. So a radical decision was made: to replace Chuck Plotkin, a regular collaborator since the mixing of *Darkness on the Edge of Town* (1978), with Brendan O'Brien, who was known for producing several major albums in the 1990s, including *Core* (1992) by the Stone Temple Pilots, *The Battle of Los Angeles* (1999) by Rage Against The Machine, and *Mirror Ball* (1995) by Neil Young and Pearl Jam. In a word, O'Brien was the best man to lead Bruce Springsteen onto a new chapter, especially since Don Ienner, the former president of Columbia Records, had previously told him that this young recording engineer had always dreamed of working with him.

The producer Brendan O'Brien began his collaboration with Bruce Springsteen with the sessions for *The Rising* album.

2002

For Springsteen Addicts

In 1998, Bruce Springsteen found out that he would soon enter the Rock & Roll Hall of Fame—a true honor. As per Hall of Fame regulations, an artist must be inducted under the name they used for their first recording, in this case, Bruce Springsteen and the E Street Band. The ceremony took place on 15 March 1999. The songwriter and his legendary group got together again for a new adventure. U2's Bono inaugurated them.

This is when the catastrophic attacks of September 11 took place. Bruce Springsteen saw the second plane hit the south tower of the World Trade Center live on television. Four suicide attacks on American soil; almost 3,000 dead. Along with the rest of America, along with the whole world, the songwriter was horrified—he spoke of a "supernatural silence."[1] In fact, even though many songs from Bruce Springsteen's 12th studio album were composed before 9/11, a large part of it bears its bloody mark. "With his new album, *The Rising*, Springsteen wades into the wreckage and pain of that horrendous event and emerges bearing 15 songs that genuflect with enormous grace before the sorrows that drift in its wake,"[70] wrote Kurt Loder in *Rolling Stone* magazine.

Bruce Springsteen wrote with subtlety, as a mark of both modesty and respect, making sure not to mention the attacks directly. Instead, he tackled them through the heartbreak experienced by the victims, such as the death of a loved one in *Lonesome Day*, *Into the Fire*, *You're Missing*, *The Fuse*, or the title song, or the refusal of a New York firefighter to be elevated to the rank of American hero in *Nothing Man*. More broadly, he wrote about the strength of the American people, which begins to recover from this act of Islamist terrorism in *My City of Ruins* and *Mary's Place*. The songwriter even mentioned a terrorist in *Paradise* and talked about the impossible love between an American soldier and an Afghan woman in *Worlds Apart*. Love also inspired him to write *Waitin' on a Sunny Day*, *Countin' on a Miracle*, *Let's Be Friends (Skin to Skin)*, *Further On (Up the Road)*, and, in a way, also *Empty Sky*, which used biblical references. The album has a wide musical range that includes folk rock, hard rock, FM rock, and a notable foray into world music.

Under the combined effects of the Bruce Springsteen and E Street Band Reunion Tour and an aggressive promotional campaign organized by Columbia, *The Rising* met with considerable success in the United States upon its release on 30 July 2002. It sold some 520,000 copies in the first week, placing the album No.1 in the *Billboard* chart on 17 August (for 15 days!). Springsteen's new discographic confession would also be a hit outside the United States, as attested by its No.1 place in Canada, the United Kingdom, and various continental European countries, including Denmark, the Netherlands, Germany, Italy, and Spain. It reached No.3 in France. Its ultimate reward was a 2003 Grammy Award for "Best Rock Album."

The jacket

A native of New Jersey (where he was born in 1964), Danny Clinch started his photography career as an assistant to Annie Leibovitz—who, among other things, shot photos for the *Born in the U.S.A.* and *Tunnel of Love* album jackets. In 1999, he

Sleeve of *The Rising*. The photograph was shot by Danny Clinch, a former assistant to Annie Leibovitz.

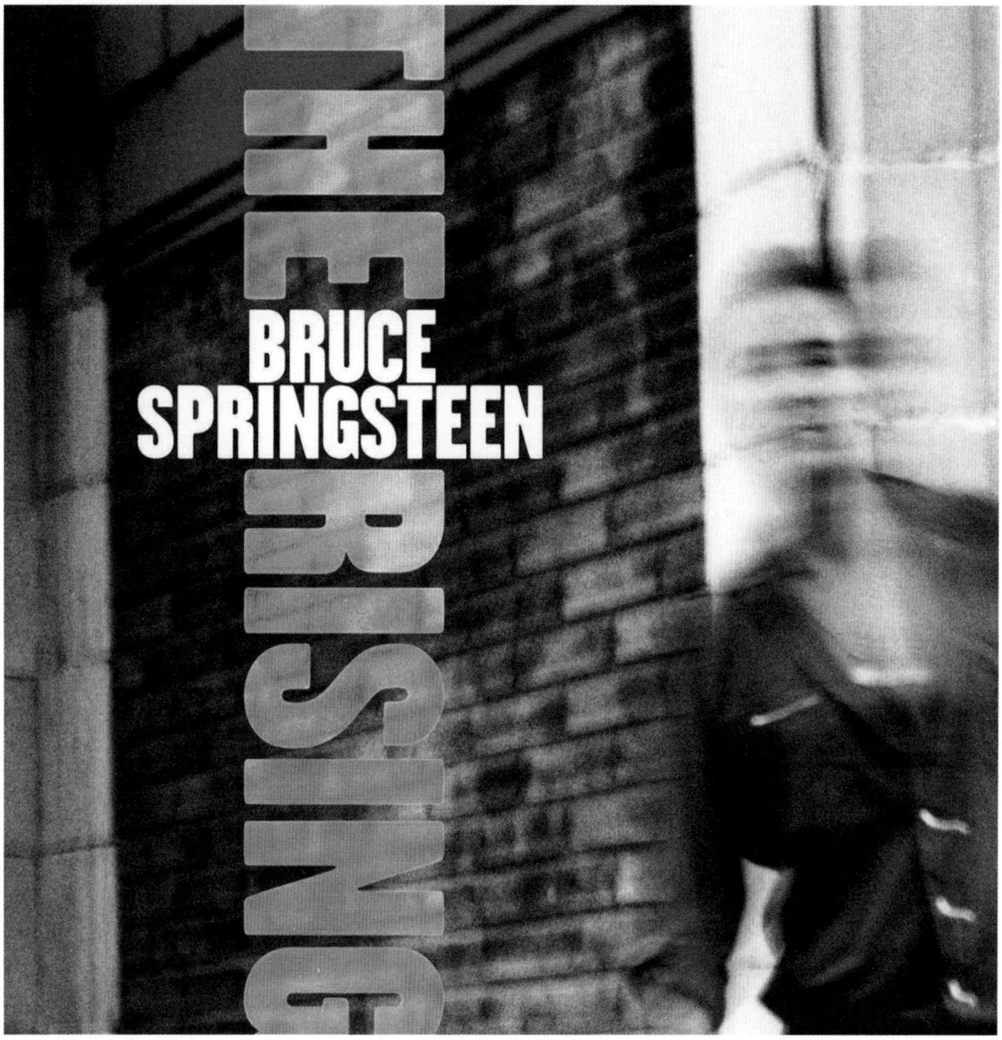

published the book *Discovery Inn* (which contained striking photos of Johnny Cash, Public Enemy, and the Smashing Pumpkins) and sent a copy of it to Bruce Springsteen. This is how Clinch was hired to shoot the cover for *The Rising*.

On the front cover is a black and white photo of a blurry man (obviously Springsteen!) standing by a brick wall. Bruce Springsteen's name is printed horizontally in white and the title of the album vertically in orange. "My first album cover for Bruce," wrote Danny Clinch on his Facebook page. "I love this image but this selection as a cover surprised me. After getting to know the music and its inspirations, it made perfect sense. Dream of life."[116] On the inside of the jacket, the songs and lyrics are illustrated with atmospheric photographs in black and white and in color—a strange, post-9/11 mood. On the back, the song titles and the producer's name, Brendan O'Brien, are written in red, like blood.

The recording

To immortalize the reunion with the E Street Band on tape, Springsteen decided to change his technical and production team. "The art of production had simply moved its center," explains the songwriter in his autobiography *Born to Run*. "Our ideas and techniques were no longer current, ear-friendly, exciting, or competent."[1] So Brendan O'Brien became both lone producer of the album and also the mixer, while the loyal Toby Scott, at the console since *The River* in 1978 (mixing), stepped aside for Nick DiDia, who would take over recording for the Boss from hereon in (Scott would, however, still work on *Let's Be Friends (Skin to Skin)*. This outstanding Philadelphia technician—who was also a producer—was a friend and colleague of Brendan O'Brien. He was also his designated sound engineer—they would work together for 20 years. Karl Egsieker and Billy Bowers were by his side to assist on certain tracks.

The album was recorded and mixed at the Southern Tracks Recording Studio in Atlanta, Georgia (except for *Worlds Apart* and *My City of Ruins*, which were mixed at the Silent Sound Studios). Many other artists would work in this recording den, founded in 1988 by Mike Clark and Bill Lowery, including Pearl Jam, the Stone Temple Pilots, Bob Dylan, and Aerosmith. It was a stronghold of Brendan O'Brien, who in 1993 outfitted it with the first SSL 4000G + Ultimation console. The studio closed in 2012.

Before invading Southern Tracks, Springsteen tried to record some new songs on his own in his home studio in Thrill Hill East between September 2000 and early 2001. Nothing survives of those sessions, except for a small part of

After having taken care of some of the Boss's sessions ever since *The River*, the faithful Toby Scott (seen here in 1999) made way for Nick DiDia on *The Rising*.

2002

For Springsteen Addicts

In 2002, Nick DiDia won a Grammy Award for "Best Recording Engineer" for *The Rising*. In 2015, he and musician Bernard Fanning founded their own studio, La Cueva Recording, based in Australia, near Byron Bay.

The Rising: Let's Be Friends (Skin to Skin). In the spring of 2001, Springsteen and the E Street Band started recording with Chuck Plotkin and Toby Scott. But the result was not up to his usual standards; only *American Skin (41 Shots)* would make it onto *High Hopes*, in 2014. So, he hired Brendan O'Brien and Nick DiDia, and booked the Southern Tracks studio. Springsteen recalls meeting his new producer in his home studio in Thrill Hill: "I met Mr. O'Brien, a youngish-looking man in his thirties. He was sane, easy to talk to and be with, without pretension, and confident. I ran by him some things I had, recent recordings, old demos, new demos. He focused on a few songs, said he'd come up just to make sure 'I was still me' and informed me that I was, and we went on to plan another meeting and a recording date in his home base of Atlanta [the Southern Tracks Recording Studio]."[1] Meanwhile, O'Brien gave a slightly different account of their meeting. "I said, 'Hey man, I've gotta tell you. We had a great day together. I'm excited about doing this...But I've just got to tell you, I'm worried. You have a history of recording things and not putting them out?'—I don't know any of this stuff, but I had always heard—and I said, 'That scares me to death, man. I don't want to do that.'"[117] Luckily, O'Brien soon confirmed that Springsteen would see the project through to the end. The pair would work together for many years.

The Boss thus recorded his 12th album flanked, once again, by his brothers in arms, the E Street Band—for the first time since the unreleased songs of *Greatest Hits* in 1995. O'Brien's technique was simple: the Springsteen quartet—including Roy Bittan, Garry Tallent, and Max Weinberg—recorded the basic tracks; then the other musicians entered as overdubs. This was a proven method for the producer, which turned out to be very effective. Only two short months were required to bag *The Rising*, from the end of January to mid-March 2002—a record time, especially since the E Street Band was known for its endless studio marathons. Seventeen songs were recorded: 15 for the album and two outtakes that would later be released on *High Hopes* (*Down in the Hole* and *Harry's Place*). Of note: although removed from production, Chuck Plotkin was responsible for recording Asif Ali Khan and Party at the Henson Recording Studios in Hollywood.

The musicians

The Rising was produced with a larger than ever E Street Band—at least on disc: in addition to Roy Bittan, Clarence

Southern Tracks recording studios in Atlanta, Georgia, founded in the 1980s by Bill Lowery (left) and Mike Clark (right).

Clemons, Danny Federici, Garry Tallent, Max Weinberg, and Steve Van Zandt—back at the Boss's side—Patti Scialfa and Nils Lofgren were also in the mix. Other participating musicians included the loyal Soozie Tyrell on backing vocals and the violin; Brendan O'Brien on the hurdy-gurdy and glockenspiel; Jere Flint, Larry LeMaster, and Jane Scarpantoni on the cello; the Nashville String Machine, conducted by Carl Gorodetzky, on strings for two of the album's songs; Asif Ali Kahn and Party for *Worlds Apart*; and, finally, the Alliance Singers choir and a brass section.

The instruments

We still can't know for sure which guitars Springsteen used in the studio in addition to his Telecaster-Esquire (this is clearly not the case in concert). There are, of course, many other 6-string guitars (and many amplifiers)—Brendan O'Brien owns a considerable collection, which he made available to the Boss, including some Gretschs for use in *The Rising*—that unfortunately remain unidentified, including a baritone guitar, likely a Danelectro Longhorn 4623 (or a Fender Bass VI).

Roy Bittan used a Mellotron, a Kurzweil, a pump organ, a Korg M1, and a Crumar. Danny Federici and his Hammond B-3 were inseparable, but he also played a Vox Continental and dusted off his Farfisa organ for the occasion.

LONESOME DAY

Bruce Springsteen / 4'08

> **For Springsteen Addicts**
>
> For the *Lonesome Day* video, shot by Mark Pellington in Asbury Park, Bruce Springsteen sang live during each take, just as he'd done for *Streets of Philadelphia* and *Brilliant Disguise*. His vocal performance might even be better than the one on the disc.

Musicians

Bruce Springsteen: vocals, guitars
Patti Scialfa: backing vocals
Steve Van Zandt: guitars, backing vocals
Nils Lofgren: guitars
Clarence Clemons: backing vocals
Roy Bittan: keyboard
Danny Federici: organ
Garry Tallent: bass
Max Weinberg: drums
Soozie Tyrell: violin, backing vocals
Jere Flint, Larry LeMaster: cellos

Recording and mixing

Southern Tracks Recording Studio, Atlanta, Georgia: February to March 2002

Technical team

Producer: Brendan O'Brien
Recording engineer: Nick DiDia
Assistant recording engineers: Karl Egsieker, Billy Bowers
Mixing: Brendan O'Brien
Mastering: Bob Ludwig

The filmmaker Mark Pellington had connections to the world of rock, notably making the video clip of Bruce Springsteen's *Lonesome Day*.

Genesis and lyrics

Lonesome Day says a lot about Bruce Springsteen's writing style at the start of the new millennium. The first verse is about a simple breakup. The narrator speaks (in his head, no doubt) to the woman who has left him: he thought he knew her, with her "tender touch," but now he admits he "didn't really know that much" about her.

Starting from the second verse, the narrator's bitter feelings of loneliness are no longer (or at least not only) related to a failed relationship, but to something far more serious. He starts to talk about hell, of a "dark sun" on the rise. Bruce Springsteen clearly wrote these words after the attacks of 9/11. "House is on fire," clearly refers to the United States, to New York, and the collapsing World Trade Center towers, while "viper's in the grass" is the new force declaring war on America: Islamist terrorism. The narrator does not, however, want to preach vengeance. He wants to ask the right questions before blowing things up.

Chosen as the title song for the second single from *The Rising* (with a live version of *Spirit in the Night*, recorded in Barcelona), *Lonesome Day* only reached No.36 and No.39 in the United States and United Kingdom, respectively. In Spain, on the other hand, the song would climb to No.6.

Production

Lonesome Day starts with Jere Flint and Larry LeMaster's cello motif and Soozie Tyrell's violin ringing out against a backdrop of acoustic guitars arpeggiated with a pick. Then the three musicians launch into the riff supported by the many saturated 6-string guitars and by the rest of the group. The sound clearly evokes Pearl Jam or the Stone Temple Pilots, and bears Brendan O'Brien's signature. This becomes even more obvious when the Boss launches into the lead vocals, as this way of compressing and integrating the voice in a mix is characteristic of the producer's musical vision. By the same token, Max Weinberg's drums sound more authentic, powerful, and modern. His performance also has a more marked groove, a tone that was already present in the previously unreleased songs on *Greatest Hits* (1995).

Although it's not among Springsteen's best songs, *Lonesome Day* has a definite charm.

INTO THE FIRE

Bruce Springsteen / 5'04

Musicians

Bruce Springsteen: vocals, guitars
Patti Scialfa: backing vocals
Steve Van Zandt: guitars, backing vocals
Nils Lofgren: dobro, backing vocals
Clarence Clemons: backing vocals, cabasa (?)
Roy Bittan: keyboard
Danny Federici: organ
Garry Tallent: bass
Max Weinberg: drums, cabasa (?)
Soozie Tyrell: violin, backing vocals
Jane Scarpantoni: cello
Brendan O'Brien: hurdy-gurdy, glockenspiel

Recording and mixing

Southern Tracks Recording Studio, Atlanta, Georgia: February to March 2002

Technical team

Producer: Brendan O'Brien
Recording engineer: Nick DiDia
Assistant recording engineers: Karl Egsieker, Billy Bowers
Mixing: Brendan O'Brien
Mastering: Bob Ludwig

For Springsteen Addicts

The live versions of *Into the Fire* are significantly different from the one on the album and include, most notably, an extraordinary introduction in Patti Scialfa's sublime voice. Among the most remarkable performances was the one from 16 October 2002 at the Palau Sant Jordi in Barcelona, Spain, which can be found on the DVD *Live in Barcelona* (released in 2003).

Genesis and lyrics

In *Born to Run*, Bruce Springsteen reveals that *The Rising* "had its origins in the national telethon we were invited to be a part of the week after September 11." He continues: "I wrote *Into the Fire* for that show (it remained incomplete, so I performed *My City of Ruins*, the song I'd written a year earlier for Asbury Park)."[1]

The program Bruce Springsteen is referring to is *America: A Tribute to Heroes*, and he is indeed paying tribute to American heroes here, specifically to firefighters and more broadly to all those who brought relief to the victims of the attacks among the ruins and the ashes of the World Trade Center. One of them was called Joe Farrelly: he was one of the 15 firefighters from Manhattan's Engine 54, ladder 4, who died on the spot. He was born in New Jersey and was a big fan of Bruce Springsteen.

Into the Fire saw the light of day after a long phone conversation between Springsteen and Stacey, Joe Farrelly's wife. In that moment he came up with some of his most emotional lyrics, such as "I need your kiss, but love and duty called you someplace higher/Somewhere up the stairs, into the fire." Bruce Springsteen sang *Into the Fire* for the first time at the Jacksonville Memorial Coliseum, in Florida, on 4 March 2002.

Production

The first song recorded with the E Street Band at the South Tracks Recording Studio, *Into the Fire* starts with Nils Lofgren playing the dobro slide guitar (on the right), accompanied by the Boss's acoustic guitar (on the left), Soozie Tyrell's violin, and Max Weinberg's decidedly modern-sounding drums. For this tribute to the victims of 9/11, the songwriter opted for a piece that fluctuates between blues, gospel, and country. The result is impressive, and the quality of the arrangements and production is exceptional—the Boss had been right to hire Brendan O'Brien. The latter also recorded a hurdy-gurdy part and glockenspiels (from 2'30). The rest of the musicians rise to the occasion for this superb song, whether in the backing vocals, rhythmic section, guitars, keyboards, or string and cello parts played by Soozie Tyrell and Jane Scarpantoni, respectively. As for the Boss, his performance is magnificent.

WAITIN' ON A SUNNY DAY

Bruce Springsteen / 4'18

For Springsteen Addicts

Waitin' on a Sunny Day came out as a single in Europe (along with live versions of *Born to Run*, *Darkness on the Edge of Town*, and *Thunder Road*), but not in the United States. It reached its highest place in the charts in Sweden, where it got to No.15.

2002

Musicians

Bruce Springsteen: vocals, guitar
Patti Scialfa: backing vocals
Nils Lofgren: guitar, backing vocals
Steve Van Zandt: guitar, backing vocals
Clarence Clemons: saxophones, backing vocals
Roy Bittan: piano
Danny Federici: organ
Garry Tallent: bass
Max Weinberg: drums
Soozie Tyrell: violin, backing vocals
Brendan O'Brien: glockenspiel, tubular bells

Recording and mixing

Southern Tracks Recording Studio, Atlanta, Georgia: February to March 2002

Technical team

Producer: Brendan O'Brien
Recording engineer: Nick DiDia
Assistant recording engineers: Karl Egsieker, Billy Bowers
Mixing: Brendan O'Brien
Mastering: Bob Ludwig

Bruce Springsteen with Nils Lofgren and Max Weinberg in Atlanta, 2002. *Waitin' on a Sunny Day* was an essential song on the tour.

Genesis and lyrics

Bruce Springsteen composed *Waitin' on a Sunny Day* well before recording *The Rising*, since he played it with the E Street Band during the onstage soundcheck at the Weserstadion in Bremen, Germany, on 17 June 1999.

The song opens with the lines: "It's raining but there ain't a cloud in the sky/Musta been a tear from your eye." On the DVD *VH1 Storytellers—On Stage*, Bruce Springsteen confessed that these types of songs—which he calls folk songs—help "free [his] mind."[13] "Now the master of this, of course, was Smokey Robinson," he says, "and when I write these sometimes I think about him singing them and it gives me an idea of the phrasing."[13]

At first glance, this is an unpretentious song whose theme contrasts sharply with that of the album. The songwriter likely included it to provide a moment of lightness between the more dramatic *Into the Fire* and *Nothing Man*. On the other hand, precisely because of the September 11 attacks, *Waitin' on a Sunny Day* seems to embody a sort of call for the American people to regain, if not immediate happiness, at least a new sense of confidence.

Production

Waitin' on a Sunny Day is among the songs Jon Landau salvaged at the last minute. Springsteen had wanted to get rid of it. It's not a masterpiece, but it's a nice song, with a twist reminiscent of *Hungry Heart*. It seems to have been initially recorded in the Boss's home studio in 1998, before being finalized in Atlanta.

Max Weinberg opens festivities with a simple and effective rock drumming. The sound of his kit is superb, his drumheads resonating to the beat of the drumsticks. The group then dives in with a very 1950s-style accompaniment, except for Soozie Tyrell's violin, which provides the melody. The Boss sings with lightness, although his performance lacks conviction. Clarence Clemons plays several saxophone parts, notably a baritone in the last chorus (at 3'16) and a tenor solo at the end. Brendan O'Brien plays the tubular bells and the glockenspiel (between 2'14 and 2'39). As for Danny Federici's organ, it seems that the producer tried to imitate the sound from *Do You Know What I Mean*, the 1971 Lee Michaels' hit. One can even hear the similarity between the two pieces in the drums during the introduction.

NOTHING MAN

Bruce Springsteen / 4'23

Springsteen performed *Nothing Man* alone on the electric piano during the Devils & Dust Solo Acoustic Tour in 2005. This version is undoubtedly better than the one on the album.

Musicians

Bruce Springsteen: vocals, guitar
Patti Scialfa: backing vocals
Steve Van Zandt: guitar, backing vocals
Nils Lofgren: guitar, backing vocals
Clarence Clemons: backing vocals, percussion instruments (?)
Roy Bittan: keyboard
Danny Federici: keyboard
Garry Tallent: bass
Max Weinberg: drums, percussion instruments (?)

Recording and mixing

Southern Tracks Recording Studio, Atlanta, Georgia: February to March 2002

Technical team

Producer: Brendan O'Brien
Recording engineer: Nick DiDia
Assistant recording engineers: Karl Egsieker, Billy Bowers
Mixing: Brendan O'Brien
Mastering: Bob Ludwig

For Springsteen Addicts

The "misty cloud of pink vapor" mentioned at the end of the first verse refers to an article by John Bussey in the *Wall Street Journal* on 12 September 2001 called *Eye of the Storm: One Journey Through Desperation and Chaos*, in which he describes the bodies falling from the World Trade Center as "pink and red vapor drifting at ground level."[118]

Genesis and lyrics

Bruce Springsteen borrowed the title of this song from Jim Thompson's book *The Nothing Man*, published in 1954, in which the master of crime fiction tells the story of Clinton Brown, a discerning journalist and unrepentant seducer who, despite his best efforts, can't seem to shake off his bad reputation. Why did he sink into alcoholism? Did he really have his wife burned alive? Was the war all for nothing?

Bruce Springsteen drafted the lyrics and recorded an initial version of this song in 1994, his "nothing man" not having fought in the Second World War but in the first Gulf War. Then the attacks of September 11 took place and the character became a hero swept up in the fury surrounding the tragedy, a reluctant hero who "never thought [he'd] live/To read about [himself] in [his] hometown paper" and whose "brave young life was forever changed/In a misty cloud of pink vapor."

Production

Nothing Man could have easily fitted into an album such as *Lucky Man* or *Human Touch*. In fact, it includes one of Springsteen's favorite stylistic tools: the synth pads. Brendan O'Brien tried his hardest to scrap this sound from the album—it was too prominent in his opinion—in favor of instruments such as the acoustic piano or Hammond organ. But the Boss had made a demo with the synths in 1994, and the producer couldn't help but admit that the song wouldn't be the same without them.

The piece starts off with brassy synth sounds, an acoustic guitar, and Max Weinberg's drums, which sound like a drum machine. Springsteen sings with a restrained voice packed with underlying emotion. The bass and a few keyboard chords enter at the first chorus (at 0'54). Then a ghostly sound emerges from a saturated fog, reinforcing the backing vocals that respond to the singer (at 1'11): it's Nils Lofgren, who once again is violining on his guitar (see *Secret Garden*, page 360).

Lastly, starting from the first choral section (at 2'21), several percussion instruments enter, notably the maracas, then the congas and a tambourine (at 2'38).

Nils Lofgren, Clarence Clemons, Bruce Springsteen, Steve Van Zandt, Max Weinberg, Patti Scialfa, and Garry Tallent at Shea Stadium, on 4 October 2003, the last concert of the Rising Tour.

COUNTIN' ON A MIRACLE

Bruce Springsteen / 4'44

Founded in the early 1980s by Carl Gorodetzky, the Nashville String Machine is a musical group based in Nashville. It's not limited to strings, and can complete its ensemble with other orchestral instruments, depending on the project. The group has worked with Neil Young, The Beach Boys, Michael McDonald, Dolly Parton, k.d. lang, Garth Brooks, and Johnny Cash, among others.

Musicians
Bruce Springsteen: vocals, guitars
Patti Scialfa: backing vocals
Steve Van Zandt: guitars, backing vocals
Nils Lofgren: guitars, backing vocals
Clarence Clemons: tambourine, backing vocals
Roy Bittan: keyboard
Danny Federici: keyboard
Garry Tallent: bass
Max Weinberg: drums
The Nashville String Machine: orchestra
- Carl Gorodetzky: first violin and manager
- Pam Sixfin, Lee Larrison, Conni Ellisor, Alan Umstead, David Davidson, Mary Kathryn Vanosdale, David Angell: violins
- Kristin Wilkinson, Gary Vanosdale, Jim Grosjean, Monisa Angell: violas
- Bob Mason, Carol Rabinowitz, Julie Tanner, Lynn Peithman: cellos
- Ricky Keller: conductor

Recording and mixing
Southern Tracks Recording Studio, Atlanta, Georgia: February to March 2002
Sound Kitchen Recording Studios, Franklin, Tennessee: February to March 2002

Technical team
Producer: Brendan O'Brien
Recording engineer: Nick DiDia
Assistant recording engineers: Karl Egsieker, Billy Bowers, Melissa Mattey (Sound Kitchen)
Mixing: Brendan O'Brien
Mastering: Bob Ludwig

2002

Genesis and lyrics

Disenchantment, bitterness, despair...these are the words that immediately come to mind when listening to *Countin' on a Miracle.* The narrator doesn't seem to believe in anything anymore, except for a hoped-for miracle. Did heartbreak plunge him into such melancholy? The mention of Sleeping Beauty emerging from her long slumber after Prince Charming's kiss, while he is now deprived of the kiss of his loved one, does indeed suggest this. Especially since he specifically mentions a fleeting happiness, "our happily ever after." But, as with the whole of *The Rising*, where the almost eschatological atmosphere of September 11 looms large, it also conjures up thoughts of the thousands of victims and of the families who waited for news of their loved ones.

Strange story, actually. Is Bruce Springsteen using *Countin' on a Miracle* to convey the message that these attacks caused the abrupt end to the fairy tale that is the history of the United States?

Production

As for production, *Countin' on a Miracle* is a rather enigmatic song, in the sense that it gives the impression that neither Bruce Springsteen nor his producer knew how to arrange it. The introduction, with its two acoustic guitars and chords, seems to be completely disconnected from the rest of the piece, which is nothing more than a hard rock against a background of saturated guitars carried by a powerful rhythmic section. This feeling is reinforced by the alternative recording of the song, which can be found among the bonus tracks from *The Essential Bruce Springsteen*, a compilation released in 2003: the songwriter sings by himself, accompanying himself on the acoustic guitar and in slide. This version is remarkably different from the one on *The Rising.* Photographer Danny Clinch, who created the album jacket, filmed the Boss on the spot in the Southern Tracks Recording Studio. The atmosphere was country blues, with Springsteen singing in falsetto. This was a very far cry from the final version, but it's very good, nonetheless. The Nashville String Machine, who recorded at the Sound Kitchen Recording Studios, enhance the sound, but the chords are unfortunately buried in the mix, except during the bridge, which inevitably brings to mind the break in *I Am the Walrus* by The Beatles (at 1'52).

Empty Sky was also the name of Elton John's first album, released in 1969, and the name of the album's opening song that launched his career.

For Springsteen Addicts

Springsteen performed some very beautiful acoustic and solo versions of *Empty Sky* accompanied only by his guitar or by Patti Scialfa's beautiful vocal harmonies, as for the 16 October 2002 concert at the Palau Sant Jordi in Barcelona, Spain (see the DVD *Live in Barcelona*, released in 2003).

EMPTY SKY

Bruce Springsteen / 3'34

Musicians

- **Bruce Springsteen:** vocals, guitar, harmonica
- **Patti Scialfa:** backing vocals
- **Steve Van Zandt:** guitar, backing vocals (?)
- **Nils Lofgren:** guitar, backing vocals (?)
- **Clarence Clemons:** maracas (?), backing vocals (?)
- **Roy Bittan:** piano
- **Danny Federici:** organ
- **Garry Tallent:** bass
- **Max Weinberg:** drums
- **Brendan O'Brien:** hurdy-gurdy

Recording and mixing

- **Southern Tracks Recording Studio, Atlanta, Georgia:** February to March 2002

Technical team

- **Producer:** Brendan O'Brien
- **Recording engineer:** Nick DiDia
- **Assistant recording engineers:** Karl Egsieker, Billy Bowers
- **Mixing:** Brendan O'Brien
- **Mastering:** Bob Ludwig

Bruce Springsteen and Patti Scialfa rehearsing at the Convention Hall, Asbury Park, in July 2002. A couple performing at their peak in *Empty Sky*.

Genesis and lyrics

"My art director had sent me a photo of clouds in an empty sky and in a few days, sitting on the edge of my hotel bed in Atlanta, I had the song,"[1] says Bruce Springsteen in his autobiography.

Empty Sky was the last song Bruce Springsteen composed for *The Rising*. Here, too, he makes the connection between a man who has been plunged into loneliness after the departure of an ex-lover and the tragedy of September 11. There's "Just an empty impression in the bed where you used to be" on the one hand, and on the other, "Blood on the streets, yeah blood flowing down." As for the title itself—*Empty Sky*—the image evokes a sense of abandonment, the collapse of the World Trade Center (which left an enormous void in New York), and even the total absence of planes in the American sky right after the attacks.

In the second part of the song, Bruce Springsteen refers to the Bible, to the river Jordan, and the Promised Land beyond, as well as the two trees in the Garden of Eden: the Tree of Life and the Tree of the Knowledge of Good and Evil (which bore the forbidden fruit). Is this a totally Springsteenian take on the radical changes taking place in the United States and the world as a whole after the September 11 attacks?

Production

Empty Sky opens to the distorted, trip hop-style sound of Max Weinberg's drums. Roy Bittan accompanies him on the piano by playing the song's melodic motif, with a relatively compressed sound. Then a wall of acoustic guitars comes out of nowhere, supported by Garry Tallent's bass line. Springsteen's voice, which is also compressed and equalized, stands out of the mix with precision, without sounding intrusive. Once again, the producer gives the songwriter a much more modern and livelier vibe. The musicians enter gradually as the song progresses, notably Roy Bittan, who returns to the piano for the second verse, and Danny Federici, on the organ at the first instrumental break (at 1'59). In the last verse, Nils Lofgren plays the electric guitar, Clarence Clemons a maracas part, and Brendan O'Brien a hurdy-gurdy accompaniment (from 2'10). As for the Boss, he plays two harmonica solos with a slightly saturated sound (at 1'59 and 3'17).

Empty Sky, which is not particularly original, was the last song to be recorded for *The Rising*.

WORLDS APART

Bruce Springsteen / 6'07

Musicians
Bruce Springsteen: vocals, guitar, harmonica (?)
Patti Scialfa: backing vocals (?)
Steve Van Zandt: guitar, backing vocals (?)
Nils Lofgren: guitar, banjo
Clarence Clemons: finger cymbals, tambourine, backing vocals (?)
Roy Bittan: keyboard
Danny Federici: organ
Garry Tallent: bass
Max Weinberg: drums
Soozie Tyrell: violin
Asif Ali Khan and Party:
- Asif Ali Khan: vocals
- Manzoor Hussain Shibli, Sarfraz Hussain, Raza Hussain, Imtiaz Shibli, Shahnawaz Hussain Khan, Bakhat Fayyaz Hussain, Omerdraz Hussain Aftab, Waheed Hussain Mumtaz: chorus
- Karamat Ali Asad: chorus and harmonies
- Haji Nazir Afridi: chorus and tabla

Recording
Southern Tracks Recording Studio, Atlanta, Georgia: February to March 2002
Henson Recording Studios, Hollywood: February to March 2002

Technical team
Producer: Brendan O'Brien
Coordinator of Pakistani musicians: Chuck Plotkin
Recording engineers: Nick DiDia, Dave Reed (Henson Studios)
Assistant recording engineers: Billy Bowers, Brian Humphrey (Henson Studios)
Mixing: Brendan O'Brien (Silent Sound Studios, Atlanta)

The musician Asif Ali Khan is originally from Pakistan. His teacher, Nusret Fateh Ali Khan, went by the moniker "emperor of the qawwalî." Qawwalîa is a type of music that expresses full devotion to Sufiism.

2002

Genesis and lyrics

Worlds Apart is only indirectly connected with the dark day of September 11, even though its world-music atmosphere might suggest that these terrorist attacks were felt well beyond the American borders—in all the countries that claim to be democratic and free. Bruce Springsteen uses the story of an American soldier and a young Afghan woman to address the war the United States and its allies waged against the Taliban and Al-Qaeda after the attacks. "I think the song started when I saw a picture of the women in Afghanistan with the veils off a few days after they'd routed the Taliban out of Kabul, and their faces were so beautiful,"[119] he explained in the magazine *Uncut* in September 2002.

Worlds Apart is the story of a forbidden love, forbidden because of what appears to be the hatred of one group and the arrogance of the other, and because civilizations are inherently divisive. There is a glimmer of hope, however, when the narrator tells the woman he loves that he will meet her "on the ridge between these worlds apart." These few sweet words became fully realized at a time when American resentment toward Arab countries was reaching its peak.

Production

Worlds Apart is nothing like any of Springsteen's previous songs: it plunges into the flow of world music, which was brought to the West by artists like Peter Gabriel with his label Real World Records, founded in 1989. Springsteen and Asif Ali Khan and Party, a Pakistani group, cheerfully dive into a happy fusion between two previously antagonistic cultures. This wasn't the first meeting of East and West in rock music—George Harrison had been pioneering this type of musical blend for The Beatles since 1966. But Springsteen, with the valuable help of Brendan O'Brien, created a particularly successful marriage of the two sounds.

The idea behind this song was to welcome "the presence of Allah," according to the songwriter, who "wanted to find a place where worlds collide and meet."[1] As Springsteen once explained to *Uncut* magazine, he also wanted to play around with mid-Eastern scales in a few of the background parts in the song. Moreover, Asif Ali Khan and Party had a record coming out with Def Jam Recordings and were in LA at the time. So, Springsteen asked Chuck Plotkin and recording

Max Weinberg successfully blended the touch and power of rock music with traditional percussion instruments in *Worlds Apart*. Here he plays his DW (Drum Workshop) kit.

engineer Dave Reed to record the Pakistani musicians at the Henson Studios with an ISDN line, a digital network of integrated services. For Springsteen it was great to hear that kind of sound in a rock song, as he wanted to look beyond the United States and push the boundaries of the song in some way.

Worlds Apart begins with Asif Ali Khan's voice ringing out against a background of harmonium playing and ethereal sounds. A drum loop soon shatters this meditative atmosphere, accompanied by tablas, finger cymbals, an organ, and multiple samples, and also by Nils Lofgren's banjo (on the right). Asif Ali Khan's group enters with vocal extemporizations before Springsteen joins them in the chorus, for which he sings some simple folkloric "la la las" (at 0'57). After a verse and another chorus, the cultures literally clash: a hard-rock sound emerges led by Max Weinberg and Garry Tallent's powerful rhythm, and the various saturated and acoustic guitars, which creates a veritable Wall of Sound (from 1'52). The Boss seems to be playing the harmonica in the third verse (far into the mix, from 2'12), and launches into the first saturated solo (at 2'30) before Danny Federici's Hammond B-3 comes in. Other instruments gradually make an appearance, notably a tambourine and Soozie Tyrell's violin, which brings a Celtic touch to this veritable cultural amalgamation (from 3'42). After an exuberant coda and a final solo on a very saturated 6-string guitar, the piece ends on the tablas, harmonium, and the voices of Asif Ali Khan and Party (at 5'41).

With *Worlds Apart*, Springsteen managed to create a formidable song with universal appeal, which he would have to defend against unfounded accusations regarding his supposedly anti-patriotic stances. But Springsteen maintained that the song was great musically and also featured some fantastic musicians and people.

For Springsteen Addicts

"I hold you in my arms" is the first line of both *Worlds Apart* and *Brilliant Disguise* (from the album *Tunnel of Love*).

LET'S BE FRIENDS (SKIN TO SKIN)

Bruce Springsteen / 4'21

THE BOSS OFF BASE

The only performance of this song, given on 16 September 2003 at the Rentschler Field in East Hartford, was a disaster. The Boss sang out of tune from start to finish. That's probably why he never sang it again! A shame, nonetheless.

2002

Musicians

Bruce Springsteen: vocals, guitar, keyboard, bass, drum-machine programming, percussion instruments (?)
Clarence Clemons: saxophone, backing vocals (?)
Roy Bittan: keyboard (?)
Soozie Tyrell: violin, backing vocals
The Alliance Singers: Corinda Carford, Michelle Moore (soloist), Tiffeny Andrews, Antoinette Moore, Antonio Lawrence, Jesse Moorer
The musicians: handclaps

Recording

Thrill Hill Studios, New Jersey: 1999–2001
Southern Tracks Recording Studio, Atlanta, Georgia: February to March 2002

Technical team

Producer: Brendan O'Brien
Recording engineer: Toby Scott (Thrill Hill), Nick DiDia
Assistant recording engineers: Karl Egsieker, Billy Bowers
Mixing: Brendan O'Brien
Mastering: Bob Ludwig

Corinda Carfora—known as Carford—is a founding member of The Alliance Singers. The choir was created right after 11 September 2001, to bring support and help to the local residents of Monmouth, New Jersey, the home county to 147 of the victims. One thing led to another, and, encouraged by Garry Tallent, the choir finally accompanied Springsteen in concert at the Asbury Park Convention Hall in December of that same year before participating in recordings for *The Rising*.

Genesis and lyrics

The theme of *Let's Be Friends (Skin to Skin)* is similar to the one from *Worlds Apart*: there is nothing to suggest the heroine is Afghani, but the subtitle of the song (*Skin to Skin*), and the line "I know we're different you and me," suggest that this song also deals with a relationship between an American and a woman from a different culture. The narrator encourages the woman to let him in and give the relationship a try, to leave the past behind and ignore criticisms, and to seize an opportunity they may never have again.

Musically, *Let's Be Friends (Skin to Skin)* brings to mind Sly Stone in his heyday, or Marvin Gaye. Bruce Springsteen only performed it once, on 16 September 2003 at the Rentschler Field in East Hartford, Connecticut.

Production

There is limited information on the precise production date of *Let's Be Friends (Skin to Skin)*, at least with regards to the basic tracks Toby Scott recorded at Thrill Hill, probably between 1999 and 2001. The song was completed in early 2002 at the Southern Tracks Recording Studio in Atlanta, and it's the only song on the album that wasn't entirely supervised by Brendan O'Brien, except for the mixing. *Let's Be Friends (Skin to Skin)* is a sort of hybrid between R&B, soul, and pop that may as well have come straight out of Motown. Springsteen provided the instrumental background virtually on his own: the drum-machine programming, keyboards, acoustic guitar, bass, and probably the few percussion intruments as well (cabasa or maracas). The lead vocals, chorus, clapping, violin, and saxophone were very likely recorded in Atlanta in early 2002.

The highlight of the piece, aside from its lovely melody, is The Alliance Singers' vocals, which inject a veritable touch of gospel into the arrangements, with Michelle Moore's lead voice being a particular point of pride. She and the Boss would cross paths again in 2012 to work on an album. Clarence Clemons brings his personal touch with some very good saxophone parts (whose sound was slightly distorted in the mixing). Soozie Tyrell's violin is practically inaudible.

FURTHER ON (UP THE ROAD)

Bruce Springsteen / 3'52

COVER
Johnny Cash did a cover of *Further On (Up the Road)* for the album *American V: A Hundred Highways* (2006), produced by Rick Rubin.

Musicians
Bruce Springsteen: vocals, guitar
Patti Scialfa: backing vocals
Steve Van Zandt: mandolin (?), backing vocals (?)
Nils Lofgren: guitar, backing vocals (?)
Clarence Clemons: maracas, backing vocals (?)
Roy Bittan: keyboard
Danny Federici: organ
Garry Tallent: bass
Max Weinberg: drums

Recording and mixing
Southern Tracks Recording Studio, Atlanta, Georgia: February to March 2002

Technical team
Producer: Brendan O'Brien
Recording engineer: Nick DiDia
Assistant recording engineers: Karl Egsieker, Billy Bowers
Mixing: Brendan O'Brien
Mastering: Bob Ludwig

The producer Brendan O'Brien. Bruce Springsteen declared that he had brought new energy to *Further On (Up the Road)*.

Genesis and lyrics

Bruce Springsteen wrote *Further On (Up the Road)* around the time of *Human Touch/Lucky Town*, or maybe later, in the late 1990s. It would seem that he worked on an initial version of the song with Chuck Plotkin. What is for sure, is that he had Brendan O'Brien listen to this song shortly before recording *The Rising*.

The main character of *Further On (Up the Road)* embodies the American hero in all his splendor. He's well-armed, and the road for him represents a sort of rite of initiation. He always has to go one step farther—it could be his motto. In any case, here he is in the desert, searching the dust for what could be gold (at least that's what we imagine). There is clearly a lot of loneliness there, while the search for gold could be a metaphor for the central role of money in war.

"Further on up the road"—could this be the ultimate expression of freedom? Or is it a subtle reference to the reformation of the E Street Band? It's worth noting that Bruce Springsteen chose *Further On (Up the Road)* to open his concert in Atlanta, on 4 June 2000, during the Bruce Springsteen and the E Street Band Reunion Tour. He then performed it on the same tour at seven of the ten concerts held at Madison Square Garden in New York (from 12 June to 1 July 2000).

Production

Springsteen recorded *Further On (Up the Road)* with the E Street Band, Chuck Plotkin, and Toby Scott in March 2001, but then scrapped it. Hence the presence of O'Brien: "Brendan brought a fresh power and focus to the band's sound and playing,"[1] explains the Boss in his autobiography. And that's exactly what we hear in this dynamic rock song: a power and a freshness.

Max Weinberg starts off the piece alone. His drums sound live, in the style of John Bonham, with the half-open hi-hat. Then come the other instruments, mainly the wall of saturated guitars. Springsteen has said that the key thing was to ensure the band sounded fresh and, as Brendan O'Brien knew exactly what he was doing, he had the opportunity to focus on the songwriting, playing, and vocals. In addition to the many guitars, Danny Federici added a powerful organ part, Clarence Clemons some maracas, and Steve Van Zandt was likely the one on the mandolin (at 1'17). In concert, Springsteen performs his song differently, in folk-rock or acoustic versions.

THE FUSE

Bruce Springsteen / 5'37

A QUESTIONABLE REMIX

In 2002, Spike Lee used *The Fuse* in the original soundtrack to his film *25th Hour.* He made sure to add chords written by Terence Blanchard, the composer of the score, and to remix the song by taking the initiative—unbeknownst to O'Brien—of removing all the delays Springsteen had added to the ends of phrases. Unfortunately, *The Fuse* was not included in the soundtrack's CD.

2002

Musicians

Bruce Springsteen: vocals, guitars, harmonica
Patti Scialfa: backing vocals
Steve Van Zandt: guitars, backing vocals (?)
Nils Lofgren: guitars (?)
Clarence Clemons: tambourine (?) backing vocals (?)
Roy Bittan: keyboard
Danny Federici: keyboard
Garry Tallent: bass
Soozie Tyrell: violin, backing vocals

Recording and mixing

Southern Tracks Recording Studio, Atlanta, Georgia: February to March 2002

Technical team

Producer: Brendan O'Brien
Recording engineer: Nick DiDia
Assistant recording engineers: Karl Egsieker, Billy Bowers
Mixing: Brendan O'Brien
Mastering: Bob Ludwig

Patti Scialfa and Bruce Springsteen take part in the *Today* show at Asbury Park, on 30 July 2002. They sang *The Fuse* with the E Street Band.

Genesis and lyrics

The Fuse was among the songs written after 11 September 2001. *Into the Fire* and *My City of Ruins* came first. Next, Springsteen wrote *You're Missing* and then he woke up one night with an idea for another song, *The Fuse.* As a result, he was delighted to find he suddenly had all the pieces of the story that he thought needed telling at the time. In fact, he has said that he felt compelled to tell this story.

This is the story of the tragic attacks on New York. "Trees on fire with the first fall's frost/Long black line in front of Holy Cross" and "Devil's on the horizon line." In this apocalyptic atmosphere, only love prevails—unless it's too late, and the fire has already destroyed everything. If this is the case, we could hazard another interpretation: that the main character of *The Fuse* met his own end in the attacks, and it's his soul, his ghost, that is now returning to his loved one. That being said, the songwriter managed to balance this description of the end of the world with explicit sensual images: "Come on let me do you right [...] On the edge of the bed you slip off your blouse [...] Your bittersweet taste on my tongue." The pulse of life is always strongest in close proximity to death: is this the Boss's message?

Production

If there is a song on this album that bears Brendan O'Brien's signature, it's this one: Springsteen and the E Street Band have never played more differently. Once again, Max Weinberg gets the ball rolling: it sounds as if his drums are coming straight out of someone's headphones before they return to a more normal sound—the trip-hop touch of the producer. The rest of the song highlights the various saturated guitars, with lyrical flights and a rhythmic section that bring to mind The Edge and U2 (at 2'31).

Springsteen's vocal performance is understated and receives tremendous support from Patti Scialfa. A break—typical of this style—falls at 3'40, immediately highlighting the Boss's vocal solo. The result is far from the Wall of Sound of *Born to Run* (see page 64), but it's a success nonetheless, all thanks to the talented producer.

MARY'S PLACE

Bruce Springsteen / 6'03

To fully appreciate the power of the E Street Band onstage and the incredible charisma of its leader, all you need to do is watch the 2003 DVD *Live in Barcelona*. This extraordinary version of *Mary's Place*, performed on 16 October 2002 at the Palau Sant Jordi in Barcelona, Spain, lasts longer than 11 minutes.

Musicians

Bruce Springsteen: vocals, guitar
Patti Scialfa: backing vocals
Steve Van Zandt: mandolin, backing vocals (?)
Nils Lofgren: guitar, backing vocals (?)
Clarence Clemons: saxophone, tambourine (?), backing vocals (?)
Roy Bittan: keyboard
Danny Federici: organ
Garry Tallent: bass
Max Weinberg: drums
Soozie Tyrell: violin, backing vocals
Jane Scarpantoni: cello
The Alliance Singers: Corinda Carford, Michelle Moore (soloist), Tiffeny Andrews, Antoinette Moore, Antonio Lawrence, Jesse Moorer
Mark Pender, Mike Spengler: trumpets
Richie "La Bamba" Rosenberg: trombone
Jerry Vivino: tenor saxophone
Eddie Manion: baritone saxophone

Recording and mixing

Southern Tracks Recording Studio, Atlanta, Georgia: February to March 2002

Technical team

Producer: Brendan O'Brien
Recording engineer: Nick DiDia
Assistant recording engineers: Karl Egsieker, Billy Bowers
Mixing: Brendan O'Brien
Mastering: Bob Ludwig

For Springsteen Addicts

"Meet me at Mary's place, we're gonna have a party," sings Bruce Springsteen in the chorus. He borrowed this line from a Sam Cooke song, *Meet Me at Mary's Place*, from his last album, *Ain't That Good News* (1964).

Genesis and lyrics

Mary's Place is an invitation to celebrate, despite a crumbling world and the September 11 attacks—that is what Bruce Springsteen wanted to express in this song. In an interview with *Uncut* magazine two months after the release of *The Rising*, the songwriter explained that he had thought at the time people were determined to celebrate and have fun, finding this to be a cathartic process. So, the song aimed to capture that spirit of celebration and to feel like home, in many ways recalling the song *Rosalita*. It's a party aimed at forgetting, or overcoming, reality while surrounded by one's own crowd. "Familiar faces around me," "everybody's here," and "Meet me at Mary's place, we're gonna have a party." It couldn't be said any better than that. And let's not forget the loved one with whom the narrator will dance.

Bruce Springsteen debuted this song onstage at the Jacksonville Memorial Coliseum, in Florida, on 4 March 2002.

Production

Soozie Tyrell opens *Mary's Place* with a violin melody. She's accompanied by Max Weinberg's drums (whose sound is the most untouched of the album), Steve Van Zandt's mandolin, and Springsteen's electric rhythm guitar. Springsteen provides very good lead vocals from the first verse, reusing hints of *Born to Run* in the chorus, to the point where some very familiar sounds can be heard in the bass and organ parts (from 0'48). This is among the Boss's songs with the highest number of musicians from outside the group: Jane Scarpantoni is on the cello, the six choralists from The Alliance Singers are involved again—after *Let's Be Friends (Skin to Skin)*—and the four members of the brass section make a memorable appearance. However, in spite of this riot of talents of all types—this "Wall of Sound" recreated for the occasion—the song remains clear and efficient, even taking on a gospel quality at the end (at 4'09). The songwriter rediscovers his powerful, rock-star voice, the choir's interventions are exhilarating, and the brass players bring an essential touch of soul, leading Clarence Clemons to deliver some very good saxophone phrasing. Just one small criticism: Brendan O'Brien didn't completely bridge the gap between his generation and that of the E Street Band, the song being too mastered to let the power and joy of the singers burst forth.

You're Missing, a very fine composition by Springsteen that is driven by Nils Lofgren's slide guitar playing.

YOU'RE MISSING

Bruce Springsteen / 5'10

Musicians
Bruce Springsteen: vocals, guitar
Steve Van Zandt: guitar
Nils Lofgren: guitar
Clarence Clemons: tambourine
Roy Bittan: keyboard
Danny Federici: organ
Garry Tallent: bass
Max Weinberg: drums
Soozie Tyrell: violin
Jere Flint, Larry LeMaster: cellos
The Nashville String Machine: orchestra
- **Carl Gorodetzky:** first violin and manager
- **Pam Sixfin, Lee Larrison, Conni Ellisor, Alan Umstead, David Davidson, Mary Kathryn Vanosdale, David Angell:** violins
- **Kristin Wilkinson, Gary Vanosdale, Jim Grosjean, Monisa Angell:** violas
- **Bob Mason, Carol Rabinowitz, Julie Tanner, Lynn Peithman:** cellos
- **Ricky Keller:** conductor

Recording and mixing
Southern Tracks Recording Studio, Atlanta, Georgia: February to March 2002

Technical team
Producer: Brendan O'Brien
Recording engineer: Nick DiDia
Assistant recording engineers: Karl Egsieker, Billy Bowers
Mixing: Brendan O'Brien
Mastering: Bob Ludwig

2002

Almost 20 years after the attacks on the World Trade Center, about 40 percent of the 2,753 people who were declared missing have yet to be identified.

Genesis and lyrics

You're Missing is the most poignant song Bruce Springsteen wrote to commemorate the victims of 9/11. It speaks directly to the missing, to all those who could never be identified by medical examiners. "Shirts in the closet, shoes in the hall/ Mama's in the kitchen [...] but you're missing." Death came knocking one September morning and an entire family was denied the chance to gather around the body.

The first verse might be a child talking about the pain of losing his father. In the second, third, and fourth verses, it seems that the mother is talking. She remembers the morning of the tragedy, the "Coffee cups on the counter, jackets on the chair/Papers on the door step." Then it's her turn to express overwhelming pain: "Your house is waiting" and "I got too much room in my bed." In the last verse, finally, we imagine the victim himself talking. He has "nothing but teardrops," with God himself "drifting in heaven" and seeming impotent, while the Devil, who hides "in the mailbox," is much closer than anyone knew.

Production

You're Missing is one of two songs, along with *Into the Fire*, that encouraged Springsteen to write more songs for the album. It's also one of the pieces he demo'ed with Brendan O'Brien at their second meeting. As Springsteen recounted, "I had *You're Missing*, and together we demo'd that and we worked together. It was something I hadn't done in a long time, to really collaborate over the structure and creation of one of my songs—I was used to doing all that myself."[115]

You're Missing starts with ethereal sounds that rise to a fade-in as Roy Bittan's piano chimes in. Springsteen composed this motif one evening in his living room and used it as the basis of the song. After the entrance of the drums, bass, and Soozie Tyrell's violin, he launches into the lead vocals with a serious voice brimming with emotion. In the chorus, Nils Lofgren takes up the melody on the slide guitar along with Jere Flint and Larry LeMaster's cellos and Soozie's violin (at 0'57). The Nashville String Machine orchestra shines in its subtlety. *You're Missing* ends on Danny Federici's superb organ.

This song is among the best on the album

THE RISING

Bruce Springsteen / 4'50

Musicians
Bruce Springsteen: vocals, guitars
Patti Scialfa: backing vocals
Steve Van Zandt: guitar, backing vocals
Nils Lofgren: guitars, backing vocals
Clarence Clemons: percussion instruments (?), backing vocals
Roy Bittan: keyboard
Danny Federici: organ
Garry Tallent: bass
Max Weinberg: drums
Soozie Tyrell: violin, backing vocals
Jane Scarpantoni: cello

Recording and mixing
Southern Tracks Recording Studio, Atlanta, Georgia: February to March 2002

Technical team
Producer: Brendan O'Brien
Recording engineer: Nick DiDia
Assistant recording engineers: Karl Egsieker, Billy Bowers
Mixing: Brendan O'Brien
Mastering: Bob Ludwig

2002

For Springsteen Addicts

A mysterious video apparently aired once only on the Australian channel ABC, on the music video show *Rage*, on 20 December 2003. Springsteen is seen recording at the Southern Tracks studio in Atlanta and playing, among other instruments, an orangey Gretsch—probably the one he uses in the solo. This video was never officially recognized, by either the songwriter or his team.

Genesis and lyrics

The Rising was written as recording for the album was coming to a close. On the DVD *VH1 Storytellers—On Stage*, Bruce Springsteen explains that after *Into the Fire* he felt a need to write more: "There's just something inside you that says it wants another song."[13] It's a song about the ultimate sacrifice, the one that leads to death, because it is dictated by a supreme sense of duty. As Springsteen once explained to *Uncut* magazine, as he got to the end of the record, he was looking to give voice to someone who had died. He wanted this voice to speak to the living. So, he created a character talking to his wife on the premise that, faced with a disaster and impending death, you would probably want to talk to your wife, your children, and other people close to you. For Springsteen, the verses gradually progress toward that final parting of the ways, toward *The Rising*. In other words, the moment when the soul leaves the body and rises up.

The main character in *The Rising*, or main characters, are the hundreds of firefighters who, on 11 September 2001, went to their deaths in the flames and rubble of the World Trade Center. "Come on up for the rising." This line from the chorus has two meanings: the climb up the stairs of the twin towers—a real-life Way of the Cross—and the rise to heaven. Similarly, "the cross of my calling" refers both to the Maltese cross (the firefighter symbol of courage since 1865) and the crucifixion of Jesus Christ.

The second part of the song leaves us in no doubt as to the spiritual aspect of *The Rising*, as the narrator says that he sees the "fiery light" of the Lord and Mary "In the garden of a thousand sighs." What's certain is that this song landed Springsteen firmly in the ranks of America's most inspired popular musicians.

Springsteen performed *The Rising* for the first time at the Jacksonville Memorial Coliseum, in Florida, on 4 March 2002. The song came out as a single (with *Land of Hope and Dreams*) in July. It went to No.24 in the United States, but reached No.5 in Norway and No.6 in Italy. It also won two Grammy Awards, one for "Best Rock Song" and one for "Best Male Vocal Performance."

Production

Springsteen's art can be confusing: while the lyrics to *The Rising* seem to call for a rather serious and collected music,

Springsteen rehearses for the 45th Grammy Awards, February 2003. He played a masterly *The Rising*, as well as The Clash's *London Calling*.

THE BOSS'S GRAMMYS

You could say that the Boss "has a subscription" to the Grammy Award for best male vocal performance: before hitting the jackpot with *The Rising* in 2002, he'd already won one for *Dancing in the Dark* in 1985 and *Streets of Philadelphia* in 1995—not to mention six other nominations in this category between 1980 and 2002.

the songwriter wrote a rock song that, while not particularly hard, has an infectious energy and a frightening efficacy. He avoids all pathos, so as not to weigh down his words. Whatever the case, this song expresses and communicates extraordinary emotion, which is enhanced by a feeling of spiritual elevation that grows progressively until the last note.

In an unusual move, the Boss launches the lead vocals in the first measure. Thus, his voice opens *The Rising* modified by a slight delay and accompanied by Soozie Tyrell's violin, Jane Scarpantoni's cello, an acoustic guitar, an electric guitar, a very pronounced quaver (on the right), another rhythm guitar (on the left), and some keyboard layers, not to mention Max Weinberg's cymbals. From the second verse, Weinberg accompanies his bandmates with his hi-hat, then—supported Garry Tallent's powerful bass line—he emphasizes the first chorus with his bass drum (at 0'35). Springsteen's incredible performance makes the chorus sound immediately like a hymn, a rock hymn to honor those who sacrificed their lives on 11 September 2001. A real success.

The song really takes off in the following verse, the drummer providing a strong beat with a clear swing (it's almost as if we are listening to Charlie Watts!), followed by several percussion parts (tambourine, maracas) and various guitars, notably Nils Lofgren's saturated slide guitar, which, once again, showcases his considerable talent. The second chorus is enhanced by Danny Federici's organ and by superb backing vocals, most notably from Patti Scialfa and Soozie Tyrell (at 1'12). *The Rising* has the intrinsic power of gospel—one might even call it a gospel rock. Springsteen then sings a short, heated, and inspired solo, picking up the melody from the vocals and generously deploying the whammy bar from his guitar—likely a Gretsch belonging to his producer (at 1'44). The rest of the song is dazzling, the Boss's vocals are decidedly among the best of his career—hence the Grammy for Best Male Vocal Performance in 2002.

The message from *The Rising* resonated particularly well within American politics, especially with Barack Obama, who asked Springsteen—and other artists—to perform on 18 January 2009 at We Are One: The Obama Inaugural Celebration at the Lincoln Memorial, which was held to celebrate his imminent investiture to the White House. Springsteen performed *The Rising* on the acoustic guitar accompanied by The Joyce Garrett Singers, a gospel choir. An amused comment from the Boss: "Once you start doing that kind of writing, it feeds off itself [...] If someone had told me in 2001 that 'you're going to sing this song at the inaugural concert for the first African-American president,' I'd have said, 'Huh?'"[120]

PARADISE

Bruce Springsteen / 5'39

2002

Musicians

Bruce Springsteen: vocals, guitar
Patti Scialfa: backing vocals
Steve Van Zandt: guitar (?)
Nils Lofgren: guitar
Clarence Clemons: percussion instruments (?)
Roy Bittan: keyboard
Danny Federici: keyboard (?)
Garry Tallent: bass
Max Weinberg: drums (?)

Recording and mixing

Southern Tracks Recording Studio, Atlanta, Georgia: February to March 2002

Technical team

Producer: Brendan O'Brien
Recording engineer: Nick DiDia
Assistant recording engineers: Karl Egsieker, Billy Bowers
Mixing: Brendan O'Brien
Mastering: Bob Ludwig

The Boss after his appearance on *Saturday Night Live*, on the occasion of the release of *The Rising*.

Genesis and lyrics

Paradise is a reflection on death seen from three different angles. In the first verse, the songwriter focuses on a young terrorist (a Palestinian suicide bomber, as Springsteen explains in his autobiography) who is preparing to launch a suicide attack. He also mentioned this in 2002 to Adam Sweeting in *Uncut*: "When I wrote *Paradise*, I was looking for something kind of really quiet, and I think it was the week there'd been the teenage girl suicide bombers. It was devastating, and so the first verse came out of thinking about that, the loss of life and the false paradise."[119]

In the second verse, the main character is the wife of a soldier: "Then I'd met a woman who had lost her husband at the Pentagon," [119] explained the songwriter. She mourned his death, which occurred during the September 11 attacks when five Al-Qaeda terrorists hijacked American Airlines Flight 77 and crashed it into the Pentagon. In the third verse, the character (the terrorist, soldier, or another character?) may be already dead. He's in paradise, sinking beneath the water to search for his love, but heaven is empty, like the eyes of death. Then he resurfaces.

One of the most touching songs the Boss has ever written, *Paradise* has seldom been performed onstage.

Production

The song's opening atmosphere resembles that of *The Wall* by Pink Floyd: a pulsing electronic sound fades in from an electro-acoustic fog, from which emerge the sound of saturated guitars—also pulsing—and synth pads. Then Springsteen's acoustic Gibson surges from the void, probably symbolizing some kind of suffering. The songwriter starts on the lead vocals with a soft voice, the melody resembling, in part, *The Sound of Silence* by Simon and Garfunkel. The second verse is marked by a cabasa (or brushes), a bass, other synths, a lone electric guitar, and the superb voice of Patti Scialfa, who adds a deep echo to the end of all the phrases (at 1'38). She also enters with a ghostly voice toward the end of the song. *Paradise* ends on the same pulsing sound from the beginning, as if the songwriter wanted to use this sound like a telephone ringing in a void to signify that nobody's home to answer, not even in heaven.

MY CITY OF RUINS

Bruce Springsteen / 5'00

For Springsteen Addicts

During the concert America: A Tribute to Heroes, Bruce Springsteen introduced *My City of Ruins* as "a prayer for our fallen brothers and sisters."[121] He also slightly modified the lyrics. He performed on the acoustic guitar and harmonica, accompanied by the superb backing vocals of Steve Van Zandt, Patti Scialfa, Layonne Holmes, Dee Holmes, Lisa Lowell, Clarence Clemons, and Soozie Tyrell. The performance was phenomenal and befitting of the occasion.

Musicians

Bruce Springsteen: vocals, guitar
Patti Scialfa: backing vocals
Steve Van Zandt: guitar, backing vocals
Nils Lofgren: guitar, backing vocals
Clarence Clemons: backing vocals
Roy Bittan: keyboard
Danny Federici: organ
Garry Tallent: bass
Max Weinberg: drums
Soozie Tyrell: violin, backing vocals
Jane Scarpantoni: cello

Recording

Southern Tracks Recording Studio, Atlanta, Georgia: February to March 2002

Technical team

Producer: Brendan O'Brien
Recording engineer: Nick DiDia
Assistant recording engineers: Karl Egsieker, Billy Bowers
Mixing: Brendan O'Brien (Silent Sound Studios, Atlanta)
Mastering: Bob Ludwig

Curtis Mayfield's band The Impressions in 1965. Meticulous soul music, which features in *My City of Ruins.*

Genesis and lyrics

Bruce Springsteen closed *The Rising* with a song influenced by gospel music. "It's like a lot of my things, like *The Promised Land*, or I had a song on the live album called *Land of Hope and Dreams*...they're all fundamentally gospel-rooted, or blues and gospel-rooted," he told *Uncut* magazine. "It seemed like that element was going to be a significant element of the record in some fashion."[119]

"There's a blood red circle on the cold dark ground/And the rain is falling down"—here, the city of ruins that Bruce Springsteen talks about is not New York after the attacks, as you might imagine. He wrote this song some time before then, for a concert at Asbury Park on 17 December 2000. So, Asbury Park is the city in question. As Springsteen explained to *Uncut* magazine, this was a city that had been struggling for a while, but was now at the point of being redeveloped, which created a real sense of anticipation and hope for the future.

Nevertheless, the songwriter performed *My City of Ruins* at the benefit concert America: A Tribute to Heroes (recorded on 21 September and broadcast on 4 December 2001), which is why this song will always be associated with the attacks. "My soul is lost, my friend/Tell me how do I begin again," sings Springsteen. *My City of Ruins* is an energetic call to resurrection.

Production

Musically, Springsteen took inspiration from "the soul gospel of my favorite '60s records,"[1] as he specifies in his autobiography. And, by all accounts, *People Get Ready* by Curtis Mayfield and The Impressions, released in 1965, was the song that inspired him the most, as one can hear in the melody in the first lines of each verse, and also in the guitar riffs that accompany the choruses, which echo Mayfield's inimitable style (for example, listen at 1'20). Sure, *My City of Ruins* is a great song, which is made all the more so by an exceptional performance from the Boss and his musicians—more specifically Max Weinberg's drumming and Danny Federici's organ—but the resemblance to *People Get Ready* spoils the impact of this sublime song. The fact remains that its production comes close to perfection, carried by luminous backing vocals that include Clarence Clemons's striking baritone (at 3'18).

Patti Scialfa was a singer with the E Street Band before she married Bruce Springsteen. Here, she is in concert at Villa Park, Birmingham, UK, in June 1988.

PATTI SCIALFA: THE FEMALE PRESENCE IN THE E STREET BAND

Following the departure of Steve Van Zandt, which was announced at the time *Born in the U.S.A.* was released in June 1984, Bruce Springsteen decided to give vocals a bigger role in the E Street Band. With this in mind, he held several auditions, and a young female singer in particular stood out. She was also a native of New Jersey and Springsteen had already met her in the mid-1970s when he was playing with The Bruce Springsteen Band. "Three days before we hit the road, Patti Scialfa joined the E Street Band [first concert in Saint-Paul, Minnesota on 29 June 1984]," he writes in his autobiography *Born to Run*. "As the first woman in the band, she sent shock waves through the troops, broke the boys' club [...]"[1] Bruce Springsteen had heard the young woman singing some time before at The Stone Pony in Asbury Park, New Jersey, and had been impressed by her rendition of *Tell Him* by the Exciters. "She had a voice filled with the blues, jazz, country, and the great girl groups of the Sixties," he writes. "Patti Scialfa had it all."[1] And so began an artistic relationship that would develop into a more personal relationship.

A Jersey girl

Vivienne Patricia Scialfa was born in Deal, New Jersey, on 29 July 1953, and raised in Long Branch. She was the daughter of Joseph, who was of Italian descent, and Patricia (née Morris) Scialfa, who is Irish. Her father owned a TV store before going on to become a real estate developer. "My dad was a very hardworking man," Patti told Lou Haviland of cheatsheet.com. "But on Sundays, he went to the Church of Sinatra... That's the soundtrack from my youth—Sinatra. In Frank Sinatra's voice, you heard all the possibilities. There's a big world out there, outside of yourself, larger than yourself, larger than the emotions that you're letting yourself feel. Sinatra's music gave me that—a gift."[34]

After graduating from Asbury High School, she studied music at the University of Miami's jazz conservatory, the Frost School of Music, then at New York University, where she obtained her degree. This was the second half of the 1970s, and Patti Scialfa had already sung in various bands on the Jersey Shore. She had also composed her first songs, submitting them to various artists, but without success. So she was working as a waitress in bars in Greenwich Village. She had not completely given up on the idea of a musical career, so she started a band called Trickster with two of her friends, Soozie Tyrell and Lisa Lowell, and they performed on the streets in the Village. She landed a few gigs in Greenwich Village clubs and in The Stone Pony in Asbury Park, where she became a member of the house band, Cats on a Smooth Surface, fronted by the singer-guitarist Bobby Bandiera. Through this, she met and worked with Southside Johnny and The Asbury Jukes, and also with David Johansen (alias Buster Poindexter), the former New York Dolls vocalist.

From music to love

Patti Scialfa joined the E Street Band in 1984. Gradually, over the course of many rehearsals, studio sessions, and world tours, her relationship with Bruce Springsteen developed into a love affair. Initially secret—although this became more and more difficult—the affair became public after the singer separated from his first wife, Julianne Phillips, whom he divorced on 1 May 1989. Two and a half years later, on 8 June 1991, Patti Scialfa and Bruce Springsteen wed. Evan James had been born a year earlier on 25 July 1990; he was followed by Jessica Rae, on 30 December 1991, and Samuel Ryan on 5 January 1994.

Solo work

Patti Scialfa became a permanent and indispensable member of the E Street Band from the mid-1980s, but nevertheless continued to pursue various personal projects. She contributed to The Rolling Stones' *Dirty Work* sessions in 1986, then Keith Richards' album *Talk is Cheap* (1988), produced by Steve Jordan, a friend of Scialfa's from the Greenwich Village years. But, most importantly of all, she recorded three albums under her own name: *Rumble Doll* (1993), coproduced by Bruce Springsteen and Mike Campbell, *23rd Street Lullaby* (2004), which Scialfa coproduced with Steve Jordan, and *Play It As It Lays* (2007), again coproduced with Jordan and also Ron Aniello; these are three albums in which her expressive voice subtly blends elements of folk, country, and rock.

Patti Scialfa was inducted into the Rock & Roll Hall of Fame in 2014.

DEVIL
ANDDUS

ALBUM

DEVILS & DUST

Devils & Dust • All the Way Home • Reno • Long Time Comin' • Black Cowboys • Maria's Bed • Silver Palomino • Jesus Was an Only Son • Leah • The Hitter • All I'm Thinkin' About • Matamoros Banks

Outtake: *It's the Little Things That Count*

RELEASE DATE

United States: 26 April 2005

Reference: Columbia Records—CSK 55416

No.1 in the United States, United Kingdom, Austria, Belgium, Denmark, Germany, Italy, the Netherlands, Switzerland, and Spain, No.3 in France

Springsteen during the *VH1 Storytellers—On Stage* acoustic concert at the Two River Theater, Red Bank, New Jersey, on 23 April 2005.

For Springsteen Addicts

For a while, Starbucks was considered as a possible distribution outlet for the *Devils & Dust* album. But the American coffee shop chain decided against it, partly because of the song *Reno*, which it felt was too suggestive, but mainly as a result of Springsteen's political beliefs, in case they offended some of Starbucks' customers.

2005

FOR SOULS IN DANGER

After the release of *The Rising*, Bruce Springsteen and the E Street Band went on a lengthy world tour—120 concerts in North America, Europe, and Australia from 7 August 2002 to 4 October 2003. Then, from 27 September to 13 October 2004, they participated in the Vote for Change Tour, which was designed to encourage Americans to register and vote for the Democrats at the November elections. It wasn't until after John Kerry conceded and the Republican George W Bush was re-elected to the White House, to Springsteen's huge disappointment, that the songwriter really began to think about his 13th studio album.

Just as the 1980 double album *The River* was the final part of the electric folk-rock trilogy begun some years before with *Born to Run* and *Darkness on the Edge of Town*, *Devils & Dust* can be considered the final chapter of the acoustic trilogy after *Nebraska* and *The Ghost of Tom Joad*. The 12 songs on the *Devils & Dust* album were written over a good ten-year period, several of them during and immediately after the Tom Joad Tour. The oldest song on the album, *All the Way Home*, dates from 1990 or 1991. The themes are very varied, although the somber atmosphere of the two previous records is often present. "I like to write about people whose souls are in danger, who are at risk,"[122] Bruce Springsteen told Jon Pareles of *The New York Times*. "In every song on this record, somebody's in some spiritual struggle between the worst of themselves and the best of themselves, and everybody comes out in a slightly different place. That thread runs through the record, and it's what gives the record its grounding in the spirit."[122]

The title track is, without a doubt, the album's biggest success in the way that it expresses the torments of America—post 9/11, and at the time of the Afghanistan and Iraq wars—through the doubts and fears of an American soldier during the Second Gulf War; torments that are revisited in *Matamoros Banks* through the eyes of a Mexican emigrant. Doubt, seen from a different angle, is also the theme of *Jesus Was an Only Son*, in which Springsteen draws a comparison between Mary's sorrow after Jesus died on the cross and the sadness and incomprehension of parents whose sons lost their lives in the mountains of Afghanistan and the deserts of Iraq.

Besides religion, the other themes that strongly inspired Bruce Springsteen on this album were the relationships between a mother or father and a son, as seen in *The Hitter*, *Black Cowboys*, the highly personal *Silver Palomino*, and *Long Time Comin'*, and love, either the memory of and/or desire for a woman in *Leah*, *Maria's Bed*, and *All I'm Thinkin' About* or the torrid eroticism of *Reno*.

The album

A largely acoustic album does not necessarily mean a solo album. *Devils & Dust* was produced by Brendan O'Brien, with the O'Brien, Springsteen, and Plotkin trio working together on two songs (*All the Way Home* and *Long Time Comin'*), and recorded at the Thrill Hill Recording Studios, in Los Angeles and New Jersey, as well as the Southern Tracks Recording Studio, in Atlanta, Georgia. The record was released on 26 April 2005, with a 30-minute bonus DVD filmed by Danny Clinch, in New Jersey, in February 2005. The DVD comprises acoustic performances of *Devils & Dust*, *Reno*, *Long Time Comin'*, *All I'm Thinkin' About*, and *Matamoros Banks*.

"The most audacious record since the home-demo American Gothic of 1982's *Nebraska*,"[123] wrote David Fricke in *Rolling Stone* magazine. Perhaps! It was nominated for the 2006 Grammy Awards in the "Best Contemporary Folk

Bruce Springsteen and the Seeger Sessions Band rehearsing at the Convention Hall, in Asbury Park, on 20 April 2005, a week before the release of *Devils & Dust*.

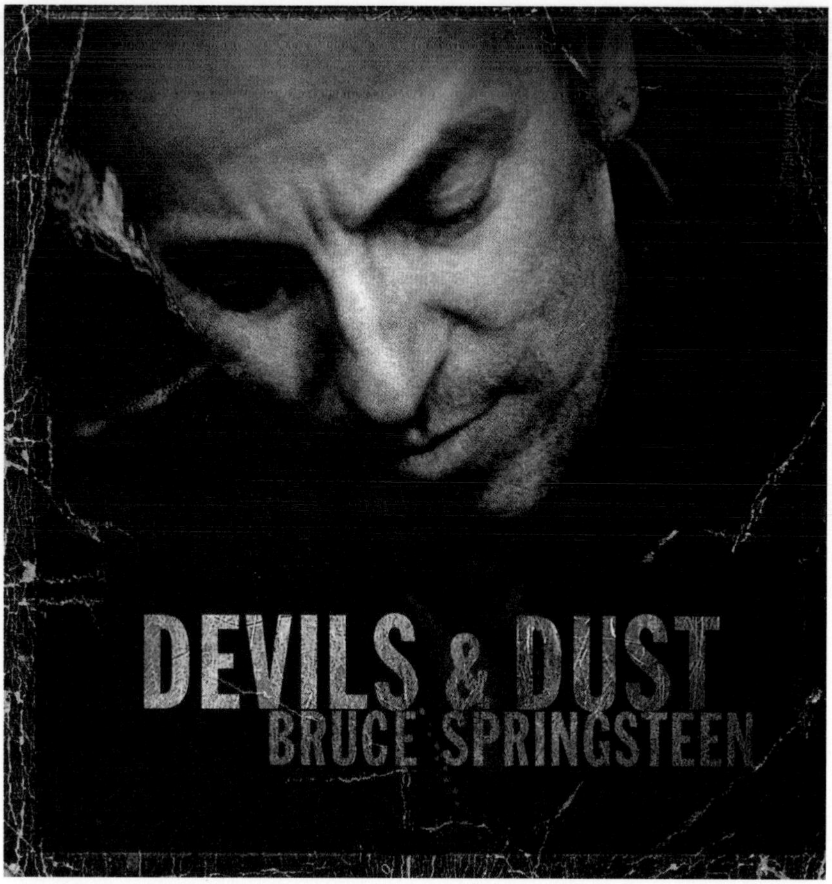

The sooty image for *Devils & Dust*, shot by Anton Corbijn.

Album" and "Best Long Form Music Video" categories, and, although it won neither, Springsteen clinched the Grammy for "Best Solo Rock Vocal Performance" for the song *Devils & Dust*. But it was what happened elsewhere that was more important: this 13th studio album received an overwhelmingly positive response from fans for whom the release of each new Springsteen album is always a huge event: *Devils & Dust* went to No.1 on both sides of the Atlantic, in the United States, the United Kingdom, Germany, Italy, the Netherlands, and Spain, No.2 in Norway, and No.3 in France, and was certified gold in a dozen countries.

On 25 April 2005, the day before the album was released, the Devils & Dust Tour kicked off in Detroit. It ended 75 concerts later on 22 November in Trenton, New Jersey, and in between, Springsteen was back performing for European audiences in venues such as the Point Theatre in Dublin, the ICC in Berlin, the Forest National in Brussels, and the Bercy Arena in Paris.

The sleeve

The cover image of *Devils & Dust* shows Springsteen with his head lowered, seemingly deep in thought. This smoky filmic shot was taken by Anton Corbijn, a native of Strijen in the Netherlands. Corbijn settled in London in the late 1970s, where he worked for the magazine *New Musical Express*. His black and white shots of various stars, ranging from David Bowie, Joy Division, and Depeche Mode to Nirvana in the States made him one of the best-known and most original photographers on the rock scene. The music videos that he has directed since 1983, the best of which include *Seven Seas* by Echo & the Bunnymen, *A Question of Time* by Depeche Mode, and *My Secret Place* by Joni Mitchell and Peter Gabriel, have also contributed to his stellar reputation, as have the five movies that he has directed to date, notably *Control* (2007), on the life of the Joy Division frontman, Ian Curtis, and *A Most Wanted Man* (2014) with Philip Seymour Hoffman and Rachel McAdams. Anton Corbijn also took the photographs that appear inside the *Devils & Dust* booklet, which contains the lyrics for the 12 songs. Chris Austopchuk, Dave Bett, and Michelle Holme were in charge of overall artistic direction.

The recording

In his autobiography *Born to Run*, Springsteen talks about how *Devils & Dust* was made, as if it were the easiest thing in the world. After the E Street Band reunion in 1999, and the two tours together (the Reunion Tour and The Rising Tour), he wanted to return to certain pieces that he had written and recorded between 1995 and 1997 during the Ghost of Tom Joad Solo Acoustic Tour. As he explains: "I went back [home after the tour]; chose the best of it; wrote a new song, *Devils & Dust*; and Brendan O'Brien helped me finish the record I'd started in my farmhouse at Joad's end. Brendan wanted to cut the songs from scratch, but I'd grown very fond of my home-recorded versions and decided to stick with those. We added some small embellishments, some subtle strings and horns; Brendan mixed; and there we were."[1]

It is easy to understand why Springsteen was not keen on rerecording the songs that had already been recorded at Thrill Hill. He is an instinctive artist, and experience has taught him that the core of a song lies in directly expressed emotion: "The minute I get the essence of something, I try to stop," Springsteen says. "If I go back to rerecord, sometimes I can hear the thinking a little more."[122] The various tracks on the album therefore date from way back, while some, such as *All the Way Home*, go back as far as 1990–1991, as mentioned earlier.

So, it was in his two home studios, Thrill Hill West and Thrill Hill East, the first in Los Angeles and the second in Colts Neck, that a large part of the Boss's 13th album was laid down. Various overdubs, such as the brass sections, were added at the Southern Tracks Recording Studio, probably between March and August 2004, as were the strings at Masterphonics in Nashville.

Devils & Dust also marked the return of Toby Scott who, having been almost entirely absent from the recording of *The Rising*, handled all the sound recordings at Thrill Hill. Nick DiDia was back in charge of the overdubs at Southern Tracks, assisted once again by Karl Egsieker and Billy Bowers. The bulk of the mixing was done by Brendan O'Brien, with Toby Scott on four of the pieces (*Black Cowboys*, *Jesus Was an Only Son*, *Leah*, and *Matamoros Banks*). And on mastering, the irreplaceable Bob Ludwig at Gateway Mastering in Portland, Maine.

Among the musicians playing alongside Springsteen, Danny Federici—the only remaining E Street Band member—is on keyboards, Chuck Plotkin pops up again on piano for one track (*All the Way Home*), and Patti Scialfa, Lisa Lowell, and Soozie Tyrell provide backing vocals, with the latter also on violin. Marty Rifkin is back on steel guitar and the string section is once again entrusted to the Nashville String Machine ensemble. The French horns are played by Brice Andrus, Donald Strand, Susan Welty, and Thomas Witte, and then there is Mark Pender, who is back on trumpet, and Steve Jordan in the drummer's seat. Jordan is a talented musician and drummer, who has worked with artists ranging from Keith Richards (and the X-Pensive Winos), Donald Fagen, and The Blues Brothers to Eric Clapton, Neil Young, and Herbie Hancock. His first encounter with Springsteen was particularly memorable: "[...] before I played a single track he gave me the book of lyrics, every lyric in *Devils & Dust*, before I played a note. And he thought it was important for me to read the lyrics to the whole album before I played on it, which is very, very, very smart. And it gave me insight into what he was thinking about and what his mindset was before we started recording. It was great."[124]

As for Brendan O'Brien, not just content to produce the album, he also plays bass, electric sarangi, hurdy-gurdy, sitar, and tambora. The arrangements for the string and brass sections were done by Eddie Horst, who worked with Springsteen up until *High Hopes* in 2014. Finally, the Boss himself is on lead vocals, guitars, keyboards, percussion, and even drums for the first time on a record (*Jesus Was an Only Son* and *All I'm Thinkin' About*).

Bruce Springsteen onstage at the Royal Albert Hall, London, on 20 May 2005, during the Devils & Dust Tour.

DEVILS & DUST

Bruce Springsteen / 4'58

2005

Musicians
Bruce Springsteen: vocals, guitar, keyboard, tambourine
Brendan O'Brien: bass
Steve Jordan: drums
Nashville String Machine: strings
Susan Welty, Thomas Witte: French horn
Recording
Thrill Hill Recording, Los Angeles and New Jersey: April 2003 to August 2004
Southern Tracks Recording Studio, Atlanta, Georgia: March to August 2004
Masterphonics, Nashville, Tennessee: March to August 2004
Technical team
Producer: Brendan O'Brien
Recording engineers: Toby Scott (Thrill Hill), Nick DiDia (Southern Tracks)
Assistant recording engineers: Karl Egsieker, Billy Bowers, Tom Tapley
Mixing: Brendan O'Brien
Mastering: Bob Ludwig (Gateway Mastering, Portland)

Springsteen considered opening the concerts on the Vote for Change Tour (which ran from September to October 2004) with the song *Devils & Dust*. But he changed his mind and opted for an instrumental version of the famous United States anthem *Star-Spangled Banner*, played on an acoustic 12-string, as immortalized by Jimi Hendrix at Woodstock in 1969.

For Springsteen Addicts

Devils & Dust is a very Dylanesque song. Bruce Springsteen even incorporates the title of one of Dylan's compositions in the lyrics: *With God on Our Side* (on the album *The Times They Are A-Changin'*, 1964).

Genesis and lyrics

As Bruce Springsteen explained to the *New York Times* journalist, Jon Pareles, in 2005, he composed and wrote this song in early 2003, shortly after the American invasion of Iraq. Although he played it for the first time with the E Street band at the Arco Arena in Sacramento, California, during a sound check on 9 April 2003, he altered the lyrics—notably the third verse, which he entirely rewrote—before recording it for his 13th album.

Here the songwriter embodies an American soldier during the Iraq war, which began in March 2003 with the invasion of the country by a military coalition led by the United States and was regarded as a preventive war instigated by George W Bush and neoconservatives like Donald Rumsfeld and Paul Wolfowitz. In the middle of the desert, far from home, the soldier in the song, his finger on the trigger in case the enemy appears, is talking with his comrade Bobbie. He is assailed by doubt: "What if what you do to survive/Kills the things you love?" is the key phrase in *Devils & Dust*. What should we understand by this? That war strips people of all humanity? That the hearts of fighting men are filled with devils? The narrator claims to have God on his side. Is he really so sure? Would God support one cause over another? These are the questions that Springsteen is asking. What he does know is that war and fear fill the "soul with devils and dust."

Officially debuted onstage on 27 September 2004 at the Convention Hall in Asbury Park, New Jersey, *Devils & Dust* was released as a single on 28 March 2005 (a month before the album). It only reached No.72 in the *Billboard* charts. In 2006, it was nominated for a Grammy award in the "Song of the Year" (2005) category, but did not win the trophy. However, Springsteen did walk away with the Grammy for the "Best Solo Rock Vocal Performance." The music video for the song was shot at the Paramount Theatre, in Asbury Park, with Springsteen singing and playing guitar and harmonica onstage in a deserted theater.

Production

With *Devils & Dust*, the only track on the album written and recorded after the American intervention in Iraq, Springsteen recaptures some of the spirit and musical texture of *The Ghost of Tom Joad*: same acoustic atmosphere, same depth in the

rendition, same quest for what is essential, same purity of sound. The difference lies partly in Brendan O'Brien's production, which is decidedly trip-hop/independent rock, and partly in the string and brass sections that enrich the track. The Boss had made a demo that he wanted to use with additional overdubs—as he did with other songs on the record—but O'Brien persuaded him to rerecord it almost entirely. And the result is an undeniable success.

In the first verse and first chorus, Springsteen accompanies himself alone on his famous Gibson J-45 acoustic guitar, as can be seen in the official music video and the DVD that accompanies the album. A highly saturated guitar comes in at the second verse (on the left, at 1'18), the remnant of an initial rock version that the songwriter had recorded in his home studio. A rhythmic motif performed by the Nashville String Machine ensemble, who had previously contributed to *The Rising*, comes in to reinforce the harmony (from 1'35). The Boss then adds organ pads, before performing a first harmonica solo (at 2'31). Steve Jordan brings in a great groove at the next verse with his characteristic drumming style, an eclectic mix of rock 'n' roll, ska, country, Britpop, and reggae. The raw sound of this track is very much in keeping with the producer's previous work. Steve Jordan's drums give way to a drum loop, an esthetic touch favored by both Springsteen and O'Brien, with O'Brien providing a solid bass line that he plays with a furious glissando on the neck of his guitar (from 3'24). The Nashville String Machine return in the final chorus, this time with a legato feel, reinforced by the extremely discreet French horns of Susan Welty and Thomas Witte (from 3'44). The piece ends on a second excellent harmonica solo from Springsteen (from 4'20).

The Boss's vocal performance on *Devils & Dust* is superb and totally deserved its Grammy Award.

2005

ALL THE WAY HOME

Bruce Springsteen / 3'38

Musicians
Bruce Springsteen: vocals, guitar, keyboard, harmonica, tambourine, maracas
Brendan O'Brien: bass, tambora, sitar, electric sarangi
Chuck Plotkin: piano
Steve Jordan: drums
Marty Rifkin: steel guitar

Recording
Thrill Hill Recording, Los Angeles and New Jersey: 1995–2004
Southern Tracks Recording Studio, Atlanta, Georgia: March to August 2004

Technical team
Producers: Brendan O'Brien, Bruce Springsteen, Chuck Plotkin
Recording engineers: Toby Scott (Thrill Hill), Nick DiDia (Southern Tracks)
Assistant recording engineers: Karl Egsieker, Billy Bowers, Tom Tapley
Mixing: Brendan O'Brien
Mastering: Bob Ludwig (Gateway Mastering, Portland)

The Boss's song *All the Way Home* was recorded by Southside Johnny in 1991. Here, the two musicians are seen at The Stone Pony, Asbury Park, in 1976.

Genesis and lyrics

All the Way Home is the oldest song on the *Devils & Dust* album. Although Bruce Springsteen recorded it at the same time as *Long Time Comin'* during *The Ghost of Tom Joad* sessions, he had composed it long before that, in 1990 or 1991, and given it to his friend Southside Johnny. The song appears on the excellent album *Better Days* (1991), produced by one Steve Van Zandt.

For his own version, Springsteen changed the lyrics slightly. For example, in the first verse, the phrase "I know what it's like to have been so sure and to wake up and find it all gone" was replaced by "I know what it's like to have soared and come crashin' like a drunk on a bar room floor"—the latter taken from the lyrics of the song *My Beautiful Reward* (on the *Lucky Town* album).

Springsteen returns here to the theme of disappointment in love. The man in the song is hoping to win back his ex-wife, or at least to alleviate his loneliness for a while. But, as he listens to a small local band trashing a Rolling Stones' number, the memories flood back and he realizes that they'll never understand one another. "Yeah love leaves nothing but shadows and vapor," Springsteen sings.

Production

For the first time in the Boss's discography, two tracks follow straight on from one another—a proven technique used since the 1960s, notably by The Beatles and Pink Floyd. Here, *Devils & Dust* segues into *All the Way Home* with a series of mellow sounds. *All the Way Home* is built around a powerful rhythm, led by Steve Jordan's excellent drumming (recorded over Gary Mallaber's drums on the first version of the song), O'Brien's very solid bass, and the Boss's Rolling Stones-style riff. It is an energetic rock number, but one that the songwriter sings in a neutral tone. He delivers two superb harmonica solos, with a saturated sound à la Little Walter. Chuck Plotkin is on piano (his second appearance after *Youngstown* on *Tom Joad*) and Marty Rifkin is back on steel guitar, but it is mainly the producer who, as well as playing bass, lets rip on a wonderful combination of oriental instruments.

RENO

Bruce Springsteen / 4'08

> **For Springsteen Addicts**
> Due to the sexual realism of the lyrics of *Reno*, the *Devils & Dust* album was released with the logo and words "Parental Guidance—Explicit Lyrics." A first for Bruce Springsteen.

Musicians

Bruce Springsteen: vocals, guitar, keyboard, tambourine
Nashville String Machine: strings
Brice Andrus, Donald Strand, Susan Welty, Thomas Witte: French horn

Recording

Thrill Hill Recording, Los Angeles and New Jersey: 1996–2004
Southern Tracks Recording Studio, Atlanta, Georgia: March to August 2004
Masterphonics, Nashville, Tennessee: March to August 2004

Technical team

Producer: Brendan O'Brien
Recording engineers: Toby Scott (Thrill Hill), Nick DiDia (Southern Tracks)
Assistant recording engineers: Karl Egsieker, Billy Bowers, Tom Tapley
Mixing: Brendan O'Brien
Mastering: Bob Ludwig (Gateway Mastering, Portland)

The city of Reno, Nevada, with Harold's casino in the foreground. *The Biggest Little City in the World*, sung by Bruce Springsteen, references the city.

Genesis and lyrics

Like Las Vegas, also in Nevada, the city of Reno owes its reputation to its thriving casinos. It is famous for having legalized prostitution, so it's no accident that the song *Reno* is about a man visiting a prostitute. "'Two hundred dollars straight in/ Two-fifty up the ass,' she smiled." No ambiguity there. The young woman selling her wares is possibly South American because she reminds the man of Maria, a woman who he once loved in a place where the sun shone on the Amatitlán, a lake in Guatemala, and where the couple went riding with *vaqueros* (cattle-herders). In an interview with Jon Pareles for *The New York Times*, the songwriter talks of a "proxy"[122] relationship and adds: "The physicality, the sexual content of the song was important, because casual sex is kind of closing the book of you. It's ecstasy, and it's release. Sex with somebody you love is opening the book of you, which is always a risky and frightening read."[122]

Production

Reno is a song that Springsteen recorded alone at Thrill Hill, between 1996 and 1997. The strings and brass sections were overdubbed between March and August 2004, at Masterphonics, in Nashville, and Southern Tracks, in Atlanta, respectively.

The song begins with Springsteen picking with his mediator on his Gibson J-45. He accompanies this on a second acoustic slide guitar (on the left in the stereo). The strings from the Nashville String Machine and the French horns from the Brice Andrus, Donald Strand, Susan Welty, and Thomas Witte quartet provide discreet support. Notice how the horns mix in almost imperceptibly with the strings, as they would in a symphony orchestra.

The timbre of Springsteen's infinitely gentle voice is somewhat reminiscent of Dylan. He adds a tambourine after the second verse—the only percussion on the song. Despite the crudeness of the images and situations described in *Reno,* the Boss's performance is no less moving. Springsteen is a great auteur as well as a great performer. Remarkable.

LONG TIME COMIN'

Bruce Springsteen / 4'17

2005

Musicians

Bruce Springsteen: vocals, guitar, keyboard
Marty Rifkin: steel guitar
Danny Federici: keyboards
Brendan O'Brien: bass
Steve Jordan: drums
Soozie Tyrell: violin, backing vocals
Patti Scialfa: backing vocals

Recording

Thrill Hill Recording, Los Angeles and New Jersey: 1995–2004
Southern Tracks Recording Studio, Atlanta, Georgia: March to August 2004

Technical team

Producers: Brendan O'Brien, Bruce Springsteen, Chuck Plotkin
Recording engineers: Toby Scott (Thrill Hill), Nick DiDia (Southern Tracks)
Assistant recording engineers: Karl Egsieker, Billy Bowers, Tom Tapley
Mixing: Brendan O'Brien
Mastering: Bob Ludwig (Gateway Mastering, Portland)

For Springsteen Addicts

The phrase "It's me and you, Rosie, cracklin' like crossed wires" is probably a friendly nod toward Neil Diamond and one of his hit records, *Cracklin' Rosie,* which reached No.1 in the United States and Canada in 1970.

Genesis and lyrics

The complex relationships between parents and children, the main theme of *Long Time Comin',* has an almost redemptive quality for Bruce Springsteen. His message here can be condensed to a single wish: that his children make their own choices and live their own lives, unburdened by the sins and mistakes of their parents. "It'd be that your mistakes would be your own/Yeah your sins would be your own." As he explains in his autobiography, "In *Long Time Comin'* I lay out the wish I've had for my children."[1] Around a campfire, beneath the constellation of Cassiopeia, the narrator reflects on his youth. He thinks about his father, who "was just a stranger/[who] Lived in a hotel downtown." Now a father himself, with two children and a third on the way, he is determined not to repeat the mistakes of his parents or the ones he may already have made himself. With his family about to expand, his emotions are running high, and as he slips his hand under his wife's shirt and feels kicking in her belly, he resolves to build genuine relationships. "I ain't gonna fuck it up this time," he says. *Long Time Comin'* is also in a way a song about second chances. A song that rejects the Christian idea of original sin.

Springsteen has sung this song quite regularly since the concert at the Paramount Theatre in Denver, Colorado, on 16 October 1996.

Production

Long Time Comin' dates from the *Tom Joad* sessions in around 1995. The version recorded at that time was the one Springsteen reworked for his 13th album, evidently keeping the earlier tracks recorded by Danny Federici, Marty Rifkin, Soozie Tyrell, Patti Scialfa, and himself. Only the rhythm section was rerecorded in 2004 by Steve Jordan and Brendan O'Brien—probably on the latter's insistence. Although the song begins with the songwriter alone on acoustic guitar, the band imbues it with a country-rock dynamic when they come in at the second verse. The bass-drums duo is definitely one of this song's great assets, their playing and the texture they create is superb. The other musicians are not to be outdone, however, particularly Rifkin on steel guitar, as well as Scialfa and Tyrell on backing vocals. Federici's keyboards are inaudible. The Boss performed some excellent live versions with The Sessions Band in 2006, but none is better than the album version.

BLACK COWBOYS

Bruce Springsteen / 4'08

Musicians

Bruce Springsteen: vocals, guitar, keyboards, percussion
Brendan O'Brien: bass
Steve Jordan: percussion
Nashville String Machine: strings
Brice Andrus, Donald Strand, Susan Welty, Thomas Witte: French horn

Recording

Thrill Hill Recording, Los Angeles and New Jersey: 1995 to 2004
Southern Tracks Recording Studio, Atlanta, Georgia: March to August 2004
Masterphonics, Nashville, Tennessee: March to August 2004

Technical team

Producer: Brendan O'Brien
Recording engineers: Toby Scott (Thrill Hill), Nick DiDia (Southern Tracks)
Assistants recording engineers: Karl Egsieker, Billy Bowers, Tom Tapley
Mixing: Toby Scott
Mastering: Bob Ludwig (Gateway Mastering, Portland)

Jonathan Kozol, writer of *Amazing Grace: The Lives of Children and the Conscience of a Nation* (1995), which made such a profound impression on the songwriter from New Jersey.

Genesis and lyrics

Bruce Springsteen was inspired to write *Black Cowboys* by the book *Amazing Grace: The Lives of Children and the Conscience of a Nation* (1995). It is a study by Jonathan Kozol of the Mott Haven neighborhood in the Bronx, New York City, and describes the ravages of drugs, Aids, and violence among children in the most underprivileged classes of American society.

Here, the songwriter tells the story of a mother and son. Rainey Williams, a young teenager, has only the dangerous streets of Mott Haven for a playground; his mother, Lynette, does not want him to go out after school. His only entertainment is television (or more accurately a channel that shows Westerns) and the books his mother brings him—also stories of the Wild West, of black cowboys on the Oklahoma range, and the Seminole scouts who fought the Native Americans of the Great Plains.

The bond between mother and son is dissolved from the day Lynette meets a man "whose business was the boulevard." This is in all likelihood a pimp and/or drug dealer. Rainey eventually leaves, boarding a train bound for Pennsylvania, Ohio, Indiana, and, finally, Oklahoma, the land of the cowboys.

Production

Black Cowboys is the first song on the album mixed by Toby Scott. Perhaps its sound comes rather closer to that of *Tom Joad*, being fuller than it would have been if Brendan O'Brien had done the mixing. Springsteen has produced a new ballad, which he sings in a rather disillusioned tone of voice. He accompanies himself on the acoustic guitar, the sound being relatively compressed. He also plays some of the other instruments, notably a piano, an organ, and synth pads which he adds to support the Nashville String Machine. The French horns are more to the fore than in the other songs on the album, but their texture appears to have been blended with sampled sounds, which creates a strange effect (listen at around 1'27). O'Brien is on bass guitar, totally under-mixed (from 1'27, it seems), and Steve Jordan produces very low-key drumming with brushes on his snare drum (at 2'04) and also his tom-toms (at 3'08). The Boss, who also receives a credit for percussion—which is hard to pick out—most certainly plays the tambourine. Finally, backing vocals can be heard, which appear to come from a keyboard (listen from 3'08).

Bruce Springsteen makes some final adjustments to the setlist for a coming concert, on 19 May 2005, at the Continental Airlines Arena, in East Rutherford, New Jersey.

MARIA'S BED

Bruce Springsteen / 5'35

2005

Musicians

Bruce Springsteen: vocals, guitars, keyboards, percussion (?)
Brendan O'Brien: bass, hurdy-gurdy, tambora
Steve Jordan: drums, percussion (?)
Soozie Tyrell: violin, backing vocals
Patti Scialfa: backing vocals

Recording

Thrill Hill Recording, Los Angeles and New Jersey: 1995–2004
Southern Tracks Recording Studio, Atlanta, Georgia: March to August 2004

Technical team

Producer: Brendan O'Brien
Recording engineers: Toby Scott (Thrill Hill), Nick DiDia (Southern Tracks)
Assistant recording engineers: Karl Egsieker, Billy Bowers, Tom Tapley
Mixing: Brendan O'Brien
Mastering: Bob Ludwig (Gateway Mastering, Portland)

A member of The Blues Bothers, and subsequently of Keith Richards' X Pensive Winos, Steve Jordan also played the drums for Bruce Springsteen.

Genesis and lyrics

Maria's Bed is the equivalent of (or sequel to?) *Further On (Up the Road)*, on the album *The Rising*. Indeed, these two songs both contain the lines: "Got on a dead man's suit and smiling skull ring/Lucky graveyard boots and a song to sing."

Like the character in *Further On (Up the Road)*, the person in *Maria's Bed* is passionate about his freedom, which the long roads of a vast America bring him. He seems to have drawn a line under his past and started again from scratch, judging by the biblical reference to the Deluge (torrential rain that lasted 40 days and 40 nights). What is he seeking? His fortune, perhaps, which is hinted at in his hope of discovering gold in the desert by sifting through the dust. More certainly he is seeking love, which is symbolized by Maria's bed. Maria offers him fulfillment through love, but he also finds light (or a sense of hope) with her, that is, an understanding of the world.

Bruce Springsteen first performed *Maria's Bed* live during the concert he gave at the Paramount Theatre in Asbury Park, New Jersey, on 21 April 2005.

Production

Maria's Bed is a song filled with light, driven by the highly effective rhythm section provided by Steve Jordan and Brendan O'Brien. Jordan provides explosive drumming, O'Brien a thumping bass line. In all likelihood, this is the first piece they recorded together for the album, and the result is quite simply excellent. It must be said that Springsteen has composed an exhilarating kind of folk-rock song, a little in the style of *Ooh La La* by Ronnie Lane and the Faces, which is fueled by a mounting energy that ends in a blaze of glory. He sings in a soft voice—sometimes verging on falsetto—that's far removed from his feats of former times, which came close to making his voice crack. The excellent backing vocals by Patti Scialfa and Soozie Tyrell bring a little more lightness to the song, while the latter's violin heightens the country-rock feel. As well as playing bass, O'Brien contributes a very fine accompaniment on the tambora and a part on the hurdy-gurdy. As for the Boss, he is at the organ, playing in a style that emulates that of Danny Federici (listen around 0'25), on acoustic guitars, including a slide guitar solo (from 0'13, on the left), and also probably on the tambourine and maracas (or is that Steve Jordan?). *Maria's Bed* is one of the most effective songs on the album.

SILVER PALOMINO

Bruce Springsteen / 3'22

Musicians
Bruce Springsteen: vocals, guitar, keyboards, percussion
Nashville String Machine: strings

Recording
Thrill Hill Recording, Los Angeles and New Jersey: 1996–2004
Southern Tracks Recording Studio, Atlanta, Georgia: March to August 2004
Masterphonics, Nashville, Tennessee: March to August 2004

Technical team
Producer: Brendan O'Brien
Recording engineers: Toby Scott (Thrill Hill), Nick DiDia (Southern Tracks)
Assistant recording engineers: Karl Egsieker, Billy Bowers, Tom Tapley
Mixing: Brendan O'Brien
Mastering: Bob Ludwig (Gateway Mastering, Portland)

The Guadalupe that Bruce Springsteen mentions in this song is a river that rises in central Texas and flows into San Antonio Bay, in the Gulf of Mexico.

Genesis and lyrics

Springsteen wrote this song after his son had told him about the sudden, premature death of the mother of two of his friends, Tyler and Oliver. Her name was Fiona Chappel.

This sad story is set in west Texas. A young boy of 13 has just lost his mother. He is alone in the world, and overwhelmed with grief, until the day she appears to him in the shape of a palomino horse. "She came out of the Guadalupe's on a night so cold/Her coat was frosted diamonds in the sallow moon's glow," sings Springsteen in the first verse. She is beautiful and cannot be tamed, not even by the *mesteñeros* (Texan cowboys who ride mustangs). Incidentally, the song's lyrics wrongly refer to "*mustañeros.*" The young teenager dreams of fleeing with her, crossing prairies and mountains. A triumph of mind over matter, in a sense...

Bruce Springsteen has performed *Silver Palomino* around 30 times to date. He first performed it live during the concert on 21 April 2005 at the Paramount Theatre in Asbury Park, New Jersey.

Production

Silver Palomino was recorded by Springsteen alone in around 1996, in his home studio at Thrill Hill. He plays all the instruments for the song, with the exception of the strings. These were provided by the Nashville String Machine, and recorded later in 2004 at Masterphonics. The Boss accompanies himself on his Gibson J-45, which has a double drop D tuning (D, A, D, G, B, D). He complements this with a second guitar—a classical acoustic with nylon strings, on which he plays a solo.

Silver Palomino is a rather nostalgic ballad, sung in a soft, moving voice. The strings come in, quite discreetly, from the second verse. From the start of the album, Springsteen systematically supported the orchestra with synth pads. However, this technique probably did not make life any easier for the arranger, Eddie Horst, who was no doubt forced to fit in with the songwriter's keyboards. Springsteen's reservations regarding this type of arrangement is well known—it was already apparent in *Secret Garden*, where he feared David Kahne's strings would eclipse his playing. The result, unfortunately, is rather linear and sometimes lacking in real buoyancy. The Boss also gets a credit for percussion on the album sleeve, but it is inaudible. Nonetheless, *Silver Palomino* is still a very fine song.

JESUS WAS AN ONLY SON

Bruce Springsteen / 2'55

2005

Musicians

Bruce Springsteen: vocals, guitar, keyboards, bass, drums, tambourine
Patti Scialfa, Soozie Tyrell, Lisa Lowell: backing vocals

Recording

Thrill Hill Recording, Los Angeles and New Jersey: 1996 to 2004
Southern Tracks Recording Studio, Atlanta, Georgia: March to August 2004

Technical team

Producer: Brendan O'Brien
Recording engineers: Toby Scott (Thrill Hill), Nick DiDia (Southern Tracks)
Assistant recording engineers: Karl Egsieker, Billy Bowers, Tom Tapley
Mixing: Toby Scott
Mastering: Bob Ludwig (Gateway Mastering, Portland)

For Springsteen Addicts

An excellent version of *Jesus Was an Only Son*, performed by Springsteen alone on piano and harmonica, was recorded on 4 April 2005 at the Joan and Robert Rechnitz Theater in Red Bank, New Jersey, for an episode of the American TV series *VH1 Storytellers—On Stage*. It went on sale a year later as part of a video featuring the other songs on the program.

Genesis and lyrics

Springsteen's Catholic upbringing clearly comes flooding back in *Jesus Was an Only Son*. All the song's originality, and its emotion, come from the fact that it deals with the Virgin Mary and expresses what she experiences following the expiatory sacrifice of Jesus, her only son. It mentions Golgotha, or the hill of Calvary, where Christ was crucified; Nazareth, the town of Jesus's birth; and the Garden of Gethsemane, where Jesus prayed before his arrest. However, it also voices doubt and incomprehension at the abandonment of the son of God by his father. "He beseeched his Heavenly Father to remove/The cup of death from his lips," sings Springsteen.

At the end of the song, Jesus turns to his mother and asks her to stop crying. "For remember the soul of the universe/ Willed a world and it appeared," he tells her. In fact, Bruce Springsteen is sending this message to everyone: that of a son who is comforting his mother, who is afflicted by the choice of a sacrifice she does not understand. At the time of the Iraq war, when young American soldiers were being sent to that country, this song took on its full meaning.

Jesus Was an Only Son is among the songs on *Devils & Dust* that has been performed live most often. Bruce Springsteen first performed the song before an audience at the Joan and Robert Rechnitz Theater in Red Bank, New Jersey, on 4 April 2005.

Production

A one-man band, Springsteen again plays all the instruments, recording the song in his home studio at Thrill Hill. In a new development, he takes care of the drums, where he would usually resort to using a drum machine. What should we make of his performance? With the best will in the world, there is no denying that it does not have the precision, the groove, or the subtlety of a Gary Mallaber, a Steve Jordan, or a Max Weinberg. His playing lacks accuracy and swing, even though the end result is very workmanlike. As for the song itself, it is a folk ballad in the manner of those by Bob Dylan, with backing vocals and an organ that create a certain religious feeling. It was, however, in live performances that Springsteen gave the song its full power, chiefly during the Seeger Sessions Band Tour in 2006, when he played it alone at the piano, as he did during the Devils & Dust Solo Acoustic Tour in 2005.

LEAH

Bruce Springsteen / 3'32

Musicians
Bruce Springsteen: vocals, guitar, keyboards, cabasa, tambourine, claves
Mark Pender: trumpet
Patti Scialfa: backing vocals (?)

Recording
Thrill Hill Recording, Los Angeles and New Jersey: 1996 to 2004
Southern Tracks Recording Studio, Atlanta, Georgia: March to August 2004

Technical team
Producer: Brendan O'Brien
Recording engineers: Toby Scott (Thrill Hill), Nick DiDia (Southern Tracks)
Assistant recording engineers: Karl Egsieker, Billy Bowers, Tom Tapley
Mixing: Toby Scott
Mastering: Bob Ludwig (Gateway Mastering, Portland)

Roy Orbison's great hit *Leah* lent its title to Bruce Springsteen's eponymous song.

Genesis and lyrics

Bruce Springsteen borrowed the title of this song from one of Roy Orbison's greatest hits (released in 1962). *Leah* is a love song. The narrator wants to build his house, live his life with Leah, and "Sleep in the same bed, search for the same proof."

But it is not only a love song; it is also a reflection on free will. "With this hand I've built and with this I've burned," Springsteen sings. In other words, there is a part of us that is good, another that is bad—and it is up to us to make the right choices. Hence, no doubt, this further biblical reference. In the book of Genesis, Leah is the cousin and first wife of Jacob, to whom she bears several children. She remains in love with Jacob, even though he has always preferred her younger sister, Rachel, whom he eventually marries.

Leah was performed regularly during 2005. Bruce Springsteen performed it live for the first time at the Paramount Theatre in Asbury Park, New Jersey, on 21 April 2005.

Production

This was a new ballad, created by the Boss practically alone, at Thrill Hill between 1996 and 1997. Springsteen begins the song with his acoustic guitar. The sound is compressed, and his rapid strumming seems to bounce along. He adds synth pads, but also several percussion instruments: cabasa, tambourine, and claves (from 0'15). The lead vocal is peaceful, the voice light. In the first verse, when he sings "li li li," which is reminiscent of *Streets of Philadelphia*, he has recorded two tracks of voices singing falsetto, positioned in stereo. But from the second verse a female voice blends with his (from 1'45), doubtless that of his wife, Patti Scialfa, even though she does not receive a credit on the album sleeve. Mark Pender, who already featured on the album *The Rising*, in the song *Mary's Place*, is officially the only musician to accompany the Boss in this piece, playing a short trumpet solo whose sound would not have been out of place in a Sergio Leone movie. Although in no way earth-shattering, *Leah* is a pleasant enough song, and one that anyway would have deserved a more sophisticated standard of production.

THE HITTER

Bruce Springsteen / 5'53

COVER
Tom Jones made a very good cover of *The Hitter* in 2008, on his album *24 Hours*. It is different from the one by the Boss, but nonetheless effective.

2005

Musicians
Bruce Springsteen: vocals, guitar, keyboards
Nashville String Machine: strings, vocals (?)
Brice Andrus, Donald Strand, Susan Welty, Thomas Witte: French horn

Recording
Thrill Hill Recording, Los Angeles and New Jersey: 1996 to August 2004
Southern Tracks Recording Studio, Atlanta, Georgia: Mar to Aug 2004
Masterphonics, Nashville, Tennessee: March to August 2004

Technical team
Producer: Brendan O'Brien
Recording engineers: Toby Scott (Thrill Hill), Nick DiDia (Southern Tracks)
Assistant recording engineers: Karl Egsieker, Billy Bowers, Tom Tapley
Mixing: Brendan O'Brien
Mastering: Bob Ludwig (Gateway Mastering, Portland)

The British pop singer Tom Jones recorded an excellent version of *The Hitter*, which is very different to the Boss's original recording.

Genesis and lyrics

Although Springsteen wrote this song in the mid-1990s, *The Hitter* is in a way the sequel, perhaps even the conclusion, to *Leah*. The narrator has now fallen onto the wrong side of the law. Having committed who knows what crime when he was just a kid, he boarded the *Southern Queen* with his mother's help in order to give the police the slip. He earned his living as a boxer in the docks of New Orleans, then in other Louisiana cities such as Baton Rouge and Lafayette. He made a name for himself, and with this came money and women.

Now the narrator has returned home and wants to see his mother. But the years have passed. There is now a chain on the front door, which symbolizes the gulf that has opened up between the mother and her son. He does not ask for his mother's forgiveness, or even a kiss. What he wants is to be allowed in to rest a little before setting off again to fight—this time no longer legally, in boxing rings, but illegally, in fields and back streets, to earn a few dollars from underground bets.

Bruce Springsteen first performed *The Hitter* live at the Landmark Theatre in Syracuse, New York State, on 13 November 1996. But it was only from April 2005, on the Devils & Dust Tour, that he regularly included it on his setlists.

Production

The Hitter is another folk ballad, written in a style that inevitably shows the influence of Bob Dylan and Woody Guthrie. There have even been rumors that Guthrie had started writing the song and Springsteen supposedly finished it on his own account. Given the Boss's integrity, this is highly unlikely.

The songwriter begins the song with only his acoustic guitar for company: in all likelihood it has an open G with drop C tuning (C, G, D, G, B, D). His lead vocals are melancholy, the timbre soft. The French horns of Brice Andrus, Donald Strand, Susan Welty, and Thomas Witte come in at the third verse. These four talented musicians, all members of the Atlanta Symphony Orchestra, are sadly undermixed, as are the strings of the Nashville String Machine—a decision that was taken by Springsteen. A voice can be heard singing discreetly at 1'32 and 5'25—this is probably one of the orchestra members. Although Springsteen gets a credit for playing percussion on the album, this is totally absent from the recording.

ALL I'M THINKIN' ABOUT

Bruce Springsteen / 4'22

Musicians

Bruce Springsteen: vocals, guitars, keyboards, drums, percussion
Brendan O'Brien: bass
Patti Scialfa, Soozie Tyrell, Lisa Lowell: backing vocals

Recording

Thrill Hill Recording, Los Angeles and New Jersey: 1997 to Aug 2004
Southern Tracks Recording Studio, Atlanta, Georgia: Mar to Aug 2004

Technical team

Producer: Brendan O'Brien
Recording engineer: Toby Scott (Thrill Hill), Nick DiDia (Southern Tracks)
Assistant recording engineers: Karl Egsieker, Billy Bowers, Tom Tapley
Mixing: Brendan O'Brien
Mastering: Bob Ludwig (Gateway Mastering, Portland)

A FAMILY AFFAIR

In the live version of *All I'm Thinkin' About*, which features on the DVD of *Devils & Dust*, the backing vocals are provided by Evan, Jess, Sam, and Patti—the Boss's children and wife.

The band Canned Heat, whose song *Going Up the Country* was one of the anthems of Woodstock and influenced the Boss's *All I'm Thinkin' About*.

Genesis and lyrics

Was Bruce Springsteen thinking about the white blues group Canned Heat when he wrote, and then sang, *All I'm Thinkin' About*? Not only does his falsetto voice call to mind that of Al "Blind Owl" Wilson, but in a way the song itself resembles the hippie anthem *Going Up the Country*.

Be that as it may, *All I'm Thinkin' About* takes us on a journey along the roads of the Carolinas. The narrator drives a flatbed truck; with him is a young woman who is drinking blueberry wine. By the side of the road a blind man makes a sign with his hand and a young boy carries a fishing rod—but the driver wants only to be by the side of the woman he loves. He is missing home terribly. "All I'm thinkin' about is you, baby," Springsteen sings. He mentions his parents—his mother going to church, his father going to town—then, once again, refers to the Bible: the phrase "Blind'll see, the lame will be healed" evokes the 37 miracles attributed to Christ in the New Testament.

Production

If *All I'm Thinkin' About* has similarities with Canned Heat and their hit *Going Up the Country*, this is chiefly because of the sound quality and boogie rhythm of the two songs, which comprise three basic chords, as should all good rock 'n' roll. Springsteen starts by counting in the band, while strumming his Gibson J-45. He plays no fewer than three guitars: in all likelihood a Dobro played with a slide on the left, a rhythm guitar in the center, and a third guitar on that right that more or less doubles the rhythm guitar. For the second time on this album, Springsteen takes care of the drums, playing them with brushes more discreetly and with better control than in *Jesus Was on Only Son*. Besides a tambourine, which he adds after the third verse (at 2'38), there are doubtless other percussion instruments buried in the mix. As for the bass guitar, it is in the hands of Brendan O'Brien.

The Boss sings this song in a falsetto voice. He certainly does not have the timbre of Prince and struggles in certain passages (listen around 1'54), but the results are convincing. As for the backing vocals of Patti Scialfa, Soozie Tyrell, and Lisa Lowell, they are highly effective, the three singers providing the ideal support for the songwriter's falsetto.

Bruce Springsteen at the Convention Hall, Asbury Park, on 20 April 2005. He included *Matamoros Banks* on his setlist.

MATAMOROS BANKS

Bruce Springsteen / 4'00

2005

Musicians
Bruce Springsteen: vocals, guitars, keyboards, percussion
Nashville String Machine: strings
Recording
Thrill Hill Recording, Los Angeles and New Jersey: 1996 to 2004
Southern Tracks Recording Studio, Atlanta, Georgia: March to August 2004
Masterphonics, Nashville, Tennessee: March to August 2004
Technical team
Producer: Brendan O'Brien
Recording engineers: Toby Scott (Thrill Hill), Nick DiDia (Southern Tracks)
Assistant recording engineers: Karl Egsieker, Billy Bowers, Tom Tapley
Mixing: Toby Scott
Mastering: Bob Ludwig (Gateway Mastering, Portland)

Unlike on the album, both in concert and on the DVD that comes with *Devils & Dust* Springsteen ends *Matamoros Banks* in a falsetto voice, thus heightening the dramatic impact of his performance.

For Springsteen Addicts

The sentence "The pale moon opens the earth to its bones" occurs almost verbatim in *Black Cowboys*: "The moon rose and stripped the earth to its bone."

Genesis and lyrics

This piece, which brings *Devils & Dust* to a close, takes its title from the name of a Mexican city on the border with the US, on the bank of the Rio Grande directly opposite the city of Brownsville, Texas. In a sense, it is an extension of several songs on the album *The Ghost of Tom Joad*, especially *Across the Border*. Once again, the theme is the journey of a Mexican in search of a better life in the land of Uncle Sam. Its distinguishing feature is that Bruce Springsteen retraces this journey in reverse, starting at the end, with the body of the unfortunate migrant at the bottom of the Rio Grande and the last words he says (in his mind) to his wife: "Goodbye, my darling, for your love I give God thanks."

The third and fourth verses describe the journey the Mexican has undertaken, under the worst of conditions: "I walk on twine and tire tread." And the song ends with his decision to leave, and his request to the woman he loves to accompany him on his odyssey: "Meet me on the Matamoros banks."

First performed live at the Paramount Theatre in Asbury Park, New Jersey, on 21 April 2005, *Matamoros Banks* was one of the high points of the Devils & Dust Tour because of its message: a plea to Washington for a humane immigration policy.

Production

The last ballad on the album, *Matamoros Banks* is in the same spirit as its predecessors, especially *Silver Palomino*, with the same understated arrangement and same sadness in the lead vocals. Springsteen begins just with his guitar, which has the open tuning D, A, D, G, A, D beloved of folk singers. He accompanies himself on a classical guitar with nylon strings, to produce rather discreet solos (for example, in the first verse at 1'05). In the third verse, the strings of the Nashville String Machine come in, most definitely supported by pads played on the Boss's keyboards (at 1'25). These are again undermixed, as was the songwriter's wish. This lack of presence on the part of the orchestra is probably the main criticism that could be leveled at the whole album. A violin solo audible in the last verse can be made out more clearly, but still with the same restraint (from 2'48). Finally, percussion, probably a cabasa or a maraca, has been recorded and mixed to a normal level (at 2'28 and from 3'30).

WESHALL
OVER

ALBUM

WE SHALL OVERCOME: THE SEEGER SESSIONS

Old Dan Tucker • Jesse James • Mrs. McGrath • O Mary Don't You Weep • John Henry • Erie Canal • Jacob's Ladder • My Oklahoma Home • Eyes on the Prize • Shenandoah • Pay Me My Money Down • We Shall Overcome • Froggie Went A Courtin' • Songs featuring on the DVD of the album • John Henry • Pay Me my Money Down • Buffalo Gals • Erie Canal • O Mary Don't You Weep • Shenandoah

Jacob's Ladder (American Land Edition version) • Froggie Went A Courtin' (American Land Edition version) • New songs for the American Land Edition (released October 2006) • Buffalo Gals • How Can I Keep from Singing • How Can a Poor Man Stand Such Times and Live • Bring 'Em Home • American Land

Bonus titles recorded live for the American Land Edition DVD (released October 2006)
How Can a Poor Man Stand Such Times and Live • Bring 'Em Home • American Land • Pay Me My Money Down

Outtakes: *Once Upon a Time in the West • Hobo's Lullaby • The Ghost of Tom Joad • If I Had a Hammer (The Hammer Song) • I Come and Stand at Every Door • Pretty Boy Floyd • Michael Row Your Boat Ashore • Worried Man Blues • Long Walk Home*

RELEASE DATE

United States: 25 April 2006; 3 October 2006 for the American Land Edition
Reference: Columbia Records – 82876 83439 1 and
82876 88231 1 for the American Land Edition
No.3 in the United States and United Kingdom

A shoot for the British magazine *Mojo*, in October 2005. This photograph was taken by Danny Clinch, who also shot the photograph for *We Shall Overcome: The Pete Seeger Sessions*.

2006

For Springsteen Addicts

Jim Musselman was a lawyer involved in humanitarian causes, especially with Ralph Nader and Michael Moore. He also founded the label Appleseed Recordings in 1997, with the aim of demonstrating that music, particularly folk music, could transform society now just as it had in the past. He was a friend of Pete Seeger; the double album *Where Have All the Flowers Gone: The Songs of Pete Seeger* was his idea, and it was Musselman who persuaded Bruce Springsteen to take part in it.

IN SEARCH OF PETE SEEGER

The plan for *We Shall Overcome: The Seeger Sessions* took shape in 1997, when Bruce Springsteen took part in the sessions for *Where Have All the Flowers Gone: The Songs of Pete Seeger*, specifically for the recording of *We Shall Overcome*. Released in March 1998, this double album was a tribute by the greatest names in folk music—from Tom Paxton to Jackson Browne, Billy Bragg, Roger McGuinn (of The Byrds), and Ani DiFranco—to the man who, in acoustic music, had been the spokesman for those excluded from the American dream ever since the dark days of the McCarthy era. Pete Seeger was not, strictly speaking, a songwriter, even though several of his songs, such as *Where Have All the Flowers Gone* and *If I Had a Hammer (The Hammer Song)* achieved worldwide renown. He was above all a singer and an ethnomusicologist who, with Woody Guthrie (and subsequently on his own account), strove to gain recognition for the North American folk music tradition, as well as for ballads from the United Kingdom and Ireland.

"Growing up a rock 'n' roll kid, I didn't know a lot about Pete's music or the depth of his influence," Bruce Springsteen writes in his autobiography *Born to Run*. "But once I started listening, I was overwhelmed by the wealth of songs, their richness, and their power. It changed what I thought I knew about folk music."[1]

In October 1997, a few weeks before *We Shall Overcome* was recorded (in November), Jim Musselman, founder of the Appleseed Recordings label (which would release the tribute double CD), sent the Boss a tape of 14 songs by Pete Seeger. Bruce Springsteen was eager to plunge into the world of folk music and, through the violinist Soozie Tyrell, contacted a New York bluegrass outfit by the name of The Gotham Playboys, whose members included Jeremy Chatzky (bass guitar), Sam Bardfeld (violin), Will Holshouser (accordion), and Larry Eagle (drums). After a few jam sessions—recorded at Thrill Hill East, in the Boss's living room in New Jersey—he decided to hire these four musicians to record his album. Holshouser had commitments to honor, and so was replaced by Charles Giordano on the accordion (and keyboards). Giordano had played with artists as varied as David Johansen (ex-New York Dolls) and Madeleine Peyroux; he would join the E Street Band following the death of Danny Federici in 2008. The lineup was then strengthened by more musicians who were equally well acquainted with traditional American music and also excellent jazz instrumentalists. These included Art Baron on tuba (recorded by overdubbing), who had played with both Duke Ellington and Buddy Rich, as well as with Lou Reed and Charlie Musselwhite; Frank Bruno on guitar and vocals; Mark Clifford on banjo; Lisa Lowell on vocals; Eddie Manion on saxophone (one of the musicians for *Mary's Place* on the *The Rising* album); Mark Pender on trumpet and vocals (who also features on *The Rising* as well as on *Devils & Dust*); Richie "La Bamba" Rosenberg, the unmissable trombonist who had first worked with Springsteen on *Born in the U.S.A.*; and, naturally, Patti Scialfa on vocals and Soozie Tyrell on violin and vocals. All were talented instrumentalists and singers who enriched the

Pete Seeger (seen here in 1982) was the guardian of the American musical tradition to whom the Boss pays homage throughout his 14th album.

traditional numbers chosen by Springsteen with a warm Dixieland touch.

The album

The 13 songs chosen to feature on *We Shall Overcome: The Seeger Sessions* were recorded by Bruce Springsteen and his musicians in three sessions: in 1997, and subsequently in 2005 and 2006. The album was released on 25 April 2006, together with a DVD produced by Thom Zimny (this features the making of certain recordings and one bonus song: *Buffalo Gals*). Although it was the first album to consist entirely of covers, it was no less appreciated by the press as a 100 percent Springsteen disc—an essential work, even, within the trend for Americana. In the 19 May 2006 issue of *Rolling Stone* magazine, Jonathan Ringen wrote: "*We Shall Overcome* [...] is his most jubilant disc since *Born in the U.S.A.* and more fun than a tribute to Pete Seeger has any right to be."[126] David Browne, in the 24 April 2006 issue of *Entertainment Weekly*, wrote that he liked Springsteen's approach, which consisted of "injecting rock 'n' roll energy into Seeger's vast repertoire."[127] *We Shall Overcome: The Seeger Sessions* won a Grammy Award for "Best Traditional Folk Album," and reached No.3 in both the United States and United Kingdom charts.

Just five days after the album went on sale, Bruce Springsteen set off on tour. Seventeen musicians—sometimes as many as 20—accompanied him onstage, most of whom had taken part in the sessions for the disc. The Bruce Springsteen with The Seeger Sessions Band Tour began on 30 April 2006 at the New Orleans Jazz & Heritage Festival, and ended on 21 November in Belfast, Northern Ireland. Between those dates, some 60 concerts were given in the United States and most European countries, especially the United Kingdom (London, 8 and 9 May), France (Paris, 10 May), Spain (Barcelona, 14 May), the Netherlands (Amsterdam, 16 May), and Germany (Frankfurt, 17 May), before audiences that were enraptured to hear an entire musical tradition revisited in depth.

The *American Land Edition*

A version supplemented with five further songs (*Buffalo Gals, How Can I Keep from Singing, How Can a Poor Man Stand Such Times and Live, Bring 'Em Home*, and *American Land*), two extra songs on the DVD (*Jacob's Ladder* and *Froggie Went A Courtin'*), as well as four bonus pieces played and filmed live (*How Can a Poor Man Stand Such Times and Live, Bring 'Em Home, American Land*, and *Pay Me My Money Down*) was released on 3 October 2006, under the title *American Land Edition*.

Please note: we do not deal with the song *American Land* in the section for this album, but in the section for *Wrecking Ball*, released in 2012, where it features as a bonus track in a studio version, rather than live.

The sleeve

The album image for *We Shall Overcome: The Seeger Sessions* is a group photo. Springsteen is surrounded by his 12 musicians and backing vocalists. Double bass, banjo, violin, brass instruments—the message is clear even before you put the record on: the Boss is inviting his listeners to return to the roots of America's musical tradition. The photo was shot—perhaps with a yellow filter applied afterward—by Danny Clinch, who had already created the sleeve for *The Rising* and directed the DVD for *Devils & Dust*. The atmosphere is reminiscent of the album sleeve of *The Basement Tapes*, by Bob Dylan and The Band released in 1975. Chris Austopchuk

On this, the sleeve of his 14th studio album, Springsteen is surrounded by his musicians. Is this a nod to *The Basement Tapes* by Dylan and the Band?

and Michelle Holme receive the credit for artistic direction, and Michelle Holme and Meghan Foley for the design.

The recording

We Shall Overcome: The Seeger Sessions required fewer sessions than any other album by the Boss: barely three! The first was on 2 November 1997, the second on 19 March 2005—more than seven years later—and the last on 21 January 2006. All the songs were recorded in Springsteen's home studio at Thrill Hill, New Jersey. As Springsteen explains: "We set up next to one another in the living room of our farmhouse (horns in the hall), counted off the opening chords to *Jesse James*, and away we went. We made a half-dozen recordings. I sat on them for almost a decade but from time to time I kept being drawn back to them. They weren't quite like anything else I'd cut before and their freshness kept commanding my ear. I set up another session in 2005 and then one more in 2006. Everything on the record was cut in those three one-day sessions ('97, '05, and '06), mostly first or second takes, all live and all with a band I'd never played a note with before they showed up at our farm barn dance. The Sessions Band was born."[1]

Springsteen and his band thus set up in the living room of his farm at Thrill Hill, with the three horns in the hall to keep a proper acoustic balance. Toby Scott was once again the chief recording engineer, isolated in an adjacent room. The Boss sang into a superb Telefunken ELA M 251 mic, his voice equalized and compressed by an Avalon Vt737sp. Recording thus went ahead in the simplest possible way, without any rehearsal, the songwriter giving his musicians only brief instructions: "All arrangements were conducted as we played, you can hear me shouting out the names and instruments of the players as we roll."[128]

During the first session, on 2 November 1997, six songs were recorded: *Jesse James*, *My Oklahoma Home*, *We Shall Overcome*, *Hobo's Lullaby*, *I Come and Stand at Every Door*, and *Pretty Boy Floyd*. However, Springsteen realized that he did not have enough material to fill an album. As he explains on the sleeve, the decision to go ahead and arrange a new recording session, on 19 March 2005, was also reached following a comment made by Jon Landau who said, "I think we've got something here..."[128] Nine songs were added to those recorded previously: *Erie Canal*, *John Henry*, *O Mary Don't You Weep*, *Pay Me My Money Down*, *Old Dan Tucker*, *Froggie Went A Courtin'*, *Shenandoah*, *Mrs. McGrath*, and *Michael Row Your Boat Ashore*. Finally, ten months later, on 21 January 2006, the last songs were recorded: *Jacob's Ladder*, *Buffalo Gals*, *Eyes on the Prize*, *How Can I Keep from Singing*, *American Land*, *Bring 'Em Home*, *If I Had a Hammer (The Hammer Song)*, and *Worried Man Blues*.

All these songs feature on the tracklisting of *We Shall Overcome: The Seeger Sessions*, with the exception of *I Come and Stand at Every Door*, *Pretty Boy Floyd*, *Michael Row Your Boat Ashore*, *Worried Man Blues*, *Hobo's Lullaby*, and *If I Had a Hammer (The Hammer Song)*—the last two having been included on compilations destined for charitable causes, respectively the albums *Give US Your Poor* (2007) and *Appleseed's 21st Anniversary: Roots and Branches* (2018), released by Appleseed Recordings.

In fact, three songs that feature on the *American Land Edition* were recorded live with the Seeger Sessions Tour Band: *How Can a Poor Man Stand Such Times and Live*, *Bring 'Em Home*, and *American Land*.

Daniel Decatur Emmett, known as Dan Emmett, was inducted into the Songwriters Hall of Fame in 1970 (Pete Seeger was inducted in 1972, and Springsteen in 1999). A movie of his life, bearing the title of one of his songs, *Dixie*, and starring Bing Crosby as Emmett, was released in 1943. *Old Dan Tucker*, performed by Bing Crosby, Billy De Wolfe, Eddie Foy Jr, and Lynne Overman, can be heard as the film credits roll.

2006

OLD DAN TUCKER

Public domain / Arrangements Bruce Springsteen / 2'31

Musicians
- **Bruce Springsteen:** vocals, guitar
- **Patti Scialfa:** backing vocals
- **Soozie Tyrell:** violin, backing vocals
- **Sam Bardfeld:** violin
- **Frank Bruno:** guitar, backing vocals
- **Mark Clifford:** banjo, backing vocals
- **Charles Giordano:** organ
- **Eddie Manion:** saxophone
- **Mark Pender:** trumpet, backing vocals
- **Richie "La Bamba" Rosenberg:** trombone, backing vocals
- **Jeremy Chatzky:** double bass
- **Larry Eagle:** drums, percussion

Recording
- **Thrill Hill, Boxwood Studios, New Jersey:** 19 March 2005

Technical team
- **Producer:** Bruce Springsteen
- **Recording engineer:** Toby Scott
- **Assistant recording engineers:** Kevin Buell, Ross Petersen
- **Mixing:** Bob Clearmountain (Mix This! Los Angeles)
- **Mixing assistant:** Brandon Duncan
- **Mastering:** Bob Ludwig (Gateway Mastering, Portland)

Bruce Springsteen at Camp Nou, Barcelona, on 20 July 2008, with Charles Giordano on keyboards for a performance of *Old Dan Tucker*.

Genesis and lyrics

Old folk tunes were handed down over decades and even centuries thanks to the oral tradition. *Old Dan Tucker*, also known by the titles *Ole Dan Tucker* and *Dan Tucker*, is no exception. The lyrics appear to have been written by Dan Emmett (1815–1904) in the early 1840s, as the music was first published in 1843.

Dan Emmett went down in the history of popular music for having founded the Virginia Minstrels. This was the first troupe of minstrels—white singers, musicians, and actors who blacked up their faces and entertained audiences by crudely imitating African-Americans. *Old Dan Tucker* was one of the best-known songs in the Virginia Minstrels' repertoire. Originally, the central character was an African-American from rural America, attracted to both sex and alcohol, who did not hesitate to use his fists. As the song was performed over time, the lyrics changed: some verses were dropped, others added, and, from the end of the 1840s and especially during the Civil War, *Old Dan Tucker* turned into a song that advocated the abolition of slavery.

It was precisely this humanist side that attracted many folk and bluegrass performers, notably Pete Seeger, who included it on the album *American Favorite Ballads* in 1957, and Bruce Springsteen half a century later.

Production

The Boss's 14th album thus begins with a very invigorating version of *Old Dan Tucker*. The songwriter counts the number in, laughing, supported by the skipping shuffle of Larry Eagle's hi-hat and Mark Clifford's typically country banjo. The whole band joins them in the first chorus, supplying enthusiastic backing vocals as well (at 0'27). Eddie Manion, Mark Pender, and Richie "La Bamba" Rosenberg heighten the song's festive quality with cheerful wind playing, as does Charles Giordano with his Hammond B-3 organ, launching into the piece's only proper solo (at 1'36).

Of course, compared with Pete Seeger, alone with his banjo, the version by Springsteen and his band is far more dynamic and entertaining, though slower. But the Boss is a born leader, and effortlessly leads his musicians in an excellent, exhilarating reinterpretation of this enjoyable song.

JESSE JAMES

Traditional / Arrangements Bruce Springsteen / 3'47

Needless to say, *Jesse James* can be heard on the soundtrack of several Westerns, such as Henry King's *Jesse James* (1939), starring Tyrone Power and Henry Fonda, and Walter Hill's *The Long Riders* (1980), starring David Carradine and Stacy Keach.

Musicians
- **Bruce Springsteen:** vocals, guitar
- **Soozie Tyrell:** violin, backing vocals
- **Sam Bardfeld:** backing vocals
- **Frank Bruno:** guitar, backing vocals
- **Mark Clifford:** banjo
- **Charles Giordano:** accordion
- **Eddie Manion:** saxophone
- **Mark Pender:** backing vocals
- **Richie "La Bamba" Rosenberg:** trombone, backing vocals
- **Jeremy Chatzky:** double bass
- **Larry Eagle:** drums, percussion

Recording
- **Thrill Hill, Boxwood Studios, New Jersey:** 2 November 1997

Technical team
- **Producer:** Bruce Springsteen
- **Recording engineer:** Toby Scott
- **Assistant recording engineers:** Kevin Buell, Ross Petersen
- **Mixing:** Bob Clearmountain (Mix This! Los Angeles)
- **Mixing assistant:** Brandon Duncan
- **Mastering:** Bob Ludwig (Gateway Mastering, Portland)

The outlaw Jesse James has won the sympathy of numerous artists, including the punk folk group The Pogues.

Genesis and lyrics

Jesse James is a late 19th-century American song, possibly dating from 1882. That was the time when Jesse James and his brother Frank were on the rampage. After fighting on the Confederate side and being expelled from Missouri to Nebraska by the victorious Yankees, they became outlaws, formed a gang, and began to attack banks, trains, and stagecoaches. In 1876, the James brothers settled in Tennessee, hoping to live a quiet life there. However, Jesse once again turned to a life of crime. He was finally betrayed, then killed, by Robert Ford, a member of his gang, in 1882.

This is exactly the story told by the song—but with a somewhat loose approach to historical accuracy. Notably, it makes Jesse James into a Robin Hood-like hero, as the words "He stole from the rich and he gave to the poor"—attributed to one Billy Gashade — attest.

This traditional number has inspired a great many performers since it was first recorded by Bentley Ball in 1919. These have included the founding fathers of the folk song, Woody Guthrie and Pete Seeger, as well as Van Morrison, Willy DeVille, The Pogues, and, of course, Bruce Springsteen. The very effective version by the British neo-skiffle band Mungo Jerry is also worthy of a mention.

Production

Jesse James was apparently the very first song recorded for the album. The recording session took place on 2 November 1997 and, as Springsteen explains in his autobiography, the song was definitely in the can after the first take.

The songwriter himself begins *Jesse James*, singing alone with an acoustic guitar—his trusty Gibson J-45. Then the banjo, double bass, and a percussion instrument come in for the second verse, before being joined by the rest of the band in the first chorus. Charles Giordano's accordion is very much to the fore and, together with the violin, banjo, and wind instruments, takes part in the various instrumental breaks typical of bluegrass.

While this recording is a fine one, the version that features on the DVD *Bruce Springsteen with The Sessions Band: Live in Dublin*, released in 2007, is undoubtedly superior (as is indeed the case with most songs on the record). Absolutely worth a listen.

For Springsteen Addicts

The Boss does not pronounce the name McGrath the Irish way: "*McGraw*."

2006

MRS. MCGRATH

Traditional / Arrangements Bruce Springsteen / 4'19

Musicians

Bruce Springsteen: vocals, guitar
Soozie Tyrell: violin
Sam Bardfeld: violin
Frank Bruno: guitar
Charles Giordano: piano
Jeremy Chatzky: double bass
Larry Eagle: drums, percussion

Recording

Thrill Hill, Boxwood Studios, New Jersey: 19 March 2005

Technical team

Producer: Bruce Springsteen
Recording engineer: Toby Scott
Assistant recording engineers: Kevin Buell, Ross Petersen
Mixing: Bob Clearmountain (Mix This! Los Angeles)
Mixing assistant: Brandon Duncan
Mastering: Bob Ludwig (Gateway Mastering, Portland)

Mrs. McGrath is an old Irish ballad, which was performed by The Clancy Brothers before Bruce Springsteen.

Genesis and lyrics

Mrs. McGrath is an Irish ballad that was written, in all probability, in the early 19th century. Indeed, the words describe the Peninsular War (1807–1814), which was fought by the First French Empire against Spain, the United Kingdom, and Portugal.

The song is set in Ireland. A British sergeant persuades a mother to allow her son to enlist and go to fight Napoleon's troops in Spain. He tempts her with the prestige of a scarlet coat and a big cocked hat. Seven years later, the lad returns to his mother, but has tragically lost both legs "on the fifth of May," so certainly during the Battle of Fuentes d'Oñoro, in which the troops of the French Marshal Masséna fought those of General Wellesley, Duke of Wellington, on 3–5 May 1811. At first, his mother does not understand, but her incomprehension gives way to anger.

Mrs. McGrath is not only a pacifist song: during the early years of the 20th century it became one of the favorite songs of the Irish Volunteers, a nationalist militia that played a decisive role in the 1916 Easter Rising, and subsequently in the Irish War of Independence (1919–1921). Naturally, many Irish artists, such as The Clancy Brothers and The Dubliners, included this song in their repertoire, but musicians on the English folk scene like Martin Carthy and those on the American one, such as Burl Ives, Pete Seeger, and, indeed, Bruce Springsteen, performed it too.

Production

The atmosphere of *Mrs. McGrath* contrasts sharply with that of the first two songs on the album: there is no longer a party spirit, but a mood of accusation instead. This protest song is performed by a reduced group of musicians: accompanying Springsteen are only Frank Bruno's acoustic guitar, Soozie Tyrell and Sam Bardfeld's violins, Jeremy Chatzky's double bass, Charles Giordano's piano, and Larry Eagle's percussion (tambourine, shell-shaker) and bass drum.

The song's "Irish folk" quality is, of course, retained, chiefly thanks to the violins, but this is less pronounced than when it was performed in concert by the Seeger Band. Also, Springsteen takes liberties with the tune, particularly the one in the chorus which, especially in Pete Seeger's version, is almost that of a children's dance. The songwriter decided to depart from that to render the song denser and more tragic.

The African-American author James Baldwin, an iconic figure in the protests of the 1950s and 1960s, also wrote an essay entitled *The Fire Next Time* (1963). The phrase comes from *O Mary Don't You Weep.*

O MARY DON'T YOU WEEP

Traditional / Arrangements Bruce Springsteen / 6'05

Musicians

Bruce Springsteen: vocals, guitar
Patti Scialfa: backing vocals
Soozie Tyrell: violin, backing vocals
Sam Bardfeld: violin
Frank Bruno: guitar, backing vocals
Mark Clifford: banjo
Charles Giordano: piano, accordion
Eddie Manion: saxophone
Mark Pender: trumpet, backing vocals
Richie "La Bamba" Rosenberg: trombone, backing vocals
Jeremy Chatzky: double bass
Larry Eagle: drums, percussion

Recording

Thrill Hill, Boxwood Studios, New Jersey: 19 March 2005

Technical team

Producer: Bruce Springsteen
Recording engineer: Toby Scott
Assistant recording engineers: Kevin Buell, Ross Petersen
Mixing: Bob Clearmountain (Mix This! Los Angeles)
Mixing assistant: Brandon Duncan
Mastering: Bob Ludwig (Gateway Mastering, Portland)

The Fisk Jubilee Singers performed for Britain's Queen Victoria in 1875. The group recorded *O Mary Don't You Weep* in 1915.

Genesis and lyrics

With this song, Bruce Springsteen demonstrates his love for African-American religious music. *O Mary Don't You Weep* is, in fact, one of the oldest spirituals, probably a song sung by slaves that predates the Civil War. It describes the Israelites' slavery in Egypt, followed by their exodus—thanks to Moses, their liberator—to the Promised Land across the Red Sea, which parts before him and then closes again, engulfing the Egyptians. It is a song full of hope.

It is only a short step from the liberation of the Israelites to the emancipation of slaves in the United States—a step that was naturally taken in the 20th century. Although the Fisk Jubilee Singers recorded *O Mary Don't You Weep* in 1915, it was only from the 1950s, and especially during the 1960s, that this song once again became topical, with African-Americans' struggle for civil rights and, more widely, protests on university campuses. After recordings by The Caravans in 1958 and the Swan Silvertones the following year, Pete Seeger gave the song its folk quality at the Newport Folk Festival in 1964. Many more versions followed—by The Soul Stirrers, Burl Ives, and Aretha Franklin—until Bruce Springsteen produced his in 2005.

Production

O Mary Don't You Weep begins with Springsteen's acoustic guitar and Sam Bardfeld's violin, the latter executing a very fine solo in the manner of the renowned Stéphane Grappelli. Soozie Tyrell joins him very soon, after which the wind instruments come in, with a New Orleans vibe. The song takes off once the drums come in with that infectious rhythm, which serves as the foundation for the Boss and his band to deliver an inspired performance. The backing vocals bring the obligatory gospel touch, while the various instrumental breaks allow the impassioned solos of the individual musicians to shine through. It appears that Charles Giordano overdubbed his accordion part, since he also plays the piano, as can be seen on the DVD of the album. As for the songwriter himself, he is visibly truly enjoying the recording—and it is one of the highlights of the disc. The result has nothing in common with Pete Seeger's version, nor even with that of Aretha Franklin—the former being a pure folk song, the latter a real spiritual. It sits halfway between the two: Springsteen has succeeded in building a bridge between these two diametrically opposed visions.

JOHN HENRY

2006

Traditional / Arrangements Bruce Springsteen / 5'07

Musicians
Bruce Springsteen: vocals, guitar
Soozie Tyrell: violin
Sam Bardfeld: violin
Frank Bruno: guitar
Mark Clifford: banjo
Charles Giordano: accordion
Eddie Manion: saxophone
Mark Pender: trumpet
Richie "La Bamba" Rosenberg: trombone
Jeremy Chatzky: double bass
Larry Eagle: drums, percussion

Recording
Thrill Hill, Boxwood Studios, New Jersey: 19 March 2005

Technical team
Producer: Bruce Springsteen
Recording engineer: Toby Scott
Assistant recording engineers: Kevin Buell, Ross Petersen
Mixing: Bob Clearmountain (Mix This! Los Angeles)
Mixing assistant: Brandon Duncan
Mastering: Bob Ludwig (Gateway Mastering, Portland)

Bruce Springsteen, on tour in the Netherlands (May 2006) during the We Shall Overcome Tour, performs *John Henry* with Jeremy Chatzky on double bass.

Genesis and lyrics

John Henry is one of the most famous heroic characters in American folklore. According to legend, he was born a slave in Alabama during the 1840s. Having been freed after the Civil War, he was hired as a steel-driver (someone who drills into rock with a hammer) for a railroad company, in all probability the Chesapeake and Ohio Railway. One day, the company acquired a steam-powered drill. In order to prove the worth of his work and not lose his job, John Henry challenged the machine. He won the contest, to the great joy of his fellow workers, but died of a heart attack shortly afterward.

Whether he was a real person or a myth, John Henry became, from the growth of industry in the second half of the 19th century, a double, contradictory symbol of both the superiority of humans over machines and of the desperate battle of manual laborers in the face of technical progress. This double symbolism was glorified by trade unions during the fight for social justice that took place throughout the 1920s. Indeed, he was the inspiration for novelists and playwrights as well as songwriters and filmmakers. The ballad *John Henry* which, it can reasonably be assumed, dates from the late 19th century, has seen an impressive number of recordings, from Woody Guthrie to Mississippi Fred McDowell, Van Morrison, and Joe Bonamassa. Bruce Springsteen's version is a real achievement—a perfect marriage of folk tradition and Dixieland.

Production

John Henry is the song that opens the DVD of the album. Springsteen could not have made a better choice, for he and his musicians deliver a superb performance—it is bright and dynamic despite its hardly joyous lyrics. The two violinists start the proceedings and are then soon joined by the band. The musicians swing, and the Boss produces excellent lead vocals, his voice as gravelly as can be. "It rocks, but it's not quite rock music,"[129] he later explained. Solos come one after the other: first the violin (at 1'29), then the accordion (at 2'56), and finally the banjo (at 3'19). The end of the album version of the song differs from the one on the DVD, because it is cut short: it lacks the Boss counting in his musicians for one last violin solo. As for the performance by Pete Seeger, accompanied only by his banjo, it is not that far from Springsteen's—at least in spirit.

COVER

When The Kingston Trio recorded *Erie Canal* in 1963, they took liberties—which worked well—compared to the more traditional versions, most notably a very spirited rhythm and vocal harmonies. All were closer to rock 'n' roll than to folk.

ERIE CANAL

Public domain / Arrangements Bruce Springsteen / 4'03

Musicians
- **Bruce Springsteen:** vocals, guitar
- **Patti Scialfa:** backing vocals
- **Soozie Tyrell:** violin, backing vocals
- **Sam Bardfeld:** violin
- **Frank Bruno:** guitar, backing vocals
- **Mark Clifford:** banjo
- **Charles Giordano:** accordion
- **Art Baron:** tuba
- **Eddie Manion:** saxophone
- **Mark Pender:** trumpet, backing vocals
- **Richie "La Bamba" Rosenberg:** trombone, backing vocals
- **Jeremy Chatzky:** double bass
- **Larry Eagle:** drums, percussion

Recording
- **Thrill Hill, Boxwood Studios, New Jersey:** 19 March 2005

Technical team
- **Producer:** Bruce Springsteen
- **Recording engineer:** Toby Scott
- **Assistant recording engineers:** Kevin Buell, Ross Petersen
- **Mixing:** Bob Clearmountain (Mix This! Los Angeles)
- **Mixing assistant:** Brandon Duncan
- **Mastering:** Bob Ludwig (Gateway Mastering, Portland)

Bruce Springsteen and the Seeger Sessions Band at Madison Square Garden, on 22 June 2006. The brass are at the heart of the groove of *Erie Canal*.

Genesis and lyrics

Thomas S Allen (1876–1919) was a Tin Pan Alley composer who gave the world a number of vaudeville and ragtime songs. *Erie Canal*, written in 1905, went by different titles, notably *Low Bridge, Everybody Down*, *Fifteen Years on the Erie Canal*, and *Erie Barge Canal*. In the song, Allen tells the story of the Erie Canal in the 19th century. This waterway, which links Lake Erie with the Hudson River, made a considerable contribution to the economic development of the eastern seaboard of the United States, at a time before barges and other craft were equipped with engines, and were hauled by mules.

"I've got a mule and her name is Sal/Fifteen miles on the Erie Canal/She's a good old worker and a good old pal," as the song has gone since the 1910s. Although the words may have changed over the decades, their nostalgic, pre-mechanization flavor has remained. *Erie Canal* is another classic of the folk repertoire, and since the 1910s numerous artists have recorded it, most notably Billy Murray in 1913, Vernon Dalhart in 1929, Pete Seeger in 1944, The Kingston Trio in 1963, and Bruce Springsteen in 2006.

Production

The DVD of the album has footage of Springsteen and his musicians putting together the intro to *Erie Canal*. The Boss is looking for the right formula for the accompaniment to his acoustic guitar. He hums a tune for the two violins, then tests the sound of the three wind instruments; finally, he opts for the violins and the banjo. The feel is that of blues mixed with Dixieland. The songwriter has a serious, inspired voice, with a rough timbre. The musicians come in one after the other, forming a sort of half-country, half-New Orleans fanfare, especially as the brass instruments are very much to the fore, including, for the first time since the beginning of the album, Art Baron and his tuba (from 1'04). The excellent backing vocals—probably supplemented by overdubbing (like the tuba)—bring a spiritual-like touch to the song. Also worth mentioning is the very fine rhythm section of Larry Eagle and Jeremy Chatzky, who are a veritable swing machine. It should also be pointed out that the version of the song by the Boss and his band remains true to the spirit of Pete Seeger's version.

Curiously, in the booklet that comes with the album, only Pete Seeger receives a credit for *Jacob's Ladder.* Even though he wrote a chorus for the song, it would have been more logical to add the word "traditional." Is this a tribute paid by the Boss?

2006

JACOB'S LADDER

Pete Seeger / 4'28

Musicians

Bruce Springsteen: vocals, guitar
Patti Scialfa: backing vocals
Liza Lowell: backing vocals
Soozie Tyrell: violin, backing vocals
Sam Bardfeld: violin
Frank Bruno: guitar, backing vocals
Mark Clifford: banjo
Charles Giordano: organ, piano, accordion
Art Baron: tuba
Eddie Manion: saxophone
Mark Pender: trumpet, backing vocals
Richie "La Bamba" Rosenberg: trombone, backing vocals
Jeremy Chatzky: double bass
Larry Eagle: drums, washboard

Recording

Thrill Hill, Boxwood Studios, New Jersey: 21 January 2006

Technical team

Producer: Bruce Springsteen
Recording engineer: Toby Scott
Assistant recording engineers: Kevin Buell, Ross Petersen
Mixing: Bob Clearmountain (Mix This! Los Angeles)
Mixing assistant: Brandon Duncan
Mastering: Bob Ludwig (Gateway Mastering, Portland)

The Staple Singers (seen here in 1960) created a superb spiritual version of *Jacob's Ladder.* Springsteen, for his part, took a folk-rock approach to the song.

Genesis and lyrics

The origins of *Jacob's Ladder* date back to between the mid-18th and early 19th centuries, among black slaves who had probably come from what is now Liberia. It is a slave song, but also a song of hope, being based on an episode in the Book of Genesis describing Jacob's ladder. Having secured his birthright, Jacob, son of Isaac and Rebecca and grandson of Abraham, is being pursued by his twin brother, Esau, who wants to kill him. Thanks to his mother, Jacob is able to take refuge in the house of his uncle Laban who lives in Haran. Jacob sets off for Haran but, during a stopover on his journey, he has a vision: a ladder leading up to the heavens, at the top of which is God.

The song *Jacob's Ladder* features a call and response. It has been recorded many times since the start of the record industry. Although most performers retained its spiritual dimension, some made it into a protest anthem, most notably on behalf of industrial trade unions during the 1930s. Pete Seeger, who recorded it in 1960, transformed it into a feminist song by adding a new chorus: "We are dancing Sarah's circle." Almost half a century later, Bruce Springsteen, in turn, recorded *Jacob's Ladder*, but without the chorus written by the folk singer from New York.

Production

Once again, it is from New Orleans that Springsteen drew inspiration for the arrangement of *Jacob's Ladder.* The wind instruments have pride of place: they begin the song, end it, and even take a solo, on the orders of the Boss: "Come on, horn section!" (at 2'00). Art Baron's tuba is overdubbed, as in all probability are the Hammond B-3 organ and piano of Charles Giordano, who has already taken care of the accordion, as can be seen on the DVD of the album. The atmosphere is totally joyful, with Larry Eagle accompanying on both washboard and drums, and the backing vocalists singing in the style of choirs that perform spirituals. However, this reinterpretation of *Jacob's Ladder* in no way resembles the gospel versions by The Famous Ward Singers and The Staple Singers, nor even the one by Pete Seeger, which can be heard on his album *Singalong: Live at the Sanders Theatre, Cambridge, Massachusetts 1980.*

Springsteen and his band offer a bright interpretation of *Jacob's Ladder*, which acquired an added dimension in concert.

MY OKLAHOMA HOME

Bill & Agnes "Sis" Cunningham / 6'03

Musicians
Bruce Springsteen: vocals, guitar
Soozie Tyrell: violin, backing vocals
Sam Bardfeld: violin, backing vocals
Frank Bruno: guitar, backing vocals
Mark Clifford: banjo, backing vocals
Charles Giordano: accordion, backing vocals
Eddie Manion: saxophone
Richie "La Bamba" Rosenberg: trombone, backing vocals
Jeremy Chatzky: double bass
Larry Eagle: drums, percussion, backing vocals

Recording
Thrill Hill, Boxwood Studios, New Jersey: 2 November 1997

Technical team
Producer: Bruce Springsteen
Recording engineer: Toby Scott
Assistant recording engineers: Kevin Buell, Ross Petersen
Mixing: Bob Clearmountain (Mix This! Los Angeles)
Mixing assistant: Brandon Duncan
Mastering: Bob Ludwig (Gateway Mastering)

The Almanach Singers in 1940: Woody Guthrie, Millard Lampell, Bess Lomax Hawes, Pete Seeger, Arthur Stern, and "Sis" Cunningham, who wrote *My Oklahoma Home*.

Genesis and lyrics

My Oklahoma Home was written by Agnes "Sis" Cunningham and her brother Bill. "Sis" Cunningham played a pivotal role in the emergence of the folk movement. With her husband, Gordon Friesen, she founded *Broadside* magazine in 1962, and for a time was a member of the Almanac Singers, the famous folk group formed by Woody Guthrie, Pete Seeger, and Lee Hays.

As an artist and intellectual, "Sis" Cunningham was politically very committed. Born and raised in Oklahoma, at the end of the 1930s she set up an agitprop theater company called the Red Dust Players; this obliged her to decamp to Greenwich Village, where the revolutionary atmosphere was more propitious. *My Oklahoma Home* is not strictly speaking a political song, however. Rather, it is a personal account: her memories of the dust storms (the Dust Bowl) that affected Oklahoma, Kansas, Arkansas, and Texas during the 1930s, and which forced almost 3 million people—the vast majority of them farmers—to leave for California.

"Sis" Cunningham recorded *My Oklahoma Home* for Folkways Records, before Pete Seeger recorded it in 1961 and Bruce Springsteen in 2006.

Production

Springsteen and his band launch into this classic of the folk repertoire with a typically country rhythm and arrangement. In contrast to those by "Sis" Cunningham and Pete Seeger, this version of *My Oklahoma Home* is driven by an enjoyable bouncing energy and an infectious enthusiasm. Cheerful backing vocals reply to the Boss at each chorus, in the best tradition of popular song. Recorded during the first 1997 session, the piece abides by the conventions of the genre, leaving it to each instrumentalist to take on a solo in turn. Thus, the violins of Soozie Tyrell and Sam Bardfeld go first (at 1'32), then the accordion of Charles Giordano (at 3'00), the banjo of Mark Clifford (at 3'54), again the accordion and violins (at 4'54), and finally the trombone of Richie "La Bamba" Rosenberg, who brings a Dixieland touch that is highly effective (at 5'11).

On listening to *My Oklahoma Home*, the extent of Springsteen's talent and eclecticism can be fully appreciated, as his performance is light years away from his own classics, such as *Born in the U.S.A.* or *Streets of Philadelphia*. Few artists can claim to have accomplished such a feat.

2006

EYES ON THE PRIZE

Traditional, Alice Wine / Arrangements Bruce Springsteen / 5'16

Musicians
Bruce Springsteen: vocals, guitar
Patti Scialfa: backing vocals
Liza Lowell: backing vocals
Soozie Tyrell: violin, backing vocals
Sam Bardfeld: violin
Frank Bruno: guitar, backing vocals
Mark Clifford: banjo
Charles Giordano: accordion
Art Baron: tuba
Eddie Manion: saxophone
Mark Pender: trumpet, backing vocals
Richie "La Bamba" Rosenberg: trombone, backing vocals
Jeremy Chatzky: double bass
Larry Eagle: drums, percussion

Recording
Thrill Hill, Boxwood Studios, New Jersey: 21 January 2006

Technical team
Producer: Bruce Springsteen
Recording engineer: Toby Scott
Assistant recording engineers: Kevin Buell, Ross Petersen
Mixing: Bob Clearmountain (Mix This! Los Angeles)
Mixing assistant: Brandon Duncan
Mastering: Bob Ludwig (Gateway Mastering, Portland)

While *Eyes on the Prize* is, in fact, an adaptation of *Gospel Plow*, the artist who recorded an astonishing version of the latter song is none other than Bob Dylan, who included it on his very first album, *Bob Dylan* (1962).

Genesis and lyrics

Eyes on the Prize is a variation of a tune entitled *Gospel Plow*—also known by the titles *Paul and Silas*, *Hold On*, and *Keep Your Hand on the Plow*—which, according to the folklorist Alan Lomax, is thought to date from the beginning of the 20th century. What is known for certain is that it was adapted by Chance McCoy and the Appalachian String Band, as well as by Mahalia Jackson and Bob Dylan. The song's title references the words of Jesus Christ in Luke 9:62 (King James Version): "No man, having put his hand to the plow, and looking back, is fit for the kingdom of God." In other words: to follow Jesus, you must be able to make a break with your past.

In 1956, a civil rights activist by the name of Alice Wine apparently wrote new lyrics to the tune of *Gospel Plow*; this became *Keep Your Eyes on the Prize* and then *Eyes on the Prize*. Also drawing on a passage from the Bible—the Acts of the Apostles and the Gospel of Luke—this song glorified resistance in the face of all oppression and suggested that tolerance would eventually prevail over tyranny. Saint Paul and Silas are central characters in *Eyes on the Prize*: arrested while preaching, they are thrown in prison, where they remain until an earthquake causes the walls of their cell to collapse, allowing them to regain their freedom.

Never give up hope—that is the message of *Eyes on the Prize*, and its many recordings are in this spirit. Pete Seeger sang it during his concert at Carnegie Hall, New York, on 8 June 1963, which has remained famous ever since.

Production

Eyes on the Prize begins in the same way as it ends: with Springsteen's Gibson acoustic and Mark Clifford's banjo. However, the rest of the song is a slow progression toward an ever-denser orchestration, which ends like a New Orleans fanfare, with the four wind instruments blowing full blast and Larry Eagle's drums beating a heavy rhythm (listen at around 3'50). The songwriter has chosen to respect Pete Seeger's original intention, that is, an interpretation that is close to blues, tinged with a touch of gospel. And that comes through clearly in his lead vocals: the timbre is hoarse, the tone confidential. As for the backing vocals—which feature Liza Lowell's second appearance on the album—they provide some very fine harmonies that have an undeniable spiritual-like color. *Eyes on the Prize* is a song that works.

SHENANDOAH

Traditional / Arrangements Bruce Springsteen / 4'52

TWO KEITHS
If you want to hear a hoarse, gritty version of *Shenandoah*, then listen to the one by Tom Waits with Keith Richards—you will not be disappointed (*Son of Rogue's Gallery: Pirate Ballads, Sea Songs, & Chanteys*, 2013). If you prefer a lyrical, gentle, jazzy reinterpretation, choose the version by Keith Jarrett (*The Melody at Night, with You*, 1999).

Musicians
Bruce Springsteen: vocals, guitar
Patti Scialfa: backing vocals
Soozie Tyrell: violin, backing vocals
Sam Bardfeld: violin
Frank Bruno: guitar, backing vocals
Mark Clifford: banjo
Charles Giordano: organ, piano, accordion
Art Baron: tuba
Eddie Manion: saxophone
Mark Pender: trumpet, backing vocals
Richie "La Bamba" Rosenberg: trombone, backing vocals
Jeremy Chatzky: double bass
Larry Eagle: drums, percussion
Recording
Thrill Hill, Boxwood Studios, New Jersey: 19 March 2005
Technical team
Producer: Bruce Springsteen
Recording engineer: Toby Scott
Assistant recording engineers: Kevin Buell, Ross Petersen
Mixing: Bob Clearmountain (Mix This! Los Angeles)
Mixing assistant: Brandon Duncan
Mastering: Bob Ludwig (Gateway Mastering, Portland)

Bela Fleck, David Grisman, and Jerry Garcia at the Squaw Valley Music Festival (1991)—three more ambassadors for the American musical tradition.

Genesis and lyrics

Shenandoah is an early 19th-century folk song. This traditional number takes its title from the name of a Native American chief of the Oneida tribe (part of the Iroquois Confederacy). The central character is an American (or Canadian) pioneer traveling on the Missouri River in a canoe—doubtless a fur trader. He wants to marry the chief's daughter. He tells the chief that he has been a wanderer for seven years: we sense that he now wishes to lead a settled life and start a family.

There are different sets of lyrics for *Shenandoah*, but all describe the hardships of daily life during the early decades of the 19th century for travelers, adventurers, sailors, and trappers of European origin. Many of them suffered from homesickness all the more because of their solitary existence. That would explain why some sought companionship among Native Americans and married young Native American women.

Ever since it was performed by John Goss and the Cathedral Male Voice Quartet in 1925, many artists have sung *Shenandoah*, notably Paul Clayton on *Whaling and Sailing Songs from the Days of Moby Dick* (1956), Pete Seeger on *American Favorite Ballads, Vol.2* (1958), Bob Dylan on *Down in the Groove* (1988), Jerry Garcia and David Grisman on *Not for Kids Only* (1993), and Bruce Springsteen during the sessions for *We Shall Overcome*.

Production

The version of *Shenandoah* recorded on 19 March 2005 by Springsteen and his musicians is one of the most poignant songs on the album. The band sing in harmony to deliver a very moving performance, heightened by wonderful, gospel-style backing vocals (which are overdubbed). The arrangement is the result of a very delicate and subtle blend of acoustic guitars, violins, banjo, accordion, piano, and the Hammond B-3 organ (both recorded by overdubbing). To those are added the various percussion instruments, double bass—whose sparing notes almost seem like the heartbeat of the piece—and the wind instruments, which carry the tune. As for the Boss, he excels in his lead vocals, with a voice that is perfectly imbued with the images described by the lyrics.

Shenandoah is the song that concludes the DVD of the album. There is footage of some takes being recorded in the studio, and of all the musicians posing outside with their Boss.

2006

PAY ME MY MONEY DOWN

Traditional / Arrangements Bruce Springsteen / 4'32

Musicians

Bruce Springsteen: vocals, guitar
Patti Scialfa: backing vocals
Soozie Tyrell: violin, backing vocals
Sam Bardfeld: violin, backing vocals
Frank Bruno: guitar, backing vocals
Mark Clifford: banjo, backing vocals
Charles Giordano: accordion, backing vocals
Eddie Manion: saxophone, backing vocals
Mark Pender: trumpet, backing vocals
Richie "La Bamba" Rosenberg: trombone, backing vocals
Jeremy Chatzky: double bass, backing vocals
Larry Eagle: drums, percussion, backing vocals

Recording

Thrill Hill, Boxwood Studios, New Jersey: 19 March 2005

Technical team

Producer: Bruce Springsteen
Recording engineer: Toby Scott
Assistant recording engineers: Kevin Buell, Ross Petersen
Mixing: Bob Clearmountain (Mix This! Los Angeles)
Mixing assistant: Brandon Duncan
Mastering: Bob Ludwig (Gateway Mastering, Portland)

For Springsteen Addicts

On 23 June 2006, Bruce Springsteen and the E Street Band performed *Pay Me My Money Down* on the NBC show *Late Night with Conan O'Brien*, with the show's presenter on guitar.

Genesis and lyrics

Lydia Austin Parrish (1871–1953), wife of the painter Maxfield Parrish, spent many winters on St Simons Island, one of the Sea Islands, and developed a passion for local history and folk tunes. In her book *Slave Songs of the Georgia Sea Islands* (1942) she listed many African-American songs, notably *Pay Me My Money Down*, a dockers' work song that was later adopted by Caribbean sailors.

The story is quite simple. Especially in the ports of Georgia and South Carolina, ships' captains only paid the African-American dockers who loaded or unloaded the ships the following day. Very often, they would leave port in the dead of night, without paying a dollar to their workers. This gave rise to the slogan: "Pay Me My Money Down."

This song has often been revisited, most notably by The Weavers, who sang it during their concert at Carnegie Hall, New York, in 1955.

Production

Springsteen and his Seeger Band made an excellent, energetic, and exhilarating cover of *Pay Me My Money Down*. The Boss begins the song alone with Gibson J-45 guitar, and is soon joined by the whole band, from the end of the first chorus (at 0'25). The rhythm is irresistible, the double bass and drums producing an infectious groove that invites the listener to tap their foot and clap their hands. The backing vocals reply to Springsteen with exuberant enthusiasm, while he delivers lead vocals that are both warm and relaxed. Solo follows solo: first the violins (at 0'47), then the trumpet—the Boss requesting: "Let's hear the trumpet!" (at 1'41)—followed by the accordion, which launches into a superb improvisation with Cajun accents (at 2'33), and then a finale in which all band members let rip (at 3'58). The piece features a key change—requested by Springsteen (at 1'57)—from G to B flat, followed by a return to the home key, also demanded by the songwriter: "Alright now, back to G" (at 3'10). *Pay Me My Money Down* is one of the album's gems, and probably superior to the superb version Pete Seeger had immortalized with The Weavers.

> **For Springsteen Addicts**
> Bruce Springsteen's version of *We Shall Overcome* was chosen to feature on the soundtrack of the documentary made by NBC on the September 11 attacks.

WE SHALL OVERCOME

Guy Carawan, Frank Hamilton, Zilphia Horton, Pete Seeger / 4'53

Musicians
Bruce Springsteen: vocals, guitar, organ (?), tambourine (?)
Patti Scialfa: backing vocals
Soozie Tyrell: violin, backing vocals
Sam Bardfeld: violin
Frank Bruno: guitar
Mark Clifford: banjo
Charles Giordano: piano, accordion
Eddie Manion: saxophone, backing vocals
Mark Pender: trumpet, backing vocals
Richie "La Bamba" Rosenberg: trombone, backing vocals
Jeremy Chatzky: double bass
Larry Eagle: drums, percussion
Recording
Thrill Hill, Boxwood Studios, New Jersey: 2 November 1997
Technical team
Producer: Bruce Springsteen
Recording engineer: Toby Scott
Assistant recording engineers: Kevin Buell, Ross Petersen
Mixing: Bob Clearmountain (Mix This! Los Angeles)
Mixing assistant: Brandon Duncan
Mastering: Bob Ludwig (Gateway Mastering, Portland)

> The version of *We Shall Overcome* that features on Bruce Springsteen's album is the same as the one on the 1998 recording for *Where Have All the Flowers Gone: The Songs of Pete Seeger.* Only the mixing is slightly different, and the counting-in only features on the 1998 record.

Genesis and lyrics

One of the most famous songs in America's folk repertoire, *We Shall Overcome* has its origins in two spirituals. *I'll Overcome Some Day* (and/or *I'll Be Allright*), written by the Rev. Charles Albert Tindley (published in 1900), is the source for the lyrics, while the musical framework comes from *No More Auction Block for Me*, a work song that predates the Civil War. Over the years, its strictly spiritual dimension evolved into a message of protest, notably when it was adopted as the battle cry of the striking workers of the American Tobacco Company in Charleston, South Carolina (they went on strike for five months from October 1945). In 1946, the folklorist and civil rights activist Zilphia Horton rewrote the lyrics; these were subsequently modified by Pete Seeger, who recorded the song and published the lyrics in the journal *Sing Out!* in 1959, under the title *We Shall Overcome*.

From then on, *We Shall Overcome* was established as one of the great protest anthems throughout the 1960s. In 1963, Pete Seeger performed it during his famous concert in Carnegie Hall and subsequently at the Newport Folk Festival, this time with the Freedom Singers, Peter, Paul & Mary, and Bob Dylan. Also, during the 1963 March on Washington for Jobs and Freedom, Bob Dylan, Joan Baez, and Peter, Paul & Mary sang it in chorus. Finally, in 1969 Joan Baez sang it to the flower children gathered at Woodstock.

"We shall overcome [...] We shall live in peace." There are dozens of recordings of this non-violent anthem. After those by Pete Seeger and Joan Baez, the version by Bruce Springsteen is the most famous.

An anthem for peace—and a copyright issue

In 2016, legal proceedings were begun against Ludlow Music and The Richmond Organization, the publishers of *We Shall Overcome*, by Isaias Gamboa—who had made a documentary about the song's history—and the producers of Lee Daniels' movie *The Butler* (released in 2013). The plaintiffs were objecting to the sum of $100,000 that Ludlow was demanding from them for using the song in their movie and were also challenging the copyright protection Ludlow was claiming. The publisher, which had registered copyrights to the song in 1960 and 1963, essentially based its case on the fact that the word "will" in the original lyrics had been changed to "shall." But federal

We Shall Overcome was sung by striking workers, and later became a 1960s protest song. Joan Baez famously sang it at Woodstock in 1969.

judge Denise L Cote, of the Southern District of New York, decided in September 2017 to place the song definitively in the public domain, on the grounds that changes made to the words of the original lyrics by artists (including Pete Seeger) were not significant enough to be taken into consideration. Thus, after the publishers had accepted the judgment, in January 2018, *We Shall Overcome* gained the same status as *Happy Birthday to You*, which in 2015 had also been declared in the public domain. However, in order to respect the credits printed on Bruce Springsteen's album, we have retained the names of the artists who appear in the record's sleeve notes.

Production

Springsteen chose to perform *We Shall Overcome* in a fairly energetic fashion—within reason, of course. If we compare his version to those of Pete Seeger and Joan Baez, it is noticeable that he takes a few slight liberties with the tune, and sings in an almost confidential voice, at a pitch that is quite low for him—perhaps even too low. In concert, he would play it at a higher pitch, which was more comfortable for him. He accompanies himself on an acoustic guitar that has nylon strings, which he plays with a pick. Alongside him can be heard a 6-string electric guitar (with tremolo), the double bass, accordion, violins, various percussion instruments (maracas, handbells), and a tom-tom drum. The other instruments then come in, one by one, with each new verse: the piano (at 0'46), the organ and tambourine (at 2'02, probably both overdubbed by the songwriter himself), the wind instruments (at 2'07), and the banjo (at 3'15). As for the backing vocals, they come in from the second verse and end the song alone, without the lead vocals. As Springsteen explained: "I wanted to keep it very, very much like parlor singing, very loose and unstructured. So basically we got parts very quick, and we rushed through everything, and that was the sound that I liked. We played the track, and then everybody came in and sang it."[10] As for solos, only the accordion plays an improvisation, after the third verse (at 2'02).

However, despite all the emotion that this cover conveys, it is probably the least effective song on the album: Springsteen's performance is not really convincing, and neither is the arrangement, which is a little too rich and formulaic, making the song sound ponderous. It would really only be in concert that the Boss would do the song justice and give it its full breadth, as is confirmed by the DVD *Bruce Springsteen with The Sessions Band: Live in Dublin*, released in 2007.

FROGGIE WENT A COURTIN'

Traditional / Arrangements Bruce Springsteen / 4'33

Musicians
Bruce Springsteen: vocals, guitar, harmonica
Soozie Tyrell: violin
Sam Bardfeld: violin
Frank Bruno: guitar
Mark Clifford: banjo
Charles Giordano: accordion
Eddie Manion: saxophone
Mark Pender: trumpet
Richie "La Bamba" Rosenberg: trombone
Jeremy Chatzky: double bass
Larry Eagle: drums, percussion
Recording
Thrill Hill, Boxwood Studios, New Jersey: 19 March 2005
Technical team
Producer: Bruce Springsteen
Recording engineer: Toby Scott
Assistant recording engineers: Kevin Buell, Ross Petersen
Mixing: Bob Clearmountain (Mix This! Los Angeles)
Mixing assistant: Brandon Duncan
Mastering: Bob Ludwig (Gateway Mastering, Portland)

Paul McCartney played *Froggie Went A Courtin'* during a rehearsal for his concert Unplugged in 1991. This rehearsal was then broadcast by the *Oobu Joobu* radio show on the American station Westwood One.

Genesis and lyrics

Froggie Went A Courtin' is a very old Scottish song. It is mentioned, under the title *The Frog Cam to the Myl Dur* ("The Frog Came to the Mill Door") in *The Complaynt of Scotland*, a nationalist work published in 1549, during the Rough Wooing war between Scotland and England (1544–1551). There is little doubt that it describes the English court—Elizabeth I had been in the habit of referring to her suitor Francis, Duke of Anjou, by the nickname "my frog." Hence this story takes the form of a nursery rhyme: the frog passionately wants to marry Miss Mousie, but the latter must ask for her uncle Rat's consent.

The first known score dates from 1611: it is in *Melismata* by the English composer Thomas Ravenscroft, who was notably famous for his collections of folk music. It subsequently crossed the Atlantic with British colonists in the early 18th century. Originally sung by Scottish shepherds, *Froggie Went A Courtin'* became a popular American song, thanks to folk singers who produced multiple versions, from Tom Glazer to Tex Ritter. Elvis Presley also made a version (*The Essential 70's Masters*, 1970), as did Bob Dylan (*Good as I Been to You*, 1992) and, in Britain, Mike Oldfield (*Mike Oldfield's Single*, 1974). Bruce Springsteen, in turn, followed what had become a tradition.

Production

This version of *Froggie Went A Courtin'* comes at the end of the first version of *We Shall Overcome: The Seeger Sessions*, released on 25 April 2006. It brings to a close a surprising album that's full of radiant, blazing energy. A few months later, the *American Land Edition*, containing five extra songs, was released. The piece is cheerful, though slower than the cover by Pete Seeger. It is Mark Clifford's banjo that starts the proceedings, supported by the sound of improvised percussion, which is soon joined by the voice of the Boss. The other instruments gradually come in: double bass, drums, accordion, violin ("Come on, Soozie!" at 2'02), and, for the first time on the album, the harmonica, which enables the songwriter to play his first solo (at 4'06). The song ends in a good mood, each instrument making a closing statement. Although revisited and adapted by countless artists, *Froggie Went A Courtin'* is rejuvenated by this new version by Springsteen and his Seeger Band.

2006

BUFFALO GALS

Public domain / Arrangements Bruce Springsteen / 3'11

Musicians
Bruce Springsteen: vocals, guitar
Patti Scialfa: backing vocals
Liza Lowell: backing vocals
Soozie Tyrell: violin, backing vocals
Sam Bardfeld: violin
Frank Bruno: guitar
Mark Clifford: banjo
Charles Giordano: organ, accordion
Art Baron: tuba
Eddie Manion: saxophone
Mark Pender: trumpet, backing vocals
Richie "La Bamba" Rosenberg: trombone, backing vocals
Jeremy Chatzky: double bass
Larry Eagle: drums, percussion

Recording
Thrill Hill, Boxwood Studios, New Jersey: 21 January 2006

Technical team
Producer: Bruce Springsteen
Recording engineer: Toby Scott
Assistant recording engineers: Kevin Buell, Ross Petersen
Mixing: Bob Clearmountain (Mix This! Los Angeles)
Mixing assistant: Brandon Duncan
Mastering: Bob Ludwig (Gateway Mastering, Portland)

On the DVD of the album, *Buffalo Gals* was not filmed in the Boss's living room, but in his garden in order to produce an entertaining acoustic version.

Genesis and lyrics

Buffalo Gals is a bonus track on the DVD that comes with *We Shall Overcome: The Seeger Sessions*, and one of the five new songs on the *American Land Edition*, which was released a few months after the original album. It is a traditional number, attributed to the blackface minstrel John Hodges, and published in 1844 under the title *Lubly Fan*. The "gals" in question are dancers who performed in bars and brothels; the song's title was changed according to where it was performed—*New York Gals*, *Boston Gals*, and so forth.

Pete Seeger first recorded the song in 1941 with the Almanac Singers, then again in 1957 for the album *American Favorite Ballads, Vol 4*. *Buffalo Gals* has deep roots in American culture: Mark Twain mentions it in his novel *Tom Sawyer* (1876) and it can be heard in the classic Hollywood movie *High Noon* (1952), as well as in the TV series *Bonanza* (1963). Moreover, the Western Writers of America added *Buffalo Gals* to the Top 100 Western Songs of All Time.

Production

Buffalo Gals begins with the Boss counting in: "One, two, three, four!" Yet the first verse features only him, on vocals and acoustic guitar. But the rest of the band soon joins him—the rhythm section of Larry Eagle and Jeremy Chatzky launching into a groove that is half zydeco, half Cajun, to the delight of Charles Giordano and his accordion. The backing vocals and wind instruments—including the tuba—join in wholeheartedly and emphasize the song's festive side. As tradition demands, the instrumentalists take turns to play solos: thus, the violin, accordion, organ, and banjo vie with each other to raise the temperature, before the brass, notably the trumpet and trombone, take over at the end of the song (from 2'27). Then, the final verse is sung only by the backing vocals and Springsteen, to bring this joyous cover to a close *a cappella* (at 2'51).

As for the version by Pete Seeger on his own, it is a folk song in the purest tradition of the genre, with only vocals and banjo, which makes it sound a little like a children's song.

HOW CAN I KEEP FROM SINGING

Traditional—Additional lyrics and musical arrangement by Doris Plenn / Musical arrangement by Bruce Springsteen / 2'20

Musicians
Bruce Springsteen: vocals, guitar
Patti Scialfa: backing vocals
Liza Lowell: backing vocals
Soozie Tyrell: violin, backing vocals
Sam Bardfeld: violin
Charles Giordano: pump organ
Eddie Manion: saxophone
Mark Pender: trumpet, backing vocals
Richie "La Bamba" Rosenberg: trombone, backing vocals
Jeremy Chatzky: double bass
Larry Eagle: drums, percussion
Recording
Thrill Hill, Boxwood Studios, New Jersey: 21 January 2006
Technical team
Producer: Bruce Springsteen
Recording engineer: Toby Scott
Assistant recording engineers: Kevin Buell, Ross Petersen
Mixing: Bob Clearmountain (Mix This! Los Angeles)
Mixing assistant: Brandon Duncan
Mastering: Bob Ludwig (Gateway Mastering, Portland)

Bruce Springsteen delivered a version of *How Can I Keep from Singing* that was highly charged with spirituality.

Genesis and lyrics

How Can I Keep from Singing is a religious song. It was first published in August 1868 in the *New York Observer* under the title *Always Rejoicing*, with lyrics attributed to the enigmatic Pauline T. The following year the Baptist preacher Robert Wadsworth Lowry published the same text in his song book *Bright Jewels for the Sunday School*, claiming that he was the author. The song's message is that singing can bring us closer to Christ—"The peace of Christ makes fresh my heart"—and that singing can act as a balm and soothe our pain.

Pete Seeger, who had learned *How Can I Keep from Singing* from a friend of his family, Doris Plenn—who had written some extra lyrics and made a musical arrangement of the song—sang it regularly during the 1960s folk revival, in a version that began thus: "When tyrants tremble, sick with fear [...] How can I keep from singing?" Those words also appear in the version by Bruce Springsteen recorded for *We Shall Overcome: The Seeger Sessions*.

Production

There is a change of atmosphere with this cover of *How Can I Keep from Singing*: Springsteen and his musicians deliver what is virtually a religious interpretation. The song begins with Charles Giordano's pump organ, in all probability a harmonium, discreetly accompanied by the songwriter's acoustic guitar, the violins of Soozie Tyrell and Sam Bardfeld, and Jeremy Chatzky's double bass, which is almost certainly bowed. The group of singers—the voices of Patti Scialfa, Soozie Tyrell, and Liza Lowell are especially prominent—perform the song's four verses with palpable emotion. Springsteen said: "So it was exciting, because when you can get a lot of people singing together, that choral sound of human voices is always something. It always ends up very personal, very human."[10] Even if the result lacks a certain accuracy in the execution, the strength of feeling is undeniable, each person singing with intense harmony. As for the wind and percussion instruments credited in the album's sleeve notes, there is no denying that they are inaudible.

HOW CAN A POOR MAN STAND SUCH TIMES AND LIVE

Blind Alfred Reed / Additional lyrics by Bruce Springsteen / 3'23

Musicians
Bruce Springsteen: vocals, guitar
Patti Scialfa: guitar, backing vocals
Liza Lowell, Curtis King Jr, Cindy Mizelle: backing vocals
Soozie Tyrell: violin, backing vocals
Sam Bardfeld: violin
Frank Bruno, Marc Anthony Thompson: guitar, backing vocals
Greg Liszt: banjo
Marty Rifkin: pedal steel guitar
Charles Giordano: organ
Art Baron: tuba
Eddie Manion: saxophone
Mark Pender, Curt Ramm: trumpet
Richie "La Bamba" Rosenberg, Clark Gayton: trombone
Jeremy Chatzky: double bass
Larry Eagle: drums, percussion

Recording
Thrill Hill Recording Remote, Asbury Park Convention Hall: 13 April 2006

Technical team
Producer: Bruce Springsteen
Recording engineer: John Cooper
Assistant recording engineer: John Bruey
Mixing: Bob Clearmountain (Metalworks Studios, Toronto, Ontario)
Mixing assistant: Giancarlo Gallo
Mastering: Bob Ludwig (Gateway Mastering, Portland)

A second live version of *How Can a Poor Man Stand Such Times and Live* features on the DVD of the *American Land Edition*, Springsteen and his band having been very probably filmed on 5 June 2006 at The Greek Theatre, in Los Angeles.

Genesis and lyrics

A pioneer of old-time music originally from Virginia, Blind Alfred Reed wrote and composed *How Can a Poor Man Stand Such Times and Live*, which he recorded in December 1929 in New York for the Victor label. In his version of the song, Springsteen adds other serious matters to those touched on by Reed, including racial segregation ("And what happened to you poor black folks, well it just ain't fair"). However, he also includes some dark humor: a doctor who prescribes humbug pills and "a dose of dope" to justify an expensive prescription and the narrator himself, who says he's "Got family scattered from Texas all the way to Baltimore," but "ain't got no home in this world no more."

Ry Cooder recorded a version of *How Can a Poor Man Stand Such Times and Live* for his eponymous album, released in 1970. It was precisely this recording that, some decades later, spurred Bruce Springsteen to perform it himself, with his Dixieland lineup. His version does not feature on *We Shall Overcome: The Seeger Sessions*; it was rehearsed at the Convention Hall in Asbury Park, in all probability on 13 April 2006, and then chosen as a bonus for the *American Land Edition* of *We Shall Overcome: The Seeger Sessions*.

Production

While the original version by Blind Alfred Reed is a country song with guitar and violin, and Ry Cooder's is more of an electric country blues, Springsteen's—accompanied by the 19 musicians of his Seeger Band in concert configuration (different from in the studio)—is a mixture of country, gospel, and blues.

Larry Eagle plays a drum rhythm from the introduction (slightly in the style of Jim Keltner), and the Boss joins him, to sing the first verse unaccompanied. The whole band then comes in, with the wind instruments and the saturated pedal steel guitar of Marty Rifkin—making a comeback to recording since his last appearance on *Devils & Dust* in 2005—being especially prominent. The song's tone color is dominated by its many gospel-inspired backing vocals and by Springsteen's superb voice, which has a rough texture and is laden with emotion. As for solos, Rifkin warms things up with his pedal steel guitar (at 1'56), as does the whole wind section (at 2'11).

Not among the best songs on the album, this deserves its place among the bonus tracks on the *American Land Edition*.

BRING 'EM HOME

Pete Seeger, with an added verse by Jim Musselman / 3'36

Although the version of *Bring 'Em Home* that was reworked in Oslo (at least as far as the lead vocals are concerned) does not feature on the album, it was nevertheless offered online for download by Sony Music from June 2006.

Musicians

Bruce Springsteen: vocals, guitar
Liza Lowell, Curtis King Jr, Cindy Mizelle: backing vocals
Soozie Tyrell: violin, backing vocals
Sam Bardfeld: violin
Frank Bruno, Marc Anthony Thompson: guitar, backing vocals
Greg Liszt: banjo
Marty Rifkin: pedal steel guitar
Charles Giordano: accordion
Art Baron: mandolin
Eddie Manion: saxophone
Mark Pender, Curt Ramm: trumpet
Richie "La Bamba" Rosenberg, Clark Gayton: trombone
Jeremy Chatzky: double bass
Larry Eagle: drums, percussion

Recording

Thrill Hill Recording Remote: 17 June 2006 (?)

Technical team

Producer: Bruce Springsteen
Recording engineer: John Cooper
Assistant recording engineer: John Bruey
Mixing: Bob Clearmountain (Mix This!)
Mixing assistant: Brandon Duncan
Mastering: Bob Ludwig (Gateway Mastering, Portland)

Bruce Springsteen and the Seeger Sessions Band were steeped in America's musical heritage, especially *Bring 'Em Home* by Pete Seeger.

Genesis and lyrics

Bring 'Em Home is, in fact, a combination of Pete Seeger's 1965 song *Bring Them Home (If You Love Your Uncle Sam)* and *When Johnny Comes Marching Home,* a pacifist tune that Patrick Gilmore (using the pseudonym Louis Lambert) wrote during the Civil War. The New York folk singer made it into a protest song against the Vietnam War, and the version Springsteen performs on the album includes an extra verse written during the Iraq war by Jim Musselman, founder of Appleseed Recordings. The songwriter then wrote two additional verses of his own. The message remains the same, a century and a half after the end of the conflict between the North and the South: the United States is a country of freedom, and peace "will make the politicians sad."

Production

Springsteen recorded a studio version of *Bring 'Em Home* on 21 January 2006, during the last session for the album. Subsequently, with the help of Toby Scott, the Boss rerecorded his voice on 18 May of the same year, not at Thrill Hill Studios but at Disclab Studios in Oslo, Norway. In the album's sleeve notes the studio that is credited is Sound One, but this appears to be the same studio. The person in charge of the premises, by the name of Grøttheim, was absent on paternity leave on the day in question, and it was his assistant, Richard Lowe, who took charge of the session, with the indefatigable Toby Scott by his side. Yet this recording of *Bring 'Em Home* does not feature on the album (although the studio and the assistant appear in the credits). Instead, a live version of the song—in all probability recorded on 17 June 2006 at DTE Energy Music Theatre in Clarkston, Michigan (the sleeve notes give Detroit, but this appears to be a mistake)—was chosen to be among the bonus tracks on the *American Land Edition.*

Springsteen begins the song alone, strumming his acoustic guitar. He is joined progressively by the bass guitar, banjo, accordion, drums, pedal steel guitar, backing vocals, and the remaining instruments. Compared to Pete Seeger's rather energetic version, Springsteen's seems more disillusioned, as if observing humanity in perpetual conflict has shattered all his illusions. His performance is no less superb or moving for all that.

ALBUM

MAGIC

Radio Nowhere • You'll Be Comin' Down • Livin' in the Future • Your Own Worst Enemy • Gypsy Biker • Girls in Their Summer Clothes • I'll Work for Your Love • Magic • Last to Die • Long Walk Home • Devil's Arcade • Terry's Song

Outtake: *Harry's Place*

RELEASE DATE

United States: 2 October 2007

Reference: Columbia Records – 88697 17060 2

No.1 in the United States, United Kingdom, Canada, Denmark, Ireland, Italy, Spain, and Sweden, No.3 in France

After the happy interlude of the Pete Seeger Sessions, Bruce Springsteen returned to political territory with the album *Magic*.

AN ANTI-WAR AND ANTI-BUSH MESSAGE

After a detour into folk music while recording *We Shall Overcome: The Seeger Sessions*, Bruce Springsteen pursued his work as a songwriter with *Magic*. In fact, this 15th studio album is made up entirely of original songs, 12 in total. The Boss started to compose these songs during the Rising Tour, which launched in August 2002 and concluded in October 2003. But he really dedicated himself to it in 2006. As he explained to *Rolling Stone* magazine: "I wrote most of this album on tour with the Sessions band. I wrote some of it the minute I came off [recording] *The Rising*. My idea was to pick up with the political and social results of what came out of the tragedy of 9/11."[130] Then, in December 2006, he got in touch with producer Brendan O'Brien. "We literally sat in his living room, he hands me a book of lyrics and he played me the songs on the guitar," O'Brien told Andy Greene of *Rolling Stone*. "He gauges people's reactions and I have to be as honest with him as I can. Some of them had a certain voice that seemed to fit all together—and some didn't have that same voice—so we decided which ones to pursue."[131]

The message of the album is clear. "*Magic* was my state-of-the-nation dissent over the Iraq War and the Bush years,"[1] says Springsteen unequivocally in his autobiography *Born to Run*. In fact, the songwriter, who never concealed his support for John Kerry during his 2004 electoral campaign, became from that moment on a determined opponent of Republican George W Bush and of his politics, which were marked both by the wars in Afghanistan and in Iraq and by the Patriot Act. But this time, Springsteen didn't tackle the issue head on: he didn't mention the president of the United States by name nor those of his lackeys. "Still, I aimed everywhere on *Magic* for the political and the personal to meld together," he says in *Born to Run*. "You can listen to the whole thing without ever thinking of the politics of the day or you can hear them ticking deadly through the internal thread of the music."[1]

Bruce Springsteen likes to make use of metaphors, as is seen, for example, in *Gypsy Biker* which, like *Born in the U.S.A.*, tells the story of an American soldier who has returned not from Vietnam, but from Afghanistan or Iraq; in *Last to Die*, a song about the "mistake" of American engagement in Southeast Asia; in *Devil's Arcade*, on the war in Iraq; or in the apocalyptic *Radio Nowhere* and *Livin' in the Future*. Not to mention the title song, which is a superb reflection on what had become of America at the start of the third millennium: it was paranoid and misinformed. The only moment of lightness comes in *Girls in Their Summer Clothes*.

The album

Despite its cold fury, *Magic* also emits a clear sense of nostalgia. The presence of members of the E Street Band, from Clarence Clemons to Steve Van Zandt, is no coincidence. In any case, the Boss makes clear references to the 1960s and 1970s, whether with *Girls in Their Summer Clothes*, which has a very 1960s' California pop sound, or with *Your Own Worst Enemy*, which masterfully evokes the work of Phil Spector and of The Beach Boys (*Pet Sounds*). Springsteen also loves to dive back into his repertoire, especially into the

Magic saw the return of the E Street Band. From left: Nils Lofgren, Clarence Clemons, Bruce Springsteen, Steve Van Zandt, Max Weinberg, Patti Scialfa, and Garry Tallent.

legendary *Born to Run*: the intro to *I'll Work for Your Love* is a clear throwback to *Jungleland*, while the atmosphere of *Livin' in the Future* recalls *Tenth Avenue Freeze-Out*. As for *Radio Nowhere*, which opens this 15th album, it singlehandedly sums up modern rock in the first decade of the 20th century.

Springsteen began working on *Magic* in earnest in February 2007. The last recording sessions took place the following May. The album came out worldwide on 2 October 2007 and shot to the top of the charts to the tempo of *Radio Nowhere*. In the United States, it reached No.1 on 20 October, then, after falling to No.2 for about a week, it returned to No.1 on 3 November. In the United Kingdom, it reached No.1 on 13 October, as it did in Canada and several continental European countries, including Denmark, Italy, Norway, and Spain. In France it got to No.3.

Critics, especially in the United States, again welcomed the good work of Bruce Springsteen and the E Street Band, as well as that of producer Brendan O'Brien. In the Chicago bureau of *Pitchfork* magazine, Stephen M Deusner wrote that "The album hides its raw disillusionment deep within the music, mingling it with a weary optimism and a thoroughly committed lustiness that have not diminished with age." He [illegible] that recalls *The River* in its heartfelt populism, *Darkness on the Edge of Town* in its small-town scope, and *Tunnel of Love* in its mature take on love and sex."[132] *Rolling Stone*, for its part, after having given it the maximum five stars, would place *Magic* at No.1 on its list of best albums of 2007 (ahead of *Graduation* by Kanye West).

The sleeve

A close-up of Bruce Springsteen. His white (or beige?) T-shirt blends into the light background of the disc. Half his face is in darkness, dark like the expression on his face. His lips are closed. He's a concerned and angry artist posing for Mark Seliger, who became one of the most emblematic photographers in rock music for shooting more than 100 magazine covers for *Rolling Stone* and portraits of some of the most important stars in music and cinema, from Mick Jagger to Susan Sarandon. On the back, there's a photo of the Boss from behind. The sleeve opens to a double-sided snapshot of Springsteen, one arm around Patti Scialfa, with the members of the E Street Band. The booklet contains several other photographs (mostly by Mark Seliger, others by Danny Clinch) of Springsteen, the E Street Band, and Terry Magovern, who died on 30 July 2007 and was among Springsteen's most trusted friends for 23 years. Michelle Holme and Chris Austopchuk [illegible]

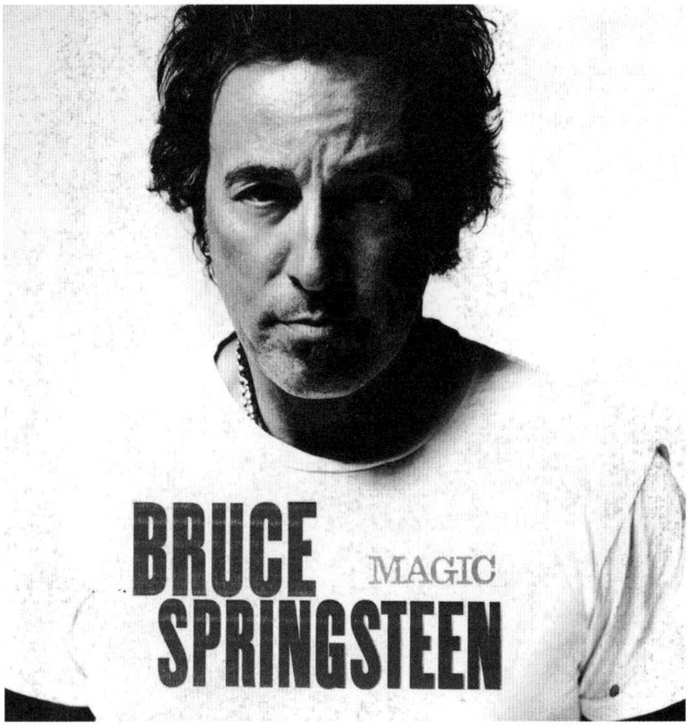

The sleeve for *Magic*. Springsteen in a white T-shirt is captured by the lens of photographer Mark Seliger.

The recording

When Brendan O'Brien visited Springsteen in December 2006, he made him listen to his new compositions. One song in particular stood out for them. They also decided to call in the E Street Band. The two men met again in February 2007 at the Southern Tracks Recording Studio in Atlanta, Georgia (O'Brien's den, where *The Rising* and *Devils & Dust* albums were partly recorded in 2002 and 2004, respectively), again with Nick DiDia on the console (backed up by Billy Bowers for additional recordings).

In this 15th album, the group's sound is centered on the guitars, much more so than with its other works, which tend to favor the keyboards. O'Brien's explanation: "I think a reason some of these earlier records were so keyboard oriented—I would have to assume, after working with Roy [Bittan] and Danny [Federici]—is that those guys are very quick at picking things up. And I would imagine that, when they recorded, maybe Roy was the first guy to pick up all the chords! [Laughs] So it became a piano song."[117] Thus the guitars, whether electric or acoustic, saturated or clean, became more prominent in songs from *Magic* (except for *Terry's Song*) than ever before on an album by the Boss and his band.

To produce the album, Brendan O'Brien recorded the basic tracks with a skeleton crew, just as he did for *The Rising*. Roy Bittan, Garry Tallent, and Max Weinberg joined Springsteen and O'Brien at Southern Tracks at the end of February to lay down the rhythmic foundations for these new songs. There was only one problem: Max Weinberg, then drummer and conductor of the Max Weinberg 7, which played during the week for the American TV show *Late Night with Conan O'Brien*, was only available on the weekend. Springsteen was forced to work within this constraint, meaning that he had to record the basic tracks on the weekend with Tallent, Bittan, and Weinberg and to record his lead vocals with different overdubs during the week.

Having completed this first phase of production, O'Brien and Springsteen appealed to the other members of the E Street Band to finish the songs. They were each called in as needed, heading to Atlanta between the end of March and beginning of May. This strategy facilitated production. "It's easier to manage the songs with less people," O'Brien says. "Once we know what we're doing, we brought the others in to do overdubs."[131]

Steve Van Zandt, Nils Lofgren, Clarence Clemons, Patti Scialfa, and Danny Federici made valuable contributions to the album. Musicians external to the group were also called in: the loyal Soozie Tyrell is on the violin and backing vocals; Jeremy Chatzky, the double bass player for the Seeger Band, is on his instrument, as is cellist Daniel Laufer and keyboardist Patrick Warren. The producer also recorded an orchestra made up of eight violins, three violas, and three cellos, with chord arrangements written by Eddie Horst, who'd already done arrangements for *Devils & Dust*.

Magic is a rock song featuring a strong guitar element, just as Springsteen and O'Brien had intended. As he told Christopher Phillips in 2007, the Boss was satisfied with the result. "We've got a record that's gonna play really great live. It's just built for it. I wrote with a lot of melody, and with a lot of hooks, and there's a lot of band power behind the stuff that I wrote this time out."[10]

Finally, in addition to the Southern Tracks Recording Studio in Atlanta, recordings were done at the Henson Recording Studios in Hollywood (with Kevin Mills, Glenn Pittman, Matt Serrecchio, and Tom Syrowski as assistant recording engineers) and at Thrill Hill Recording in New Jersey (still with Toby Scott at the controls).

2007

RADIO NOWHERE

Bruce Springsteen / 3'19

Musicians

Bruce Springsteen: vocals, guitar, maracas (?)
Patti Scialfa: backing vocals
Steve Van Zandt: guitar, backing vocals
Nils Lofgren: guitar, backing vocals
Roy Bittan: keyboards
Danny Federici: keyboards
Clarence Clemons: saxophone, backing vocals
Garry Tallent: bass
Max Weinberg: drums

Recording

Southern Tracks Recording Studio, Atlanta, Georgia: March to May 2007

Technical team

Producer: Brendan O'Brien
Recording engineer: Nick DiDia
Assistant recording engineer: Tom Tapley
Mixing: Brendan O'Brien
Mastering: Bob Ludwig (Gateway Mastering, Portland)

For Springsteen Addicts

Aside from the Grammy Awards for "Best Vocal Performance", the Boss is also a frequent winner of the Grammy Awards for "Best Rock Song": before winning this trophy for *Radio Nowhere* in 2008, he'd already won one for *The Rising* in 2003 and for *Streets of Philadelphia* in 1995. He would later win another one in 2009 for *Girls in Their Summer Clothes*, another song from *Magic*.

Genesis and lyrics

Magic starts off with a supercharged rock sound, a testament to how glad Bruce Springsteen was to play with the E Street Band and work with producer Brendan O'Brien again. The lyrics, on the other hand, give no reason for optimism. The narrator dances "down a dark hole/Just searching for a world with some soul." In an interview with Joe Levy of *Rolling Stone*, the songwriter explained that "It's an end-of-the-world scenario—[the narrator is] seeing the apocalypse. All communications are down."[130]

So, there is no more radio, no way for people to contact each other. All their sources of entertainment and happiness are gone, along with those "thousand guitars" that have gone silent and that he longs to hear. In this end-of-the-world atmosphere, the narrator searches in vain to make contact. Is Bruce Springsteen alluding to the Bush administration's politics of security (the Patriot Act) and their destructive impact on the spirit of America? Maybe. In any case, a certain sense of nostalgia pervades the piece. *Radio Nowhere* is, in fact, scattered with innuendo: "I was driving through the misty rain" and "Dancing down a dark hole," respectively, allude to *Downbound Train* and *Dancing in the Dark*, two songs from *Born in the U.S.A.*, while "Searchin' for a mystery train" is a nod to *Mystery Train* written by Sam Phillips and Junior Parker and performed by Elvis Presley in the mid-1950s.

The *Radio Nowhere* single came out on 28 August 2007, a little more than a month before the album's release. The song was first distributed over the Internet, then on satellite radio, and then on FM radio. Then, on 4 September, the video, directed by Thom Zimny, became available on Amazon. The song would not reach the *Billboard* Hot 100, but this wouldn't stop it from winning two Grammy Awards, one for "Best Solo Rock Vocal Performance" and one for "Best Rock Song." It would reach its highest ranking in Norway, where it was No.2 in the charts.

Production

Radio Nowhere, the first song of Springsteen's new album, fits in perfectly with the album's parameters: it's definitely a rock song, one of the hardest in the discography of the Boss and his group. "It's a pretty straight-ahead rocker," O'Brien says. "The most straightforward song I've heard [Springsteen]

Tommy Heath and Jim Keller, from the band Tommy Tutone. The intro of their song *867-5309/ Jenny* and that of *Radio Nowhere* are strangely similar. However, no legal action was taken.

do in years."[131] He explained that the album version was similar to the demo made in the songwriter's home studio. However, O'Brien's hand in it is clear: this is the hand that helped define the sound of groups such as the Stone Temple Pilots, Rage Against the Machine, and Pearl Jam. His influence is obvious from the intro: the sound is clearly that of an assertive alternative rock song.

Speaking of the intro, its chords raised controversy upon *Magic*'s release: they clearly resembled those of *867–5309/ Jenny*, a song by Alex Call and Jim Keller released in 1981 and performed by the American rock group Tommy Tutone. Nevertheless, Tommy Heath, lead singer of the band, did not file a suit, despite some initial hesitation. As he said at the time, "Everybody's calling me about it, I think it's close enough that if I wanted to, I could work with it."[133] A few months later, he clarified his position. "I'm really honored at a similarity, if any. I think there's too much suing in the world now, and I'm writing Bruce's manager [Jon Landau] now a letter to assure him that I'm not taking any action."[133] While Tommy Heath and his group's attitude was honorable, it must be said that even though the harmonic progression of the verses in the two songs is similar (with a half-tone difference), it's a rather banal progression that has been used in many songs before (like *Good-Bye Bad Times* by Philip Oakey and Giorgio Moroder in 1985). Because of this, it would have been hard to justify a plagiarism lawsuit.

Radio Nowhere begins with a riff played by various saturated guitars—in garage-rock style—and supported by an acoustic guitar (on the right), percussion instruments, and Max Weinberg's hi-hat. After four measures, the whole group joins in. The song is powerful, the 6-string guitars take center stage, while the drums and bass line provide an incandescent rhythm, everything amplified by a very strong compression and a frenetic—albeit it undermixed—maracas part. The Boss returns with a very energetic lead vocal with rugged accents. Patti Scialfa, Steve Van Zandt, Nils Lofgren, and Clarence Clemons's backing vocals support him in the chorus. Clemons performs an excellent (dubbed) saxophone solo alongside Lofgren's brilliant lead guitar improvisation (from 1'56).

Although not one of Springsteen's best songs, *Radio Nowhere* is among the most successful of the album—hence the Grammy Award in 2008. However, despite an impeccable production and a clearly catchy tune, it lacks the magic that powers the Boss's greatest songs—which explains its near absence from the charts.

2007

YOU'LL BE COMIN' DOWN

Bruce Springsteen / 3'45

You'll Be Comin' Down's melody would have a real impact on the group One Direction. It inspired their 2014 hit *Night Changes.*

Musicians
- **Bruce Springsteen:** vocals, guitar, tambourine
- **Patti Scialfa:** backing vocals
- **Steve Van Zandt:** guitar
- **Nils Lofgren:** guitar
- **Roy Bittan:** keyboards
- **Danny Federici:** keyboards
- **Clarence Clemons:** saxophone
- **Garry Tallent:** bass
- **Max Weinberg:** drums

Recording
- **Southern Tracks Recording Studio, Atlanta, Georgia:** March to May 2007

Technical team
- **Producer:** Brendan O'Brien
- **Recording engineer:** Nick DiDia
- **Assistant recording engineer:** Tom Tapley
- **Mixing:** Brendan O'Brien
- **Mastering:** Bob Ludwig (Gateway Mastering, Portland)

Brendan O'Brien, who produced *Magic* and mixed *You'll Be Comin' Down*, onstage with Barry Bailey of the Atlanta Rhythm Section, 1988.

Genesis and lyrics

With *You'll Be Comin' Down*, Bruce Springsteen revisits a theme Bob Dylan had developed brilliantly in *Like a Rolling Stone* a few years before: the fall of a woman who used to have everything. "You'll be fine long as your pretty face holds out/ Then it's gonna get pretty cold out." These two lines in the fourth verse sum up the song perfectly: you can't live in the present and in the past at the same time, and the narrator assures the heroine that she will learn this at her peril. The high life, the easy money, all that will end; the years will pass and she will no longer be as seductive as she was. Who is this woman who will lose her "pretty face?" Bruce Springsteen doesn't say.

One can also glean from *You'll Be Comin' Down* a veiled criticism of President George W Bush, who "Like a thief on a Sunday morning/It all falls apart with no warning." What's for sure, is that Bruce Springsteen has only performed this song once, to date: on 24 March 2008 in Columbus, Ohio, during the Magic Tour.

Production

Despite the power and dynamism that emanate from the recording, despite the compression of the mixing, despite Max Weinberg's John Bonham-style drumming, and despite the wall of saturated guitars concocted by Brendan O'Brien, *You'll Be Comin' Down* is a 1960s-style song that O'Brien updated for a modern audience. Yet the intro starts off with a curious mix of guitars, bringing to mind The Byrds as well as The Who. Then, from the first verse on, driven by the heavy drums of "The Mighty Max" and Garry Tallent's Bill Wyman-style bass line, Springsteen delivers a sweet, British-style melody that comes to a head in the chorus.

The guitars take center stage: their almost suffocating presence and their various entrances literally invade the song, notably with the Andy Summers-style guitar mutes in the second verse (at 1'09). The keyboards—Danny Federici's organ or Roy Bittan's piano—are equally up to the task. Clarence Clemons performs a very good solo by revolving around the melody (at 2'11).

If you were to sum up *You'll Be Comin' Down* in two words, they would be simple and efficient—but maybe a little too compressed.

LIVIN' IN THE FUTURE

Bruce Springsteen / 3'56

For Springsteen Addicts

Just this once, the Boss, and not Danny Federici, is on the glockenspiel (from the first chorus at 0'27). How times have changed!

Musicians

Bruce Springsteen: vocals, guitar, glockenspiel, tambourine
Patti Scialfa: backing vocals
Soozie Tyrell: violin
Steve Van Zandt: guitar, backing vocals
Nils Lofgren: guitar, backing vocals
Roy Bittan: keyboards
Danny Federici: keyboards
Clarence Clemons: saxophone, backing vocals
Garry Tallent: bass
Max Weinberg: drums

Recording

Southern Tracks Recording Studio, Atlanta, Georgia: March to May 2007

Technical team

Producer: Brendan O'Brien
Recording engineer: Nick DiDia
Assistant recording engineer: Tom Tapley
Mixing: Brendan O'Brien
Mastering: Bob Ludwig (Gateway Mastering, Portland)

Bruce Springsteen and Danny Federici in Boston, on November 2007, attack George W Bush's America with *Livin' in the Future*.

Genesis and lyrics

Livin' in the Future is one of the first songs Bruce Springsteen wrote during the Rising Tour. He set it aside while recording *Devils & Dust* and *We Shall Overcome: The Seeger Sessions*, then reworked it with Brendan O'Brien. "*Livin' in the Future* was the genesis, the little starting point of the record,"[5] he explained in 2011. It's a dark song, distressing, and full of allusions to post-9/11 America. This America is at war, but the narrator refuses to accept it. "Don't worry darling, now baby don't you fret/We're living in the future and none of this has happened yet," he tells the woman he loves. His denial of reality is first and foremost a way to protect her and conceal a sinister picture: "the sea [that] rose towards the sun" and "the groundskeeper [who] opened the gates and let the wild dogs run." All this happened on election day or right after—and refers to the re-election of George W Bush to the White House. "It's a song about apathy, and how what you never thought could happen has happened already,"[130] Springsteen told Joe Levy.

Livin' in the Future is a plea to return to the America of yesterday, the one that had human rights and Habeas Corpus.

Production

From the introduction, the Boss invites us to turn back the clock: *Livin' in the Future* is an emphatic nod to *Tenth Avenue Freeze-Out*, written in 1975 for *Born to Run*. The result is a complete success: Clarence Clemons' sax tenor introduction brings back warm memories, and the rest of the song is a veritable breath of nostalgia. Springsteen sings with a joy and freshness not seen in years, and the group supports him with infectious dynamism and enthusiasm. Max Weinberg and Garry Tallent provide a Stax Records-style groove, with the Boss and his musicians backing it up with many excellent guitar parts. Clemons takes center stage once more with three tenor solos and some riffs on the baritone (at 0'55). Finally, among the many keyboards, Danny Federici's superb solo stands out (at 1'57) on the B3—enough to rival Steve Winwood himself!

2007

YOUR OWN WORST ENEMY

Bruce Springsteen / 3'18

AN INSPIRING ENEMY
Your Own Worst Enemy inspired other songwriters, including Lit (*A Place in the Sun*, 1999), Janet Bates (*A Time Has Come...*, 2004), and Alice Cooper (*Dirty Diamonds*, 2005).

Musicians
Bruce Springsteen: vocals, guitar, percussion instruments
Patti Scialfa: backing vocals
Steve Van Zandt: guitar, backing vocals
Nils Lofgren: guitar, backing vocals
Roy Bittan: keyboards
Danny Federici: keyboards
Clarence Clemons: backing vocals
Garry Tallent: bass
Max Weinberg: drums
Patrick Warren: Chamberlin, tack piano
Eddie Horst: chord arrangements
Karen Freer, Charae Kruege, Daniel Laufer: cellos
Amy Chang, Tania Maxwell Clements, Lachlan McBane: violas
Justin Bruns, Jay Christy, Sheela Lyengar, John Meisner, William Pu, Christopher Pulgram, Olga Shpitko, Kenn Wagner: violins

Recording
Southern Tracks Recording Studio, Atlanta, Georgia: March to May 2007

Technical team
Producer: Brendan O'Brien
Recording engineer: Nick DiDia
Assistant recording engineer: Tom Tapley
Mixing: Brendan O'Brien
Mastering: Bob Ludwig (Gateway Mastering, Portland)

Composer and instrumentalist Patrick Warren's collaborations range from cinema to the silver screen and rock music (Eric Clapton, Chris Isaak, Stevie Nicks, and so on). He's known as a Chamberlin specialist. This electronic keyboard was precursor to the Mellotron. Incidentally, in addition to his performance for the Boss, he also starred in *Road Trippin'*, by the Red Hot Chili Peppers (1999).

Genesis and lyrics

We are our own worst enemy: the meaning of this title is clear. As Bruce Springsteen told Joe Levy of *Rolling Stone*, "The lyrics are 'we're always teetering on the edge,' and it's all about self-subversion. You can take it personally or politically."[130] On the personal side, *Your Own Worst Enemy* is the story of a man who sinks into insanity or paranoia. Either way, what he does had irreversible consequences, for himself and for his wife. He can no longer "dream [his] dream"—the dream he could have if he were sleeping, but also the American dream, which has now become inaccessible to him. And still he dares not stare truth in the face, to the point where he removes "all the mirrors."

On the political side, President George W Bush is again in the crosshairs: "Your flag it flew so high/It drifted into the sky." This is a criticism of the wars the United States waged in the early 2000s and of the Patriot Act, which was seen as oppressive.

Production

How can this song not bring to mind Brian Wilson's legendary album *Pet Sounds*? The tone is set in the introduction: after two measures of bells and piano, Springsteen launches into his vocals supported by violins, an arpeggioed electric guitar, and, last but not least, a handbell, the key tool of The Beach Boys' front man. The Boss had written in a style that was relatively new for him, and he did not hide his satisfaction. "I always loved those little pop symphonies, so on this record, I had a chance to play around with some of that. *Your Own Worst Enemy* was one of my big pop productions."[130] He was not afraid to enhance the arrangements with various instruments: strings—which, unlike those of *Devils & Dust* and *The Rising*, are actually audible—a tack piano (in the background on the left at 0'51) and a Chamberlin for the trumpets, in the style of *Penny Lane* (in the bridge at 1'53), both played by Patrick Warren; Beach Boys-style unisons (at 1'33); and multiple percussion instruments, including orchestra timbales (at 1'16). As for the lead vocals, Springsteen adopts Roy Orbison-like intonations, notably in his vibrato (for example, at 2'55).

"We pulled your cycle out of up back to the garage and polished up the chrome," in the third verse of *Gypsy Biker*, echoes the line about the Ford in *Shut Out the Light*.

GYPSY BIKER

Bruce Springsteen / 4'31

Musicians
Bruce Springsteen: vocals, guitar, maracas (?)
Patti Scialfa: backing vocals
Steve Van Zandt: guitar, backing vocals
Nils Lofgren: guitar, backing vocals
Roy Bittan: keyboards
Danny Federici: keyboards
Clarence Clemons: backing vocals
Garry Tallent: bass
Max Weinberg: drums

Recording
Southern Tracks Recording Studio, Atlanta, Georgia: March to May 2007

Technical team
Producer: Brendan O'Brien
Recording engineer: Nick DiDia
Assistant recording engineer: Tom Tapley
Mixing: Brendan O'Brien
Mastering: Bob Ludwig (Gateway Mastering, Portland)

Steve Van Zandt rehearses at the Convention Hall, New Jersey, on 24 September 2007. His bond with the Boss on *Gypsy Biker* was total.

Genesis and lyrics

With *Gypsy Biker*, Bruce Springsteen revisits a theme developed some 20 years before in *Born in the U.S.A.* and *Shut Out the Light*: the return of an American soldier, or rather of his body, since the man has died in combat. Time has passed, and the United States has gone from one war to the next. One can therefore assume that the "gypsy biker" in question is a soldier who fought in Afghanistan or Iraq. But the message remains the same: *Gypsy Biker* is a resolutely antiwar song. The songwriter takes aim at those responsible: the government, army generals, and the military industrial complex that "made their money on the blood you shed." He condemns the same authorities that decorate the soldiers who died in combat and organize ridiculous parades to give them their final honors.

Gypsy Biker debuted onstage at the Convention Hall in Asbury Park, New Jersey, on 24 September 2007. It was performed throughout the 2007–2008 tour in the United States and in Europe.

Production

Gypsy Biker is close to Springsteen's usual style, in the sense that it is neither alternative rock nor a pop song like *Pet Sounds*. The piece begins with a harmonica line buried in a deep reverberation, a bit like in *Man with a Harmonica*, by Ennio Morricone. An acoustic guitar and maracas accompany it. The Boss launches into the lead vocals in the first verse before the whole group joins in for the following verse. The rhythm is again spectacularly supported by the Weinberg-Tallent duo and by the multiple saturated guitars of the three guitarists. This song gives Steve Van Zandt and Springsteen the opportunity to challenge each other to a superb duel on the 6-string guitars, with "Miami Steve" opening hostilities (from 1'46) followed by the Boss (at 2'01). Roy Bittan's piano emerges in places, as does Danny Federici's Hammond B-3. Regarding the piano, which is rather discreet in the entire album, Brendan O'Brien later explained its essential role: "It's not as distinguishable as the higher stuff, but if you pulled it out of the mix, you'd go, what happened to the whole bottom end?"[117]

2007

Girls in Their Summer Clothes references the Beach Boys, but also the version performed by The Walker Brothers of *The Sun Ain't Gonna Shine Anymore* by Frankie Valli.

GIRLS IN THEIR SUMMER CLOTHES

Bruce Springsteen / 4'19

Musicians

Bruce Springsteen: vocals, guitar, keyboards (?), glockenspiel, percussion instruments
Patti Scialfa: backing vocals
Steve Van Zandt: guitar, backing vocal
Nils Lofgren: guitar, backing vocals
Roy Bittan: keyboards
Danny Federici: keyboards
Clarence Clemons: saxophone (?), backing vocals
Garry Tallent: bass
Max Weinberg: drums, percussion instruments (?)
Patrick Warren: Chamberlin, tack piano (?)
String arrangements: Eddie Horst
Karen Freer, Charae Kruege, Daniel Laufer: cellos
Amy Chang, Tania Maxwell Clements, Lachlan McBane: violas
Justin Bruns, Jay Christy, Sheela Lyengar, John Meisner, William Pu, Christopher Pulgram, Olga Shpitko, Kenn Wagner: violins

Recording

Southern Tracks Recording Studio, Atlanta, Georgia: March to May 2007

Technical team

Producer: Brendan O'Brien
Recording engineer: Nick DiDia
Assistant recording engineer: Tom Tapley
Mixing: Brendan O'Brien
Mastering: Bob Ludwig (Gateway Mastering, Portland)

For Springsteen Addicts

Made available on iTunes on 15 January 2008 (in a remix called *Winter Mix*) and accompanied by a video by Mark Pellington, *Girls in Their Summer Clothes* reached No.27 in the US *Billboard* Mainstream Rock category. It was the first Springsteen song to place in the charts since *Devils & Dust* in 2005.

Genesis and lyrics

This song, which sounds like 1960s pop, was inspired by an Irwin Shaw novel called *The Girls in their Summer Dresses*, published in 1939. The story in a few words: a couple is walking through the streets of New York, but the narrator can't keep himself from looking at the young women passing by. Springsteen's song doesn't take place in New York, but in a small town in the United States, perhaps a little seaside town with a charming atmosphere—sparkling lamplights, lovers walking hand in hand, the breeze that crosses the porch. "I don't think I've written as romantically as I allowed myself to do on that song maybe since *Born to Run*,"[130] he told Joe Levy for *Rolling Stone* magazine.

Romantic, yes, but *Girls in Their Summer Clothes* also emits a pronounced sense of nostalgia, as if it were a bittersweet meditation on times gone by, on getting old. A bit like Proust with his madeleine, the mere sight of pretty girls in light dresses thrusts the narrator into his past, when he was young and had his life in front of him. "It is the most insightful song about aging,"[134] said Bono, of U2. Lines such as "Things been a little tight" makes one wonder. But it's also a song about a painful breakup—"She went away, she cut me like a knife."

Girls in Their Summer Clothes won a Grammy Award for "Best Rock Song" in 2008.

Production

Acoustic guitars, including some 12-strings, open the piece, supported by a string motif arranged by Eddie Horst and by a tambourine mixed into the distance.

An electric guitar and a bass guitar with a slightly saturated sound come in with the Boss's lead vocals. He sings with a light, suave, and gentle voice. The recording of this voice caused Brendan O'Brien some problems: the basic track had already been recorded when the songwriter noticed a tonality problem, causing the musicians to have to rerecord all of their parts—at least the guitars. Moreover, Springsteen used a rather common studio technique for this album. "I doubled my voice, I sang in a bigger voice,"[130] he explained. This is noticeable in the first chorus, for example, where his voice rises to high pitches with characteristic confidence and ease—it's a technique that achieves clarity and presence while remaining at a relative distance in the mix.

The rest of the group enters in the second verse, led by Max Weinberg's Hal-Blaine style drumming (from 1'08). The arrangements are rather dense, making it hard to identify the different instruments, O'Brien having clearly chosen to reproduce the Wall of Sound dear to Phil Spector (see page 69). One can, however, pick out the keyboards, Roy Bittan's piano, and the strings.

The chorus and bridge follow (at 1'59). Again, the Boss pays tribute to The Beach Boys as they were in their *Pet Sounds*' period. The various percussion instruments, saxophone, organ, glockenspiels, and other arrangements rightly bring to mind songs such as *Pet Sounds*, the instrumental version of the previously mentioned album.

Additional percussion instruments enter in the last part of the song (a second tambourine and some maracas), along with a chorus line that is mixed into the background.

While *Girls in Their Summer Clothes* clearly brings to mind The Beach Boys, especially in the bridge, the feel of the verses and choruses more closely resembles songs like *The Sun Ain't Gonna Shine Anymore*, written by Frankie Valli in 1965 and updated the following year by The Walker Brothers—at least in the spirit and arrangements of the adaptation.

"*Girls in Their Summer Clothes*, that was fun," said Springsteen. "I like that big production style, I haven't done that in a long, long time."[10] And, as he added in 2007, "I'm actually looking forward to writing a little bit more in that style, to picking up some of those elements that I discarded because I wanted to make sure that the music was tough enough for the subjects I was interested in dealing with."[130]

The Boss also sang this song solo with the guitar in a rather surprising but successful version on 7 February 2014 at the Perth Arena, in Australia, during the High Hopes Tour.

2007

I'LL WORK FOR YOUR LOVE

Bruce Springsteen / 3'34

Musicians

Bruce Springsteen: vocals, guitar, harmonica, keyboards, glockenspiel, percussion instruments
Patti Scialfa: backing vocals
Steve Van Zandt: guitar, backing vocals
Nils Lofgren: guitar, backing vocals
Roy Bittan: keyboards
Danny Federici: keyboards
Clarence Clemons: percussion instruments, backing vocals
Garry Tallent: bass
Max Weinberg: drums
Soozie Tyrell: violin

Recording

Southern Tracks Recording Studio, Atlanta, Georgia: March to May 2007

Technical team

Producer: Brendan O'Brien
Recording engineer: Nick DiDia
Assistant recording engineer: Tom Tapley
Mixing: Brendan O'Brien
Mastering: Bob Ludwig (Gateway Mastering, Portland)

For Springsteen Addicts

Since 2007, Springsteen has been participating each year in the Stand Up for Heroes concert to raise funds for the Bob Woodruff Foundation, which helps wounded veterans and their families. He performed *I'll Work for Your Love* many times. To raise the stakes, the Boss even added personal bonuses, such as a private dinner with him (homemade lasagna!), guitar lessons, and a ride in his Cadillac to get hamburgers together in Freehold.

Genesis and lyrics

Something in the melody of *I'll Work for Your Love* brings to mind that of *Positively 4th Street* by Bob Dylan. But the lyrics are completely different. The narrator is in a bar talking to a barmaid named Theresa who tells him that unlike other people, he will have to work hard to be loved. The dramatic tension in *I'll Work for Your Love* essentially resides in the contrast between the location of the scene and the narrator's use of Christian imagery: "And I'll watch the bones in your back like the Stations of the Cross/'Round your hair the sun lifts a halo, at your lips a crown of thorns," "The pages of Revelations lie open in your empty eyes of blue," and "Well tears, they fill the rosary at your feet." Lastly, the name Theresa could be a reference to Saint Theresa of Lisieux, who used prayer and sacrifice to save souls until her death in 1897 at the age of 24. None of this is a coincidence. "Our book of faith's been tossed," adds the narrator. Bruce Springsteen performed this profound song some 30 times between 2007 and 2016.

Production

Another nod to the songwriter's past: the piano intro to *I'll Work for Your Love* recalls that of *Jungleland* on the *Born to Run* album. Springsteen accompanies Roy Bittan on the glockenspiel, an instrument that is emblematic of this glorious era and which had previously been reserved exclusively for Danny Federici. But times change, and the Boss plays this percussion instrument himself with obvious delight as he revisits the sounds that forged his group's identity.

I'll Work for Your Love is halfway between pop and punchy rock. On the one hand, the melody is catchy; on the other, the rhythmic section, percussion instruments (tambourine, maracas), keyboards, and guitars give power and energy to the piece, enhanced by Brendan O'Brien's assertive production style. As for solos, Soozie Tyrell launches into a brief violin performance (at 1'00) before Springsteen joins in on a saturated sounding harmonica, all while being doubled by a lead guitar, likely that of Nils Lofgren (at 1'48 and 3'17).

MAGIC

Bruce Springsteen / 2'45

Musicians

Bruce Springsteen: vocals, guitar, percussion instruments, pump organ
Steve Van Zandt: mandolin
Nils Lofgren: guitar
Roy Bittan: keyboards (?)
Danny Federici: keyboards (?)
Clarence Clemons: percussion instruments (?)
Max Weinberg: drums
Soozie Tyrell: violin, backing vocals (?)
Jeremy Chatzky: double bass
Patrick Warren: Chamberlin

Recording

Southern Tracks Recording Studio, Atlanta, Georgia: March to May 2007

Technical team

Producer: Brendan O'Brien
Recording engineer: Nick DiDia
Assistant recording engineer: Tom Tapley
Mixing: Brendan O'Brien
Mastering: Bob Ludwig (Gateway Mastering, Portland)

For Springsteen Addicts

Bruce Springsteen speaks of "bodies hanging in the trees." He's most certainly referring to the lynching of African-Americans, which persisted well beyond the Civil War. The *Strange Fruit* Billie Holiday sang about.

Pages 518–519 Bruce Springsteen and Clarence Clemons in Atlanta, 2007. *Magic* is an album filled with a cold anger, but it is also tinged with nostalgia.

Genesis and lyrics

It's no coincidence that *Magic* is the title song of Bruce Springsteen's 15th album. It embodies the driving idea of the disc, which is that the truth presented to Americans is nothing but a lie. Bruce Springsteen clearly references the war in Iraq, which began in 2003, launched by the United States and a large coalition under its thumb with the excuse of neutralizing weapons of mass destruction that existed only in the minds of certain Washington leaders. As explained to Joe Levy of *Rolling Stone*: "The song *Magic* is about living in a time when anything that is true can be made to seem like a lie, and anything that is a lie can be made to seem true. There are people that have taken that as their credo. The classic quote was from one of the Bushies in *The New York Times*: 'We make our own reality. You guys [the journalists] report it, we make it.'"[130]

The narrator is depicted as an illusionist able to make a coin disappear, or to make a card appear behind someone's ear. But it's all just deception. "And the freedom that you sought's/Driftin' like a ghost amongst the trees/This is what will be," sings Bruce Springsteen during the 2007–2008 tour.

Production

This fantastic song has an acoustic, restrained ambience; it's a veritable hymn to the refusal to be manipulated. The song starts with an unusual sound, likely the songwriter's pump organ. Then two fingerpicked acoustic guitars appear, supported by the bass drum and a tambourine serving as a snare drum. Lastly, Springsteen's superb voice gushes forth in a clear and precise tone, enhanced by a subtle reverberation. Jeremy Chatzky's double bass enters in the second verse with an uncharacteristic sound for the instrument. Steve Van Zandt follows suit, launching into a very good reverberated mandolin solo (at 1'09) that is soon followed by Soozie Tyrell's violin—strangely, she is also credited for some inaudible backing vocals. As for Patrick Warren, he's probably on the strings with his Chamberlin, unless he used it to increase density in various parts of the song, the strings in that case being the work of samplers.

LAST TO DIE

Bruce Springsteen / 4'16

Bruce Springsteen mentions Truth or Consequences in the first verse. This is a town in New Mexico whose name comes from a radio and television show from the 1950s hosted by Ralph Edwards. It was no coincidence the songwriter chose this town!

Musicians
Bruce Springsteen: vocals, guitar, percussion instruments (?)
Patti Scialfa: backing vocals
Steve Van Zandt: guitar, backing vocals
Nils Lofgren: guitar, backing vocals
Roy Bittan: keyboards
Danny Federici: keyboards
Clarence Clemons: percussion instruments (?), backing vocals (?)
Garry Tallent: bass
Max Weinberg: drums
Soozie Tyrell: violin

Recording
Southern Tracks Recording Studio, Atlanta, Georgia: March to May 2007

Technical team
Producer: Brendan O'Brien
Recording engineer: Nick DiDia
Assistant recording engineer: Tom Tapley
Mixing: Brendan O'Brien
Mastering: Bob Ludwig (Gateway Mastering, Portland)

Neil Tennant and Chris Lowe of the Pet Shop Boys, backstage. They recorded an inspired version of *Last to Die*.

Genesis and lyrics

Bruce Springsteen wrote this song based on a speech made by John Kerry in 1971. Before losing against George W Bush in the 2004 presidential elections, Kerry, who fought in Vietnam, was brought to testify before a commission overseen by Senator JW Fulbright, whose objective was to put an end to the Vietnam War. "We are asking Americans to think about that, because how do you ask a man to be the last man to die in Vietnam? How do you ask a man to be the last man to die for a mistake?"[135]

Thirty-five years later, John Kerry's words remain a painful truth, with the attacks on September 11 and the wars waged in Afghanistan and Iraq. Now, as then, the incompetence of those in power trumps their humanity and judgment. This is anyway Bruce Springsteen's point when he says: "We just stack the bodies outside the door," "The sun sets in flames as the city burns," and "Faces of the dead at five."

Production

Last to Die is a medium rock song marked by a prevalence of acoustic and electric guitars. Only Soozie Tyrell's violin is able to breach this wall of 6-strings, most notably in the intro: she plays the piece's excellent riff, likely with the help of Steve Van Zandt's guitar.

Max Weinberg hammers on his kit with the vigor and determination of a lumberjack, supported by Garry Tallent's excellent bass line, which is both melodious and rhythmic. The keyboards are literally ensconced in the sound mass, from which only the piano occasionally stands out. Springsteen's performance is dignified and superb, doing justice to his lyrics.

Last to Die is one of the best songs on the album. It contains undeniable energy and vigor, which reach their height in concert.

To note: the Pet Shop Boys made a very good cover of this song in 2013 for their album *Electric*. This version is very different from that of the Boss, but it deserves a listen.

LONG WALK HOME

Bruce Springsteen / 4'34

For Springsteen Addicts

Thom Zimny directed the video for *Long Walk Home* on the same day as the one for *Radio Nowhere*. Shooting took place at the Convention Hall, in Asbury Park, and in a restaurant (Tony's Freehold Grill) in Freehold. The E Street Band makes a few fleeting appearances.

Musicians

Bruce Springsteen: vocals, guitar, keyboards (?), percussion instruments
Patti Scialfa: backing vocals
Steve Van Zandt: guitar, backing vocals
Nils Lofgren: guitar, backing vocals
Roy Bittan: keyboards
Danny Federici: keyboards
Clarence Clemons: saxophone, percussion instruments (?), backing vocals (?)
Garry Tallent: bass
Max Weinberg: drums
Patrick Warren: Chamberlin, tack piano (?)

Recording

Southern Tracks Recording Studio, Atlanta, Georgia: March to May 2007

Technical team

Producer: Brendan O'Brien
Recording engineer: Nick DiDia
Assistant recording engineer: Tom Tapley
Mixing: Brendan O'Brien
Mastering: Bob Ludwig (Gateway Mastering, Portland)

Ralph and Carter of the Stanley Brothers. They sing about "going home" in *Rank Strangers to Me*, as the Boss does in *Long Walk Home*.

Genesis and lyrics

Bruce Springsteen most certainly wrote *Long Walk Home* in 2006, since he performed it on 11 November 2006 during the Seeger Sessions Band Tour, explaining to the audience at Wembley that it was not yet finished. The songwriter was revisiting the "homecoming" theme, taking inspiration from *Rank Strangers to Me*, a song by Albert E Brumley that has been covered by the Stanley Brothers and Bob Dylan. The line "I looked in their faces, they were all rank strangers to me," in any case, was taken directly from that song.

Like Ulysses, the narrator in *Long Walk Home* returns home after a long trip. He finds that everything has changed, that the restaurant he used to go to is now shuttered, and that no one recognizes him. No doubt he too is returning from the war in Afghanistan or Iraq, and this transformed town is actually a post-9/11 America.

Long Walk Home came out as a single in October 2007. *Rolling Stone* magazine named it No.8 out of the 100 best songs of that year.

Production

The first versions performed with the Seeger Band in late 2006 were rather sweet and melancholy, albeit with a country feel. When the Boss performed the song alone on the acoustic guitar, as he did in Pittsburgh, Pennsylvania, in September 2016, the result fitted in well with *The Ghost of Tom Joad*. But when he recorded it with the E Street Band, it went from delicate song to aggressive rock, supported by the same wall of guitars that had prevailed since the opening of the album. The piece starts off relatively calmly, but after the first chorus, it's carried by a powerful rhythmic section and by multiple saturated 6-string guitars—Brendan O'Brien's calling card. Springsteen's voice is enhanced by a fairly long delay, making his performance more open and perhaps more moving. He performs two guitar solos ahead of the bridge and at the end of the song, each followed by Clarence Clemons' saxophone (at 1'57 and 4'06).

Long Walk Home is a fabulous song, but was it necessary to infuse it with so much rock energy? Each to their own.

2007

DEVIL'S ARCADE

Bruce Springsteen / 5'20

Michael Dickes performed *Devil's Arcade* for the comedy-drama *Henry Poole is Here* (2008), by Mark Pellington and starring Luke Wilson.

Musicians

Bruce Springsteen: vocals, guitar, keyboards, percussion instruments
Steve Van Zandt: guitar
Nils Lofgren: guitar
Roy Bittan: keyboards
Danny Federici: keyboards
Clarence Clemons: percussion instruments (?)
Garry Tallent: bass
Max Weinberg: drums
Patrick Warren: Chamberlin, tack piano
Daniel Laufer: cello

Recording

Southern Tracks Recording Studio, Atlanta, Georgia: March to May 2007

Technical team

Producer: Brendan O'Brien
Recording engineer: Nick DiDia
Assistant recording engineer: Tom Tapley
Mixing: Brendan O'Brien
Mastering: Bob Ludwig (Gateway Mastering, Portland)

Cellist Daniel Laufer is part of the Atlanta Symphony Orchestra, whose members include Brice Andrus, Donald Strand, Susan Welty, and Thomas Witte, the French horn players who participated in the *Devils & Dust* recording.

Genesis and lyrics

Devil's Arcade is another song about the war waged by American soldiers in the vast desert expanses of Iraq and is a sort of follow-up to the album *Devils & Dust*. The soldier was seriously wounded, and his wife is the one to recount the path that led him to the Devil's arcade, to hell. She remembers what happened to him: "Just metal and plastic where your body caved," then the recovery in the hospital, poker games with other wounded soldiers, and, finally, the return home and physical love as the last escape from reality.

It's clear that *Devil's Arcade* is a new indictment by Democrat Bruce Springsteen against the Republican administration of George W Bush, who thought it legitimate to wage a preemptive war in Iraq without really understanding the consequences. The America Springsteen describes wanted to make unwilling heroes of its young combatants.

Devil's Arcade was one of the mainstays of the 2007–2008 world tour, during which it was performed more than 70 times.

Production

This last song from *Magic—Terry's Song* was a bonus track—is another little masterpiece from Springsteen.

The piece starts with a fade-in marked by nearly unidentifiable keyboard sounds (sampler, Chamberlin, pump organ?). A strongly saturated guitar immediately appears in an electronic fog (on the right). Then Daniel Laufer performs a melancholic cello motif accompanied by an acoustic guitar. Finally, Springsteen's voice comes in. The arrangements evolve throughout the song to become increasingly dense, notably thanks to Max Weinberg's superb drumming (first on the brushes, then on the drumsticks). The cello motif reemerges after the only bridge of the song, doubled by the lead guitar and by Patrick Warren's Chamberlin (at 2'17).

The end of *Devil's Arcade* is particularly successful, with an extraordinary Max Weinberg (from 3'40) ending the piece alone. This move resonated strongly with the songwriter after a journalist had pointed out that in *Radio Nowhere*, the title song of the album, he sings that he just wants to hear rhythm, and that "I want pounding drums." A subliminal link, in short.

TERRY'S SONG

Bruce Springsteen / 4'11

For Springsteen Addicts
Because of the way in which Bruce Springsteen recorded *Terry's Song*, certain preordered copies of *Magic* were released without it. The album available on iTunes also did not contain this song.

Musician
Bruce Springsteen: vocals, guitars, harmonica, piano, organ
Recording
Southern Tracks Recording Studio, Atlanta, Georgia: August 2007 (?)
Thrill Hill Recording, New Jersey: August 2007 (?)
Technical team
Producer: Brendan O'Brien
Recording engineer: Nick DiDia (?) Toby Scott (?)
Mixing: Brendan O'Brien
Mastering: Bob Ludwig (Gateway Mastering, Portland)

Terry's Song is the last on the *Magic* album. Bruce Springsteen wrote and recorded it in memory of his assistant Terry Magovern.

Genesis and lyrics

The recording, mixing, and announcement of *Magic* had already been completed when Terry Magovern, Bruce Springsteen's personal assistant since 1987, passed away. The pair met in 1972 in a club called the Captain's Garter in Neptune, New Jersey, and a strong friendship had developed. Terry himself had been a musician in the 1970s as the front man for the Sundance Blue Band, which had appeared at the Captain's Garter. Bruce Springsteen described Terry Magovern as "a strange New Jersey version of 'the catcher in the rye,' [a reference to JD Salinger's famous 1951 novel, *The Catcher in the Rye*] out on the edge of some windswept cliff keeping children from rushing over the edge."[136]

A few days after Terry Magovern's death, Bruce Springsteen took up his guitar again and recorded *Terry's Song*, a tribute to his friend. "Now your death is upon us and we'll return your ashes to the earth," he sings. "But love is a power greater than death," he adds. A love and a friendship that the songwriter elevates to the rank of masterpiece, like the *Mona Lisa* by Leonardo da Vinci or the Sistine Chapel.

Production

This bonus song succeeds *Devil's Arcade* after a 15-second pause. It was likely recorded in the Boss's home studio at Thrill Hill Recording, in Colts Neck, rather than at Southern Tracks in Atlanta, Georgia.

A piano part opens this folk-like song. Then the songwriter takes up his Gibson J-45 and launches into the vocals with a taut voice that betrays a very emotional state. He gradually adds to the arrangements, notably with a second guitar, vocal harmonies, an organ, and an instrumental break with a short harp solo (at 2'13). Finally, after the last verse, he ends the song on a second harp solo.

What to say about this recording, other than the fact that it reveals the pain of its author? The music is simple, clear, and direct. The lyrics are simple, clear, and beautiful. Before recording *Terry's Song*, Springsteen played it at his friend's funeral on 2 August 2007 in Red Bank, New Jersey. He later performed it in concert with an emotion that was difficult to hide, as he did during the High Hopes Tour on 8 February 2014 in Perth, Australia.

Alejandro Escovedo and Springsteen sing *Always a Friend* during the 11th Light of Day concert, 15 January 2011, in Asbury Park, New Jersey.

ALWAYS A FRIEND

Alejandro Escovedo, Chuck Prophet / 4'49

EP: *Magic Tour Highlights: Always a Friend, The Ghost of Tom Joad, Turn! Turn! Turn!, 4th of July, Asbury Park (Sandy)* EP (only available for download) **Release date:** United States: 15 July 2008 **Reference:** Columbia Records **Musicians:** Bruce Springsteen: vocals, guitar / Alejandro Escovedo: vocals, guitar / Steve Van Zandt: guitar, backing vocals / Nils Lofgren: guitar, backing vocals / Clarence Clemons: percussion, backing vocals / Roy Bittan: piano / Garry Tallent: bass guitar / Max Weinberg: drums / Soozie Tyrell: violin, backing vocals / Charles Giordano: organ **Recording:** Toyota Center, Houston, Texas: 14 April 2008 **Technical team:** Producer: John Cooper / Recording engineer: John Cooper / Assistant recording engineer: Brett Dixon / Mixing: Bob Clearmountain, Brandon Duncan (assistant) / Mastering: Bob Ludwig

Genesis and lyrics

During the concert in Houston on 14 April 2008, part of the Magic Tour, Bruce Springsteen invited Alejandro Escovedo, a Texan singer and composer of Mexican descent whose managers at the time were Jon Landau and Barbara Carr, to join him onstage. A few hours earlier, Alejandro Escovedo had received a text message informing him that Bruce Springsteen wanted to sing *Always a Friend* with him. There was no sound check—just two acoustic run-throughs before the arrival of the E Street Band. A little later, Bruce Springsteen and Alejandro Escovedo sang *Always a Friend* together (the latter had just recorded the song for his album *Real Animal*, released in June 2008). A very fine song that celebrates love.

Always a Friend was chosen, together with *The Ghost of Tom Joad, Turn! Turn! Turn!, 4th of July*, and *Asbury Park (Sandy)*, to feature on the EP aptly entitled *Magic Tour Highlights* (comprising videos of the concerts), which was available to download from 15 July 2008.

Production

Even though the version of *Always a Friend* delivered by Springsteen and Alejandro Escovedo gets off to a shaky start, it is quite simply excellent: it is a real surge of positive energy. It must be said that the song is a superb rock number, custom-made for the E Street Band. The Boss and his guest share the lead vocals, even though Escovedo has the lion's share, with the songwriter replying to him with pleasant-sounding "ooh oohs," among other things.

Always a Friend is above all a number for guitarists (the original version is a must-listen): it brings together Springsteen, Alejandro Escovedo, Nils Lofgren, and Steve Van Zandt, each playing a 6-string guitar, with "Miami Steve" even delivering a few solo phrases toward the end of the song. Soozie Tyrell takes an active part in the piece's riff with her violin, while also contributing backing vocals. As for keyboards, Roy Bittan is on piano and Charles Giordano, who already featured on *We Shall Overcome: The Seeger Sessions*, replaced Danny Federici from 25 November 2007, the latter having become ill and made way for him (Federici's last concert would be on 20 March 2008).

For Springsteen Addicts

All the proceeds from downloads of the EP, including royalties, were donated to the Danny Fund—which supports research into melanoma—set up by the E Street Band's talented and much-mourned keyboard player, who died three days after the 14 April 2008 concert.

Turn! Turn! Turn! is one of Pete Seeger's compositions, which was transformed into a manifestly folk-rock song by The Byrds in 1965. Pictured is Roger McGuinn in 2009.

TURN! TURN! TURN!

Pete Seeger / 4'51

Musicians: Bruce Springsteen: vocals, guitar / Roger McGuinn: vocals, guitar / Steve Van Zandt: guitar / Nils Lofgren: guitar, backing vocals / Clarence Clemons: percussion / Roy Bittan: keyboards / Garry Tallent: bass guitar / Max Weinberg: drums / Soozie Tyrell: violin, backing vocals (?) / Charles Giordano: keyboards **Recording:** Amway Arena, Orlando, Florida: 23 April 2008 **Technical team:** Producer: John Cooper / Recording engineer: John Cooper / Assistant recording engineer: Brett Dixon / Mixing: Bob Clearmountain, Brandon Duncan (assistant) / Mastering: Bob Ludwig

Genesis and lyrics

Turn! Turn! Turn! (To Everything There Is a Season) is a song by Pete Seeger that dates from the folk revival of the late 1950s but was not recorded until 1962 for the album *The Bitter and the Sweet*. The folk singer drew inspiration from the Bible's book of Ecclesiastes, especially its third chapter, which begins with the words: "To every thing there is a season, and a time to every purpose under the heaven." (Ecclesiastes 3:1, King James Version.) Three years after Pete Seeger, The Byrds added this song to their repertoire, producing a gem of folk rock. The song even lent its title to their second album, which was released in 1965.

Having already devoted a whole album to the songs of Pete Seeger, Bruce Springsteen once again drew on the New York folk singer's repertoire. He sang *Turn! Turn! Turn!* for the first time at the Convention Hall in Asbury Park, on 25 April 2006, during rehearsals for the upcoming Bruce Springsteen with The Seeger Sessions Band Tour, then, on 23 April 2008, at the Amway Arena, Orlando, Florida, during the Magic Tour. The cherry on the cake came when Roger McGuinn, the leading light of The Byrds, came onstage in person to sing it as a duet with the Boss (followed by Bob Dylan's *Mr. Tambourine Man*).

Production

Initially planned for 19 April, the concert was postponed until 23 April following the death of Danny Federici on 17 April. Despite the tragic news, the E Street Band and Springsteen put on a brave face and delivered the show with an energy and enthusiasm that were doubtless cathartic. The star of this precious moment was clearly Roger McGuinn, with his legendary 12-string Rickenbacker—the sound of The Byrds, forever etched into the history of folk rock. It is in all probability a 620/12 model, and he is accompanied by Steve Van Zandt's Rickenbacker 660/12 and Nils Lofgren's Takamine 12-string acoustic. As for the Boss, he plays his Telecaster-Esquire, the only 6-string guitar in the song.

As well as the sound of the Rickenbacker, *Turn! Turn! Turn!* features the mellow voice of Roger McGuinn and the sublime vocal harmonies that support it. He and Springsteen take turns in singing lead vocals and supporting vocals. The result is a fine song, and a resounding tribute to The Byrds—not forgetting Pete Seeger.

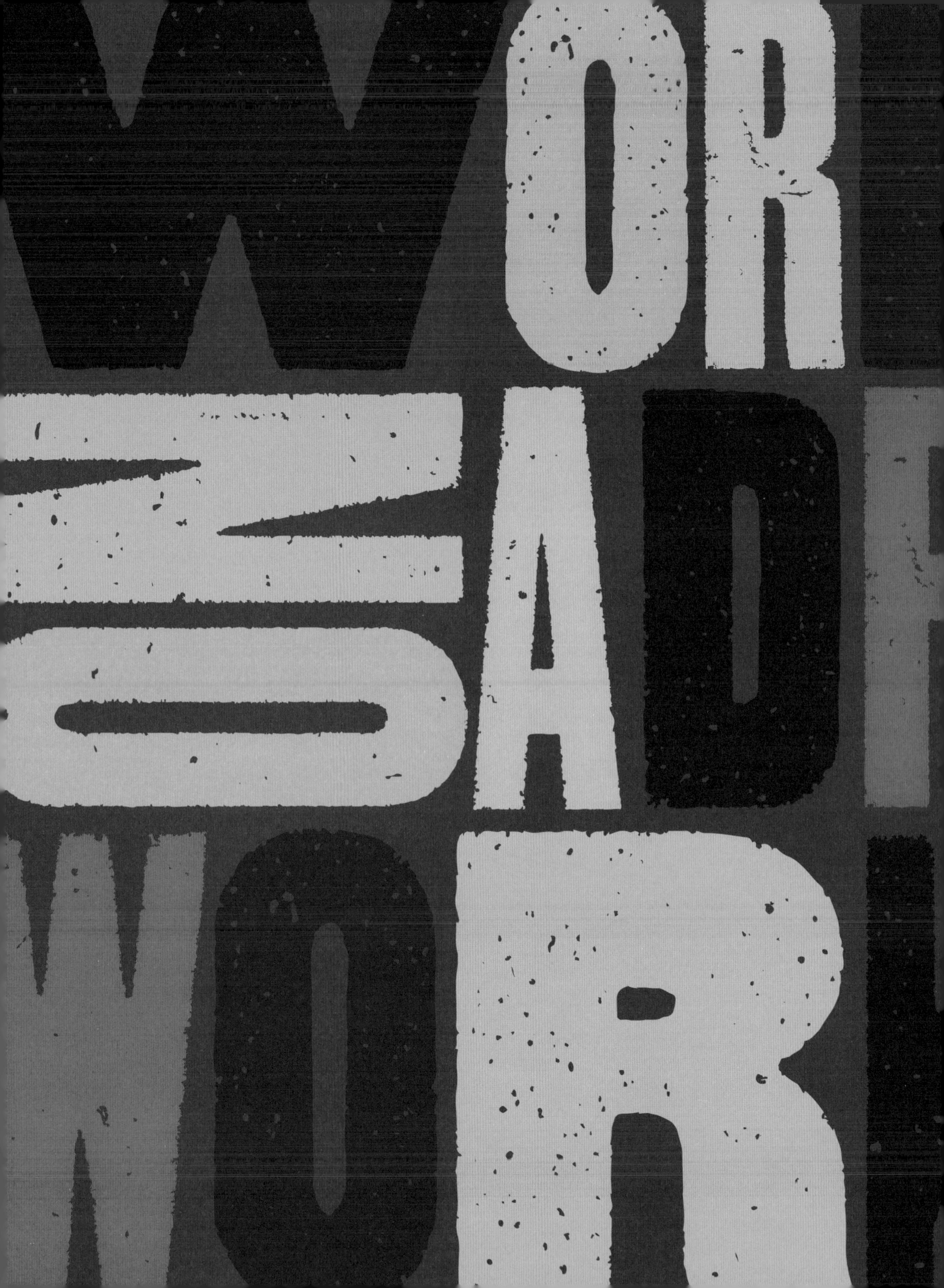

ALBUM

WORKING ON A DREAM

Outlaw Pete • My Lucky Day • Working On a Dream • Queen of the Supermarket • What Love Can Do • This Life • Good Eye • Tomorrow Never Knows • Life Itself • Kingdom of Days • Surprise, Surprise • The Last Carnival • The Wrestler

Outtakes: *A Night with the Jersey Devil* • *Frankie Fell in Love*

RELEASE DATE

United States: 27 January 2009

Reference: Columbia Records – 88697 41355 2

No.1 in the United States, United Kingdom, Canada, Denmark, Germany, the Netherlands, Ireland, Italy, Spain, Sweden, and Switzerland, No.2 in France

For Springsteen Addicts

The Deluxe version of *Working On a Dream* contains, as well as the CD, a 30-minute documentary DVD made by Thom Zimmy about recording the album, and demos of several songs, as well as the song *A Night with the Jersey Devil*. The French version includes a bonus CD on which Antoine de Caunes retraces the life story of the New Jersey songwriter.

Bruce Springsteen at the Convention Hall, Asbury Park, on 23 March 2009, photographed for the *Los Angeles Times*. He made a strong comeback in 2009 with *Working On a Dream*.

AN ALBUM DEDICATED TO DANNY FEDERICI

Fourteen months after the release of *Magic* and four months after the end of the promotional world tour, Bruce Springsteen was once again working hard composing *Working On a Dream*. The songwriter started work on this 16th album while he was still putting the finishing touches to *Magic* with Brendan O'Brien in Atlanta, Georgia. In his hotel room, he went back to composing, with new ideas going through his head. The result was five songs—*This Life*, *My Lucky Day*, *Life Itself*, *Good Eye*, and *Tomorrow Never Knows*—which were to become the backbone of the future album. Like the other numbers on the album, they were recorded with the E Street Band.

The album

Perhaps because this was Springsteen's first record of the post-Bush era—and therefore of the Obama era—the subject matter of *Working On a Dream* in no way resembles that of any of the last few albums he had made. The anti-Bush tirades, the pacifist manifestos against US military action in Afghanistan and Iraq, and the sadness, even anger, at seeing the ideas of America's founding fathers flouted in the early 2000s, here give way to more personal, intimate reflection, focusing especially on relationships, love that endures over the years, the passage of time, and, implicitly, the inescapable approach of death. No fewer than seven songs on the album deal with such themes—*My Lucky Day*, *This Life*, *Good Eye*, *Tomorrow Never Knows*, *Life Itself*, *Kingdom of Days*, and *Surprise, Surprise*—and also, in a sense, the more light-hearted *Queen of the Supermarket*. *Outlaw Pete*, for its part, combines Western epic with biblical imagery, while *The Last Carnival* is dedicated to Danny Federici, who died on 17 April 2008. Only the title track and *What Love Can Do* have a more political character, directly descended from the songs on *Devils & Dust* and *Magic*: the former deals with social injustice and an alarming erosion of democracy, while the latter questions the very definition of the word "love" during the Bush years. As for *The Wrestler*, which was added to the album as a hidden song, it is the song that features in the eponymous movie, directed by Darren Aronofsky and starring Mickey Rourke.

Working On a Dream is the fourth and last album Bruce Springsteen recorded with Brendan O'Brien. The producer unquestionably left his mark on it—even more, probably, than on *The Rising*, *Devils & Dust*, and *Magic*. Essentially, it is an ambitious album—over-produced, some might say—with orchestration that could be described as copious (guitars, strings, choruses), as in *My Lucky Day* and *What Love Can Do*. It is certainly an album packed with revisited references. *Outlaw Pete* sounds like a Calexico-style Americana/Tex-Mex song, with a harmonica in the style of Ennio Morricone, while *Good Eye* is a blues number that draws deeply on the Mississippi delta, and *Tomorrow Never Knows* is very much in the spirit of Nashville country pop. Also worthy of mention are *Surprise, Surprise*, a pop song with a Phil Spector-style (or Moby-style) Wall of Sound (see page 69), *Life Itself*, which brings to mind The Byrds' *Eight Miles High*, *This Life*, which is an emphatic tribute to The Beach Boys, and *Kingdom of Days*, which pays homage to the California sound in general. The album draws to a close with two ballads that might well be the finest on this 16th record: *The Last Carnival*, which features a very beautiful melody and choruses expressing all the sadness of a man who has lost someone he loves, and *The Wrestler*, where the most luminous facet of the New Jersey songwriter reappears—that of the folk singer...

Bruce Springsteen and E Street Band at half-time at the Super Bowl, at the Raymond James Stadium, in Tampa, Florida, on 1 February 2009.

Photograph by Danny Clinch on the sleeve of *Working On a Dream*.

The dream becomes reality

Although its release had been announced for 17 November 2008, *Working On a Dream* did not go on sale until January 2009: on 23 January in Germany and Ireland, and on 27 January in the United States and the rest of the world. This time, the critics were fairly divided. Ann Power, writing in the *Los Angeles Times* (26 January 2009), felt that it was a "boisterously scatterbrained"[137] album, and was disappointed that Bruce Springsteen had taken a wrong turn by "recalling the radio hits of his youth and applying their glitter to his template"[137] By contrast, Brian Hiatt of *Rolling Stone* magazine wrote: "*Working On a Dream* is the richest of the three great rock albums Springsteen has made this decade with the E Street Band."[138]

The public agreed more with Brian Hiatt's complimentary view, largely as a result of highly effective promotion: Bruce Springsteen was present at the 66th Golden Globe Awards (11 January) and took part in a concert celebrating the inauguration of Barack Obama (18 January), as well as a concert with the E Street Band, The Miami Horns, and a gospel choir at half-time at the Super Bowl (1 February). In the United States, *Working On a Dream* reached No.1 on 14 February 2009, before being certified a gold record. The album also got to No.1 in the United Kingdom, on 7 February, and stayed there for two weeks, as it did in other European countries, including Belgium, Sweden, Germany, and Spain, as well as in Canada. In France it got to No.2 and sold more than 50,000.

The sleeve

The photograph that appears on the sleeve of *Working On a Dream* was shot by Danny Clinch. Bruce Springsteen is looking down, with a hint of a smile. His hair has been neatly combed, and he is wearing a dark jacket with red accents. Behind him, above the Atlantic Ocean—one assumes the picture was shot on the Jersey Shore—is a cloudy, almost nighttime sky, dotted with stars around a crescent moon. The image has been edited to look like an illustration, almost as if in a graphic novel.

On the back of the sleeve there is a twilight atmosphere, with a tree and bushes in the background, and again those enigmatic red accents.

On the double-page spread inside, Bruce Springsteen is walking in a field, in the middle of nowhere, carrying a guitar whose neck is pointing downward. Solitude, again...

All the photographs inside the album, including those from the booklet—with the exception of the portraits of the E Street Band (which were also by Clinch)—are by Jennifer Tzar, a fashion photographer who also worked for *Rolling Stone* magazine.

The recording

While Springsteen was mixing *Magic* with Brendan O'Brien, in May and June 2007, he wrote *What Love Can Do*, a new song that did not seem to fit the album they were making. However, it gave him the idea for another project, and the

The website Pitchfork listed the visual imagery on the album sleeve of *Working On a Dream* as among the worst of the year 2009 (along with, among others, *Graffiti* by Chris Brown, *21st Century Breakdown* by Green Day, and *Fork in the Road* by Neil Young).

concept of *Working On a Dream* gradually took root—all the more so because songs such as *Girls in Their Summer Clothes*, written toward the end of the work on *Magic*, revived his desire to launch into more pop-oriented, ambitious projects: a kind of orchestral rock. "That brings you to come up with another song," he explained. "And then you go home that night and think, man, I'd really like to make something big, and rich, and romantic, but that carries with it the concerns of somebody at my age. Innocent and kind of knowing at the same time. And take that sound—the sound of which is basically the sound of innocence in those days of The Beach Boys and [Phil] Spector—and take that sound and combine it with my 60 years of experience on the planet Earth. And so you have *Working On a Dream*."[10]

The production method chosen by Brendan O'Brien was identical to the one used for the two preceding albums: in the first instance, Bruce Springsteen, Roy Bittan, Garry Tallent, and Max Weinberg recorded the basic tracks of each song. "We do whatever we want to interpret the song when we cut the basics. He [Bruce] does rely on us for that. But as far as sweetening the tracks [by means of overdubs], he's interested in trying to eke out the song's potential that he hears in his head. Which is evident on this new record. It's almost a little shocking to hear the songs at first, because the album is different than our classic E Street records, which were recorded mostly live."[139]

The rest of the process involved bringing in the other musicians to record the various overdubs. Steve Van Zandt described the method the producer used: "Brendan O'Brien has become his [Bruce's] partner, and by the time I get involved now, it's no longer in the early stages of arrangement and discussion. It's been arranged; the stuff is there. You play whatever they have in mind for you, and you add whatever you have as an idea. I think it's probably the way most normal bands record."[139] The guitarist regarded *Working On a Dream* as the last in a trilogy comprising *The Rising* and *Magic*: "They make sense together in terms of sound, concept, and writing style. The three records have been a projection more toward the pop-rock form—this one more than the other two."[139] To Van Zandt's ears, *Working On a Dream* was a blend of *The River* and The Rolling Stones' *Exile on Main St.*

Workers in the dream factory

Springsteen made this 16th album with the same team who made *Magic*: the same production and technical personnel. He recorded with the E Street Band during breaks on the Magic Tour, from October 2007 to the fall of 2008. This album was also recorded at the Southern Tracks Recording Studio in Atlanta, Georgia, at least for the basics—again, with Nick DiDia at the controls, assisted by Billy Bowers. Then, four more studios were also booked for further recording sessions: Avatar Studios and Clinton Recording Studios in New York, Henson Recording Studios in Hollywood, and Thrill Hill Recording at Colts Neck, New Jersey. The recording engineers were Rick Kwan, Tom Syrowski, and Toby Scott. For mastering, Bob Ludwig was always on the case, at Gateway Mastering in Portland, Maine.

As well as the members of the E Street Band, other musicians lent a helping hand in recording *Working On a Dream*: Soozie Tyrell was always there on violin and backing vocals; Patrick Warren was on keyboards, and Eddie Horst was once again in charge of string arrangements and wind harmonies. The only new arrival was the son of Danny Federici, Jason Federici, who recorded a timid but moving accordion part in *The Last Carnival*, the song written in tribute to his father.

In memory of Danny Federici

As is stated in the sleeve notes to the album, *Working On a Dream* is dedicated to the memory of Danny Federici. Springsteen writes of his friend with warmth and respect, recalling that they had a permanent bond from having shared, every evening at 8 pm, minor miracles onstage. "Of course,

Danny Federici (seen here 17 April 2001, at the Houston Ship Channel, Houston, Texas), to whom Bruce Springsteen dedicated *Working On a Dream.*

we all grow up, and we know 'it's only rock 'n' roll'...but it's not. After a lifetime of watching a man perform his miracle for you, night after night, it feels an awful lot like love."[1]

For his part, Roy Bittan regretted not having realized more clearly to what extent Danny was unique: "We appreciated him, but I think a lot of people didn't realize exactly what he did in the band until it wasn't there. We were always more than the sum of our parts. But when you take one of those parts out, the machine is not working in quite the same way."[140]

As for Clarence Clemons, he remembered Danny as a generous, extraordinary, and uncontrollable man. He recalled one day in particular, when he was sharing a bedroom in Boston with Danny and Springsteen that the mother of an ex-manager had allowed them to use: "Suddenly, Danny sat up in his bed, wide awake, said, 'Semicomasomadoma,' and went back to sleep." [...][140] Clemons and the Boss looked at each other, perplexed. Years later the "Big Man," who had come to visit his ill friend, asked him: "Danny, tell me, before you go, what was that 'Semicomasomadoma' thing?" Clemons laughs. "He didn't tell me. It remains a mystery."[140]

Danny Federici's funeral took place on 21 April 2008 in the Methodist church in Red Bank, in the presence of his entire family, his friends, and the E Street Band.

OUTLAW PETE

Bruce Springsteen / 8'00

For Springsteen Addicts

On 4 November 2014, Springsteen published a book entitled *Outlaw Pete*, which was inspired by his song and illustrated with drawings by Frank Caruso. The hero is a combination of *The Wild, the Innocent, and the E Street Shuffle*, the story of *Brave Cowboy Bill*, and the Spaghetti Westerns that left their mark on the Boss's youth.

Musicians

Bruce Springsteen: vocals, guitar, harmonica, keyboards, percussion, glockenspiel
Patti Scialfa: backing vocals (?)
Steve Van Zandt: guitar, mandolin, backing vocals
Nils Lofgren: guitar, backing vocals
Clarence Clemons: saxophone, backing vocals (?)
Roy Bittan: keyboards
Danny Federici: organ
Garry Tallent: bass
Max Weinberg: drums
Soozie Tyrell: violin, backing vocals (?)
Patrick Warren: keyboards
Edward (Eddie) Horst: string and wind arrangements

Recording

Southern Tracks Recording Studio, Atlanta, Georgia: October 2007 to fall 2008
Avatar Studios, New York: October 2007 to fall 2008
Clinton Recording Studios, New York: October 2007 to fall 2008
Henson Recording Studios, Hollywood: October 2007 to fall 2008
Thrill Hill Recording, Colts Neck, New Jersey: October 2007 to fall 2008

Technical team

Producer: Brendan O'Brien
Recording engineers: Nick DiDia, Bill Bowers (Southern), Toby Scott (Thrill Hill), Tom Syrowski (Clinton and Henson)
Assistants recording engineers: Tom Tapley, Darren Tablan (Southern), Rick Kwan (Avatar), Tim Mitchell (Clinton), Kevin Mills, Derek Karlquist, Paul Lamalfa (Henson)
Mixing: Brendan O'Brien
Mastering: Bob Ludwig (Gateway Mastering, Portland)

Genesis and lyrics

Outlaw Pete is a return to Bruce Springsteen's earliest youth. The song's story is inspired by a book called *Brave Cowboy Bill*, by Kathryn and Byron Jackson, which his mother read to him as a child. To this Springsteen added another world—one not far removed, in truth, and to which he is particularly attached—that of Sergio Leone's and Clint Eastwood's Spaghetti Westerns.

Pete the outlaw "was born a little baby on the Appalachian Trail/At six months old he'd done three months in jail." Then, aged 25, he stole a Mustang. He led the life of a killer and a thief, until he had a vision: that of his own death. It produced a total metamorphosis. He galloped into the West, married a Navajo girl, settled down on a reservation, and became the father of a little girl. But one day he found himself face to face with a bounty hunter. So, he killed him, and fled to the top of a mountain. What became of him? It remains a mystery. The songwriter's message in this tale of the Far West is clear: we cannot escape our destiny; the most we can do is make the best of it.

Outlaw Pete, Springsteen's longest song since *Drive All Night* (on the *The River* album), was first performed live at the Convention Hall, in Asbury Park, on 23 March 2009, then played regularly throughout the Working On a Dream Tour.

Production

Springsteen declared that he had wanted to write a short opera, "[...] something fantastic with a cartoon character, like *Rocky Raccoon*, by The Beatles."[140] Although his hero is unquestionably a cowboy, as in the song by McCartney, the music is rather more inspired by The Beach Boys, at least in its form: *Outlaw Pete* sounds like a series of interwoven songs, in the style of Brian Wilson. Yet the influences are more diverse than they appear: from the introduction, *Friday On My Mind* by the Easybeats comes to mind, while Eddie Horst's cellos provide a movement that is reminiscent of George Young, the Australian group's guitarist. As for the melody of the first two verses, this brings a certain confusion because, apart from a vague resemblance to that of the Easybeats, it more definitely calls to mind the chorus in Kiss's *I Was Made for Lovin' You*. And this is even more striking when the Boss adds vocals between verses (listen at 0'46). However, he dis-

The glam-metal group Kiss. Their hit *I Was Made for Lovin' You* probably influenced Bruce Springsteen when he wrote *Outlaw Pete.*

puted this: "*Outlaw Pete*—people said I was ripping off a Kiss song, actually I thought I was ripping off [Van Dyke Parks and Brian Wilson's] *Heroes and Villains* [laughs]."[10] Gene Simmons, the band's outspoken leader, did not sue Springsteen for plagiarism, simply because he had always liked him.

Although the song consists of a series of different sections, the same basic melody is developed throughout *Outlaw Pete*—with the exception of certain instrumental parts, such as the motif played by the string ensemble just before the last verse (from 4'58). In order to produce this long musical picture, lasting more than eight minutes, Brendan O'Brien employed a very precise technique: "We actually cut it in pieces, one step at a time," he explained. "In Bruce's mind, it was 'Let's make every moment as interesting as we can.'"[141] Thus, the musicians recorded the basic tracks for the different sections of the song, one after the other. Only once these were put together were the additional overdubs recorded. This way of working may be surprising, for the group had already recorded long pieces in one go, such as *Jungleland* in 1975 (9'33 in length). But times and techniques had changed, and, despite the help of computers, it was now easier to proceed in stages—at least as far as O'Brien's approach was concerned.

It is difficult to pick out the different instruments that make up the song precisely, as the producer had a vision fairly similar to that of Phil Spector with his Wall of Sound (see page 69). Nevertheless, multiple keyboards can be heard (piano, organ, tack piano, etc.), as well as a multitude of acoustic and electric guitars, numerous percussion instruments (glockenspiel, tambourine, shaker, rattle, and so forth), not forgetting the strings and wind harmonies arranged by Eddie Horst and the superb rhythm section of Max Weinberg and Garry Tallent. The Boss's lead vocals are excellent, with occasional hints of Roger Waters in *Vera* on *The Wall* (for example, listen around 6'23); perhaps his voice is a little too compressed, and slightly under-mixed, to allow all the nuances of his performance to be audible. Also, he does not hesitate to turn to his harmonica for some Ennio Morricone-style sequences, with reverb and twanging guitar (from 5'35, for example).

But what were the reasons that drove Springsteen to place such a long musical picture at the beginning of the album? It is all the more surprising because O'Brien was apparently against the idea. It appears that he sought to embark on a new musical adventure, far removed from everything he had done before. By making it the first track on the album, he was making *Outlaw Pete* into a sort of artistic manifesto. This unquestionably required courage, and he was right to do it.

LONG-PLAYING SONGS

Although *Outlaw Pete* is one of Bruce Springsteen's longest songs, several of the Boss's studio recordings last longer than eight minutes: *New York City Serenade* (9'56), *Jungleland* (9'33), *Drive All Night* (8'26), and, from the outtakes of the *Tracks* box set, *Thundercrack* (8'25).

MY LUCKY DAY

Bruce Springsteen / 4'00

> **For Springsteen Addicts**
> Like *Born to Run, My Lucky Day* features in the American version of the video game *Guitar Hero: World Tour*, from the company Activision Blizzard.

Musicians
Bruce Springsteen: vocals, guitar, percussion
Steve Van Zandt: guitar, vocal harmonies
Nils Lofgren: guitar
Clarence Clemons: saxophone
Roy Bittan: keyboards
Danny Federici: organ
Garry Tallent: bass
Max Weinberg: drums

Recording
Southern Tracks Recording Studio, Atlanta, Georgia: October 2007 to fall 2008
Avatar Studios, New York: October 2007 to fall 2008
Clinton Recording Studios, New York: October 2007 to fall 2008
Henson Recording Studios, Hollywood: October 2007 to fall 2008
Thrill Hill Recording, Colts Neck, New Jersey: October 2007 to fall 2008

Technical team
Producer: Brendan O'Brien
Recording engineers: Nick DiDia, Bill Bowers (Southern), Toby Scott (Thrill Hill), Tom Syrowski (Clinton & Henson)
Assistant recording engineers: Tom Tapley, Darren Tablan (Southern), Rick Kwan (Avatar), Tim Mitchell (Clinton), Kevin Mills, Derek Karlquist, Paul Lamalfa (Henson)
Mixing: Brendan O'Brien
Mastering: Bob Ludwig (Gateway Mastering, Portland)

> **ALL BECAUSE OF A TATTOO**
> On 30 June 2013, as he was about to perform *Thunder Road* before an audience at Queen Elizabeth Olympic Park, in London, the Boss caught sight of a little girl perched on her father's shoulders—he had a tattoo with the words: "You're my lucky day." So, he immediately changed his plan, and played an acoustic version of *My Lucky Day* for them.

Genesis and lyrics

My Lucky Day is one of the first songs Bruce Springsteen wrote for what would become *Working On a Dream*. He composed the song in May or June 2007, while mixing *Magic* in Atlanta with Brendan O'Brien. It is also the first love song on the album. Everything seems to be falling apart around the narrator, as in this "room where fortune falls." His loneliness "In the dark of this exile" is ended thanks to this woman whom he loves, who is his "lucky day." She stops him from foundering and enables him to bear "the burdens of the day." In return, he brings her comfort: "I have waited at your side/ I've counted the tears you've cried." A love story like countless others and, one might logically assume listening to those words, that it is the story of Bruce Springsteen and Patti Scialfa.

My Lucky Day is the second song from *Working On a Dream* that was available to download from amazon.com on 1 December 2008. It came with a video which showed Bruce Springsteen arranging and recording the song. It was first performed live on 23 March 2009 at the Convention Hall, in Asbury Park, but has rarely been played since then.

Production

What else can one say about *My Lucky Day* other than that Springsteen has written a rock song of ferocious energy? Unusually, all the band's members are together in the studio to record the basic track, and the bond they share is palpable. Each contributes his part with vigor, the hardest-hitting being unquestionably Max Weinberg, with his explosive, savage drumming—as requested by the Boss.

The piece starts with the song's riff, played by Steve Van Zandt, with a very garage-rock saturated sound. The songwriter then takes up the same tune with the lead vocals, in an extremely powerful voice. Once again, the Boss appears to have drawn inspiration from other musicians, in this case the chorus of AC/DC's *You Shook Me All Night Long*. But he has perfectly adapted this borrowing to his personal style, to create something that clearly bears his hallmark. This rock number also appeals by virtue of the vocal harmonies of "Miami Steve," whose piercing voice is perfectly in tune with Springsteen's. Finally, there is Clarence Clemons with his tenor saxophone, delivering a superb, incandescent, passionate solo (at 2'17).

WORKING ON A DREAM

Bruce Springsteen / 3'30

Musicians

Bruce Springsteen: vocals, guitar, keyboards, percussion, glockenspiel
Patti Scialfa: backing vocals
Steve Van Zandt: guitar, backing vocals
Nils Lofgren: guitar, backing vocals
Clarence Clemons: saxophone, backing vocals
Roy Bittan: keyboards
Danny Federici: organ
Garry Tallent: bass
Max Weinberg: drums
Soozie Tyrell: violin (?), backing vocals

Recording

Southern Tracks Recording Studio, Atlanta, Georgia: October 2007 to fall 2008
Avatar Studios, New York: October 2007 to fall 2008
Clinton Recording Studios, New York: October 2007 to fall 2008
Henson Recording Studios, Hollywood: October 2007 to fall 2008
Thrill Hill Recording, Colts Neck, New Jersey: October 2007 to fall 2008

Technical team

Producer: Brendan O'Brien
Recording engineers: Nick DiDia, Bill Bowers (Southern), Toby Scott (Thrill Hill), Tom Syrowski (Clinton & Henson)
Assistant recording engineers: Tom Tapley, Darren Tablan (Southern), Rick Kwan (Avatar), Tim Mitchell (Clinton), Kevin Mills, Derek Karlquist, Paul Lamalfa (Henson)
Mixing: Brendan O'Brien
Mastering: Bob Ludwig (Gateway Mastering, Portland)

For Springsteen Addicts

Working On a Dream was released as a single on 24 November 2008, and was then free to download on iTunes and brucespringsteen.net on the same day. From the following day, and until 9 December, the song was paid-only, exclusively on iTunes.

Genesis and lyrics

Working On a Dream dates from the summer of 2008 and is one of the six songs that Bruce Springsteen performed at the Change We Need Rally with Barack and Michelle Obama on 2 November 2008 in Cleveland, Ohio—two days before the presidential election. Initially, it was not, strictly speaking, a political song, but rather a philosophical reflection, the description of a dream that would not come true unless one worked at it. "That was just the simple idea of effort—the ongoing daily effort to build something," Springsteen explained to journalist David Fricke, "and that you can't give up. I write my songs. I go around the world to sing 'em, about a particular place that I have imagined, that I have hopes is real. I don't see that often. A lot of what I see is the opposite—less economic justice, democracy eroded."[140] It was only after Barack Obama's election victory, and in the light of the hopes it raised, that *Working On a Dream* became emblematic of a new America.

"I'm working on a dream/And our love will make it real someday," sings Bruce Springsteen. *Working On a Dream* is also, and above all, about love's triumph in a hostile world, "a Pete Seeger work song sweetened with the mid-Sixties Roy Orbison,"[140] as David Fricke rightly wrote.

Production

In *Working On a Dream* the songwriter explores a musical style that is a cross between The Beach Boys—listen to the verse choruses (for example, at 1'10)—and Roy Orbison, whose influence on the writing and the singing of the choruses is obvious. The arrangement is rich, being colored by a multitude of instruments, notably handbells, a glockenspiel, very probably a saturated bass (at 1'20, on the left), guitars, keyboards, and a saxophone, played by Clarence Clemons as an accompaniment to the instrumental break, in which the Boss can be heard whistling the tune (listen from 1'44). As for Roy Bittan, he recalled of his piano part: "*Working On a Dream*—there's a spot in the chorus when he sings 'Working on a dream,' a little space immediately after that where I go down to the bottom of the piano and do a double hit on the real low end. It seemed to work itself into the final arrangement, almost as a tiny hook."[139]

Bruce Springsteen in Vancouver on 26 November 2012 during the Wrecking Ball World Tour, with Cindy Mizelle who may be the mysterious voice in *Queen of the Supermarket.*

QUEEN OF THE SUPERMARKET

Bruce Springsteen / 4'39

Musicians

Bruce Springsteen: vocals, guitar, keyboards, percussion, glockenspiel
Patti Scialfa: backing vocals
Steve Van Zandt: guitar, backing vocals
Nils Lofgren: guitar, backing vocals
Clarence Clemons: backing vocals
Roy Bittan: keyboards
Danny Federici: organ
Garry Tallent: bass
Max Weinberg: drums
Soozie Tyrell: violin, backing vocals

Recording

Southern Tracks Recording Studio, Atlanta, Georgia: October 2007 to fall 2008
Avatar Studios, New York: October 2007 to fall 2008
Clinton Recording Studios, New York: October 2007 to fall 2008
Henson Recording Studios, Hollywood: October 2007 to fall 2008
Thrill Hill Recording, Colts Neck, New Jersey: October 2007 to fall 2008

Technical team

Producer: Brendan O'Brien
Recording engineers: Nick DiDia, Bill Bowers (Southern), Toby Scott (Thrill Hill), Tom Syrowski (Clinton & Henson)
Assistant recording engineers: Tom Tapley, Darren Tablan (Southern), Rick Kwan (Avatar), Tim Mitchell (Clinton), Kevin Mills, Derek Karlquist, Paul Lamalfa (Henson)
Mixing: Brendan O'Brien
Mastering: Bob Ludwig (Gateway Mastering, Portland)

A MYSTERIOUS VOICE

A voice that is not Springsteen's can be heard singing the chorus, at 2'59 precisely. It is hard to know to whom this voice belongs, as no information has come to light to date. Of course, Steve Van Zandt, Patti Scialfa, and Soozie Tyrell come to mind, but so does Cindy Mizelle, the highly talented backing vocalist of the E Street Band. For all that, it is not certain that she is the one heard on the record.

Genesis and lyrics

In an interview with *Observer Music Monthly* in January 2009, Bruce Springsteen explained how he got the idea for this song after visiting a grocery store that had just opened near where he was living, in New Jersey: "Patti and I would go down, and I remember walking through the aisles—I hadn't been in one in a while—and I thought this place is spectacular...it's a fantasy land!"[142]

In this land of a thousand fantasies, Bruce Springsteen has imagined a tender romance. The narrator goes from one display to another with his shopping cart—where "the cool promise of ecstasy fills the air"—but he has eyes only for a beautiful assistant whose boredom is barely concealed. "I'm in love with the queen of the supermarket": the words are clear enough. And, at night, he prays for the courage to declare his love to her.

Queen of the Supermarket is therefore not a song that denounces the excesses of consumerism, exalted as the supreme guiding principle. It is not simply a love story either. What is also clear is that grocery stores—places full of dreams—can give an almost sensual pleasure.

Production

From the very first notes of the song, the listener is surprised by the romantic atmosphere. Acoustic guitar, organ, piano, glockenspiel—all the Springsteen ingredients are present in *Queen of the Supermarket.* One might have expected a muscular rock number, but the Boss opted to express the dreams and emotions triggered by this grocery store, newly opened near his home, through the most lyrical music. When he starts the first verse, the dichotomy between the lyrics and the music is striking, all the more since the string pads, supported by Soozie Tyrell's violin, reinforce this impression (listen at 1'03). The songwriter leans toward a performance in the style of Roy Orbison and does not hesitate to sprinkle the song with Spector-like touches, such as the tambourine, which could have come straight out of a Crystals record (around 1'10), or Beatles-style touches, with the very Fab Four choruses in the bridge (listen from 2'06). But the biggest surprise comes at the end of the song when, after the last verse, a complete rhythmic and harmonic break plunges *Queen of the Supermarket* into a totally dreamlike atmosphere (from 3'17), which, it must be admitted, does not really seem in keeping with the lyrics.

WHAT LOVE CAN DO

Bruce Springsteen / 2'56

Musicians
Bruce Springsteen: vocals, guitar, harmonica, percussion
Patti Scialfa: backing vocals
Steve Van Zandt: guitar, backing vocals
Nils Lofgren: guitar, backing vocals
Clarence Clemons: backing vocals
Roy Bittan: keyboards
Danny Federici: organ
Garry Tallent: bass
Max Weinberg: drums
Soozie Tyrell: backing vocals

Recording
Southern Tracks Recording Studio, Atlanta, Georgia: October 2007 to fall 2008
Avatar Studios, New York: October 2007 to fall 2008
Clinton Recording Studios, New York: October 2007 to fall 2008
Henson Recording Studios, Hollywood: October 2007 to fall 2008
Thrill Hill Recording, Colts Neck, New Jersey: October 2007 to fall 2008

Technical team
Producer: Brendan O'Brien
Recording engineers: Nick DiDia, Bill Bowers (Southern), Toby Scott (Thrill Hill), Tom Syrowski (Clinton & Henson)
Assistant recording engineers: Tom Tapley, Darren Tablan (Southern), Rick Kwan (Avatar), Tim Mitchell (Clinton), Kevin Mills, Derek Karlquist, Paul Lamalfa (Henson)
Mixing: Brendan O'Brien
Mastering: Bob Ludwig (Gateway Mastering, Portland)

Genesis and lyrics

What Love Can Do is one of the songs that dates back to the spring of 2008, when *Magic* was being mixed in Atlanta. "It was sort of a 'love in the time of Bush' meditation," the songwriter wrote on his website, brucespringsteen.net. "It was a great track but felt more like a first song of a new record rather than something that would fit on *Magic*."[143] He added: "And usually I don't write that quickly. But that night I went back to my hotel in Atlanta and over the next week, I wrote several songs (*This Life*, *My Lucky Day*, *Life Itself*, along with *Good Eye*, and *Tomorrow Never Knows*) that formed the beginnings of our new album."[143]

In this song, which clearly references The Byrds musically, the narrator addresses his beloved. Love is the sole remedy for the ills of the world—a world in which "it's blood for blood and an eye for an eye" and where "our memory lay corrupted and our city lay dry." He admits he cannot stop the rain, or a train "When it comes crashing through," but he assures her that he can show her "what love can do." Love lightens our burden, for we all bear the mark of Cain—that is, the seal of our own perdition.

Curiously, Bruce Springsteen has played *What Love Can Do* live only once, at the Wachovia Spectrum in Philadelphia, Pennsylvania, on 14 October 2009.

Production

What Love Can Do is a very fine rock number that is driven by the excellent Max Weinberg and Garry Tallent. Acoustic guitars essentially give the piece its tone color, which is in the spirit of country rock. However, the Boss's tune sounds rather like the British pop of the 1960s, with a touch of The Kinks and a coating of The Byrds (in the vocal harmonies). One of the song's most interesting passages is perhaps its bridge—one of the songwriter's specialities—as Brendan O'Brien explained in 2007: "Bruce is a great bridge or great middle-8 writer [...] A lot of these things he was writing for the bridges in my mind were perfect opportunities to actually have a little 40-second song... in the middle of the song."[117]

An instrumental section follows this sequence, with a solo delivered both by the Boss's saturated harmonica and by several lead guitars, particularly that of Steve Van Zandt (at 1'36).

Springsteen felt that *What Love Can Do* was not a good fit for *Magic*, but this was probably on account of the lyrics, not the music, which is in keeping with the spirit of this album.

THIS LIFE

Bruce Springsteen / 4'30

Musicians
Bruce Springsteen: vocals, guitars, harmonica, keyboards, percussion
Patti Scialfa: backing vocals
Steve Van Zandt: guitar, backing vocals
Nils Lofgren: guitar, backing vocals
Clarence Clemons: saxophone, backing vocals
Roy Bittan: keyboards
Danny Federici: organ
Garry Tallent: bass
Max Weinberg: drums
Soozie Tyrell: violin (?), backing vocals
Patrick Warren: keyboards

Recording
Southern Tracks Recording Studios, Atlanta, Georgia: October 2007 to fall 2008
Avatar Studios, New York: October 2007 to fall 2008
Clinton Recording Studios, New York: October 2007 to fall 2008
Henson Recording Studios, Hollywood: October 2007 to fall 2008
Thrill Hill Recording, Colts Neck, New Jersey: October 2007 to fall 2008

Technical team
Producer: Brendan O'Brien
Recording engineers: Nick DiDia, Bill Bowers (Southern), Toby Scott (Thrill Hill), Tom Syrowski (Clinton & Henson)
Assistant recording engineers: Tom Tapley, Darren Tablan (Southern), Rick Kwan (Avatar), Tim Mitchell (Clinton), Kevin Mills, Derek Karlquist, Paul Lamalfa (Henson)
Mixing: Brendan O'Brien
Mastering: Bob Ludwig (Gateway Mastering, Portland)

Genesis and lyrics

Springsteen first sketched out *This Life* at the end of the mixing for the *Magic* album, in May or June 2008. As David Fricke pointed out in *Rolling Stone* magazine: "Most of *Working On a Dream* takes place far from newspaper headlines, in darkened bedrooms, under starlight. There is ecstasy and pleading, promises made and broken (...)."[140]

This song is most certainly one of ecstasy, of supreme adoration. When the beloved appears, darkness flees and millions of stars twinkle. The narrator is madly in love, and has been for some time: "This life, this life and then the next/With you I have been blessed" and there's "A beauty in the neighborhood/This lonely planet never looked so good." Has there ever been a more passionate declaration of love? One that Bruce Springsteen is making, in all probability, to Patti Scialfa, who has shared his life for almost 30 years. To date, Bruce Springsteen has played *This Life* live only three times. The first was at Asbury Park on 23 March 2009.

Production

Who exactly was Springsteen thinking about when he wrote the intro to *This Life*? In all probability it was The Beach Boys. On listening, one has the impression of hearing something out of *Pet Sounds*. Indeed, there's the same kind of percussion, similar choruses (though not to the same standard...), an organ played in the style of Brian Wilson, and a bass guitar that bears the hallmark of the extraordinary Carol Kaye. The rest of the song is different, but still displays various influences—every listener can make their own connections: to The Walker Brothers, ELO, George Harrison, and so forth. In praising his beloved, the Boss sings with ardor, his voice doubled and harmonized with, riding a wave of interwoven instruments from which one really stands out: Clarence Clemons's saxophone, as it plays a clear solo (at 3'51). The end of the song marks a return to the world of The Beach Boys, with choruses that answer each other in a sort of sugar-coated attempt at counterpoint—the specialty of the leader of The Beach Boys, whose characteristic falsetto voice does not fail to make an appearance (listen at 3'34).

This Life is a fine ballad, but above all it gives the impression that Springsteen has sought to indulge himself, completely without inhibitions, without worrying about the E Street Band's musical identity. After all, there is nothing wrong with that.

Bruce Springsteen at the Pinkpop Festival in the Netherlands, on 30 May 2009, with Jay Weinberg (son of Max), who was present for some live performances of *Good Eye*.

GOOD EYE

Bruce Springsteen / 3'00

Musicians

Bruce Springsteen: vocals, guitar, harmonica, percussion
Patti Scialfa: backing vocals (?)
Steve Van Zandt: mandolin, backing vocals
Nils Lofgren: guitar, backing vocals
Clarence Clemons: backing vocals (?)
Roy Bittan: keyboards
Danny Federici: organ
Garry Tallent: bass
Max Weinberg: drums
Soozie Tyrell: violin (?), backing vocals (?)

Recording

Southern Tracks Recording Studios, Atlanta, Georgia: October 2007 to fall 2008
Avatar Studios, New York: October 2007 to fall 2008
Clinton Recording Studios, New York: October 2007 to fall 2008
Henson Recording Studios, Hollywood: October 2007 to fall 2008
Thrill Hill Recording, Colts Neck, New Jersey: October 2007 to fall 2008

Technical team

Producer: Brendan O'Brien
Recording engineers: Nick DiDia, Bill Bowers (Southern), Toby Scott (Thrill Hill), Tom Syrowski (Clinton & Henson)
Assistant recording engineers: Tom Tapley, Darren Tablan (Southern), Rick Kwan (Avatar), Tim Mitchell (Clinton), Kevin Mills, Derek Karlquist, Paul Lamalfa (Henson)
Mixing: Brendan O'Brien
Mastering: Bob Ludwig (Gateway Mastering, Portland)

For Springsteen Addicts

Jay Weinberg, Max Weinberg's son, played the drums in *Good Eye* when it was first performed live on 23 March 2009 at the Convention Hall in Asbury Park, New Jersey.

Genesis and lyrics

Here is another song that Bruce Springsteen wrote at the end of the making of *Magic*. Whether it comes from the Mississippi delta or the clubs and studios of Chicago, blues is immortal. That is what the Boss's music is conveying here. The lyrics sound like a declaration of love, in the manner of other songs on *Working On a Dream*. The narrator reveals that he possesses "all the earthly riches, I had each and every one," but in the end all that counts for nothing alongside the love he feels for a woman.

The is also chorus in the old blues tradition, for it is well known that bluesmen have always liked a double entendre. "I had my good eye to the dark and my blind eye to the sun." What is Bruce Springsteen saying here? Maybe that for a long time the narrator has sought happiness where there was none to be found, when all the while it was right in front of him?

Bruce Springsteen has played *Good Eye* live only three times. The first was at the Convention Hall, in Asbury Park, on 23 March 2009. This is surprising, as this song could have achieved its full potential onstage in the same way as another blues song in the Springsteen repertoire, *Ain't Got You* (on the *Tunnel of Love* album).

Production

Springsteen has never flirted with Chicago blues, except in the very fine song *Good Eye*. The piece begins with a saturated harmonica in the manner of Little Walter, calling to mind, to some extent, that of Mick Jagger on The Rolling Stones' album *Blue & Lonesome* (2016). The Boss has recorded a loop with the "harp" (the bluesman's name for the harmonica), which comes back throughout the introduction, accompanied by an electric guitar featuring the obligatory tremolo (on the right). As the drums and bass come in, a tambourine, maracas, and Steve Van Zandt's mandolin provide support. On the vocals side, the Boss uses his most raucous voice to record his part, the effect heightened by the same saturation used for the harmonica. The instrumental bridge brings an atmosphere that is more psychedelic rock than blues, with melodious choruses that contrast with the song's supercharged ambience (listen at 1'09).

Good Eye ends with an instrumental coda punctuated by breaks, where the mandolin and harmonica also feature. One criticism: the rhythm section of Max Weinberg and Garry Tallent noticeably lack groove; surprising coming from them.

TOMORROW NEVER KNOWS

Bruce Springsteen / 2'13

Although The Beatles' *Tomorrow Never Knows* was written by John Lennon in 1966, the song's title is an expression invented by Ringo Starr, who had a gift for coming up with new words or curious phrases, such the famous "A hard day's night."

Musicians
Bruce Springsteen: vocals, guitar
Patti Scialfa: backing vocals
Steve Van Zandt: guitar
Nils Lofgren: guitar
Roy Bittan: keyboards (?)
Danny Federici: organ (?)
Garry Tallent: bass
Max Weinberg: drums
Soozie Tyrell: violin, backing vocals
Patrick Warren: keyboards
Eddie Horst: string arrangements

Recording
Southern Tracks Recording Studios, Atlanta, Georgia: October 2007 to fall 2008
Avatar Studios, New York: October 2007 to fall 2008
Clinton Recording Studios, New York: October 2007 to fall 2008
Henson Recording Studios, Hollywood: October 2007 to fall 2008
Thrill Hill Recording, Colts Neck, New Jersey: October 2007 to fall 2008

Technical team
Producer: Brendan O'Brien
Recording engineers: Nick DiDia, Bill Bowers (Southern), Toby Scott (Thrill Hill), Tom Syrowski (Clinton & Henson)
Assistant recording engineers: Tom Tapley, Darren Tablan (Southern), Rick Kwan (Avatar), Tim Mitchell (Clinton), Kevin Mills, Derek Karlquist, Paul Lamalfa (Henson)
Mixing: Brendan O'Brien
Mastering: Bob Ludwig (Gateway Mastering, Portland)

Genesis and lyrics

Dating from spring 2007, and the final phase of the making of the *Magic* album in Atlanta, *Tomorrow Never Knows* is not to be confused with John Lennon's masterpiece, which brings the album *Revolver* to a close. Musically, it is indeed a long way from the psychedelic avant-garde of The Beatles. The reference here is rather to country music—the Nashville sound—as in Dylan's album *Nashville Skyline*.

As the title indicates, the words of the song express a doubt, or rather, a call to live for the present moment—specifically, the love that unites a couple—given that the future is unknown. "You and me we been standing here my dear/Waiting for our time to come." Is this "time" the arrival of death? In all probability. The narrator then plunges back to a carefree, happy past: "In the field your long hair flowed/Down by the Tildenberry tracks/There 'neath the water tower/I carried you on my back." What Bruce Springsteen is trying to say is that we should take advantage of the good times that come our way. "Well he who waits for the day's riches will be lost/In the whispering tide," he sings in the last verse, by way of a moral.

Tomorrow Never Knows has never been played live. Is The Beatles reference too heavy-handed?

Production

Obviously, to a listener who knows The Beatles' *Tomorrow Never Knows*, with its tape loops of effects featuring reversed sounds and its highly compressed drums, Springsteen's composition comes as something of a surprise. Midway between Bob Dylan and Johnny Cash, the Boss's song is a pleasant country ballad, which opens with two strummed acoustic guitars, their strings muffled. The song then starts in earnest with the entry of Max Weinberg's drums, played with brushes, Garry Tallent's bass guitar, and a slide guitar, probably played by Nils Lofgren. The songwriter begins his lead vocals with a soft, almost murmured voice—the opposite of his savage performance in *Good Eye*. The superb strings arranged by Eddie Horst come in at the third verse (from 0'52). Women's voices then come in to harmonize with the Boss, at the end of the following verse, before Soozie Tyrell delivers a violin solo accompanied by a second slide guitar and a sort of organ sound that is totally deformed by a flanger/chorus effect.

LIFE ITSELF

Bruce Springsteen / 4'00

Musicians

Bruce Springsteen: vocals, guitar, percussion
Patti Scialfa: backing vocals
Steve Van Zandt: guitar
Nils Lofgren: guitar
Roy Bittan: keyboards
Danny Federici: organ
Garry Tallent: bass
Max Weinberg: drums
Soozie Tyrell: violin (?), backing vocals

Recording

Southern Tracks Recording Studios, Atlanta, Georgia: October 2007 to fall 2008
Avatar Studios, New York: October 2007 to fall 2008
Clinton Recording Studios, New York: October 2007 to fall 2008
Henson Recording Studios, Hollywood: October 2007 to fall 2008
Thrill Hill Recording, Colts Neck, New Jersey: October 2007 to fall 2008

Technical team

Producer: Brendan O'Brien
Recording engineers: Nick DiDia, Bill Bowers (Southern), Toby Scott (Thrill Hill), Tom Syrowski (Clinton & Henson)
Assistant recording engineers: Tom Tapley, Darren Tablan (Southern), Rick Kwan (Avatar), Tim Mitchell (Clinton), Kevin Mills, Derek Karlquist, Paul Lamalfa (Henson)
Mixing: Brendan O'Brien
Mastering: Bob Ludwig (Gateway Mastering, Portland)

For Springsteen Addicts

Life Itself was the fourth song on *Working On a Dream* to be released as a single in the United States, available only for download on amazon.com, on 28 December 2008.

Pages 546–547 Bruce Springsteen in his New Jersey studio, photographed by Danny Clinch for *Mojo* magazine in 2010.

Genesis and lyrics

Life Itself, which also dates from May to June 2007 in Atlanta, is musically one of the most singular songs in Bruce Springsteen's repertoire. Its atmosphere is, in fact, rather psychedelic—at least for a musician who is the blue-collar worker's singer par excellence. It thus takes a new musical direction, but the theme is one that recurs in the work of the New Jersey songwriter: the disintegration of a couple over time.

Life Itself begins with a meeting "down in the valley, where the wine of love and destruction flowed" and "where flowers of temptation grow." A love story was born: "it was you and nothing else", a woman of many secrets who "squandered...[her] beauty and [her] wealth." Then the years passed, and with them a certain monotony and then a lack of understanding—and more, perhaps—set in. *Life Itself* is the admission of failure in a couple's life together, which leads inexorably to mental confusion.

Production

It is quite difficult to describe the style of *Life Itself,* as it is so totally original is its blend of genres. Just as many songs on the album clearly display their sources of inspiration, so this superb psychedelic, alternative, country-rock ballad is an oddity in the Boss's oeuvre.

The song begins with a combination of acoustic guitars and saturated electric guitars. Max Weinberg provides a cross-stick rhythm, supported by a tambourine. Brendan O'Brien's skill and production are, on this occasion, truly precious: they allow him to subtly fuse tradition and modernity.

Springsteen begins his lead vocals in an intimate, confidential, and astonishingly clear voice. Garry Tallent's bass guitar supports it, like a pedal point. The various instruments, particularly the guitars, amplify a sensation of permanent oppression. "This thing is based around its retaining tension, so you've got to be careful. It's all sort of a taut wire, you know?"[5] the Boss explained to his musicians. Influences are inescapable: Nils Lofgren takes an excellent guitar solo, played back through a reverse tape effect—a device first used by The Beatles on *Revolver* in 1966 (listen at 1'54 and 3'34).

Life Itself is one of the most effective tracks on the album, and one of Springsteen's most surprising songs.

KINGDOM OF DAYS

Bruce Springsteen / 4'02

Musicians
Bruce Springsteen: chant, guitar, percussion, glockenspiel
Patti Scialfa: backing vocals
Steve Van Zandt: guitar, backing vocals (?)
Nils Lofgren: guitar, backing vocals (?)
Clarence Clemons: backing vocals (?)
Roy Bittan: keyboards
Danny Federici: organ
Garry Tallent: bass
Max Weinberg: drums
Soozie Tyrell: violin, backing vocals (?)
Eddie Horst: string arrangements

Recording
Southern Tracks Recording Studios, Atlanta, Georgia: October 2007 to fall 2008
Avatar Studios, New York: October 2007 to fall 2008
Clinton Recording Studios, New York: October 2007 to fall 2008
Henson Recording Studios, Hollywood: October 2007 to fall 2008
Thrill Hill Recording, Colts Neck, New Jersey: October 2007 to fall 2008

Technical team
Producer: Brendan O'Brien
Recording engineers: Nick DiDia, Bill Bowers (Southern), Toby Scott (Thrill Hill), Tom Syrowski (Clinton & Henson)
Assistant recording engineers: Tom Tapley, Darren Tablan (Southern), Rick Kwan (Avatar), Tim Mitchell (Clinton), Kevin Mills, Derek Karlquist, Paul Lamalfa (Henson)
Mixing: Brendan O'Brien
Mastering: Bob Ludwig (Gateway Mastering, Portland)

Genesis and lyrics

Here is another declaration of love, one that is all the more authentic in that it directly involves Bruce Springsteen and Patti Scialfa. "Patti and I have been together for 20 years," he told David Fricke at *Rolling Stone* magazine after *Working On a Dream* was released. He continued: "*Kingdom of Days* is something you write after having a long, long life with somebody, where you see how much you've built together. You also see its finiteness, the passing of the day's light on your partner's face. The song is about taking the fear and terror out of those things."[140]

The lyrics of *Kingdom of Days* show great elegance in the writing. They demonstrate that love felt for another is stronger than the passage of time. The first few verses, particularly the first sentence ("With you I don't hear the minutes ticking by"), bear witness to this. At the end of the song, the man and the woman have, naturally, become aware that the years have passed, but they don't care: "And I count my blessings that you're mine for always/We laugh beneath the covers/and count the wrinkles and the grays."

Kingdom of Days is one of the most beautiful songs about the beauty of true love transcending the ravages of time. Bruce Springsteen performed it regularly during the first part of the Working On a Dream Tour.

Production

This subtle ballad marks another plunge into romanticism. The tone is set from the start: Soozie Tyrell plays a delicate melodic line on the violin, supported by an acoustic guitar, bass guitar, and piano. Max Weinberg then joins in with the snare drum. Springsteen sings with conviction, his voice both firm and tender.

Other instruments come in as the song develops: electric guitars, an organ, a glockenspiel, and a tambourine, not forgetting Eddie Horst's strings, which coat the song in syrupy lines. A guitar solo strikes a more rock-like note, although it, too, is supported by the strings.

Max Weinberg recalled the perfect unity among the musicians in the studio: "My son, Jay, who is a drummer, came to the session in New York where we did *Kingdom of Days*. He was in the control room. He was amazed at how it sounded like a record as we were playing it..."[139] As for Garry Tallent, he was straight to the point: "One of the best songs he's ever written."[5]

SURPRISE, SURPRISE

Bruce Springsteen / 3'24

> **For Springsteen Addicts**
>
> Steve Van Zandt was treated to the surprise of being presented, onstage, with an enormous birthday cake on the occasion of his 59th birthday, on 22 November 2009, at the HSBC Arena, in Buffalo, New York State. Once the candles had been blown out, the Boss and the E Street Band launched into *Surprise, Surprise!*

Musicians

Bruce Springsteen: vocals, guitar, keyboards, percussion
Patti Scialfa: backing vocals
Steve Van Zandt: guitar, backing vocals (?)
Nils Lofgren: guitar
Clarence Clemons: saxophone (?)
Roy Bittan: keyboards
Danny Federici: organ
Garry Tallent: bass
Max Weinberg: drums
Soozie Tyrell: violin, backing vocals
Eddie Horst: string arrangements
The band: handclaps

Recording

Southern Tracks Recording Studios, Atlanta, Georgia: October 2007 to fall 2008
Avatar Studios, New York: October 2007 to fall 2008
Clinton Recording Studios, New York: October 2007 to fall 2008
Henson Recording Studios, Hollywood: October 2007 to fall 2008
Thrill Hill Recording, Colts Neck, New Jersey: October 2007 to fall 2008

Technical team

Producer: Brendan O'Brien
Recording engineers: Nick DiDia, Bill Bowers (Southern), Toby Scott (Thrill Hill), Tom Syrowski (Clinton & Henson)
Assistant recording engineers: Tom Tapley, Darren Tablan (Southern), Rick Kwan (Avatar), Tim Mitchell (Clinton), Kevin Mills, Derek Karlquist, Paul Lamalfa (Henson)
Mixing: Brendan O'Brien
Mastering: Bob Ludwig (Gateway Mastering, Portland)

Genesis and lyrics

Having previously borrowed a title from The Beatles (*Tomorrow Never Knows*), here Springsteen raids the repertoire of The Rolling Stones during the Brian Jones' era (*Surprise, Surprise* was written by Mick Jagger and Keith Richards for the American album *Now!*, released in 1965). There is another musical reference, too: *Surprise, Surprise* seems to be a second nod (after *What Love Can Do*) to the psychedelic folk rock of The Byrds and, in particular, to their third album, *Fifth Dimension* (1966).

The lyrics, though, bear no relation to the glorious 1960s. This is a day for celebration: "Well today is your birthday, we traveled so far we two/So let's blow out the candles on your cake and we'll raise a glass or two," the narrator says to his wife. A little later, when the party's over, his words become more tender: "May the rising sun caress and bless your soul for all your life." *Surprise, Surprise*, therefore, is another song that deals with profound love standing the test of time.

Bruce Springsteen has performed *Surprise, Surprise* only around a dozen times, between 2009 (in Asbury Park) and 2014 (in Hershey, Pennsylvania).

Production

Surprise, Surprise begins with a Byrds-like introduction—12-string electric and acoustic guitars, and chords played in the style of Roger McGuinn; the Boss is paying tribute to one of the bands he admired in his youth. The chorus that follows is in an enjoyable pop vein, a trip back in time that is quite surprising coming from the creator of *Streets of Philadelphia*. It is true that *Born to Run* flirted with Phil Spector's Wall of Sound (see page 69), but never before had the songwriter from New Jersey gone to such lengths in paying tribute to the 1960s. And it was the right thing to do, for *Surprise, Surprise* is an effective song in all respects: the tune is very catchy, the harmonies and backing vocals are superb, the sound of tubular bells in the verses is well judged (for example, around 0'46), and the organ in the style of Gary Brooker is an inspired idea (listen between 1'38 and 1'45). The instrumental part is magnificently executed, with a 12-string electric guitar solo, as well as excellent strings by Eddie Horst, sustained by handclaps. At the end of the piece, voices answer each other in the finest tradition of vocal groups from the days of psychedelic pop. Of all the pastiche songs on the album, *Surprise, Surprise* is probably the most successful.

18 SECONDS

The Last Carnival ends with a silence lasting 18 seconds. Is this a way of drawing the listener's attention to the next song, *The Wrestler*, which is, in fact, a hidden bonus track (like *Terry's Song* on the *Magic* album)? Or is it simply a silence intended for remembrance, in memory of Danny Federici?

THE LAST CARNIVAL

Bruce Springsteen / 3'29

Musicians

Bruce Springsteen: vocals, guitar, keyboards
Patti Scialfa: backing vocals
Steve Van Zandt: guitar (?)
Roy Bittan: keyboards (?)
Soozie Tyrell: backing vocals (?)
Jason Federici: accordion

Recording

Southern Tracks Recording Studios, Atlanta, Georgia: fall 2008
Thrill Hill Recording, Colts Neck, New Jersey: fall 2008

Technical team

Producer: Brendan O'Brien
Recording engineer: Nick DiDia, Bill Bowers (Southern), Toby Scott (Thrill Hill)
Assistant recording engineers: Tom Tapley, Darren Tablan (Southern)
Mixing: Brendan O'Brien
Mastering: Bob Ludwig (Gateway Mastering, Portland)

Danny Federici in 2001. *The Last Carnival* was written in his memory (his son Jason played accordion).

Genesis and lyrics

The Last Carnival is the last song Bruce Springsteen wrote for *Working On a Dream*. He recorded it during the fall of 2008, as the mixing of the album was drawing to a close. It is a song in the folk idiom, composed in memory of Danny Federici, who had been his friend and the keyboard player of the E Street Band since the early 1970s (and the recording of *The Wild, the Innocent, and the E Street Shuffle*). "It started out as a way of making sense of his passing. He was a part of that sound of the boardwalk the band grew up with and that's something that's going to be missing now,"[142] Springsteen explained to *Observer Music Monthly*.

"We won't be dancing together on the high wire/Facing the lions with you at my side anymore." Bruce Springsteen's words ring true, and reflect a real sadness, a profound wrench: it is the loss of a friend, of course, but also the end of an era, the epic of the E Street Band, which had begun almost 40 years earlier on the Jersey Shore. It was nevertheless down to Bruce Springsteen to persevere on his journey: "We'll be riding the train without you tonight/The train that keeps on moving its black smoke scorching the evening sky." Above him, and above the musicians of the E Street Band, thousands of stars shine. Among them, perhaps, is that of Danny Federici...Jason, the son of the E Street Band's much-missed keyboard player, symbolically accompanied Bruce Springsteen on the accordion.

Production

The Last Carnival is probably the greatest song on the album—sober and powerful. It starts with the sound of a barrel organ fading in, a direct reference to *Wild Billy's Circus Story* (on the second album, *The Wild, the Innocent, and the E Street Shuffle*) in which Danny Federici was on accordion. Springsteen then launches into each verse accompanying himself on the acoustic guitar, recorded on two tracks positioned in stereo. His voice is not sorrowful, just sad and dignified. In the third verse, a flute is heard in the distance (at 1'14). There follows a bridge colored by vocal harmonies and, above all, Jason's accordion, in a nod to his father (from 1'38). After a final verse, superb celestial choirs come in, with reverb, the barrel organ audible in the background. Presumably a certain idea of paradise...

THE WRESTLER

Bruce Springsteen / 3'50

A video of *The Wrestler* was made in January 2009. It shows the Boss singing the song in a ring in New Jersey. This version, lasting 5'20, is longer than the one on the album, the intro and coda being more extensively developed. The video also featured on a promotional CD.

Musician
Bruce Springsteen: vocals, guitar, synthesizer, piano, percussion
Recording
Thrill Hill Recording, Colts Neck, New Jersey: May to July 2008
Technical team
Producer: Bruce Springsteen
Recording engineer: Toby Scott
Mixing: Bob Clearmountain (Mix This!, Los Angeles)
Mixing assistant: Brandon Duncan

For Springsteen Addicts

In 2009, *The Wrestler* won "Best Song" at the 14th Critics' Choice Awards and "Best Original Song—Motion Picture" at the 66th Golden Globe Awards.

Mickey Rourke and Bruce Springsteen at the 66th Golden Globes, in January 2009. *The Wrestler* received an award.

Genesis and lyrics

The last song on *Working On a Dream*—a hidden bonus track, in fact—*The Wrestler* was especially written by Bruce Springsteen for the eponymous movie by Darren Aronofsky. The movie was shown at the Venice International Film Festival, on 5 September 2008, and at the New York Festival the following month, before being released in the United States in December. Mickey Rourke plays a wrestler who, having achieved a certain degree of fame, is obliged to appear in small venues. Having fallen out with his daughter, he tries to reconnect with her following a heart attack, which prevents him returning to the ring.

"While on tour in Ireland, I received a call from my old friend Mickey Rourke," the songwriter writes on his website, brucespringsteen.net. "He talked about the film he was working on, said it was a picture that meant a great deal to him, and asked if I might have a song. He explained the character to me. I always felt there was a place where the best of our work crossed over, so I told him I'd give it a shot. I wrote the song quickly, recorded it with Toby Scott [...]"[144]

"My only faith is in the broken bones and bruises I display," Bruce Springsteen sings at the end of *The Wrestler*. The songwriter, too, has been able to get inside the skin of the character, Randy "The Ram" Robinson, and lay bare his scars—which are not only physical.

Production

Springsteen probably wrote this song after 25 May 2008, the date of the last concert that the band played in Ireland. The Boss recorded all the instruments in his home studio at Colts Neck—a habit that dated back to *Nebraska*—with the faithful Toby Scott by his side.

Airy, ethereal keyboard pads begin *The Wrestler*, as if linking back to *The Last Carnival*, which ended with celestial choirs. The Boss is on acoustic guitar and sings with his tremendous storyteller's voice. The arrangement is understated: on the left, a mono piano picks out notes drowned in reverberation (at 1'18), before a second piano, in stereo this time, comes in to support the acoustic guitar (at 1'54). Scattered cymbals are also heard, as are backing vocals.

Springsteen has the gift of writing extraordinary songs for film, and he proves that once more with *The Wrestler*.

PRO
THEP

ALBUM

THE PROMISE

Racing in the Street ('78) • Gotta Get that Feeling • Outside Looking In • Someday (We'll Be Together) • One Way Street • Because the Night • Wrong Side of the Street • The Brokenhearted • Rendezvous • Candy's Boy • Save My Love • Ain't Good Enough for You • Fire • Spanish Eyes • It's a Shame • Come On (Let's Go Tonight) • Talk to Me • The Little Things (My Baby Does) • Breakaway • The Promise • City of Night • The Way (hidden song)

RELEASE DATE

United States: 16 November 2010

Reference: Columbia Records - 88697 76177 2

No.16 in the *Billboard* chart, No.7 in the United Kingdom, No.1 in Germany, Spain, and Sweden, No.14 in France

The R&B and disco group The Pointer Sisters performed *Fire* by Bruce Springsteen in 1979.

From 1978 the neo-rockabilly singer Robert Gordon included *Fire* in his repertoire. The Boss had intended it for the King.

A PROMISE KEPT

The period after *Born to Run* was a particularly fertile one for the songwriter Bruce Springsteen. So, by the time he went into the studio with the E Street Band at the beginning of June 1977 to record his fourth album, he had composed and/or written several dozen songs. The 22 recordings collected together for *The Promise* date from that period: in discographic terms, they complement *Darkness on the Edge of Town*, of course, but also the *Tracks* box set (1998) and *18 Tracks* (1999). "I was still held in thrall by the towering pop records that had shaped my youth and early musical education," Springsteen writes in the liner notes to the double CD, *The Promise*. "Echoes of Elvis, Dylan, Roy Orbison, the full-voiced rockabilly ballad singers of the '50s and '60s along with my favorite soul artists and Phil Spector, thread throughout."[68] This applies especially to *Fire*, which would be recorded by The Pointer Sisters, reaching No.2 in the United States in December 1979 into the bargain. Although he had originally written *Fire* for Elvis Presley, he eventually offered it to Robert Gordon, after the death of the King.

Musically, therefore, the 22 songs on *The Promise* are fairly different from those that feature on *Darkness on the Edge of Town* which, to differing degrees, show the influence of punk rock from Britain. The only exceptions are the alternative versions of *Racing in the Street* (which has a new violin part recorded by David Lindley), *Come On (Let's Go Tonight)* before it became *Factory*, *Ain't Good Enough for You*, and *Spanish Eyes*—as well as the title track and *Because the Night*. We have chosen to highlight these last two songs here: the first for its artistic value, the second because of its global success, thanks to the version recorded by Patti Smith. Nevertheless, all the tracks on *The Promise* deserve careful listening. In his notes, the songwriter compares them to old girlfriends that you would visit after a long wait...

After the addition (by overdubbing) of vocals and several instruments to the original recordings, *The Promise* was released on 16 November 2010 on two CDs or three LPs. Extremely well received by the specialist press, Springsteen's work was also acclaimed by the public, reaching No.16 and No.7 in the US and UK, respectively. It was in continental

Photograph for *The Promise* shot by Eric Meola during his journey through the American West with Bruce Springsteen and Steve Van Zandt, August 1977.

Europe, however, that it would have its greatest success, especially in Germany, Spain, and Sweden, where it climbed to No.1. In France, *The Promise* got to No.14.

It should also be noted that the same year, 2010, saw the release of a box set with the title *The Promise: The Darkness on the Edge of Town Story*, which comprised the album *Darkness on the Edge of Town*, remastered, all the songs on *The Promise*, and three DVDs. These featured *The Promise: The Making of Darkness on the Edge of Town* and also three concerts: Bruce Springsteen and The E Street Band: Darkness on the Edge of Town, Paramount Theatre, Asbury Park, 2009; Bruce Springsteen and The E Street Band: Thrill Hill Vault, 1976–1978; and Bruce Springsteen and The E Street Band: Thrill Hill Vault Houston '78 Bootleg House Cut. It also included notes written by Springsteen himself (either by hand or on a typewriter), studio recording notes, and some very fine black and white photographs taken notably by Frank Stefanko and Eric Meola.

The sleeve

The photo chosen for the sleeve of *The Promise* shows Bruce Springsteen leaning against a convertible car in the middle of a dusty road, with a threatening sky in the background. It was shot by Eric Meola on 22 August 1977 during his road trip with Springsteen and Steve Van Zandt. In his book *Streets of Fire: Bruce Springsteen in Photographs and Lyrics 1977–1979*, published in 2012, Eric Meola writes: "I spent days looking at maps, and then settled on a stretch of Route 80 between Salt Lake City, Utah, and Reno, Nevada. Finally, the plans came together—we would fly out to Salt Lake City, find an old car, and drive it across the desert to Reno. Then, the day before we were due to leave, Elvis died. We flew to Salt Lake City on schedule, and spent an afternoon in used car lots, finally settling on a red convertible—a 1965 Ford Galaxy 500XL with bucket seats."[69] On the back of the sleeve is the same dusty desert landscape, with the Ford Galaxy set back a little farther from Eric Meola's lens.

GOTTA GET THAT FEELING

Bruce Springsteen / 3'19

Musicians: Bruce Springsteen: vocals, guitar / Steve Van Zandt: guitar / Clarence Clemons: saxophone, percussion instruments / Roy Bittan: piano / Danny Federici: organ / Garry Tallent: bass / Max Weinberg: drums / Unidentified musicians: brass, backing vocals **Recording:** Atlantic Studios, New York: 12 August 1977 / The Record Plant, New York: 30 August 1977 / Thrill Hill Recording, Colts Neck: 2010 **Technical team:** producers: Jon Landau, Bruce Springsteen / recording engineers: Jimmy Iovine (Atlantic, Record Plant), Toby Scott (Thrill Hill) / assistant recording engineers: Thom Panunzio (Atlantic, Record Plant), Rob Lebret (Thrill Hill) / mixing: Bob Clearmountain (Mix This!), Brandon Duncan (assistant mixing) / mastering: Bob Ludwig (Gateway Mastering, Portland)

This song had been around for a long time as a bootleg before reaching the public at large with the release of the box set *The Promise: Darkness on the Edge of Town Story* (2010). The narrator asks a young woman to come "where the stars are shining bright" and to "get that feeling" again with him. It doesn't matter that they have no money, that it's raining, or that a storm's coming; as long as they're in each other's arms, love will prevail! Musically, Phil Spector's influence looms large over the arrangements, with a characteristic syncopated rhythm, castanets, a sax solo, and a striking piano part, not to mention the brass section, backing vocals ("sha la la!"), and lead vocals recorded in 2010.

OUTSIDE LOOKING IN

Bruce Springsteen / 2'18

Musicians: Bruce Springsteen: vocals, guitar / Steve Van Zandt: guitar, backing vocals / Clarence Clemons: saxophone, percussion instruments, backing vocals / Roy Bittan: piano / Danny Federici: organ / Garry Tallent: bass / Max Weinberg: drums **Recording:** The Record Plant, New York: 27 September 1977 **Technical team:** producers: Jon Landau, Bruce Springsteen / recording engineer: Jimmy Iovine / assistant recording engineer: Thom Panunzio / mixing: Bob Clearmountain (Mix This!), Brandon Duncan (assistant mixing) / mastering: Bob Ludwig (Gateway Mastering, Portland)

Bruce Springsteen never denied the artistic debt he owed The Animals, so it's very likely that he got the idea for *Outside Looking In* from *Inside Looking Out*, the single the group from Newcastle released in 1966—at least for the title.

It's about yet another breakup, this time with the narrator accusing the woman he used to love of having changed, of "looking for some strange new games." In the end, he becomes a spectator and loses interest in his ex-partner: "Those pretty eyes that they all adore/But baby not me, not anymore."

This song was recorded for the first time at Atlantic Studios on 1 June 1977, then the group met on 27 September at the Record Plant to record the album version. As for the musical inspiration, it doesn't come from The Animals, but from Buddy Holly. A completely authentic-sounding Max Weinberg plays a rhythm in the style of *Peggy Sue*, while the Boss quavers on his Telecaster-Esquire. A special mention goes to Clarence Clemons's excellent sax solo.

SOMEDAY (WE'LL BE TOGETHER)

Bruce Springsteen / 5'38

Musicians: Bruce Springsteen: vocals, guitar / Steve Van Zandt: guitars / Clarence Clemons: percussion instruments / Roy Bittan: piano / Danny Federici: organ, glockenspiel / Garry Tallent: bass / Max Weinberg: drums / Tiffeny Andrews, Corinda Carford, Michelle Moore, Antoinette Savage (Antionete Moore), Patti Scialfa, Soozie Tyrell: backing vocals **Recording:** The Record Plant, New York: 26 (?), 29–30 September 1977 / Thrill Hill Recording, Colts Neck: 2010 **Technical team:** producers: Jon Landau, Bruce Springsteen / recording engineers: Jimmy Iovine (Atlantic, Record Plant), Toby Scott (Thrill Hill) / assistant recording engineers: Thom Panunzio (Atlantic, Record Plant), Rob Lebret (Thrill Hill) / mixing: Bob Clearmountain (Mix This!), Brandon Duncan (assistant mixing) / mastering: Bob Ludwig (Gateway Mastering, Portland)

Someday (We'll Be Together) is a song about loneliness. The narrator says that he can't sleep because the woman he loves is far away. So, he walks aimlessly through the streets. But this song is also a message of hope because, deep down, he knows that one day they'll be together, and their love will prevail.

Bruce Springsteen signs autographs at the preview of the rockumentary *The Promise: The Making of Darkness on the Edge of Town* at the Toronto International Film Festival, on 14 September 2010.

To illustrate his point, the Boss wrote a ballad that is once again permeated with Phil Spector's techniques, notably the handbells, castanets, and drumming in the style of *Be My Baby*, by The Ronettes. Some of The Alliance Singers who contributed to *The Rising*—notably to *Let's Be Friends (Skin to Skin)*—returned in 2010, but despite their best efforts, they greatly weighed down the song with a poorly written chorus part. The version in *The Promise* was significantly revised compared to the 1977 one, for better and for worse.

ONE WAY STREET

Bruce Springsteen / 4'20

Musicians: Bruce Springsteen: vocals, guitar / Steve Van Zandt: guitar (?) / Clarence Clemons: saxophone / Roy Bittan: piano / Danny Federici: organ, glockenspiel / Garry Tallent: bass / Max Weinberg: drums / unidentified musicians: brass instruments **Recording:** Atlantic Studios, New York: 17 July 1977 / Thrill Hill Recording, Colts Neck: 2010 **Technical team:** producers: Jon Landau, Bruce Springsteen / recording engineers: Jimmy Iovine (Atlantic), Toby Scott (Thrill Hill) / assistant recording engineers: Thom Panunzio (Atlantic), Rob Lebret (Thrill Hill) / mixing: Bob Clearmountain (Mix This!), Brandon Duncan (assistant mixing) / mastering: Bob Ludwig (Gateway Mastering, Portland)

What happened to this daredevil couple? What mistakes must they atone for? Maybe laziness. Maybe lies. Now, the narrator says he wants to change and stop going down this one-way street that only leads to failure. What he wants is to turn a page, to change course.

Springsteen wrote this R&B ballad on the organ, glockenspiel, and a few key brass instruments. The latter were added as overdubs in 2010, as were the lead vocals. The Boss can be heard fully forcing the timbre of his voice in order to find the right grain, rugged and rough, but the result clearly lacks authenticity. As for Clarence Clemons, he performs two good saxophone solos, which serve as a reminder of his prominent role in the heyday of the E Street Band.

BECAUSE THE NIGHT

Patti Smith/Bruce Springsteen / 3'25

Musicians
Bruce Springsteen: vocals, guitars
Steve Van Zandt: guitars, vocal harmonies
Clarence Clemons: saxophone, percussions
Roy Bittan: piano
Danny Federici: organ, glockenspiel
Garry Tallent: bass guitar
Max Weinberg: drums

Recording
The Record Plant, 321 West 44th St, New York: 27 September 1977
Thrill Hill Recording (Stone Hill Studio), 132 Muhlenbrink Rd, Colts Neck, New Jersey: 2010

Technical team
Producers: Jon Landau, Bruce Springsteen
Recording engineers: Jimmy Iovine (Record Plant), Toby Scott (Thrill Hill)
Assistant recording engineers: Thom Panunzio (Record Plant), Rob Lebret (Thrill Hill)
Mixing: Bob Clearmountain
Assistant: Brandon Duncan

Fred "Sonic" Smith, the guitarist of MC5. The future husband of Patti Smith is at the heart of the lyrics for *Because the Night*.

Genesis and lyrics

Bruce Springsteen composed *Because the Night* in 1977, possibly during the first day's recording of *Darkness on the Edge of Town* on 1 June at Atlantic Studios in New York (source: Sony). The fact that this song became one of the most famous in the repertoire of Patti Smith is thanks to Jimmy Iovine, who at the time was producing, in the same studios, both *Darkness on the Edge of Town* and Smith's album *Easter* (1978). In fact, Iovine told Springsteen that he needed a powerful song, a single that could make Patti Smith's third album a big commercial success. He brought up a piece recently composed by the songwriter: "'You know that song you don't think fits your album?' the recording engineer asked him. 'You think that would be good for Patti?' replied the Boss. 'I'm positive,' answered Iovine. The recording engineer—and future successful producer—sensed the piece's enormous potential [...] 'I knew a girl singing that song, to a guy, was the sexiest thing in the world [...] And I knew that chord change—minor to major—was going to work. And then the chorus, "Because the night belongs to lovers"—a girl singing that? A winner.'"[35] As for Springsteen, he elaborates on why he discarded the song in Thom Zimny's documentary: "A real love song, like *Because the Night*, I was reticent to write. I think I was too cowardly to write at the time."[54]

Captivated by the bewitching music of the songwriter from New Jersey, Patti Smith immediately set about modifying some of the words and adding others (although nobody knows exactly which ones). As she explained: "I was in my apartment and I was having a long-distance romance with Fred "Sonic" Smith, who later became my husband. He was supposed to call me up and I waited for him to call me for hours."[54] And she was singing: "Because the night belongs to lovers/Because the night belongs to lust/Because the night belongs to lovers/Because the night belongs to us." Patti Smith's version of *Because the Night* is certainly the flagship song on *Easter*. It was also released as a single (with *God Speed* on the B-side) on 2 March 1978, reaching No.13 in the *Billboard* charts and No.5 in the UK charts. Bruce Springsteen, for his part, performed it for the first time with the E Street Band on 30 May 1978, at the Boston Music Hall, during the Darkness Tour. The version performed onstage at the Nassau Veterans Memorial Coliseum in Uniondale, New York state,

Patti Smith with Fred Smith—not Fred "Sonic" Smith, whom *Because the Night* references, but Fred Smith the bass player of Television.

For Springsteen Addicts

Patti Smith first played *Because the Night* in public at the CBGB, in New York, on 30 December 1977—her 31st birthday—with Bruce Springsteen playing guitar.

on 28 December 1980 (which features on the *Live/1975–85* box set), also deserves a special mention.

Production

The first takes for *Because the Night* were recorded at Atlantic Studios on 1 June and 1 July 1977. However, it appears that the recording which served as the basis for the 2010 version—completed (for the lead vocal) in the Boss's home studio at Colts Neck—is the result of a session on 27 September 1977 at the Record Plant.

Compared to the version by Patti Smith, Springsteen's is more lyrical and less aggressive. Only in live versions would he give it a more dynamic, rock-like dimension, with some performances lasting eight minutes. Nevertheless, it possessed neither the power nor the charm that Patti Smith, the future author of *Just Kids*, was able inject into it. The version on *The Promise* is nevertheless excellent and notably features that fabulous introduction, once again entrusted to the magic of Roy Bittan's piano and to the glockenspiel of Danny Federici.

Although Springsteen removed this song from the tracklist of *Darkness on the Edge of Town*, that was partly on account of its commercial potential. Ever since the first demos, everyone had regarded it as a hit in the making, but, since the Boss was seeking pure, austere emotion for his new album, in no way making compromises for the record industry, he preferred to leave it out. Yet the version by the E Street Band is impressively effective, and the musicians are in perfect harmony. Clarence Clemons plays multiple percussion instruments, including a tambourine and castanets, but also a saxophone solo, which Springsteen hastens to support with the lead guitar (from 2'01).

In the final chorus, the songwriter chose to change key by going up a whole tone (from 2'40). Although very unusual for the Boss, this is a device widely used by arrangers to increase the tension in a piece. This seems to suggest that, from the start, Springsteen envisaged this as a song destined for radio stations, before he changed his mind.

Because the Night is an excellent song, which doubtless would have made *Darkness on the Edge of Town* an album with wider popular appeal, at least on its initial release. But the reasons that led Springsteen not to include it on his fourth album and to offer it to Patti Smith are entirely to his credit.

WRONG SIDE OF THE STREET

Bruce Springsteen / 4'20

Musicians: Bruce Springsteen: vocals, guitar / Steve Van Zandt: guitar, backing vocals (?) / Clarence Clemons: saxophone, percussion instruments, backing vocals (?) / Roy Bittan: piano / Danny Federici: organ / Garry Tallent: bass / Max Weinberg: drums **Recording:** The Record Plant, New York: 14 October 1977 / Thrill Hill Recording, Colts Neck: 2010 **Technical team:** producers: Jon Landau, Bruce Springsteen / recording engineers: Jimmy Iovine (Record Plant), Toby Scott (Thrill Hill) / assistant recording engineers: Thom Panunzio (Record Plant), Rob Lebret (Thrill Hill) / mixing: Bob Clearmountain (Mix This!), Brandon Duncan (assistant mixing) / mastering: Bob Ludwig (Gateway Mastering, Portland)

This song was called *Endless Night* in a bootleg. It was also given the title of *English Sons*, no doubt under the influence of the 1977 British punk invasion.

Day breaks after a night of love. The narrator tells his partner that she has to leave because they're "on the wrong side of the street." The young woman, who clearly belongs to the upper classes, had ventured into troubled waters out of boredom and a naïve sense of confusion between fear and desire. But it's time for her to open her eyes and realize that she doesn't belong there with him. Of note: the lines "You get bored of every day bringing the same/So you go out looking for some strange new game" are almost the same as the ones from *Outside Looking In:* "Well, every day just brings the same/You go out looking for some strange new games."

With an intro worthy of The Who, *Wrong Side of the Street* is a good rock song with clear potential. With a bit more work, it could have made it onto the tracklist of an album. The E Street Band's accompaniment lives up to its reputation, expertly supporting the Boss and Clarence Clemons in their respective solos. The lead vocals were recorded in 2010.

THE BROKENHEARTED

Bruce Springsteen / 5'19

Musicians: Bruce Springsteen: vocals, guitars / Steve Van Zandt: guitars, backing vocals / Clarence Clemons: saxophone, percussion instruments, backing vocals / Roy Bittan: piano / Danny Federici: organ, glockenspiel / Garry Tallent: bass / Max Weinberg: drums / Barry Danielian, Curt Ramm: trumpets / Stan Harrison: tenor saxophone / Dan Levine: trombone / Eddie Manion: baritone saxophone **Recording:** The Record Plant, New York: 29 November 1977 / Thrill Hill Recording, Colts Neck: 2010 **Technical team:** producers: Jon Landau, Bruce Springsteen / recording engineers: Jimmy Iovine (Record Plant), Toby

The singer in concert in New Jersey, December 1977. It was a punk year—and a Springsteen year.

Scott (Thrill Hill) / assistant recording engineers: Thom Panunzio (Record Plant), Rob Lebret (Thrill Hill) / mixing: Bob Clearmountain (Mix This!), Brandon Duncan (assistant mixing) / mastering: Bob Ludwig (Gateway Mastering, Portland)

This tender ballad has a Latin pop spirit that is very different from the ambience of the ten songs in *Darkness on the Edge of Town*. So, it was rightly scrapped (to later evolve into *Fade Away* on *The River* album).

The story is summarized in the title. A couple has a fight. His words make her leave. He hopes she'll forgive him so they can resume their beautiful love story, and that she'll forget his shameful disregard. He doesn't want to add to the endless list of broken hearts. But is it too late?

Springsteen finished *The Brokenhearted* in 2010, notably by adding brass instruments and recording new lead vocals. They're easily spotted: he modified the bridge (between 2'39 and 3'01) and the end of the coda (at 4'38). His voice is no longer the same: its timbre is much scratchier after many years spent singing on stages around the world.

CANDY'S BOY

Bruce Springsteen / 4'39

Musicians: Bruce Springsteen: vocals, guitar / Steve Van Zandt: guitar / Clarence Clemons: percussion instruments / Roy Bittan: glockenspiel (?) / Danny Federici: organ, glockenspiel (?) / Garry Tallent: bass / Max Weinberg: drums **Recording:** Atlantic Studios, New York: 3, 6, and 27 June, 24 August, 2 September 1977 **Technical team:** producers: Jon Landau, Bruce Springsteen / recording engineers: Jimmy Iovine (Atlantic), Toby Scott (Thrill Hill) (?) / assistant recording engineers: Thom Panunzio (Atlantic), Rob Lebret (Thrill Hill) (?) / mixing: Bob Clearmountain (Mix This!), Brandon Duncan (assistant mixing) / mastering: Bob Ludwig (Gateway Mastering, Portland)

Candy's Boy is the first iteration of *Candy's Room*, which made the cut for *Darkness on the Edge of Town*. The heroine is the same: a young woman who turns tricks in her small apartment. The lyrics, however, differ starting from the second verse, with Bruce Springsteen referencing "Mongolian gangs," who were California biker gangs made up of Hispanic Vietnam veterans and adversaries of the Hell's Angels. A few lines written for *Candy's Boy* are in *Drive All Night* (in *The River*): "Well, there's machines and there's fire waiting for us on the edge of town."

Candy's Boy is a beautiful song that deserved to be released at the time of *Darkness*. The organ dominates the arrangements and performs the only real solo of the piece—an extraordinary Hammond B-3 solo. All the idiosyncrasies of the E Street Band come together: glockenspiels (no doubt played by Roy Bittan, since there's no piano), multiple percussion instruments (cowbell, maracas), and the Boss's superb voice. This song doesn't seem to have been reworked in 2010.

SAVE MY LOVE

Bruce Springsteen / 2'36

Musicians: Bruce Springsteen: vocals, guitars, percussion instruments, glockenspiel (?) / Steve Van Zandt: guitars, vocal harmonies (?) / Clarence Clemons: percussion instruments / Roy Bittan: piano, organ (?) / Charles Giordano: organ (?) / Garry Tallent: bass / Max Weinberg: drums **Recording:** Thrill Hill Recording, Colts Neck: 22 July 2010 **Technical team:** producers: Jon Landau, Bruce Springsteen / recording engineer: Toby Scott (Thrill Hill) / assistant recording engineer: Rob Lebret (Thrill Hill) / mixing: Bob Clearmountain (Mix This!), Brandon Duncan (assistant mixing) / mastering: Bob Ludwig (Gateway Mastering, Portland)

Bruce Springsteen wrote *Save My Love* while thinking about the first time he heard one of his songs on the waves, in this case *Spirit in the Night* (from the album *Greetings from Asbury Park, N.J.*). He later said it was too upbeat for a firmly serious album like *Darkness on the Edge of Town*. The songwriter and the E Street Band practiced it in the fall of 1976, but only practiced, it would seem. *Save My Love* for *The Promise*, in any case, was recorded on 22 July 2010.

This song seems like a declaration of love where the radio symbolizes the narrator's link to the woman he loves ("So turn up your radio and baby dial me in close").

Save My Love came out as a promotional single in November 2010. The video combines scenes filmed at the time of *Darkness on the Edge of Town* with scenes shot for *The Promise*.

When the E Street Band was practicing *Save My Love* in 1976, Danny Federici was on the organ and glockenspiel. Not so in 2010, when he was succeeded by Charles Giordano. Whatever the case, this is a very good song, and it was thanks to the insistence of Thom Zimny, who accidentally discovered it while watching video rushes of practices, that the Boss decided to record it in earnest in his home studio in 2010.

AIN'T GOOD ENOUGH FOR YOU

Bruce Springsteen / 4'01

Musicians: Bruce Springsteen: vocals, guitar / Steve Van Zandt: guitar / Clarence Clemons: saxophone, percussion instruments / Roy Bittan: piano / Danny Federici: organ / Garry Tallent: bass / Max Weinberg: drums / The group: clapping, backing vocals **Recording:** The Record Plant, New York: 26 September 1977 **Technical team:** producers: Jon Landau, Bruce Springsteen / recording engineer: Jimmy Iovine / assistant recording engineer: Thom Panunzio / mixing: Bob Clearmountain (Mix This!), Brandon Duncan (assistant mixing) / mastering: Bob Ludwig (Gateway Mastering, Portland)

Ain't Good Enough for You was initially called *What's the Matter Little Darling*, as seen in the bootleg *Deep Down in the Vaults*. It evolved from *This Little Girl*, which the songwriter had given to Gary U.S. Bonds (reaching No.5 in the *Billboard* chart's Mainstream Rock category in 1981).

It's another story about a struggling couple. A man makes the bitter discovery that the woman he lives with doesn't think he's good enough for her. She doesn't love anything about him, anything at all, not his way of talking or walking or even the clothes he wears. Some comic relief from Bruce Springsteen: "I bought a shirt uptown in Bloomingdales [...] Hitting cool just like Jimmy Iovine"—the recording engineer from *Born to Run* and *Darkness on the Edge of Town* shopped at that store at the time.

This is an upbeat rock song, a boogie that brings to mind Elton John's *Crocodile Rock*. The E Street Band is in tiptop shape, the musicians responding to the Boss with enthusiastic backing vocals. Roy Bittan takes center stage on the piano, performing the solo. As for Clarence Clemons, he supports his bandmates with his baritone.

FIRE

Bruce Springsteen / 4'08

Musicians: Bruce Springsteen: vocals, guitars / Steve Van Zandt: guitars / Clarence Clemons: saxophone, percussion instruments / Roy Bittan: piano / Danny Federici: organ / Garry Tallent: bass / Max Weinberg: drums **Recording:** Atlantic Studios, New York: 17 June 1977 / Thrill Hill Recording, Colts Neck: 2010 **Technical team:** producers: Jon Landau, Bruce Springsteen / recording engineers: Jimmy Iovine (Atlantic), Toby Scott (Thrill Hill) / assistant recording engineers: Thom Panunzio (Atlantic), Rob Lebret (Thrill Hill) / mixing: Bob Clearmountain (Mix This!), Brandon Duncan (assistant mixing) / mastering: Bob Ludwig (Gateway Mastering, Portland)

Bruce Springsteen wrote *Fire* hoping that Elvis Presley would turn it into a hit. The King reportedly received a demo of it but died before recording the song. In the end, Robert Gordon (in *Fresh Fish Special* with Link Wray, 1978) and The Pointer Sisters (in *Energy*, 1978) added it to their repertoire, The Pointer Sisters even reaching No.2 in the *Billboard* charts in December 1978. Bruce Springsteen performed it for the first time onstage on 23 May 1978 in Buffalo, New York. The version on the *Bruce Springsteen & The E Street Band Live 1975–85* box set (1986) was recorded at the Winterland Arena, in San Francisco, on 16 December 1978. It would take *The Promise* in 2010 to reveal the studio version, which dates back to June 1977, aside from Bruce Springsteen's rerecorded vocals telling the story of the narrator's partner, who denies loving him even though her burning kisses prove the opposite.

Fire is an excellent song, mainly based on a bass guitar riff and on the superb performance of the Boss, who relishes the opportunity to sing like Elvis. The solos are shared between the lead guitar and the saxophone. The simple and airy arrangements make this one of the best songs of *The Promise*.

SPANISH EYES

Bruce Springsteen / 3'50

Musicians: Bruce Springsteen: vocals, guitars / Steve Van Zandt: guitars, backing vocals / Clarence Clemons: saxophone, percussion instruments, backing vocals / Roy Bittan: piano / Danny Federici: organ, glockenspiel / Garry Tallent: bass / Max Weinberg: drums **Recording:** Atlantic Studios, New York: 30 June, 13 July or August 1977 / Thrill Hill Recording, Colts Neck: 2010 **Technical team:** producers: Jon Landau, Bruce Springsteen / recording engineers: Jimmy Iovine (Atlantic), Toby Scott (Thrill Hill) / assistant recording engineers: Thom Panunzio (Atlantic), Rob Lebret (Thrill Hill) / mixing: Bob Clearmountain (Mix This!), Brandon Duncan (assistant mixing) / mastering: Bob Ludwig (Gateway Mastering, Portland)

Also known as *New Spanish*, *Spanish Eyes* evolved into *I'm On Fire*, which is on *Born in the U.S.A.* It contains the same lyrics: "Hey little girl, is your daddy home, did he go away and leave you all alone." Bruce Springsteen and the E Street Band performed it on 19 May 1978 at the Paramount Theatre, in

Bruce Springsteen with Steve Van Zandt and Max Weinberg in concert in Oslo, 21 July 2012. *Ain't Good Enough for You* was on the setlist.

Asbury Park, a few days before the official launch of the Darkness Tour, then much later, in Madrid, Spain, in June 2012.

The musical inspiration for *Spanish Eye* came from *Spanish Harlem*, by Ben E King, a passionate song with all the trappings: a languorous voice, simple and effective arrangements, idiosyncratic maracas. The Boss has a romantic soul, and it's obvious.

IT'S A SHAME

Bruce Springsteen / 3'14

Musicians: Bruce Springsteen: vocals, guitar / Steve Van Zandt: guitar, backing vocals / Clarence Clemons: percussion instruments, backing vocals / Roy Bittan: piano / Danny Federici: organ / Bob Chirmside: bass / Jon Landau: drums / Barry Danielian, Curt Ramm: trumpets / Stan Harrison: tenor saxophone / Dan Levine: trombone / Eddie Manion: baritone saxophone / Unidentified singer: backing vocals **Recording:** Atlantic Studios, New York: 14 June 1977 / Thrill Hill Recording, Colts Neck: 2010 **Technical team:** producers: Jon Landau, Bruce Springsteen / recording engineers: Jimmy Iovine (Atlantic), Toby Scott (Thrill Hill) / assistant recording engineers: Thom Panunzio (Atlantic), Rob Lebret (Thrill Hill) / mixing: Bob Clearmountain (Mix This!), Brandon Duncan (assistant mixing) / mastering: Bob Ludwig (Gateway Mastering, Portland)

The working title of this song was *Jon's Jam*, which obviously refers to Jon Landau who is on the drums (Bob Chirmside, Springsteen's road manager, is on the bass). The music later evolved into *Prove It All Night*, which explains why *It's a Shame* didn't make it onto *Darkness on the Edge of Town* (*Prove It All Night* was on the same album).

The main character could be the same one from *Ain't Good Enough for You*. But what can we say about this exceptional drum contribution from the Boss's coproducer, manager, and friend? Only good things: Jon Landau plays a respectable drum part with a good installation. The same goes for Bob Chirmside, whose bass line lives up to this lively rock song and its R&B influences. Springsteen sings with enthusiasm, supported in the backing vocals of the chorus by an unidentified voice: is it Landau, Chirmside, or, according to some rumors, Southside Johnny? The brass section was recorded in 2010.

Talk to Me is a composition by Bruce Springsteen that was recorded by Southside Johnny in 1978. Here, the two musicians are seen in concert at the Capitol Theatre, in Passaic, New Jersey, on 31 December 1977.

COME ON (LET'S GO TONIGHT)

Bruce Springsteen / 2'20

Musicians: Bruce Springsteen: vocals, guitars / Steve Van Zandt: guitars, vocals harmonies (?) / Clarence Clemons: tambourine / Roy Bittan: piano / Danny Federici: organ / Garry Tallent: bass / Max Weinberg: drums / David Lindley: violin **Recording:** The Record Plant, New York: 9 and 29 December 1977 / Thrill Hill Recording, Colts Neck: 2010 **Technical team:** producers: Jon Landau, Bruce Springsteen / recording engineers: Jimmy Iovine (Record Plant), Toby Scott (Thrill Hill) / assistant recording engineers: Thom Panunzio (Record Plant), Rob Lebret (Thrill Hill) / mixing: Bob Clearmountain (Mix This!), Brandon Duncan (assistant mixing) / mastering: Bob Ludwig (Gateway Mastering, Portland)

As with *It's a Shame*, *Come On (Let's Go Tonight)* is the original version of *Factory*, the second track on the B-side of *Darkness on the Edge of Town*. Bruce Springsteen seems to have written it in the spring. He reused several lines with minimal modifications for *Out in the Street* (in *The River*), notably "Put on your black dress baby, and put your hair up right/There's a party way down in factory town tonight," and for the single *Johnny Bye-Bye*, "There's a party way down in factory town tonight/I'll be going down there if you need a ride."

As for the recording, the first takes were done at Atlantic Studios in June 1977, but the version in *The Promise* dates back to December of the same year, with a violin part by David Lindley recorded in 2010. The music and arrangements are identical to the ones in *Factory*, but not the tempo, which is slightly slower. The lead vocals of *Come On (Let's Go Tonight)* were recorded in 1977, not 2010.

TALK TO ME

Bruce Springsteen / 4'21

Musicians: Bruce Springsteen: vocals, guitar / Southside Johnny: backing vocals (?) / Steve Van Zandt: guitar, backing vocals (?) / Clarence Clemons: saxophone, percussion instruments, backing vocals (?) / Danny Federici: organ, glockenspiel / Garry Tallent: bass / Max Weinberg: drums / Rick Gazda, Bob Mucklin: trumpets / Stan Harrison: tenor saxophone / Richie "La Bamba" Rosenberg: trombone / Eddie Manion: baritone saxophone **Recording:** The Record Plant, New York: 14 October 1977 / Thrill Hill Recording, Colts Neck: 2010 **Technical team:**

producers: Jon Landau, Bruce Springsteen / recording engineers: Jimmy Iovine (Record Plant), Toby Scott (Thrill Hill) / assistant recording engineers: Thom Panunzio (Record Plant), Rob Lebret (Thrill Hill) / mixing: Bob Clearmountain (Mix This!), Brandon Duncan (assistant mixing) / mastering: Bob Ludwig (Gateway Mastering, Portland)

Talk to Me is one of the songs Bruce Springsteen gave his friend Southside Johnny, who recorded it with The Asbury Jukes during sessions for *Hearts of Stone* (1978).

The narrator is desperate to talk to the young woman he loves. But she doesn't want to see him. Through the window, "Late at night [he sees] the two of [them] softly swaying." He just wants to know "what did [he] do, what did [he] say, what must [he] pay" to touch her (or reach her).

Musically, *Talk to Me* is a light and breezy rock, with a bit of Latin color in the chorus. The brass section, recorded in 2010, dominates the arrangements. Clarence Clemons recorded an excellent saxophone solo in 1977. Lastly, it would seem that Southside Johnny himself is the one who replies to the Boss in the coda (from 3'40).

THE LITTLE THINGS (MY BABY DOES)

Bruce Springsteen / 3'18

Musicians: Bruce Springsteen: vocals, guitar / Steve Van Zandt: guitars, vocal harmonies (?)/ Clarence Clemons: saxophone, percussion instruments / Danny Federici: organ, glockenspiel / Garry Tallent: bass / Max Weinberg: drums / Roy Bittan: backing vocals **Recording:** Atlantic Studios, New York: 15 August 1977 (?) / The Record Plant, New York: 15 August 1977 (?) / Thrill Hill Recording, Colts Neck: 2010 **Technical team:** producers: Jon Landau, Bruce Springsteen / recording engineers: Jimmy Iovine (Atlantic, Record Plant), Toby Scott (Thrill Hill) / assistant recording engineers: Thom Panunzio (Atlantic, Record Plant), Rob Lebret (Thrill Hill) / mixing: Bob Clearmountain (Mix This!), Brandon Duncan (assistant mixing) / mastering: Bob Ludwig (Gateway Mastering, Portland)

This is another song in which the narrator talks about being happy at his partner's side. The way she kisses him, the way she loves him, are like gifts from God. Is it an autobiographical song?

This song was a bit too intimate to include in *Darkness on the Edge of Town* or to perform onstage. However, it doesn't lack charm, Springsteen having written a medium-tempo rock song typical of the *Born to Run* era, with a Phil Spector-style rhythm, a glockenspiel, tambourine, maracas, a piano, an organ, his Telecaster-Esquire, and the mandatory saxophone solo. As for his voice, it was recorded in 2010, with a scratchier timbre than in 1977, with the Boss being a lot more comfortable in his falsetto, as can be heard several times throughout the piece.

BREAKAWAY

Bruce Springsteen / 5'32

Musicians: Bruce Springsteen: vocals, guitars / Steve Van Zandt: guitars / Clarence Clemons: saxophone, percussion instruments / Roy Bittan: piano / Danny Federici (?): organ, glockenspiel / Garry Tallent: bass / Max Weinberg: drums / Barry Danielian, Curt Ramm: trumpets / Stan Harrison: tenor saxophone / Eddie Manion: baritone saxophone / Dan Levine: trombone / Tiffeny Andrews, Corinda Carford, Michelle Moore, Antoinette Savage (Antoinette Moore), Patti Scialfa, Soozie Tyrell: backing vocals **Recording:** Atlantic Studios, New York: 1 June 1977 (?) / Thrill Hill Recording, Colts Neck: 2010 **Technical team:** producers: Jon Landau, Bruce Springsteen / recording engineers: Jimmy Iovine (Atlantic), Toby Scott (Thrill Hill) / assistant recording engineers: Thom Panunzio (Atlantic), Rob Lebret (Thrill Hill) / mixing: Bob Clearmountain (Mix This!), Brandon Duncan (assistant mixing) / mastering: Bob Ludwig (Gateway Mastering, Portland)

Breakaway is about three people who decided to burn their bridges and break with a life they couldn't stand anymore: Sonny takes off in a sky-blue Monterey (a Mercury) and gambles away his life in a hotel room; Janie quits her waitressing job at a bar and loses herself in the streets; and Bobby dies beneath the stars. Three broken hearts shattering.

A demo of the song was made at Atlantic Studios on 1 June 1977, but the recording date of *Breakaway* is uncertain. As for the rest, it's hard to know whether this version was fully—or in part—rerecorded for *The Promise*. We know the brass instruments, backing vocals, and the Boss's voice were recorded in 2010. However, as a whole, this romantic song bears no traces of the 1977 recordings. The drumming is more warlike than lyrical in this Spector-inspired song, while The Alliance Singers' choral singing is perfectly in line with the arrangements this time, unlike in *Someday (We'll Be Together)*. A special mention goes to Clarence Clemons's sax solo. As for the organ and glockenspiel, unless they were recorded in 1977, unfortunately Danny Federici did not play them.

THE PROMISE

Bruce Springsteen / 5'52

Musicians
Bruce Springsteen: vocals, guitars
Steve Van Zandt: guitar
Roy Bittan: piano
Danny Federici: organ, glockenspiel
Garry Tallent: bass guitar
Max Weinberg: drums
Ken Ascher: string arrangement

Recording
The Record Plant, 321 West 44th St, New York: 28 September 1977
Thrill Hill Recording (Stone Hill Studio), 132 Muhlenbrink Rd, Colts Neck, New Jersey: 2010

Technical team
Producers: Jon Landau, Bruce Springsteen
Recording engineers: Jimmy Iovine (Record Plant), Toby Scott (Thrill Hill)
Assistants recording engineers: Thom Panunzio (Record Plant), Rob Lebret (Thrill Hill)
Mixing: Bob Clearmountain
Assistant: Brandon Duncan

The Challenger mentioned by Bruce Springsteen is a Dodge "muscle car" launched in 1970. As for Route 9, also mentioned in the song, it runs along the East Coast of the US, from Delaware to New York state.

Genesis and lyrics

Bruce Springsteen composed *The Promise* long before the sessions for *Darkness on the Edge of Town*, first performing it live on 3 August 1976, at the Monmouth Arts Center in Red Bank, New Jersey. In the Thom Zimny documentary *Bruce Springsteen, The Promise: The Making of Darkness on the Edge of Town*, he reveals what guided his writing: "It's a song about fighting and not winning. It was just about the disappointments of the time."[54] These words might give the impression that *The Promise* describes the end of a friendship, as a result of the legal dispute then taking place between Bruce Springsteen and Mike Appel, and the arrival of Jon Landau as producer. "Johnny works in a factory/Billy works downtown/Terry works in a rock and roll band/Looking for that million-dollar sound," Springsteen sings at the very beginning of his song. Beyond that, *The Promise* is a reflection on the role of the songwriter. In his book *Two Hearts, The Definitive Biography, 1972–2003*, Dave Marsh quotes the remarks of the *Chicago Reader* critic John Milward: "The song's metaphor is 'The Challenger,' a race car that the singer has built by hand to 'carry the broken dreams of all those who have lost.' But the real twist comes during the song's bridge, when he sings the words 'thunder road' and immediately transforms his car into his rock 'n' roll dreams."[16] With *The Promise*, it is important to understand that the singer-songwriter's vocation is as intoxicating and dangerous as that of the racing driver.

Once again, this song places Bruce Springsteen somewhere between Bob Dylan and Van Morrison—and, certainly, it could have been worthy of a place on *Darkness on the Edge of Town* (probably even in place of *Racing in the Street*) if the singer-guitarist and the E Street Band had put the finishing touches to it. "Bruce cut that song every way possible," recalls the recording engineer Thom Panunzio in Thom Zimny's documentary. "It just was, you know, unheard of not to put a song that great on the record."[54]

Production

Tracing the history of the recordings on *The Promise* is a rather tricky exercise. Several versions were put in the can over a period of three months, according to Thom Panunzio, who asserts this in Thom Zimny's documentary. But the song had probably been worked on over a longer period because

Springsteen at the Boston Music Hall during the Darkness on the Edge of Town Tour.

versions exist that were recorded between June and August 1977, at Atlantic Studios, while others were recorded in September 1977 and January 1978 at the Record Plant. There was also a new recording made on 9 and 12 February 1999 in the Boss's home studio, Stone Hill Studio. The one that features on *The Promise* comes from a session at the Record Plant on 28 September 1977, which was reworked and completed in 2010—again in Springsteen's home studio.

The Promise is a superb, deeply melancholy rock ballad, such as only the songwriter from New Jersey could have produced. He expresses his emotions without restraint or modesty, a little like John Lennon with the Plastic Ono Band in 1970. This time, and unlike in the songs on *Darkness on the Edge of Town*, he does not seek to shatter the softness of his voice with more savage, rock-like outbursts. The tone is sober, calm, almost nostalgic. It is noticeable that Springsteen's voice changes in the third verse (starting at 3'20); this is very probably a new recording made in 2010, as the first two verses feature a medium tone of voice, which the recording engineer at Stone Hill Studio, Toby Scott, has tried to recapture as best he can. It is worth noting that in this version the last line of the final verse (before the chorus)—"And when the promise was broken I was far away from home sleeping in the back seat of a borrowed car"—has disappeared.

As regards arrangements, Roy Bittan's piano is as luminous and ubiquitous as ever. His lyricism works wonders, all the more because he is accompanied in a remarkable fashion on the organ and glockenspiel by the no less talented Danny Federici. The rhythm section, consisting of Garry Tallent and Max Weinberg, supplies the metronomic and majestic beat of the E Street Band, as usual. As for the various guitar parts, some were overdubbed in 2010. This is especially noticeable in the introduction, where their sound in no way resembles that from the sessions for the *Darkness* album. Finally, it is worth highlighting the string section, which was arranged for the occasion by Ken Ascher, a composer, keyboard player, and arranger, who notably collaborated with John Lennon and Paul Simon.

The Boss onstage at the Capitol Theatre, in Passaic, New Jersey, 31 December 1977.

CITY OF NIGHT

Bruce Springsteen / 3'21

Musicians: Bruce Springsteen: vocals, guitars / Steve Van Zandt: guitars, backing vocals / Clarence Clemons: saxophone, percussion instruments, backing vocals / Roy Bittan: piano, backing vocals / Danny Federici: organ, glockenspiel / Garry Tallent: bass / Max Weinberg: drums **Recording:** The Record Plant, New York: 14 October 1977 / Thrill Hill Recording, Colts Neck: 2010 **Technical team:** producers: Jon Landau, Bruce Springsteen / recording engineers: Jimmy Iovine (Record Plant), Toby Scott (Thrill Hill) / assistant recording engineers: Thom Panunzio (Record Plant), Rob Lebret (Thrill Hill) / mixing: Bob Clearmountain (Mix This!), Brandon Duncan (assistant mixing) / mastering: Bob Ludwig (Gateway Mastering, Portland)

This song had many working titles—*Taxi Driver* (a nod to Martin Scorsese), *Taxi Cab*, and *City of Night*—before finally landing on *City of Night*.

The narrator asks his taxi driver to take him across town. His final destination: his girlfriend, who starts her work at closing time. Is she a prostitute, or does she have something to do with drugs? It's a mystery! In the second verse, Bruce Springsteen mentions 12th and Vine (the Kansas City neighborhood where the clubs are), in a reference to the famous song *Kansas City*, written in 1951 by Jerry Leiber and Mike Stoller. As for the line "Some people wanna die young and gloriously," which means life should only be lived dangerously, the songwriter would later use it again almost word for word in *All That Heaven Will Allow* (on the *Tunnel of Love* album).

Recorded on the same day as *Talk to Me*, *City of Night* is a superb soulful and jazzy rock song. Composed on simple instrumentals, it is primarily built around the Telecaster-Esquire and its pronounced quaver, the bass drum, and Max Weinberg's hi-hat. The Boss tells the story with an extraordinary voice. The instruments enter one after the other, ending on Clarence Clemons' very good saxophone solo. At the end of the song, there are 21 seconds of silence, then comes *The Way*, a hidden track (which brings the length of this track, on the disc, to 7'08 for both songs). This song was retouched in 2010, notably in the intro, which was shortened.

THE WAY

Bruce Springsteen / 3'47

Musicians: Bruce Springsteen: vocals, guitars / Steve Van Zandt: guitars, backing vocals / Clarence Clemons: saxophone, percussion instruments, backing vocals / Roy Bittan: piano, backing vocals / Danny Federici: organ, glockenspiel / Garry Tallent: bass / Max Weinberg: drums **Recording:** Atlantic Studios, New York: 15 August 1977 (?) / The Record Plant, New York: 15 August 1977 (?) **Technical team:** producers: Jon Landau, Bruce Springsteen / recording engineer: Jimmy Iovine / assistant recording engineer: Thom Panunzio / mixing: Bob Clearmountain (Mix This!), Brandon Duncan (assistant mixing) / mastering: Bob Ludwig (Gateway Mastering, Portland)

The Way is a hidden track on *The Promise*. Bruce Springsteen explained why, on 15 November 2010, to the E Street Radio station: "Because I never liked it." He added, "I would like to see it placed in a David Lynch film over a sexually perverse scene."[42] The theme, once again, is a couple. The narrator lists all the reasons he loves his partner: "the way your heart beats," "the way you sigh," and especially "the way you make my blood rush in my veins." Two of the lines can be found almost in their entirety on *The River*: "Sometimes at night I lie awake/I pull you close and feel each breath you take."

The last song of *The Promise*, *The Way* is a hidden track that doesn't start until 3'21 into *City of Night*. It bears Springsteen's typical style and is phenomenally enriched by the E Street Band. The only solo of the piece is another saxophone solo, proof that in 1977 the "Big Man" was central to the group. While the Boss never liked this song, Jimmy Iovine loved it.

ALBUM

WRECKING BALL

We Take Care of Our Own • Easy Money • Shackled and Drawn • Jack of All Trades • Death to My Hometown • This Depression • Wrecking Ball • You've Got It • Rocky Ground • Land of Hopes and Dreams • We Are Alive

Bonus tracks on the Special Edition: *Swallowed Up (In the Belly of the Whale), American Land*

Outtakes: *American Skin (41 Shots) • American Man*

RELEASE DATE

United States: 6 March 2012

Reference: Columbia Records – 88691 94254 2

No.1 in the United States, United Kingdom, Belgium, Denmark, the Netherlands, Germany, Ireland, Italy, Spain, and Switzerland

Bruce Springsteen speaks to the media during the sound check for the concert in Brisbane, Australia, on 14 March 2013.

PUTTING THE SPOTLIGHT ON THE SORCERER'S APPRENTICES OF WALL STREET

Following the release of *Working On a Dream* in January 2009, Bruce Springsteen was already getting new ideas, and even had several songs that were well past the preliminary stage. He was thinking particularly of a movie, featuring pieces of gospel music. He also decided to work with a new producer, having collaborated with Brendan O'Brien on four out of his past five albums. His choice was Ron Aniello who, as well as having coproduced Patti Scialfa's *Play It as It Lays* (2007) had been both producer and recording engineer to artists and bands as varied as Jude (*I Don't Know Why I Act this Way*, 1995), Lifehouse (*Stanley Climbfall*, 2002), and Candlebox (*Into the Sun*, 2008).

The album

It was thus with Ron Aniello that Bruce Springsteen, putting aside his feature film, began working on his 17th studio album. He had three songs ready to go: *We Take Care of Our Own*, *Shackled and Drawn*, and *Rocky Ground*. Then came *Easy Money*, after the first two lines came to him while driving: "You put on your coat, I'll put on my hat/You put out the dog, I'll put out the cat." As Springsteen writes in his autobiography *Born to Run*: "Bing...the light went on. The muse had materialized along the roadside. *Easy Money* was the key to a record I needed to make."[1]

The other songs on the album followed immediately afterward. Like *Easy Money*, the songs on *Wrecking Ball* are among the most politically committed the New Jersey songwriter has ever written. Firmly taking the side of social outcasts, the excluded, and blue-collar workers—as he has always done—he proclaims his loathing of what the United States has become at the dawn of the third millennium. This time, his target is not the Bush administration's foreign policy, but rather globalization, the commodification of the world, and their multiple consequences—in short, the financialization of the economy. The subprime mortgage crisis of 2007, which was followed by the financial crisis of 2007–2008—as well as the deregulation that preceded them—demonstrated the limits of capitalism. There was a torrent of bankruptcies, not only of banks (notably, Lehman Brothers), but also of households, along with impoverishment and even annihilation of the middle classes. All this took place while a tiny minority of financiers and traders—the sorcerer's apprentices of Wall Street—shamelessly enriched themselves: it was precisely this almost apocalyptic downward spiral of capitalism that outraged Bruce Springsteen. "I'd been following and writing about America's post-industrial trauma, the killing of our manufacturing presence and working class, for 35 years. So I went to work."[1] To work, certainly, but with a disgust and an anger that were only growing as a result of the gulf that, from now on, separated the American dream from the reality of the 2000s. Springsteen felt the same sense of rebellion as his character in *Jack of All Trades*, with the difference that the songwriter expressed it through words instead of dreaming of letting his gun do the talking—hence the "wrecking ball" of the album's title and title track.

Bruce Springsteen, armed with his guitar, on the sleeve of *Wrecking Ball.*

Still a working-class hero, despite success and fame

Some might question Bruce Springsteen's credibility: having been an icon of American popular music since the mid-1970s, and one of the biggest-selling artists in the record industry, could he be sincere in defending the weak, the homeless, and those exploited by a system from which he had profited to boot? In fact, as far as he was concerned, this was not even an issue. Fame and fortune had never deflected him from the path he had followed ever since *Greetings from Asbury Park, N.J.*, released in 1973. The songwriter from New Jersey was an authentic working-class hero. Not only had he not forgotten the world he came from, but he had also always extolled its values. In an interview with Jon Stewart for *Rolling Stone* magazine, Springsteen noted that he had witnessed a rise in inequality for most of his life, although it had only become widely discussed since Occupy Wall Street. He explained that "it was something that I never forgot. I experienced what happens when, say, the male figure in your house struggles to work, can't find work, and the woman in the house becomes the primary breadwinner. That was my house."[149]

Wrecking Ball was released on 6 March 2012 and went to No.1 in the *Billboard* chart on 24 March—Springsteen's 10th No.1 in his native country. In the United Kingdom, the album climbed to the top of the charts on 17 March, as it did in some 15 other countries, including Belgium, the Netherlands, Germany, Italy, Spain, and Switzerland. In France, where it sold more than 50,000, it was certified a gold record. This commercial success was matched by critical acclaim, as the Boss's 17th studio album was awarded five stars by *Rolling Stone* and the British newspaper *The Independent.*

The sleeve

Against a black background, Bruce Springsteen, with his head bowed—perhaps by the cares of this world—firmly grasps his Fender guitar, its neck pointing upward, dead straight. The artist's name and the album title are superimposed in large, white letters, like spray-painted graffiti, proclaiming the denunciation of an America that is adrift, where social classes that have hitherto been spared are now in their turn plunged into crisis, for the benefit of a few. On the back of the sleeve, Springsteen, his guitar in the playing position suspended by its strap, clutches his shoulder with a grimace of pain.

The sleeve notes contain more photographs, this time in black and white, the last of which shows Springsteen and Clarence Clemons saluting the crowd. There are the song's lyrics, and some lines about Clarence Clemons, who died a few months before the release of the album. The photographs were shot by Danny Clinch and Jo Lopez. The design and artwork are by Michelle Holme and Dave Bett.

Clarence Clemons. In the sleeve notes for *Wrecking Ball*, Bruce Springsteen wrote movingly about the saxophonist, who died on 18 June 2011.

Paying tribute to the "Big Man"

Although this album is not dedicated to Clarence Clemons—as *Working On a Dream* is to the late Danny Federici—the Boss wrote a glowing tribute to him in the album's sleeve notes. The last sentence is especially moving: "Clarence doesn't leave the E Street Band when he dies, he leaves when we die."[150] In an interview in February 2012 with Antoine de Caunes at the Théâtre Marigny, Paris, the songwriter recalled the death of his friend: "Losing Clarence is like losing something elemental. It's like losing the rain, or air. And that's a part of life."[151]

Clarence Clemons died on 18 June 2011 following a stroke. Jackson Browne and the E Street Band paid him a musical tribute when he was buried, on 21 June at the Royal Poinciana Chapel, in Palm Beach, Florida. Nils Lofgren even wrote *Miss You, "C"* in his memory. The Boss ended his funeral oration with these words: "How big was the Big Man? Too fucking big to die."[53] However, fortunately, the replacement for "C" was his nephew, Jake Clemons, who joined the Wrecking Ball Tour in 2012. There, he found his place and his own identity, even though his uncle's shadow always hovered over the stage when the E Street Band played.

The recording

Wrecking Ball is thus a coproduction by Springsteen and Ron Aniello, and, for the first time since *The Ghost of Tom Joad* in 1995, Jon Landau rejoined the team, though now as executive producer. Recording took place during 2011, mostly in the songwriter's hideaway, the famous Stone Hill Studio at Colts Neck, New Jersey. Two other studios were also booked: MSR Studio B in New York, for recording the strings, and Very Loud House Studio in Woodland Hills, California, for some additional recordings.

One might nevertheless wonder why Springsteen wanted to change producer and interrupt—albeit temporarily—his collaboration with Brendan O'Brien. The songwriter has explained that it was somewhat by chance that he had opted for Aniello, whom he knew because he had worked with Patti Scialfa, and also because Aniello had helped him make his

Bruce Springsteen and Tom Morello during the 25th Rock & Roll Hall of Fame concert in Madison Square Garden, New York, on 29 October 2009.

gospel album, a project that was temporarily postponed. Springsteen said: "He came in to help me finish that one, and as we went along, a few of the songs started to come up for this record; he had a lot of fresh ideas about the way the music could sound, and he had a large library of sounds—alternative and hip-hop elements—and we used quite a bit of different looping techniques."[151]

Aniello was quite impressed by Springsteen when they started working together, and gradually discovered the direction the songwriter wanted to take for this new project: "Much of it was going on in Bruce's mind, and my role was to give him the tools he needed to help him get on the right level with each song. We started a new song practically every day. It was a great experience."[153]

Aniello recalled that there were hundreds of musical instruments strewn around the Boss's home studio—guitars, keyboards, percussion instruments, synthesizers, vintage instruments, and even toy instruments. For his part, the producer brought his soundbanks, which were packed with orchestra and strings samples.

Wrecking Ball—a working manual

Their way of working was simple: Springsteen came into the studio with a new song, which he played to Aniello on the guitar, the rhythm provided by a click track or a drum loop. They would then put the piece together, following the songwriter's guiding idea and instructions. If he had come with a song that was barely finished, and not yet fully mastered, they would assemble the arrangement together: "We experimented a lot, finding different ways to sculpt and build his ideas," Aniello recalled. "I'd play something on upright bass, for example, and he'd go to the xylophone and play along. Other times, I'd jump on the drums, record a beat, and loop it as the basic rhythm track for a song. The real drum tracks came later."[153] Only once Springsteen and Aniello had recorded all the backing tracks did the other musicians become involved, overdubbing their respective parts. However, since *Wrecking Ball* was more a solo project by the songwriter than an album by the E Street Band, the only members of the band's lineup who took part were Patti Scialfa, Max Weinberg, Clarence Clemons, and Steve Van Zandt.

In an interview with *Rolling Stone* magazine in March 2012, Bruce Springsteen mentioned Occupy Wall Street. This movement, started in September 2011, denounces the excesses of capitalism. The demonstrators' rallying point, Zuccotti Park, which is not far from Wall Street, was renamed Liberty Square by them for the occasion.

The other musicians

Numerous other musicians contributed to the album: Matt Chamberlain on drums, Charlie Giordano on accordion, celesta, and keyboards, Soozie Tyrell on violin and backing vocals, Lisa Lowell and Michelle Moore on backing vocals, Cindy Mizelle on vocals, Tom Morello and Rob Lebret on guitar, Greg Leisz on banjo, mandocello, and lap steel guitar, Marc Muller on pedal steel guitar, Kevin Buell on marching drum, Clif Norrell on tuba, and Steve Jordan on tambourine. Not forgetting the brass section, consisting of Curt Ramm, Clark Gayton, Stan Harrison, Eddie Manion, Dan Levine, and Art Baron (who also played the penny whistle), with Curt Ramm and Darrell Leonard playing solo trumpet. A vocal group consisting of Ross Petersen, Ron Aniello, Clif Norrell, and Rob Lebret features on some songs, as do the Victorious Gospel Choir, conducted by Lilly "Crawford" Brown, and the New York Chamber Consort, a string ensemble put together and conducted by Rob Mathes. This was the first time so many musicians had featured on a Springsteen album. This was a long way from *Nebraska*.

It is worth noting that Ron Aniello declared in an interview that the credits which appear on the album sleeve are simply disastrous. While awaiting future corrected editions of *Wrecking Ball*, we give them here as they appear, commenting wherever possible in the light of our research.

Technical details

To record Springsteen's voice, Ron Aniello positioned the mic in the main room of the home studio, facing the Boss. He used a Telefunken ELA M 251 E (which can be seen in the DVD of *We Shall Overcome: The Seeger Sessions*), passing it through a UA 1176 limiter and a AMS Neve pre-amp. The console used was again an SSL 4000 with Ultimation and a Pro Tools workstation was used for recordings.

As for recording engineers, they were proportional to the number of musicians: Ross Petersen, Ron Aniello, Rob Lebret, Clif Norrell, and Toby Scott took care of recording, while Bob Clearmountain, Chris Lord-Alge, Mark "Spike" Stent, and Rich Costey did the mixing. Finally, Bob Ludwig, as ever, was in charge of mastering.

Telefunken ELA M 251 E mics identical to the ones Ron Aniello used for the sessions for *Wrecking Ball.*

WE TAKE CARE OF OUR OWN

Bruce Springsteen / 3'54

Musicians
Bruce Springsteen: vocals, guitar, piano, drums, loops (?), percussion
Ron Aniello: guitar, bass guitar, keyboards, drums, loops, backing vocals
Patti Scialfa, Lisa Lowell, Soozie Tyrell: backing vocals
New York Chamber Consort: strings

Recording
Stone Hill Studio, Colts Neck, New Jersey: 2011
MSR Studio B, New York: 2011

Technical team
Producers: Ron Aniello, Bruce Springsteen
Executive producer: Jon Landau
Recording engineers: Ross Petersen, Ron Aniello, Rob Lebret, Clif Norrell, Toby Scott
Mixing: Mark "Spike" Stent (The Mix Suite), Matty Green (assistant)
Mastering: Bob Ludwig (Gateway Mastering, Portland)

The expression "from sea to shining sea" (meaning from the Pacific Ocean to the Atlantic, or vice versa) is taken from the hymn *America the Beautiful*, a poem by Katharine Lee Bates (1895) set to music by Samuel A Ward. Is that a nod to Woody Guthrie, who sang: "This land is your land, this land is my land, from California to the New York Island"?

For Springsteen Addicts

Bruce Springsteen first performed *We Take Care of Our Own* live at the 54th Grammy Awards, at the Staples Center, Los Angeles, on 12 February 2012.

Genesis and lyrics

During a press conference in Paris on 16 February 2012, Bruce Springsteen revealed that he had written *We Take Care of Our Own* in 2009 or 2010. There is no hidden message in the lyrics, the song's very title being a call for a general awareness. We must take care of our own, all the more so in this every-man-for-himself society: "There ain't no help, the cavalry stayed home," as Springsteen sings. The narrator desperately seeks compassionate hearts. And he asks himself: "Where's the work that set my hands, my soul free/Where's the spirit that'll reign, reign over me." *We Take Care of Our Own* is a song about the death of illusions—or the birth of others. It is doubtless no coincidence that it was played during Barack Obama's 2012 presidential election campaign, and during his victory speech (delivered from his Chicago headquarters). For it was full of optimism and was a call for renewal.

Although nominated for two Grammy Awards—for "Best Rock Performance" and "Best Rock Song"—*We Take Care of Our Own* won neither. On the other hand, the rock journalist Robert Christgau named it the best single of 2012. The single was available to download on iTunes and amazon.com from 18 January 2012, and it reached No.6 in the United States. The video of the song was shot in Asbury Park, especially in the Savoy Theatre, and the surrounding area.

Production

We Take Care of Our Own, which opens the album, is the first taste of the fruit of Springsteen's collaboration with Ron Aniello. It is clear that the latter was a wind of change blowing through the Boss's work, bringing to it a welcome dynamism. The difference with Brendan O'Brien may reside in a production approach that is less Wall of Sound (see page 69) and less linear. The song begins with a tribal rhythm, played simultaneously on drums by both musicians by taking charge of part of the drum kit. Numerous instruments then join the dance: guitars, bass guitar, keyboards, glockenspiel, various samples, percussion, and so forth. The Boss sings with enthusiasm, rather like Joe Strummer. Aniello joins in with the backing vocals (for example, around 2'41), as do the trio of Patti, Lisa, and Soozie, at the end of the song (at 3'01). Finally, the strings of the New York Chamber Consort provide a (very) discreet pop touch to the whole.

EASY MONEY

Bruce Springsteen / 3'37

For Springsteen Addicts

Initially, to put together the loop for *Easy Money*, Ron Aniello had the idea of sampling an extract from the distinctive rhythm of Queen's *We Will Rock You*, which consists of the sound of footsteps and handclaps. But the Boss was against the idea, and a platform was specially built to record the sound of their own footsteps.

Musicians

- **Bruce Springsteen:** vocals, guitars, organ, drums (?), loops (?), percussion
- **Ron Aniello:** guitars, bass guitar, keyboards, drums (?), loops
- **Steve Jordan:** tambourine
- **Soozie Tyrell:** violin
- **Patti Scialfa, Lisa Lowell, Soozie Tyrell:** backing vocals
- **Ross Petersen, Ron Aniello, Rob Lebret, Clif Norrell:** vocal group
- **New York Chamber Consort:** strings
- **Unidentified musicians:** foot-stomping, drums

Recording

- **Stone Hill Studio, Colts Neck, New Jersey:** 2011
- **MSR Studio B, New York:** 2011

Technical team

- **Producers:** Ron Aniello, Bruce Springsteen
- **Executive producer:** Jon Landau
- **Recording engineers:** Ross Petersen, Ron Aniello, Rob Lebret, Clif Norrell, Toby Scott
- **Mixing:** Rich Costey (Eldorado Recording Studios, Burbank)

The No Banker Left Behind Coalition demonstrates on Wall Street against the financialization of the economy.

Genesis and lyrics

After his wakeup call in *We Take Care of Our Own*, Bruce Springsteen cuts to the heart of the matter with *Easy Money*, which probably dates from February 2011. The narrator, a small-time crook, sees all around him a tiny minority of wealthy people making money easily. He wants a share of the cake, and he aims to get hold of it armed with a Smith & Wesson .38—accompanied by his girlfriend wearing her best dress. "That's the street criminalization of the big-money Wall Street hustle," Bruce Springsteen explained to Jon Stewart of *Rolling Stone* magazine. "That's the guy that's saying, 'Everybody else is getting theirs, and not paying for it, I'm going out to get mine.' That hustle has been legitimized over the past four years, when you have the level of risk and greed at the top of the financial industry, and people basically walking away, relatively scot-free, completely unaccountable. That lack of accountability is the poison shot straight into the heart of the country. It goes back to Watergate."[149]

Bruce Springsteen first performed *Easy Money* live at a concert on 18 March 2012 in Atlanta, Georgia.

Production

Easy Money was the first song Springsteen wrote for *Wrecking Ball*—the one that lit the spark, as he said himself, "[...] and then the rest of the songs came pretty quickly, one day at a time."[151]

The song starts with an "urban loop," a rhythm loop consisting largely of handclaps and footsteps recorded on a platform. The tune has a slight Irish tinge, heightened by Soozie Tyrell's violin, the strings of the New York Chamber Consort, and the various acoustic guitars. Oddly, the song has points in common with *Into the Fire*, on *The Rising* album, as the rhythmic sequence and the tune of the verses are quite similar. But *Easy Money* has a more folk-like sound, even though Ron Aniello plays a lead guitar that has very probably been saturated at the console (Steve Van Zandt would play it live). Also, there are drums on the recording. The drummer is not named in the credits, and it is unlikely to be Springsteen or Ron Aniello.

Backing vocals from the trio of Patti, Lisa, and Soozie come in after the third verse (at 1'16), supported by the vocal group, consisting of the four recording engineers, and end the song, accompanied by the piano, organ, violin, rhythm loop, and tambourine.

SHACKLED AND DRAWN

Bruce Springsteen / 3'46

Musicians

Bruce Springsteen: vocals, guitar, banjo, keyboards, percussion
Ron Aniello: guitar, bass guitar, keyboards, loops
Cindy Mizelle: vocals at the end of the song
Charles Giordano: piano, accordion
Matt Chamberlain: drums, percussion
Soozie Tyrell: violin
Curt Ramm, Clark Gayton, Stan Harrison, Eddie Manion, Dan Levine, Art Baron: brass section
Clif Norrell: tuba
Patti Scialfa, Lisa Lowell, Soozie Tyrell: backing vocals
Ross Petersen, Ron Aniello, Rob Lebret, Clif Norrell: vocal group

Recording

Stone Hill Studio, Colts Neck, New Jersey: 2011

Technical team

Producers: Ron Aniello, Bruce Springsteen
Executive producer: Jon Landau
Recording engineers: Ross Petersen, Ron Aniello, Rob Lebret, Clif Norrell, Toby Scott
Mixing: Bob Clearmountain (Mix This!, Los Angeles), Brandon Duncan (assistant)

Lyn Collins in London, 1989. An extract from her song *Me and My Baby Got Our Own Thing Going* brings *Shackled and Drawn* to a close.

Genesis and lyrics

In all probability, *Shackled and Drawn* dates from 2010. Bruce Springsteen explained to *Rolling Stone* journalist Jon Stewart that it is similar to the field songs and chants of African-American slaves.[149] It is certainly a protest song, a veritable shout of rage: "I woke this morning shackled and drawn." The narrator is working class, and every passing day brings him closer to the grave. He is oppressed—the victim of an unjust society: "Gambling man rolls the dice, working man pays the bill." Meanwhile, the banker, at the top of the hill, makes piles of dollars and parties, indifferent to the woes of his fellow humans. But anger is boiling up. "I want everybody to stand up and be counted," Springsteen sings. Is he calling for revolution?

The Boss has performed *Shackled and Drawn* almost 150 times, from his concert at the Apollo Theater, New York, on 9 March 2012, to the one in Göteborg, Sweden, on 25 June 2016.

Production

Shackled and Drawn is one of the three songs on *Wrecking Ball* that Springsteen originally earmarked for his gospel album. The piece has the sound quality of an Irish Celtic dance, with violin, foot-stomping, and even a banjo (from 1'27). The song begins with the Boss's acoustic guitar, which he strums while muffling the strings. Then a vigorous bass drum with an invasive sound heralds the drumming of Matt Chamberlain. Electric guitars, a bass guitar, an accordion, a piano, several synthesizers, samples, and percussion instruments gradually come in, rendering the sound texture thicker, as does the brass section, which discreetly makes itself heard from the fourth verse (at 1'04)—not forgetting Clif Norrell's tuba.

As regards vocals, the Boss lays it on a little too thick, rendering his performance somewhat overdone. Accompanying him throughout is the trio of female singers, as well as the vocal group comprising the four recording engineers, who warm the piece with a saloon-bar atmosphere, especially toward the end.

Shackled and Drawn ends with an extract from *Me and My Baby Got Our Own Thing Going* (1972), a song written by Lyn Collins with James Brown, Fred Wesley, and Charles Bobbitt. However, it is not her voice that is heard, but that of Cindy Mizelle, the talented backing vocalist who accompanied the E Street Band in live performances.

2012

JACK OF ALL TRADES

Bruce Springsteen / 6'00

"Now sometimes tomorrow comes soaked in treasure and blood," Springsteen sings. The expression "treasure and blood" refers to the cost of war in human lives and money. It was used by President Theodore Roosevelt in 1900, with reference to the American War of Independence, and again by Senator Carl Levin in 2006, with reference to the Iraq war.

Musicians
- **Bruce Springsteen:** vocals, guitar, banjo, mandolin (?), piano, organ, drums (?), tambourine
- **Ron Aniello:** guitar, bass guitar, keyboards, drums (?), loops
- **Tom Morello:** lead guitar
- **Soozie Tyrell:** violin
- **Curt Ramm, Clark Gayton, Stan Harrison, Eddie Manion, Dan Levine, Art Baron:** brass section
- **Curt Ramm:** solo trumpet
- **New York Chamber Consort:** strings
- **Rob Mathes:** conductor

Recording
- **Stone Hill Studio, Colts Neck, New Jersey:** 2011
- **MSR Studio B, New York:** 2011

Technical team
- **Producers:** Ron Aniello, Bruce Springsteen
- **Executive producer:** Jon Landau
- **Recording engineers:** Ross Petersen, Ron Aniello, Rob Lebret, Clif Norrell, Toby Scott
- **Mixing:** Bob Clearmountain (Mix This!, Los Angeles), Brandon Duncan (assistant)

The trumpet player Curt Ramm joined Bruce Springsteen for the recording of *Jack of All Trades*.

Genesis and lyrics

The narrator of this song declares that he can mow the lawn, clear leaves from the drain, mend the roof, hammer in nails, set stones, and more. In short, take all the work that God provides. Here, again, Bruce Springsteen is describing the America he sees around him: "The banker man grows fat, the working man grows thin." To be sure, "It's all happened before and it'll happen again," but you sense that the socio-economic situation in the United States has deteriorated since the 2000s.

Jack of All Trades sounds like a call to show fighting spirit, even to revolt: "If I had me a gun, I'd find the bastards and shoot 'em on sight." The songwriter from New Jersey points to the culprits—the bankers and other vultures in finance who with impunity have plunged thousands of families into despair when they lost their homes. Doubtless he is also implicitly referring to his own past, specifically to the financial difficulties his parents encountered during his childhood.

Production

Jack of All Trades is a rather somber ballad, but superb nonetheless. After a short intro consisting of electronic sounds, it is driven on by insistent arpeggios played on an acoustic piano. The tune, which Springsteen sings in a resigned voice, is a sort of refrain, simple and persistent. The various instruments appear in turn: synth pads, bass guitar, brass, organ, and so forth. The instrumental bridge is especially effective, with the brass and Curt Ramm's trumpet, which takes up the tune lyrically and with melancholy (from 2'16). A banjo, and probably a mandolin (on the right) can be heard, as well as a violin and accordion, with the whole supported by a bass drum and snare drum. Who is the drummer? It's hard to say. The strings, conducted by Rob Mathes, come in discreetly in the fifth verse. The song appears to end with the following verse, but the instruments come in again, allowing Tom Morello, the guitarist of Rage Against the Machine, to deliver an excellent solo, accompanied by Ramm's trumpet and supported by the drums, played in a manner curiously reminiscent of Nick Mason's.

DEATH TO MY HOMETOWN

Bruce Springsteen / 3'29

The extract from *The Last Words of Copernicus* that was chosen for *Death to My Hometown* begins most certainly at 0'53 on the original recording by Alan Lomax.

Musicians

Bruce Springsteen: vocals, guitars, banjo
Ron Aniello: guitars, bass guitar, keyboards, loops
Charles Giordano: accordion (?)
Soozie Tyrell: violin
Matt Chamberlain: drums
Kevin Buell: marching drum
Ross Petersen, Ron Aniello, Rob Lebret, Clif Norrell: vocal group
Art Baron: penny whistle (?)
Unidentified musician: hurdy-gurdy

Recording

Stone Hill Studio, Colts Neck, New Jersey: 2011

Technical team

Producers: Ron Aniello, Bruce Springsteen
Executive producer: Jon Landau
Recording engineers: Ross Petersen, Ron Aniello, Rob Lebret, Clif Norrell, Toby Scott
Mixing: Chris Lord-Alge (Mix LA, Los Angeles), Keith Armstrong and Nik Karpen (assistants)

The ethnomusicologist Alan Lomax recorded *The Last Words of Copernicus*, which features in *Death to My Hometown*.

2012

Genesis and lyrics

Bruce Springsteen has never clarified when he wrote *Death to My Hometown*. It was probably after the financial crisis of 2008, in all likelihood in 2011. Musically, the songwriter is here reconnecting with the folk tradition, which he had revisited so successfully with the recording of *We Shall Overcome: The Seeger Sessions*. *Death to My Hometown* bathes in an atmosphere that harks back to an eternal Ireland, as if the songwriter had spent interminable nights listening to The Dubliners or The Pogues.

However, the song is also topical. "*Death to My Hometown* sounds like an Irish rebel song, but it's all about what happened four years ago. I want to give people a sense that this is something that's happened over and over and over again; what happened in 2008 happened before the turn of the century, and just after the turn of the century—it's a repetitive, historical cycle that has basically landed on the heads of the same people."[149] These "same heads" are the working and middle classes, who were hit hard by the 2008 financial crisis. The culprits? Those "vultures" who "destroyed our families, factories, and they took our homes," the "robber barons"—that is, traders and other financiers on Wall Street—whom Springsteen hopes to see go straight to hell. Thus, the death visited upon the town has not come from cannonballs, rifles, or bombs, but from financiers.

Production

The song begins with the beat of a bass drum, handclaps, very probably a hurdy-gurdy, and a sample from *The Last Words of Copernicus*, a poem by the mid-18th-century poet Philip Doddridge, which was set to music by Sarah Lancaster in 1869. It is a recording of the Alabama Sacred Harp Singers, made by the ethnomusicologist Alan Lomax on 12 September 1959. Adapted by Ron Aniello at Springsteen's request, the performance by this fabulous choir fits perfectly with the rhythm of the song, which is given by Matt Chamberlain, an excellent drummer who has worked with musicians ranging from David Bowie to Joe Cocker and The Who. His drumming is both supple and powerful, hammering the tempo with impressive bass drumbeats (doubtless reinforced by a drum sample put together by the producer). To heighten the piece's Celtic flavor, a penny whistle—a small Irish flute—

The Alabama Sacred Harp Singers in Double Springs, Alabama, 1944.

accompanies the Alabama Sacred Harp Singers, apparently played by Art Baron, who was more often employed as a trombonist, at least on records by the Boss. Probably Charlie Giordano's accordion also makes a contribution.

The first two verses alternate with extracts from *The Last Words of Copernicus*. Springsteen sings with energy, and a sort of suppressed rage, accompanied by the sounds of banjos, acoustic guitars, bass guitar, and violin (for example, at 1'10). After a bridge there follows a third verse, again with the choir in the background, reinforced by numerous handclaps (at 1'59). To accompany Springsteen in the last lines of the song, the vocal group comprising the four recording engineers is pressed back into service (this is their third contribution to the album!), again with its distinctive live, mocking tone (from 2'33).

The song ends with a reprise of the sample, supported by all the musicians (especially Kevin Buell, Springsteen's guitar technician, with a marching drum), who play with enthusiasm and exaltation, thus giving the impression that they are in the same studio as the Alabama Sacred Harp Singers—a real feat of production on the part of Ron Aniello. Also of note is the excellent mixing executed by Chris Lord-Alge, a recording engineer who was already known to the Boss because he remixed three of his songs: *Dancing in the Dark*, *Cover Me*, and *Born in the U.S.A.*

The live version of *Death to My Hometown* does not include the sample of *The Last Words of Copernicus*, but showcases saturated guitars, a muscular brass section, and, as at the 15 March 2012 performance at the Moody Theater in Austin, Texas, Tom Morello's blazing lead guitar.

Death to My Hometown is a very fine song which, incidentally, would not have been at all out of place on the tracklisting of *We Shall Overcome: The Seeger Sessions*, were it not for the fact that it was never performed by Pete Seeger...

HEADPHONES AT THE READY

At 2'42, the firing of an AK-47, the famous Kalashnikov Soviet rifle, one of the most emblematic weapons of the 20th century, is heard. This sound effect is from an open-access soundbank.

2012

A muscular wind section on the Wrecking Ball Tour, in Wrigley Field, Chicago, in September 2012.

THIS DEPRESSION

Bruce Springsteen / 4'08

For Springsteen Addicts

Tom Morello, the guitarist of Rage Against the Machine who took part in the recording of *This Depression*, had struck up a friendship with Bruce Springsteen when he sang *The Ghost of Tom Joad* with him in 2008—a song that RATM had recorded during the sessions for *Renegades* (2000).

Musicians

Bruce Springsteen: vocals, guitars, piano, drums, loops (?), percussion
Ron Aniello: guitars, bass guitar, keyboards
Tom Morello: lead guitar
Soozie Tyrell: violin
Patti Scialfa, Lisa Lowell, Soozie Tyrell: backing vocals

Recording

Stone Hill Studio, Colts Neck, New Jersey: 2011

Technical team

Producers: Ron Aniello, Bruce Springsteen
Executive producer: Jon Landau
Recording engineers: Ross Petersen, Ron Aniello, Rob Lebret, Clif Norrell, Toby Scott
Mixing: Bob Clearmountain (Mix This!, Los Angeles), Brandon Duncan (assistant)

Genesis and lyrics

The narrator is in danger of plunging into the abyss at any moment. "Baby, I've been down but never this down," he sings. He feels the need to confide in the woman he loves, saying: "This is my confession, I need your heart." A short time later, he adds: "I've been without love but never forsaken." Clearly, this suffering is not only romantic. Like the other characters Bruce Springsteen introduces throughout the dramatic sequence of *Wrecking Ball*, the narrator of *This Depression* could be one of the many victims of the banking and financial crisis of 2008. His is therefore a dual bitterness. What is certain is that his salvation will come—if there can be any salvation—from love, understanding, and a shared bond with the woman he loves. This song is also perhaps an expression of the songwriter's own depressive state.

Despite its delicate melody and dreamlike atmosphere (due to Tom Morello's guitar), *This Depression* has been performed live only seven times, the first performance taking place in Bergen, Norway, on 23 July 2012.

Production

Of course, *This Depression* is not a joyous song. Springsteen sings with a subdued, pained voice. It is impossible not to think of his own depression, which he revealed in his autobiography, *Born to Run*. He appears to play the drums, with a relatively simple rhythmic pattern which, nevertheless, requires a decent dose of groove. Mission accomplished. The sounds from his drum kit are resolutely modern. Here, Ron Aniello has done a remarkable job—even though the snare drum is a little too prominent. The producer has left his stamp especially clearly on the instrumental arrangements, systematically working on most of the instruments, keyboards, guitars, and even the fabulous backing vocals of the vocal trio led by Patti Scialfa. However, the most interesting part of the song is without a doubt the instrumental bridge, led by Tom Morello's lead guitar, in which the playing and instruments' entries are superb (from 1'29)—there are up to three guitar tracks, which answer each other, giving an ethereal feel that inevitably brings to mind David Gilmour and Pink Floyd.

Bruce Springsteen and the E Street Band in Chicago, September 2012, with Tom Morello as guest star.

WRECKING BALL

Bruce Springsteen / 5'49

Musicians

Bruce Springsteen: vocals, guitars, keyboards, percussion
Ron Aniello: guitars, bass guitar, keyboards, loops
Charles Giordano: accordion, celesta, piano, organ
Rob Lebret: guitar, backing vocals
Soozie Tyrell: violin
Curt Ramm: trumpet solo
Curt Ramm, Clark Gayton, Stan Harrison, Eddie Manion, Dan Levine, Art Baron: brass section
Max Weinberg: drums
Patti Scialfa, Lisa Lowell, Soozie Tyrell, Steven Van Zandt: backing vocals
Ross Petersen, Ron Aniello, Rob Lebret, Clif Norrell: vocal group
New York Chamber Consort: strings
Unidentified musicians: handclaps

Recording

Stone Hill Studio, Colts Neck, New Jersey: 2011
MSR Studio B, New York: 2011
Very Loud House Studio, Woodland Hills, California: 2011

Technical team

Producers: Ron Aniello, Bruce Springsteen
Executive producer: Jon Landau
Recording engineers: Ross Petersen, Ron Aniello, Rob Lebret, Clif Norrell, Toby Scott
Mixing: Bob Clearmountain (Mix This!, Los Angeles), Brandon Duncan (assistant)

A WRECKING BALL TO SUIT EVERY TASTE

Wrecking Ball is a title (and a subject) that appears to have inspired a number of singer-songwriters and/or performers. To name but a few, it is the title of an album by Emmylou Harris (1995), one by the band Dead Confederate (2008), a song by Neil Young (1989), and another by Miley Cyrus (2013).

Genesis and lyrics

Bruce Springsteen wrote *Wrecking Ball* during the summer or fall of 2009. On 30 September of that year, during the first of five concerts played at the Giants Stadium in East Rutherford, New Jersey—as part of the Working On a Dream tour—he told the audience that he had just written the song, following the announcement of the planned demolition of the famous stadium where the Giants and Jets American football teams from New York had played. "I was raised out of steel here in the swamps of Jersey," are the opening words of *Wrecking Ball.*

The demolition of the Giants Stadium is, of course, a metaphor. For the songwriter, *Wrecking Ball* in fact describes the disappearance of the American dream from the collective imagination, under the onslaught of neoliberalism, which led to the banking and financial crisis of 2008 and to unprecedented social inequality. Faced with this carnage, his feelings are ambivalent. "Bring on your wrecking ball/Come on and take your best shot, let me see what you got." These few words could well be heralding the start of a revolt by the downtrodden. And the injunction to "Hold tight to your anger, don't fall to your fears" is an incitement to stand firm.

Wrecking Ball is one of the most powerful songs Springsteen has written.

Production

Wrecking Ball begins with just Springsteen's guitar, very probably his Telecaster-Esquire. As soon as he attacks the lead vocals, the listener feels that they are rediscovering the Boss's old voice, the one from a time when he sang in a less restrained manner, and doubtless with more freshness. This impression is also due to the recording and mixing, with less compression as a bonus—or at least that is how it sounds.

Charlie Giordano very quickly joins them, accompanying discreetly on the accordion. The song's tune follows, somewhat reminiscent of that of *Secret Garden* from the *Greatest Hits* album, and probably played on the trumpet by Curt Ramm, on the violin by Soozie Tyrell, and on the celesta by Giordano. The sounds interweave, with equalization leveling out the different frequencies relative to each other (at 0'37).

The drums enter in the second verse, and it is Max Weinberg who is on the case. This is the first song on the album in which three members of the E Street Band take

A poster advertising the concert by Bruce Springsteen and the E Street Band before the demolition of the Giants Stadium in East Rutherford, New Jersey.

part—the other being Steve Van Zandt on backing vocals. It is also the only song on the album that features Weinberg. In a return to the method that the group always used in recording sessions, the basic track was recorded live with Springsteen on guitar, Giordano on keyboards, Aniello on bass guitar, and Weinberg on drums. And it must be admitted that the groove is different—more airy, supple, and effective. This is noticeable in the second verse, where they embark on a rhythm that is especially energetic, rock-like, and exhilarating (from 1'41). An organ, a piano, saturated guitars, and a brass section can be heard supporting them. There follows a bridge section, before the riff returns, which has a lighter atmosphere, with violin, guitars, tambourine, and handclaps (at 2'39). In the following verse, three tracks of electric rhythm guitars come in, one after the other, with the organ in the background, pushing Springsteen's voice a little more into the limelight (from 2'55).

The last section of the song is perhaps the one that works best. There is an irresistible crescendo from the various elements, especially the backing vocals, where the voices of the women's trio blend with those of the four recording engineers—not forgetting, of course, the voice of Steve Van Zandt—as well as the strings of the New York Chamber Consort, conducted by Rob Mathes.

The grand finale explodes when the Boss utters a loud "one, two, a-one-two-three-four" (at 4'30), literally giving rein to Max Weinberg, who rushes headlong into an excellent, frenetic bout of drumming. Weinberg is surrounded by all the musicians, who are equally frenzied, singing "whoa whoa" like the E Street Band in full cry, the whole electrified by riffs in the manner of Earth Wind & Fire, played by the brass.

It had been a long time since Springsteen had produced such a song, such a totally joyous and liberating burst of adrenalin. *Wrecking Ball* is truly one of the great successes of the album—even of the songwriter's last five records. The live versions of the song are, of course, extraordinary, though not, it must be admitted, to the high standard of the studio version, which is remarkable—and that is rare enough to be worth pointing out.

For Springsteen Addicts

After the five concerts performed at the Giants Stadium in East Rutherford, Bruce Springsteen and the E Street Band were on the bill at the Wachovia Spectrum, in Philadelphia, on 13, 14, 19, and 20 October. During the first and last of those four concerts, they performed *Wrecking Ball* with modified lyrics, referencing the planned demolition of that stadium as well. Pearl Jam were the last band to perform there, on 31 October.

YOU'VE GOT IT

Bruce Springsteen / 3'48

Marc Muller has played with Alain Bashung, Steve Forbert, Shania Twain, and Branford Marsalis, among others.

Musicians

Bruce Springsteen: vocals, guitar, claviers, percussions
Ron Aniello: guitar, bass guitar, keyboards
Matt Chamberlain: drums
Greg Leisz: lap steel guitar
Marc Muller: pedal steel guitar
Curt Ramm, Clark Gayton, Stan Harrison, Eddie Manion, Dan Levine, Art Baron: brass section
Unidentified musicians: handclaps

Recording

Stone Hill Studio, Colts Neck, New Jersey: 2011

Technical team

Producers: Ron Aniello, Bruce Springsteen
Executive producer: Jon Landau
Recording engineers: Ross Petersen, Ron Aniello, Rob Lebret, Clif Norrell, Toby Scott
Mixing: Bob Clearmountain (Mix This!, Los Angeles), Brandon Duncan (assistant)

Greg Leisz, on pedal steel guitar in *You've Got It*, performs in An Evening with the Majestic Silver Strings, Los Angeles, in March 2011.

Genesis and lyrics

After the extremely somber *Wrecking Ball*, Bruce Springsteen pauses in his criticism of early 2000s America. Here, he returns to the fine old tradition of the love song, midway between rock and folk. The woman the narrator is addressing possesses something that cannot be found anywhere else—at any rate not in books. It cannot be taught, manufactured, or bought. It cannot be broken either, and it is impossible to steal or imitate it. What is it? Obviously, the song's heroine possesses supernatural powers—the power of love, which clearly elevates her to the heights of sensuality.

You've Got It could be described as an optimistic song, in striking contrast to the others on *Wrecking Ball*. Yet Bruce Springsteen has performed it live only once, to date, at a concert on 24 July 2012 in Bergen, Norway.

Production

You've Got It is a song in the rockabilly blues vein, a genre that has always inspired Springsteen to produce very fine songs. This is no exception—the results are excellent. Certainly, in terms of originality, it is in a very well-worn style, but that doesn't really matter. The Boss delivers it with talent, and that is the main thing.

The first verse begins with the songwriter's voice, with a slap-back echo. He accompanies himself by strumming a guitar whose acoustic tone is quite odd—doubtless his Telecaster-Esquire, but highly compressed. In the second verse, a piano, which is equally compressed, and a tambourine come in. Matt Chamberlain's drums make their first appearance, with bass drum and hi-hat, in the following verse, supported by handclaps. But it is in the following instrumental break that the song literally explodes, again with a highly compressed sound, and alongside the brass section performing a very fine R&B accompaniment (from 1'49). *You've Got It* is also an opportunity to hear some excellent solo guitar parts—played on the lap steel guitar by Greg Leisz and on the pedal steel guitar by Marc Muller. The final solo is superb; it is a shame that the fade-out is too quick, cutting short the improvisation.

ROCKY GROUND

Bruce Springsteen / 4'41

Musicians
Bruce Springsteen: vocals, guitars, keyboards, percussion
Ron Aniello: guitar, keyboards, drums (?), loops
Michelle Moore: vocals
Charles Giordano: piano, organ
Curt Ramm, Clark Gayton, Stan Harrison, Eddie Manion, Dan Levine, Art Baron: brass section
Victorious Gospel Choir: backing vocals

Recording
Stone Hill Studio, Colts Neck, New Jersey: 2011

Technical team
Producers: Ron Aniello, Bruce Springsteen
Executive producer: Jon Landau
Recording engineers: Ross Petersen, Ron Aniello, Rob Lebret, Clif Norrell, Toby Scott
Mixing: Ron Aniello, Ross Petersen(Thrill Hill), Rob Lebret (assistant)

In the Parable of the Sower, Jesus tells the story of a farmer who scatters some grain. Some falls by the wayside and is eaten by birds; some falls on stony ground or among brambles; and some is lost. But some grain lands on good earth and bears fruit. The grain is, of course, the word of God. Each of us is free to hear it.

Genesis and lyrics

Rocky Ground was written for a gospel movie Bruce Springsteen was thinking of making in 2009–2010, and there is no doubt that here we are immersed in the heart of African-American religious tradition, which is both solemn and spellbinding. The song begins with a sample of *I'm a Soldier in the Army of the Lord*, performed by the congregation of The Church of God in Christ and recorded in 1942 by the ethnomusicologists Alan Lomax, John W Work, and Lewis Wade Jones. The song then continues with a ballad, also in a very gospel spirit.

Is Bruce Springsteen asking God for help, having seen the disaster caused by the financial crisis? At any rate, there are numerous biblical references in this song. The title itself refers to the Parable of the Sower, which is found in three gospels—those of Matthew, Mark, and Luke. Bruce Springsteen also mentions the Deluge ("Forty days and nights of rain have washed this land"), the Promised Land ("we're Canaan bound"), and the day of the Last Judgment. As for the reference to "money changers," these are the merchants and money changers in the Temple in Jerusalem who were accused by Jesus of perverting it through their commercial activities. Doubtless Bruce Springsteen sees them reincarnated in the Wall Street traders of today.

Two singles of *Rocky Ground* were released as limited editions (7-inch vinyl and CD) on 21 April 2012, with a live version of *The Promise* recorded at the concert performed in Carousel House, Asbury Park, on 7 December 2010.

Production

Rocky Ground begins with a gloomy, deep synth pad that fades in. Suddenly, a sample of a male voice shouts: "I'm a soldier!" According to the album's sleeve notes this is an extract from *I'm a Soldier in the Army of the Lord*, performed by The Church of God in Christ, as described above. The problem is that the recording in question does not contain the phrase used by Springsteen, unless it is from another version of the spiritual, recorded by Alan Lomax in 1942, or simply an extract that is not identified. Be that as it may, a drum loop made by Ron Aniello comes in after this sample. The sound is deliberately light, equalized, hip-hop style. Then the voice of Michelle Moore suddenly attacks the first verse—full of feeling, its

2012

Bruce Springsteen and the E Street Band in concert in East Rutherford, New Jersey, during the Wrecking Ball World Tour.

timbre pure. The singer was not a newcomer to Springsteen's circle, as she had already featured in *Let's Be Friends (Skin to Skin)* and *Mary's Place* on *The Rising* album (2002), with the vocal group The Alliance Singers. She also took part in the Wrecking Ball Tour as a backing vocalist, alongside the E Street Band. In the first verse, it is Springsteen who sings, again with the fragility and magnetic power that make him such a unique artist who comes across as deeply sincere. He is accompanied by the airy chords of a piano and by a discreet pulse, most certainly produced by an arpeggiator.

An organ, brass chords, and a real drum kit come in at the third verse—it would appear that Ron Aniello is playing the last of those (at 1'50). There follows an instrumental passage, led by the brass section, which plays an elegant melodic motif (from 2'15). Springsteen is playing a guitar with a wah-wah pedal—a rare example of his making use of this effect pedal—the previous one being in *Missing* in 1996 (on an EP containing four songs). It isn't a Jimi Hendrix-style performance, obviously, but rather a rhythm guitar mixed somewhat in the background, which is undeniably effective.

The fourth chorus is followed by a rap passage, written by the Boss (from 3'02)—something completely new from him. Originally, he had thought of performing it himself. Then, as he did not feel ready for such an exercise, various names were mentioned, including Al Green and Mavis Staples. In the end, it was once again Michelle Moore who was called upon, and it must be said that the result—with help from Aniello, who adjusted her diction during editing so that it fitted with the rhythm—is gorgeous and all the more since her performance is supported by brass and backing vocals that are exquisite.

Finally, the piece ends in a masterly fashion, with the Victorious Gospel Choir (of which Michelle Moore is incidentally a member), conducted by Lilly "Crawford" Brown. Springsteen joins the singers, with deeply moving results. And this astonishing song ends with just Michelle Moore, simply accompanied by a church organ.

With this piece, Springsteen proved that he could still surprise and pull off a real feat. Independently of his religious beliefs, he expresses a certain spirituality just by virtue of his talent and humanity, touching everyone's heart.

And we should also pay tribute to Ron Aniello, whose production of this song is luminous, intelligent, and superb.

For Springsteen Addicts

A video of *Rocky Ground* was shot in 2012 and released on 24 May that year. It shows a hand writing the words as the song plays, against the background of an urban landscape, all filmed in black and white.

LAND OF HOPE AND DREAMS

Bruce Springsteen / 6'58

This song references *People Get Ready* (1965) by the Impressions, a soul masterpiece of the 1960s, in which Curtis Mayfield uses the metaphor of a train to describe the legitimate fight for freedom by African-Americans.

Musicians

Bruce Springsteen: vocals, guitars, keyboards, loops (?)
Ron Aniello: guitars, bass guitar, keyboards, loops
Michelle Moore: vocals, backing vocals
Clarence Clemons: saxophone
Steve Van Zandt: mandolin, backing vocals
Soozie Tyrell: violin
Curt Ramm, Clark Gayton, Stan Harrison, Eddie Manion, Dan Levine, Art Baron: brass section
Charles Giordano: piano, organ
Matt Chamberlain: drums
Patti Scialfa, Lisa Lowell, Soozie Tyrell: backing vocals
Ross Petersen, Ron Aniello, Rob Lebret, Clif Norrell: vocal group
Victorious Gospel Choir: backing vocals

Recording

Stone Hill Studio, Colts Neck, New Jersey: 2011

Technical team

Producers: Ron Aniello, Bruce Springsteen
Executive producer: Jon Landau
Recording engineers: Ross Petersen, Ron Aniello, Rob Lebret, Clif Norrell, Toby Scott
Mixing: Chris Lord-Alge (Mix LA, Los Angeles), Keith Armstrong and Nik Karpen (assistants)

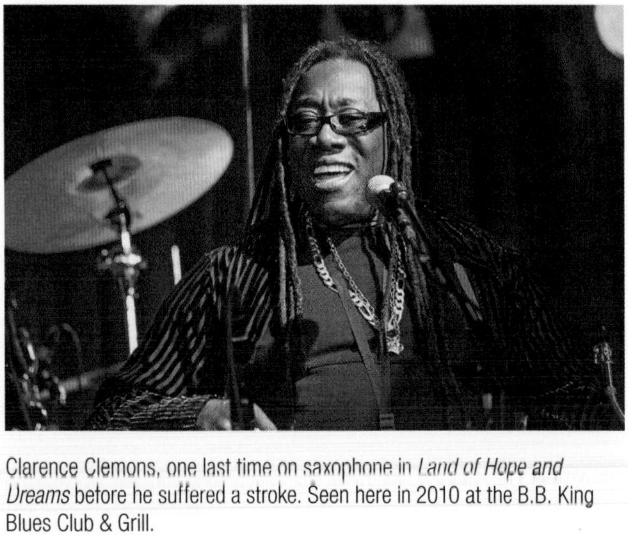

Clarence Clemons, one last time on saxophone in *Land of Hope and Dreams* before he suffered a stroke. Seen here in 2010 at the B.B. King Blues Club & Grill.

Genesis and lyrics

Land of Hope and Dreams is the earliest composition on *Wrecking Ball*. Bruce Springsteen wrote it in 1998, to celebrate the re-forming of the E Street Band. He first performed it live at a concert in the Convention Hall, Asbury Park, on 18 March 1999, and has played it regularly since, notably onstage at Madison Square Garden on 29 June and 1 July 2000.

Incidentally, it is the 1 July recording which features on a two-track CD, along with *The Rising* (1999), and on *Live in New York City* (2001), which apparently led Bruce Springsteen and his producer, Ron Aniello, to produce a studio version. Although the rhythm and atmosphere are different from those of the live version of *Land of Hope and Dreams*, the message is the same. It is a manifesto against injustice, in the past as well as in the present and future. As Bruce Springsteen explained to Jon Stewart of *Rolling Stone* magazine: "But it was a funny song because the voices in it sort of do come from beyond the current moment, they're talking about that other world: 'People, get ready, there's a train coming'—everybody knows what that refers to. It refers to both something that's present, whether it's a train of equality, justice, fairness, whatever, good times, joy, struggle—that train is coming into your life every single day of your life."[149] This train carries "saints and sinners," "losers and winners," and "whores and gamblers," sings Bruce Springsteen. No one, then, is barred from the journey. Utopia is where it's headed.

Production

Land of Hope and Dreams begins with two gospel singers and a church organ in the background. They are quickly joined by the members of the Victorious Gospel Choir, accompanied by the mandolin of Steve Van Zandt, before electronic drums, programmed by Ron Aniello, herald a much more hard-rock passage, featuring Matt Chamberlain on a real drum kit, Charlie Giordano on a Hammond B-3 organ, and Springsteen on saturated guitars. Then the song's brilliant riff bursts forth, led by the mandolin and recorded on several tracks (at 0'48). In fact, this riff is a motif that the Boss himself had recorded on the mandolin for *Labour of Love*, a song by his friend Joe Grushecky, for the album *American Babylon* for which he produced most of the tracks in 1995.

2012

The Boss with Joe Grushecky in 2012. In 1995, Springsteen recorded a mandolin part for Grushecky's song *Labor Of Love* in a similar style to the part in *Land Of Hope And Dreams*.

For Springsteen Addicts

During the recording of *Wrecking Ball*, Clarence Clemons suffered a stroke, on 12 June 2011, and then fell into a coma. Bruce Springsteen immediately flew to Palm Beach, Florida. In the hospital, he played *Land of Hope and Dreams* on the guitar for his friend as he lay dying.

From the first verse, it is clear that the songwriter is driven by the same conviction and energy that he deployed when he started out. Despite success, awards, and the passage of time, Springsteen throws himself into the song completely, without restraint, as if his career depended on it. This first verse, which he accompanies with an acoustic guitar, is followed by a short chorus, with bass guitar and Hammond B-3. Then the mandolin riff explodes again, supported by Chamberlain's extraordinary drumming (at 1'51). His spirited, funky playing, with its syncopated groove, is very different from the first live version the E Street Band had played at Madison Square Garden in 2000 (which was excellent all the same), but Aniello has chosen to inject an energy and dynamism into the piece that are closer to his own canons, which are ultimately quite different from those of the E Street Band.

After two more verses comes the most poignant moment in the song. This is Clarence Clemons' saxophone solo (from 3'46)—his sole contribution to the album. Since the start of the recording sessions for *Wrecking Ball*, Clemons, who was ill, had postponed coming into the studio for as long as possible. Sadly, he died on 18 June 2011, without having had the time to record a single note. While some of the musicians were devastated by the loss of their friend, Aniello remained focused on the album. Springsteen finally joined him. The songwriter had said: "[...] when we were finished mixing, there's a part in *In the Land of Hope and Dreams* where the sax solo was supposed to be [...] I wish we had Clarence on there [...]"[154] This remark gave Aniello an idea: he looked for an old live recording of Clemons. He found one, but the key and tempo did not match exactly (the live and studio versions were a semitone apart). No problem. Aniello managed to resolve the issue and incorporated the result into the song. "[Then] I literally forgot to bring it up to Bruce [...],"[154] he explained. One day, he remembered, and he told Springsteen as a surprise. Caught totally off guard, the latter could not hold back his tears. "We were lucky to get him on *Land of Hope and Dreams*, which was essential—really essential." Springsteen said. "When he comes up, it's just a lovely moment for me."[151] Aniello commented: "It was really a special moment for all of us. It's a moment I'll remember the rest of my life."[154]

The rest of the song is a crescendo toward the final climax, with a second saxophone solo (at 5'14). For the final part of the song, Springsteen decided—in contrast to the live version of 2000—to use an extract from the lyrics of *People Get Ready* by the Impressions, a song that had left a profound impression on him and to which he had already paid tribute in *My City of Ruins* on *The Rising* album. Initially, Springsteen shares the lead vocals with Michelle Moore, but then leaves her to end alone, accompanied by the gentle harmonies of the brass section (from 6'36).

Land of Hope and Dreams is an essential song in Springsteen's career, and a gem of his oeuvre—if only because of the Big Man's final appearance. Superb.

WE ARE ALIVE

Bruce Springsteen / 5'36

Musicians
Bruce Springsteen: vocals, guitars, drums (?), tambourine, maracas, glockenspiel
Ron Aniello: guitar, bass guitar, drums (?), keyboards, loops
Greg Leisz: banjo, mandocello
Darrell Leonard: trumpet
Soozie Tyrell: violin
Max Weinberg: drums (?)
Patti Scialfa, Lisa Lowell, Soozie Tyrell: backing vocals
Unidentified musicians: handclaps
Recording
Stone Hill Studio, Colts Neck, New Jersey: 2011
Technical team
Producers: Ron Aniello, Bruce Springsteen
Executive producer: Jon Landau
Recording engineers: Ross Petersen, Ron Aniello, Rob Lebret, Clif Norrell, Toby Scott
Mixing: Bob Clearmountain (Mix This!, Los Angeles), Brandon Duncan (assistant)

Johnny Cash and his wife June Carter. Their song *Ring of Fire* is omnipresent in *We Are Alive*, which brings the album *Wrecking Ball* to a close.

Genesis and lyrics

Bruce Springsteen ends *Wrecking Ball* with another song about the burning need to stand up to injustices—the eternal battle of David against Goliath. In *We Are Alive*, as in *Jack of All Trades* and *Rocky Ground*, the songwriter brings characters out from the shadows: "It's a party filled with ghosts," he explained to Jon Stewart of *Rolling Stone*. "It's a party filled with the dead, but whose voices and spirit and ideas remain with us and go on and on. That's why I talk about the girls in Birmingham, the workers in Maryland, and the new immigrants crossing the southern border. It's just the recurrence and how the blood and spirit of all those people regenerate the country and what America is, generation after generation, so I end the record with a party of ghosts. Ghosts who are speaking to the living."[149]

Aside from biblical references—"There's a cross up yonder up on Calvary Hill"—with *We Are Alive* Bruce Springsteen plunges into the history of the United States. "A voice cried I was killed in Maryland in 1877" is a reference to the strikes, which were almost revolts, by the workers on the Baltimore and Ohio Railroad. These strikes later spread to virtually the entire country. The line "I was killed in 1963 one Sunday morning in Birmingham" refers to the bomb that exploded on 15 September that year on the steps of a Baptist church in Alabama, killing four young African-American girls.

Production

We Are Alive begins with the crackling sound of a vinyl record. An organ pad then fades in, as does the tune of Johnny Cash's *Ring of Fire*, whistled by Springsteen who is accompanying himself on acoustic guitar. The next verse is totally different, with the songwriter singing his own tune alone with his guitar. There follows an instrumental break, which repeats the tune of *Ring of Fire*, again whistled by the Boss, and doubled by Greg Leisz's mandocello for a Spaghetti Western atmosphere (at 1'28).

The style of *We Are Alive* is country rock, though Max Weinberg revealed in 2012 that the song's first version was punk, in the style of the Ramones. It is not, incidentally, certain whether Max Weinberg played drums on the version that features on *Wrecking Ball*.

The rest of *We Are Alive* is energetic, with a mariachi touch toward the end, supplied by Darrell Leonard's trumpet, ending as it began, with the Boss whistling the *Ring of Fire*.

2012

Greg Leisz (banjo, mandocello), who was present during the recording of *We Are Alive*, is an excellent instrumentalist on the California scene (he was born in Buffalo, New York State). He has played with the greats of rock, country, and folk, from Jackson Browne to Eric Clapton, Emmylou Harris, Joni Mitchell, Randy Newman, and Lucinda Williams. He took part in the tour for The Seeger Sessions, as can be seen on the DVD *Bruce Springsteen with The Sessions Band: Live in Dublin* (2007).

Darrell Leonard is a renowned trumpet player who, throughout his career, has rubbed shoulders with prestigious artists, including, among many others, B.B. King, Taj Mahal, Elton John, The Rolling Stones, and Stevie Ray Vaughan. He is also an arranger and composer.

African-Americans' houses reduced to ashes during race riots in 1963. This is a central theme of *We Are Alive*.

SWALLOWED UP (IN THE BELLY OF THE WHALE)

Bruce Springsteen / 5'28

Musicians
Bruce Springsteen: vocals, guitar, keyboards, percussion, loops (?)
Ron Aniello: keyboards, loops, backing vocals
Charles Giordano: accordion (?)
Rob Lebret, Lisa Lowell, Ross Petersen, Patti Scialfa: backing vocals
Mark Romatz, Dan Shelly: bassoon
Jeremy McCoy: bass violin
Soozie Tyrell: violin, backing vocals
Clif Norrell: tuba, backing vocals
New York Chamber Consort: strings (?)

Recording
Stone Hill Studio, Colts Neck, New Jersey: 2011
MSR Studio B, New York: 2011

Technical team
Producers: Ron Aniello, Bruce Springsteen
Executive producer: Jon Landau
Recording engineers: Ross Petersen, Ron Aniello, Rob Lebret, Clif Norrell, Toby Scott
Mixing: Ron Aniello, Ross Petersen (Thrill Hill), Rob Lebret (assistant)

Genesis and lyrics

Swallowed Up (In the Belly of the Whale) is the first bonus track on the Special Edition of the *Wrecking Ball* album. In writing this song, Bruce Springsteen once again drew on the Bible. Indeed, it calls to mind the prophet Jonah. Having disobeyed God, Jonah fled by boat toward Tarshish. Blamed by the other sailors on board for being responsible for the storm that had blown up, Jonah was thrown overboard and then swallowed by a great fish, which eventually vomited him up three days later. Back on terra firma, Jonah now obeyed God. What are we to learn from these adventures? First of all, it is wise to obey God. Second, all people should show mercy to their fellows. This is in all likelihood what Bruce Springsteen means when he sings: "We trusted our skills and our good sails/Our faith that with God the righteous in this world prevail."

This humanist message takes on its full meaning at the start of the third millennium. However, Bruce Springsteen has never sung it onstage.

Production

From the very first seconds of the song, Springsteen plunges us into a distinctive ambience: strange sound effects which, without a doubt, evoke the sound of the sea heard from inside the stomach of the whale. The sea sound was equalized to produce this effect and is punctuated by timpani, probably from Ron Aniello's soundbank. Claustrophobia, oppression, isolation—in this strange climate, the songwriter launches into the first lines of his song. He sings in a deep, serious, almost lugubrious voice, but what a feat! He accompanies himself on acoustic guitar before being progressively joined by a bass violin, finger cymbals, and, in the first bridge (at 3'05), by a piano, various samples, effects, and synthesizers. A tuba and sounds of woodwind or strings, probably partly from samples, appear in the third verse (from 3'54). In the second bridge, his voice blends with other voices, some of them from samples, for a kind of finale that is reminiscent of the music of Danny Elfman (at 4'39).

Once again, Springsteen surprises with his eclecticism, as with this unclassifiable *Swallowed Up (In the Belly of the Whale)* he proves that he is still far from reaching the end of his creative journey and has lost none of his amazing talent. Ron Aniello's incredible production is also worth mentioning.

AMERICAN LAND

Bruce Springsteen / 4'25

For Springsteen Addicts
The immigrant workers that Bruce Springsteen mentions in *American Land* include the Zerillis. This surname was his mother's maiden name. The songwriter's maternal grandmother was from the Naples area, and arrived at Ellis Island on 3 October 1900.

Musicians
Bruce Springsteen: vocals, guitar, banjo, keyboards, percussion
Ron Aniello: guitar, bass guitar, keyboards, loops, backing vocals, hurdy-gurdy (?)
Steve Van Zandt: mandolin, backing vocals
Soozie Tyrell: violin, backing vocals
Max Weinberg: drums
Charles Giordano: keyboards, accordion
Art Baron: penny whistle, sousaphone (?)
Ross Petersen, Ron Aniello, Rob Lebret, Clif Norrell: vocal group
Recording
Stone Hill Studio, Colts Neck, New Jersey: 2011
Technical team
Producers: Ron Aniello, Bruce Springsteen
Executive producer: Jon Landau
Recording engineers: Ross Petersen, Ron Aniello, Rob Lebret, Clif Norrell, Toby Scott
Mixing: Chris Lord-Alge (Mix LA, Los Angeles), Keith Armstrong and Nik Karpen (assistants)

Bruce Springsteen and the E Street Band at the Glastonbury Festival, 27 June 2009. The Boss sings *American Land.*

Genesis and lyrics

In the liner notes to the CD *We Shall Overcome: The Seeger Sessions—American Land Edition*, Bruce Springsteen writes that *American Land* is "an original song inspired by *He Lies in the American Land*, a poem by immigrant steelworker Andrew Kovaly and set to music by Pete Seeger."[128]

Five years after recording the first version of *American Land*, during the last session of The Seeger Sessions Band on 21 January 2006, Bruce Springsteen decided to make a new version for *Wrecking Ball.* The story is the same—that of Andrew Kovaly, a young worker originally from Czechoslovakia, who has decided to try his luck in the United States. He bids farewell to his wife, hoping she will join him soon in that country where "Gold comes rushing out the rivers." He is at Ellis Island (the main entry point for immigrants to the United States until the mid-1950s), then in the "valley of red-hot steel and fire" (probably a reference to the steelworks of Pittsburgh, the main center of the USA steel industry). There, he soon realizes that the earthly paradise does not exist. Wherever they have come from, these workers "died building the railroads, they worked to bones and skin." Others were treated worse than dirt, even though it was "Their hands that built the country."

A veritable hymn to blue-collar workers, *American Land* has become an essential song in Bruce Springsteen's setlists, as evidenced by some 250 performances since the one at Madison Square Garden, on 22 June 2006, with a special mention for the performance at the Glastonbury Festival on 27 June 2009.

Production

Springsteen definitively ends *Wrecking Ball* with a song worthy of The Pogues—this second and final bonus on the album is in the same vein as the Seeger Sessions. *American Land* begins just with Max Weinberg's drumming, before some of the musicians launch into the main theme, with violin, hurdy-gurdy, accordion, penny whistle—the whole Celtic-Irish panoply is out in force. The piece then takes a more rock-like turn with, in particular, saturated guitars and bass guitar. Springsteen sings with an energy that electrifies his companions, and he is joined in the choruses by enthusiastic backing vocals. Steve Van Zandt is in the thick of it with his mandolin, and in all likelihood the Boss is playing the banjo. *American Land* is an invitation to party, and an invitation to share.

ALBUM

HIGH HOPES

High Hopes • Harry's Place • American Skin (41 Shots) • Just Like Fire Would • Down in the Hole • Heaven's Wall • Frankie Fell in Love • This Is Your Sword • Hunter of Invisible Game • The Ghost of Tom Joad • The Wall • Dream Baby Dream

Outtakes: *Cold Spot*

RELEASE DATE

United States: 14 January 2014

Reference: Columbia Records – 88843015462

No.1 in the United States, United Kingdom, Belgium, the Netherlands, Germany, Ireland, Italy, Spain, and Sweden, No.2 in France

Bruce Springsteen at a press conference in Perth, during his 2014 Australian tour.

Zack de la Rocha, Tim Commerford, Brad Wilk, and Tom Morello of Rage Against the Machine, Los Angeles, in June 1992. The guitarist played a pivotal role in the making of *High Hopes*.

TOM MORELLO'S STAMP

Less than two weeks after the release of *Wrecking Ball*, Bruce Springsteen and the E Street Band embarked on an 18-month tour that would take them across the United States, Europe, Mexico, Australia, and South America (Chile, Argentina, and Brazil). This was a total of 133 concerts, starting in Atlanta on 18 March 2012 and ending in Rio de Janeiro on 21 September 2013. It was during this Wrecking Ball World Tour—the first without Clarence Clemons (who died on 18 June 2011)—that the songwriter started working on what would become his new album, *High Hopes*. "When I'm on tour, I'll often carry with me a collection of my unfinished music," he explains in his autobiography *Born to Run*. "I'll bring a few unfinished projects along that I'll pop on in the wee wee hours after the show and listen to."[1]

This 18th studio album has a special place in Springsteen's discography, in that it can be divided into four parts. The first part consists of the original compositions that he mentions above. These were the songs that he worked on with Brendan O'Brien, who produced his albums from *The Rising* (2002) to *Working On a Dream* (2009). Tom Morello, the guitarist from Rage Against the Machine, played a major role in these compositions. The second part consists of the three songs without Morello (*Down in the Hole*, *Frankie Fell in Love*, and *This Is Your Sword*). The third part consists of tracks that are already known but were rerecorded with different arrangements, such as *The Ghost of Tom Joad*. And, finally, the three cover versions: *High Hopes*, the title track by Tim Scott McConnell that Springsteen had previously recorded for an EP released in 1995, *Just Like Fire Would* by The Saints, and *Dream Baby Dream* by Suicide.

Springsteen's incursions into Australian punk (*Just Like Fire Would*) and the New York minimal wave (*Dream Baby Dream*) might seem slightly surprising, but they show that he was willing to venture down new and unusual musical paths, with no guarantee of success. Likewise, his over seven-minute-long reinterpretations of *The Ghost of Tom Joad*, the title track of one of his best albums, and *American Skin (41 Shots)*, played live for the first time in June 2000 on the Bruce Springsteen and the E Street Band Reunion Tour, both feel like an auspicious change of direction from a musical standpoint.

As for the new songs, the relationship between the New Jersey songwriter and Tom Morello works wonderfully, whether on the very modern rock *Harry's Place*, the Dylan-style folk track, *Hunter of Invisible Game*, or on *Heaven's*

With his 18th studio album, a new musician entered Bruce Springsteen's world: Tim Scott McConnell, composer and leader of The Havalinas.

Wall, with its pronounced gospel flavor. Three other compositions, recorded without the Rage Against the Machine guitarist, are pure Springsteen: *Down in the Hole*, which bears a passing resemblance to *I'm On Fire* from *Born In The U.S.A.*, *Frankie Fell in Love*, which is typical of the sound of the E Street band during the *Born to Run* era, and *This Is Your Sword*, whose Celtic-rock atmosphere is a clear nod to *We Shall Overcome: The Seeger Sessions*. Finally, the lyrics show that Springsteen is still a political songwriter. This can be seen in the previously mentioned *The Ghost of Tom Joad* and *American Skin (41 Shots)*, as well as in *The Wall*, a new song about Vietnam. He is clearly still driven—and inspired—by the hope of a better future. That is the overarching theme of his 18th album.

High Hopes was released worldwide on 14 January 2014, the same day that the entire *Late Night with Jimmy Fallon* show was dedicated to Bruce Springsteen. The Boss and the E Street Band performed *High Hopes*, *Heaven's Wall*, and *Just Like Fire Would* on the show. Those wishing to denigrate *High Hopes* could accuse it of being a hotchpotch album scraped from the bottom of the barrel. However, this 18th album received largely positive reviews, with *Rolling Stone* magazine in the United States giving it four and a half stars and, in an article in the UK's *Independent* newspaper, music critic Andy Gill drawing attention to "the way that Rage Against the Machine guitarist Tom Morello has reinvigorated old material"[155] (notwithstanding the lack of thematic unity). By late January, *High Hopes* had topped the *Billboard* charts—Springsteen's 11th No.1 in the United States—and climbed to No.1 in the United Kingdom. It went on to become No.1 in a dozen other countries, including Australia, Spain, Belgium, the Netherlands, Germany, and Italy. In France, it reached No.2 and was certified gold.

On 26 January 2014, the album had been out in stores for 12 days when Bruce Springsteen and the E Street Band hit the road again with Tom Morello as their special guest. The tour kicked off in Cape Town, South Africa, and continued in Australia and New Zealand. This was followed by 17 dates in the United States, from Dallas, Texas, to Uncasville, Connecticut, with a particularly notable stop in New Orleans at the Jazz & Heritage Festival on 3 May. Both in the studio and onstage, Bruce Springsteen was still very much the Boss!

The cover

Enveloped in an orange-tinted halo are two Bruce Springsteens for the price of one; one Bruce is looking at the other. Is there a hidden message? Is today's Springsteen saying goodbye to yesterday's Springsteen? Listening to the record

The visual for *High Hopes* or the expression of duality. The photograph was shot by the faithful Danny Clinch.

For Springsteen Addicts

Steve Van Zandt did not participate in the Australian concerts on the Wrecking Ball Tour because he was in the middle of filming the first series of *Lilyhammer*. This also explains why his only guitar contribution to the *High Hopes* album is *American Skin (41 Shots)*.

and considering the major role played by Tom Morello, this could well be the case. And there is Springsteen's look too—at 64, he now sports a very smart haircut but still wears the characteristic jeans and shirt that proclaim loud and clear that the Boss will always be the Boss. The guitar is blurred, which is another mystery. The back cover features Springsteen with his back turned.

The cover photos, along with the ones in the booklet (which also features the lyrics for the 12 songs), were taken by Danny Clinch, a long-standing Springsteen collaborator, assisted by Edward Smith and Nyra Lang. Artistic direction was by Michelle Holme.

The recording

After years of writing and composing, Springsteen had accumulated a huge number of songs that he had not always had the time to finish or record, although he had worked on some with the help of Toby Scott and Brendan O'Brien: "I still had a nice set of songs from my production work with Brendan," he writes in his autobiography *Born to Run*, "and night after night, they'd call to me, looking for a home."[1] He chose a few of the unfinished tracks, and decided to contact Ron Aniello, the producer that he had worked with on *Wrecking Ball*. "I remember that Bruce called me on my birthday, so it was December 9th, 2012," Aniello explained. "He said to me, 'I have some songs. I want to get together.' Knowing Bruce, that just meant a conversation. He doesn't do things cavalierly, so I just assumed, 'OK. I'll get the songs and I'll listen to them.'"[156] Aniello thought he would just be improving a few demos, but instead found himself producing the Boss's next album. The *High Hopes* project therefore took shape throughout the Wrecking Ball World Tour, forcing the producer to record parts during the band's breaks between dates. It was a complicated and unusual method for Springsteen. As Aniello explained in an interview with *Rolling Stone* magazine, a lot of the discussion took place in Europe, while some recording was done using iChat when the band was in Australia. Overall, however, they had less time to work on this album than *Wrecking Ball*.[156]

These constraints meant that the entire team had to juggle between different studios in Los Angeles, New York, Colts Neck, and Australia. So, the producer recorded many overdubs, often with a single musician: "I was in Los Angeles and so was Roy [Bittan], so we put a bunch of piano on some of the songs. Max [Weinberg] would fly to New Jersey or we'd record him in Los Angeles. Bruce flew to Los Angeles a few times, which is unusual for him. Garry [Tallent] lives in Nashville. Charlie [Giordano] lives in New York, so he'd record

TUMBLING DICE
On 15 December 2012, Bruce Springsteen shared the mic with Mick Jagger to sing *Tumbling Dice* at the Prudential Center in Newark, New Jersey. The Rolling Stones had invited the Boss to help them celebrate the band's 50th anniversary on the 50 & Counting Tour.

Bruce Springsteen goes onstage during The Rolling Stones' concert in Newark, on 15 December 2012, to perform *Tumbling Dice*.

at the farm [Colt's Neck]. Honestly, however it would work, it just worked."[156] In the end, no fewer than 16 different studios were used to complete the album—an absolute record for the songwriter! Twenty tracks were cut during the many sessions, but only 12 of them found their way onto the album. Four (*American Beauty*, *Mary Mary*, *Hurry Up Sundown*, and *Hey Blue Eyes*) would be used to make an EP, released three months after the album, four remain unreleased to date, and in the case of one, *Cold Spot*, only the title is known.

When it came to the mixing and mastering, Ron Aniello recollects that the band was touring in Europe—in Milan to be precise (this was early June 2013)—and that Springsteen didn't like the result he was hearing. Aniello asked him what he was listening to the mixing and mastering on, and realized when he said Dr. Dre Beats headphones that these were probably dialing up the bass in the music. To fix the problem, Aniello promptly sent over a recording engineer to set up a pair of decent speakers in Springsteen's hotel room in Italy!

The musicians

The Boss is, of course, accompanied by members of the E Street Band: Roy Bittan, Nils Lofgren, Patti Scialfa, Garry Tallent, Steve Van Zandt, and Max Weinberg. But the album also features Clarence Clemons's saxophone and Danny Federici's organ, recorded on tracks that were produced back in the day by Brendan O'Brien. Clemons appears on *Harry's Place*, Federici on *The Wall*, and both musicians on *Down in the Hole*. Soozie Tyrell is still present, along with Charlie Giordano and Ron Aniello who, once again, does more than just produce the album.

Other musicians include: Everett Bradley on percussion and backing vocals; Jake Clemons, Barry Danielian, Clark

Bruce Springsteen and his musicians in concert in Cape Town, South Africa, during the High Hopes Tour, on 26 January 2014. Jake Clemons is on saxophone.

Gayton, Stan Harrison, Eddie Manion, and Curt Ramm on brass; Jeff Kievit on the piccolo trumpet; Scott Tibbs for the brass arrangements; Tawatha Agee, Keith Fluitt, John James, Curtis King, Cindy Mizelle, Michelle Moore, Al Thornton, and Brenda White on backing vocals—as well as Evan, Jessie, and Sam Springsteen, the Boss's three children; the Atlanta Strings, with eight violins, three violas, and three cellos, conducted by Eddie Horst; the New York Chamber Consort Strings, with 11 violins, four violas, and three cellos, conducted by Rob Mathes; Sam Barfeld on violin; Josh Freese on drums; and, finally, Cillian Vallely on the uilleann pipes (Irish bagpipes) and the high and low whistles. But the musician who really puts his stamp on eight of the 12 tracks on the album is none other than Tom Morello, on guitar and vocals. Springsteen expresses his utmost gratitude in the album booklet: "Tom and his guitar became my muse, pushing the rest of this project to another level. Thanks for the inspiration Tom."[157]

The recording studios

As previously mentioned, 16 studios, including two in Australia, were used to complete the Boss's 18th studio album. Obviously, if we compare this album with how *Nebraska* was produced—using little more than a humble Portastudio—the gap could not be wider! These are the studios: Thrill Hill Recording (Colts Neck, NJ), Stone Hill Studio (the Boss's new studio in Colts Neck, NJ), Very Loud House (Los Angeles, CA), Renegade Studios (New York), Veritas Studios (Los Angeles, CA), Southern Tracks Recording Studio (Atlanta, GA), EastWest Studios (Hollywood), NRG Recording Studios (Los Angeles, CA), The Village Studios (Los Angeles, CA), Studios 301 (Byron Bay and Sydney, Australia), the Record Plant (Los Angeles, CA), Electric Lady Studios (New York), Avatar Studios (New York), Sear Sound (New York), and Berkeley Street Studio (Santa Monica, CA).

For Springsteen Addicts

Ron Aniello has revealed that Bruce Springsteen composed between 30 and 40 songs during the production of *Wrecking Ball*. However, none of these were selected for *High Hopes*.

Tim Scott McConnell, a guitarist who founded a blues style that could be described as Gothic, and who wrote the song *High Hopes*.

HIGH HOPES

Tim Scott McConnell / 4'57

Musicians

Bruce Springsteen: vocals, guitar, vibraphone, percussion
Ron Aniello: drum loops
Nils Lofgren: guitar
Tom Morello: guitar
Roy Bittan: piano
Charles Giordano: accordion
Barry Danielian, Clark Gayton, Stan Harrison, Eddie Manion, Curt Ramm: brass
Garry Tallent: bass
Max Weinberg: drums
Everett Bradley: percussions, backing vocals
Curtis King, Cindy Mizelle, Michelle Moore, Patti Scialfa, Soozie Tyrell: backing vocals

Recording

Studios 301, Sydney and Byron Bay, Australia: March 2013
Studios not precisely identified (see page 605): 2013

Technical team

Producers: Ron Aniello, Bruce Springsteen
Recording engineers: Nick DiDia, Ross Petersen, Toby Scott
Assistant recording engineers: Sean Astill, Tom Astill, Jordan Power, Jack Prest, Luke Yeoman (Studios 301)
Mixing: Chris Lord-Alge (Mix LA, Los Angeles); Nik Karpen, Keith Armstrong, Brad Townsend, Andrew Schubert (assistants)
Mastering: Bob Ludwig (Gateway Mastering, Portland)

High Hopes is also the name of a song by Pink Floyd, released in 1994 on the album *The Division Bell.*

Genesis and lyrics

High Hopes was composed by Tim Scott McConnell and recorded for his solo album *The High Lonesome Sound* (1987), then again with his band The Havalinas (for an album of the same name, 1990). Bruce Springsteen loved The Havalinas' version and did three studio takes in January 1995 at The Hit Factory in New York during the *Greatest Hits* sessions. One of these recordings was released on the *Blood Brothers* EP (1996). Then, in 2014, he decided to record it again, following the shrewd advice of Tom Morello, who had heard it on SiriusXM's E Street Radio channel. "I thought that might be a fun one to play," Morello explained to Andy Greene for *Rolling Stone* magazine. "So in the middle of the night I sat in my driveway and I texted Bruce and said, 'What do you think about *High Hopes* for the upcoming thing?'"[158]

After adding it to his setlist, Springsteen performed a new version of *High Hopes* in Sydney, Australia. "I was drawn to the song because it's very good lyrically without being sort of didactic or too direct," he said to Andy Greene. "It's got a really good lyric about struggling. And also it's got a great chorus."[113]

In the same vein as some of the songs on *Wrecking Ball*, *High Hopes* urges people to fight back and refuse to be cowed. Faced with the onslaught of a "breathless army" bent on stifling all hope, the narrator asks for help and strength. He wants a wife and kids, and he wants to be able to look in their eyes and know they stand a chance. "Before the meek inherit they'll learn to hate themselves," sings Springsteen. These words sound like the exact opposite of the Gospel According to St Matthew (Matthew 5:5): "Blessed are the Meek, for they will inherit the Earth." All very symbolic!

High Hopes was released as a single on 25 November 2013, and shortly after reached No.15 in the *Billboard* Adult Alternative Songs Chart.

Production

So it was Tom Morello who suggested that Springsteen include *High Hopes* on his setlist (along with *Just Like Fire Would*): "As we gathered in Australia at our first rehearsal for the Wrecking Ball Tour's resumption, I had an arrangement [for *High Hopes*] that I thought might work. This was going to be Tom's first stint subbing for Steve, who was busy with his acting commitments, so I wanted him to be able to put his

imprint on the show."[1] After performing it for the first time onstage on 16 March 2013 at the Brisbane Entertainment Center, in Brisbane, Australia, the Boss realized that it really grabbed the fans, and that his guest guitarist was a major asset. So, during a break from the live performances, he took his musicians along to Studios 301 to record it. By then Nick DiDia, Brendan O'Brien's former recording engineer, was working at the studio. Tom Morello recalls: "I got a message one night saying, 'Hey, can you be in the studio at noon tomorrow?' And I'm like, 'OK, [laughs] what are we doing?' And I was sent to some studio [in Byron Bay] and played on X number of tracks. There may have been something I played on before where Bruce wanted me to add a solo with some direction. And then the whole band went into the studio to cut *High Hopes*, which had become a staple of the live set at that point."[158]

Back in the United States, Ron Aniello followed the recording live, as he explains: "I was listening in online. I wasn't part of the tracking session. I was listening via Knifecast, which is a program we use through iTunes where I can listen anywhere in the world. And then for overdubs and stuff, I was on iChat talking to the musicians. Then we linked in via satellite or something. It was a very interesting record, a very modern record."[156] And in order to remain neutral in his production choices, Aniello preferred not to listen to the 1996 recording made for the *Blood Brothers* EP.

Compared to the version by The Havalinas, which is a kind of alternative folk rock with a hint of rockabilly, Springsteen's version sounds more like E Street band rock with a hint of Cajun, peppered with a touch of Rage Against the Machine. The Boss and his team have kept the amazing rhythmic pulse from the original, based this time on an inimitable drum groove and muted guitar chords. The main difference lies in the brass section and the backing vocals in the choruses (there's an example at 1'55), as well as the very obvious percussion ensemble (and, of course, the drum loop concocted by Aniello). Charlie Giordano's accordion also brings a Cajun color to the verses, as does Roy Bittan's piano played Allen Toussaint-style. And, of course, there is the incredible guitar part from Tom Morello, who delivers an amazing solo that combines rhythmic wah-wah with biting lead phrases (from 2'14). The Boss, on acoustic guitar and lead vocals, sets the pace as always.

However, despite the excellent contributions, this version is not as good as the original. It lacks the simplicity and sense of urgency that were the great strength of *High Hopes* by The Havalinas.

HARRY'S PLACE

Bruce Springsteen / 4'04

Musicians

Bruce Springsteen: vocals, guitar
Clarence Clemons: tenor saxophone
Nils Lofgren: guitar
Tom Morello: guitar
Roy Bittan: piano
Garry Tallent: bass
Max Weinberg: drums
The Atlanta Strings, Eddie Horst: string arrangements, conductor
Justin Bruns, Jay Christy, Sheela Iyengar, John Meisner, Christopher Pulgram, William Pu, Olga Shpitko, Kenn Wagner (violins); Amy Chang, Tania Maxwell, Lachlan McBane (violas); Karen Freer, Charae Krueger, Daniel Laufer (cellos)

Recording

Southern Tracks Recording Studio, Atlanta, Georgia: January to March 2007
Veritas Studios, Los Angeles, California (?): 2013

Technical team

Producer: Brendan O'Brien
Recording engineers: Nick DiDia, Ross Petersen, Toby Scott
Assistant recording engineers: Karl Egsieker, Tom Tapley, Billy Bowers (Southern Tracks)
Mixing: Chris Lord-Alge (Mix LA, Los Angeles); Nik Karpen, Keith Armstrong, Brad Townsend, Andrew Schubert (assistants)
Mastering: Bob Ludwig (Gateway Mastering, Portland)

2014

Genesis and lyrics

Bruce Springsteen wrote the text for *Harry's Place* when *The Rising* was produced in 2002. "I had those lyrics at that time," he said to Andy Greene in an interview for *Rolling Stone* magazine. "It's not uncommon for lyrics to sit in a notebook for a very long time sometimes. I might not know what to do with them, and then suddenly it's there. So that song was a classic one that had a long gestation."[113] The music dated from the *Magic* sessions in 2007.

Harry's Place is like a kind of brothel or cocaine den. A strange resemblance to the America of the 2000s, perhaps? In the same interview for *Rolling Stone*, the songwriter explained that *Harry's Place* was another song about his "take on the Bush years."[113] Of note are the lines: "You don't fuck with Harry's money, you don't fuck Harry's girls/These are the rules, this is the world." We understand that Harry, and Harry alone—in other words, the occupant of the White House (?)—decides the rules and presides over a country in decline. A police officer checking IDs, a character called Bobby, dressed as a drag queen, who is about to torture the narrator as a voice whispers, "We do what we must do." This is the picture painted by Springsteen, a macabre scene that he is afraid might become real.

Production

Harry's Place is a kind of rock FM-alternative-disco-funk, which is hard to define as it comprises so many disparate elements. "It initially started out as just me on the piano," the songwriter said in 2014. "[Producer] Brendan [O'Brien] heard it and I believe he may have turned it into this rhythmic piece and made the sound that's very compelling." Max Weinberg's drumming style here is very robotic, rather like a drum machine, and is supported by Garry Tallent's electronically distorted bass. The Boss sings in a monotonous voice, except for the chorus lines that use an equalizer to create a telephone effect (for example, at 0'35). Clarence Clemons's saxophone (recorded during the *Magic* sessions) also puts in an appearance, with a rather jazz-rock feel (listen to his solo at 1'48). And, finally, Tom Morello's many guitar contributions color the piece with wild, delirious resonances, giving *Harry's Place* a unique dimension that is quite simply unclassifiable. Morello's were the only overdubs recorded in LA over the original 2007 recording.

AMERICAN SKIN (41 SHOTS)

Bruce Springsteen / 7'23

Musicians

Bruce Springsteen: vocals, guitar, percussion
Ron Aniello: bass, synths, guitar, drum loops, percussion, organ, vibraphone
Steve Van Zandt: guitar, backing vocals
Nils Lofgren: backing vocals
Tom Morello: lead guitar, backing vocals
Roy Bittan: piano
Charles Giordano: organ
Max Weinberg: drums
Jake Clemons: tenor saxophone
Barry Danielian, Clark Gayton, Stan Harrison, Eddie Manion, Curt Ramm: brass
Scott Tibbs: brass arrangements
Curtis King, Cindy Mizelle, Patti Scialfa, Soozie Tyrell: backing vocals

Recording

Veritas Studios, Los Angeles: 2013
Studios not precisely identified (see page 605): 2013

Technical team

Producers: Ron Aniello, Bruce Springsteen
Recording engineers: Ross Petersen, Toby Scott
Assistant irecording engineers: Mike Bauer (Avatar)
Mixing: Chris Lord-Alge (Mix LA, Los Angeles); Nik Karpen, Keith Armstrong, Brad Townsend, Andrew Schubert (assistants)
Mastering: Bob Ludwig (Gateway Mastering, Portland)

For Springsteen Addicts

Bruce Springsteen was honored with an award from the National Association for the Advancement of Colored People (NAACP) for *American Skin (41 Shots)*.

Genesis and lyrics

Bruce Springsteen wrote this song in the spring of 2000, several months after the Amadou Diallo affair. Amadou Diallo was born in Liberia and had come to New York in 1996 with plans to study computer engineering. On 4 February 1999, as he was returning home, he was stopped by four police officers looking for a serial rapist who matched his description. They then fired 41 shots at him. The four police officers were brought to trial in February 2000—they blamed their salvo of shots on stress and the belief that Diallo was pulling a weapon out of his pocket (it turned out to be his wallet). Their acquittal sparked huge controversy, less than ten years after the Rodney King affair.

American Skin (41 Shots) tells the story of Amadou Diallo's tragic destiny, but it does more than that. Bruce Springsteen also points the finger at a particular attitude in America that makes it impossible for WASP [White Anglo-Saxon Protestant] and African-American communities to live in harmony—namely that the former believes all black people are potential criminals. Seen from this angle, the second verse, where a mother gets her son ready for school and tells him to be polite if he is stopped by the police, is both sad and very revealing.

Bruce Springsteen has denied that *American Skin (41 Shots)* is an anti-cop song. "Though the song was critical, it was not 'anti-police' as some thought," he claims in *Songs*. "The first voice you hear after the intro is from the policeman's point of view." [6]

Bruce Springsteen played *American Skin (41 Shots)* onstage for the first time in Atlanta on 4 June 2000, then again at Madison Square Garden (where one of his concerts was attended by Amadou Diallo's parents). This version features on the album *Bruce Springsteen & The E Street Band: Live in New York City* (2001). The studio version was recorded at The Hit Factory, in New York, on 2 March 2001, and subsequently released as a promotional single in June. In 2013, Bruce Springsteen recorded it again, profoundly transforming it thanks to Tom Morello.

Production

Springsteen has said that a song does not have authority until it has been recorded in the studio. This is one of the reasons

The Boss faces a rapt audience in Cape Town with, in the foreground, the saxophonist Jake Clemons (nephew of Clarence).

The sleeve for the DVD *Bruce Springsteen & The E Street Band: Live in New York City*, released in 2000.

why he did a different version of *American Skin (41 Shots)* on *High Hopes*, after he and the E Street Band had performed a fantastic live version on 29 June and 1 July 2000 at Madison Square Garden in New York. Ron Aniello also later explained that Springsteen felt this song was one of his best and that he would really appreciate having a recording of it.[156]

Once the decision was made, the first step involved cutting a basic track; so, Springsteen, Max Weinberg, and the producer (on bass) laid down the foundations for the piece. Then overdub followed overdub—drum loops for the intro, synth pads, guitar inversions, palm-muted guitars, percussion instruments, and the Boss's vocals, which emerge from the mix like a ghostly cry, carried by an ample delay to stress the chilling 41 shots (at 0'19). In the first verse, Springsteen's voice sounds brittle and emotional with a somewhat meditative tone. In the chorus, his voice takes on gospel intonations, backed by choirs that are probably created on synthesizers.

The arrangements progressively become more complex with each verse and chorus, with bass, drums, piano, organ, vibraphone, percussion, and backing vocals alongside Scott Tibbs's brass arrangements, which are unfortunately too deeply buried in the mix (listen from 4'07). For the first time on a record, we hear Jake Clemons on tenor saxophone, and it has to be said that the uncle's spirit is present in the nephew's instrument (at 5'53).

American Skin (41 Shots) is also Tom Morello's first guitar contribution to the album, recorded in Veritas Studios, his own studio in Los Angeles, as he explained in 2014: "That song to me was the most challenging one. It was also the first one I did. Normally, I'll go in there and tinker with a song a bit and try to capture inspiration and see if the world likes it or not. But that song just didn't come together for me. I went back to it a couple of times, and I'm glad that I did because at the end of the day I was really pleased with how the guitar solo and the rhythm stuff came out. But that one felt like it was work. I had to really work on that one."[158] However, several years later, Morello admitted that the song was a little too heavy on the guitars and arrangements.

Lyrically and musically, *American Skin (41 Shots)* is without a doubt one of Springsteen's greatest tracks. But despite the hard work put in by the Boss, the producer, and the musicians, the song lacks the sheer power of the live version performed with the E Street Band in 2000. As the songwriter himself has recognized, referring to *American Skin (41 Shots)* and *The Ghost of Tom Joad*, it is "very, very hard to top any E Street Band live recordings of any of these songs."[5]

For Springsteen Addicts

Following the first public performances of *American Skin (41 Shots)* in 2000, the police commissioner, Howard Safir, and Patrick Lynch, the president of the Patrolmen's Benevolent Association, called for a boycott of Springsteen's concerts. But there was very little response.

Marshall

Chris Bailey, guitarist of the Saints and composer of *Just Like Fire Would*, rehearses for the I'm Not There concert at the Beacon Theatre, New York, on 6 November 2007.

JUST LIKE FIRE WOULD

Chris Bailey / 3'56

Musicians

Bruce Springsteen: vocals, guitar
Ron Aniello: 12-string guitar
Nils Lofgren: guitar
Tom Morello: guitar
Roy Bittan: piano
Charles Giordano: organ
Jake Clemons, Barry Danielian, Clark Gayton, Eddie Manion, Curt Ramm: brass
Jeff Kievit: piccolo trumpet
Garry Tallent: bass
Max Weinberg: drums
Everett Bradley: percussion, backing vocals
Curtis King, Cindy Mizelle, Michelle Moore, Patti Scialfa, Steve Van Zandt: backing vocals
New York Chamber Consort Strings: Rob Mathes (arranger and conductor), Lisa Kim (first violin); Quan Ge, Hyunju Lee, Jessica Lee, Ann Lehman, Joanna Mauer, Suzanne Ornstein, Annaliesa Place, David Southorn, Jeanine Wynton, Sharon Yamada (violins); Maurycy Banaszek, Desiree Elsevier, Shmuel Katz, Robert Rinehart (violas); Maria Kitsopoulos, Alan Stepansky, Ru Pei Yeh (cellos)

Recording

Studios 301, Sydney and Byron Bay, Australia: March 2013
Studios not precisely identified (see page 605): 2013

Technical team

Producers: Ron Aniello, Bruce Springsteen
Recording engineers: Nick DiDia, Ross Petersen, Toby Scott
Assistant recording engineers: Sean Astill, Tom Astill, Jordan Power, Jack Prest, Luke Yeoman (Studios 301)
Mixing: Bob Clearmountain (Mix This!, Los Angeles), Brandon Duncan, Sergio Ruelas Jr (assistants)
Mastering: Bob Ludwig (Gateway Mastering, Portland)

2014

Genesis and lyrics

The Saints started writing a punk manifesto with their very first album, *(I'm) Stranded*, which was released in 1977. Six albums and over a decade later, they produced another major album, *All Fools Day* (1986), which introduced them to America and American fans. The single *Just Like Fire Would*, composed by the singer Chris Bailey, was taken from this album.

Just Like Fire Would is a song that "I've had on my radar for 20 years or so that I always liked,"[113] Bruce Springsteen said to Andy Greene of *Rolling Stone*. He first played it with the E Street Band in Brisbane on 14 March 2013 during the Wrecking Ball Tour, and because the crowd was so enthusiastic about it, he decided to record it in Studios 301. He possibly recognized something of himself in the narrator, who is hoping that wine and cigarettes, a motel room, and, in particular, the exhilaration of the open road will alleviate his burden of solitude and sense of futility: "Five hundred miles I've gone today/And tomorrow's five hundred more." And so, his life flashes by, just as the world flashes by beyond his car window while he burns up "just like fire would."

Just Like Fire Would was released as a single on 22 January 2014, at the same time as a video on Springsteen's website, shot during rehearsals at the SIR Studios in New York.

Production

As previously mentioned, *Just Like Fire Would* was recorded at Studios 301 in Australia at the same session as *High Hopes*. The musicians recorded nearly all of the piece live in Sydney—with the exception of Tom Morello who laid down his guitar parts in Byron Bay. This explains why the song hangs together so well and has so much energy. *Just Like Fire Would* is perfectly suited to Springsteen—pure rock with an irrepressible riff (played on an electric 12-string guitar), a thumping but subtle rhythm section, keyboards that light up the arrangements, a wealth of backing vocals (with what appears to be Steve Van Zandt responding to the Boss in the fourth verse, at 1'48), a *Penny Lane*-style piccolo trumpet in the instrumental bridge, strings and brass instruments to plump up the riff (although they are quite far back in the mix), and the calm, solid voice of the Boss.

The version by Springsteen and his troops is more than a match for The Saints' version.

Down in the Hole inspired rock songwriters, including The Rolling Stones (*Emotional Rescue*, 1980), James Taylor (*New Moon Shine*, 1991), Tom Waits (*Way Down in the Hole* on the album *Frank's Wild Years*, 1987), and Alice in Chains (*Down in a Hole* on *Dirt*, 1992).

DOWN IN THE HOLE

Bruce Springsteen / 4'59

Musicians
Bruce Springsteen: vocals, guitar, percussion, banjo
Clarence Clemons: tenor saxophone
Danny Federici: organ
Soozie Tyrell: violin
Garry Tallent: bass
Max Weinberg: drums
Patti Scialfa, Evan Springsteen, Jessica Springsteen, Sam Springsteen: backing vocals

Recording
Southern Tracks Recording Studios, Atlanta, Georgia: February to March 2002
Studios not precisely identified (see page 605): 2012–2013

Technical team
Producer: Brendan O'Brien
Recording engineers: Nick DiDia, Toby Scott, Ross Petersen
Assistant recording engineers: Karl Egsieker, Tom Tapley, Billy Bowers (Southern Tracks)
Mixing: Brendan O'Brien (Henson Recording Studios, Hollywood), Tom Syrowski (assistant)
Mastering: Bob Ludwig (Gateway Mastering, Portland)

The Springsteen family participated in the song *Down in the Hole*. From left: Sam, Patti Scialfa, Evan, Bruce, and Jessica.

2014

Genesis and lyrics

Down in the Hole was written at the time of *The Rising* album. "Sometimes you end up with a choice between two things that you like a lot and I think I had maybe that and *Empty Sky*," Springsteen explained to Andy Greene at *Rolling Stone*. "*The Rising* had 15 songs on it and it felt long enough. [*Down in the Hole*] is basically as it was written and mixed at that time by Brendan. That's sort of very original."[113]

"The rain it keeps on falling on twisted bones and dirt" and a "Dark and bloody autumn pierces my heart." Here, Springsteen is referring to the cataclysmic events of 11 September 2001, while the "Radio's crackling with the headlines, wind in the phone lines" alludes to the media reaction to the attacks. Springsteen recounts the drama from the viewpoint of a man searching for the remains of a woman, or maybe a loved one. He will carry on digging in the rubble of Ground Zero until he retrieves his loved one from down in the hole.

Production

Down in the Hole opens with a somber atmosphere, created with percussion sounds from Brendan O'Brien's sample store, which echo one another in the stereo and reverb. A shaker quickly comes in to establish a spirited rhythm overlaid by the celestial voices of Springsteen's wife and three children. Several notes on a banjo can be heard, as well as an organ, which sounds like the harmonium. The Boss's vocals emerge from this troubling atmosphere, as if from nowhere; this impression is further accentuated by the use of a telephone effect. Springsteen was asked whether this filter had any particular significance, but he said that he could not remember.

Max Weinberg's drums come in at the second verse, sounding similar to a drum machine, backed by Garry Tallent's barely audible bass. The lead vocals sound more normal again from the second verse (at 1'43). A bridge with another saturated rhythm sample is followed by a good instrumental section, dominated by the excellent organ from the late Danny Federici, as well as two violin tracks from Soozie Tyrell (at 2'40).

The subtle backing vocals from the Springsteen clan rule supreme at the end of the song, along with a return to the telephone-filter effect on the paterfamilias' voice.

Clarence Clemons's saxophone is credited on the album but is inaudible.

HEAVEN'S WALL

Bruce Springsteen / 3'50

Musicians

Bruce Springsteen: vocals, guitar, additional bass, percussion loops, organ, synth
Ron Aniello: percussion loops, synth, Farfisa organ
Tom Morello: lead guitar
Sam Barfeld: violin
Garry Tallent: bass
Max Weinberg: drums
Everett Bradley: percussion
Tawatha Agee, Keith Fluitt, John James, Curtis King, Cindy Mizelle, Patti Scialfa, Al Thornton, Soozie Tyrell, Brenda White: backing vocals
New York Chamber Consort Strings: Rob Mathes (arranger and conductor); Lisa Kim (first violin); Quan Ge, Hyunju Lee, Jessica Lee, Ann Lehman, Joanna Mauer, Suzanne Ornstein, Annaliesa Place, David Southorn, Jeanine Wynton, Sharon Yamada (violins); Maurycy Banaszek, Desiree Elsevier, Shmuel Katz, Robert Rinehart (violas); Maria Kitsopoulos, Alan Stepansky, Ru Pei Yeh (cellos)
The band: handclaps

Recording

Southern Tracks Recording Studio, Atlanta, Georgia: January to March 2007
Studios not precisely identified (see page 605): 2012–2013

Technical team

Producers: Brendan O'Brien, Ron Aniello, Bruce Springsteen
Recording engineers: Nick DiDia, Ross Petersen, Toby Scott
Assistant recording engineers: Karl Egsieker, Tom Tapley, Billy Bowers (Southern Tracks)
Mixing: Bob Clearmountain (Mix This!, Los Angeles); Brandon Duncan, Sergio Ruelas Jr (assistants)
Mastering: Bob Ludwig (Gateway Mastering, Portland)

Genesis and lyrics

Bruce Springsteen probably composed *Heaven's Wall* in early 2007 and recorded an initial version during the *Magic* sessions. The definitive version, with Tom Morello and the New York Chamber Consort Strings, dates from 2013. The lyrics once again explore biblical stories. The first verse announces the coming of Jesus, who will "heal the blind [and] raise the dead..." It then calls upon Gideon's men (Gideon was a judge and warrior who sinned against God, then saved the Israelites from the oppression of Saul, the first king of Israel), the sons of Abraham, waiting outside heaven's wall, and "Jonah in the belly of the whale" to all "raise your hand" and "walk [together] into Canaan land." The song alludes to the story of the enslavement of the Israelites in Egypt and the crossing of the Sinai Desert to the Promised Land. From the emancipation of the Jews to the protests of the rank and file in the United States at the turn of the 21st century is but a small step, and it is tempting to see a connection between the two when you listen to *Heaven's Wall*. Bruce Springsteen performed the song for the first time on 14 January 2014 on *Late Night with Jimmy Fallon*.

Production

The basic structure of *Heaven's Wall*, dating back to the *Magic* sessions, was used as the foundation for the rest of the song. Ron Aniello has explained that for *Heaven's Wall* they added overdubs to the basic track, which means that the song is very close to the original drums, bass, and vocals.[156]

The song opens with percussion loops, concocted by the Boss and Aniello. They are swiftly joined by real percussion instruments, as well as backing vocals that have been equalized to give a radio effect (the sound returns to normal when the band comes in at 0'19). Here, Springsteen has composed a kind of folk-rock gospel structured around choral vocals, a rhythm section, a saturated organ, and several acoustic guitars. Sam Barfeld's violin can occasionally be heard (for example, at 2'53), as can the New York Chamber Consort Strings. But the standout feature of *Heaven's Wall* is Tom Morello's guitar contributions. The two 6-string tracks, responding to one another across the stereo as if they were playing a demented game, heavily reinforced by various effects (there are examples at 2'02 and 3'08), could not be farther from traditional gospel.

FRANKIE FELL IN LOVE

Bruce Springsteen / 2'48

Musicians

Bruce Springsteen: vocals, guitar, percussion, organ, mandolin
Ron Aniello: bass, guitar
Roy Bittan: piano
Sam Barfeld: violin
Max Weinberg: drums
Steve Van Zandt: backing vocals

Recording

Southern Tracks Recording Studios, Atlanta, Georgia: 2007–2008 (?)
Studios not precisely identified (see page 605): 2012–2013

Technical team

Producers: Ron Aniello, Bruce Springsteen
Recording engineers: Nick DiDia, Ross Petersen, Toby Scott
Assistant recording engineers: Karl Egsieker, Tom Tapley, Billy Bowers (Southern Tracks) (?)
Mixing: Chris Lord-Alge (Mix LA, Los Angeles); Nik Karpen, Keith Armstrong, Brad Townsend, Andrew Schubert (assistants)
Mastering: Bob Ludwig (Gateway Mastering, Portland)

Bruce Springsteen and Steve Van Zandt sing *Frankie Fell in Love* in Perth, Australia, on 15 February 2014.

Genesis and lyrics

Frankie Fell in Love was composed and recorded during the *Magic* sessions. Springsteen put this initial version aside, along with a demo that he also liked. "I just loved it lyrically, and I thought that it's a great thing for Steve and myself," he said to Andy Greene in an interview for *Rolling Stone*. "It's just a great little Faces-type rock song."[113] Producer Ron Aniello has said that he thinks the song contains some of the best lyrics Springsteen has ever written.

The main character in *Frankie Fell in Love* is a young woman whom everybody seems to know and like. This particular morning, everyone's talking about her: "News is out all over town, Frankie fell in love." Total metamorphosis! Bruce Springsteen plays around with a few surrealistic lyrics in the style of 1960s Dylan. Suddenly, everything becomes possible, even Einstein and Shakespeare having a beer together, with the first "trying to figure out the number that adds up to bliss" and the second telling him that "Man, it's just one and one make three/Ah, that's why it's poetry." Frankie is in love and "World peace's gonna break out." No less!

Production

While the basics of *Frankie Fell in Love* date from the *Magic* period, a promotional video filmed in 2008 during the Wrecking Ball sessions shows the band working on the song in the studio. However, the album credits for the song make no mention of Brendan O'Brien on production, and it seems to have been completely reworked in 2012–2013.

"It's just a great, playful, rowdy rock 'n' roll song," Ron Aniello commented in 2013. The producer couldn't have found a better way to sum up *Frankie Fell in Love*. The song gets off to a gentle start with the Boss's vocals surrounded by guitars and percussion instruments, before it delivers a huge adrenalin hit in the third verse, with the thunderous entry of drums, bass, organ, and a wall of saturated guitars (at 0'37). A 6-string takes on some slide phrases, Springsteen plucks a mandolin (listen at around 2'22), and Barfeld is on violin. But it is Steve Van Zandt's vocal harmonies that are a real bonus. Not forgetting, of course, the songwriter's excellent lead vocals that express a contagious joy.

THIS IS YOUR SWORD

Bruce Springsteen / 2'52

The first time *This Is Your Sword* was performed onstage, on 29 January 2014 at the Bellville Velodrome in Cape Town, Steve Van Zandt had clearly not learned the lyrics. Amateur videos from that night show him laughing and trying to hang on in there. At the same concert, Tom Morello played an acoustic 12-string that doesn't appear on the album version.

Musicians

Bruce Springsteen: vocals, guitar, synth, piano, banjo, mandolin
Ron Aniello: bass, synths, guitars
Roy Bittan: piano, organ
Sam Barfeld: violin
Josh Freese: drums
Cillian Vallely: uilleann pipes, high and low whistles
Patti Scialfa, Soozie Tyrell, Steve Van Zandt: backing vocals

Recording

EastWest Studios, Hollywood: 2012–2013
Studios not precisely identified (see page 605): 2012–2013

Technical team

Producers: Ron Aniello, Bruce Springsteen
Recording engineers: Toby Scott, Ross Petersen, David Shiffman (drums at EastWest)
Assistant recording engineer: Brendan DeKora (EastWest)
Mixing: Chris Lord-Alge (Mix LA, Los Angeles); Nik Karpen, Keith Armstrong, Brad Townsend, Andrew Schubert (assistants)
Mastering: Bob Ludwig (Gateway Mastering, Portland)

Josh Freese plays drums in *This Is Your Sword* in a concert with the Vandals in San Diego, California, in October 2017.

Genesis and lyrics

This Is Your Sword dates from the early 2010s, possibly from a project on spirituality for which Springsteen had composed *We Take Care of Our Own*, *Shackled and Drawn*, and *Rocky Ground* (all of which ended up on the *Wrecking Ball* album).

Musically, the song would not have been out of place on the *We Shall Overcome: The Seeger Sessions* album, as the atmosphere is predominantly Celtic folk. Even the lyrics are imbued with a similar spirit: they could have been taken from one of the stories of King Arthur. A father, who we could easily imagine as a knight of the Round Table, is talking to his children. He is bequeathing them "The sword of our fathers with lessons hard taught" and "The shield strong and sturdy from battles well fought." Because now his offspring must continue the fight with the power of love bestowed upon them by the sword and shield in a world where "The times they are dark [and] darkness covers the earth." The demonic forces must be vanquished and the world "filled with the beauty of God's work."

This Is Your Sword is a superb song with more than a passing nod to the Celtic rock of Big Country and The Waterboys. It has only been performed onstage three times, the first at a concert in Cape Town, South Africa, on 29 January 2014.

Production

This Is Your Sword opens with sounds inspired by Irish Celtic music: Cillian Vallely, an Irish musician and member of the band Lúnasa, plays the uilleann pipes (Irish bagpipes) and the high and low whistles (Irish flutes), while Springsteen is on mandolin, banjo, acoustic guitars (probably assisted by Ron Aniello), and tambourine, and Sam Barfeld is on violin. The piece takes on a Celtic folk-rock color with the appearance of saturated guitars, organ, piano, synths, bass, and drums. The latter are played by Josh Freese rather than Max Weinberg. As the producer has explained, Springsteen was on tour and he was in Los Angeles. Weinberg was also on tour, which meant that he had to ak Freese to play the drums instead. Freese's drumming technique is powerful and subtle in equal measure, which has led him to work with artists such as Devo, The Vandals, Guns N' Roses, Nine Inch Nails, Sting, Lenny Kravitz, and many others.

Backing vocals provide the Boss with efficient support, and it is very probably the voice of Steve Van Zandt responding to Springsteen in the choruses (for example, at 1'11).

With Tom Morello onstage at the Convention Center, Los Angeles, during the MusiCares Person of the Year award in honor of Bruce Springsteen, on 8 February 2013.

HUNTER OF INVISIBLE GAME

Bruce Springsteen / 4'42

Musicians
Bruce Springsteen: vocals, guitar
Tom Morello: guitar
Soozie Tyrell: violin
Garry Tallent: bass
Max Weinberg: drums
The Atlanta Strings, Eddie Horst: string arrangements, conductor
Justin Bruns, Jay Christy, Sheela Iyengar, John Meisner, Christopher Pulgram, William Pu, Olga Shpitko, Kenn Wagner (violins); Amy Chang, Tania Maxwell, Lachlan McBane (violas); Karen Freer, Charae Krueger, Daniel Laufer (cellos)
Unidentified musicians: electric piano, backing vocals

Recording
Southern Tracks Recording Studio, Atlanta, Georgia: January to March 2007–2008
Avatar Studios, New York: 2007–2008
Studios not precisely identified (see page 605): 2012–2013

Technical team
Producer: Brendan O'Brien
Recording engineers: Nick DiDia, Ross Petersen, Toby Scott
Assistant recording engineers: Karl Egsieker, Tom Tapley, Billy Bowers (Southern Tracks), Mike Bauer (Avatar)
Mixing: Bob Clearmountain (Mix This!, Los Angeles); Brandon Duncan, Sergio Ruelas Jr (assistants)
Mastering: Bob Ludwig (Gateway Mastering, Portland)

2014

For Springsteen Addicts

On 9 July 2014, Springsteen unveiled the music video for *Hunter of Invisible Game* on his official website. Working with the ever-loyal Thom Zimny, he directed this 10'12 short film himself, which includes a new 5'35 musical intro. The Boss takes us on a kind of personal quest, like a tramp wandering through the countryside.

Genesis and lyrics

Hunter of Invisible Game is one of the high points of *High Hopes*. "I wrote [the title] down years ago, and I don't remember a lot about it except I said, 'That's a nice title,'" Springsteen explained to Sean Sennett of *Rolling Stone* magazine in 2014. "I wrote it down and it sat there. Then I did more reading of other things. And I started to get into this sort of post-apocalyptic idea."[160]

The main character in the song is a survivor of a world that has collapsed, where the cities are empty and the plains are burning. He must do what Noah did in the Bible—build "an ark out of gopher wood and pitch" and, with other travelers, create a new world from the ruins of the old and restore lost human values. "Now there's a kingdom of love waiting to be reclaimed," sings Bruce Springsteen at the end of the piece. Is this a message of hope or a hopeless wish? Springsteen gives us a partial answer to this question by having the hero describe himself as the hunter of invisible game.

To date, this remarkable song has only had one outing onstage: on 12 February 2014 in Adelaide, Australia.

Production

Hunter of Invisible Game was probably recorded during the sessions for *Working On a Dream* between 2007 and 2008. Ron Aniello only altered the original recording slightly and ensured that the editing had a light touch. This was out of respect for Brendan O'Brien and his approach to production. As Aniello didn't want to interfere too much, they only touched things up, while Springsteen tweaked a couple of lyrics. Seemingly, the only addition (apart from perhaps one or two changes Springsteen made to his lead vocal) is Tom Morello's guitars. Morello loved this track and persuaded Springsteen to finish it.

The piece opens with the string section playing an elegant melodic motif that recurs throughout the song, Soozie Tyrell's violin or Tom Morello's (very restrained) guitar. *Hunter of Invisible Game* is a superb ballad, driven by acoustic guitars, an uncluttered rhythm section, and a wonderful rendition from the Boss. Female voices (at 3'12) and an electric piano can be heard, all of which are unidentified.

Springsteen later said that *Hunter of Invisible Game* is one of his favorite songs on the album. He is not alone in thinking that.

THE GHOST OF TOM JOAD

Bruce Springsteen / 7'33

Musicians
Bruce Springsteen: vocals, guitar
Tom Morello: vocals, guitar
Ron Aniello: bass, synth
Nils Lofgren: pedal steel guitar, mandolin
Soozie Tyrell: violin
Roy Bittan: piano
Charles Giordano: accordion
Max Weinberg: drums

Recording
Studios not precisely identified (see page 605): March 2013

Technical team
Producers: Ron Aniello, Bruce Springsteen
Recording engineers: Ross Petersen, Toby Scott
Mixing: Chris Lord-Alge (Mix LA, Los Angeles); Nik Karpen, Keith Armstrong, Brad Townsend, Andrew Schubert (assistants)
Mastering: Bob Ludwig (Gateway Mastering, Portland)

THE TWO TOMS

Tom Morello performed *Tom Joad* for the first time with Springsteen on 7 April 2008 at the Honda Center in Anaheim, California. And as the guitarist later explained, it was a real first for him, as he had never before sung while holding a guitar!

Genesis and lyrics

This recording is totally different from the one that gave its name to the 1995 album. *The Ghost of Tom Joad* was originally intended as a rock song for the *Greatest Hits* album before it became the title track of one of Bruce Springsteen's major acoustic albums. But it still had rock potential, and the New Jersey songwriter was not the only one who thought so. Rage Against the Machine produced an alternative metal-rap version that was released as a single in 1997, and subsequently on the *Renegades* album in 2000. In an interview with *Rolling Stone* magazine's Andy Greene, Tom Morello said that *The Ghost of Tom Joad* "was one of Bruce's best songs. [...] The song tells a very human tale and the musical accompaniment of the song invokes the very different ends of the struggle for social justice spectrum. There's a plaintive ballad, which feels like a lament. And there's the full-bore rocker that feels like a threat."[158] So it was thanks to Tom Morello, as Springsteen explains, that the "*Ghost of Tom Joad* ends up on this record as the rock song it was, perhaps, intended to be 15 years ago. That's a pretty good idea of the way I go with these things."[113]

(For a more indepth analysis of the song, see pages 374–377.)

Production

This version of *Tom Joad* was recorded in California, as Tom Morello explains: "The day before I left for Australia, we tracked *The Ghost of Tom Joad* in Los Angeles. It was me, Max [Weinberg], and Ron Aniello. We just did the basic tracks for that song and I sang my verse."[158] The session took place a few days before the first concert on the fourth leg of the Wrecking Ball Tour, on 14 March 2013 at the Brisbane Entertainment Center. Once the basic track had been laid down, the other musicians recorded the overdubs, notably Springsteen who shares vocals and some of the lead guitar parts with Morello. The two men deliver an excellent 6-string duel after the second verse, with the Boss playing on the left channel and Morello on the right (from 2'39). But the star attraction of the piece is the solo at the end, where the Rage Against the Machine guitarist is given full scope to express himself unaccompanied (from 5'22). He improvises for over two minutes on often identical double tracks, sometimes harmonizing with himself. Great artistry! Morello is an outstanding guitarist—the Boss wasn't mistaken!

THE WALL

Bruce Springsteen / 4'20

Musicians

Bruce Springsteen: vocals, guitar, drums
Ron Aniello: synths, accordion
Nils Lofgren: guitar
Roy Bittan: piano
Danny Federici: organ
Curt Ramm: cornet
Garry Tallent: bass
Max Weinberg: percussion
Patti Scialfa: backing vocals

Recording

Thrill Hill Recording, New Jersey: 1998–1999
Studios not precisely identified (see page 605): 2012–2013

Technical team

Producers: Ron Aniello, Bruce Springsteen
Recording engineers: Nick DiDia (?), Ross Petersen, Toby Scott
Mixing: Bob Clearmountain (Mix This!, Los Angeles); Brandon Duncan, Sergio Ruelas Jr (assistants)
Mastering: Bob Ludwig (Gateway Mastering, Portland)

It was Joe Grushecky—seen here January 2015 at Asbury Park, New Jersey—who inspired the title of the Boss's song.

2014

Genesis and lyrics

In December 1997, Bruce Springsteen and Patti Scialfa were in Washington to attend the Kennedy Center Honors ceremony. While they were there, they visited the Vietnam Veterans Memorial. On the memorial wall, they spotted the name Walter Cichon, who was the lead singer of The Motifs, a Jersey Shore band who had left a powerful mark on Springsteen in the 1960s. The songwriter wrote this song in tribute to Walter Cichon and Bart Haynes (the drummer of The Castiles, one of the first bands that the future Boss had played in), who were both killed in the Vietnam War. The idea for the title came from the ex-guitarist of the Iron City Houserockers, Joe Grushecky, whose 1995 album *American Babylon* was produced by Springsteen; Grushecky had sent him a newspaper clipping about The Wall.

"*The Wall* is something I'd played onstage a few times and remains very close to my heart,"[157] writes Springsteen in the album's booklet. Unlike Walter Cichon, who fought in the 3rd Battalion of the 8th Infantry, Billy, the character in *The Wall,* is a Marine. And the words directed at those who sent him to his death pull no punches: "Now the men that put you here eat with their families in rich dining halls/And apology and forgiveness got no place here at all, here at the wall." The songwriter even mentions Robert McNamara, who was the Secretary of Defense at the time of the Vietnam War.

Production

This superb ballad probably emerged from the recording sessions for the additions to the *Tracks* box set (1998) and was finalized in 2012–2013 by Ron Aniello, as he states: "I think that's just the band playing in a room. It's haunting. Danny [Federici] is there, too. We had a couple of guitars, but we wound up just using one [...] I didn't know who was playing what, and I added some touches to it [on the synths and the accordion]." [156]

Springsteen's rendition is once again characterized by an unparalleled emotional power. You can feel the musicians communing perfectly, and they perform together magnificently. Federici leaves his imprint with his subtle contributions on the organ. Curt Ramm ends the song with a kind of Last Post on the cornet.

DREAM BABY DREAM

Martin Rev, Alan Vega / 5'00

Musicians

Bruce Springsteen: vocals, guitar, synth, piano, mandolin, harmonium
Ron Aniello: percussion, loop, bass, synths, guitar
Tom Morello: guitar
Roy Bittan: piano
Barry Danielian, Clark Gayton, Stan Harrison, Eddie Manion, Curt Ramm: brass
New York Chamber Consort Strings: Rob Mathes (arranger and conductor); Lisa Kim (first violin); Quan Ge, Hyunju Lee, Jessica Lee, Ann Lehman, Joanna Mauer, Suzanne Ornstein, Annaliesa Place, David Southorn, Jeanine Wynton, Sharon Yamada (violins); Maurycy Banaszek, Desiree Elsevier, Shmuel Katz, Robert Rinehart (violas); Maria Kitsopoulos, Alan Stepansky, Ru Pei Yeh (cellos)

Recording

Studios not precisely identified (see page 605): 2013

Technical team

Producers: Ron Aniello, Bruce Springsteen
Recording engineers: Ross Petersen, Toby Scott
Mixing: Bob Clearmountain (Mix This!, Los Angeles); Brandon Duncan, Sergio Ruelas Jr (assistants)
Mastering: Bob Ludwig (Gateway Mastering, Portland)

Alan Vega, the singer of Suicide, the avant-garde rock duo whose song *Dream Baby Dream* Bruce Springsteen recorded.

Genesis and lyrics

"I've liked Suicide for a long time," Springsteen said in an interview for the British magazine *Mojo* in 2006. "I met the guys late in the '70s in New York City, when we were in the studio at the same time. You know, if Elvis came back from the dead I think he would sound like Alan Vega."[162] The New Jersey songwriter liked Alan Vega and Martin Rev's minimalist rock so much that he added *Dream Baby Dream* to his repertoire in 2005. It had originally been released as a single in 1979 out of the recording sessions for the duo's second album, *Suicide: Alan Vega and Martin Rev* (1980). Springsteen ended the shows on the Devils & Dust Tour with a version of this song. Accompanied by Alan "Fitz" Fitzgerald on the synthesizer, Springsteen turned to the crowd and repeated this line: "I just wanna see you smile"; followed by "Come on dream on, dream baby dream."

Eight years after the Devils & Dust Solo Acoustic Tour and five years after the release of a vinyl single, Bruce Springsteen rerecorded *Dream Baby Dream* for *High Hopes*, and today the lyrics sound like a mantra. "We gotta keep the light burning," "We gotta keep the fire burning," and "Come on and open up your heart."

Production

Springsteen later explained that the live performances of *Dream Baby Dream* were an experience for him. As Ron Aniello has pointed out, it required a lot of work to recreate the live experience on a record. This meant that they had to do lots of different versions of the song until Springsteen was happy with the final result. The reason Springsteen struggled to produce this piece is because of its repetitiveness—Suicide's version is based on the repetition of a musical formula that the song keeps returning to with very few changes, either to the lyrics or the music. Nevertheless, it is a unique and utterly hypnotic song—a "mantra," as Springsteen said. And this is what he was trying to replicate, with Ron Aniello's help. Based on chords played on the harmonium, he sings in a delicate, fragile voice, full of emotion. With each new verse, the arrangements are progressively enriched with guitar effects, 6-string acoustics, percussion, loops, keyboards, brass, strings, and sublime vocals from Patti Scialfa. The Boss can be satisfied with what he created: Alan Vega said that he wanted this version played at his funeral.

EP

AMERICAN BEAUTY

American Beauty • Mary Mary • Hurry Up Sundown • Hey Blue Eyes

RELEASE DATE

United States: 19 April 2014

Reference: Columbia Records – 88843 041497

AMERICAN BEAUTY

Bruce Springsteen / 4'06

For Springsteen Addicts

Thom Zimny and Springsteen produced a music video for *American Beauty*, which was filmed on 19 April 2014. Max Weinberg, Tom Morello, Nils Lofgren, and Roy Bittan can all be seen playing in the video even though none of them was involved in the recording of the song!

Musicians

Bruce Springsteen: vocals, acoustic and electric guitars, slide guitar, keyboards, tambourine
Ron Aniello: bass, piano
Charles Giordano: organ
Josh Freese: drums, timpani

Recording

Thrill Hill Recording and Stone Hill Recording, New Jersey: 2012–2013
EastWest Studios, Hollywood: 2012–2013

Technical team

Producers: Ron Aniello, Bruce Springsteen
Recording engineers: Toby Scott, Ross Petersen, Rob Lebret, David Shiffman (drums at EastWest)
Assistant recording engineer: Brendan DeKora (EastWest)
Mixing: Chris Lord-Alge (Mix LA, Los Angeles); Nik Karpen, Keith Armstrong, Brad Townsend, Andrew Schubert (assistants)
Mastering: Bob Ludwig (Gateway Mastering, Portland)

The sleeve for the EP *American Beauty*. The title track pays homage to American women as portrayed in *American Girl* by Tom Petty.

Genesis and lyrics

When does *American Beauty* date from? In the booklet notes for the EP, Bruce Springsteen states that it is a collection of songs "I cut at home. Upon revisiting them for *High Hopes* I recognized their potential and Ron Aniello and I worked on them until we'd turned them into the music before you."[163]

Some lines from older compositions are recycled in the song *American Beauty*: "Radio's cracklin' with the headlines/ Something on your shoulder, winds in the phone line" comes from *Down in the Hole* (*High Hopes*), while "Out on this highway counting white lines" is very similar to "Now I'm out countin' white lines in *Gypsy Biker* (on the *Magic* album). The melody has a hint of *Lucky Day*, from the *Working On a Dream* album.

Beyond these various references, *American Beauty* is an energetic rock 'n' roll tribute to American women that is very much driven by Bruce Springsteen's vocals. It was chosen as the first track on the EP of the same name, which was released on 19 April 2014 as a limited edition of 7,500 copies.

Production

The song opens with a strings riff on the Mellotron—the hallmark of many prog-rock bands. Josh Freese, who again replaces Max Weinberg after contributing to *This Is Your Sword* on *High Hopes,* accompanies the Mellotron with a powerful drumbeat recorded at the EastWest Studios in Hollywood. The band then dives into the first verse, supported by the Boss's high-pitched vocals and a veritable wall of guitars. The songwriter later explained that his lead vocal, sung in a high register that was fairly unusual for him, and this kind of Wall of Sound (see page 69), which included 6- and 12-string acoustic guitars, makes the song sound a bit like parts of *Exile On Main St.*, the legendary 1972 Rolling Stones album.

While the melody of *American Beauty* does recall that of *Lucky Day* in some ways, it particularly resembles the one on *Affection*, a song by The Lost Boys that features a certain Steve Van Zandt. The song appears only in season three of *The Sopranos* series and was officially released on the compilation *The Sopranos—Peppers & Eggs—Music from The HBO Original Series* (2001).

MARY MARY

Bruce Springsteen / 2'48

Musicians

Bruce Springsteen: vocals, guitar, synth, bass, percussion, pump organ
Ron Aniello: synth
Patti Scialfa: backing vocals
Charles Giordano: Farfisa organ
Songa Lee: violin
Steve Richards: cello
Scott Tibbs: conductor and string arrangements
Toby Scott: drum-machine programming

Recording

Thrill Hill Recording and Stone Hill Recording, New Jersey: 2012–2013
EastWest Studios, Hollywood: 2012–2013

Technical team

Producers: Ron Aniello, Bruce Springsteen
Recording engineers: Toby Scott, Ross Petersen, Rob Lebret, David Shiffman (drums and strings at EastWest)
Assistant recording engineer: Brendan DeKora (EastWest)
Mixing: Bob Clearmountain (Mix This!, Los Angeles), Sergio Ruelas Jr (assistant)
Mastering: Bob Ludwig (Gateway Mastering, Portland)

Before Springsteen, Michael Nesmith used *Mary Mary* as the title for one of his songs, covered by the Butterfield Blues Band in 1966, The Monkees in 1967 (he was the guitarist in the band), as well as Run-DMC in 1988. It is also the name of a 1963 American movie directed by Mervyn LeRoy.

Genesis and lyrics

Mary Mary was composed, but not selected, for the *High Hopes* album. "A lovely mystery, a small piece of heartbreak poetry that sneaks up on you with its slippery groove, punctuated string section, and spectral lyrics,"[163] writes Springsteen in the booklet for the *American Beauty* EP. The lyrics refer to a mysterious young woman. "Where have you run to?" the narrator wonders. He has no idea and feels that the story resembles a "book of love with pages worn through" like "torn and tattered pieces of a love gone wrong." The years may have passed, but the narrator has not forgotten the woman that he loved and still loves. And he grasps at any straw he can, even if it's just rumors: "I heard they seen you yesterday in Charlestown." Which Charlestown is it? The one in Indiana, Maryland, or Massachusetts? No doubt Springsteen deliberately chose this name to add to the mystery.

Production

The reason that *Mary Mary* was not chosen for *High Hopes* was probably because of its melody, which is too similar to that of *We Take Care of Our Own* on the *Wrecking Ball* album. It's a real shame because it is a beautiful ballad composed as only Springsteen knows how.

Mostly recorded by Toby Scott, it bears the recording engineer's distinctive stamp, a warm analog sound. The songwriter accompanies himself on acoustic guitar, singing in a gentle and calm voice, supported by the sound of an organ—probably a harmonium. Patti Scialfa joins him on backing vocals at the end of the verse, before the other instruments come in. Toby Scott programmed the drum machine, and it is one of the few times that his name appears in the credits for this type of contribution. Songa Lee on violin and Steve Richards on cello, directed and orchestrated by Scott Tibbs, deliver a rhythmic and melodic motif (on the right, from 0'45), echoed by Charles Giordano's Farfisa organ (on the left).

After an instrumental bridge, dominated by the cello, the song ends on a final verse with the backing vocals of Springsteen and Scialfa.

HURRY UP SUNDOWN

Bruce Springsteen / 3'17

Musicians
Bruce Springsteen: vocals, acoustic and electric guitars, bass, keyboards, glockenspiel, percussion, piano
Josh Freese: drums
Recording
Thrill Hill Recording and Stone Hill Recording, New Jersey: 2012–2013
EastWest Studios, Hollywood: 2012–2013
Technical team
Producers: Ron Aniello, Bruce Springsteen
Recording engineers: Toby Scott, Ross Petersen, Rob Lebret, David Shiffman (drums at EastWest)
Assistant recording engineer: Brendan DeKora (EastWest)
Mixing: Chris Lord-Alge (Mix LA, Los Angeles); Nik Karpen, Keith Armstrong, Brad Townsend, Andrew Schubert (assistants)
Mastering: Bob Ludwig (Gateway Mastering, Portland)

The drummer Josh Freese (seen here in Philadelphia, 2011) is the only musician to have recorded *Hurry Up Sundown* with Bruce Springsteen.

2014

Genesis and lyrics

Like *American Beauty*, *Hurry Up Sundown* was originally recorded when Bruce Springsteen was working with Brendan O'Brien. It is a pop song that picks up on a theme Springsteen had already thoroughly explored on his early albums. "It's the end of another working day/Come on and pack your blues away," he sings at the very start of the track. After a tough, monotonous day at the factory or office, sundown arrives and it's time to have fun. "We'll go for a ride/To the other side." Is this an allusion to the days of his youth, when he would head out of New Jersey for the dazzling lights of New York? One thing is for sure—only the night brings freedom for the narrator and his friend (male or female?), who one can easily imagine as a blue-collar worker. Springsteen has never performed this song onstage.

Production

Springsteen initially worked on *Hurry Up Sundown* back in the days of Brendan O'Brien, but then finished it with Ron Aniello. He handles all the instruments except the drums, which are once again played by Josh Freese in the absence of Max Weinberg.

The piece begins with sound effects that appear to simulate the screeching of a siren. The drummer then launches into an intro fill on snare and tom-toms, before continuing with a contagious groove on drums, supported throughout by the Boss on a frenetic tambourine. Springsteen launches into lead vocals, a joyous double-tracked voice, but this is arguably a tad lackluster and has no real sense of conviction. Once again, he has recorded a veritable wall of guitars that is suffocatingly dense, particularly as the instruments are heavily compressed. He also plays a melodic motif on guitar in two instrumental sections (at 1'35 and 2'50).

The choruses have a 1960s pop feel and are sung with two harmonizing voices (there's an example at 0'24). The songwriter sings the second voice in falsetto (at 2'11). And, in the final verse, he can be heard delivering Beach Boys-style choral vocals (from 2'32).

Springsteen summed up the song perfectly in the notes in the CD booklet: "*Hurry Up Sundown* is a fun piece of modern power pop."[163]

HEY BLUE EYES

Bruce Springsteen / 4'33

Musicians
Bruce Springsteen: vocals, guitar, organ, percussion
Nils Lofgren: guitars, pedal steel guitar
Roy Bittan: piano
Patrick Warren: keyboards
Soozie Tyrell: fiddle
Garry Tallent: bass
Max Weinberg: drums
Patti Scialfa: backing vocals
Recording
Southern Tracks Recording Studio, Atlanta, Georgia: 2007
Technical team
Producer: Brendan O'Brien
Recording engineer: Nick DiDia
Assistant recording engineer: Tom Tapley
Mixing: Brendan O'Brien (Southern Tracks); Nick DiDia, Tom Tapley (assistants)
Mastering: Bob Ludwig (Gateway Mastering, Portland)

Two young Iraqis photographed outside the walls of the Abu Ghraib prison, 19 miles (30km) from Baghdad, where inmates were tortured and humiliated during the Iraq war.

Genesis and lyrics

Hey Blue Eyes is by far the darkest song on the *American Beauty* EP. "Written during the Bush years, it's a metaphor for the house of horrors our government's actions created in the years following the invasion of Iraq," Springsteen states in the notes for the booklet accompanying the record. "At its center is the repressed sexuality and abuse of power that characterized Abu Ghraib prison."[163]

The picture that Springsteen paints of America during the Bush administration has a twilight feel to it, which in some senses evokes a Stalinist dictatorship from the Cold War period more than it does the nation of the *Rights of Man*. "In this house we've abandoned history, in this house there are no laws" and "In this house there's just the dust of bones." The lyrics of violence. And then, this terrible line: "Tonight I'll have you naked and crawling at the end of my leash." This is an explicit reference to a shocking image that was broadcast worldwide in 2004 of a female American soldier holding a prisoner on a leash in a corridor at Abu Ghraib prison in Baghdad.

Production

Hey Blue Eyes is the only track on the EP produced by Brendan O'Brien, and was most likely recorded during the *Magic* sessions in 2007. The presence of Patrick Warren, who played the Chamberlin during the sessions, seems to confirm this.

The song begins with the Boss alone on acoustic guitar, before he gets going on the first verse. His tone is both neutral and sarcastic, intimate and accusing. Most of the E Street Band are on duty here, notably the Weinberg-Tallent duo, who deliver a solid rhythm section, with the first on brushes and the second producing a deep sound like a double bass. The arrangements are subtle, and the composition is based on relatively sober and nuanced instrumental textures, a sound palette that includes Nils Lofgren on pedal steel guitar, Patrick Warren on keyboards (and what appears to be a vibraphone from 2'00), and Springsteen on organ. Soozie Tyrell also contributes with the plaintiff sound of the fiddle, which glides over the final chorus. And, finally, note the backing vocals from Springsteen and Scialfa that resonate like groans from the depths of a prison cell (listen from 3'14).

OVER

ALBUM

CHAPTER AND VERSE

Baby I • You Can't Judge a Book by the Cover • He's Guilty (The Judge Song) • The Ballad of Jesse James • Henry Boy • Growin' Up • 4th of July, Asbury Park (Sandy) • Born to Run • Badlands • The River • My Father's House • Born in the U.S.A. • Brilliant Disguise • Living Proof • The Ghost of Tom Joad • The Rising • Long Time Comin' • Wrecking Ball

RELEASE DATE

United States: 23 September 2016

Reference: Columbia Records – 88985 35820 2

No.5 in the United States, United Kingdom,
No.2 in Italy, No.9 in France

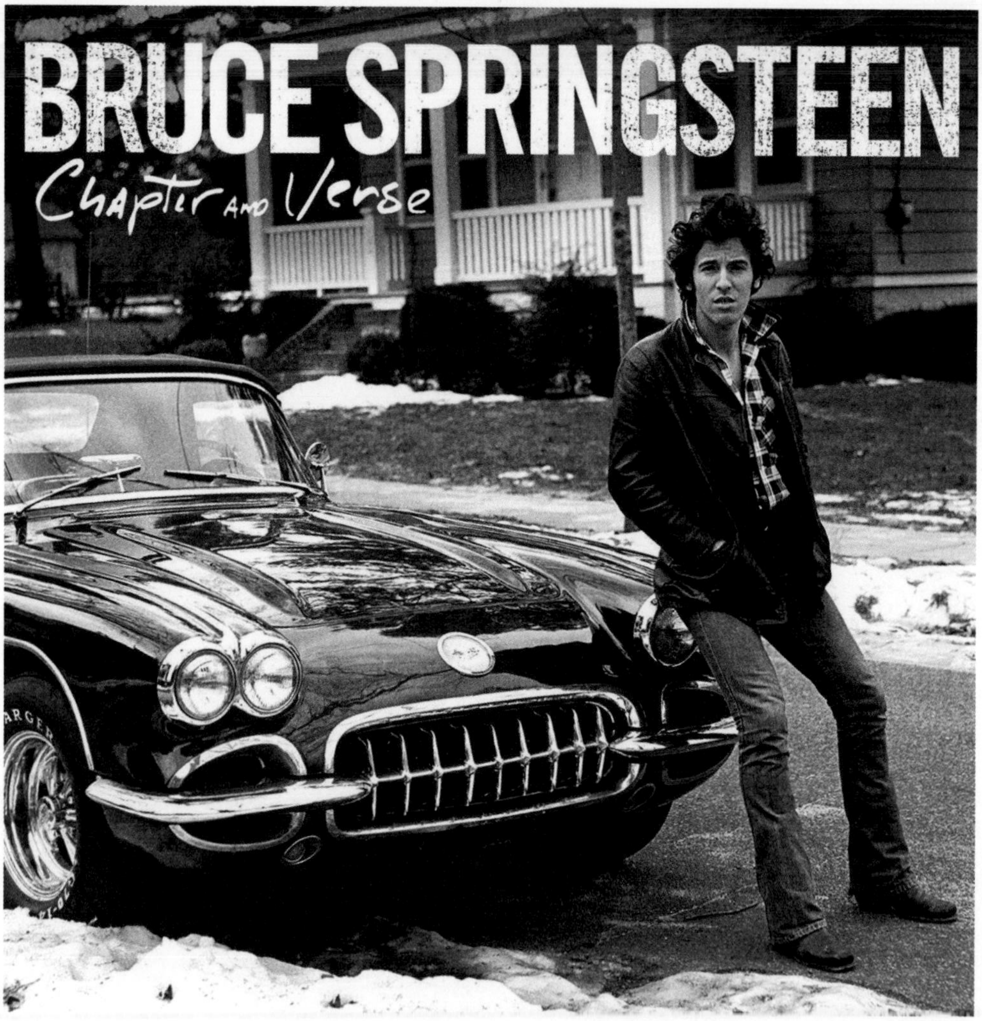

Bruce Springsteen at the Barclays Center, Brooklyn, on 25 April 2016, a few months after *Chapter and Verse* went on sale.

The same photograph was used for the compilation *Chapter and Verse* and Bruce Springsteen's autobiography, the aptly entitled *Born to Run*.

2016

AN AUTOBIOGRAPHY IN 18 SONGS

Chapter and Verse is the compilation album that accompanied the publication of Bruce Springsteen's autobiography, *Born to Run*, on 27 September 2016 in the United States. Incidentally, the same image features on the book's cover and the album sleeve.

The album contains 18 songs in total. Twelve of these are from albums that were released between the *The Wild, the Innocent, and the E Street Shuffle* (1973) and *Wrecking Ball* (2012), plus a version of *Growin' Up*—not the version on *Greetings from Asbury Park, N. J.*, but the demo that features on the box set *Tracks* (1998). The other five are previously unreleased recordings that date from the start of Bruce Springsteen's career: *Baby I* and *You Can't Judge a Book by the Cover* with The Castiles, *He's Guilty (The Judge Song)* with Steel Mill, *The Ballad of Jesse James* with the Bruce Springsteen Band, and *Henry Boy* with the songwriter singing alone with his guitar.

Chapter and Verse was a worldwide hit, reaching No.5 in the United States and, in particular, No.2 in the United Kingdom, Austria, Italy, and Sweden, and No.4 in Belgium, Spain, and Germany. In France, the compilation got to No.9.

BABY I

Bruce Springsteen, George Theiss / 1'56

Musicians: Bruce Springsteen: vocals, guitar / George Theiss: vocals, guitar / Paul Popkin: vocals, tambourine, maracas / Curt Fluhr: bass / Vinnie Manniello: drums **Recording:** Mr. Music, Brick Township, New Jersey: 18 May 1966 **Technical team:** Producer: Bruce Springsteen (?) / Recording engineer: (?) / Mastering: Bob Ludwig (Gateway Mastering, Portland)

The Castiles were Bruce Springsteen's first proper band, with which he played several concerts during the mid-1960s and, above all, recorded his first single. Interviewed by *Backstreets* magazine, George Theiss recalled: "*Baby I* and *That's What You Get* were written in the back seat of Tex's car [Tex Vinyard, The Castiles' manager, owned a 1961 Ford Mercury at the time] on the way to the studio to record them."[30]

It is a very (British) pop song, in which the narrator declares to his girlfriend—or rather ex-girlfriend—that he no longer wants her love or her kisses, because he has found someone better.

Springsteen has explained how in the studio they had been obliged to turn the amps down to the minimum to avoid upsetting the neighbors, which had the effect of removing all distortion. And that is indeed noticeable on hearing the piece, the band sounding a little like the Dave Clark Five, with some verses calling to mind *Gloria* by Van Morrison, and a guitar solo that could be straight out of The Beatles' *Please Please Me*. The Boss's first studio recording, *Baby I* contains some awkward moments, but also the freshness and enthusiasm of an aspiring star. Only one of the band's musicians would make the big time...

2016

YOU CAN'T JUDGE A BOOK BY THE COVER

Willie Dixon / 2'58

Musicians: Bruce Springsteen: vocals, guitar, harmonica (?) / George Theiss: vocals, guitar / Paul Popkin: vocals, tambourine, maracas / Bob Alfano: organ / Curt Fluhr: bass / Vinnie Manniello: drums **Recording:** The Left Foot, Freehold, New Jersey: 16 September 1967 **Technical team:** Producer: Bruce Springsteen (?) / Recording engineer: Fred Coleman / Mastering: Bob Ludwig (Gateway Mastering, Portland)

You Can't Judge a Book by the Cover is a song by Willie Dixon, immortalized by Bo Diddley in 1962 (it was, incidentally, the rock 'n' roll pioneer's last hit).

One should not be deceived by appearances—that is the main idea of this standard, which has been played by countless bands, from The Rolling Stones to Jerry Garcia, The Yardbirds, and Roy Buchanan. So, it is not surprising that The Castiles also included it in their repertoire. This live version was recorded in September 1967 in a club in Freehold called The Left Foot. The sound quality is fairly average, but the result is incandescent and energetic, fully reflecting The Castiles' reputation at the time. A special mention for Bob Alfano's organ accompaniment and the harmonica intro, in all probability played by Springsteen.

HE'S GUILTY (THE JUDGE SONG)

Bruce Springsteen / 4'39

Musicians: Bruce Springsteen: vocals, guitar / Danny Federici: organ, piano, backing vocals / Vinnie Roslin: bass, backing vocals / Vini Lopez: drums **Recording:** Pacific Recording Studio, San Mateo, California: 22 February 1970 **Technical team:** Producer: Bruce Springsteen / Recording engineer: (?) / Mastering: Bob Ludwig (Gateway Mastering, Portland)

Before the formation of the E Street Band, Bruce Springsteen served his apprenticeship in a number of groups, such as The Castiles, Earth, and Child, which was later renamed Steel Mill (to avoid confusion with an eponymous band). With Steel Mill, Bruce Springsteen went to perform in California, notably at the Matrix, as the opening act for the Elvin Bishop Group. He also recorded three songs there: *Goin' Back to Georgia*, *The Train Song*, and *He's Guilty (The Judge Song)*.

The last of these was the result of a rather unpleasant experience the young songwriter had when he was arrested for trying to access a beach without paying the $1 entry fee. "He's guilty, he's guilty, send that boy to jail"—the jury was hardly soft-hearted. So, many years later, Springsteen used this song to look back and mock his own experience of being arrested by the police for doing something very minor.

Musically, the song is a rock number showing influences ranging from Cream to the Doobie Brothers (especially in the very fine vocal harmonies). Springsteen leads the band with energy, delivering lead vocals that are not really recognizable, and also an excellent 6-string guitar part, with the obligatory riff and solo. This is also a chance to hear Danny Federici on record for the first time (with an excellent organ solo at 2'57), as well as Vini Lopez, who gets out his cowbell for the occasion.

THE BALLAD OF JESSE JAMES

Bruce Springsteen / 5'30

Musicians: Bruce Springsteen: vocals, guitar / Steve Van Zandt: guitar, backing vocals / David Sancious: organ, piano / Garry Tallent: bass / Vini Lopez: drums **Recording:** Challenger Eastern Surfboards, Highland,

New Jersey: 14 March 1972 **Technical team:** Producer: Bruce Springsteen / Recording engineer: Carl "Tinker" West / Mastering: Bob Ludwig (Gateway Mastering, Portland)

Accompanied by the Bruce Springsteen Band—soon to be renamed the E Street Band—Springsteen turns the spotlight on two mythical outlaws from American history. They are Jesse James, an unrepentant Confederate who, with his brother Frank, demonstrated his hatred of Yankees through multiple attacks on banks and trains, and also Billy the Kid, who was shot dead by sheriff Pat Garrett after killing no fewer than 21 men (the same number as his age in years).

Springsteen's message? Probably that life is only worth living if we go beyond our limits—climb mountains, climb the tallest tree, and, above all, give our beloved all the love we can.

This song also goes by the title *Don't You Want to Be an Outlaw*. It is worth noting that, many years later, Springsteen would again sing about the outlaw's bloody career (the song *Jesse James*), this time during the Pete Seeger Sessions.

For now, though, *The Ballad of Jesse James* is a rock-blues number, driven by Springsteen's guitar, which plays the riff, rhythm guitar, and solos, and by that of Steve Van Zandt, who plays slide guitar. Danny Federici has been replaced by David Sancious who, like Garry Tallent, makes his first appearance on record alongside the songwriter. This song already contains seeds of the Springsteen style—both lyrical and rock. Only a few months later, the 914 Sound Recording Studios in Blauvelt, New York State, would be booked—the start of the path to glory.

HENRY BOY

Bruce Springsteen / 3'13

Musician: Bruce Springsteen: vocals, guitar **Recording**: Mediasound Studios, New York: June 1972 **Technical team:** Producers: Bruce Springsteen, Mike Appel / Recording engineer: Harvey J Goldberg / Mastering: Bob Ludwig (Gateway Mastering Studios, Portland)

This demo, which dates from June 1972, is the original version of what would become *Blinded by the Light*, the first single from *Greetings from Asbury Park, N. J.* Bruce Springsteen performed it at Max's Kansas City, New York, on 10 August 1972.

It tells the story of Henry, who discovers the big city—New York—probably after leaving his native New Jersey. But life is not as easy as he had hoped: "It's a hard world when you're the new kid in town," Springsteen sings.

What can we say about *Henry Boy* from a musical standpoint? It is a song in the making, certainly written in an overly complicated way, but Springsteen rewrote it to arrive at a perfectly finished form in *Blinded by the Light*. Furthermore, his talent is already abundantly apparent in this demo, where he accompanies himself, alone, on the guitar. John Hammond and Mike Appel were not mistaken.

"Wanted" poster for Billy the Kid, dead or alive. Bruce Springsteen brought this legendary outlaw back to life in *The Ballad of Jesse James*.

WESTE
SWES
SER

ALBUM

WESTERN STARS

Hitch Hikin' • The Wayfarer • Tucson Train • Western Stars • Sleepy Joe's Café •
Drive Fast (The Stuntman) • Chasin' Wild Horses • Sundown • Somewhere North of Nashville •
Stones • There Goes My Miracle • Hello Sunshine • Moonlight Motel •
Rhinestone Cowboy (only on the CD for the movie soundtrack)

RELEASE DATE

United States: 14 June 2019

Reference: Columbia Records—19075941972

No.1 in the United Kingdom, Australia, Belgium, the Netherlands, Germany, Italy, Spain, and Switzerland, No.2 in the United States, No.3 in France

Bruce Springsteen at home in Colts Neck, New Jersey, on 26 September 2019, one month before the release of the movie *Western Stars* in the United States.

The entrance of the Walter Kerr Theatre, New York, where Bruce Springsteen performed during June 2018.

2019

ALMIGHTY BRUCE

More than five years after *High Hopes*, Bruce Springsteen ended his recording silence with *Western Stars*. Not that he had been doing nothing during the long interval—as demonstrated by the High Hopes Tour (2014) and the River Tour (2016–2017), the publication of his autobiography, *Born to Run*, and the Springsteen on Broadway show—but a new album from the Boss is nevertheless always eagerly awaited.

The album

If Springsteen's intention was to surprise his fans, then he succeeded. Musically, his 19th album is totally unlike any other. It sounds like a tribute to 1960s California pop, and to three songwriters/composers in particular. Firstly, Jimmy Webb who composed and wrote *By the Time I Get to Phoenix* and *Wichita Lineman* for Glen Campbell, and also *MacArthur Park* for the actor Richard Harris. Secondly, Burt Bacharach, to whom Dionne Warwick owes her biggest hits (*Anyone Who Had a Heart*, *I Say a Little Prayer for You*, *I'll Never Fall in Love Again*). Thirdly, BJ Thomas who composed *Raindrops Keep Fallin' on My Head*, the song from George Roy Hill's 1969 movie, *Butch Cassidy and the Sundance Kid*. From *Hitch Hikin'* through to *Moonlight Motel*, this album is lushly orchestrated and often languid, falling somewhere between Phil Spector's Wall of Sound (see page 69) and the soundtracks from the great Hollywood Westerns composed by Max Steiner (*The Searchers*), Jerry Fielding (*The Wild Bunch*), and John Hammond Jr (*Little Big Man*). The vocals are also unusual, as the rock and folk elements are replaced by a pop-crooner style that resembles Roy Orbison at the height of his powers (*In Dreams* and *Oh, Pretty Woman*).

The themes in *Western Stars*, however, are not that far removed from those that have inspired the songwriter since the 1970s. These are the open road, be it at the wheel of a car, astride a motorbike, or simply on foot; vast open spaces; and the West Coast. His characters are also familiar—noble losers, actors, stuntmen down on their luck, hitchhikers who want to break with the past and change their lives, or just lonely souls. What makes Springsteen's approach unique is the stage that he sets for his antiheroes. This album is either a kind of road trip toward a mythical promised land, crossing stunning landscapes, immense deserts, and dusty, sun-baked roads or, conversely, set in the intimate atmosphere of a motel or bar on Route 66—in many ways, it is an *Easy Rider* road drama. If you close your eyes and listen to the voice, you are rapidly transported to the heart of the stories that Bruce Springsteen meditated on at length before putting pen to paper. Throughout *Western Stars*, Springsteen is the portraitist and scriptwriter of an America as we imagine it to be, an America of our fantasies, and, occasionally, an America as it really is.

Is this an introspective album? Undoubtedly. On the cusp of 70, Bruce Springsteen clearly wanted to record an album of redemption, an album that to some extent marks his emergence from the depression rooted in his childhood, a journey of recovery that had begun in his book *Born to Run*. It is also the album of an artist who has been around and seen a lot, the album of an artist who draws his inspiration from the golden

Bruce Springsteen at the London Film Festival, where there was a preview screening of *Western Stars*.

age of the 1960s in order to carve his path into the future. Produced by Ron Aniello, but recorded without the E Street Band (with the exception of Patti Scialfa), *Western Stars* was released worldwide on 14 June 2019 to widespread media acclaim. *Rolling Stone* magazine and the allmusicguide website gave it four stars, while the online British newspaper, *The Independent*, awarded it the maximum of five stars.

So, it was a hit with the critics, but also very much a commercial success, too: *Western Stars* reached No.2 in the *Billboard* charts in the United States from the week of 29 June 2019. In the United Kingdom, the album went to No.1 on 27 June. It was also No.1 in 13 other countries, including Belgium, the Netherlands, Germany, Italy, and Spain. In France, it reached the No.3 spot.

An album and a film

Western Stars is a feature film as well as an album. The film was produced and directed by Bruce Springsteen and his friend Thom Zimny. It was presented at the Toronto International Film Festival on 12 September 2019, followed by the London Film Festival on 11 October, before being released in American movie theaters on 25 October and in UK cinemas on 28 October. It is an autobiographical, acoustic, and symphonic concert, recorded in a barn with a bar on the songwriter's ranch, Stone Hill Farm in Colts Neck, New Jersey. Bruce Springsteen, with his band and a classical orchestra, performed the songs from the album to an audience of around a hundred. The movie's particular interest lies in the photos and home movies from the family archives that show Springsteen as a child, a teenager, a father, and on his honeymoon with Patti Scialfa, as well as in the songwriter talking about his vision of the American dream. The *Western Stars* movie, so Springsteen claims, is the last part of his autobiographical trilogy, after the book *Born to Run* and the Springsteen on Broadway concert residence.

The sleeve

Western Stars is the third album after *Nebraska* and *The Ghost of Tom Joad* that does not feature Springsteen on the cover—and the first with an image of an animal. A mustang (a wild horse from the American West) is shown galloping toward a mountainous horizon, set to the backdrop of a cloudy sky. The symbolism is easy to decipher: the indomitable mustang setting out to conquer the wide-open spaces represents freedom in all its glory, the expression of the American dream. On the back cover, Bruce Springsteen in jeans, brown jacket, cowboy hat, and cowboy boots leans against what appears to be a Dodge pickup (1979 model) in the carport of a house. It gives the impression that, like the mustang, the songwriter is also about to head out to wherever the fancy takes him. The sleeve was designed by Michelle Holme in association with the photographers Kalle Gustafsson (Trunk Archive) and Danny Clinch.

The recording

Western Stars was produced over several years and constantly put on the back burner in favor of new projects. Springsteen began working on it in 2010 in his home studio, Stone Hill in Colts Neck. The ever-loyal Toby Scott was there to help him bring his songs to life. The songwriter, very accustomed by then to recording alone, laid down basic, stripped-down tracks of several pieces. "Some of the parts were good, but they were only an indication of what they could be,"[43] the recording engineer later explained. The Boss used his

The superb sleeve for *Western Stars*—a mustang at full gallop toward the great open spaces of the American West.

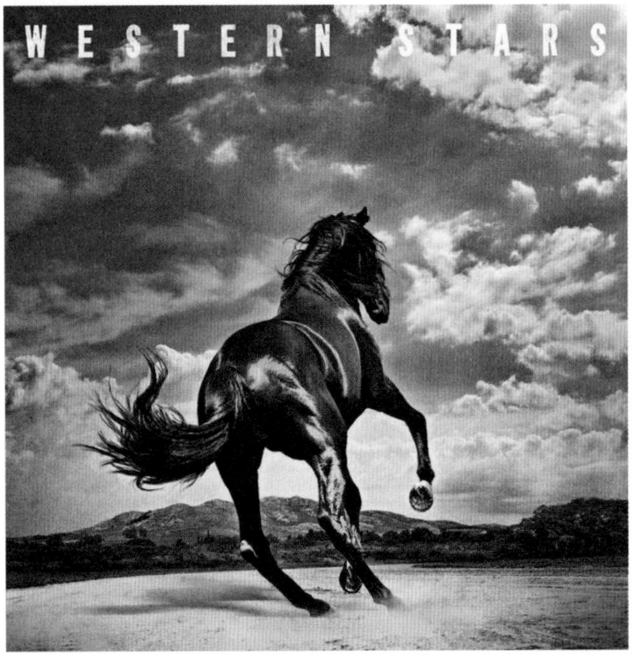

WESTERN STARS, SONGS FROM THE FILM

The original movie soundtrack was released on 25 October 2019. It features the live versions of all the songs on *Western Stars*, as well as Glen Campbell's *Rhinestone Cowboy*. It was produced by Bruce Springsteen and Ron Aniello. Bob Clearmountain did the mixing, and Bob Ludwig the mastering.

Mellotron and various samplers to record ideas for string and brass instruments, the main elements of which would later become the fabric of *Western Stars* (largely re-orchestrated and reinterpreted by real musicians and two string orchestras). Although he was the only musician creating and recording the pieces, the result is closer to a master than a demo. Something that Scott confirms: "We don't really do demos. What am I gonna do? Use the bad microphones? As I said to Bruce, 'You don't do demos either. You sing in key and in time while playing the guitar. We just make recordings that don't get released.'"[43] Which fortunately was not the case here.

When Ron Aniello started working with the songwriter in 2012, he noticed that Springsteen had accumulated a lot of unreleased material: "There were about 30 or 40 songs. They were very unique for him, unlike anything I'd ever heard [...]."[156] Aniello even went as far as comparing them to the work of Aaron Copland, one of the great American composers, mostly known for his ballet *Appalachian Spring* (1943). "It has a very open landscape feel and I guess...You wouldn't call it country. It's just very hard to describe. You'll just have to wait. I'm actually working on some of the songs now [...] [Bruce] is looking for a way to approach that album."[156]

So, in between the *Wrecking Ball* and *High Hopes* albums, his autobiography *Born to Run*, three tours with the E Street Band (Wrecking Ball Tour, High Hopes Tour, and The River Tour), and his solo performances for Springsteen on Broadway, the songwriter gradually managed to complete production of *Western Stars*, culminating in the release of his 19th album in April 2019. His long-standing friend, Steve Van Zandt, expressed his admiration for Bruce's creative power: "Well, he's the most prolific guy I know of. Bob Dylan is right there with him, those [two] are just ridiculous. Bruce is very good at a lot of different things. He's very versatile. He can do whatever he puts his mind to. I really hate him for it. He decides to write a book—he writes a fantastic book. He decides to do Broadway—he does a fantastic Broadway show. So this record is an interesting, different part of his personality. It has a Jim Webb quality to it. And I like it a lot and I think people will like it. But it's not...it's not a rock album. Don't judge it as a rock album. Just take it as it is."[152]

The recording studios

Although *Western Stars* was mainly produced at Stone Hill Studio in Colts Neck, New Jersey, other studios were also booked to record the overdubs. In California: Ocean Way Studios, Burbank; Very Loud House Studio, Woodland Hills; and Sage and Sound, Hollywood. In New York: Avatar Studios and Electric Lady Studios (for the mixing).

The musicians

Patti Scialfa is the only other member of the E Street Band to participate on the album. Besides the Boss himself and Ron Aniello, numerous other musicians are involved: David Sancious, an ex-E Streeter, is back on piano, Soozie Tyrell on violin and backing vocals, Charles Giordano on accordion, Matt Rollings on piano, Jon Brion on drums, timpani, guitar, keyboards, and celeste, Gunnar Olsen and Matt Chamberlain on drums, Marc Muller on lap steel and pedal steel guitar, Rob Lebret on guitar, Marty Rifkin and Greg Leisz on pedal steel guitar, Lenny Castro on percussion, Toby Scott on programming and loops, Michelle Moore, Curtis King, Cindy Mizelle, and Matthew Koma on backing vocals, Curt Ramm, Barry Danielian, Clark Gayton, Dan Levine, and Eddie Manion on brass, Rachel Drehmann and Leelanee Sterrett on French horn, Alden Banta on bassoon, Andrew Sterman on alto flute, Charles Pillow on oboe, and Luis Villalobos on violin. Thirty-one musicians, including the Boss. Not forgetting the Avatar Strings, conducted by Rob Mathes, with nine violins, three violas, and two cellos, and the Stone Hill Strings, conducted by Scott Tibbs, with three violins, two violas, and a cello. A total of 52 musicians!

HITCH HIKIN'

Bruce Springsteen / 3'37

The hitchhiking theme has inspired other artists besides the Boss, notably Marvin Gaye who released a single called *Hitch Hike* in 1962, which was covered by The Rolling Stones in 1965. Roger Waters also called one of his albums *The Pros and Cons of Hitch Hiking* (1984).

2019

Musicians

Bruce Springsteen: vocals, guitar, glockenspiel, keyboards, banjo, percussion, orchestra samples
Ron Aniello: bass, keyboards, percussion, orchestra samples, drums, loops
The Avatar Strings: Rob Mathes (arranger and conductor); Lisa Kim, Hyunju Lee, Liz Lim, Joanna Maurer, Suzanne Ornstein, Annaliesa Place, Emily Popham, Sharon Yamada, Jung Sun Yoo (violins); Desiree Elsevier, Vivek Kamath, Robert Reinhart (violas); Alan Stepansky, Nathan Vickery (cellos)

Recording

Stone Hill Studio, New Jersey: 2010–2019
Avatar Studios, New York: 2014–2019

Technical team

Producers: Ron Aniello, Bruce Springsteen
Recording engineers: Rob Lebret, Ross Petersen, Toby Scott, Ron Aniello
Mixing: Tom Elmhirst (Electric Lady Studios, New York), Joe Visciano (assistant)
Mastering: Bob Ludwig (Gateway Mastering, Portland)

The orchestral conductor Rob Mathes (with Michael Feinstein on the left) before a concert in Carnegie Hall, in 2017. He conducted the Avatar Strings in *Hitch Hikin'*.

Genesis and lyrics

Bruce Springsteen's road trip begins with *Hitch Hikin'*. The character in the song is a drifter on the highway, probably heading out West. He talks about folks who understand him, those who stop and pick him up on the roadside. Like the couple who are expecting a child—to whom he says, "children are a gift"—or the truck driver who has a photo of a pretty girl on his dashboard. Is it his daughter or his wife?

Tom Joad obviously comes to mind, the character from Steinbeck's *Grapes of Wrath* that Springsteen brought back to life in his masterful folk album *The Ghost of Tom Joad*. The difference being that the character from the novel was heading for California in the hope of finding work, whereas the narrator of *Hitch Hikin'* clearly feels that the journey itself, and his many encounters along the way, is the ultimate symbol of freedom.

Production

The live version recorded for the soundtrack of the film isn't that far removed from the album version; the main difference being the Boss's voice and the overall sound, which is slightly harsher and not quite as smooth.

Hitch Hikin' is a success and proves that after an exceptionally rich 46-year career, Springsteen is still as inspired and talented as ever.

THE WAYFARER

Bruce Springsteen / 4'18

Musicians

Bruce Springsteen: vocals, guitar, keyboard, percussion, orchestral samples, organ
Ron Aniello: double bass, keyboards, guitar, percussion, vibraphone, celeste, loops, orchestral samples
David Sancious: piano
Rachel Drehmann, Leelanee Sterrett: French horn
Curt Ramm: trumpet, flugelhorn
Matt Chamberlain: drums
Patti Scialfa, Soozie Tyrell: backing vocals
Stone Hill Strings: Scott Tibbs (conductor); Lisa Kim, Hyunju Lee, Joanna Maurer (violins); Schmuel Katz, Rebecca Young (violas); Alan Stepansky (cello)

Recording

Stone Hill Studio, New Jersey: 2010–2019

Technical team

Producers: Ron Aniello, Bruce Springsteen
Recording engineers: Rob Lebret, Ross Petersen, Toby Scott, Ron Aniello
Mixing: Tom Elmhirst (Electric Lady Studios, New York); Joe Visciano (assistant)
Mastering: Bob Ludwig (Gateway Mastering, Portland)

For Springsteen Addicts

Matt Chamberlain is a studio drummer as well as songwriter and producer who started out in the music business with Soundgarden. He played on three tracks for *Wrecking Ball* (2012), and after the *Western Stars* sessions, he joined Bob Dylan's orchestra on the Fall Tour in October 2019.

Genesis and lyrics

Once again, Bruce Springsteen writes a story about a traveler, and once again "It's the same old cliché, a wanderer on his way, slipping from town to town," as he sings. Unlike other folks who prefer a home, a fire, and slippers tucked under the bed, the traveler feels the irresistible pull of the open road. And at night, when the whole world is sleeping, he can't count sheep because of the white lines in his head. He wanders from town to town, tires squealing up the highway. But perhaps the imagery goes further. Indeed, the music gives the impression that this diehard wayfarer is a solitary hero, a character from a Western for whom crossing vast open spaces is a voyage of (self-) discovery.

Production

Listening to *The Wayfarer* is to experience the full measure of Springsteen's incredible eclecticism. This song is a kind of pop-jazz ballad and is so unusual compared to his previous body of songs—which is already astonishingly diverse—that it is hard to believe they were composed by the same artist. Bruce Springsteen is an extraordinary songwriter, composer, and performer, and few of his peers can hold a candle to him.

The piece begins with Springsteen playing a palm-muted acoustic guitar, accompanied by David Sancious playing staccato on the piano. Sancious is a former E-Streeter who last worked with Springsteen on the *Human Touch* (1992) and *Tracks* box set (1998) sessions. The musicians from the Stone Hills Strings, conducted by Scott Dibbs, then come in with a melodic, rhythmic motif, before the Boss's superb vocals resonate in a deep reverb. The arrangements are progressively stacked up with, notably, a drum loop, a vibraphone, a celeste, electric guitars, a double bass, timpani, a shaker, a triangle, and many other percussion instruments. Not forgetting the contributions from Curt Ramm on bugle and trumpet, Matt Chamberlain on drums, Patti Scialfa and Soozie Tyrell on backing vocals, and the Boss's organ solo (from 3'47). Great artistry!

TUCSON TRAIN

Bruce Springsteen / 3'31

For Springsteen Addicts

Gunnar Olsen is a New York drummer who played with the electronic music band Big Data in 2014, reaching No.1 in the *Billboard* alternative charts with *Dangerous*. He also founded the group Mother Feather.

2019

Musicians

Bruce Springsteen: vocals, guitar, keyboard, percussion
Ron Aniello: bass, keyboards, guitars, percussion
Matt Rollings: piano
Barry Danielian, Curt Ramm: trumpet
Dan Levine: trombone
Alden Banta: bassoon
Rachel Drehmann, Leelanee Sterrett: French horn
Charles Pillow: oboe
Andrew Sterman: alto flute
Gunnar Olsen: drums
Toby Scott: programming, loops
Stone Hill Strings: Scott Tibbs (conductor); Lisa Kim, Hyunju Lee, Joanna Maurer (violins); Schmuel Katz, Rebecca Young (violas); Alan Stepansky (cello)

Recording

Stone Hill Studio, New Jersey: 2010–2019

Technical team

Producers: Ron Aniello, Bruce Springsteen
Recording engineers: Rob Lebret, Ross Petersen, Toby Scott, Ron Aniello
Mixing: Tom Elmhirst (Electric Lady Studios, New York), Joe Visciano (assistant)
Mastering: Bob Ludwig (Gateway Mastering, Portland)

Little Steven & The Disciples of Soul perform an exhilarating version of *Tucson Train* at the Rialto Theatre, in Tucson, Arizona, on 15 September 2019.

Genesis and lyrics

Like many bluesmen and folk singers before him, from Robert Johnson to Woody Guthrie, Bruce Springsteen turned to the metaphor of the train and the railroad as a way of talking about his characters' love relationships. A notable example is *Downbound Train* (on the *Born in the U.S.A.* album), where the protagonist's girl boards a train and leaves him, and he subsequently gets a job on the railroad.

Tucson Train is not the story of a couple breaking up, but of a couple getting back together—or at least, hoping to do so. Without a dollar to his name, the man quit "the pills and the rain" of San Francisco, leaving behind him a love that "was in vain." He is now in Arizona working as a crane operator on a building site. And a lot of water seems to have flowed under the bridge since he left. In the past, the couple "fought hard over nothing" and work was a struggle, too. Today, the narrator says that he has changed, and he is as impatient as a lovesick teenager to see his sweetheart who is "coming in on the Tucson Train."

Tucson Train is the third single taken from *Western Stars*. The accompanying black and white music video was directed by Thom Zimny; Springsteen performs the song alongside Patti Scialfa and an orchestra in the best tradition of music for Westerns.

Production

Tucson Train begins with a rhythm loop programmed by Toby Scott to sound like the chugging of a train. The brass and woodwind sections then come in with a melodic motif that would not have felt out of place in a John Wayne Western. The Boss confidently launches into his lead vocal, backed by bass, acoustic and electric guitars, synth pads, drums played by Gunnar Olsen (who had been recommended for the sessions by his friend Ross Petersen), and numerous percussion instruments. Matt Rollings, a highly skilled pianist who has worked with artists ranging from Mark Knopfler to Willie Nelson and Brian Setzer, makes a few sparse but effective piano contributions. The spirited and lively passages from the Stone Hill Strings reinforce the motif played by the brass section. The song ends with the same rhythm loop as the intro.

Tucson Train takes Springsteen closer to the world of Glen Campbell or Burt Bacharach than that of the E Street Band. Proof again of his astonishing eclecticism.

Fun fact: all Springsteen's albums from *Born to Run* in 1975 to *Western Stars* in 2019 feature a song with the same title as the album.

WESTERN STARS

Bruce Springsteen / 4'41

Musicians

Bruce Springsteen: vocals, guitars, keyboards
Ron Aniello: bass, keyboards, guitars, loops
Jon Brion: guitar, Moog synthesizer
Rob Lebret: guitar, baritone guitar
Marc Muller: lap steel guitar
Matt Rollings: piano
Barry Danielian, Curt Ramm: trumpet
Dan Levine: trombone
Alden Banta: bassoon
Rachel Drehmann, Leelanee Sterrett: French horn
Charles Pillow: oboe
Andrew Sterman: alto flute
Lenny Castro: congas, tambourine
Matt Chamberlain: drums
Curtis King, Cindy Mizelle, Michelle Moore: backing vocals
Stone Hill Strings: Scott Tibbs (conductor); Lisa Kim, Hyunju Lee, Joanna Maurer (violins); Schmuel Katz, Rebecca Young (violas); Alan Stepansky (cello)

Recording

Stone Hill Studio, New Jersey: 2010–2019
Ocean Way Studios, Burbank: 2014–2019

Technical team

Producers: Ron Aniello, Bruce Springsteen
Recording engineers: Rob Lebret, Ross Petersen, Toby Scott, Ron Aniello (Stone Hill), Brett Rouche, Greg Koller (Ocean)
Mixing: Tom Elmhirst (Electric Lady Studios, New York), Joe Visciano (assistant)
Mastering: Bob Ludwig (Gateway Mastering, Portland)

For Springsteen Addicts

Lenny Castro, a Los Angeles musician and former member of the band Toto, plays the congas on this song (as well as *Sleepy Joe's Café* and *There Goes My Miracle*).

Genesis and lyrics

Of all the compositions, *Western Stars* is without a doubt the one that best reflects the air of nostalgia that sweeps through this 19th studio album—a nostalgia for the Golden Age of Hollywood during the era of the big studios.

The narrator is a former actor. He recalls the good old days when the makeup girl used to bring him two raw eggs and a shot of gin before a day's shooting in the deserts and canyons somewhere in the American West, including California and perhaps also Nevada or Arizona, in Monument Valley or Death Valley. "Tonight the western stars are shining bright again," sings Bruce Springsteen in the chorus. A woman sipping a mojito in a bar thinks she recollects seeing the actor in a commercial for a credit card. Back in the day, he worked with the great John Wayne and was even shot by him in one memorable scene. But that was a long time ago—too long. Nowadays, only Viagra (the little blue pill mentioned at the start of the song) gives the narrator his thrills.

Western Stars is the fourth single released from the album, and the fourth song to be filmed as a video directed by Thom Zimny. The Boss sits at a bar, and the barman serves him a whisky. We then see him singing with his musicians, and behind the wheel of his Dodge pickup.

Production

Western Stars begins with a lap steel guitar, drowned in a mesmerizing spatial reverb, played by Marc Muller, who had previously appeared on *Wrecking Ball*. It is accompanied by a rhythmic section performed by the Boss on his acoustic guitar and by Matt Rollings on piano. Springsteen has written a superb and lavishly orchestrated ballad, tinged with nostalgia. The instruments come in one after the other—electric guitars, strings, drum, brass, woodwind, synths, and percussion. Lenny Castro recorded the percussion parts at the Ocean Way Studios: "This was my first time working for Bruce," he later said. "My sessions were really quick. I don't sit around and overthink things. If you can't grab it off the top of your head, then it's not worth it as far as I'm concerned."[43]

Western Stars is an absolute gem, elevated by Ron Aniello's exceptional production.

An acoustic and symphonic concert is recorded for *Western Stars* in a bar set up in a barn on Bruce Springsteen's ranch, Stone Hill Farm, at Colts Neck, New Jersey.

SLEEPY JOE'S CAFÉ

Bruce Springsteen / 3'14

More than 60 years before Bruce Springsteen and his version of *Sleepy Joe's Café*, Jerry Leiber and Mike Stoller had written a song called *Smokey Joe's Cafe*, recorded by The Robins (who later became The Coasters) in 1955. Smokey Joe's, on the corner of Beverly Boulevard and La Cienaga Boulevard in Los Angeles, later lent its name to a 1955 Broadway musical, featuring songs by the famous duo.

2019

Musicians
Bruce Springsteen: vocals, guitars, glockenspiel, keyboards, banjo
Ron Aniello: bass, keyboards, guitars
Jon Brion: keyboards
Charles Giordano: accordion
Barry Danielian, Curt Ramm: trumpet
Clark Gayton: trombone
Ed Manion: saxophone
Lenny Castro: congas, shaker
Gunnar Olsen: drums

Recording
Stone Hill Studio, New Jersey: 2010–2019
Ocean Way Studios, Burbank: 2014–2019

Technical team
Producers: Ron Aniello, Bruce Springsteen
Recording engineers: Rob Lebret, Ross Petersen, Toby Scott, Ron Aniello (Stone Hill), Brett Rouche, Greg Koller (Ocean)
Mixing: Tom Elmhirst (Electric Lady Studios, New York), Joe Visciano (assistant)
Mastering: Bob Ludwig (Gateway Mastering, Portland)

Bruce Springsteen and the accordionist Charles Giordano had a total rapport, both onstage and in the studio, in *Sleepy Joe's Café*.

Genesis and lyrics

Does Sleepy Joe's Café exist? Bruce Springsteen may well have stumbled across a bar like this when he was riding the highways of California on his motorbike. It's a dance-bar where truckers and bikers gather every evening, and the songwriter places it not far from San Bernadino. The atmosphere is good, pretty hot in fact, with "summer girls [...] flirting the night away"; it's a place where the narrator can drown all his worries in a few pints of beer and some live music. Joe was an army cook who was demobbed after the Second World War. He used his army loan to open this bar in a peaceful little corner of California. He married May, and the money started rolling in after the highway was built. So, thanks to Joe, the regulars have a place where "Monday morning is a million miles away."

Production

Gunnar Olsen gets the song underway with a drum fill. Unlike the previous tracks on the album, *Sleepy Joe's Café* is in a traditional format—mid-tempo country rock, with Latino and Cajun flavors. It's a piece that would better suit the E Street Band's repertoire.

Springsteen is on acoustic guitar, probably the 12-string, and banjo (on the right). On the left of the stereo, he is accompanied by strings played by Jon Brion on the Moog synthesizer. It's not the best sound, especially as Springsteen and Ron Aniello have accustomed us to hearing real orchestras since the start of *Western Stars*. Fortunately, on the live version of the album (from the movie), the Moog parts are played by actual musicians.

Charles Giordano's accordion comes in on the first verse, while a piano and some discreet glockenspiels join in on the following verse (at 0'39). Brion performs a solo on the Farfisa organ at the instrumental bridge, echoed by a Hank Marvin-style electric guitar (from 1'33). The brass section appears on the final verse, bringing a mariachi color to the piece.

For the rhythm section, Gunnar Olsen later explained that there were originally two other versions of the song, with Matt Chamberlain and Steve Jordan on drums. But the Boss invited him to give it a shot, and ended up keeping his take. "And it had nothing to do with what those guys were doing. He wanted another option."[159]

DRIVE FAST (THE STUNTMAN)

Bruce Springsteen / 4'17

Musicians
Bruce Springsteen: vocals, guitars, glockenspiel, keyboards, percussion
Ron Aniello: double bass, keyboards, guitars, percussion
Marc Muller: pedal steel guitar
David Sancious: organ
Luis Villalobos: violin
Gunnar Olsen: drums
Stone Hill Strings: Scott Tibbs (conductor); Lisa Kim, Hyunju Lee, Joanna Maurer (violins); Schmuel Katz, Rebecca Young (violas); Alan Stepansky (cello)

Recording
Stone Hill Studio, New Jersey: 2010–2019

Technical team
Producers: Ron Aniello, Bruce Springsteen
Recording engineers: Rob Lebret, Ross Petersen, Toby Scott, Ron Aniello
Mixing: Tom Elmhirst (Electric Lady Studios, New York), Joe Visciano (assistant)
Mastering: Bob Ludwig (Gateway Mastering, Portland)

Bruce Springsteen at the 13th Stand Up for Heroes concert at Madison Square Garden, New York, on 4 November 2019.

Genesis and lyrics

Like *Western Stars, Drive Fast (The Stuntman)* shines the spotlight on Hollywood's Golden Age. But this time Springsteen tells the story of a stuntman rather than a supporting actor. A stuntman who now has, as he says in the lyrics, "two pins in my ankle and a busted collarbone"; such are the dangers of the job, the hard reality of action films. But back then, he enjoyed the risks. Even as a child, he was oblivious to fear and vertigo, and would climb high into the boughs of the tallest trees. Some years later, he was employed by a Hollywood studio. He was paid to leap obstacles at top speed for the cameras, without worrying about tomorrow. While shooting a B movie in Hollywood, the intrepid stuntman met a woman, an actress. They headed off into the desert to try and make a go of it together. Did it all end in bitter disappointment? It seems that way, especially as Springsteen's voice sounds desperately sad and the orchestration touches a raw nerve of nostalgia.

Production

A single acoustic guitar and a few piano chords open *Drive Fast (The Stuntman)*. The songwriter's voice then echoes out in a Roy Orbison-style vibrato, carried by a short reverb. As always, the sincerity and authenticity in Springsteen's voice cannot be faulted, even though he is about to turn 70.

The Stone Hill Strings subtly glide in among the other instruments at the end of the first verse (at 0'44). The string arrangements are lavish, with Scott Tibbs conducting his musicians totally intuitively. Ron Aniello is on double bass, joined by Marc Muller on pedal steel guitar and Gunnar Olsen on drums (in the second verse), probably accompanied by maracas. On the instrumental bridge, a piano and an electric guitar can be heard playing a melodic motif in unison, with a pedal steel guitar in the background (from 2'06). This same motif returns a bit further on in the song, this time enhanced by soaring orchestral strings. Worth noting: David Sancious, credited on the Hammond B-3, is barely audible, except in the final bars (at 3'58).

CHASIN' WILD HORSES

Bruce Springsteen / 5'03

For Springsteen Addicts

Marc Muller specializes in the pedal steel guitar, as well as acoustic instruments like the guitar, Dobro, and mandolin. He has also performed and recorded with Shania Twain and Steve Van Zandt.

2019

Musicians

Bruce Springsteen: vocals, guitars, keyboards, banjo, piano, percussion
Ron Aniello: upright bass, keyboards, guitars, drums
Barry Danielian: trumpet
Rachel Drehmann, Leelanee Sterrett: French horn
Marc Muller: pedal steel guitar
The Avatar Strings: Rob Mathes (arranger and conductor); Lisa Kim, Hyunju Lee, Liz Lim, Joanna Maurer, Suzanne Ornstein, Annaliesa Place, Emily Popham, Sharon Yamada, Jung Sun Yoo (violins); Desiree Elsevier, Vivek Kamath, Robert Reinhart (violas); Alan Stepansky, Nathan Vickery (cellos)

Recording

Stone Hill Studio, New Jersey: 2010–2019
Avatar Studios, New York: 2014–2019

Technical team

Producers: Ron Aniello, Bruce Springsteen
Recording engineers: Rob Lebret, Ross Petersen, Toby Scott, Ron Aniello
Mixing: Tom Elmhirst (Electric Lady Studios, New York), Joe Visciano (assistant)
Mastering: Bob Ludwig (Gateway Mastering, Portland)

Leelanee Sterrett and Rachel Drehmann of the New York Youth Symphony play the French horn in *Chasin' Wild Horses*.

Genesis and lyrics

In *Chasin' Wild Horses*, the narrator looks back on his life and regrets the decision he took to leave his home and his friends and head out to Montana without saying goodbye. He found work with the Bureau of Land Management. His job was to chase wild horses. But today he is haunted by the memory of the woman that he left behind, and he works himself to death to avoid thinking about it.

The fact that Bruce Springsteen chose the state of Montana as a backdrop to this song is no accident. He is following in the footsteps of writers like Richard Brautigan, Raymond Carver, and Thomas McGuane who often set their books in the natural open spaces of Montana. This can be seen in lines such as "A fingernail moon in a twilight sky/I'm riding in the high grass of the switchback" and "The winter snow whites out the plains/Till it can turn you blind."

Production

Chasin' Wild Horses is a magnificent ballad, written by an inspired songwriter and brilliantly served by the production. While fans of *Born to Run* or *Born in the U.S.A.* probably won't find what they're looking for here, it is hard not to be moved by the Boss's new musical language, a language that is neither bound to a particular era nor musical form.

The piece begins with an acoustic guitar, acompanied by a cello. Springsteen sings energetically, and avoids falling into the trap of melodrama. The arrangements are superbly elegant and never overdone (except perhaps in the instrumental lyricism at 2'18). Every instrument—be it the second acoustic guitar (at 1'02), the various keyboards, the banjo (at 1'47), the double bass, the drums played with brushes, the piano, the electric 6-strings, or the wonderful strings conducted by Rob Mathes and supported by the two French horns played by Rachel Drehmann and Leelanee Sterrett—contributes to what is a unique soundscape. Not forgetting Barry Danielian's trumpet (at 4'02), as well as the superb contributions from Marc Muller, whose pedal steel guitar ends the piece, drowned in a resounding intergalactic reverb!

SUNDOWN

Bruce Springsteen / 3'17

> **For Springsteen Addicts**
> The pianist Matt Rollings contributes to several songs on *Western Stars*. He is mainly known as a member of Lyle Lovett's Large Band, but has also played with Larry Carlton, Mary Chapin Carpenter, Mark Knopfler, and Johnny Hallyday. He won a Grammy Award in 2016 for producing Willie Nelson's *Summertime: Willie Nelson Sings Gershwin.*

Musicians

Bruce Springsteen: vocals, guitars, glockenspiel, keyboards, banjo, percussion
Ron Aniello: bass, keyboards, guitars, percussion, loops, backing vocals (?)
Matt Rollings: piano
Barry Danielian, Curt Ramm: trumpets
Clark Gayton: trombone
Gunnar Olsen: drums
Patti Scialfa, Soozie Tyrell: backing vocals
The Avatar Strings: Rob Mathes (arranger and conductor); Lisa Kim, Hyunju Lee, Liz Lim, Joanna Maurer, Suzanne Ornstein, Annaliesa Place, Emily Popham, Sharon Yamada, Jung Sun Yoo (violins); Desiree Elsevier, Vivek Kamath, Robert Reinhart (violas); Alan Stepansky, Nathan Vickery (cellos)

Recording

Stone Hill Studio, New Jersey: 2010–2019
Avatar Studios, New York: 2014–2019

Technical team

Producers: Ron Aniello, Bruce Springsteen
Recording engineers: Rob Lebret, Ross Petersen, Toby Scott, Ron Aniello
Mixing: Tom Elmhirst (Electric Lady Studios, New York), Joe Visciano (assistant)
Mastering: Bob Ludwig (Gateway Mastering, Portland)

The pianist Matt Rollings during the Sundance Festival, in 2014. His playing in *Sundown* was very lyrical.

Genesis and lyrics

Many of the characters in *Western Stars* find themselves somewhere that they don't want to be. This is the case of the narrator in this song: "Just wishing you were here with me, in Sundown." *Sundown* here is a town and also the sunset. Does this imagery imply that something is about to finish and something else is about to start? The main character is struggling to cope with loneliness in Sundown, where "It's all long, hot, endless days and cold nights," as he drifts from bar to bar, drowning his sorrows in alcohol. But he is hoping that the woman he loves will come back to him once summer's through.

Production

Sundown begins as the Dantesque reverb at the end of *Chasin' Wild Horses* (the previous track on the album) tails off. The Avatar Strings play a melodic motif, supported by Matt Rollings' highly lyrical piano part. A counterpoint on the electric guitar, colored by a very obvious tremolo effect, stands out from the arrangements, leaving Springsteen to add a banjo part (on the right). The talented Gunnar Olsen then starts with a drum fill on the tom-toms, before fully launching into the piece. He is accompanied by a bass guitar, small handbells (absent on the live version for the film), a shaker, several keyboards, and a recurrent and insistent phrase from the Avatar Strings.

The Boss energetically launches into his lead vocal, channeling both Roy Orbison and Glen Campbell. In fact, the entire song—the arrangements, the songwriter's soaring vocals (listen at 2'29), and even the very kitsch "sha la la, sha la la la" backing vocals from Patti Scialfa and Soozie Tyrell (there are examples at 1'11 and 2'33)—sounds like a homage to Glen Campbell.

Worth noting: a George Harrison-style solo electric guitar part (at 1'24) and the brass contribution on the bridge (at 1'42).

Sundown is unlikely to excite early Springsteen fans, but its indisputable quality will certainly attract new admirers.

SOMEWHERE NORTH OF NASHVILLE

Bruce Springsteen / 1'52

Musicians
Bruce Springsteen: vocals, guitar, keyboards (?)
Ron Aniello: keyboards (?)
Charles Giordano: piano
Marty Rifkin: pedal steel guitar
Soozie Tyrell: violin, backing vocals
Patti Scialfa: backing vocals

Recording
Stone Hill Studio, New Jersey: 2010–2019

Technical team
Producers: Ron Aniello, Bruce Springsteen
Recording engineer: James Brown
Mixing: Tom Elmhirst (Electric Lady Studios, New York), Joe Visciano (assistant)
Mastering: Bob Ludwig (Gateway Mastering, Portland)

2019

UNDER TWO MINUTES

At 1'52, *Somewhere North of Nashville* is one of only three Springsteen songs that are less than two minutes long, making it one of the shortest songs in his repertoire. The other two tracks are: *Held Up Without a Gun* (the B-side of *Hungry Heart*, 1980), at 1'15, and *Johnny Bye-Bye* (the B-side of *I'm On Fire*, 1985), at 1'50.

Genesis and lyrics

In the profusion of strings and brass instruments that characterize the *Western Stars* album, *Somewhere North of Nashville* sounds slightly out of place. Bruce Springsteen has played the restraint card here, restraint being one of his greatest qualities as a songwriter, the kind that characterized *Nebraska* and *The Ghost of Tom Joad,* and made him Bob Dylan's soul brother. When it comes to the lyrics, it's all about the emotion. The narrator's dreams have crashed and burned "somewhere north of Nashville," one of America's musical meccas. He says that he went there "with a pocketful of songs," but was unsuccessful. He is now wandering the highway with no destination in mind. And he's thinking about his failures, this time in his love relationships. His heart is unsteady, and the night is far from over.

Production

Musically, *Somewhere North of Nashville* is a short folk ballad that is particularly reminiscent of early Dylan on the 1963 *The Freewheelin' Bob Dylan* album.

The song begins with Springsteen nonchalantly playing arpeggios on an acoustic guitar. He then launches into his lead vocal, which is strikingly evocative of the troubadour of Duluth. His voice is sad, drawling, and full of nostalgia.

In the second verse, Marty Rifkin's superb pedal steel guitar produces some phrases that sound like moans, amplified by a wonderful, long, deep reverb (from 0'29). Rifkin is one of the Boss's long-standing musicians, and has been with him since 1995. He is also a member of The Sessions Band.

Charles Giordano's piano comes in at the following verse (at 0'55) to accompany the two musicians. Soozie Tyrell's violin puts in an appearance at the end of the song (at 1'18), and she also provides backing vocals alongside Patti Scialfa, who was in charge of the vocal arrangements for the whole album. We can also hear something that sounds like synth pads, used to bolster the sound texture of the piece.

What can we say about *Somewhere North of Nashville* apart from the fact that it is a short song that stands out for its simplicity and emotion? It is also timeless: Springsteen could have chosen to include it on albums like *Nebraska* or *The Ghost of Tom Joad.* It's hard to believe that when *Western Stars* was made, over four decades had passed since the recording of the oldest of the two albums. The Boss is truly immortal...

A still from *Western Stars*: Bruce Springsteen and Patti Scialfa sing *Somewhere North of Nashville* together.

STONES

Bruce Springsteen / 5'38

Musicians

Bruce Springsteen: vocals, guitars, glockenspiel, percussion
Ron Aniello: bass, keyboards, guitars, percussion, loops, piano, backing vocals (?)
Jon Brion: timpani
Rachel Drehmann, Leelanee Sterrett: French horn
Luis Villalobos: violin
Gunnar Olsen: drums
The Avatar Strings: Rob Mathes (arranger and conductor); Lisa Kim, Hyunju Lee, Liz Lim, Joanna Maurer, Suzanne Ornstein, Annaliesa Place, Emily Popham, Sharon Yamada, Jung Sun Yoo (violins); Desiree Elsevier, Vivek Kamath, Robert Reinhart (violas); Alan Stepansky, Nathan Vickery (cellos)

Recording

Stone Hill Studio, New Jersey: 2010–2019
Avatar Studios, New York: 2014–2019

Technical team

Producers: Ron Aniello, Bruce Springsteen
Recording engineers: Rob Lebret, Ross Petersen, Toby Scott, Ron Aniello
Mixing: Tom Elmhirst (Electric Lady Studios, New York), Joe Visciano (assistant)
Mastering: Bob Ludwig (Gateway Mastering, Portland)

2019

The violinist Luis Villalobos in 2017. Two years later, he would bring all his musical ability to the recording of *Stones* with Bruce Springsteen.

Genesis and lyrics

The stones that the narrator had in his mouth when he woke up this morning were lies, the ones that he told his partner. It is easy to imagine that these stones are the symbols of a relationship falling apart. Outside the home, the symbols of this failing relationship are everywhere: "The dirt-brown winter field, a thousand black crows [that] cover the ground," "The autumn wind [that] blows through the trees," and "the dark leaves [that] come tumbling down." There seems to be no way back for the narrator. He is unable to express his feelings and wanders along a sun-washed highway like a soul in torment.

Production

Stones starts with the Avatar Strings and Rachel Drehmann and Leelanee Sterrett on French horns playing a recurring three-note motif, a technique that Springsteen has often used, notably in *Secret Garden*. Jon Brion's timpani come in after several bars (at 0'10), along with the piano, probably played by Ron Aniello (there is no accurate information available about this), and the acoustic guitar, strummed by the songwriter.

The latter sings in a dynamic but gentle voice, with an omnipresent Roy Orbison-style vibrato. He is accompanied in the third verse by the producer on bass, Gunnar Olsen on drums, numerous percussion instruments (tambourine, shaker), and a second acoustic guitar, very probably a 12-string (from 1'15). This verse is followed by an instrumental section, with a melodic motif played on strings, French horns, and electric guitars colored by a slight tremolo (at 1'34).

In the last part of the song, a voice can be heard responding to Springsteen. It is most likely that of Ron Aniello, unless it is the Boss himself singing in a rather unusual register (between 3'13 and 3'35).

After a final instrumental section, led by Luis Villalobos' violin solo (at 3'46), the main motif is reprised by all the musicians, and Springsteen harmonizes with the second voice to bring *Stones* to a close.

THERE GOES MY MIRACLE

Bruce Springsteen / 4'05

Musicians
Bruce Springsteen: vocals, guitars, glockenspiel, keyboards
Ron Aniello: bass, keyboards, guitars, loops
Jon Brion: Moog synthesizer, timpani
Barry Danielian, Curt Ramm: trumpet
Clark Gayton: trombone
Lenny Castro: tambourine, shaker
Gunnar Olsen: drums
Patti Scialfa, Matthew Koma, Michelle Moore: backing vocals
Stone Hill Strings: Scott Tibbs (conductor); Lisa Kim, Hyunju Lee, Joanna Maurer (violins); Schmuel Katz, Rebecca Young (violas); Alan Stepansky (cello)

Recording
Stone Hill Studio, New Jersey: 2010–2019
Ocean Way Studios, Burbank: 2014–2019

Technical team
Producers: Ron Aniello, Bruce Springsteen
Recording engineers: Rob Lebret, Ross Petersen, Toby Scott, Ron Aniello (Stone Hill), Brett Rouche, Greg Koller (Ocean)
Mixing: Tom Elmhirst (Electric Lady Studios, New York), Joe Visciano (assistant)
Mastering: Bob Ludwig (Gateway Mastering, Portland)

The singer (and composer) Matthew Koma (seen here in Auburn Hills, Michigan, in May 2012) sings backing vocals in *There Goes My Miracle*.

Genesis and lyrics

Although Bruce Springsteen's voice here sounds so much like Roy Orbison that we struggle to recognize him, the theme of the song is a long-established part of the Springsteenian universe. "Heartache, heartbreak/Love gives, love takes/The book of love holds its rules." And when someone flouts those rules, they will probably live to regret it. This is exactly what has happened to the main character in the song. He did not obey the rules of love, and his love has walked away. Now all he has is regrets. He is searching for his lost love, but the "miracle" has left town.

There Goes My Miracle was released on 17 May 2019 as the second single from *Western Stars*.

Production

Along with *Tucson Train* and *Drive Fast (The Stuntman)*, this is one of the fastest paced songs on the album. It is also the most pop-like in style. Springsteen has composed a very different song from the usual E Street Band canon, in a style that borrows from Glen Campbell (for the arrangements), Elton John (for the pop chorus), and even David Bowie (for the vocals).

Strings also have pride of place here, but with a smaller-than-usual line-up of six musicians from the Stone Hill Strings, conducted by Scott Tibbs. A multitude of instruments contribute to this piece, notably several acoustic and electric guitar tracks, a bass, keyboards, brass (far back in the mix), and even tubular bells from a soundbank (for example, at 2'45). On percussion, Lenny Castro plays tambourine and shaker. The piece begins with a rhythmic drum loop, probably constructed by Ron Aniello, joined in the second verse by Gunnar Olsen's C&C Gladstone Maple Kit. Olsen spoke highly of the Boss after participating in these sessions, even though he thought that his contributions would not be kept: "He's a very loyal person [...] He's not interested in session people. He's interested in players. I'd like to think that's what he saw in me."[159] Finally, Patti Scialfa handles the vocal arrangements, which include some wonderful choral parts that she sings alongside Matthew Koma and Michelle Moore (for example, at 1'24).

HELLO SUNSHINE

Bruce Springsteen / 3'56

A music video of *Hello Sunshine* shot in a CinemaScope-type format was used as the opening to *Western Stars*. A Chevrolet El Camino Super Sport 454 can be seen driving across the Mojave Desert (in Southern California), but the driver remains hidden from view. Madonna also used this mythical site in the music video for her song *Frozen* in 1998.

Musicians

Bruce Springsteen: vocals, guitars, percussion, organ (?), piano (?)
Ron Aniello: bass, keyboards, guitar (?), organ (?), piano (?)
Marc Muller: pedal steel guitar
Matt Chamberlain: drums
The Avatar Strings: Rob Mathes (arranger and conductor); Lisa Kim, Hyunju Lee, Liz Lim, Joanna Maurer, Suzanne Ornstein, Annaliesa Place, Emily Popham, Sharon Yamada, Jung Sun Yoo (violins); Desiree Elsevier, Vivek Kamath, Robert Reinhart (violas); Alan Stepansky, Nathan Vickery (cellos)

Recording

Stone Hill Studio, New Jersey: 2010–2019
Avatar Studios, New York: 2014–2019

Technical team

Producers: Ron Aniello, Bruce Springsteen
Recording engineers: Rob Lebret, Ross Petersen, Toby Scott, Ron Aniello
Mixing: Tom Elmhirst (Electric Lady Studios, New York), Joe Visciano (assistant)
Mastering: Bob Ludwig (Gateway Mastering, Portland)

2019

The singer Harry Nillson in 1972. Bruce Springsteen was doubtless recalling his song *Everybody's Talkin'* when he composed *Hello Sunshine*.

Genesis and lyrics

Hello Sunshine is a thinly disguised homage to 1960s American pop music. This song bears a slight resemblance to *Everybody's Talkin'*, the Fred Neil composition that was covered by Harry Nilsson in 1969 and features in John Schlesinger's 1969 film *Midnight Cowboy*, starring Dustin Hoffman and Jon Voight.

Like the character in *Hitch Hikin'*, the narrator in *Hello Sunshine* has been around and traveled through many places, always in an attempt to leave the pain and heartbreak behind him. Solitude is not a problem for him. On the contrary, he likes walking along empty streets, traveling for miles and miles, discovering that it is possible to "fall in love with lonely." His words are directed at the sun, which could be the symbol of a divinity or some kind of powerful force that has cured him of his heartbreak and stopped him sinking into madness.

Hello Sunshine was released on 26 April 2019 as the first single from *Western Stars*.

Production

Hello Sunshine starts with Matt Chamberlain playing drums with brushes to create a rhythm that is very similar to Fred Neil's composition. The drums are accompanied by Springsteen's acoustic guitar (or Telecaster-Esquire?) and Ron Aniello's bass. This trio are enough to carry the piece, which stands out for its simplicity and the color of the instruments. The songwriter's voice is gentle and melancholic, a combination of Jimmy Webb and Glen Campbell. The arrangements progressively become more complex, a second acoustic guitar, a piano, and an organ in the second verse, a spellbinding pedal steel guitar in the following verse, and the Avatar Strings that soar lyrically in the instrumental bridge (at 1'45).

Hello Sunshine is without a doubt the most accessible track on *Western Stars*, obviously due to its resemblance to Nilsson's *Everybody's Talkin'*, as mentioned earlier, but also because it sounds remarkably similar to the wonderful *Good Time Charlie's Got the Blues* by Danny O'Keefe (1972). The general atmosphere also has a Mark Knopfler-magic guitar feel to it.

For all these reasons, *Hello Sunshine* grabs listeners the first time they hear it and is likely to stick in the minds of all Springsteen fans for a long time.

MOONLIGHT MOTEL

Bruce Springsteen / 4'16

Musicians
Bruce Springsteen: vocals, guitar, keyboards, percussion
Ron Aniello: bass, keyboards, loops
Matt Rollings: piano
Greg Leisz: pedal steel guitar
Jon Brion: drums, celeste
Recording
Stone Hill Studio, New Jersey: 2010–2019
Technical team
Producers: Ron Aniello, Bruce Springsteen
Recording engineers: Rob Lebret, Ross Petersen, Toby Scott, Ron Aniello
Mixing: Tom Elmhirst (Electric Lady Studios, New York), Joe Visciano (assistant)
Mastering: Bob Ludwig (Gateway Mastering, Portland)

Greg Leisz, pedal steel guitar virtuoso, is the Boss's sideman in *Moonlight Motel*. Here he is seen in Golden Gate Park, San Francisco, on 1 October 2016.

Genesis and lyrics

The concluding song of *Western Stars* perfectly sums up the whole album—nostalgia for a golden age and past loves. The narrator revisits his past with a certain melancholy. The Moonlight Motel was a place hidden from prying eyes where he used to meet his lover (we imagine a married woman). Their romantic trysts were a way for both of them to escape the hard realities of life.

Years and decades have passed and yesterday's secret love affair is no more. The symbols are highly meaningful. There's the musty smell in a room, wilted flowers, an empty swimming pool, a half-rusted chain-link fence. In his mind, the narrator talks to the woman he once loved: "Last night I dreamed of you, my lover." And, suddenly, he feels the need to return to the Moonlight Motel. He pulls into the parking lot and pulls out a bottle of Jack Daniel's, pouring one shot for the love of his life, one for himself, and another onto the ground. End of story at the Moonlight Motel.

Production

Moonlight Motel is first and foremost a wonderful ballad that is further enhanced by Ron Aniello's superb production. No single instrument dominates the arrangements, apart from perhaps Springsteen's guitar arpeggios, which create a motif somewhat reminiscent of *Falling Slowly* by Glen Hansard and Marketa Irglova (2006). The overall feel eclipses any individual instrument. Various keyboard pads, strings created on synths, Greg Leisz's delicate pedal steel guitar part (Leisz had already contributed to two tracks to *Wrecking Ball*), the stripped-back piano from Matt Rollings, and the (hard to hear) celeste from Jon Brion all come together to carry the Boss's nostalgic voice along in a kind of dream-like fog of sound. Even Jon Brion's drums remain in the background, with the drummer using mallet drumsticks and probably a cloth on his drumheads to muffle the sound (listen from 1'42).

Note: the live version recorded for Thom Zimney's film packs a more powerful emotional punch, as the songwriter's voice is particularly moving. The only negative point being overly present backing vocals.

With this last song on *Western Stars*, Bruce Springsteen brilliantly demonstrates that, as he approaches his 70th year, he has lost nothing of his talent. Respect.

RHINESTONE COWBOY

Larry Weiss / 3'20

2019

Musicians

Bruce Springsteen: vocals, guitar
Patti Scialfa: guitar, backing vocals
Ben Butler: guitar
Marc Muller: pedal steel guitar
Rob Mathes: keyboards
Charles Giordano: keyboards
Henry Hey: keyboards
Barry Danielian, Curt Ramm: trumpets
Rachel Drehmann, Zohar Schondorf: French horn
Kaveh Rastegar: bass
Gunnar Olsen: drums
Soozie Tyrell, Lisa Lowell, Vaneese Thomas, Surrenity XYZ: backing vocals
Joanna Maurer (first violin); Monica Davis, Maggie Gould, Joyce Hammann, Elizabeth Lim-Dutton, Laura Lutzke, Annaliesa Place, Emma Sutton, Robin Zeh (violins); Maurycy Banaszek, Will Frampton, Celia Hatton (violas); Andrew Janss, Maureen McDermott, Alan Stepansky (cellos)

Recording

Stone Hill Farm, New Jersey: April 2019

Technical team

Producers: Ron Aniello, Bruce Springsteen
Recording engineers: Rob Lebret, Ron Aniello, John Cooper, John Harris, Joel Singer
Mixing: Bob Clearmountain (Mix This!, Los Angeles)
Mastering: Bob Ludwig (Gateway Mastering, Portland)

Genesis and lyrics

Rhinestone Cowboy is a song written by Larry Weiss, a native of Newark, New Jersey. As a composer, he worked with the lyricist Scott English, and also made a major contribution to the success of British rock in the 1960s with *Hi Ho Silver Lining*, sung by Jeff Beck, and *Help Me Girl* by Eric Burdon & The Animals. However, his biggest hit was *Rhinestone Cowboy*, as sung by Glen Campbell. Campbell was on tour in Australia when he heard the song for the first time. The recording that he did once he returned to the United States whisked him to the No.1 spot in the *Billboard* pop charts in June 1975.

Larry Weiss' composition is largely autobiographical. It is the story of a country singer who tries everything to find fame, traveling from the sidewalks of Broadway to star-spangled rodeos—the metaphor speaks for itself. The image speaks volumes, as rhinestones are the cheap gems worn by certain country singers. This is an image that clearly appealed to the Boss—45 years after Glen Campbell sang about him, the "star-spangled cowboy" joined the pantheon of characters in *Western Stars.*

Bruce Springsteen didn't record this song for the album, but performed it live at Stone Hill Farm in Colts Neck, in April 2019, for the film *Western Stars.*

Production

Listening to *Rhinestone Cowboy*, the last song recorded for the *Western Stars* movie soundtrack, it is easy to understand why Springsteen didn't want to include it on the tracklist for his studio album because, for the first time in his career as a recording artist, he lowers himself to singing middle of the road music with saccharine violins and heavy-going choir vocals. The result is pretty good quality, but it is a song from a universe so far removed from Springsteen's usual world that it comes as quite a shock. This kind of easy listening is enough to make fans of *The River* or *The Ghost Of Tom Joad* shudder. Yet, it is the best tribute that Bruce Springsteen could pay to Glen Campbell, as their respective versions are very similar. So, listeners can make of it what they will. The Boss is always a surprising artist, which is one of the reasons for his huge talent.

Bruce Springsteen, hero of the movie *Western Stars*. He ends his album with *Rhinestone Cowboy*, a song by Larry Weiss.

Pages 660–661 A highly symbolic still from *Western Stars*. Bruce Springsteen has been out of the shadows for more than 50 years.

GLOSSARY

Bend A guitar technique in which a string is pushed to raise a note's pitch by a semitone or more.

Bottleneck A glass (or metal) tube that the guitarist places over a finger and slides over the strings to produce a metallic sound. This style of playing comes from the pioneers of the blues, who used the neck of a bottle. Bottleneck is most often used with open tuning; that is, the guitar's six strings are tuned to a chord (for example, G or D).

Break An instrumental interlude that interrupts a song's development, thus allowing a new part to be launched and giving the song new impetus.

Bridge A passage between two parts of a song. The bridge links the verse to the chorus.

Chicago blues There are several forms of blues in Chicago. Electric Chicago blues, which is an amplified version of Delta blues, is chiefly played by artists signed up to the Chess Records label, from Willie Dixon to Howlin' Wolf, Muddy Waters, and Sonny Boy Williamson II.

Coda This Italian term denotes the passage that brings a piece of music to an end. Its length varies, according to the piece.

Compressor An electronic circuit used to increase low volumes or, alternatively, decrease high volumes during recording or mixing.

Cover A term denoting a new performance or recording of a previously recorded and commercially released song by another artist, generally in a different arrangement from the original version

Cowbell A percussion instrument that features both in rock and R&B, and in European classical music (Gustav Mahler, Richard Strauss) and avant-garde music (Karlheinz Stockhausen, Olivier Messiaen).

Delay An effect produced by electronic means to shift a sound in time, by reinjecting it into the original signal and repeating it as desired. It is related to the echo.

Distortion see *Fuzz*.

Double stopping A guitar effect that consists of playing two notes simultaneously during a solo or riff.

Drumming A term that denotes the playing of a drummer.

Effect pedal A small electronic box that makes it possible to add an effect to an instrument's sound. It is generally operated by the musician's foot, like a fuzz box or the Octavia. There are wah-wah pedals, distortion pedals, chorus, delay, flanger pedals, etc.

Fade-in A process consisting of progressively increasing the sound (generally at the beginning of a piece).

Fade-out A process consisting of gradually decreasing the sound (generally at the end of a piece).

Fills A rhythmic figure played on the drums to start a song or mark a transition.

Finger-picking A guitar technique used chiefly in folk and blues music, consisting of playing certain strings of the instrument using the right hand (in the case of right-handed musicians) with different fingers independent from each other (the opposite of strumming), generally allowing the song's tune and bass line to be brought out.

Flanger see *Flanging*.

Flanging A sound effect that is obtained by adding, to the original signal, that same signal, but delayed by a few milliseconds.

Fuzz A distorted sound effect obtained by saturating the sound signal, notably through the use of a distortion pedal (fuzz box). The Rolling Stones were pioneers of the fuzz box with *(I Can't Get No) Satisfaction*. This effect is used chiefly for guitars. Jimi Hendrix made it a signature feature of his guitar playing.

Gimmick A series of notes aimed at getting the listener's attention. This method, which originated with jazz, has found its logical extension in rock.

Groove It is quite difficult to give a precise definition of groove in music. The term applies to the moment when musicians, in total communion, give a piece its particular atmosphere, an alchemy that is created around rhythm and harmony. All the musicians experience this feeling. People talk about a song "moving forwards."

Jam An improvised, rather informal get-together of several musicians, most often driven by the pleasure of playing together. In French, it is called *faire un bœuf* (literally "making an ox").

Lead A term denoting the main voice or instrument in a song (lead vocal or lead guitar, for example).

Leslie A cabinet fitted with a rotating speaker, generally used with Hammond organs. The sound's rotating effect can be adjusted according to the effect desired.

Lick A short musical phrase played to support or accompany the arrangement and/or the melodic line of a piece in a clearly defined style (blues, rock, country, jazz, etc.).

Low-down In music, this term applies to authentic rural blues, untouched by any external influences.

Mute A technique for cutting off sound on a channel strip.

Open tuning A different way of tuning a guitar, generally in order to obtain—with open strings—a chord consisting of six notes. It is a technique widely used in blues, notably with open tunings in G, D, A, etc.

Outtake A piece (or song), recorded in the studio or onstage, that did not make it onto an official album. It is either an unreleased or an alternative version of an existing song.

Overdubbing/Overdub A process whereby new sounds (for example, a guitar part or a second voice) are recorded onto an existing recording. See also Rerecording.

Palm mute A guitar technique which consists of muffling, to a greater or lesser extent, the instrument's strings with the right hand (in the case of right-handed musicians), while playing the notes with a pick.

Pattern A fragment that returns during the course of a song and that can be repeated indefinitely by "looping."

Pedal point Sustained notes, generally in the bass.

Phasing An electronic effect that treats the sound signal using different filters and oscillators, and which makes it possible to obtain a richer, more colored sound, especially with saturated guitars.

Play-back The instrumental part of a song that is partially or totally recorded, enabling a singer or instrumentalist to have a musical base that is sufficient for recording his or her part.

Power chord This is used on the guitar. It consists of two notes: the tonic and the fifth. It is highly effective in rock music, often in conjunction with distortion.

Premix A preliminary mix or stage in the recording process that consists of mixing—not definitively—the various tracks of a multi-track tape recorder to have an overview of the work done so far. It is sometimes called mise à plat ("complete review").

Rerecording This false friend denotes a technique that makes it possible to record one or more tracks while listening to the track or tracks that have already been recorded.

Reverberation A reverberation effect used in the studio either via an electronic device or through a natural echo chamber, which makes it possible to "lighten" and give relief to certain sounds (especially a solo voice or instrument) while recording or mixing.

Riff Abbreviation of "rhythmic figure"; it is a short motif (or ostinato)—a series of notes or chords that regularly returns during a piece.

Rimshot A drumming technique that consists of striking the rim of the snare drum (or tom-tom) at the same time as the head. The sound thus obtained is deliberately incisive.

Roots The term references the return to the "roots" of popular music, from blues to Appalachian music.

Score Synonymous with orchestral score.

Shuffle A musical style that developed in the 1950s in Jamaica; a kind of R&B precursor of ska. It was also a slow rhythm practised by slaves.

Slap-back echo Typical echo used by the pioneers of rock 'n' roll, such as Elvis Presley, Gene Vincent, and Buddy Holly.

Strumming A guitar technique that generally consists of striking all the guitar's strings using the right hand (in the case of right-handed musicians), with or without a pick. It is one of the instrument's most widely used techniques.

Sustain An instrument's capacity to continue over time a note that has been played. It is an effect used especially on electric guitars, often prolonged by means of various devices (saturation, feedback, sustainer, etc.).

Tracklisting The list of songs that feature on an album.

Wah-wah The wah-wah pedal was one of the first electronic effects designed for electric guitar players, popularized from 1967 by such masters of the 6-string guitar as Eric Clapton and Jimi Hendrix. The musician operates the pivoting part of the device with his or her foot, to modulate the frequencies from low to high, thus producing a very distinctive sound effect—hence the device's name. The wah-wah has also been widely used in funk and adapted for use with other instruments such as electric keyboards.

BIBLIOGRAPHY

1. Springsteen (Bruce), **Born to Run**, Simon & Schuster (Kindle edition).

2. Zimny (Thom), **Springsteen on Broadway**, 16 December 2018.

3. Eliot (Marc) and Appel (Mike), **Down Thunder Road: The Making of Bruce Springsteen**, Renaissance Literary & Talent, 2013 (and Kindle edition).

4. Hammond (John), Townsend (Irving), **John Hammond on Record**, Ridge Press, 1977.

5. White (Ryan), **Springsteen: Album by Album**, Palazzo Editions (and Kindle edition).

6. **Bruce Springsteen Songs**, Avon Books, New York, 1998.

7. Burger (Jeff), **Springsteen on Springsteen**, Omnibus Press, 2013 (and Kindle edition).

8. Werbin (Stuart), "Bruce Springsteen: It's Sign Up a Genius Month," **Rolling Stone**, 26 April 1973 (https://www.rollingstone.com/music/music-news/bruce-springsteen-its-sign-up-a-genius-month-90635/)

9. Bangs (Lester), "Greetings from Asbury Park, NJ," **Rolling Stone**, 5 July 1973 (https://www.rollingstone.com/music/music-album-reviews/greandings-from-asbury-park-nj-249992/).

10. Phillips (Christopher) and Masur (Louis, P), **Talk About a Dream: The Essential Interviews of Bruce Springsteen**, Bloomsbury Publishing (and Kindle edition).

11. Luerssen (John D), **Bruce Springsteen FAQ**, Backbeat Books (and Kindle edition).

12. Guandta (Eldad), "Luis Lahav: Dispatch from Israel...," **Tape Op**, no.56, November to December 2006 (https://tapeop.com/interviews/56/luis-lahav/).

13. Bruce Springsteen, DVD **VH1 Storytellers—On Stage**, 2005.

14. Spelling (Ian), "Laying Down History: New Milford's Phil Giambalvo," **(201) Magazine**, eu.northjersey.com, 5 April 2017.

15. www.springsteenlyrics.com/lyrics.php?song=foryou

16. Marsh (Dave), **Bruce Springsteen: Two Hearts**, Taylor & Francis, 2003 (and Kindle edition).

17. Clemons (Clarence) and Reo (Don), **Big Man: Real Life & Tall Tales**, Grand Central Publishing, New York, 2009.

18. Emerson (Ken), "The Wild, the Innocent & the E Street Shuffle," **Rolling Stone**, 31 January 1974 (https://www.rollingstone.com/music/music-album-reviews/the-wild-the-innocent-the-e-Street-shuffle-247900/).

19. Simons (David), **Studio Stories**, Backbeat Books, London, 2004.

20. Cianci (Bob), "Phil Petillo: Master Luthier, Engineer, Scientist & Inventor," **Premier Guitar**, 21 April 2009 (https://www.premierguitar.com/articles/Phil_Petillo_Master_Luthier_Engineer_Scientist_Inventor).

21. Tellone (Albee), **Upstage, Springsteen and Me**, 2012, Kindle edition.

22. Concert, Gaston Hall, Georgetown University, Washington DC, 3 March 1974.

23. Allan (Steven), Interview with Suki Lahav, **Backstreets Magazine**, December 1985.

24. "Diane Lozito, **La Rosalita de Bruce Springsteen**," **Summer of Girls**, Arte.

25. https://www.springsteenlyrics.com/lyrics.php?song=newyorkcityserenade

26. Muchetti (Luca), "David Sancious: From Monk to Sting," allaboutjazz.com, 8 June 2018 (https://www.allaboutjazz.com/david-sancious-david-sancious-from-monk-to-sting-by-luca-muchetti.php).

27. Tootell (Rod), "E Street Serenade: Bruce Springsteen, David Sancious, and the E Street Shuffle," **Rock's Back Pages**, December 2012 (https://www.rocksbackpages.com/Library/Article/e-Street-serenade-bruce-springsteen-david-sancious-and-the-e-Street-shuffle).

28. Landau (Jon), "Growing Young with Rock and Roll," **The Real Paper**, 22 May 1974 (http://www.brucespringsteen.it/Other/real.htm).

29. Zimny (Thom), **Wings for Wheels: The Making of Born To Run**, 2005.

30. Santelli (Robert), **Backstreets**, no.20, Spring 1987.

31. Santelli (Robert), "Ernest 'Boom' Carter, batteur" (https://www.bruce-springsteen.fr/Ernest-Boom-Carter_a1204_2.html).

32. Marcus (Greil), "Born To Run," **Rolling Stone**, 9 October 1975 (https://www.rollingstone.com/music/music-album-reviews/born-to-run-87675/).

33. Larkin (Colin), **All-Time Top 1000 Albums**, Virgin Books, London, 1998.

34. Haviland (Lou), "Bruce Springsteen's Wife Patti Scialfa—Get Ready to Be Surprised At Her Incredible Musical Chops," cheatsheet.com, 1 December 2019 (https://www.cheatsheet.com/entertainment/bruce-springsteens-wife-patti-scialfa-get-ready-to-be-surprised-at-her-incredible-musical-chops.html/).

35. Fricke (David), "Jimmy Iovine: The Man With the Magic Ears," **Rolling Stone**, 12 April 2012 (https://www.rollingstone.com/music/music-news/jimmy-iovine-the-man-with-the-magic-ears-120618/).

36. Gold (Adam), "Behind the Song: Thunder Road," **American Songwriter**, 21 October 2011 (https://americansongwriter.com/behind-the-song-thunder-road/).

37. Schoof (Dustin), "Trumpet player Randy Brecker discusses working with Aerosmith and Bruce Springsteen," lehighvalleylive.com, 28 February 2013 (https://www.lehighvalleylive.com/music/2013/02/trumpet_player_randy_brecker_d.html).

38. Junior (Chris M), "When Van Zandt joined Springsteen's E Street Band," **Goldmine**, 30 July 2010. (https://www.goldminemag.com/articles/when-van-zandt-joined-springsteens-e-Street-band).

39. Hiatt (Brian), **Rolling Stone**, 5 October 2016 (https://www.bruce-springsteen.fr/Rolling-Stone-05-October-2016_a2537.html).

40. Scott (Roger) and Humphries (Patrick), **Hot Press**, 2 November 1984.

41. "Mighty Max Turns On The Music Machine—The 2018 Backstreets Interview with Max Weinberg," backstreets.com, 29 August 2018 (http://www.backstreets.com/jukebox.html).

42. http://www.backstreets.com/newsarchive41.html

43. Deusner (Stephen), **Uncut Magazine**, August 2019.

44. Guesdon (Jean-Michel), Interview with Suki Lahav, 2019.

45. Greene (Andy), "40 Years of E Street: Roy Bittan on Bruce, Beach Pics, and **Born to Run**," **Rolling Stone**, 22 January 2015 (https://www.rollingstone.com/music/music-news/40-years-of-e-Street-roy-bittan-on-bruce-beach-pics-and-born-to-run-240923/).

46. Hiatt (Brian), "Bruce Springsteen on Making **Born to Run**: We Went to Extremes," **Rolling Stone**, 25 August 2015 (https://www.rollingstone.com/music/music-news/bruce-springsteen-on-making-born-to-run-we-went-to-extremes-50232/).

47. "Randy Brecker—Around the Horn," Yamaha Entertainment Group of America (http://www.yamahaentertainmentgroup.com/all-access/item/328-randy-brecker-around-the-horn).

48. Miriello (Ralph A), "The Philosophy of the Spiritual—Part Two of an Interview with the Bassist Richard Davis," **Notes on Jazz**, 2 September 2014 (http://notesonjazz.blogspot.com/2014/09/the-philosophy-of-spiritual-part-two-of.html).

49. "100 Greatest Singers of All Time," **Rolling Stone**, 3 December 2010 (https://www.rollingstone.com/music/music-lists/100-greatest-singers-of-all-time-147019/).

50. McCall (Tris), "Roy Bittan Interview: Spotlight on key member of the E Street Band," **nj.com**, 16 September 2012 (https://www.nj.com/entertainment/music/2012/09/roy_bittan_interview_spotlight.html).

51. **Backstreets, The Boss Magazine**, no.91, Autumn/Winter 2013 (http://www.backstreets.com/Merchant2/merchant.mvc?Screen=PROD&Product_Code=BBI91&Category_Code=110).

52. BBC News, 19 June 2011.

53. "Bruce Springsteen's Eulogy for Clarence Clemons," **Rolling Stone**, 29 June 2011 (https://www.rollingstone.com/music/music-news/bruce-springsteens-eulogy-for-clarence-clemons-62867/).

54. Zimny (Thom), **Bruce Springsteen, The Promise: The Making of Darkness on the Edge of Town**, 2010.

55. "Exclusive: The Complete Text of Bruce Springsteen's SXSW Keynote Address," **Rolling Stone**, 28 March 2012 (sshttps://www.rollingstone.com/music/music-news/exclusive-the-complete-text-of-bruce-springsteens-sxsw-keynote-address-86379/).

56. Marsh (Dave), "Darkness on the Edge of Town," **Rolling Stone**, 27 July 1978 (https://www.rollingstone.com/music/music-album-reviews/darkness-on-the-edge-of-town-197342/).

57. Ruhlmann (William), **AllMusic**, 2 June 1978 (https://www.allmusic.com/album/darkness-on-the-edge-of-town-mw0000191913).

58. Dombal (Ryan), "Take Cover: Darkness on the Edge of Town—Photographer Frank Stefanko talks about his iconic 1978 Springsteen album cover," **Pitchfork**, 12 November 2010 (https://pitchfork.com/news/40570-take-cover-darkness-on-the-edge-of-town/).

59. Fish (Scott K) "Max Weinberg—Good Time on 'E' Street," moderndrummer.com (https://www.moderndrummer.com/article/april-1982-max-weinberg-good-time-e-Street/).

60. Herman (Dave), Interview with Bruce Springsteen, **King Biscuit Flower Hour**, 9 July 1978, D.I.R. Radio Network.

61. Saunders (Mike), "Steve Paraczky: The Backstreets Interview," backstreets.com, 30 November 2017 (https://www.backstreets.com/paraczky.html).

62. "Ed Norton Interviews Bruce Springsteen On **Darkness**," National Public Radio Inc., 15 November 2010 (https://www.npr.org/transcripts/131272103?storyId=131272103&t=1583786546899).

63. Hiatt (Brian), "**Darkness Revisited**," **Rolling Stone**, 25 November 2010 (https://www.rollingstone.com/music/music-news/bruce-springsteen-darkness-revisited-94429/).

64. Glynn (Michael), **The National Enquirer**, 9 March 2002.

65. Marsh (Dave), **Musician**, February 1981.

66. Fuzek (John), "Garry Tallent Full Interview," motifri.com, 19 April 2017 (https://motifri.com/garry-tallent-full-interview/).

67. Kandell (Steve), "Win Butler-Bruce Springsteen: The Conversation on the Early Days, the Glory Days, and the End of Days," **Spin** (US), 4 December 2007 (https://www.spin.com/featured/win-butler-and-bruce-springsteens-2007-cover-story-on-the-early-days-the-glory-days-and-the-end-of-days/).

68. Notes from the CD **The Promise**.

69. Meola (Eric), **Streets of Fire: Bruce Springsteen in Photographs and Lyrics 1977–1979**, It Books, 2012.

70. Loder (Kurt), "The Rising," **Rolling Stone**, 30 July 2002 (https://www.rollingstone.com/music/music-album-reviews/the-rising-248610/).

71. **Live /1975–85** box set.

72. Introduction to **Prove It All Night** during the Darkness Tour, Largo, 15 August 1978.

73. Meldrum (Molly), Interview, **Sunday Night**, Seven Network (Australia), 20 November 2010, quoted by Burger (Jeff), **Springsteen on Springsteen**, Omnibus Press (and Kindle edition).

74. Nelson (Paul), "Let Us Now Praise Famous Men," **Rolling Stone**, 11 December 1980.

75. Chiu (David), "Bruce Springsteen Photographer Looks Back on 40 Years of Shooting the Singer—Frank Stefanko discusses some of the now-legendary images collected in his new book **Further Up the Road**," **Rolling Stone**, 1 November 2017 (https://www.rollingstone.com/music/music-lists/bruce-springsteen-photographer-looks-back-on-40-years-of-shooting-the-singer-122906/the-indian-king-haddonfield-new-jersey-1978-123011/).

76. Crane (Larry), **Tape Op**, no.127, September to October 2018 (https://tapeop.com/issues/127/).

77. Cote (James B), Salama (Marc), Alessandri (Pier), Interview with Bob Clearmountain, "The Prince of Mixers," pieralessandri.com, 4 December 2011 (http://pieralessandri.com/Interview-with-Bob-Clearmountain).

78. Droney (Maureen), "Classic Tracks: Bruce Springsteen's **The River**," mixonline.com, 1 October 2003 (https://www.mixonline.com/news/classic-tracks-bruce-springsteens-river-425283).

79. Buskin (Richard), "Bruce Springsteen **Born in the USA**/Classic Tracks," **Sound on Sound**, March 2010 (https://www.soundonsound.com/people/bruce-springsteen-born-usa-classic-tracks).

80. Hyden (Steven), "Steven Van Zandt On Why He Thinks The Rock 'Renaissance' Has Been Over Since The Mid-'90s," uproxx.com, 23 May 2017 (https://uproxx.com/music/steven-van-zandt-soulfire-interview/).

81. Humphries (Patrick), **Record Mirror**, February 1999.

82. "Turtle Talk with Howard Kaylan"(interview), **Rock Cellar Magazine**, 4 June 2013 (https://www.rockcellarmagazine.com/turtle-talk-interview-howard-kaylan-turtles/).

83. Strauss (Neil), "The Springsteen Interview," **Guitar World**, October 1995.

84. Zimny (Thom), **The Ties That Bind**, 2015.

85. Pond (Steve), **Rolling Stone**, 28 October 1982.

86. Simmons (Sylvie), **Mojo**, January 2006.

87. www.snapgalleries.com

88. Keller (Daniel), "Bruce Springsteen's **Nebraska**—a PortaStudio, two SM57's, and Inspiration," tascam.com, 25 July 2007 (https://tascam.com/us/support/news/481).

89. Loder (Kurt), **Rolling Stone**, December 1984.

90. Flippo (Chand), **Musician**, November, 1984.

91. http://brucebase.wikidot.com/1984

92. Terich (Jeff), treblezine.com, July 2016 (https://www.treblezine.com/author/jterich/).

93. Cameron (Keith), **Mojo**, January 2006.

94. Kirkpatrick (Rob), **The Words and Music of Bruce Springsteen**, Praeger Singer-Songwriter Collection, Praeger Publishers, 2006 (and Kindle edition).

95. Gross (Terry), "Springsteen's **Born to Run** Redone—with Video," National Public Radio, 15 November 2005 (https://www.npr.org/templates/story/story.php?storyId=5012820).

96. Lambert (Mel) and Borgerson (Sam), "RE/P Files: An Interview with Bob Clearmountain," prosoundweb.com, 27 May 2016.

97. Greatest Hits booklet.

98. Pond (Steve), "Bruce Springsteen's **Tunnel Vision**," **Rolling Stone**, 5 May 1988 (https://www.rollingstone.com/music/music-news/bruce-springsteens-tunnel-vision-246390/).

99. Hiatt (Brian), **Bruce Springsteen: The Stories Behind the Songs**, Abrams, New York, 2019.

100. Loss (Robert), "Bruce Springsteen: **The Ties That Bind: The River Collection**," **PopMatters**, 7 December 2015 (https://www.popmatters.com/bruce-springsteen-the-ties-that-bind-the-river-collection-2495463081.html).

101. Prato (Greg), "Nils Lofgren of the E Street Band," **Songfacts**, 17 December 2015 (https://www.songfacts.com/blog/interviews/nils-lofgren-of-the-e-Street-band).

102. Interview with Max Weinberg, **Rolling Stone**, 1989.

103. Appleford (Steve), "Bruce Springsteen: See Intimate Eighties and Nineties Portraits From New Gallery Show," **Rolling Stone**, 23 May 2018 (https://www.rollingstone.com/music/music-lists/bruce-springsteen-see-intimate-eighties-and-nineties-portraits-from-new-gallery-show-627995/).

104. Bruce Springsteen's Speech After Being Inducted into the Rock & Roll Hall of Fame, 15 March 1999. (https://www.youtube.com/watch?v=r96COJZ5nnU)

105. Beninate (Tom), Interview with Lisa Lowell, **Master Seven**, 2012 (http://www.masterseven.com/pages/interviews/lisa_lowell.html).

106. Puterbaugh (Parke), "Greatest Hits," **Rolling Stone**, 6 April 1995 (https://www.rollingstone.com/music/music-album-reviews/greatest-hits-8-206019/).

107. Kinos-Goodin (Jesse), CBC Radio, 26 April 2017 (https://www.cbc.ca/radio/q/blog/jonathan-demme-on-how-he-got-bruce-springsteen-and-neil-young-on-the-philadelphia-soundtrack-1.4086586).

108. https://www.springsteenlyrics.com/lyrics.php?song=Streetsofphiladelphia

109. Hilburn (Robert), "Q&A; with Bruce Springsteen," **Los Angeles Times**, 6 March 1995 (https://www.latimes.com/archives/la-xpm-1995-03-06-ca-39397-story.html).

110. Fritz (Ernie), **Blood Brothers**, 1996.

111. De Caunes (Antoine) and Manœuvre (Philippe), "Springsteen speaks!," **Rock & Folk**, May 1995.

112. Gilmore (Mikal), **Rolling Stone**, 28 December 1995.

113. Greene (Andy), "A 54-Minute Conversation with Bruce Springsteen," **Rolling Stone**, 9 January 2014 (https://www.rollingstone.com/music/music-news/a-54-minute-conversation-with-bruce-springsteen-181303/).

114. Hart (Ron), "Celebrating Bruce Springsteen's dark folk masterpiece," The A.V. Club, 10 June 2015 (https://music.avclub.com/celebrating-bruce-springsteen-s-dark-folk-masterpiece-1798285013).

115. Hiatt (Brian), "Bruce Springsteen Talks Steel Mill, **Human Touch**, What Prince Taught Him," **Rolling Stone**, 17 October 2016 (https://www.rollingstone.com/music/music-features/bruce-springsteen-talks-steel-mill-human-touch-what-prince-taught-him-126267/).

116. Danny Clinch's Facebook page.

117. Willman (Chris), "Brendan O'Brien: Springsteen Magic Man," ew.com, 16 October 2007 (https://ew.com/article/2007/10/16/brendan-obrien-springsteen-magic-man/).

118. Bussey (John), "Eye of the Storm: One Journey Through Desperation and Chaos," **The Wall Street Journal**, 12 September 2001 (https://www.wsj.com/articles/SB1000265058230898329).

119. Sweeting (Adam), "Bruce Springsteen: 'I think I just wanted to be great,'" **Uncut**, September 2002.

120. Pareles (Jon), "The Rock Laureate," **The New York Times**, 28 January 2009 (https://www.nytimes.com/2009/02/01/arts/music/01pare.html).

121. Concert America: A Tribute to Heroes, 21 September 2001.

122. Pareles (Jon), "Bruce Almighty," **The New York Times**, 24 April 2005 (https://www.nytimes.com/2005/04/24/arts/music/bruce-almighty.html).

123. Fricke (David), **Rolling Stone**, 5 May 2005.

124. Leslie (Paul), "Steve Jordan: Drummer, Composer & Record Producer," **The Paul Leslie Hour**, 13 May 2014 (https://www.thepaulleslie.com/steve-jordan-drummer-composer-record-producer/).

125. Concert at Berkeley Community Theater, Berkeley, 2 March 1973.

126. Ringen (Jonathan), "We Shall Overcome: The Seeger Sessions," **Rolling Stone**, 19 May 2006 (https://www.rollingstone.com/music/music-album-reviews/we-shall-overcome-the-seeger-sessions-189797/).

127. Browne (David), **Entertainment Weekly**, 24 April 2006.

128. We Shall Overcome: The Seeger Sessions booklet.

129. DVD **We Shall Overcome: The Seeger Sessions.**

130. Levy (Joe), "Bruce Springsteen: The Rolling Stone Interview," **Rolling Stone**, 1 November 2007 (https://www.rollingstone.com/music/music-news/bruce-springsteen-the-rolling-stone-interview-238478/).

131. Greene (Andy), "More On New Bruce Springsteen Album: Producer Brendan O'Brien Reveals All," **Rolling Stone**, 17 August 2007 (https://www.rollingstone.com/music/music-news/more-on-new-bruce-springsteen-album-producer-brendan-obrien-reveals-all-101485/).

132. Deusner (Stephen M), "Bruce Springsteen: Magic," **Pitchfork**, 3 October 2007 (https://pitchfork.com/reviews/albums/10733-magic/).

133. Horowitz (Carl F), "Sue Me, Sue You: Musical 'Plagiarism' in Court," National Legal and Policy Center, 5 October 2007.

134. Wenner (Jann S), "Bono: The Rolling Stone Interview," **Rolling Stone**, 27 December 2017 (https://www.rollingstone.com/music/music-features/bono-the-rolling-stone-interview-3-203774/).

135. Sevy (Grace), **The American Experience in Vietnam: A Reader**, University of Oklahoma Press, 1981.

136. Remembering Terry (https://www.springsteenlyrics.com/lyrics.php?song=terryssong).

137. Powers (Ann), "Bruce Springsteen and the E Street Band **Working On a Dream**," **Los Angeles Times**, 26 January 2009 (https://www.latimes.com/archives/la-xpm-2009-jan-26-and-springsteen26-story.html).

138. Hiatt (Brian), "Working On a Dream," **Rolling Stone**, 21 January 2009 (https://www.rollingstone.com/music/music-album-reviews/working-on-a-dream-188863/).

139. Fricke (David), "The Band on Bruce: Their Springsteen," **Rolling Stone**, 21 January 2009 (https://www.rollingstone.com/music/music-news/the-band-on-bruce-their-springsteen-243261/).

140. Fricke (David), "Bruce Springsteen: Bringing It All Back Home," **Rolling Stone**, 5 February 2009 (https://www.rollingstone.com/music/music-news/bruce-springsteen-bringing-it-all-back-home-95067/).

141. Fricke (David), "The E Street Band Keep Rolling in '09," **Rolling Stone**, 22 January 2009 (https://www.rollingstone.com/music/music-news/the-e-Street-band-keep-rolling-in-09-68021/).

142. Hagen (Mark), "Meet the new Boss," **Observer Music Monthly**, 18 January 2009 (https://www.theguardian.com/music/2009/jan/18/bruce-springsteen-interview).

143. brucespringsteen.net, 23 December 2008.

144. brucespringsteen.net, 22 September 2014 (https://brucespringsteen.net/news/2014/video-of-the-week-the-wrestler).

145. Billboard, November 1998.

146. Hilburn (Robert), "Some Glory Days, Revisited," **Los Angeles Times**, 8 November 1998 (https://www.latimes.com/archives/la-xpm-1998-nov-08-ca-40494-story.html).

147. Concert, Shrine Auditorium, Los Angeles, 16 November 1990.

148. Hagen (Mark), **Mojo**, 1998.

149. Stewart (Jon), "Bruce Springsteen's State of the Union," **Rolling Stone**, 29 March 2012 (https://www.rollingstone.com/music/music-news/bruce-springsteens-state-of-the-union-172644/).

150. Booklet from the **Wrecking Ball** album.

151. De Caunes (Antoine), "An American in Paris," backstreets.com, 2 March 2012 (https://backstreets.com/paris.html).

152. Fricke (David), **Mojo**, no.309, August 2019.

153. Gallant (Michael), "Ron Aniello, doing whatever it takes to make the record great," mmusicmag.com, November 2012 (http://musicmag.com/m/2012/11/ron-aniello/).

154. Clarke (Norm), "Springsteen got wish for sax solos," **Las Vegas Review-Journal**, 17 December 2012. (https://www.reviewjournal.com/news/springsteen-got-wish-for-sax-solos/).

155. Gill (Andy), **The Independent**, 7 January 2014.

156. Greene (Andy), "Bruce Springsteen Producer Breaks Down **High Hopes**: Exclusive," **Rolling Stone**, 30 December 2013 (https://www.rollingstone.com/music/music-news/bruce-springsteen-producer-breaks-down-high-hopes-exclusive-231926/).

157. Booklet from the **High Hopes** album.

158. Greene (Andy), "Tom Morello: 'Springsteen Concerts Are Orthopedically Exhausting,'" **Rolling Stone**, 3 January 2014 (https://www.rollingstone.com/music/music-news/tom-morello-springsteen-concerts-are-orthopedically-exhausting-188775/).

159. Berkery (Patrick), **Modern Drummer Magazine**, January 2020.

160. Sennett (Sean), "Bruce Springsteen Q&A: On Top Down Under," **Rolling Stone**, 11 March 2014 (https://www.rollingstone.com/music/music-news/bruce-springsteen-qa-on-top-down-under-52877/).

161. Movieline, December 1991.

162. Sutcliffe (Phil), **Mojo**, January 2006.

163. Booklet from **American Beauty**.

INDEX

Bruce Springsteen's songs, albums, and singles being analyzed are highlighted in bold

Bruce Springsteen
photographed by
Danny Clinch, in
October 2005.

PICTURE CREDITS

Getty Images France : © Aaron Rapoport/Corbis 122, 223, 267, 393 • © Afro American Newspapers/Gad 453 • © Al Pereira/WireImage 588, 642 • © Al Seib/Los Angeles Times 420 • © Alison Buck/WireImage 53 • © Allan OlCharlie Ley/Mirrorpix 277 • © Allan Tannenbaum 55, 117, 119, 147 l • © Andy Katz/Corbi 341 • © Apic 192 • © Araya Diaz/WireImage 82 • © Arnaldo Magnani 327, 505 • © ArtCo-Berlin/Ullstein Bild 36 • © Bettmann 11, 52, 198, 201, 224, 363, 465 • © Bill Eppridge/The LIFE Picture Collection 193 l • © Bill O'Leary/The Washington 242 • © Birmingham Post and Mail Archive/Mirrorpix 455 • © Bobby Bank 108, 123, 147 r, 158 r, 228, 592 • © Bob Carey/Los Angeles Times 178 • © Bob Riha Jr/WireImage 375 • © Bradley Kanaris/Afp 556 • © Brian Alpert/Keystone 206 • © Brian Quigley/The Life Images Collection 249 • © Brian Rasic 32, 597 • © Brooks Kraft LLC/Corbis 225 • © Brooks Kraft LLC/Sygma 291, 336 • © Bruce Glikas/FilmMagic 614 • © Burton Mcneely/The Life Images Collection 595 • © CA/Redferns 120 • © Caroline Gillies/BIP 286 • © Carolyn Cole/Los Angeles Time 579, 629 • © CBS Photo Archive 9 • © Charles Bertram/Lexington Herald-Leader/Tribune News Service 245 • © Chris Felver 15 l • © Chris Gabrin/Redferns 134 • © Chris McKay 581 • © Chris Walter/WireImage 405 • © Cindy Ord/NY & Company/Afp 361 • © Clayton Call/Redferns 179, 319 • © Corbis/Corbis 582 • © Daniel Boczarski 153 • © Danny Clinch 469, 546, 671 • © Danny Clinch/Contour 481, 518 • © David M. Benett/Dave Benett/WireImage 640 • © David Corio/Redferns 145, 157, 176, 580 • © David Gahr 25, 29, 43, 44, 80, 104, 142, 144, 247, 272, 395, 398, 401 • © David M. Benett/Steinway & Sons 59 • © David Redfern/Redferns 177, 209, 372, 486 • © David Reed/Redferns 219 • © David Tan/Shinko Music 167 • © Debra L. Rothenberg/FilmMagic 339, 438, 449, 506, 622 • © Derek Storm/FilmMagic 385 • © Dimitrios Kambouris/WireImage 347, 377 • © Don Paulsen/Michael Ochs Archives 12, 42 • © Ebet Roberts 79, 129, 196, 237, 413, 482 • © Ed Perlstein/Redferns 133 • © Eric Catarina/Gamma-Rapho 335, 417 • © Éric Robert/Sygma/Sygma, 305 l., 309, 322, 342 • © Eric Schaal/The Life Picture Collection 193 r • © Erica Echenberg/Redferns 68 • © Fin Costello/Redferns 66, 81, 91, 93 r, 99 • © Found Image Holdings/Corbis 20 • © Fototeca Gilardi 635 • © Fotos International 37, 496 • © Francesco Castaldo\Archivio Francesco Castaldo\Mondadori 160 • © Frank Micelotta/ImageDirect 443 • © Frans Schellekens/Redferns 33, 485 • © Franziska Krug 288 • © Fred Hayes/Sundance 651 • © Fryderyk Gabowicz/Picture Alliance 255 • © GAB Archive/Redferns 166 • © Gai Terrell/Redferns 343 • © Gary Gershoff/WireImage 306 • © Gems/Redferns 150, 475 • © George Pimentel/WireImage 557 • © Georges De Keerle 302 • © Getty Image 210 • © Gie Knaeps 402, 543 • © Gijsbert Hanekroot/Redferns 87, 158 l • © Gilles Petard/Redferns 71 • © Harmony Gerber/WireImage 644 • © Harry Scott/Redferns 200, 281, 303, 463, 648 • © Henry S. Dziekan II 202 • © Herbert Schulze/Ullstein Bild 299 • © Hiroyuki Ito 650 • © Hulton-Deutsch/Hulton-Deutsch Collection/Corbis 65, 78, 487 • © Ian Dickson/Redferns 325 • © J.-C. Olivera/Mastercard/Afp 109 • © James Devaney/WireImage 452 • © James Keivom/NY Daily News Archiv 489 • © James Leynse/Corbis 8 top l and r • © Jamie McCarthy/New York Fashion Week : The Shows/Afp 344 • © Jazz Archiv Hamburg/Ullstein Bild 185 • © Jeff Kravitz/FilmMagic, Inc 365, 529 • © Jeff Fusco 121, 621 • © Jeff Vinnick 539 • © Jeffrey Mayer/WireImage 276 • © Jim Steinfeldt/Michael Ochs Archives 374 • © Jemal Countess/WireImage 613 • © Jerod Harris 617 • © John Mead/Mirrorpix/Mirrorpix 105 l • © Jon Sievert/Michael Ochs Archives 231, 236, 239 • © Jordi Vidal/Redfern 250, 484 • © Joseph Branston/Future Music Magazine/Futur 271 • © Joyce Rudolph/Fotos International 421 ; © June McKim/Afp 441 • © Justin Sullivan/Afp 243 • © Kevin Mazur/WireImage 51, 235, 446, 459, 461, 477, 511, 513, 530, 576, 591, 604, 618, 633 • © Kevin Winter/DMI/The Life Picture Collection 172, 367 • © Kevork Djansezian/The Recording Academy 387 • © Larry Busacca/WireImage 312, 408 • © Larry Hulst/Michael Ochs Archives 131 • © Leni Sinclair/Michael Ochs Archives 64 • © Linda Cataffo/NY Daily News Archive 523 • © Lindsay Brice 600 • © LMPC 112, 180 • © Loomis Dean/The Life Picture Collection 467 • © Lynn Goldsmith/Corbis/VCG 19, 103, 125, 126, 191, 234, 269, 320, 404 • © Oliver Morris 75 • © M. Caulfield/WireImage 451 • © Marie Hansen/The Life Picture Collection 583 • © Mark Cuthbert/UK Press 474 • © Mark Weiss/WireImage 174 • © Mark Sullivan/WireImage 316 • © Marlin Levison/Star Tribune 386 • © Matt Kent/Afp 241 • © Michael Childers/Sygma/Sygma 230 • © Michael Kovac/WireImage 252 • © Michael Ochs Archives 22, 23, 30, 39, 57, 85, 90, 105 r, 106, 111, 159, 205, 240, 274, 314, 428, 490, 491, 509, 515, 521, 554 l, 558 • © Michael Putland 49, 293, 560, 564, 569, 656 • © Michael Rougier/The Life Picture Collection 594 • © Michael S. Williamson/The Washington Post 639 • © Michael Tighe/Donaldson Collection 208 • © Michael Zorn/FilmMagic 292 • © Michel Linssen/Redferns 313 • © Michelly Rall/WireImage 605, 611 • © Mitchell Layto 285 • © Mick Hutson/Redferns 211, 520 • © Mike Coppola/The Bob Woodruff Foundation/Afp 649 • © Mike Windle/SiriusXM/Afp 445 • © Mirrorpix 535 • © Nick Elgar/Corbis/VCG 207 • © Nigel Osbourne/Redferns 149 • © Norman Potter/Daily Express 217 ; © Pam Francis 533, 550 • © Paul Bergen/Redfern 199, 488 • © Paul Harris 323 • © Paul Kane/Afp 616 • © Paul Morigi/WireImage for Naras 358, 584, 585 • © Paul Natkin 161, 212, 251, 345, 554 r • © Paul Warner 213 • © Peter Noble/Redferns 623 • © Peter Stackpole/The Life Picture Collection 31 • © POP-EYE/Ullstein Bild 352 • © Popperfoto 113 • © Randy Bachman 226 • © RB/Redfern 473 • © Ragnar Singsaas/WireImage 563 • © Ray Avery 69 • © Rebecca Sapp/WireImage 332, 589 • © Richard E. Aaron/Redferns 83, 88, 95, 96, 138, 139, 233, 297, 464 • © Richard Ecclestone/Redferns 470 • © Rick Diamond 433, 510 • © Rick Diamond/WireImage 436 • © Rick Diamond/WireImage for The Recording Academy 430 • © Rita Barros 287 • © Rob Verhorst/Redferns 181, 203, 261, 321, 378 • © Robert Alexander 638 • © Robert Gauthier/Los Angeles Times 371 • © Ron Galella, Ltd./Ron Galella Collection 290, 304, 354 • © Ross Gilmore/Redferns 128 • © Ross Marino 151, 156, 163, 164 • © Scott Gries/Afp 127 • © Sean Gardner/Afp 215 • © Scott Dudelson 657 • © Scott Legato 655 • © Sherry Rayn Barnett/Michael Ochs Archives 278 • © Shirley/Ullstein Bild 382 • © Simon Ritter/Redferns 317 • © Sergione Infuso/Corbis 182, 183 • © Stan Grossfeld/The Boston Globe 567 • © Stephen Lovekin/WireImage for New York Post 499 • © Steve Granitz/WireImage 551 • © Steve Thorne/Redferns 525 © Sunset Boulevard/Corbis 110 • © Taylor Hill 34, 47 • © Taylor Hill/FilmMagic 524, 593 • © Terry O'Neill/Iconic Images 73 • © The Life Picture Collection 187, 337, 379 • © The Washington Post 380, 381 • © Theo Wargo/WireImage 48 • © Tim Mosenfelder 162, 244, 493 • © Time Life Pictures/DMI/The Life Picture Collection 333 • © Tom Hill/WireImage 20, 77, 137 • © Tom Sheehan/Sony Music Archive 102 • © Ulf Andersen 384 • © United Artists 282 • © Universal History Archive/UIG 370 • © Universal Pictures/Sunset Boulevard/Corbis 232 • © VCG Wilson/Corbis 170 • © Walt Disney Television 422 • © Walter Leporati 38 • © Will Russell/Afp 601 • © William Campbell/Sygma 388. **Hemis :** © AF Archiv /Alamy 434 • © Allstar Picture Library/Alamy 359 • © CBW/Alamy Stock Photo 72, 227, 284 • © David Parker/Alamy Stock Photo 289 • © Gonzales Photo/Alamy Stock Photo 169, 173 • © Historic Collection/Alamy Stock Photo 326 • © Iconographic Archive/Alamy Stock Phot 334 l • © John Ares/Alamy Stock Photo 115 • © Landmark Media/Alamy 646, 653, 659, 660 • © Movies/Alamy Stock Photo 204 • © Phillip Harrington/Alamy Banque d'images 27 • © Posters/Alamy Stock Photo 268 • © Records/Alamy Stock Photo 194, 270 • © Robert Landau/Alamy Stock Photo 132 • © Roberto Finizio/Alamy Stock Photo 154 • © Roger Garfield/Alamy Stock Photo 8 bas • © Ronald /Grant Archiv/Alamy 222 • © Texas Country/Alamy Stock Photo 124 • © TheCoverVersion/Alamy Stock Photo 146 • © Universal/Ronald Grant Archiv/Alamy 279 • © UPI/Alamy Stock Photo 253 • © Yarvin World Journeys/Alamy Stock Photo 50 • © Wenn Rights Ltd/Alamy Stock Photo 94, 423 • © Zuma Press, Inc./Alamy Stock Photo 10, 505, 555, 575. **Dalle :** © 1978 Robert Matheu 559 • © Bob Gruen 7 • © Christian Rose 61, 93 l • © Cunningham 15 • © Dave Plactik 60 • © Ebet Roberts 118, 432 • © Gibert-Retna Ltd 429 • © Greg Allen/Cache 602, 607 • © Jay Good/Frank White agency 74 • © Marc Bruxelle/Alamy Live 654 • © Michael Putlan 349 • © Phil Taka 315 • © Preston-Retna UK/Avalon 357. **Leemage :** © Writer Pictures 389.

An Hachette UK Company
www.hachette.co.uk

Original title: *Bruce Springsteen, La Totale*
Texts: Philippe Margotin and Jean-Michel Guesdon
Published by Editions EPA – Hachette Livre 2020

This edition first published in Great Britain in 2020 by Cassell,
an imprint of Octopus Publishing Group Ltd
Carmelite House
50 Victoria Embankment
London EC4Y 0DZ
www.octopusbooks.co.uk

Distributed in the US by
Hachette Book Group
1290 Avenue of the Americas
4th and 5th Floors
New York, NY 10104

Distributed in Canada by
Canadian Manda Group
664 Annette St.
Toronto, Ontario, Canada M6S 2C8

ISBN 9781784726492

A CIP catalogue record for this book is available from the British Library.

Printed and bound in China

10 9 8 7 6 5 4 3 2 1

For this edition:
Commissioning Editor: Joe Cottington
Senior Editor: Pollyanna Poulter
Senior Designer: Jaz Bahra
Senior Production Controller: Allison Gonsalves
Translators: Simon Jones, Andrea Reece, Elettra Pauletto
Copy Editor: Caroline West
Proofreader: Jane Birch
Typesetter: Jeremy Tilston

Disclaimers:
All information correct at time of printing.
Details that are unknown are marked by "(?)", for example the second recording date on page 32.